FRANCE
A GEOGRAPHICAL SURVEY

FRANCE

A Geographical Survey

PHILIPPE PINCHEMEL

Professor of Human Geography at the Sorbonne

Translated by
CHRISTINE TROLLOPE
and
ARTHUR J. HUNT

LONDON
G. BELL AND SONS LTD
1969

Originally published as
Géographie de la France
by Armand Colin, Paris
© 1964
English translation,
revised from the French second edition,
Copyright © 1969
G. BELL AND SONS LTD.
York House, Portugal Street
London, W.C.2

SBN 7135 1536 8

Printed in Great Britain by Richard Clay (The Chaucer Press), Ltd.,
Bungay, Suffolk

FOREWORD

The publication of a book on the geography of France is no easy undertaking. To begin with, the author is well aware of his great predecessors, and knows that his work naturally invites comparison with the incomparable writings of such men as Vidal de La Blache, Demangeon and de Martonne.

Then, since the middle of this century, everything in and around France has been changing extremely rapidly. We cannot hope to present a definitive picture of France; we can only show, at one point in time, the changes which recent times have wrought on the face of our country.

Lastly, the author, even more than his predecessors, has every reason to question the value of such a work.

The expression 'Geography of France' suffers, in fact, from three series of false images which have become attached to it: memories of school geography with its lists of names and figures; the almost encyclopaedic presentation of every possible aspect and every possible phenomenon, from physical features to overseas trade and from river regimes to the pyramids of past ages; and the poetic description of France's landscapes and beauty spots which is primarily intended as a lure for tourists.

Geography has nothing to do with such distortions of reality. It is in the strictest sense the science of spatial organisation visibly expressed in landscape. Geography should aim to show first how a part of the earth's surface—in this case France—is laid out, and then to establish the distribution of the principal features; to trace their origins, natural or man-made, and show how similarities or differences in location can lead to a real differentiation.

We have thus aimed, throughout the various chapters of this book, at giving as coherent a picture as possible of the land of France, its organisation, its transformations and the factors which go to make it up. We ran many risks; we might have produced a general handbook of geography illustrated by French examples only, or become bogged down in a mass of trivial examples, examining regional differences so minutely that we lost sight of the whole.

We do not anticipate that every reader will find here what he is looking for: we can only hope that he will come across some things which he did not expect. We have decided not to pursue purely economic questions, either agricultural or industrial, with which we were not directly concerned.

We have felt it necessary to make our standpoint clear, in the first place because since 1945, profound changes in the demographic and economic spheres have brought about a fundamental alteration in the organisation of the country, both national and regional; and in the second place because during this same period geography has ceased to be a purely academic, theoretical discipline and has become an applied science. The 'delocalised' type of economic planning associated with the early national plans is being increasingly replaced by geographical methods of which the planned development of the country, decentralisation and budgeting at regional level are only three examples.

Official publications, parliamentary debates, the agenda and proceedings of commissions and committees, whenever they propose a balanced distribution of men and materials among the various regions, or put forward plans for regional development, are all contributions to an ideal man-made geography of France for the year 2000. Just as Monsieur Jourdain was unwittingly speaking prose, so many Frenchmen today are, in the same way, unwitting geographers. We shall have fulfilled our purpose if this book has given them a better understanding of the scene of their actions and of the possible consequences of these on the indivisible whole which is their country.

Although this book bears the name of only one author, it reflects innumerable researches carried out by generations of geographers from Vidal de La Blache onwards, who have devoted the best years of their lives to describing and explaining one aspect or another of the geography of France or of one of her regions.

We have found an exceptional wealth of information in theses, regional geographical reviews and the major general text-books. We have tried to give a glimpse of this wealth by means of extensive quotations and by reproducing a large number of maps and diagrams, but if we have misused or misinterpreted any of them, the responsibility is ours alone. We must also acknowledge our great debt to all those sciences, natural, social and economic, without whose contribution the picture would not be complete.

The plan of the work follows naturally upon these considerations. There is a general introduction, then six parts falling into two groups of three each. The first three parts analyse the spatial distribution of phenomena under the influence of both natural and man-made conditions. They examine successively the roles of nature, man and the man-imposed framework or infrastructures. Many factors contribute to these phenomena, from the nature of the soil to investments, from physical features to economic planning, from population to infrastructures; all these play their part, according to where they occur, in differentiating between regions, endowing them with varying importance and giving each its distinctive individuality. The last three parts deal with the three types of geographical environment resulting from these processes whether natural or purposive: rural areas, industrial districts and towns.

Publisher's Note

This English edition is based on the second French edition with the inclusion of some of the author's revisions for the third French edition which is in preparation. The Bibliography has been adapted by the author for this edition and brought up to date.

CONTENTS

*

INTRODUCTION

FRANCE: GENERAL CHARACTERISTICS

By what means did a fragment of the earth's surface, neither a peninsula nor an island, which no physical geographer could ever consider a whole, become a political unity and finally reach the status of a nation?

P. VIDAL DE LA BLACHE

INTRODUCTION

1. HISTORY

The 551,695 km.[2] of metropolitan France, the boundaries of which are usually shown as a hexagon in sketch-maps, do not represent an ancient, unchangeable entity; the whole of French history bears witness to the constant movement of her frontiers. Some frontiers were fixed early, while others were not stabilised until later.

After Brittany and Auvergne had become part of the Crown lands of Francis I, and after the treaties of Vervins (1598) and Lyons (1601), the edict of Henry IV in 1607, which joined together the Crown lands and the king's personal domain, gave French territory some element of cohesion which had not existed earlier. Only the northern and eastern frontiers were still to be moved and fixed in their present positions.[1]

The existing northern frontier, from the North Sea to the Sambre, dates from the Treaty of Utrecht (11th March 1713);[2] that between the Sambre and the Rhine was finally established by the second Treaty of Paris (1815) with the loss of Philippeville, Marienbourg and Bouillon in the Ardennes, Sarrebourg and Landau.

In the east, the Treaty of Rastadt (1714) brought the frontier up to the Rhine for the whole length of Alsace (the Treaty of Westphalia in 1648 had given France only the Sundgau and the advocacy of ten imperial cities not including Strasbourg and Mulhouse). But the duchy of Lorraine was not finally annexed until 23rd February 1766, after the death of Stanislas Leczinski, and the area around Montbéliard did not become part of France until 1793.

Alsace and part of Lorraine (corresponding to the department of Moselle) ceased to be part of France for half a century, between the Treaty of Frankfurt (10th May 1871) and the Treaty of Versailles (28th June 1919).

In the South, Corsica, which had already been a French possession for four separate periods from Charles VI to Henry II, finally became French in 1768; Comtat Venaissin and Avignon joined on 14th September 1791.

Savoie and the county of Nice were annexed at the Revolution, but lost as a result of the Napoleonic Wars; they returned to France in 1860 (Treaty of Turin). Roquebrune and Menton were ceded to France by the Prince of Monaco on 2nd February 1861.

The latest modifications of French frontiers date from the Second World War; in 1947 Italy gave up to France the two communes of Brigue and Tende.[3]

France thus became a politically united country long before the other great powers of the continent of Europe. From the 16th and 17th centuries onwards, the wide expanse of France was sharply contrasted with the small rival states into which Italy, central and northern Europe were divided.

As the territory of France progressively increased, it came under the sway of an autocratic monarchy with a strongly centralising tendency, which steadily pressed on with the task of unification and economic planning before the term was even invented. This peculiar territorial and political situation is one of the prime factors of the radiating power, the attraction and the dynamic qualities of France.

We must not, however, neglect the importance of the late entry of certain provinces into the political and administrative territory of France. It explains certain psychological peculiarities affecting relationships between provinces, which continue to exist more or less consciously.

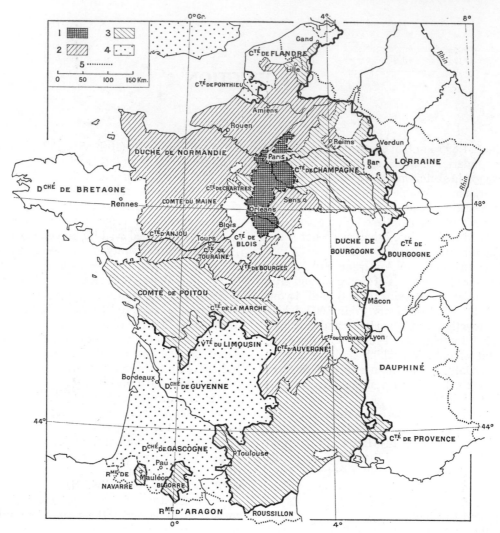

Fig. 1.   Territorial growth of France: extension of the royal domain up to Philip the Fair.   (Source: A. Demangeon, *Géographie Universelle*, A. Colin, Vol. VI)

1. Royal domain at the beginning of the reign of Henry I.   2. Acquisitions made under Philippe-Auguste.   3. Acquisitions from the reign of Louis VIII to that of Philip the Fair.   4. English possessions. 5. Present frontiers of France.

This historical geography still has an important part to play in the landscapes and in the organisation of present-day France. It is impossible to understand the distribution of certain forests, or contrasts in population and settlement, or the sites of many towns, without reference to the political history of France, to the network of political frontiers which once crossed her territory and to the strongpoints built for her protection.

The boundaries of the ancient Gallic city-states, the provinces and the duchies, once marked by forest barriers, have not completely vanished from the French landscape.

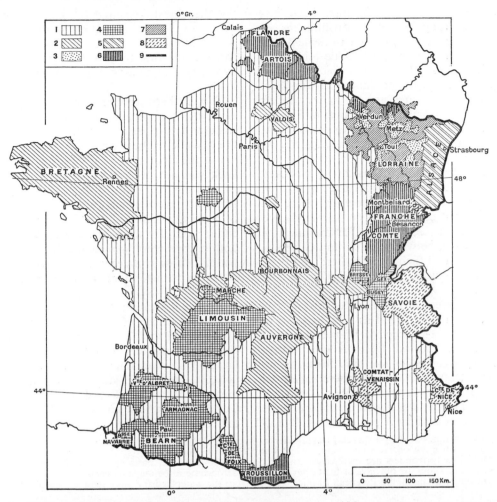

Fig. 2. Territorial growth of France from 1515 to the present day. (After A. Demangeon, *Géographie Universelle*, A. Colin, Vol. VI)

1. Royal domain in 1515. 2. Acquisitions of Francis I. 3. Acquisitions of Henry II. 4. Acquisitions of Henry IV. 5. Acquisitions under the Treaty of Westphalia (1648). 6. Acquisitions following the treaties of the Pyrenees (1659), Aix-la-Chapelle (1668) and Nijmegen (1678). 7. Acquisitions under Louis XV. 8. Acquisitions of the late 18th and 19th centuries. 9. Present frontier.

The frontier forest of Arrouaise, which separated the Veromandui from the Atrebates and the Nervii, and which served to mark the boundary of the kingdom allocated to Charles the Bald at the Peace of Verdun (843), is still visible to a great extent in the countryside between Saint-Quentin and Cambrai.

The persistence of extensive forests in France can thus be explained by reference to both history and environment at the same time; the forests of the West, of Perche and of Maine marked the boundaries of Brittany. French territory was thus divided into a series of vast fertile areas largely cleared of forest, bounded by wooded regions, moorland, high ground or watersheds, with infertile soils (fig. 3).

The Pays de Bray and the neighbouring

regions show very sharp contrasts in the distribution of population; the dividing line between the zone of dispersed settlement and that of village settlement is none other than the old frontier of Normandy, which ceased to exist at the Treaty of Saint-Clair-sur-Epte. Certain large estates are the relics of fiefs granted in the past by the kings of France, which carried the obligation to defend what were then frontier zones (Boulonnais is an example).

The siting of many towns can be explained only by their strategic importance in relation to a frontier which no longer exists. Here and there on the frontiers between Normandy and the Ile-de-France, between Brittany and the Crown lands, between Poitou and Guyenne, fortresses stood facing each other; and these formed the nuclei of towns like Gisors and Cholet.

This progressive extension of French territory, political in origin as it is, helps us to realise that the concept of France as a state bounded by 'natural' frontiers is a relative one. This is not to say that there are no 'natural' features in these frontiers; of a total of 5,500 km., more than 2,100 are sea-coast, and 1,000 km. coincide with mountain ranges (the Pyrenees and the Alps) and generally follow their crest-lines, and 160 km. follow the course of a river, the Rhine.[4] But there is probably nothing more artificial than such a frontier allotting to two different states the two banks of a river, with their adjoining lowlands.

The northern frontier alone has no natural element; it is peculiar in that it cuts across rivers and river basins, one after another, from the Moselle to the Yser.

But the land on which France has engraved itself was not predestined in any way by its natural configuration to give rise to a state. It might have become quite a different type of political organisation, with its frontiers on either side of the present ones. There was nothing predetermined about this hexagonal pattern whose symmetry and balance, so often stressed, belong rather to geometry than to geography.

Thus constituted, France covers 551,695 km.[2], that is, 5% of the continent of Europe and 0·428% of the land area of the globe. Apart from Russia in Europe, France is the largest European state, coming before Spain (449,000 km.[2]). On the other hand, it is, in area, the thirty-fourth largest country in the world, ranking between Kenya (583,000 km.[2]) and Thailand (514,000 km.[2]).

1. In the south, Roussillon was still lacking; it was joined to France in 1659 (Treaty of the Pyrenees).
2. Except for a few enclaves (Warneton) which disappeared in 1769.
3. Occasionally frontiers are rectified by mutual consent (for example, plots of land were exchanged with Switzerland to allow the runways of the Geneva–Cointrin aerodrome to be made longer).
4. On the other hand, the Pyrenean frontier diverges from the watershed for more than a third of its length.

2. GEOGRAPHICAL ADVANTAGES

A. Advantages of Situation

Continental France lies between latitude 42° 30′ N. and 51° N., approximately halfway between the Equator and the North Pole. No other European state has this range of latitude, which gives France the advantages both of the subtropical Mediterranean climate and of the temperate climate of north-west Europe. The Étang de Lacanau in the Landes, the Bec d'Ambès, the confluence of the Rhône and Isère, and the summit of the Meije are all on the 45th parallel.[5] As for longitude, France lies between 4° W. and 8° E. (Bastia 9° 30′ E.).

The country thus forms a relatively compact mass, without any very considerable projections. The distance from Dunkirk to Le Canigou and from Ouessant to Strasbourg is 950 km., from Hendaye to Lauterbourg 1,000 km. and from Brest to Menton 1,050 km. Not one point in the whole country is more than 500 km. from the coast as the crow flies.

These proportions are a quite exceptional asset for France.

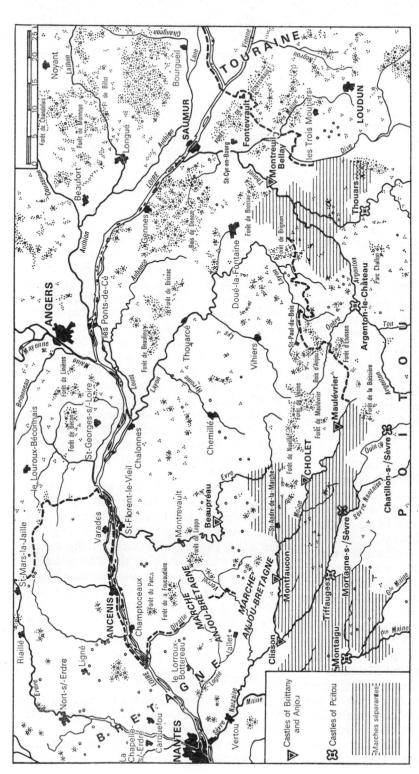

Fig. 3. The Marchland Divides (*Marches séparantes*) of Poitou, Brittany and Anjou. (Sources: R. Dion, *Les Frontières de la France*, Paris, 1947. Map after Chénon (E). 'Les Marches séparantes', *Nouvelle Revue Historique de droit français et étranger*, XVI, 1892).

'The joint possession in which the territories known as *Marches* were held in the Middle Ages in the region represented by this map was the result of the incessant conflicts between the masters of Anjou, Brittany and Poitou.

'As war was here the reason for the lack of definite frontiers, it is natural that they should be least clearly defined in regions which are natural routes for armies, and that it should be less marked elsewhere. The marches are broader in populated and largely cleared areas (between Thouars and Montreuil-Bellay, for example), and they disappear in forest zones less suitable for troop movements, as in the region east of Cholet, on the high ground, still thickly wooded today, from which the Layon and the Moine flow down.

'This particular case brings out the disturbances in the territorial division of France caused by the feudal system. The way indefinite frontiers and relatively precise ones are distributed is exactly the opposite of what it is in the case of primitive frontiers, where uncultivated, wooded districts remain in joint possession, while open, busy regions contain very ancient landmarks showing precisely how the sovereignty was divided' (R. Dion).

AT THE CENTRE OF THE LAND MASSES OF THE WORLD

The central point of the hemisphere with the greatest area of land is near Nantes. This gives France, and western Europe in general, a most valuable advantage.

France, like all western Europe, lies in the centre of the vast zone of damp, cold, temperate and subtropical climates, bounded on the periphery of the continental hemisphere by a crescent-shaped zone of dry climate curving inwards at the ends which separates it from tropical Africa and eastern and southern Asia.

AT THE WESTERN EXTREMITY OF EUROPE

Lying within this damp and temperate zone, France, while closely bound to the peninsula of Europe, is at the same time open to the Atlantic Ocean. This situation, enjoyed by no other European state, means that France is divided by two separate influences, a continental influence whose effects are felt mainly in the eastern half of the country, and a maritime or oceanic influence, felt chiefly in the west. But this twofold division is complicated by other gradations.

Maritime France faces three very different seas: the land-locked Mediterranean; the wide Atlantic Ocean, spanned by communications to distant America; and the North Sea, which has taken over the role of the Mediterranean as a focus of civilisation.

These seas, centres of civilisation as they are, can most easily communicate one with another across France. Across the basin of Aquitaine and Languedoc, and through the Carcassonne gap, the Atlantic is only 400 km. from the Mediterranean. This in turn is linked with the North Sea by the Rhône and Rhine valleys, or by a route through the Rhône valley, Champagne and Flanders.

It can be seen that this involves differences between eastern and western France in the general direction of lines of communication. In the East, they run north–south between centres of development in inland areas. In the West, on the other hand, they run from east to west, providing inland regions with outlets to the Atlantic ports.

B. Orographical Advantages

By a rare coincidence, France is favoured both by its situation and by its relief. Many parts of the world have an advantageous situation, full of possibilities which are however rendered useless by high mountain ranges which make communications difficult, and restrict agricultural lowlands or large centres of population; an example is the west of North America. There is no such difficulty in France, where more than 60% of the land is less than 250 m. above sea-level. Size for size, only the British Isles have a lowland area of comparable extent, but that is less favoured in situation.

These plains, very wide in the North and West and long and narrow in the East, are so placed as to give France more open country than is found almost anywhere else. We should, however, note that they are irregularly distributed. They predominate in the northern half of France, where the plains and plateaux of the Paris basin and Armorican massif are interrupted only by the Vosges massif and the Morvan.

In the southern half, too, there are widespread plains, from Poitou and Vendée to the Pyrenees. But from the Central Massif to the Alps and the Mediterranean they become wide coastal strips (such as Languedoc), broad corridors (such as the Rhône–Saône valley) or are reduced to intermontane basins (such as the Limagne) or narrow valley corridors (as in the Alps). Orographically France must thus be divided into two sectors (fig. 4).

C. Advantages of Climate

Most of France lies in the temperate zone; the South is on the northern fringe of the Mediterranean subtropical zone.

France, because of her situation and relief, has climatic characteristics which are unique in Europe: oceanic, continental and Mediterranean influences are found side by side or in combination. The result is a range of climates all with the characteristic advantage of moderation; extremes of climate are rarely found. Of all continental climates, with their extreme contrasts between seasons, those of France are the least continental; of all Mediterranean climates, with their fearsome summer droughts, those of France are the least 'Mediterranean'.

This advantage of climate has many and varied consequences. The moderate climate of France is one of the most favourable in the world, particularly in the temperate and sub-tropical zones. It is favourable not only to human life but also to plant and animal life and to economic life.

This threefold advantage of situation, relief and climate has, from time immemorial, made France the meeting-place for foreign influences, oceanic and continental, Nordic, Anglo-Saxon and Mediterranean.

French territory was a melting pot for the most varied influences, and from it came the new gleaming metal of a civilisation and a philosophy in which each race was to some extent reflected.

5. At the southern extremity of Corsica, Bonifacio is at latitude 41° 24′ N.

3. THE UNITY AND DIVERSITY OF FRANCE

The foregoing remarks give the impression that France is characterised by a high degree of unity, facilitated by ease of communications and strengthened by her achievement of unification at an early date and its accompanying centralisation.

France appears to be largely homogeneous; but this impression must be corrected at once. Unity is not the same thing as uniformity. There may be few lands which show so many kinds of unity, but there are also few which show so many differences between one part and another. France is a mosaic of regions and *pays* whose own peculiar characteristics are expressed in their landscapes, their buildings and the ways of life and activities of their people.

Nature and man have worked together to make this diversity. Variations in geology, morphology, climate, soil and plant life combine to produce contrasting environments. Man has turned these natural divisions into regions, accentuating natural differences by differences in the way the land is organised and used. One cannot travel a hundred kilometres without passing through several of them.

Going from Dunkirk to Lille, for example, the traveller does not simply cross the wide plain of Flanders, as might be expected; he passes through four regions—maritime Flanders, Houtland, which lies around the Cassel hills, the plain of the river Lys and the district of Weppes.

It is impossible to understand France without starting from this patchwork of regions which was laid down long ago and has become more and more apparent with the passing of centuries. For a long time this partitioning of French territory was forgotten, but awareness of the reality of regional differentiation has recently been revived. The revival of regional patriotism (in Brittany, Alsace, the South-west and the North) has brought to light the inequalities of revenue, equipment and potentialities between the regions.

We may take this to mean that a better balance has been regained between centripetal and centrifugal forces, that is, between central and regional influences; for centuries the second element in this balance of forces had been dismissed as negligible.

4. THE WORK OF MAN

A. A Civilised Country

The most characteristic feature of the geography of France is the large extent to which the landscape has been modified by man. Natural landscapes of forest, moorland or bare rock are very little in evidence. The dominant pattern is that of a many-coloured patchwork of cultivated fields, meadowland and built-up areas, so that landscapes show the imprint of long and intensive human activity. The impression of a garden is the one which occurs most often to travellers as soon as they pass over French frontiers, whether they are coming by air from the Mediterranean countries where the areas of parcelled-out land are smaller and less distinct, or from the New World with its vast open spaces either undivided or divided into immense fields. They can see differences in the scale and in the nature of man–land relationships between France and their own countries. Similar characteristics can no doubt be found outside France in all western European states, but the man-made landscape of France displays some unexpected features:

1. In the small size of its unit of land use: the parcel, or plot.
2. In the great variety of types of land use and organisation; open fields, *bocage*, arable fields and meadows are unevenly mingled to produce landscapes of great complexity.
3. In certain archaic features, which are very easily seen. One of the most conspicuous is the small size of the plots of land in a world where mechanisation of farming requires fields to be as large as possible to make economic use of machines. Another is the survival of archaic settlement forms, both rural and urban.

B. An Underpopulated Country

On 1st January 1968 the population of metropolitan France was more than 50 million (1·5% of the world's population in 1964).

In actual numbers, the population of France is the fourth largest in Europe (excluding the U.S.S.R.), after West Germany, the United Kingdom and Italy. It represents 10·68% of the population of Europe (excluding the U.S.S.R.) concentrated on 5% of the area of the continent, which would seem to indicate a dense population.

In reality, with 88·5 inhabitants per square kilometre (1964), France comes fourteenth in density of population among the European nations, immediately before Austria (85·8). She comes far behind the Netherlands (360·7), Belgium (307·3), West Germany (248), the United Kingdom (222) and Italy (168·5).[6]

This low density of population is an important feature of France. Considered in relation to the country's advantages, it poses a serious problem; at the same time it raises other issues. Is France under-populated? If so, might not this under-population be responsible for bad organisation and use of land? How has this low density of population affected the economy and the changes that have taken place in it?

Nevertheless, France may contain only 1·5% of the population of the world, but 2·7% of the world's active industrial population and 2·6% of those engaged in commerce, transport and services are found there. This indicates a particularly high level of economic and social development.

6. Figures for 1964.

5. THE BALANCE OF THE ECONOMY

In 1964 the gross national product, corresponding to the value of goods produced and services performed, was 432,000 million francs. This figure places France among the 'secure' countries, with a product of $1,920 *per capita*. France ranks alongside Belgium, Denmark, Western Germany, before Great Britain (1,810), Italy (1,100), but appreciably behind Switzerland (2,330), Sweden (2,500) and the United States (3,560).

A. Comparative List of Products

Table I shows the position of France in the total production of the world, giving the products in descending order of importance.

TABLE I. FRENCH PRODUCTION IN RELATION TO THE REST OF THE WORLD AND TO COMMON MARKET EUROPE

Products	Production (1,000 tons) U = units, 1963	% of world production 1961	% of world production 1963	% of Common Market production 1961	% of Common Market production 1963
Wine . . .	46,715	21·7	19·5	46·0	48·4
Iron ore . .	23,302	10·2	9·1	75·2	77·4
Cars and lorries .	1,350,000 U	9·0	8·3	33·2	30·6
Bauxite . .	2,182	9·0	6·5	86·3	88·0
Aluminium. .	322·8	6·7	6·8	48·1	49·8
Barley . .	5,377	6·1	7·2	57·9	61·0
Cast iron and iron alloys	14,808	5·5	5·0	26·1	27·0
Beet sugar . .	2,728	5·1	3·9	23·0	35·0
Cement . .	15,660	4·8	4·9	23·1	23·7
Rayon . .	56·5	4·8	4·8	22·0	21·4
Steel . . .	17·568	4·8	4·5	24·0	24·0
Oats . . .	2,486	4·5	5·6	43·9	43·0
Staple fibre. .	67·3	4·3	4·5	19·3	19·8
Wheat . .	9,430	4·1	4·1	45·4	41·4
Refining capacity	43·25	3·2	3·1	27·1	24·6
Electric power .	76,200 (million kWh.)	3·1	3·2	26·4	25·4
Coal . . .	52,356	2·6		22·7	
Timber . .	42·0 (million m.²)	2·4	2·3		47·5
Cattle . .	19,500 (thousand head)	2·1	2·0		40·8
Synthetic rubber .	41	2·0	2·8		
Pigs . .	8,526 (thousand head)	1·6	1·6	25·2	25·4
Maize . .	2,813	1·3	1·5	42·2	49·5
Rye . . .	346	0·9	0·9	8·5	8·3
Potatoes . .	14,894			30·1	30·4
Woollen yarns .	142·9			7·8	26·7	27·7
Natural gas .	44·8 (million m.²)			9·0	23·3	35·7
Butter . .	380			35·4	36·8
Meat . .	2,780			39·8	38·6
Wood pulp. .	1,144		1·8	33·9	34·8

It provides a great deal of interesting information; agricultural and industrial products are equally well represented, showing the characteristic balance of the French economy. The fertility of the soil and climatic diversity make agriculture one of the bases of national economic development; but the abundance of mineral resources and sources of power, and extensive connections with countries supplying raw materials, have all been favourable to the development of industry.

The highest percentages obtain for agricultural products, minerals, semi-manufactured products, yarns, cast-iron, aluminium; but also for the production of cars and lorries, the only finished manufactures to appear in this list.

B. Recent Progress

These production figures are the expression of an economic life which is developing from year to year and whose dynamic character has been a feature of the last twenty years; in fact the population and the economy of France are and have been growing particularly fast since the Liberation. From 1950 to 1961 gross national production increased by 60%; from 1950 to 1960 the increase in the gross national production per head of the working population was 47% in France (Others: Western Germany, 64%; Italy, 48%; Netherlands, 42%; United Kingdom, 24%; United States, 21%).

TABLE II. CONSUMPTION *PER CAPITA*
(in kilograms *per capita*)

	France	United Kingdom	Germany	U.S.A.
Steel, 1963 . .	326	368	473	540
Aluminium, 1955 .	2·5	5·7	3·5	9·8
Cement, 1955 . .	190	228	275	280
Nitrogen, 1955 . .	7·4	9·3	13·5	9·2
Plastics, 1955 . .	2·5	6·6	7·6	10
Power used—in coal equivalent, 1963 .	2,788	5,090	4,121	8,507

But this expansion, dating from after the last war, followed a long period of stagnation and regression in both the economy and the population. That is why, despite her recent brilliant achievements, France in the second half of the 20th century bears, and will bear for a long time yet, the marks of her past.

The long-term rate of growth shows France to have fallen behind other countries. From 1929 to 1954, for example, industrial production increased by 18%, as against 61% in Great Britain, 70% in Italy, 99% in the Netherlands, 111% in the United States, 136% in Norway.

The same sequence of events explains the differences, which are sometimes surprising, between the level of consumption and of industrial construction of France and that of other countries.[7]

C. Weakness of External Trade

Richly endowed by nature with an economy in which the balance is maintained between agriculture and industry, and relatively underpopulated, France passed through the 19th and the first half of the 20th century without having to deal with the problems of employment and foreign exchange which her neighbours faced. In Germany, England and the Netherlands there was an urgent need to export industrial products in large quantities in order to import foodstuffs; the economy of these countries developed in accordance with this pressing necessity.

In France the circumstances were different and these explain the unusual features of French trade. In 1964 the value of imports was $7,520 million, and that of exports was $8,990 million. In 1962 the proportion of French exports in the gross national product was 10·3%, as against 3·8% in the United States, 14% in the United Kingdom, 22% in Denmark, 32·7% in Belgium–Luxembourg and 34·9% in the Netherlands.

Imports represented (1964) 5·7% of world trade, and exports 5·3%, which placed France in the fourth rank among the commercial nations of the world behind the United States, Federal Germany and Great Britain.

Table III gives a breakdown of imports and exports under four headings for four years.

France imports coal, petroleum, raw materials, foodstuffs (tropical produce) and to an increasing degree manufactured goods.

TABLE III. COMPOSITION OF EXTERNAL TRADE (%)

	Imports				Exports			
	1934	1950	1960	1964	1934	1950	1960	1964
Foodstuffs . .	32·3	27·7	20·3	10·9	14·4	10·8	13·2	16·0
Power . .	{49·3	15·6	17·0	14·4	{28·8	6·1	3·8	3·4
Raw materials . .		31·1	24·2	18·7		10·1	8·4	8·0
Manufactured goods . .	18·4	24·3	38·4	55·5	56·7	66·9	75·0	72·6

She exports raw materials (bauxite, iron ore), foodstuffs and agricultural produce (wine, timber), and manufactured goods which represent three-quarters of her exports.

But these four headings do not stress sufficiently certain weaknesses and anomalies in external trade. France imports goods which French agriculture and industry could and should produce in larger quantities. Agricultural exports appear low in view of the fertility of French soil. In 1959 the value of these agricultural exports rose to $769,700,000. Denmark, with one twelfth of the area of France and with much less favourable climatic and soil conditions, exported agricultural produce to the value of $869,700,000 in the same year.

In the realm of industry, France exports more ores (iron ore, bauxite), pig iron and steel products (sheets and bars) than manufactured metallurgical and engineering products. For several years now, attention has been drawn to France's serious deficiency in production of industrial equipment, and of machine-tools in particular.

From these facts, two characteristics emerge. France is not an industrial nation comparable to other highly industrialised states; and she does not seem to have taken advantage of her rich potentialities in agriculture.

The balance of French external trade was permanently negative from 1928 to 1964 inclusive, except for the years 1955, 1959, 1960 and 1961.

---

7. See also Part Three, Chapter II.

PART ONE

THE ROLE
OF NATURE

France is certainly one of the least isolated countries in Europe.
A. DEMANGEON

I

RELIEF AND MINERAL RESOURCES

1. ALTIMETRY AND THE PRINCIPAL LINES OF THE RELIEF

France as a whole is a lowland country in which lowlands, low plateaux and mountains of moderate height predominate over high mountainous regions. This characteristic is clearly shown by the average altitude of France (excluding Corsica), which is 342 m. (Europe, 297 m.). Table IV shows the area of France divided into six altimetric zones.

TABLE IV. ALTIMETRIC ZONES

Altimetric zones (metres)	Area (km.²)	%
0–100	135,524	25·4
100–250	192,301	36·4
250–500	110,453	20·4
500–1,000	64,730	11·0
1,000–2,000	28,830	5·3
2,000	8,425	1·5

One quarter of mainland France is thus less than 100 m. above sea level, more than 60% lying between sea-level and 250 m. It is surprising to find that only 17·8% of France lies above 500 m. (not counting Corsica) and that only 6·8% of the country is higher than 1,000 m. These figures are scarcely in accord with what we know about the presence of Hercynian massifs and mountain chains of more recent formation whose highest point in Europe is in France.

Where are these lowlands situated? The 100-m. contour line has some very large re-entrants, notably in the Aquitaine basin and the Armorican massif (Rennes, Laval and Le Mans region) (fig. 4). The 250-m. contour line forms a convenient dividing line between the French lowlands and the regions with high plateaux and mountains; it describes a sine curve cutting France in two and passing through Fourmies, Saint-Dizier, Auxerre,

Nevers, La Châtre, Confolens, Cahors, Toulouse and Pau.

To the west of this curve there are only two hilly regions of any size. One of these consists of the hills of Perche (with Mont d'Amain, 309 m.), which are a continuation of the hills of Normandy (highest point Mont Pinçon, 365 m.) and the heights of Maine (highest point the Avaloirs beacon in the forest of Écouves, 417 m.); and the other is the uplands of interior Brittany (Tuchenn Gador in the Monts d'Arrée, 384 m.). The rest of this sector reaches a height of 200 m. at only a few points, for instance, in the hills surrounding the Boulonnais and in the Pays de Bray.

To the east of this 250-m. contour, lowlands are rare; they are found in the Mediterranean South, in the Rhône valley and the plains of the Saône and the Rhine.

But this contour is merely a conventional line with no topographical significance. The great dividing line of the relief lies farther east.

A. The Backbone of the Relief

The major relief features of France are distributed around a very important divide (*ligne directrice*) with a threefold significance —altimetric, hydrographic and structural.

This divide begins in the south of France to the east of Revel, with the first spurs of the Montagne Noire. It then continues through the Monts de l'Espinouse and follows the great escarpment of the Cévennes and the Vivarais and the crest-line of the mountains of Lyonnais, Beaujolais and Charolais. From there it continues through the plateaux of the

Fig. 4. The relief of France. (Source: A. Demangeon, *Géographie Universelle*, A. Colin, Vol. VI) Altitudes: 1. 0–100 m.   2. 100–250 m.   3. 250–500 m.   4. 500–1,000 m.   5. Above 1,000 m.   6. Cols.

Côte-d'Or, the plateau of Langres and the 'Monts Faucilles' to meet the Ballon d'Alsace.

This great S-shaped divide, which extends in a mainly southerly direction, marks the division between two different structural areas; the Hercynian and the Pyreneo–Alpine provinces.   To the north and west of the divide the two types of Hercynian structure are spread out in large separate units: the ancient massifs—the Vosges, the Ardennes, the Armorican massif and the Central Massif; and the sedimentary basins—the Anglo-Flemish basin, the Paris basin and the basin of Aquitaine.   To the east and south are mountains formed by the mountain-building movements of the Tertiary period, which in some cases affected new sedimentary material (as in the Jura and the Alps), and in others carried up bodily fragments of the Hercynian core (as in the Pyrenees), or left these fragments merely as relict blocks (Maures–Estérel massif and Serre mountains), while the other blocks of the core have subsided and are buried under huge masses of sedimentary rocks (Alsace, Saône).

This line is remarkable for its high altitudes,

for the height from which it dominates the lands lying on either side and for its significance as a watershed. It includes the highest points in the whole of the zone stretching thence to the western coasts of France.[1] For the still higher peaks found in Auvergne are in fact recent additions of volcanic origin (Plomb du Cantal, 1,858 m.). On the fringes of the divide there are crystalline blocks which are already part of the intense upthrust on the east of the Central Massif (1,640 m. at Pierre-sur-Haute in the Monts du Forez).

This divide is interrupted by very occasional cols (*seuils*) and corridors: for example, the cols of the plateau of Langres, of Charolais and of Jarez in the latitude of Vienne. All these heights rise suddenly from a broad corridor of plains and plateaux, from the Burgundy gate which opens into Alsace to the Carcassone gap which gives access to the Aquitaine basin. Seen from the plains of the Bas-Languedoc and the Rhône–Saône corridor, the fall in height from the divide is considerable, very often exceeding a thousand metres. The extent and steepness of this rise isolates the highlands to the west of the divide from the series of depressions developed along it and prevents them from sharing the easy flow of traffic which the lower parts enjoy, since links with the western side in a crosswise direction exist at long intervals or even not at all, especially from the Montagne Noire to Mont Pilat.

The topographical importance of this divide, which has no passes and through which communications are so difficult, is due to its role as a watershed. It is, in fact, the main watershed of France. A great number of rivers, from the Moselle to the Thore, a tributary of the Agout, rise there. It separates the river-basins draining to the Atlantic Ocean, the Channel and the North Sea from those flowing to the Mediterranean.

To the west the streams collect in large river-basins draining along the slopes which lead down to the sea: those of the Seine, the Garonne and the Loire. To the east of this line the Rhône, which collects, in the Rhône–Saône corridor, a large number of rivers converging upon it from the Jura, the Alps and the Cévennes, is the master-stream.

To the west the great arterial valleys of the drainage systems which come down from this watershed cut more or less deeply into a topography of plateaux and plains. Apart from the disturbances caused in the upper Loire valley by volcanic eruptions and the subsidence of the Limagne, these plains and plateaux correspond broadly to a system of slopes inclined in various directions towards the north and the west, starting at the watershed. To the east the rivers show a less regular course, and tend more to conform to pre-existing corridors, rift valleys and valleys of dominantly structural origin. These features are attributable to the extreme youth of the watershed.

B. Hercynian and Alpine France

This divide not only separates two different geological formations; it also separates two areas which have undergone different types of morphological and topographical evolution.

In the west is a France of great plains and plateaux, where the relief appears hollowed out, and where the valleys are cut into a landscape which always bears, in differing degrees, the marks of earlier bevellings and erosional cycles which have followed one upon the other since the Hercynian structure came into existence.

The average heights of the various geological units show clearly how low the general altitudes are: Paris basin, 178 m.; Aquitaine basin, 135 m.; Armorican massif, 104 m.; Central Massif, 715 m.; Vosges, 530 m.

In the east is the France of youthful mountains, recent subsidences and strong topographic contrasts; mountains, ranges of hills, escarpments, plains and troughs are found side by side. It is a younger France, where Tertiary mountain-building resulted in the uplift of huge masses which erosion has only just begun to reduce. In this region structural morphology, because of the multiplicity of folds and faults, plays a much greater part than in the Hercynian France of the west. In order to analyse the relief of Alpine France we must be guided not by drainage patterns but by geological maps.

Average altitudes are of course greater:

Alps, 1,121 m.; Pyrenees, 1,008 m.; Jura, 660 m.; Corsica, 570 m.; these mountains appear side by side with very low-lying areas such as Bas-Languedoc, 122 m., and the Rhône corridor, 279 m.

1. The Ballon d'Alsace (1,248 m.), the Ballon de Servance (1,189 m.), the Mont des Fourches (504 m.), points as high as 516–512 m. in the Plateau de Langres, Mont Tasselot (606 m.), Mont St.-Rigaud (1,012 m.) in Maconnais; Mont Boussièvre (1,004 m.) near Tarare; Mont Pilat (1,434 m.) to the south-east of Saint-Étienne; Grand Felletin (1,390 m.), Mont de Mézenc (1,754 m.) and the Gerbier de Jonc (1,551 m.) in Vivarais; Mont Lozère (1,702 m.) and the Aigoual (1,567 m.); the Pointe de Nore (1,210 m.) in the Montagne Noire.

2. THE MORPHOLOGICAL EVOLUTION OF HERCYNIAN FRANCE

Traditionally, the Hercynian massifs are contrasted with the sedimentary basins occupying the depressed areas of the Hercynian platform; in actual fact they are as closely bound up with each other in their morphological evolution as they are different lithologically; they are analysed separately merely for convenience of presentation.

A. Ancient Massifs

The ancient massifs are veritable palimpsests, bearing the more or less legible traces of a long succession of episodes in their complex tectonic, sedimentary and morphological history. The present forms of the relief are a reflection of a part of these episodes.

ROCK FORMATIONS AND THE
    POST-HERCYNIAN SURFACE

The building of these massifs dates from the Primary era, when geologically composite blocks were formed; we find, side by side, crystalline and metamorphic formations and Palaeozoic sediments. Most of these blocks date from the Hercynian folding, which was extremely violent, with fractures and overthrusting. However, certain regions of the Central Massif are considered to be fragments of the older Caledonian block, the Hercynian 'consolidation' having affected the regions on the edges of a Caledonian structure in the centre of the massif.

The geological structure of the ancient massifs is very varied. It comprises:

1. Vast outcrops of crystalline rocks with granite batholiths and metamorphic aureoles (as in the Central Massif).

2. Banded structure corresponding to folds of the Hercynian chain, levelled to their roots; also bands of crystalline rocks (the cores of the anticlines) alternate with primary sediments preserved in synclinal positions. This is the case in the south of Brittany and the Normandy *Bocage*.

3. Folded Palaeozoic sedimentary cover completely masking the crystalline blocks.

From the end of Palaeozoic (Permian) times onwards, these blocks underwent very considerable erosion resulting in the post-Hercynian peneplanation. These processes went on for periods of unequal length as is shown by the variety of early sedimentary deposits of lagoonal or marine facies beneath which they are buried. For example, from south-east to west the south side of the post-Hercynian surface of the Ardennes massif is pre-Triassic in Luxembourg, pre-Liassic from the north of Virton, pre-Cretaceous north of Hirson, pre-Eocene between Hirson and Fumay. In Morvan the post-Hercynian surface developed under the influence of tilting along a north–south axis. From north to south the eastern edge of the Armorican massif is pre-Triassic, pre-Liassic, pre-Jurassic and pre-Cretaceous; the surface is pre-Cenomanian in western Vendée.

The morphology of this post-Hercynian surface is of course very varied. Sometimes it is a perfectly bevelled surface the outline of which can be followed despite later earth movements (Vosges border). Marine transgressions, by their erosive action, have at many points helped to complete the levelling action of continental erosive systems.

Elsewhere the surface shows traces of a topography of mature or senile valleys fossilised by deposits either from accumulation of debris or marine transgression (Vendée). Finally, in certain regions, where structure and lithology are favourable, we can observe how true ridge-crests persist, coming to the surface in the midst of Triassic sediments (regions of Falaise, Valognes and the Carentan marshes) or Liassic sediments.[2]

EVOLUTION AFTER THE FORMATION OF THE POST-HERCYNIAN SURFACE

Since the peneplanation of the late Palaeozoic, the Hercynian blocks have been affected by phenomena of three types: marine transgressions and sedimentation, earth movements, and cycles of erosion acting differentially.

Transgressions

It is very difficult to determine the existence or the exact extent of marine transgressions in the absence of any considerable sedimentary remains. In the Armorican massif a very small Cenomanian deposit on the summit of Mont Pinçon is evidence of a transgression of the Cretaceous sea, which extended also over Vendée (witness fragments of the Cenomanian at Challans). The whole of the Vosges–Black Forest area was covered by the sea in the Jurassic period, as proved by the limestone expanses of the Vosges foothills, now down-faulted above the plain of Alsace. Although no secondary deposits have been found in the greater part of the Central Massif, the south was affected by the Jurassic transgression which deposited in a geosyncline the series of thick Triassic, Liassic and Jurassic limestones found in the plateaux of the Causses (1,500 m. thick in the Grands Causses). The limestone covering is continuous from Quercy to the Causses de Rodez, interrupted

only by a 20-km. 'bridge' of older rocks to the south of Decazeville.

Off the coasts of Brittany, surface rocks of the Cretaceous periods show that at that period the coastline was not very different from the present one. (Certain deposits are *in situ*, but others, consisting of gravel, are cargoes of ballast discharged by ships in the past).

In the second half of the Tertiary, the Armorican massif, like all western France, was affected by relatively extensive Miocene and Pliocene transgressions. In the middle Miocene period a great gulf of the 'Crag' sea stretched over Anjou, Touraine, Vendée and part of Brittany, depositing sands, shelly sands and limestone. These deposits survive in topographical and structural depressions. A preliminary tectonic phase led to a regression.

The Pliocene transgression in the Hercynian regions of western France sets us some delicate problems. It has been possible in many places to identify Pliocene deposits, sometimes fossiliferous (Redonian in the Rennes basin, for example), and whose marine origin is indicated by the presence of glauconite. Lithologically these deposits are very varied: sands (often red), gravels, shingle, clays and limestones have been identified in many places. The landscape they have fossilised is still a very sharply defined one of valleys and rias, and they sometimes encroach on the interfluves. But later earth movements make it difficult to determine with any accuracy the maximum heights reached by this transgression. A. Guilcher, in his thesis, is of the opinion that this did not exceed 100 m. But deposits have been identified at much greater altitudes. Near Mayenne, at Champéon, there is a Pliocene (?) bed at 291 m.

Deformations

Since the post-Hercynian planation, and between the periods of transgression, the Hercynian massifs have undergone deformations, tectonic in origin, which have continued up to a very recent period. These deformations have occurred to an unequal degree, depending on distance from the orogenic zones and the nature of the materials, which are brittle and not plastic (fig. 5).   They take the following forms:

Mass movements. Uplift, warping, tilting in asymmetric blocks and subsidence forming great sedimentary basins, but also small, more localised basins, such as those floored by Miocene and Upper Pliocene lacustrine deposits in the Velay and Allier valleys.

The Armorican massif was affected in this way by two up-warpings in Basse-Bretagne and in the Normandy–Perche *Bocage*, while the zone formed by the Mont-Saint-Michel bay and the Rennes–Nantes basin subsided

The subsidences and faults doubtlessly occurred during the times when the Alpine thrusts temporarily abated, resulting from a relaxation, not a compression, in a west–east direction.

Small-scale undulations.   Though fractures are the type of deformation most often observed because of their rectilinear form, we must recognise the existence of anticlinal or synclinal undulations, although evidence of this is difficult to produce.   Here, analysis of river patterns may be very helpful (fig. 8).

These deformations, according to their nature and extent, distinguish between three types of ancient massif.

The Armorican type.   The Hercynian struc-

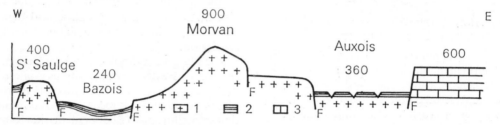

Fig. 5.   Diagrammatic profile of the major deformations of the post-Hercynian surface.   (Source: J. Beaujeu-Garnier, *Le Morvan et sa Bordure*, P.U.F.)

1. Ancient rocks.   2. Liassic rocks.   3. Jurassic rocks.

between the two masses.   This accounts for the two highland zones in western France.

Later the whole of Brittany was tilted from north to south, giving rise to the orographic and hydrographic asymmetry of the peninsula.

Fractures.   The southern rim of the Rennes basin is formed by a system of faults originating or revived in recent times.   Guilcher considers that occurrences in the Tertiary played an important part in the formation of the islands off the south coast of Brittany; the Montagne de Locronan is believed to be a Tertiary horst; in Vendée the asymmetric basin of Chantonnay was formed in the Tertiary.   The Vosges began to rise in the Oligocene, and the movement was continued, and according to some authors accentuated, in the Quaternary, when the rift-valley of the Rhine was being formed.

ture still predominates, and Tertiary structures appear only in wide deformations and isolated fractures which never form a large fault zone, but give rise to a structure of tilted blocks (fig. 6).   Corresponding to these faults are escarpments separating two large plateau sectors; the fractures determine the direction of the rivers.   The Armorican massif, the Ardennes and the west of the Central Massif illustrate this type.

The Vosges type.   In this type the Tertiary structure is evident in strongly tilted fault blocks, with several series of faults breaking the continuity of the post-Hercynian surface. The Hercynian structure is incorporated in a system of structural slopes dating from the Tertiary.   The Vosges, caught up in the great Vosges–Black Forest up-warping and fractured on their eastern side, and the southern part of the Central Massif belong to this category, which exists through proximity to the Pyreneo-Alpine orogenies.

The Forez type. Here the Tertiary structure is the determinant factor, even in particular details. A large number of structural disturbances of the fault type—new faults of Tertiary age or Palaeozoic ones along which posthumous movements occurred—breaks up the block into steps, horsts and graben. The eastern Central Massif and the extensive faulted zone stretching from the Sancerrois across the Limagne to the Causses are of this type. Alsace is in a sense a hypertrophied

basalt from the summit. It differs from Mont Dore and Cantal only by its smaller accumulation of conglomerates.[3]

(*b*) The phonolithic volcanoes of eastern Velay.

(*c*) The extensive basaltic effusions of Velay and the Cézallier mountains.

All these volcanic formations provide unusually valuable morphological evidence, thanks to the rocks and the deposits which they fossilise, and the faults which may or may not have affected them.

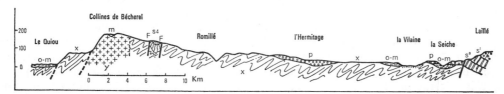

Fig. 6. An example of a tilted block in the Armorican massif. Section N.W.–S.E. from the Tertiary basin of Quiou to the southern escarpment of the Rennes basin. (Source: A. Meynier, *Ann. de Géog.* no. 303, 1947, p. 173)

p. Pliocene detrital sand. o–m. Miocene and Oligocene limestone and clay. S⁴. Upper Silurian shales. S¹. Armorican sandstone. Sᵃ. Shales and red sandstones of Pont-Réan (Cambrian). x. Brioverian schists (pre-Cambrian). y. Granite. Solid lines, faults (F) recognised by geologists; broken lines, probable faults. The surface from the Bécherel hills to the Rennes basin has all the appearance of a tilted block. At Bécherel the Hercynian fault, now levelled, is several kilometres away from the Alpine disturbances (note the small fragment of Tertiary shelly sand (m) in a small valley on the Bécherel hills).

example, as the zone of subsidence is as large as the two fragments of the massif after its fracture.

Volcanic eruptions have taken place in those parts of the Central Massif which were most affected by displacements in the Tertiary. The vulcanism of this region dates from the Oligocene (the basalt hills of the Limagne) to the Holocene (Le Pariou, in the Dômes chain, dates from less than 8,000 years ago) with periods of very considerable activity. Mont Dore (1,884 m.) and Cantal (1,858 m.) date from the Pontian and the Lower Pliocene; the cones of Velay belong to the Upper Pliocene.

The volcanoes of the Central Massif are of many different types:

(*a*) The great Strombolian volcanoes of Mont Dore and Cantal. Le Cézallier was an explosive volcano before the discharge of

These various volcanic phenomena have added a whole range of different relief forms to the morphology of ancient massifs: the blister-like formations of the Dômes chain, flattened cones in the Cézallier mountains, the great masses of Cantal, the lava flows, either linear or in sheets, with their rough or smooth surfaces, which are to be found in Aubrac or Velay. Erosion acting on these recently formed masses has created still more variety of shapes. It has fragmented the cones and divided their flanks into *planèzes*, and freed the necks of the volcanoes from the accumulation of scoria and ash with which they were covered, as in the Bassin du Puy, and freed the mesas and lava flows from the softer materials into which the lava had flowed, as in the lava fields of the Limagne. Volcanic morphology has caused unaccustomed changes in the topography of a rock formation, artificially increasing heights, altering hydrographic systems by volcanic barrier lakes and by changes in the course of rivers such as the Truyère, and either creating extensive zones of repellent uniformity, permeable and without valleys, or, on the contrary, breaking up the landscape into a disordered array of compartments.

Cycles of erosion and erosion surfaces

Since the post-Hercynian erosional surface was formed, alternate marine transgressions and tectonic movements have set off cycles of erosion starting at different base-levels and acting on differing amounts of available relief. There has thus been a very large number of contrasting ways in which the initial surface of the ancient massifs could be destroyed or altered; evidence of this is still seen in the complexity of the erosion surfaces and the difficulty of reconstructing them.

The Palaeogene surface is one of the largest erosion surfaces affecting the ancient massifs. Under the influence of the tropical climate of the Eocene, the rocks were subjected to intense soil-forming processes. The crystalline rocks were decomposed into very thick beds of sand, more or less lateritic in type. This has been referred to as a 'Tertiary disease' of the rocks. This surface has its characteristic deposits: ferruginous residual sands (*sidérolithique*), lateritic clays, aeolian deposits and basin deposits. The morpho-climatic conditions suggest that these surfaces are of the pediplain type with residual inselbergs rather than a peneplain brought about by erosion in a temperate climate.

This intensely eroded topography began to take shape as far back as the Jurassic and the Cretaceous, when the ancient massifs appeared above the sea as islands, peninsulas and archipelagos, or were temporarily covered by seas whose waters contributed to the levelling of the relief.

In certain parts of the Central Massif this Palaeogene surface can be divided into a sub-Oligocene surface [4] and a late Oligocene surface. [5] We can make this distinction because they are separated by the episode of Oligo-

cene sedimentation which followed the downfaulting of fragments of the core. This Palaeogene surface plays a dominant part in the present morphology of the Central Massif.

Since the Palaeogene, the erosional surfaces which have been recognised are more localised and less clearly marked, as they were formed between mountain-building phases which limited, in both time and space, the stable conditions necessary for the perfect formation of an erosional surface. In the Central Massif a Miocene surface, which had only begun to evolve, has been noted in the crystalline rocks on the western edge of the Limagne; it is contemporary with the deposition of the Sologne sands. On the western edge of the rift-valley of Montbrison, stepped Miocene surfaces, slotting into the Aquitanian surface, are covered by gravel containing angular quartz and heavily encrusted flints. This surface is of the same age as that which bevelled the Causses and the neighbouring crystalline regions before they were uplifted. On the eastern border of the Central Massif an extensive area with gentle slopes between 480 and 320 m. above sea-level, below Mont Pilat and above the Rhône valley, is taken to be a pediment of the Middle and Upper Miocene, which succeeded a primitive fault-scarp.

Finally, evidence of a Mio-Pliocene morphology has been found, in the form of surfaces in the crystalline Bourbonnais, associated with the deposition of the Bourbonnais sands; also evidence of wide valleys dominating the Quaternary valleys in the Forez region.

The periphery of the Armorican massif carries erosion surfaces of more recent times (the Sainte-Anne and Ploermel surfaces of A. Guilcher). They are found between 80 and 100m. above sea-level to the west and to the east of Quimper in Trégor and Goello, and at the bottom of the Brest roadstead.

It is, however, the post-Hercynian surface which very often remains the dominant surface of the ancient massifs. Certain authors have recently shown that all the cycles of erosion following that which resulted in the post-Hercynian surface together removed only a minute thickness of the land. In western Vendée, for example, 'since the lower Cenomanian, the entire morphological history has taken place in a layer nowhere more than 70 m. thick' (M. Ters). More often than not, the surfaces of unconformity of various ages are juxtaposed in a composite surface to which all cycles contribute, with the post-Hercynian surface as the archetype. On the Grands Causses the Palaeogene surface was replaced at a lower altitude by broad surfaces of Pontian age attributed by some authors to pediplanation processes.

The example of Limousin

The topography of Limousin shows a series of broad, stepped plateaux culminating in the Plateau of La Montagne (or Millevaches); each step is reached from the one below by slopes which, according to the sector in which they occur, are rectilinear and homogeneous, or sinuous, even preceded by outliers. Limousin is a veritable laboratory for morphological research and has continually attracted scholars since 1910, when a first article by A. Demangeon appeared. Later, H. Baulig and A. Perpillou saw the general topography of Limousin as a succession of erosion surfaces arranged in steps. A. Perpillou sees it as a stepped succession of four erosion surfaces (Baulig had distinguished two): the highest surface, pre-Liassic, of La Montagne, from 950 to 750 m.; the sub-Cretaceous surface (650–580 m.), which is particularly well developed in the south-east (Haute Marche, Monts de Blond); the

Palaeogene surface (460–360 m.), covered by ferruginous sands (*sidérolithique*); the surface of the Basse Marche plateaux (340–200 m.), belonging to the Miocene and connected with the Sologne sands. This interpretation postulates a polycyclic evolution with no local tectonic movements, but only large-scale warping. The hills which subsist on lower surfaces are, according to these ideas, residual monadnocks.

Recently, J. Beaujeu and B. Bomer brought forward an interpretation on mobilist lines. Close study of scarps shows that most of them cannot be explained by lithological contrasts or by contacts between successive erosion levels. On the contrary, their appearance suggests a tectonic origin, the eroded surfaces having been folded and faulted. The Monts de Blond and the Monts d'Ambazac, and probably the whole of La Montagne too, are thus considered as horsts. But we still have to solve the problem of the number and the dating of the surfaces. B. Bomer thinks they all belong to the Palaeogene surface; J. Beaujeu and A. Meynier distinguish the post-Hercynian and pre-Triassic summit surface from the lower ones, which they consider to be Palaeogene. Both these authors, though they differ on a few points, see the morphological evolution as a rhythmic succession of phases of deformation and cycles of erosion.

Structural morphology and differential erosion in the ancient massifs

Even though erosion surfaces truncate the ancient massifs, that is not to say that there is

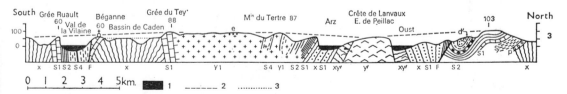

Fig. 7. Section across the Armorican massif in the lower Vilaine region. (Source: A. Guilcher, *Le relief de la Bretagne méridionale*, folder III, section 3)
1. Recent alluvium. 2. Eocene surface. 3. Surface of the Caden basin. F. Primary fault. y′. Lanvaux granite. y1. granulite. x. Brioverian schists. P. Montfort puddingstone. XS1. Shales and arkoses of Bains. S1. Armorican sandstone. S2. Angers shales. S4. Gothlandian shales. d′. Gedinnian shales and quartzites.

B

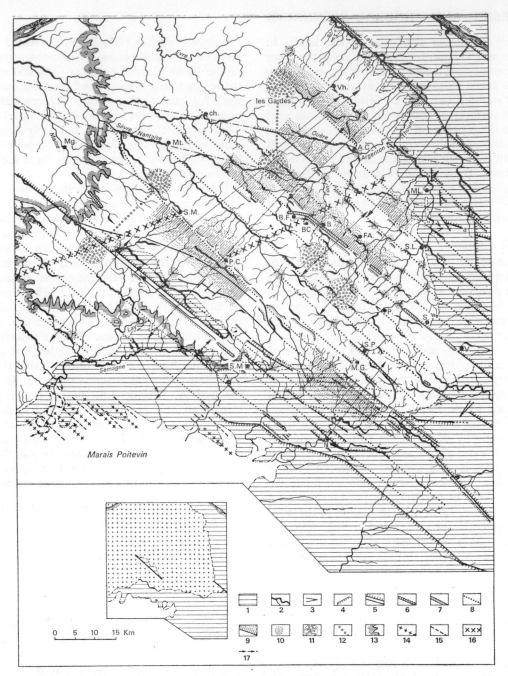

Fig. 8.   Structure of the eastern part of the Bocage of Vendée and the Gâtine de Parthenay.   (Source: M. Gautier, *Ann. de Géog.*, no. 320, 1951, pp. 188–9)

1. Liassic, Jurassic and Cretaceous.   2. Watercourses the direction of which is adjusted to Primary disturbances.   3. Dry valleys and structural valleys.   4. Structural escarpments.   5. Known faults. 6. Known flexures.   7. Quartz veins.   8. Structural alignments.   9. Tilted blocks.   10. Aligned confluence zones.   11. Principal poles of drainage dispersal.   12. Water partings linking these poles.   13. 80 m. contour line in Vendée.   14. Tertiary anticlines.   15. Tertiary synclines.   16. Axes of Tertiary upwarp-

no structural morphology. Sometimes a line of hills or a ridge breaks the uniformity of the surface in an abnormal way, obscuring the horizon, and separates two plateaux of the same height, or joins two stepped surfaces (fig. 7).

Appalachian morphology has long been recognised in ancient massifs. Ridges, often rectilinear but sometimes bent into a hairpin shape, formed of quartzite and Palaeozoic limestones, alternate with depressions eroded in the schists. The Appalachian relief is particularly well developed in the Armorican massif (Normandy *Bocage*, Vannetais, Finistère).

Modern research has stressed the importance, hitherto neglected, of recent tectonic movements in the ancient massifs, and as a result of these, of scarp formation connected with Tertiary faults, folding, tilted blocks, inclined planes or, more simply, fractures which changed the course of the rivers in recent times (fig. 8). In the Central Massif, for example, certain scarps date from the Pliocene (such as that of Espinouse, above the Orb and the Taur). Velay and the Limagne d'Issoire were affected by movements in the Upper Pliocene. It would also be well to discover whether these deformations belong to the Tertiary both in age and form, or whether they date from the Tertiary but follow Hercynian lines.

Moreover, laboratory studies have shown that crystalline and metamorphic rocks show a very unequal degree of sensitivity to the action of the various systems of erosion. Granite, for example, may behave as a resistant rock, producing uplands (such as Sidobre), or as a weak rock, giving rise to depressions (such as Vénazès and the south of Aurillac), depending on its chemical composition, its porosity, the number of joints, the slopes and the system of erosion which attacks it. In Corsica the granitic landscapes—rounded hills, convex slopes, slowly weathered surfaces—differ from the more rugged granulitic landscapes with their ridges and sharp peaks.

The rounded topographical forms for which the landscapes of Sidobre and Huelgoat are famous are explained by the exposure either on the surface or more deeply of granite blocks bounded by an orthogonal network of joints in a coarse-grained granite.

As a result of these detailed studies, we are now beginning to recognise in the ancient massifs the existence of a double framework, structural and lithological, and relatively subtle, and not merely uniform expanses of confused topography.

We must not forget, moreover, that the topography of the ancient massifs, as used and organised by man, consists of valleys, large and small, rather than of escarpments and ridges, which are relatively uncommon. In these Hercynian regions of impermeable rocks

TABLE V. HYDRO-MORPHOLOGICAL INDICES IN ANCIENT MASSIFS

Region	Rock	Drainage density* (km./km.²)	Density of thalwegs† (km./km.²)
Limousin .	Granite	1·94	2·61
Morvan .	Granite	0·35	2·54

* Drainage density = Total length of water courses, divided by the surface area of the basin (or surface area otherwise defined).

† Density of thalwegs = Total length of valleys, whether drained or not, divided by the surface area of the basin.

there is a very high density of valleys that divide the surfaces into hills and interfluves of reduced size, 'breaking up' the topography.

The above hydro-morphological indices

ing. 17. Former course of the Lay. Abbreviations: A.C., Argenton-Château; B., Bressuire; B.C., Breuil-Chaussée; B.F., Brétignolles-la-Faye; Bo., Boussais; C., Chantonnay; Ch., Cholet; F.A., Faye-l'Abbesse; F.C., Fontenay-le-Comte; L., Lezay; M., Mareuil; M.G., Mazières-en-Gâtine; Mg., Montaigu; Ml., Maulais; Mt., Mortagne; N., Niort; P., Parthenay; P.C., Puy-Crapeau; Pi., Pissotte; S., Saumur (to the north-east, on the Loire), Saurais (in the east of the map); S.L., Saint-Loup; S.M., Saint-Maixent (in the south-east), Saint-Michel-Mont-Mercure (in the centre); S.M.C., Saint-Michel-le-Cloucq; S.P., Saint-Pardoux; T., Thouars; V., Vasles; Vh., Vihiers. The lines with double arrows indicate the direction of sections.

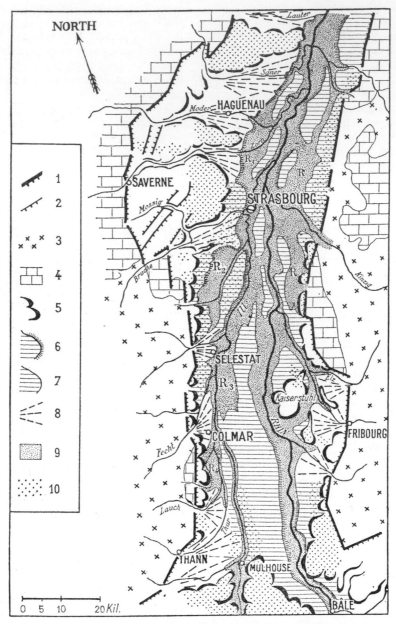

Fig. 9. The Alsace–Baden plain. Morphological sketch. (Source: E. Juillard, 'Une carte des formes de relief dans la plaine d'Alsace–Bade', *L'Information Géographique*, J.-B. Baillière, May–June 1949, p. 117)

1. Main boundary fault.   2. Other fault influencing the topography.   3. Ancient massif.   4. Sedimentary covering.   5. Border of a hilly area.   6. Low terrace with a clear edge.   7. Low terrace without a clear edge.   8. Alluvial cone grading to the low terrace.   9. Present alluvial plain and *ried* (R₁, Ried of Hoerdt; R₂, of the Andlau; R₃, of Sélestat; R₄, of Rouffach).   10. Loess covering.

clearly show the extent to which the relief is broken up. It can be seen that dry valleys play an important part; the water is in fact easily absorbed by the sandy mantle and forms a shallow aquifer which feeds the springs.

In complete contrast to this topography of the ancient massifs is that of subsidence zones and fault troughs such as the Causses or the plain of Alsace (fig. 9).

B. Sedimentary Basins

The relief forms of sedimentary basins derive from a more recent morphological history than those of the ancient massifs; this history began with periods of marine regression. Cycles of continental erosion then re-modelled the warped and uplifted sediments.

Like the ancient massifs, the basins were subjected to cycles of erosion, transgressions and deformations. Each progressively took on its own individual character, depending on the degree to which its borders were raised or depressed and its central area subsided, and on the erosional stripping of the sedimentary mantle covering the uplifted ancient massifs.

The sedimentary regions of Hercynian France are divided between two great basins; the Aquitaine basin and the Paris basin. North of the Artois axis which marks the northern boundary of the Paris basin, the Flanders area belongs to another basin, called the Anglo-Flemish basin.

SEDIMENTATION

The history of sedimentation affects the morphological analysis of the basins, since the lithology and the thickness of the beds depend on it. The Paris basin is characterised by the large scale of subsidence, the migration of the centre of the subsidence zone and the preponderance of limestone and chalk.

The Jurassic beds are more than 1,000 m. thick in Lorraine and Champagne; but the subsidence was a progressive one. The idea of *subsidence* was defined in 1930 by P. Pruvost, following E. de Margerie: the sea bottom gradually subsides, largely beneath the weight of the sediment deposited; the depth

of the sea, and thus the conditions in which sedimentation takes place, remain in this way relatively constant. For this reason limestone, particularly coral limestone, predominates in Jurassic sedimentation. After a phase of regression and emergence at the end of the Jurassic and the beginning of the Cretaceous, the Cretaceous seas invaded the whole of the Paris basin, depositing essentially chalky material. Chalk, either pure or with varied facies—marly chalk, glauconitic chalk, sandy chalk and even micaceous chalk— belongs specifically to this period. It is the result of the sedimentation of calcareous materials of no great depth (100–500 m.) and with no terrigenous deposits of any significance. But as subsidence continued, the chalky beds could be deposited in great thickness. However, the centre of subsidence moved from Lorraine to the Paris region, where borings have shown the greatest thicknesses ever found in Cretaceous rocks.

After a long period of emergence at the end of the Cretaceous, the sea once more invaded the Paris basin, but with much less regularity, advancing, then retreating, leaving lakes and lagoons; Eocene and Oligocene sedimentation provides alternations of sand, clay and limestone in a succession which has now become classic; in the centre of the Paris basin the Oligocene period ends with the lacustrine limestone of Beauce (fig. 11).

Then in the Miocene the sedimentation moved south-westwards as shelly sand was brought by the sea along a synclinal trough along the line of the lower Loire.

The extent of the Pliocene transgression in the Paris basin is a problem as yet unsolved. Some authors consider that the basin was completely unaffected by this transgression, which was limited, on the one hand, to an 'English Channel', which deposited fossiliferous sediments in Basse-Normandie and on the South Downs, and, on the other hand, to a North Sea, the sediments of which are found no farther south than the northern slopes of Artois and the summits of the Monts de Flandre (Diestian conglomerate).

Other geographers, on the other hand, think

it probable that there was an extensive transgression starting with these epicontinental
seas and occurring particularly in the Picardy
synclinorium, or at least a river-borne sedimentation connected with this transgression
(A. Cholley).

The geological history of the Aquitaine
basin is rather different, and more varied,
because its surrounding areas are of such
diverse types—the Central Massif to the north
and east, the Pyrenees to the south. In the
northern half, between the Garonne and the
Central Massif, the subsidence of the basement remained limited all through the
Secondary and Tertiary periods, and the sea
was never very deep, so that in the Jurassic
the sedimentation was of limestone similar to
that of the Paris basin—the limestone of
Quercy and Périgord. In the Cretaceous it
comprised sand, marl, gritty limestone and
limestone beds sandwiched between these
weaker beds.

In the south of the Aquitaine basin, on the
other hand, the palaeogeography depends on
the history of the Pyrenean range. A trench
which first began to form in the Cretaceous
and was accentuated in the Tertiary, when it
varied in size and position, became the re-
pository for the flysch, sandstones, schists and
limestones resulting from the erosion of the
Pyrenees. In the Tertiary, after the Pyrenean
folding, the sedimentation was threefold:
marine deposits from seas which reached the
basin by way of the wide oceanic front, and
which were particularly extensive in the
Middle Oligocene and the Burdigalian, but
which did not pass the meridian of Bordeaux;
lacustrine deposits, either calcareous or
detrital (sandstones, molasse, conglomerates),
laid down under more or less endoreic conditions in tropical climates; continental
deposits, either river-borne or detrital, and
taking the form of sheets of alluvium, and
nappes caused by mass flow, coming either
from the Central Massif or the Pyrenees (such
as the Pliocene sands underlying the plain of
the Landes). The main deposits came from
the Pyrenees; the great quantities of debris
forming the plateau of Lannemezan, spread

out in several cones between the valleys of the
Aspe and of the Salat, have fossilised the
sedimentary rocks of the Aquitaine basin, and
built up a remarkable piedmont feature.

DEFORMATIONS AND STRUCTURE OF THE
    BASINS

Deformations of the beds in sedimentary
basins are closely dependent on those of the
blocks on which they rest and also on the
depth of the blocks. If the sedimentary
covering is thin, the deformations of the basement, which is rigid and brittle, are reflected
in it; the basement faults, when posthumous
movement occurs, bring about distortion of
the sedimentary mantle expressed in faults or
folds according to the degree of plasticity of
the beds. In the north-east of the Paris basin
the Triassic and Liassic beds are intensely
faulted and folded in the Variscan direction;
this applies also in the Nivernais, Artois and
Boulonnais; the faults in Artois are almost all
Hercynian faults of Armorican trend along
which posthumous movement occurred in the
Tertiary, breaking the Cretaceous cover.

Where, on the other hand, the sedimentary
cover is very thick, the recent movements of
the basement have not been transmitted to it
and the sedimentary material has behaved
autonomously, folding independently. The
independence of the sedimentary rocks can
even go as far as an actual inversion. The
anticline of the Pays de Bray was formed on
the site of a subsidence zone which had
existed from the beginning of the Secondary,
and where the sedimentary beds were at their
thickest (the Primary was reached at Ferrières-
en-Bray at a depth of 1,205 m.).

In the structure of a sedimentary basin mass
deformations and secondary deformations are
superimposed. We will take the Paris basin
as an example.

Major deformations of the Paris basin

First of all there are *subsidence zones*, the heart
of the basin, where the Cretaceous and Tertiary deposits are particularly thick, and the
English Channel.

The Channel. The fact that this epicontinental sea (100 m. deep at Hurd's Deep, to the
north of Guernsey) cuts through both the
Paris and Hampshire basins and the ancient
massifs of Cornwall and Brittany might suggest that the Channel is of recent origin, and
that it came in at a late date to interrupt the
continuity of a unified geological structure.
In fact, the Channel is an ancient and stable
feature of the palaeogeography of western
Europe. It corresponds to a subsidence zone
underlain, between Cornwall and Brittany, by
almost 1,000 m. of Secondary and Tertiary
beds, mainly Cretaceous in the west, and
Tertiary between the sedimentary basins.

These depressed regions are separated by
anticlinal zones; from Basse-Normandie to
Haut-Boulonnais, Haute-Normandie and
western Picardy correspond to an anticlinal
zone between the Channel depression and the
Paris basin; this regional uplift is shown in
altitudes exceeding 100 m. and reaching 200 in
several places. There are also uplifts along
the periphery of the basin where erosion of
the sedimentary cover following differential
uplift of the Hercynian borders defines its
limits. The western borders of the Paris
basin have been only moderately uplifted and
there is no visible break in relief between the
basin and the ancient massif.

The southern and eastern borders, on the
contrary, being near the Alpine regions, have
been very strongly uplifted; the regional
slope from south-east to north-west, with the
rivers following the same direction, dates from
the Tertiary. The northern border—the
Ardennes massif—was formed later, after the
Miocene; movement probably occurred
along the Artois anticlinal axis during the
Pliocene.

If we compare these mass deformations
with the general dip of the beds, we notice a
curious contrast: on the one hand, a general
dip of all the sedimentary beds of the Paris
basin from north to south, the Tertiary rocks
reaching their lowest point in the Loire depression; on the other hand, the differential uplifts of surrounding areas which have formed
a slope not quite in the opposite direction, but
oblique to the dip of the beds, following the
S.E.–N.W. direction.

Secondary features

To this picture of major deformations we can
add minor deformations of very varied type
and extent: anticlinal and synclinal undulations in the form of continuous folds, short
folds, domes or small basins.

The old conception of perfectly continuous
folds running south-east to north-west across
the whole of the Paris basin has been superseded by the more realistic conception of a
structure made up of basins, large and small,
with more complex deformations resulting
from the truncation of undulations running in
various directions. Though many features
run from south-east to north-west throughout
Hercynian France, where the prevailing direction is that of the Armorican massif, there are
also some trending north to south and west to
east. West to east features are particularly
important in the western Paris basin, Perche,
Maine (the Merlerault anticline) and the
borders of Picardy and Normandy. In this
region the anticlinal axis of Bray, running
south-east to north-west, is crossed near
Forges-les-Eaux by a large anticlinal up-
warping running west to east, which can be
followed from the western extremity of the
Pays de Caux as far as Picardy. The river
system depends on this axis, which is more
recent than the Bray anticline.

Faults also play their part in the more detailed structure of the sedimentary basins;
they accompany folds, like the faults of Bray
or those of the northern flank of the Artois
anticline, or appear in isolation; intermediate
forms, such as asymmetric folds and flexures,
are the most common.

RECENT CYCLES OF EROSION AND EROSION
    SURFACES

Like the ancient massifs, the sedimentary
basins bear witness to numerous episodes
of erosional planation interpolated between
the episodes of transgression and those of
emergence and deformation. The erosion

surfaces appearing in the present morphology of these basins belong essentially to the Tertiary.

Some of them were formed before the major Alpine phases, by pre-Tertiary and Palaeogene planations. Others are later than the deformations connected with the Alpine folding; these are Neogene surfaces.

Pre-Tertiary and Palaeogene surfaces

Even more than in the ancient massifs, the surfaces belonging to the Cretaceous and the beginning of the Tertiary appear as the basic element of the morphology. These planations occurred on Jurassic and Cretaceous rocks between the end of the Cretaceous transgressions and the beginning of the Eocene transgressions. The resulting surface can be identified thanks to the presence of Eocene deposits, which are relics of its fossilisation and later exhumation, and which are unconformable with the Mesozoic sedimentary rocks on which they lie. This surface, then, was fossilised by Eocene seas and lagoons which filled up the valleys, and also fossilised a Karst topography in certain limestone and chalk areas. It is particularly well developed in the chalk plains of Picardy and Normandy.

Clay with flints is often considered to be a deposit which can be correlated with this early Tertiary surface, and to be evidence of the decalcification of chalk on exposure to air. In fact the expression 'clay with flints' embraces several different types of formation: black clay with flints, found in very thin layers between chalk and Tertiary rocks, is a true product of decalcification, but can be formed below the surface; red clay with flints, which is very often transformed into residual clay with flints, never found under Tertiary rocks, incorporates flows of Eocene sedimentary clay and smoothed pebbles; it was laid down from the end of the Cretaceous to the Eocene and Oligocene, spreading over the flanks of anticlinal zones in the process of upheaval.

Phosphorites were formed in the cavities of the karstic Jurassic limestone plateaux of the Aquitaine basin, from the upper Eocene to the Oligocene. This erosion surface is covered by the reddish clay of the Cainozoic (*sidérolithique*).

Neogene planation

In the Paris basin, after the Middle Oligocene sea had receded (leaving the sands of Fontainebleau), and after the Oligocene deformations, a new cycle of erosion set in. It took place in a tropical or subtropical climate, tending towards aridity which gave rise to savanna or steppe morphology. The Upper Oligocene limestones of the Beauce Lake are contemporaneous with this phase. Rivers (*oueds* or *fumare*) coming from the south and bringing kaolinic terrigenous elements (such as the molasse of the Gâtinais) flowed into the Beauce lake. The upper part of the Beauce limestone was silicified and transformed into 'millstone' (*meulière*), a rock with cavities. West of the Paris basin the Miocene surface is marked out by the vast expanses of the Lozère sands, a granitic sand characterised by large blunt quartz crystals and smaller quartz grains, and containing granite shingle (blocks embedded in a flow of mud). Long trains of this sand occur from Sologne to Basse-Seine, and are found as far as the north bank of the Seine, to the north of the Seine fault-fold, which must, therefore, have been planed off at this period. These Lozère sands belong to a type of arid fluviatile sediment brought by a proto-Loire, a tributary of the Seine, flowing down the alluvial cone of the Sologne sands. Later the accentuation of the Basse-Loire depression and the transgressions of the Crag sea caused this Loire to be diverted.

In the Aquitaine basin the Upper Oligocene '*meulière*' surface accounts for the forms of erosion: it was created at the expense of the Cretaceous and Tertiary limestones, and its silica is derived from the sand formations of Périgord.

Ancient surfaces

We cannot, however, leave out of account the traces of some older planations which can be observed on the periphery of the basins. The seas receded generally at the end of the Portlandian (Upper Jurassic), and as the land emerged, a complex of Purbeckian and Wealden lakes and lagoons was substituted. The transgressive Cretaceous deposits rest unconformably on the extremely varied Jurassic levels. This post-Jurassic and pre-Cretaceous surface is found on the periphery of sedimentary basins in Barrois, the eastern Paris basin and the Jurassic limestone plateaux disposed around Morvan, and in the nuclei of breached anticlinal domes (*boutonnières*) such as Bray and the Boulonnais, where it plays a fundamental part. This surface is pre-Cenomanian in Périgord.

These erosion surfaces are very distinct in the centre of the sedimentary basins, where they are separated, and the oldest ones fossilised, by the sedimentary series left by intervening transgressions; but their projections intersect one another on the peripheral aureoles at very small angles and they are much more difficult to distinguish there. For this reason, the farther away these surfaces are from the centre of the basins, the greater is the tendency to interpret them as polycyclic. This crowding of the erosion surfaces, combined with the uplift of the borders, has exposed the aureoles of the sedimentary basins.[6]

After the Miocene planations, the topography of the sedimentary basins has been modified only locally by erosion levels connected with the Pliocene sedimentation or transgressions (see above), or with the various epicycles which are landmarks in the formation of the river systems.

A close and objective study shows the importance of valley-side benches and erosion levels. H. Baulig drew attention to their development as early as 1928, but the inadequacy of the methods concerned with their identification and explanation and the lack of field mapping, then later the greater interest in research into climatic morphology, has caused us to lose sight of this aspect of morphology.

The erosion levels are no less present than in the ancient massifs, and they represent one of the most familiar forms of the topography of the basins; erosional floors exist in the

Boulonnais, the Pays de Bray and Flanders (where, at 60 m., they testify to the stripping of the enormous mass of weak sediments in the Flemish basin of Eocene to Pliocene age).

STRUCTURAL AND LITHOLOGICAL
    MORPHOLOGY

Recent cycles of erosion have brought out the lithological and structural contrasts shown by the sedimentary rocks in the basins. In the Paris basin the structural morphology is particularly well developed in the Jurassic and Tertiary rocks, owing to the frequently alternating layers of hard and soft rock.

The resistant beds of the Jurassic in the east of the basin are found in many areas from the newest to the oldest stages (fig. 10):

(a) The Barrois limestone (Portlandian) lying on Kimmeridgian clay.

(b) The corallian limestone of the Sequanian lying on Oxfordian and Callovian clay, forming the Côtes de Meuse cuesta.

(c) The crinoidal limestone of the Bajocian, lying on Liassic sands and marls, forming the Côtes de Moselle.

(d) Limestone with Gryphaea, frequently dividing the cuestas of the Bajocian (as in the Plaine).

(e) The shelly limestone of the Middle Trias and the Bunter Sandstone of the Lower Trias which lie directly on the basement, or are separated from it locally by weak Permian rocks (as in the Saint-Dié basin).

The series of Tertiary rocks shows a similar alternation (fig. 11): the Beauce limestone resting on the Fontainebleau sands, the Brie limestone on Middle Oligocene marls and gypsum, the Saint-Ouen limestone on the Beauchamp sands, Lutetian limestone on Eocene sands and clays.

The structural morphology consists here essentially of structural planes more or less tilted, either plains (as in Beauce) or plateaux (as in Soissonnais) and systems of cuestas accompanied by outliers. Fault-scarps, and monoclinal hills, play a strictly local role or are found in association with cuestas, while the very occasional anticlinal depressions

have developed on the most accentuated anticlines. The Pays de Bray and the Boulonnais are only two outstanding examples of a
'Wealden' morphology with a great variety of
size, origin and development.

Secondary structural features appear in the
outline of the cuestas (as in Lorraine) and in
the position of some outliers (as in the Paris
region).

beds, as in the Agen region. But there is
nothing corresponding to the structural
morphology of the Paris basin. Similarly, a
morphology of sand and clay, without a limestone backbone, predominates in Flanders.

But, independently of structural conditions,
lithological differences are responsible for
contrasts in the morphology of the sedimentary basins.

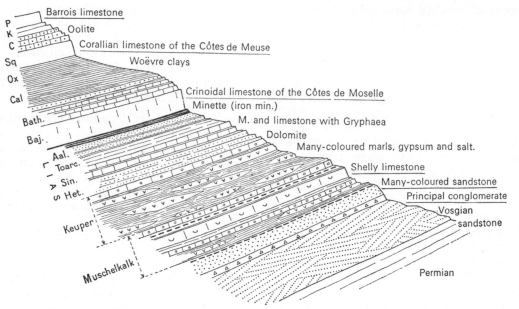

Fig. 10. Schematic section of secondary formations in the east of the Paris basin. (Source: E. De
Martonne, *Géographie Universelle*, A. Colin, Vol. VI)
Abbreviations: Het., Hettangian; Sin., Sinemurian; Toarc., Toarcian; Aal., Aalenian; Baj., Bajocian;
Bath., Bathonian; Cal., Callovian; Ox., Oxfordian; Sq., Sequanian; C., Corallian; K., Kimmeridgian;
P., Portlandian.

The Cretaceous rocks, on the other hand,
show little contrast; the very slight lithological differences between the chalk and the
marls result in a very subdued structural
morphology.

In the Aquitaine basin the structural morphology is much less clear-cut, because uncemented sediments predominate, and because the limestone horizons are often discontinuous. Structural forms appear mainly
in the limestones of Quercy and Périgord, or
are associated with certain Tertiary limestone

The varied nature of the outcrops has
brought with it a large number of different
types of hydro-morphological features; the
number of valleys and the importance of dry
or intermittently dry valleys varies considerably from one outcrop to the next. Besides
the lithology, slope and climatic conditions
act as complementary factors.[7] Beauce,
which is a sub-horizontal limestone region, is
most lacking in valleys; over wide tracts of
land they are either non-existent or present
only in the form of very shallow dry valleys.

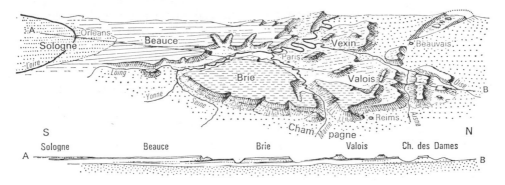

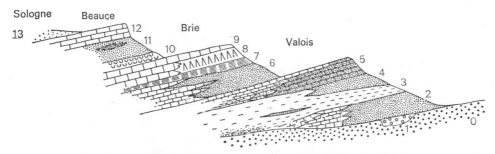

Fig. 11. Composition and morphological role of the Tertiary rocks of the Paris basin. (Source: J. Goguel, *Géologie de la France*, P.U.F.)
Top, perspective diagram showing the relationship between the main structural surfaces; and profile along the line A–B. Bottom, stratigraphical profile.

O. Chalk. 1. First marine deposits of the Tertiary in the depressions in the infra-Eocene surface. 2. Thanetian (Bracheux sands). 3. Sparnatian (plastic clay and lignites). 4. Ypresian (nummulitic sand). 5. Lutetian (coarse limestone). 6. Bartonian (Beauchamp sands with limestone intercalations, Saint-Ouen limestone). 7. Sannoisian (gypsiferous clay, gypsum and freshwater limestone). 8. Sannoisian (supergypsiferous marl). 9. Sannoisian (Brie limestone). 10. Stampian (oyster marl). 11. Stampian (Fontainebleau sands). 12. Chattian (lacustrine limestone of Beauce). 13. Miocene (river sand appearing in belts).

On the Jurassic plateaux the drainage is interrupted to varying degrees; dry valleys predominate in the limestone areas to the east of the Paris basin, and karstic forms are found on the interfluves (in the form of closed depressions). In Quercy and Périgord the karstic forms are much more highly developed. Secondary and also Tertiary marl, sand and clay terrains have more highly developed hydrographic systems. Contrasts are conspicuous on the maps and create a great variety of topographic forms: river-valleys may be many or few, long or short, and the length of the interfluves varies too. The figures given in Table VI serve to emphasise the contrasts in the hydrography of the sedimentary regions.

TABLE VI. HYDRO-MORPHOLOGICAL
INDICES IN SEDIMENTARY REGIONS

Region	Rock	Drainage density (km./km.²)	Density of thalwegs (km./km.²)	$\frac{DD}{DT}$
Houtland (Flanders).	Clay and sand	0·58	0·80	72%
Beauce . .	Limestone	0	0·83	0%
Champagne .	White chalk	0·17	1·10	15%
Picardy plateau .	Chalk	0·08	0·95	8%
Woëvre . .	Clays	0·78	1·67	47%

C. The Morphological Interdependence of the Ancient Massifs and the Sedimentary Basins

It can be seen from the foregoing pages that the morphological evolution of the ancient massifs and that of the sedimentary basins go hand in hand. The broad lines of their relief have been determined by the same deformations, the same erosion surfaces and the same river systems. In the history of Hercynian France the Central Massif, acting as a dispersal centre for the rivers, played an important part, particularly in the Eocene and Oligocene. Its weathering provided materials which were spread in sheets of varying thickness over the sedimentary rocks of the basins (such as the formations of Lozère, Sologne and Brenne), even fossilising subsequent depressions and Eocene, Oligocene or pre-Tertiary cuestas (as in Berry).

Hydrographic Unity

The hydrographic unity of Hercynian France is truly remarkable. The main rivers and their tributaries, the Loire, the Seine, the Meuse, the Moselle, the Garonne and its right-bank tributaries, and the Charente, take no account of the distinction between basins and massifs. The great river axes run north-west, west and south-west from the main divide of the relief which we defined at the beginning of this chapter. The Seine, with the Tertiary hollow of the Paris basin, the lower Loire, rising in the depression made by the Crag sea, and the Garonne, in the central vale of the Aquitaine basin, collected the greater part of the run-off. The complete picture is that of an immense slope, which was already half formed in the Palaeogene and accentuated in the Neogene, but with local disturbances; north–south trough-faulting and volcanic activity in the Central Massif created a secondary central watershed.

The small number of watersheds in Hercynian France is remarkable. They are: the Monts d'Arrée, the Gâtine, Perche, the Pays de Bray, the ridge of Artois, Cantal, which we have already mentioned, and the crystalline Vosges, which form an extension of the major watershed. These watersheds correspond to the axes of recent uplifts, probably Pliocene in age.

Hydrographic anomalies are rare and strictly local, each involving not a river system but one single river; one of the most important problems is that of how the Meuse crosses the Ardennes massif. The most probable explanation is that of antecedence; the Meuse must have been established on an Oligo-Miocene slope before the uplifting of the massif.

Contact Zones of Massifs and Basins

These offer a great variety of morphological types because numerous factors are involved; lithology of the basement, lithology of the sedimentary rocks, structural dip irregularities and the nature of the erosion surfaces.

The three main morphological types peculiar to transitional zones are found in Hercynian France:

The type under slope (*en glacis*). The topography of the massif is continued into the basin without any differential erosion, either because the rocks are equally resistant on both sides, as on the margins of the Armorican massif, or because the zone of unconformity has been fossilised by sheets of detritus, such as the Eocene ferruginous sands (*sidérolithique*) on the north-western border of Limousin, in the *pays* of Brenne (fig. 12).

The classic type of peripheral depression hollowed out of weak Permo-Triassic rocks, limited on the side of the massif by the eroded slope of the exposed post-Hercynian surface, and on the side of the basin by the cuesta formed by the first limestone bed of the Jurassic (as on the northern border of Morvan).[8]

The transitional type, broken by structural irregularities, either folds or faults. Beyond a depression which may be no more than a fault-line valley, a fault-line scarp rises facing the ancient massif. This occurs on the south-western border of the Central Massif, in Auxois and in Bazois (fig. 5).

Cols

Cols (*seuils* = 'gates' or 'gaps') represent another type of contact between the sedimentary mantle and the basement. The sedimentary series are generally less thick, the

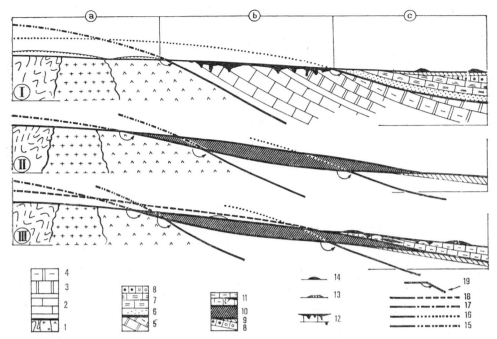

Fig. 12.   Morphological evolution of Brenne.   (Source: C. Klein, *Norois*, 1962, p. 250)

I. Infra-Siderolithic surface (diagrammatic section): (*a*) Area of residual sands and siderolithic materials *in situ*, associated with the crystalline rocks of Limousin.   (*b*) Area of pisolitic red clay (with or without flints) associated with Jurassic limestone outcrops.   (*c*) Area of clay with flints and Spongiae remains associated with Turonian and Senonian chalk outcrops.
II. Late Siderolithic surface (diagrammatic section).
III. Post-Siderolithic surface (diagrammatic section).

1. Crystalline basement.   2–8. Mesozoic series.   2. Triassic and Liassic.   3. Bajocian–Bathonian. 4. Callovian–Oxfordian.   5. Rauratian (Corallian)–Sequanian.   6. Cenomanian (Vierzon sands and oyster marl).   7. Turonian.   8. Senonian.   9. Clay with flints.   10. Tertiary detrital series of Brenne (upper Eocene).   11. Lacustrine limestone of Poitou and Touraine (Tongrian: Lattorfian and Sannoisian) with interbedded lenses of pisolitic clayey sand (1).   12. Pockets of pisolitic red clay (some on Jurassic limestone and others on Tongrian limestone).   13. Surface silifications (heterochronous).   14. Granitic sand (continental Helvetian).   15. Post-Hercynian surface.   16. Infra-Cenomanian surface.   17. Infra-Siderolithic surface.   18. Late Siderolithic surface.   19. Angle formed by the intersection of two buried erosion surfaces.

basement rocks lie nearer the surface, and there have been many transgressions which have contributed to the morphological evolution of their two margins.

The Poitou gate is the most characteristic of those in Hercynian France.   Here the post-Hercynian surface, fossilised by the Liassic marine deposits, appears on the margins of the old blocks, but the Primary rocks penetrate the cover at fifteen points along the ridge. The col itself was above sea-level from the Argovian to the Upper Cenomanian.   As there are no deposits left by transgressions of the Upper Cretaceous, we still have to consider the question of a pre-Cretaceous surface. In the Tertiary, deformations and epicycles of erosion resulted in multiple local erosion surfaces on which rest continental sediments. These deposits are partly of clay and residual clay with flints, and Cainozoic deposits (*sidérolithique*) such as multi-coloured clay, lacustrine formations and reddish-brown clay, forming divisions in an Eocene surface, and partly cavernous siliceous limestone with red clay filling the cavities, and Aquitanian and Burdigalian sandstone forming patches on an Oligo-Miocene surface. This surface was created by the action of the first of the two marine episodes which the area was still to experience; the transgression of the sea bearing Middle Miocene shelly sands provided, in fact, the base-level for the deposition of Miocene continental sands. This surface is polycyclic; it was begun in the Oligocene in a damp tropical climate and completed in the sub-arid climate of the Miocene. The Pliocene transgression transformed the threshold into a gulf in which the rivers spread out the Miocene deposits to form a base-level plain. After the Pliocene the region received Plio-Quaternary deposits, sand and shingle, quartz and flint of fluviatile origin which came down from the Central Massif. These formations have been disturbed by faulting. The Oligo-Miocene surface was up-warped along a line joining Gâtine to Confolentais, and faulted.

D. The Morphological Heritage of the Quaternary

CLIMATIC CONDITIONS

Only three regions of Hercynian France were directly glaciated; the highlands of Auvergne (Cantal and Forez), the Vosges and Corsica.

Scholars have identified two to four glaciations in the Central Massif. The forms of relief associated with these glaciations are not found in any great quantity, but some do exist: the glacial trough of Haut-Fossat in Forez, the ice-smoothed rocks and the confused topography of Artense, on which the glaciers coming down from the neighbouring volcanoes formed an ice-plateau, and the basin of Bort-les-Orgues. The Vosges glaciation, fed by an ample supply of ice, was relatively wide in scope, and covered all the crystalline blocks of the Vosges; tongue-like glaciers carved out trough-shaped valleys, thrusting their moraines forward as far as Épinal.

Apart from these regions, the rest of France experienced 'peri-glacial' conditions of morphology and climate, as they were only a short distance not only from the glaciers of the Pyrenees and the Alps but also from the glaciers covering part of England and the Netherlands.

During the glaciations, Hercynian France experienced climatic conditions very like those of the present taiga and tundra: cold oceanic climates with abundant snowfalls, causing great fluctuations in the glacial fronts. Fierce winds blew from the north and the east. The ground was frozen to a depth of several metres; the surface thawed only during the short summers or during the retreat phases of the glaciers. Vegetation was sparse, though the north and south of France certainly had different kinds of vegetation and there were periodic variations.

These peri-glacial conditions did not obtain uniformly throughout the older Quaternary. Phases of greater warmth alternated with cold phases, contemporaneously with the advance and retreat of the glaciers.

The problem of Quaternary chronology has been studied for almost a century by geologists, pre-historians, palaeobotanists, palaeontologists, sedimentologists and geomorphologists. It is less important to geographers than knowledge of the forms of relief associated with it. Some understanding of the chronology is, however, essential.

The chronology of the Quaternary in France is linked with the four glacial stages identified in the Alps—Gunz, Mindel, Riss and Wurm—but the glaciations of Great Britain and the Netherlands do not show an equivalent number of phases. Each of the glacial and interglacial periods, which must have lasted 200,000–250,000 years, can be broken down into a succession of smaller climatic oscillations called stadials and interstadials, each lasting some tens of thousands of years, each with a different area of influence and each having its own character (Wurm I–Wurm II). The curve of each stadial and interstadial shows still shorter oscillations. Differences of opinion between specialists are exaggerated by this theoretical hierarchy, since apart from the Alpine regions which were directly glaciated, confusion between phases and stadials is possible, especially as the last glacial stage—the Wurm—was the longest and thus the most intense. Table VII, drawn up after Franck Bourdier, sums up the Quaternary chronology.

the level of the seas, connected with the alternation of glacial and inter-glacial phases.

Deposits and the accumulation of superficial deposits

Gravity plays an essential part in peri-glacial erosion. Slopes were covered with a mantle

TABLE VII. SYNOPTIC TABLE OF THE QUATERNARY
(after F. Bourdier) [9]

Alpine glacial stages	Climate	Soil	Sea-level	Fluviatile deposits	Cultures
POST-WURM	Temperate	As at present	Dunkirkian transgression +5 m. Late Pleistocene (Flandrian) transgression 0 to +15 m.	Peat Marsh	Age of metals (Neolithic) Mesolithic
WURM	Cold	Recent loess (upper) Residual clay (*lehm*) Recent loess (lower)	Pre-Flandrian regression	Gravels Climatic terraces	Magdalenian Aurignacian Mousterian (cave dwellings)
RISS–WURMINTER-GLACIAL	Temperate	Decalcified yellow loams (*limon fendillé*)	Monastirian transgression	Low levels	Levalloisian Acheulean
RISS	Cold	Ancient loess	Regression	Climatic terraces	
MINDEL–RISS INTER-GLACIAL	Warm	Red soils	Tyrrhenian +30 m.	Medium levels	
MINDEL	Cold		Regression (Sicilian II)	High levels	Abbévillian
PRE-MINDEL	Temperate Warm	Indurated loess	Sicilian transgression		
GUNZ	Cold				

PERI-GLACIAL SURFACE RELIEF

The influence of the history of the Quaternary on the relief of Hercynian France cannot be denied and has some most unusual features. But sculptural forms predominate over relief forms proper, excepting those which are the product of accumulation.

Peri-glacial erosion operates by means of a number of different processes:

Gelivation (frost-cracking), which splits solid rocks into fragments through which water can circulate.

Permafrost (permanently frozen ground), which hardens loose ground and brings about landslides by solifluction of the active (thawed) layers on the surface.

Variations in the flow of rivers, bound up with climatic oscillations, and variations in

of materials which had disintegrated through frost and then had been set in motion by solifluction: screes, boulder spreads (as in the Margeride mountains and the Montagne Noire), various slope deposits ranging from gravelly marl to silt, mud flows and screes with a regular alternation of coarse and fine material, all of which can be explained by a succession of years with differing degrees of cold and differing amounts of snow.

The chalk region of Champagne, due to the ease with which chalk is split by frost, sank beneath sheets of gravel which came down from the interfluves and the hill slopes, or were brought by the rivers.[10]

The uneven distribution of these deposits must not be overlooked. Their presence is significant, but their extent and development should not be overrated. They lie on the floors of tributary river-valleys, above valleys or valley-heads which have been opened out into nivation hollows, and they occur on the slopes where the thaw was most marked, while they are absent on the opposite slopes.

Asymmetric valleys

These are among the most widespread legacies of the peri-glacial system of erosion. This asymmetry, mainly affecting valleys running north–south (and especially north-west to south-east), means that hillsides facing west have steep slopes and those facing east have gentle slopes. It is explained by the combined action of west winds and snow.

Limons

These are another type of superficial deposit. (*Limon* is best regarded as a modified form of loess occasionally approximating closely to loess but usually altered, true loess having been preserved only in much drier climates— *Note*, A. J. Hunt.) Minute particles torn from moraines by the wind were deposited in the form of loess, whose dispersal was limited by the presence of vegetation or by zones with heavier rainfall; sometimes these particles accumulate to a depth of several metres. Limon covers wide areas of the Paris basin and certain parts of the Armorican massif, particularly the northern coast of Brittany; the district of Léon owes its fertility to it (fig. 27). Not all limons are of aeolian origin; recent analyses have definitely shown that unconsolidated Tertiary deposits have played an important part in their formation.[11]

Depositional land-forms

In the downstream sectors of the river-basins, variations in sea-level have led to the formation of alluvial plains (eustatic terraces). The sea invaded the lower parts of the valleys, transforming them into rias and estuaries: the rivers progressively filled these with alluvial deposits brought from upstream to build an alluvial base-level plain. When the sea retreated and the sea-level was lower (during the glacial stages) the river regraded itself by cutting into the alluvial deposits, leaving

them preserved only in the terraces. Flights of 'eustatic' terraces are found along many valleys, such as those of the Somme and Garonne: their relative heights remain constant, so that we can distinguish higher, middle and lower terraces. But the process by which eustatic terraces are formed does not operate beyond a certain distance from the marine base-level. It gives way to the formation of climatic terraces. During a glacial period or stadial, the material loosened by frost and soliflucted was heaped up in quantity on the lower slopes and in the valley bottoms. At this time the flow of the rivers was greatly reduced, and their capacity to transport solid material was thereby limited. During the inter-glacial periods or interstadials, the rivers, better supplied by rain or by the summer melting of the snows, were able to erode, and by cutting deeper could carve terraces in part of the accumulated material. Climatic and eustatic terraces are clearly asynchronous.

Peri-glacial materials transported by the rivers were deposited when the slopes changed or when the valleys narrowed. Thus the watergaps in Champagne and Lorraine are often blocked and partly fossilised by these deposits, which built up some really remarkable plains, sometimes later cut into terraces (fig. 13). The Aube, leaving the Jurassic plateaux, built up a true 'peri-glacial piedmont cone' (J. Tricart), 20 km. long and 8 km. wide (the plain of Brienne).

The determining influence of the erosion systems of the Quaternary was most recently confirmed with respect to the surface form of the Aquitaine basin (fig. 14). H. Enjalbert brought out the idea of 'morphogenetic crises' associated with pre-glacial, glacial and interglacial phases.

Geographically, these episodes of the Quaternary played a considerable part. They fossilised the hillsides, reducing the gradients of slopes to the angle of rest of frost-shattered materials, and they filled up the valleys. Occasionally they added new topographical features, and they always remodelled the relief so that a new surface form was created. This peri-glacial remodelling

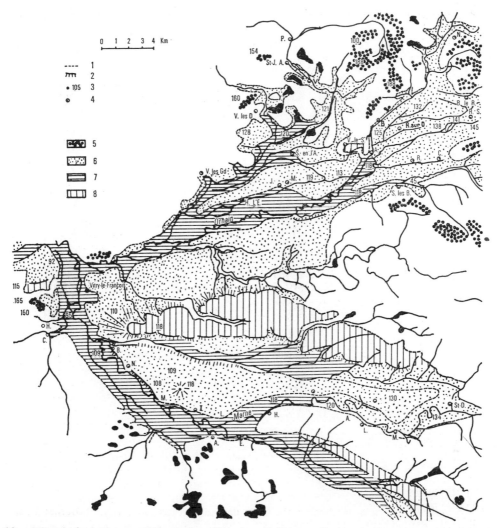

Fig. 13. Morphological map of Perthois. (Source: J. Tricart, *Le Bassin Parisien Oriental*, Vol. II)
1. Edge of alluvial terrace. 2. Edge of terrace. 3. Spot heights. 4. Village. 5. Upper level (1st interglacial). 6. Upper surface of Grève II terrace deposits. 7. Upper surface of the Grève III terrace. 8. Slopes cut into the Grève II terrace when the Grève III terrace was formed. (*Grève* is a geological name for sand and gravel alluvium—*Note*, Author.)

was carried to the point where a landscape of old age was created (J. Beaujeu-Garnier).[12]

Wide valleys filled with alluvial material, with very gentle slopes separated by some tens of metres or even several kilometres of waterlogged ground, marshes and peat bogs, with ox-bow lakes and sluggish rivers, are a legacy of the Quaternary. Such valleys are a very

special feature of Hercynian France; these episodes have superimposed on the solid geology of the rock outcrops a drift geology of uncemented superficial deposits, covering the former with a discontinuous mantle which is almost always present, although of uneven thickness.

These deposits covering the slopes are the

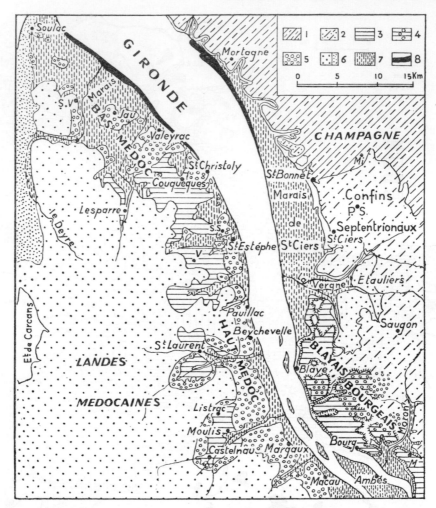

Fig. 14. A typical Quaternary landscape: the Gironde and northern Bordelais. (Source: P. Barrère, H. Enjalbert, L. Papy, G. Viers, *Ann. de Géog.*, no. 370, 1959, p. 495)

1. The *champagnes* of Charente (soft limestone of the Upper Cretaceous). 2. The northern borders of the Bordelais (Eocene continental sands). 3. Limestone domes of Listrac and Couquèques in Médoc (Tertiary limestone). 4. The limestone plateaux of Blayais-Bourgeais (Tertiary limestone) and their covering of old gravels. 5. Gravel terraces of Médoc (Early Quaternary alluvium). 6. *Landes* of Médoc and coastal dunes (Landes sands). 7. Bordelais lowlands (fluvio-marine silt and peat marshes). 8. Recent silts of Mortagne and Jau. Abbreviations: M., Marcamps; Mi., Mirambeau; P.S., Pleine Selve; S.S., Saint-Seurin-de-Cadourne; S.V., Saint-Vivien; V., Valeyrac.

basic material from which has evolved the soil cultivated and worked by man. 'It is to periglacial action that the plains owe their most distinctive younger physical features; and it is to them that our soil owes all its character' (A. Cailleux).

PRESENT SYSTEMS OF EROSION

Are plains, plateaux and hills actively undergoing erosion at present? In a temperate climate, under a covering of forest or grass-covered soil, erosion is obviously reduced. A large number of authors have stressed its insignificance, drawing attention to the way carpets of dead leaves remain undisturbed from one autumn to another. Other factors explain why relief appears to be little affected by the agents of erosion:

1. The recent rise of sea-level has displaced the base-level upstream. Rias, estuaries and valleys as they filled up have reduced the length of slopes and the available relief.

2. Most of the slopes correspond to the natural slopes of the Quaternary deposits, which are, moreover, stabilised by vegetation.

3. Linear erosion carried out by rivers is limited by the large number of undrained valleys; the progressive lowering of the water-tables leads to springs emerging at lower levels downstream, thus limiting the field of action of erosion.

It exists nevertheless; and we can see its effects as soon as the altitude becomes greater; then the rivers scour their beds, undermine their banks and hollow out the concave portions of incised meanders. The solid matter transported by the rivers is clear proof of this erosive action even though part of this material is merely due to the loosening of alluvium already deposited farther upstream. Every year the Loire transports 700,000 tons of solid matter and the Seine 150,000–200,000 tons, not counting the much greater amount of material in solution.

But above all we must not forget that erosion works mainly spasmodically; its periods of activity are sudden, and as short as they are intense; they are bound up with changes in climatic conditions. A storm or an exceptionally heavy rainfall will swell the streams, which take on the colour of the sediment set in motion, while the flow of water is temporarily restored in dry valleys. Violent rain tears up the earth in fields not protected by plant growth.

In the same way, exceptionally cold winters prepare the ground for the mobility which ensues when warm weather returns, causing innumerable landslips.[13] These erosive activities are a useful reminder of the equilibrium rather than stability which exists even in temperate climates.

2. With this in mind, A. Guilcher has stressed the danger of giving the name 'Appalachian' to every ridge of an ancient massif.

3. The Dôme mountains have a volcanic structure whose complexity belies their appearance. They were built up in the course of several phases, and consist of scoria injected into domitic cones of fine scoria.

4. Also called pre-Oligocene, Eocene central plateau (by P. Glangeaud) and Eocene surface (by Baulig).

5. Or 'Aquitanian'.

6. The morphological map of the Paris basin, compiled by A. Cholley and his pupils, well expresses this complexity.

7. In the Landes, Haute-Lande, for lack of slope, is a district with no surface run-off (the 'aréïsme humide' of Enjalbert).

8. The small sedimentary basins found locally along the margins of the massifs give exactly the same morphological result. Examples are the basins of Brive and Saint-Dié.

9. *Compte-Rendus de l'Académie des Sciences* (Paris), 31st March 1947.

10. Those morphological paradoxes the 'Monts de Champagne' correspond to areas of sand which, being less affected by frosts, protected the chalk beneath.

11. The vast sandy covering of the Landes is a product of wind erosion deposited during a recent cold phase of the Quaternary; the material is said to come from the continental shelf which was uncovered by the sea during a phase of marine regression.

12. The wide synclinal valleys, often with marshy bottoms, of Haut-Limousin are known as '*pex*' or '*rebières*'.

13. In our present climate, polygonal and striped soils are formed above 1,750 m. in Mézenc.

3. THE MORPHOLOGICAL EVOLUTION OF PYRENEO-ALPINE FRANCE

This evolution is entirely dependent on the formation of the young mountain ranges which rose in the Tertiary, with repercussions on their forelands and the surrounding regions.

A. Tectonics and Structure

THE PYRENEES

The Pyrenees, joined to the highlands of the Iberian peninsula, may appear, falsely, to be a 'mere marginal protuberance of the Iberian Meseta' (E. de Martonne). They are lithologically and structurally distinct, forming a particular type of young mountain range.

In the greater part of the range the material is that of a Hercynian chain—Primary sediments metamorphosed by contact with vast granitic massifs—levelled, and having a Secondary sedimentary covering which is not very thick, and incomplete.

'Embryonic' mountain-building movements appear from the Cenomanian onwards, as shown by the abundant orogenic sediments such as breccia and conglomerate. Then the basement was split, and great fractures divided it into blocks which all behaved quite differently one from another. The sedimentary mantle was also faulted, and, according to circumstances, was folded, pinched or affected by gravity flows; this produced very complex folds.

The paroxysmal phase of the Pyrenees is 'traditionally' dated from the Eocene (post-Lutetian and post-Bartonian) and is thus considered to be earlier than the building of the Alps. But recent research suggests an interpretation which brings forward the main episodes of the folding to the end of the Oligocene and the beginning of the Miocene. J. Ph. Mangin has in fact noted that in the Eocene there was no change in the nature of the sediments which might have borne witness to the proximity of a mountain chain.

Tectonic movements in the Eocene and Oligocene did not merely affect the Pyrenees; they extended into the regions of Languedoc and Provence, where the folds are of the same type and direction as those of the Pyrenees. In the plain of Languedoc the folds of the Gardiole, Montpellier and Pic Saint-Loup, contemporary with the Pyrenean and Provençal mountain-building, rose in the Bartonian.

A large part of Provence and the lower Rhône valley at that time formed the Durancian isthmus, separating the Pyrenean and Provençal regions from the Alpine region proper, into which the sedimentation continued.[14]

In the western Mediterranean the massif of the Pyrenees, Corsica and Sardinia subsided slowly, from the Upper Eocene to the Upper Miocene, with interruptions.

The building of the Pyrenees continued all through the Tertiary, and, as some think, through the Quaternary also. In the eastern Pyrenees the thickness of the marine Pliocene in Roussillon (780 m.) and the dips bear witness to an uplift of 1,000 m. (P. Birot), which is post-Upper Miocene and probably post-Upper Pliocene, confirming the recent nature of certain fault scarps.

THE ALPS

History of the Alpine uplift

This began with the vast Mediterranean geosyncline formed as early as the pre-Cambrian. Hercynian tectonic movements built ranges which were deformed again in the Lower Permian; the coal deposits appear trapped in the synclines of the basement rocks. From the Permian—or the Triassic—onwards, the Alpine area was divided into a piedmont geosyncline in the east, and a zone of shoals (Vindelician gate) in the west, situated on the present site of the crystalline massifs of Belledonne and Mont Blanc.

During the Secondary, in the piedmont geosyncline there was a very fluid alternation of abyssal troughs (deeps), where thick sedimentary beds were deposited, and cordilleras,

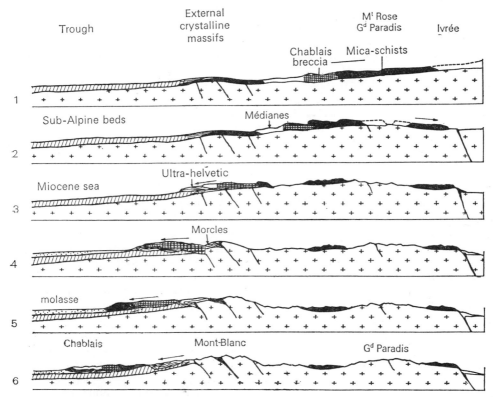

Fig. 15.   Formation and evolution of nappes in the northern Alps: the formation of the pre-Alpine nappes of Chablais.   (Source: M. Gidon, *Bull. Soc. Géol. France*, 1958, p. 153)
1. End of Eocene.   2. Oligocene.   3, 4, 5. Miocene.   6. Post-Miocene.

where sedimentation was reduced. One of the cordilleras is that of Briançonnais, separating the great piedmont geosyncline in the east from a subsiding trough (Vocontian deep in the south, ultra-Dauphiné deep in the west).

In the Middle Cretaceous, then in the Lower Eocene (pre-Lutetian), the preliminary movements began, mainly affecting the external, non-geosynclinal zone; they caused the sub-Alpine massifs to emerge during part of the Upper Cretaceous. Thus Diois and the Baronnies, down-faulted in the Jurassic and the Cretaceous as apophyses (tongues) of the Vocontian deep, were uplifted from the Upper Cretaceous onwards, largely escaping the Tertiary sedimentation.

The paroxysmal movements came in the Oligocene. The rock masses of the geosyncline rose to form a geotumour—an enormous swelling—which moved from east to west (as a result of tectonic movements in depth).

As it developed, this swelling, made up of the rocks of the substratum and their sedimentary cover, caused this cover to be displaced and to flow gravitationally down the slopes (surface tectonics). This was the origin of the great nappes, their separation occurring at the stratigraphical level of the Triassic, which acted as a lubricating sliding plane (fig. 15).

But only the internal zone was affected by mountain-building in the Oligocene; the external regions were not involved until later, with the persistence of deformations during the Miocene (Chablais nappes covering the Miocene molasse) and the Pliocene,[15] and the late uplift of the external crystalline massifs, whose sedimentary cover became detached to form the sub-Alpine folds (Eocene marine deposits corresponding to the sediments of the ultra-Dauphiné zone).

These movements were not independent of the paroxysmal movements. They can be interpreted as the last stage of the east to west translation of the axis of the Alpine intumescence. Between the first appearance of the swelling in the east (in the Eocene) and its most westerly position (in the Miocene) the nappes must have taken 20 million years to complete their motion. The slow displacement of the axis of the intumescence explains the stratigraphical complexity of the nappes. For example, it accounts for the breaks which have been observed in the continuity of a nappe, the passage of the intumescence initiating flow phenomena downstream and counter-flow upstream. The 'crossing' of the external massifs by these nappes can be simply explained by the fact that these massifs did not yet form topographical protuberances.

In the maritime Alps the major tectonic phase of the Nice arc dates from the Upper Miocene; the sedimentary cover (which was in process of uplift) slipped at that time, pushing before it the beds which had slid along a Triassic junction plane. These piled up in overfolded festoons abutting on the ancient Tyrrhenian–Maures–Estérel massif which was subsiding in the south.

After the long history of the building of the Alps, there was a readjustment in the course of the Pliocene which raised the whole massif by between 1,500 and 2,000 m.

It has been proved that very recent deformations have actually taken place in the maritime Alps; thus the Nice arc shows a compacting from east to west which dates from after the Upper Pliocene and before the Pleistocene; the effects of diapirism, capping and overthrusting were superimposed on to a relief which was already strongly differentiated, producing an extremely complex structure.

Structural zones

A geological map of the Alps, even a diagrammatic one, shows a characteristic zoning non-existent in the Pyrenees. The following divisions are recognised: Ivrée zone, internal Alpine zone (or Pennine zone), external Alpine zone.

The Ivrée zone. Above the piedmont subsidence the Alpine swelling begins with a discontinuous zone of crystalline massifs— Dora Maira and Grand Paradis. These massifs form the counterpart of the external crystalline massifs. They are unrooted and do not belong to the system of westward-flowing nappes as was envisaged in the 'ultranappist' hypotheses according to which the nappes had their original roots in the plain of the Po.

The internal Alpine zone consists, from east to west, of:

(*a*) *The zone of mica-schists.* Mica-schists result from intense metamorphism in the Alpine geosyncline which affected not only sedimentary rocks from the Triassic to the Eocene but also the granites and gneiss of the Hercynian blocks. These mica-schists suffered intense fracturing and were thrust in successive layers from the underlying eastern crystalline massifs.

(*b*) *The Briançonnais zone* is formed by a sedimentary series stretching from the Carboniferous to the Cretaceous with thick beds (3,000–4,000 m.) of unmetamorphosed Carboniferous and Permian rocks. These beds were displaced westwards, without the crystalline core appearing to have participated in the movement. The Mesozoic cover, which was mainly calcareous (showing elements of structural morphology), was carried along with the underlying Carboniferous and came to rest as a series of superposed lenses along the front of the translated wave (fig. 16).

(*c*) *The sub-Briançonnais zone.* This is distinguished from the Briançonnais zone by the relative absence of Permo-Carboniferous rocks. From east to west it consists of a gypsum zone, the Pas du Roc nappe and the nappe of the Tarentaise breccia (the former nappe of Embrunais) in a complex system of imbricate scales. The flysch bed of Ubaye–Embrunais flowed freely between the Pelvoux and the Argentera massifs, pushing back the limestone masses which now form the structurally very complicated massifs of Morgon and Chabrière, on either side of the Durance.

The external Alpine zone consists, from east to west, of:

(*a*) *The crystalline massifs.* These are, from north to south: the Mont Blanc and Aiguilles Rouges massifs, the Belledonne

the uplifting of the massifs and was facilitated by the plasticity of the Triassic and Liassic beds.

(*c*) *The sub-Alpine chains* (pre-Alps).[17] These represent the autochthonous covering of the external crystalline massifs, which has either slid down their western flank or been folded above the very slightly uplifted core. Moving westwards by force of gravity, this zone was folded without overthrusting. The pre-Alps were built of thick Jurassic and Cretaceous beds strengthened by two great limestone series—that of the Tithonic, which appears in the north, beginning at Vercors,

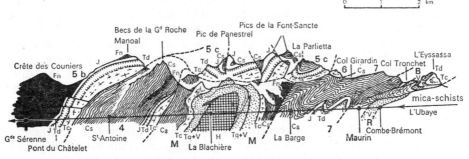

Fig. 16. Example of structure in the inner Alps: section taken on the right bank of the upper Ubaye. (Source: J. Debelmas and M. Gidon, *Bull. Soc. Géol. France*, 1958, p. 643)
M., Marinet anticline. R., Siliceous wedge of Roure. 5. Chatelet and Peyre-Haute nappe (the letters b and c indicate the digitations of the nappe). 6. Assan nappe. 7. Ceillac-Chiappera zone.
V., Verrucano series. Tq., Triassic quartzites. Tc., Virglorian limestone. Td., Ladinian dolomite.
J., Jurassic (Dogger and Malm). Cs., Cretaceo-Eocene. Fn., black Flysch.

range, the Grandes Rousses, Pelvoux and Mercantour or Argentera massifs.[16]

The Mont Blanc, Aiguilles Rouges, Belledonne and Pelvoux massifs can be schematically considered as pieces of a block forming a frame for a narrow synclinal zone filled with Carboniferous and Secondary rocks.

(*b*) *The sub-Alpine furrow.* This was, for a long time, considered to be a wide depression exposed by erosion on contact with the pre-Alpine sediments which were in unconformity with the external crystalline massif. According to the new conception of tectonics, it is interpreted as a structural rent caused by the removal of the autochthonous covering of the sub-Alpine zone, a removal which followed on

and that of the Urgonian. In the southern pre-Alps, south of Drôme, Urgonian limestones are missing; this is the Vocontian deep.

In the northern Alps the sub-Alpine secondary chains are divided into massifs separated by wide transverse valleys or *cluses*: Chablais, Faucigny (Arve valley), Bornes, Cluse d'Annecy, Bauges, Cluse de Chambéry, Grande Chartreuse, Cluse de Grenoble, Vercors. The *cluses* provide exceptional facilities for traffic and communications between the interior and the outer parts of the Alps. Together with the sub-Alpine furrow they give access to the northern Alps to an extent unknown in the southern Alps. The *cluses*

are not mere depressions or transverse synclines breaking the continuity of the pre-
Alpine folds; they are structural breaks which
differ in tectonic origin and form from one
place to another.   One structuralist interpretation, by P. Veyret, considers the pre-Alpine
massifs as blocks placed independently of
each other; thus the *cluses* would be caused by
structural rents occurring at the time of the
tectonic landslides.[18]

The structure of the pre-Alpine massifs of
Savoie is complicated by the presence of overthrust nappes taking the form either of fairly
large *klippes* (as at Sulens and Annes in the
Bornes) or of nappes entirely covering the sub-
Alpine sedimentary series (as in Chablais).
Geologists distinguish several nappes (three or
four) which came from the Briançonnais and
sub-Briançonnais zones before the uplift of
the central massifs.   The morphology of
Chablais is thus very different from that of the
other massifs, without Urgonian structural
relief and without the north–south orientation
of relief (fig. 15).

In the southern Alps, south of Vercors, the
folded Secondary and Tertiary sub-Alpine
sediments form two large and widely extended
chains separated by the gulf of the Valensole
plateau, a depression in which Pliocene gravel
accumulated to a thickness of more than 1,000
m.   In the west the first chain includes the
massifs of Diois, Dévoluy and the Baronnies.
They are not as simply disposed as the
northern pre-Alps, and the sub-Alpine furrow
no longer exists.   To the east lies the zone of
the pre-Alps of Digne and the maritime pre-
Alps, closed by the Maures massif.

The sub-Alpine folds show a chequerboard
formation of domes and basins.   The west–
east direction, already very apparent in the
south of the Baronnies, predominates in the
maritime pre-Alps.   These west–east orienta-
tions probably owe as much, if not more, to the
influence of dislocations of the block as to the
interference of folding in the Pyrenean era.[19]

THE JURA AND PROVENCE

The Jura could easily be regarded as a third
Alpine festoon bordering the Alpine axis on
its north-western side, exactly in the angle of
the eastward bend.   But it differs from the
preceding chains in that it is not continuous
with the Alpine system.   The Dent du Chat,
to the west of lake Bourget, is an authentically
Jurassic secondary ridge, independent of the
pre-Alps; farther to the south, the Mont de
l'Épine area is separated from the Grande
Chartreuse by a synclinal zone.   Between the
pre-Alps and the Jura is the wide crescent of
molasse which opens out in Switzerland.[20]
This zone corresponds to a sector of continuous, thick sedimentation, a sort of pre-
Alpine trough.   Probably the enormous
weight of Oligo-Miocene conglomerates forming the Swiss plain prevented the folding of
the underlying rocks, and caused the folding
to take place to the west of the Tertiary basin;
only a few isolated Urgonian folds emerge
through the molasse, in Salève.

The tectonic history of the Jura can be
schematically reduced to four phases:

1. A period of deformation in the Oligocene which affected a sedimentary basin
abutting against the Vosges–Black Forest and
the Central Massif.   Its fringes corresponded
symmetrically with those of the Paris basin
beyond the Langres plateau.   The basement
block lying close beneath the sedimentary
rocks had a profound influence on the structure of the terrain and its deformations.[21]
This basement was then split into a 'mosaic of
fault-blocks' (L. Glangeaud) which inter-
acted, folding and crumpling the sedimentary
cover.   At the same time the Bresse depression was formed by subsidence.

2. A phase of deformation in the Miocene
with its paroxysm in the Pontian or the pre-
Pontian (according to Glangeaud).   A wave
of upheaval, comparable, on a smaller scale,
to the Alpine swelling, moved from east to
west, causing a very complex structure in
which small, very localised nappes were
formed by gravity; the western edge of the
Jura thus thrust forward on Bresse; the
Tertiary formation in Bresse was covered, for
some 10–15 km., by a true nappe with its
thrust plane in the Trias.

3. A phase of post-Pontian and pre-Plaisantian folding which led to new tectonic slips.

4. A final phase of Plio-Quaternary deformations with upheavals and reactivated folds, and, in particular, a mass upheaval in the Upper Pliocene.

South of the Alps, Provence had an analogous evolution, punctuated by multiple mountain-building phases. According to J. Aubouin and G. Mennessier, the succession of episodes was as follows:

The first orogenic phase took place in the Albian (end of the Lower Cretaceous), giving rise to the Durancian isthmus; at the end of the Upper Cretaceous a phase of folding formed the broad structural features of present-day Provence: great synclinal basins and anticlinal zones. At the end of the Middle Eocene a phase of mountain-building in Provence caused first the breaking away of the cover and then the subsidence of the basins (Oligocene sedimentation). At the end of the Oligocene a fifth phase (pre-Aquitanian) emphasised earlier structures and uplifted the Maures massif. Finally, in the Pontian, a widespread movement warped the whole of Provence, tilting it towards the Mediterranean. A part of the Maures massif collapsed into the Mediterranean.

THE PLAINS IN FRONT OF THE YOUNG MOUNTAINS

From Alsace to Roussillon, plains of various forms and dimensions lie in front of the mountains, or between two branches of the mountain mass: the plain of Alsace, the Belfort Gap, the Saône plains, the plains and basins of the Rhône (Valence, Montélimar), the plains of the lower Rhône, the plain and plateaux of Languedoc and the triangular plain of Roussillon. Their formation is bound up with that of the Pyrenees and the Alps and their accompanying subsidences. These depressions in front of the newly built mountains marked the episodes of an extremely complex morphological history showing a great variety of evolution over a short distance, a succession of transgressions, deformations, the depositing of debris from the erosion of new mountain chains and phases of emergence.

In front of the Alpine zones, both internal (geosynclinal) and external (Dauphiné deep), there was, in the Secondary, a system of epicontinental seas similar to that of the Paris and Aquitaine basins; transgressions alternated with periods of regression during which planation took place.

The Palaeogene seas, after the Stampian, deposited thick beds of molasse (soft calcareous sandstone). In the Oligocene, that is to say, directly after the end of the Pyreneo-Provençal movements, a series of subsidences in a southerly direction affected the peri-Alpine regions; these were filled up with lakes which deposited thick sedimentary beds. At this time the depressions of the Saône, of Bresse, Bas-Dauphiné and Gard were initiated (the pre-Burdigalian erosion surface is clear in certain parts of the Rhône valley).

Contemporaneously with these the border escarpments were uplifted. In the Bartonian the Montagne Noire underwent a great upheaval, as a result of which it dominates the marginal depressions, which were drowned by the Palaeogene sea and the Lutetian lakes. From the Oligocene onwards the Cévennes massif was uplifted, with the greatest uplift in the south. Several upheavals occurred, particularly at the end of the Miocene. The subsidence of the central part of the Pyreneo-Provençal chain and the formation of the Gulf of Lions occurred in the Miocene, leading to a vast marine transgression in the Lower and Middle Miocene.

The depression of the Rhône shows a great diversity of structural conditions, partly masked by recent morphological evolution: the bedrock of the plain of Valence is entirely Tertiary; the plain of Montélimar is developed on Quaternary alluvium resting directly on Lower Cretaceous rocks. Finally, the floor of the plain of Comtat Venaissin belongs to the Cretaceous in the west and the Tertiary elsewhere. The various compartments thus behaved in different ways. Until

the Lower Miocene that of Montélimar behaved like a dome which underwent further
upheavals on several occasions. It did not
subside until the Middle Miocene, whereas
the neighbouring sectors were affected by
these negative movements as early as the
Oligocene.

As the Alps were uplifted and the axis of
the swelling came nearer, the sediments
deposited in the peri-Alpine zone became
coarser and coarser, providing evidence of the
demolition of the chain; they are conglomerates and torrential deposits of the Miocene. Farther west, the Miocene sea, in the
Middle Miocene transgression, deposited
several hundred metres of calcareous sand,
fossilising round its coast the secondary
ranges of the Jura and the edge of the Central
Massif, which was already markedly precipi-
tous.[22] This Miocene marine transgression
ended with the deposition of conglomerates
with pitted pebbles (Pontian).

This was succeeded by a continental phase
in the Rhône valley, following on tectonic
movements during which the ria of the Rhône
began to be cut below the present sea-level.
The continental phase ended with a fluvio-
lacustrine alluviation, which filled up the ria
(Pierrelatte beds and Saint-Restitut terrace
gravel).

In the Pliocene, Roussillon, Languedoc, the
region of the lower Rhône and the Rhône corridor were affected by the Pliocene (Plaisantian) transgression; this transgression formed
a gulf penetrating more than 200 km., with
offshoots, and alternately wide and narrow.
The Pliocene transgression covered all beds
from the Jurassic to the Tertiary with unconformable and thick beds of grey clay with
sand, limestone appearing only in the upper-
most strata. It was a 'powerful marine transgression which drowned a very strongly
marked relief and established a fairly deep and
stable sea in basins which had been formed by
subsidence as early as the Oligocene'. This
transgression drowned a very vigorous system
of escarpments and mountain chains. The
filling up of the sea produced a flat, almost
horizontal surface, representing the stable sea-

level which marked the highest point of the
transgression. This surface was later broken
up or tilted *en bloc*. In the Camargue the
Pliocene reaches a thickness of 1,500 m., while
its highest fragments are found actually at
+180 m.

Above Lyons the Bresse lake was filled up
by Pliocene deposits to a depth of more than
200 m. (Middle and Upper Pliocene) and the
sedimentation submerged some valleys and
depressions in the south of the Jura. In
Provence the low-lying valleys of the Argens
and the Siagne were also invaded by the
Plaisantian transgression.

Large masses of gravel and fluvio-conti-
nental deposits, resulting from the breaking
down of the upland borders, alternated with
these marine deposits and covered them. In
Bas-Dauphiné the Pliocene deposits end in a
sheet of water-worn gravel reaching 0·6 m. in
diameter.

The absence of forms comparable to the
Pyrenean piedmont is explained by the disposition of the structural units, the complex
history of sedimentation around the French
Alps, the importance of the pre-Alpine limestone massifs and the position of the rivers.
The piedmonts of the Alps are more fragmented, more varied from the Dombe to the
Crau, an enormous Pliocene alluvial cone
built by the Durance and extending beneath
the Rhône delta.

The Valensole plateau, which suddenly
breaks the continuity of the mountain relief,
forms a sort of 'internal piedmont', resulting
from the deposition of Miocene conglomerates in a subsidence zone. Beneath a
morainic cover the substratum of the Dombe
is covered by a sheet of pebbly alluvium of
Alpine origin and dating from the Pliocene.

During these episodes of sedimentation the
eastern edge of the Central Massif continued
to rise by a succession of uplifts. The
volcanic flows of the Coiron make it possible
to analyse closely the morpho-tectonic evolution of this sector. The Coiron is not one
great flow but sheets discharged by volcanoes
of the Hawaiian type. There were several
phases of volcanic activity—pre-Pontian,

Pontian and Lower Pliocene. These sheets fossilised a Plaisantian topography, a complex of north–south valleys, tributary to the Pliocene Ardèche. As the Plaisantian sediments of the Rhône valley are 400 m. lower than those of the same age in the Ardèche, we must postulate a throw of this order at the fault bordering the Rhône. On the western side these alluvia have a particle size incompatible with the presence of the escarpment of the Central Massif; the great fault of Vivarais and the Cévennes must, then, have strongly thrown posthumously in the Middle or Upper Pliocene; in any case, the formation of the escarpment in this sector must date from after the Plaisantian.

As far as the Cévennes are concerned, analysis of the heavy minerals and sediments of Languedoc allows us to date their uplift from the Oligocene to the Miocene, continuing less rapidly in to the Pliocene.

B. Morphology

In the Pyreneo-Alpine domain in general, folding has produced a topography on the grand scale; subsidence and fractures have led to considerable contrasts between structural units, juxtaposing massifs and depressions in a 'piano-keys' type of tectonics, and creating great numbers of escarpments; all of these were formed at quite a recent epoch.

We can thus understand the intensity of erosion throughout this domain, in the sector with a Mediterranean climate as well as in the temperate one. There are innumerable modifications in the hydrography, such as the river captures by the mountain streams of the Cévennes. But demolition was carried on during the Quaternary by other systems of erosion, which are nowadays confined to high mountain regions where frost, snow and ice still occur.

CYCLIC MORPHOLOGY

In these recently formed regions the size and chronology of erosion surfaces are obviously very different from those of Hercynian France. It is still possible, though difficult, to identify the post-Hercynian surface on the blocks incorporated in the Tertiary foldings or reshaped by them. We find fragments of this surface which play a secondary but by no means negligible part in the topography; such is the plateau of Chamrousse in the Alps. In the Pyrenees the axial zone east of the Garonne shows numerous fragments of surfaces between 2,000 and 2,900 m.; isolated areas of mature topography are left perched at about 2,000 m. in the Cauterets region. The dating of these surfaces is obviously uncertain, owing to the warping and fracturing which may have deformed and stepped the level of any one surface. Several levels have been identified, both pre-Pontian and Pliocene. According to L. Solé Sabaris, the higher surfaces belong to the Palaeogene, and are perhaps contemporary with the surfaces of Hercynian France.

In Diois, which remained emerged during the Miocene transgression, a fairly highly developed pre-Pontian erosion surface evolved. The river system was formed on the slopes of this erosion surface, before the Ponto-Pliocene deformations (fig. 20).

In the Jura, erosion surfaces are much more important, and the morphology of the plateaux and folds bears the mark of numerous planations. Pre-Pontian surfaces were formed in relation to the base-levels of the Molasse sea in the east and the Bresse lake in the west. These surfaces provided a starting-ground for more localised Pliocene planations (fig. 17).

Let us consider an example of a polygenetic surface (fig. 17). The Molard de Don massif is truncated by an erosion surface which is tilted westwards and was initiated in the Eocene or the Oligocene (it was fossilised by a cover of Burdigalian sandstone). This surface was then remodelled and deformed in the Middle Miocene (pre-Vindobonian surface) and completed at the end of the Miocene (the Vindobonian intersects the surface, which is dotted with ferruginous sands (*sidérolithique*).

In Provence we find, in the same way, evidence of a very highly developed pre-Pontian

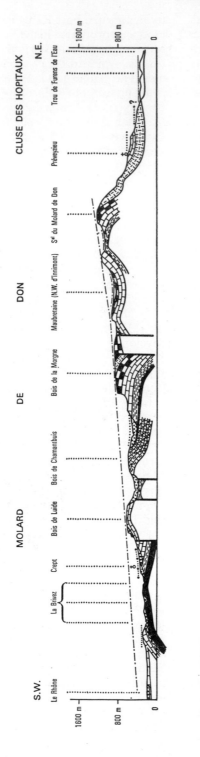

Fig. 17. Section across the Molard de Don massif. (Source: M. Dubois, *Le Jura Méridional, étude morphologique*, Paris, 1959, Fig. 20)

1. Bathonian. 2. Callovian. 3. Oxfordian. 4. Rauratian. 5. Astartian. 6. Kimmeridgian. 7. Portlandian. 8. Glacial and fluvio-glacial.

'The structure is both faulted and folded. The whole is asymmetrical, raised by a great flexure in the east, above the Belley basin. The major relief derives from a Neogene surface tilted westwards. The minor relief is Appalachian, shaped by Pliocene and Quaternary erosion. In the east is the syncline of Innimont or Maubretaine and the anticlinal valley of Molard, karstic depressions which may be a re-modelling of Vindobonian incisions.'

surface, and also of a surface dating from the end of the Cretaceous or the beginning of the Eocene. In Corsica, too, there is a Palaeogene surface which is recognisable by the planations to be seen in the topography, and in its effect on the direction of the rivers.

Side by side with these remains of vast erosion surfaces, the hillsides and slopes of these regions often show flats and benches which have not been systematically listed and which are very difficult to interpret; the Grenoble and Paris schools of geography have long been at variance over their presence and significance in the Alps. J. Chardonnet considers that these levels are of great morphological importance in the southern Alps. Although geomorphologists have recently turned their minds towards other fields of interest, forms are nevertheless present which geographers must take into account in analysing relief.

LITHOLOGICAL AND STRUCTURAL MORPHOLOGY

The variety of conditions under which sedimentation took place, the incorporation of ancient structures in recent folds, the complexity and texture of structural features, the extent of erosion by torrents, rivers and ice, all serve to explain why young mountains are veritable museums of lithological and structural morphology.

Granite gives rise either to massive domes (Maladetta and Mercantour) chiselled by glaciers, where fractures play an important part in determining the direction of the rivers and the minor landforms, or regions of low relief (as in the massif of Ercé on the Salat) or peaks and crest-lines as in the massifs of Mont Blanc, Pic d'Aneto and Balaïtous.

Weak beds, which are numerous owing to the conditions of sedimentation, are easy prey to erosion. Both within and outside the mountains, shale, marls, clays, sands, flysch and molasse are carved into spectacular 'bad lands'.

But in this structural morphology the dominance of limestone is incontestable, in the Alps, the Jura and the Pyrenees as well as in Provence and Languedoc. Where it has been preserved in extensive outcrops it appears as high limestone plateaux of a deeply tunnelled karstic character: such are the plateaux of the Jura (fig. 18), Parmelan,

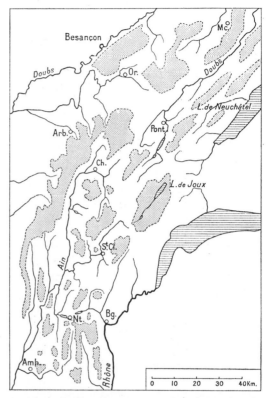

Fig. 18. Extent of areas without surface run-off in the Jura. (Source: E. De Martonne, *Géographie Universelle*, A. Colin, Vol. VI)

Abbreviations: Amb., Amberieu; Arb., Arbois; Bg., Bellegarde; Ch., Champagnole; M., Moert; Mc., Maîche; Nt., Nantua; Or., Ornans; Pont., Pontarlier; St Cl., Saint-Claude.

Vercors, Vivarais and the flats (*plans*) of Provence. When sandwiched in beds of varying thickness, it gives rise to structural forms related to all known types, according to the dip: low hills, cuestas, ridges, vertical rock-faces, fault-scarps and discordant, normal, derivative and inverted forms.

In the Jura, the Plantaurel and the Petites-

Pyrénées, the present structural morphology has been evolved from erosion surfaces whose development in the Tertiary indicates the variety of morphological evolution; ridges, cuestas and limestone back-slopes are, properly speaking, Appalachian forms; thus all morphological combinations are possible.

In the interior Alps the very complex surface tectonics leads, curiously enough, to structural or pseudo-structural forms, such as ridges, cuestas, marginal depressions and knife-edges, as erosion acts differentially on the rock materials, without taking into account the overthrusts and unconformities.

In the pre-Alps the limestones of the Tithonic (Upper Jurassic) and the Urgonian (Lower Cretaceous), separated by Hauterivian-Valanginian marls and marly limestones, produce the forms of structural relief which give them their beauty: the height of vertical walls, the massive shapes of the mountains and the slenderness of the crests and perched synclines.

In the Pyrenees 'the most common structural landscape is the result of the combination of bands of Urgonian limestone, sometimes reinforced by Jurassic dolomites (in Béarn), with long subsequent vales opened either in Lower Aptian shales or in Liassic marl and ophitic Keuper' (G. Viers).

The characteristic of these structural forms is their lack of continuity: the sudden breaks in structural forms can be explained by faults, layers which have slipped independently of each other, transverse disruptions, the uneven height of the beds and the extent of sedimentation.

CLIMATIC MORPHOLOGY

Glaciations, glaciers and peri-glacial forms

North of a line joining the middle reaches of the Vésubie to the Bourne in Vercors the Alpine massif was entirely glaciated.[23] South of this line the Alps as a whole were free from glaciers apart from a few valley glaciers, the largest of which reached as far as Sisteron.

This great mass of ice overflowed from the Alpine massif, advancing farthest at the latitude of the Mont Blanc massif, where the Rhône glaciers met those coming from the pre-Alpine *cluses*; ice reached the Rhône at Lyons, covered the Dombe as far as Bourg-en-Bresse and invaded the southern Jura; a tongue of ice crept along the Isère valley to Saint-Marcellin.

The Pyrenean glaciers, unlike those of the Alps, spread out from the range at two points only: at Arudy (Gave d'Ossau) and at Lourdes. The absence of great Pyrenean glaciers in the Quaternary can be explained by the facts that the latitudes are lower than those of the Alps, the chain is narrow and there are few large concentrations of water. Most authors recognise no more than one glacial oscillation there.

At present, glaciers cover a relatively small area: 21 km.^{2} in the Pyrenees and 300 km.^{2} in the Alps. But there is a great variety of types, giving rise to mountain landscapes of indescribable beauty, a great attraction to tourists.

The glaciers of the Mont Blanc massif form the largest group; ice caps (Mont Blanc, Dômes de Miage), corrie glaciers (Tour) and valley glaciers (Mer de Glace, Trè la Tête) are found there side by side. There are still glaciers in the Vanoise massif, where plateau glaciers predominate (as at Chasseforêt), and in the Pelvoux massif, where various types of glaciers are to be found, such as the vast plateau glaciers of the Mont de Lans, and valley glaciers, the 'Black' and the 'White'. In the Pyrenees glaciation is more restricted to summits and cirques.

The mountain massifs thus show a very highly developed glacial morphology:

1. Glacial valley erosion; the valleys of the northern Alps are a succession of glacial troughs and rock-bars. Fresh glacial landforms are exposed by the glaciers, which are everywhere receding, as the terminal ice-tongues retreat from the splendid frontal moraines into which the pro-glacial torrents incise themselves, as at Bossons.

2. Glacial accumulation; moraines and morainic deposits cover large areas and mantle the slopes. This favours agriculture and makes for increased population. Frontal moraines at valley entrances are characteristic of the Alps but rarer in the Pyrenees.

The glaciers have spread their moraines outside the mountain massifs. Morainic deposits stretch from the Dombe to the plateau of

Slopes

The most important forms of relief associated with the peri-glacial climate are the erosion slopes (*glacis d'érosion*) which have developed in weak rock at the foot of escarpments. These *glacis d'érosion* can be found in the

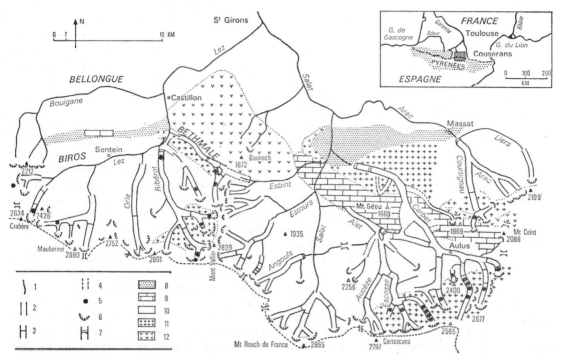

Fig. 19. Glacial morphology of Haut Couserans. (Source: M. Chevalier, *R. Géog. Pyr. et S.O.*, 1954)
1. Unglaciated valley. 2. Glacial valley. 3. Main rock steps of the glacial valleys. 4. Diffluence and transfluence zones. 5. Lake and lacustrine steps. 6. Large cirque and cirque zone. 7. Frontal moraine. 8. Cretaceous Flysch. 9. Infra-Secondary limestone. 10. Primary sedimentary material. 11. Granite. 12. Migmatites.

Chambaran in three series of frontal moraines and fluvio-glacial terraces. In the Pyrenees some very fine series of frontal moraines and sheets of fluvio-glacial deposits occupy fan-shaped series of river and dry valleys that radiate from the Lourdes basin.

In the South-east Languedoc and Provence had peri-glacial climatic conditions during the cold phases of the Quaternary, giving rise to loessic limons, and to the head deposits of the Nîmes *garrigue*.

interior of the southern Alps (Durance valley), round the mountain spurs of the lower Rhône (from the Montagnes de Lure to the Coiron), in the Corbières, the Basque Country and Languedoc. Sometimes there are several tiers of *glacis d'érosion* on one slope; there are five in Diois and the Baronnies.

Present-day erosion

On this highly accidented part of France, all under slope and with abrupt changes in height, the phenomena of erosion occur in many forms: rock-falls, landslips, gullying and subsidence.[24] This present-day erosion can be explained by steep slopes, relief contrasts, accumulations of snow and continental or Mediterranean rainfall.

The most exact information on the intensity of erosion is furnished by the solid matter transported by the rivers. Figures showing the specific amount of degradation are very high for mountain basins (the Drac at Grenoble shows 615 tons per km.[2] per year).

In Mediterranean France erosion is more vigorous than in the temperate zone and strengthens the contrasts between slopes and flats, strips the limestone mountains to the bone and spreads the eroded material over the plains and in the beds of the seasonal torrents. Gullying, of the 'bad-lands' type, appears south of Clermont-Ferrand in the uncompacted materials of the Limagne. It increases in amount as we move south, becoming spectacular in the shale and clay terrains of the Alps.

Glacial and peri-glacial erosion persists at high altitudes, due to heavy snowfall and to seasonal climatic contrasts.

But erosive agents often find a ready helper in man, who is responsible for disrupting the equilibrium of the natural environment. Clearings, deforestation, the extension of fields and vineyards on slopes which are too steep, neglect of the upkeep of terraces or drainage systems, the extension of fallow lands and the substitution of crops which do not bind the soil, such as flowers, for those which do, such as olives and grapes, have often started erosion processes which cannot easily be stopped.

The Menton region suffered multiple landslides in April 1952. These landslides occurred in the afternoon of 24th April and the night of 24th to 25th April as a result of exceptionally heavy rainfall, amounting locally to as much as 300 mm. in 72 hours. This water turned the friable sandy earth on which houses were built, and on which terraced vineyards were held up by low stone walls, into a sea of mud. On the valley slopes

126 landslides of various proportions were counted. They tore up and destroyed vineyards and terraces, demolishing 17 houses and killing or injuring 46 people.

In the Vésubie valley, on 24th November 1926, a mud flow estimated at 2 million m.[3] also caused great damage.

THE RIVER SYSTEMS

The conditions under which the river systems originated and developed in this Alpine and peri-Alpine world were very different from those of Hercynian France. The deformed erosion surfaces on which the river systems established themselves were often wiped out by later episodes.

There has been a succession of drainage systems, very different one from the other, and relative to changing shorelines, positive and negative changes of sea-level, phases of complex deformation, heterogeneous, lithological and structural patterns, and fundamental changes caused by the river systems incising themselves into different superimposed structural units.

The river systems are thus more recent (pre-Pontian) in their courses than those of Hercynian France, and less consistent in the shape of their basins, their types of drainage and the details of their courses. The very large number of tilting movements has often caused a complete reversal of drainage (as in Provence). In this miniature basin and range country with its slopes and back-slopes, the rivers were formed segment by segment under the influence of natural obstacles, proximity of the sea, the presence of a col or a temporary base-level. In matters of detail, minor streams are adapted to structure and follow the lines of maximum slope determined by primitive structures.

Only the largest rivers could remain integrated through all the structural changes, which is why there are so many examples of epigenesis, either by superimposition or by antecedence. The extent of the sedimentation in the Rhône valley, fossilising the relief features of the margins, accounts for the importance of superimposed drainage, of

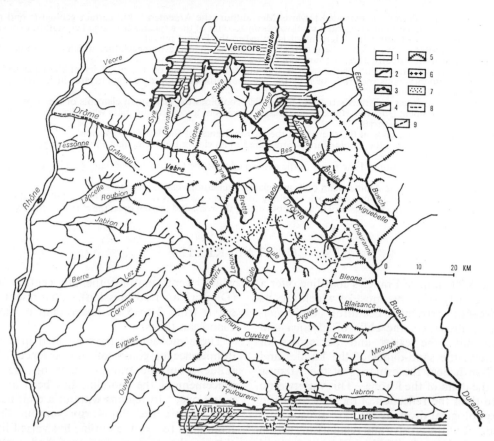

Fig. 20. River system of Diois, the Baronnies and the foothills. (Source: J. Masseport, *Le Diois, les Baronnies et leur avant pays rhodanien*, Grenoble, 1960)

1. Urgonian plateaux of Vercors and Provence. 2. North-west, south-west and north–south parallel courses unadjusted to the structure. 3. Course which has recently been adjusted. 4. Course which is adjusted, though very old because faults have consistently been revived along pre-existing trend lines. 5. Courses which are particularly unadjusted, other than 2. 6. Original water parting, limiting in the south the Southern Baronnies fault, and in the north the fold separating Diois from Bochaine. 7. Zone corresponding to the highest point of the compound Miocene surface. 8. Former course before capture (Roubion-Grânette). 9. Sault faults.

which the Rhône and the Saône furnish several examples.

In certain cases the abnormal unadjusted course of the rivers is an enigma for geomorphologists, and different interpretations have been advanced.

The best-known example is probably the river system of the Gap dome. The two principal rivers, the Durance and the Avance, flow, paradoxically as it seems, along the axes of maximum elevation of the dome. Whereas the earliest explanations invoked 'traditional' causes—river capture, antecedence and superimposition—P. Veyret explains these courses by primitive tectonic rents caused by tension of the dome surface.

14. This isthmus stretched as far as the Montpellier region.
15. This delay explains how the external sub-Alpine regions were affected by marine transgressions of the Oligocene and the Miocene.

C

16. Traditionally Pelvoux is extended towards Mercantour (the Argentera), but certain geologists and geographers (such as J. Chardonnet) extend it southwards on account of the appearance of small crystalline exposures and of domes (such as Gap), while Mercantour is linked to the Estérel massif.

17. The geographers' pre-Alps are the geologists' sub-Alpine chains, a nomenclature which is more accurate from the point of view of structure, but not adopted by geographers.

18. The westward progression of the massifs was uneven, depending on the plasticity of the beds and the resistance of autochthonous materials such as the accumulation of Miocene conglomerates in Bas-Dauphiné, opposite Grande-Chartreuse.

19. Corsica constitutes a distinct structural unit which combines the Hercynian elements of the Alps. Separated from the continent from the Miocene onwards, it consists of a vast granite mass which has been overthrust on the east, by a schistose series.

20. This molasse zone ends in the south with the narrow trench of the *Vallée de Vercors*.

21. In one interpretation the tabular Jura is considered as an element of Hercynian France, comparable to the plateaux of the Haute-Saône.

22. The first manifestations of the rising of the eastern edge of the Central Massif date from the Upper Cretaceous.

23. In the interior of the Alpine chain only two glacial oscillations can be recognised.

24. On 30th March 1963 a mass of rock weighing more than 200 tons came away from a hillside above the village of Plan du Var, wrecking several houses, obstructing the road and tearing open the channel of the Vésubie.

4. COASTAL RELIEF

The 6,200 km. of France's coastline offer a great variety of forms most of which are, as landscapes, extremely beautiful: the *calanques* of Provence, the cliffs of Corsica and Normandy, the capes and peninsulas of Brittany, the sand-dunes of the Landes and the North Sea, the estuaries of the Atlantic and the delta of the Rhône. This variety is no more than the reflection of the structural and morphological diversity we have already analysed. But the erosive and regularising action of the sea shows up lithological and structural contrasts, exposing rocks which, on land, are covered with a mantle of regolith and soil.

The seas which wash these coasts show as great a variety in the depth of the sea-bed as in the direction of the currents and in the range of the tides, which are practically non-existent in the Mediterranean, but which reach 4–12 m. in the Atlantic, with a maximum of 15 m. in Mont-Saint-Michel bay.

The present course of the shoreline dates from the last episodes of the Quaternary, which caused variations in sea-level: these were the Monastirian transgression, contemporary with the last inter-glacial stage, which raised the sea-level to +15 to 20 m.; the pre-Flandrian regression, during the Wurm glacial stage, which is estimated to have lowered the sea-level to −100 m.; and the post-Wurmian (Flandrian) transgression,

which went on until the 5th century A.D. (Dunkirkian transgression). At present the sea is from 2 to 5 m. lower than it was in Flandrian times.

These movements have resulted in a predominance of coasts of submergence. The influence of the transgressions on the displacement of the shoreline has been an unequal one. In regions without a continental shelf, where the slopes run without break from land to sea, the outline has varied little; this is the case in Provence and western Corsica, where variations result rather from very recent tectonic deformations, such as continental flexures. In those more numerous regions where there is a continental shelf there have been considerable changes in the outline of the coasts.

Coastal topography shows the state of the relief at the time of its submergence: we find archipelagos off the north coast of Brittany, rias in Brittany, *calanques* in Provence and estuaries bringing the sea and its agents of erosion into the interior of the land, as in the gulf of Morbihan and the Seine estuary. On low-lying coasts the advancing sea created gulfs which river-borne sediments turned into marshes, which may or may not be sheltered by off-shore bars built on the continental shelf. Maritime Flanders was formed in this way, in front of a coastline running west to east from Cape Blanc-Nez to the region north of Saint-Omer, then bending round towards Bergues. England was probably separated from the continent of Europe by a pro-glacial barrier lake, at the foot of the North Sea ice sheet, discharging through the area between the Boulonnais and the Weald.

Modifications of the coastline by accumulation are evidently rare in coasts of submergence, and the Rhône delta is all the more exceptional for that, although certain rivers flowing into the Atlantic have submarine deltas, such as the mudbanks at the mouth of the Gironde and the Loire.

Structural conditions and the degree of morphological evolution reached on the land itself, are more responsible for the coastal topography than erosion by the sea. The islands and peninsulas fringing the Armorican peninsula correspond to portions of higher ground which are often considered to be of structural origin (fault-blocks); the islands of Charente are anticlines continuing the structural folds of the hinterland.

The work of the sea was in the field of differential erosion; this is reflected on all scales, whether we consider the outline of the coast as a whole, with its bays corresponding to weak rocks and capes to resistant rocks, or its detailed form, with the undercutting of dykes and the opening up of joints. There are great differences in the part played by cliffs in the morphology of the French coasts; their role is all important on the sedimentary coasts of Picardy, Boulonnais and Normandy, and minimal in the least exposed and most recently submerged crystalline coasts. Rocky and cliffed coasts are in fact far from synonymous; often the rocky coast falls into the sea before marine erosion has had the time or the strength to carve out a cliff. Regions with cliffs which have receded to any large extent are rare; there are the Vaches Noires cliffs in Normandy, the chalk cliffs of the Pays de Caux and the Jurassic sandstone cliffs of Boulonnais. Marine erosion has worked more quickly than normal erosion, transforming the valleys into hanging valleys or notches.

The function of the sea in transporting and accumulating deposits is no less important. It has built, all along the low-lying coasts of Languedoc, the Landes, Cotentin and Picardy, long off-shore bars, usually covered with dunes, as for 200 km. from Bayonne to the Gironde estuary; their heads move in the direction of the off-shore currents, displacing the mouths of the estuaries, as in Picardy, closing lagoons, as in Languedoc, and joining islands to the shore, as at Quiberon, Batz and the Hyères. But the sea accumulates sand in every bay and every inlet, forming beaches which contrast with the rocky headlands.

Salt-marshes are an important type of coastal scenery both because of their size (the Poitevin marsh is 9,500 km.^{2}) and because of the unusual landscapes they offer. They occur in the sheltered part of an estuary such as the Gironde, behind an off-shore bar like the coastal plain of Picardy or in the landward part of a bay like the Poitou marshes (fig. 14).

Since the Flandrian transgression, the effect of tidal currents and combined sedimentation by the sea and the rivers, where rivers flow into the sea, has led to the deposition of mud. These marshes, like the margins of the estuaries, consist of a zone covered with vegetation called *schorre* or *herbu*, occasionally submerged by the sea, and a zone of soft mud without vegetation, regularly covered by the sea; this is the *slikke* or *tangue* of the marshes of north-eastern Brittany, and the *terre de bri* of the marshes of west-central France.

Variations in sea-level have led to complex types of coastal morphology. The recession of the sea at the time of the Würm glaciation exposed Monastirian cliffs and estuaries, differentially remodelled by continental erosion systems and fossilised by peri-glacial flows and dune formations. The rising seas were quick to clear away these loose sediments mantling the rocks *in situ*; they rapidly carved out cliffs, exhumed the buried Monastirian cliffs and exposed granite boulders which had lain submerged in the sand and the silt (north coast of Brittany). This explains

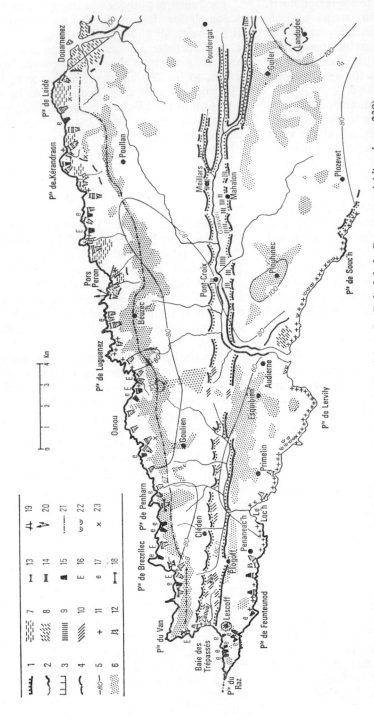

Fig. 21.   Morphological map of Cap Sizun.   (Source: A. Guilcher, *Le Relief de la Bretagne méridionale*, p. 230)

1. Escarpment of hard rock.   2. Coastline (thickened line along the high cliffs).   3. Fault which appears to have been revived in the Tertiary.   4. Limits of an ancient surface farther inland (more or less worn away abandoned cliff—*falaise morte*).   5. Contours of the Eocene surface.   6. Fragment of this surface (which may have been slightly modified in places and incorporated in a more recent planation).   7. Sainte-Anne bench (50–65 m.).   8. 30–35 m. bench.   9. Benches along the Goayen.   10. Benches along the Loc'h-Laoual.   11. Monastirian beaches.   12. Small coastal valley filled with head and in process of exhumation.   13. Coastal hanging valley in the Monastirian surface.   14. Coastal hanging valley in the 30–35 m. bench.   15. Coastal valley still filled with head and not exhumed.   16. Epigenesis on head in a coastal valley.   17. Embryonic coastal valley.   18. Structural break of slope in a coastal valley.   19. Hanging valley due to cliff recession.   20. Diffluence.   21. Watershed in the north of Cap Sizun.   22. Dunes.   23. Residual Eocene quartzitic sandstone.

why marine erosion appears more active in some sheltered bays than on exposed headlands.

Analysis of the relief often reveals the presence of staged fossil coastlines—such as cliff and abrasion platform—at uniform heights. These forms are the relics of marine still-stands at higher levels during the Quaternary. The most widespread of these, at about $+2$ to $+5$ m., correspond to a retreat stage after the Monastirian (Lower Monastirian or Normannian) transgression. But higher sea-levels can be recognised at $+40$ m. to the east of Cherbourg, at $+60$ m. to the south of Cape Gris-Nez, and at $+85$ m. in the maritime Alps.[25]

25. The interpretation of very much higher levels raises some tricky problems.

5. MORPHOLOGICAL AREAS AND TYPES IN FRANCE

If we refrain from taking into account single structural units, which should never be allowed to influence attempts to classify geographical regions, and consider only types of relief or groups of closely associated forms resulting from the morphological history of France, we can distinguish these main zones:

1. The plains and plateaux of Hercynian France.
2. The faulted and folded regions of Hercynian and Alpine France.
3. The great valleys of the young mountains.

A. The Plains and Plateaux of Hercynian France

This zone includes all of Hercynian France which does not show in its morphology visible evidence of the sudden and intense deformations of the Tertiary. Its distance from the mountain-building movements of the Pyrenees and the Alps has given it a gentle, unexciting structure, livened simply by deformations with a large radius of curvature, by warping and by some sharper irregularities which are, however, very isolated and localised.

This is the domain of plain and plateau relief forms in the sedimentary basins as well as on the ancient massifs; both show evidence of the number and magnitude of the cycles of erosion which have planed down upland masses which were already comparatively reduced in size and uplifted to only modest heights.

Plains and plateaux develop on rocks which outcrop over vast areas, and are relatively homogeneous: the Cretaceous Series is a result of the uniformity of the chalk itself and of the wide extent of its clay-with-flints cover, crystalline and limestone rocks, and the uncemented Tertiary rocks of the Aquitaine basin.

In this area, hills and scarps are rare, and ridges even rarer. Usually they only appear as isolated morphological features, such as the hills which form the boundary of inland Brittany, the Artois ridge, the inward-facing scarps of Bray, the cuesta of Auge, the Appalachian ridges of the Armorican massif, the Monédières escarpment. They often occur at the junction of two plains or two plateaux at different levels, and only rarely are they found associated in such a way as to give rise to varied morphology.

There are, of course, morphological differences of lithological or structural origin; there are large or small basins complementary to the uplands, and depressions breaking the continuity of plateaux, but these contrasts are relative; the Rennes basin and that of Châteaulin in the Armorican massif are distinguished from the surrounding regions by characteristics which have been progressively acquired. Often the contrast is strongly emphasised along only one of the edges of the basin.

In this homogeneous type of area the essential quality of the relief is determined by valley network depressions. It is a concave type of relief, graded and divided into large basins which are, however, not very deep.

Regional contrasts stem from differences in the density of valleys. The morphology of the valleys determines the type of relief in the plains and *bocages* of this part of France. The higher ground, drier because it is well drained, more windswept but easier to work, contrasts with the damp valley bottoms, where ground water is nearer the surface and where the soil is heavier but more fertile, and sometimes marshy. Between them, and very different one from the other, are the hillsides with their benches and their gentle slopes, concave or convex, incised by small valleys. Peasant toponymy has given us precise words for these elements of the countryside, emphasising their peculiar characteristics: valley, mountain, upland plain and bottom. The thousandfold repetition of these elements gives us the fabric into which these regions are woven. The texture of this fabric is uneven, depending on the density of valleys within a given area, but it is a difference of degree rather than of kind. There are many centres of population and agricultural districts, and one type of countryside is repeated an infinite number of times.

Northern and western France is wide open for communications, or at least if there are obstacles they cannot be attributed to the relief, but rather to the type of soil, the activities of man and natural vegetation. Limestone and chalk plains have an especial advantage owing to the ease of communication they allow.

There are no real obstacles to traffic anywhere, and roads and railways radiate in the same way from every town. On the whole, if there is any natural distinction between regions, we should not normally exaggerate its significance. There are certainly differences between Valois and Soissonnais, between Vimeu and the plateau of Picardy and between Trégorrois and Léon, but they are not very sharply defined; lithological differences are responsible for the most evident regional contrasts, and often we have to fall back on historical boundaries to distinguish and delimit the various regions.

B. The Uplifted, Faulted and Folded Regions of Hercynian and Alpine France

As we leave the western plains and move eastwards, altitudes increase; we are entering another zone whose frontiers are not easily defined, but whose component parts share many common characteristics.

The skeleton, as it were, of this zone is the great escarpment-divide and watershed we have already discussed. It consists of the east of the Paris basin, the greater part of the Central Massif, Languedoc, Provence apart from the Alpes-Maritimes, the Rhône–Saône valley, the plateaux of the Jura, the Vosges and Alsace, and part of the folds of the Jura and the pre-Alps.

The first characteristic is the importance of morphological contrasts of structural origin. All these regions, whether they are structurally old or young, were displaced, faulted and folded during the various orogenic episodes of the Tertiary. From the fracture belt of Saverne to the tilted block of the Montagne Noire and the Escandorgue lava-flow, there is a continuous succession of rift-valleys and horsts, plateaux and scarps, subsidence zones and faulted minor ranges, massifs and depressions. The patchwork appearance of the geological maps reflects a morphological patchwork, juxtaposing sharply contrasting topographical units. The concave relief of the valleys plays an important part in limestone plateaux and up-warped crystalline massifs such as the Central Massif, but it is soon broken by scarps and changes of slope such as do not exist in northern and western France.

This is also an area of limestone plateaux and long cuesta dip slopes from Lorraine to the Grands Causses, through the plateaux of Langres, Haute-Saône and the Jura, the limestone fault-blocks of Mâconnais, the table-lands (*plans*) and the folds of the pre-Alps, the plateaux of Vivarais and the *plans* of Provence. These limestone masses show karstic development to an unequal degree, and they vary in height above their crystalline or sedimentary surrounds, but they play a leading part in regional division and in the contrast between different *pays*.

The drainage pattern of this area is unusual in more than one respect; on each side of the main watershed the flow is southerly; valleys, corridors, depressions and structural troughs all run in the same direction.

The scale of relief and of relief forms is greater than in northern and western France. There are mountain summits, round-topped masses (*ballons*), *puys* and the elongated ridges of the Cévennes, none of which can be seen west of the divide. Broken relief predominates and structural irregularities tend to overshadow the minor relief forms, although these are still visible in the detailed pattern. Moreover, relief forms are more sharply differentiated than in the north and in particular localities west. There are districts with special advantages, whose attraction is derived from their aspect, their soils or their micro-climates. Hill-slopes, cuestas and fault-line scarps are the most widespread types of relief forms. People have settled at the base of these slopes, helped by the greater variety and fertility of the soil and by sheltered and sunny climates.

Apart from the distinction between high *pays* and low-lying *pays* we must also distinguish between good districts and cantons, and poor ones. This contrast does not exist so markedly in western and northern France. Such a morphological environment facilitates the delimitation of clearly defined regions, with sharply contrasting characteristics.

The pattern of relief in this zone thus predetermines in large measure the pattern of communications. Axes of communication are canalised in the valleys or along the interfluves. Cross-country communications are therefore limited and difficult.

C. Alpine France and the Mountain Slopes

This third zone has only a limited area: the Pyrenean and Alpine valleys. Their unique characteristics are twofold:

1. Their great height, which increases the available relief and results in an altitudinal zoning of relief forms, climatic conditions, vegetation and soils. These differences have a strong influence on the development and use of land.

2. The predominance of valleys and vast mountainsides. In fact, in this area flats and other such features not normally associated with great valleys are rare; where they do exist they are too high and too inaccessible from the valleys to be developed and used by man. The geographical *milieu* consists in effect of the pattern of valley bottoms and the great slopes which rise from them.

All settlement and human activity is concentrated in the valleys and thus distributed in a characteristic linear and vertically zoned pattern. Whereas in the area previously discussed there are still topographical areas not directly connected with the river systems, here everything depends on the valleys. This is the land of great intramontane valleys in the strict sense of the term. The region does not necessarily coincide with geological divisions, which in both the Alps and the Pyrenees include part of the surrounding country. We need hardly stress the close connection between the main valley bottoms and the road and rail networks in this area.

Lucien Gachon has made a subtle analysis of the contrast between the last two mentioned zones, the zone of broken relief with innumerable rounded uplands separated by more or less open valleys, and the zone of great Alpine valleys. He gives an excellent description of the repercussions of these regional relief contrasts on the human geography of the area:

'In the Alps, the physical unit is the valley . . . human life has taken refuge in these deep narrow trenches. This is because in the Alps the improved area (*ager*) strictly speaking is localised and narrowly confined by the highly integrated systems of relief and drainage. In the Central Massif, on the other hand, the improved area (*ager*) can be extended or reduced to a quite extraordinary degree . . . mainly because the integra-

tion of relief and drainage systems is less well advanced.'[26]

The soils of these mountain areas are very different from those of the plains. They are governed by altitude, aspect and slope.

26. L. Gachon, 'Les Alpes françaises et le Massif Central', *R. Géog. Alpine* (1955), Part IV, pp. 685–96; the *ager* means the cultivated area (cf. p. 278).

6. MINERAL RESOURCES

The geographical composition of France endows it with a range and variety of mineral resources that few other nations possess. The combination of ancient massifs and sedimentary basins, together with metamorphic and volcanic activity, has increased this variety both in the ancient massifs and in the young mountains.[27]

Thus every region is endowed with mineral wealth, even if of unequal value; this has, at one epoch or another of French history, contributed to the economic life of each region, made easier the establishment of its infrastructures, given it a settled population and brought in its industries. In 1959, 51 departments had mines with a production of more than 10 million francs.

The value of mineral production in France amounted in 1959 to 6,785 million francs, distributed as follows:

Quarried materials	1,231·6
Fuel and power	4,023·6
Metallic ores	1,101·3
Non-metallic ores	428·1

A. Quarried Materials

The value of production can be broken down as follows:

Constructional and ornamental materials	380·9
Alluvial sand and gravel	373·1
Materials for embanking and road maintenance	298·2
Flux for iron smelting	30·6
Agricultural fertilisers	18·8
Filling for mines	18·4
Other materials for industrial use	111·6

We need only think of the materials used in traditional building before the age of concrete and prefabrication in order to realise how rich France is in building stone: hard stone provided by granite, sandstone, lava and millstone (from Brie and Beauce), freestone from the Jurassic limestone rocks of Lorraine, Burgundy (Côte-d'Or Comblanchian), Poitou, Charente and Caen, and the Tertiary rocks of the Paris region (*calcaire grossier*), and slates from Maine-et-Loire. France also possesses numerous marble quarries in the Pyrenees, which form the principal source of supply (green marble from Campan), also in Provence (pink marble from Brignoles), the Alps (green from Barcelonnette and blue from Hauteville), Burgundy (pink from Burgundy), the Boulonnais (beige from Lunel) and the West (from Sablé-sur-Sarthe).

But the subsoil also provides limestone and gypsum (from the Paris region and Ariège), marl and marly chalk for cement: chalk from the edge of the Boulonnais depression, chalk from the Oise valley, marl from the Vivarais (le Teil), clay and limons for brick and tile works and potteries, refractory clays, and flux for ironworking (limestone flux from the Meuse). Alluvial land yields sand and gravel which are used in considerable quantities for building and metalling.[28]

Most of these resources are relatively scattered and obtainable all over the country. There are only 6 departments without brick or tile works. All departments have sand quarries. In 1956, 22 departments produced less than 100,000 tons of sand and gravel; all the others exceeded this figure. The main regions producing these materials are naturally the sedimentary areas, flat or gently un-dulating, where these heavy products can easily be transported. Such regions are the Paris basin, Alsace, the Aquitaine basin, the Rhône valley, Languedoc and Provence.

The centres of production of materials for refractory products are less scattered; they are localised in the Paris basin and the North, the Rhône corridor and the Digoin–Mont-chanin region, and the Aquitaine basin.

B. Metallic and Non-metallic Ores

A complete inventory of mineral ores would assume encyclopaedic proportions, for the list of French mineral resources is very long indeed. The most important ones are indicated in Table VIII. Later we will

TABLE VIII. PRINCIPAL ORES MINED
IN FRANCE

(1959: in millions of francs)

Metallic ores

Iron ore	.	. 1,034·5	Gold ore .	. 2·7
Bauxite	.	. 36	Copper ore .	. 0·6
Lead ore	.	. 14·4	Magnesite .	. 0·5
Zinc ore	.	. 8·3	Manganese ore	. 0·1
Tungsten ore	.	4·2		

Non-metallic ores

Potassium	.	233·3	Feldspar .	. 3·5
Salt (rock salt and				
sea salt)	.	. 80·7	Barytes .	. 3·3
Sulphur	.	. 41·3	Asphalt .	. 2·3
Iron pyrites	.	17·1	Bentonite .	. 1·8
Kaolin	.	. 16·6	Phosphates .	. 1·3
Talc	.	. 12·2	Oil-shales .	. 0·04
Asbestos	.	. 8·6	Mica . .	. 0·04
Fluorine	.	. 6		

return to the great sources of fuel and power; here we will consider only uranium deposits.

As uranium ores are very numerous, de-posits are naturally many. Moreover, the potentialities of French territory in this respect have by no means been fully explored. The deposits at present being mined are scattered throughout the Central Massif, in Morvan, Forez, Velay, Mont Lozère, Rouer-gue, Margeride, Dordogne, Limousin, in the Vendée massif, the Montagne de la Serre, the Vosges, Bas-Languedoc, Morbihan and eastern Provence.

But the map showing these deposits is
*

continually changing and their distribution can only become more widely dispersed in the future.

It is convenient to divide the production of ores into metallic ores (1,101·3 million francs in 1959) and non-metallic ores (428 million francs).

The two crowning glories of French mineral production are iron and bauxite.

IRON

In 1964 France produced 60·9 million tons, coming third in the world after the U.S.S.R. and the United States.[29] Reserves are esti-mated at more than 8,000 million tons. Lor-raine and the Armorican massif contain most of it, with the Pyrenees a long way behind.

The iron deposits of Lorraine are among the largest in the world. It is an oolitic ore, above the Liassic and just below the Bajocian limestone (Inferior Oolite). It outcrops on the flank of the escarpments of the Côtes de Moselle for more than a hundred and twenty kilometres, from Longwy to Neuves-Maisons (with a break of 15 km. at Pont-à-Mousson) and for 30 km. west to east, owing to the valleys which cut through into the dip-slope of the cuesta. This *minette* ore, which has a limestone or siliceous gangue, contains 27–35% iron; it is characterised by the presence of phosphorus. The reserves are said to be about 6,000 million tons of ore (containing 1,950 million tons of iron).

The deposits in the Armorican massif appear in a very different form. They are found in two sedimentary beds, the Ordovi-cian Armorican sandstone (*Grès Armoricains*) and the Calymene shales. The sandstone beds are found in the ore-basin in the south of the massif, from Anjou into Brittany; the basin is divided into three large Silurian synclines formed between the Sarthe and the Vilaine. The shales form the ore-basin of Normandy, divided between four synclines, from the May Saint-André syncline south of Caen to the Domfront–Mortain syncline (with, in addition, a small deposit at Diélette on the north-west coast of the Cotentin). The iron-bearing beds are folded and faulted, and are therefore mined under very different conditions from those of Lorraine. The ores, on the other hand, have a higher iron content (45–50%) and little or no phosphorus.

The reserves of these western basins are also very large—with an iron content of about 730 million tons. The great difference between the production of Lorraine (62 million tons in 1960) and that of the Armorican massif (3,800,000) is all the more astonishing. But the Armorican basins suffer from their situation, which exposes them to competition from foreign ores, also from the absence of large iron works in the neighbourhood, and from an inadequate transport system (the mines of Diélette were closed in 1962).

The 360,000 tons of ore mined in the Pyrenees makes an even more sorry total. These deposits are divided between three places: Barburet, near Ferrières, on the boundary between the Hautes-Pyrénées and the Basses-Pyrénées; Puymorens, where mining is carried out at a height of 2,100 m.; and Le Canigou, where ten concessions are responsible for most of the production in the Pyrenees.[30] The Pyrenean ores have the advantage of a high iron content and a good quality (3–4% manganese), but reserves are low.

Apart from such deep deposits, there are surface deposits scattered through many of the regions of France. These deposits, spread out in sheets or localised in pockets, are found on the surface of Upper Jurassic limestone, in a more or less diffused state, or concentrated in granular form in residual clays (argiles rouges). At one time they were worked intensively and exclusively, but most are now abandoned. However, surface working is still going on in the Armorican massif, to the north-west of Chateaubriant, with a production in the region of 300,000 tons.

BAUXITE AND OTHERS

Bauxite is the result of pedological modification of limestone which emerged in the Cretaceous. It is mined in Var (Brignoles), Hérault (Bédarieux) and Ariège. The Var workings represent 80% of the production of France. Total production is 2,424,000 tons

(1964),[31] placing France fifth in the world.[32] Reserves are not exactly known but are said to represent about sixty years' production.

There are, on French territory, about forty lead and zinc deposits, which either are or could be worked. They are associated with the metamorphic rocks of the ancient massifs, particularly the slightly metamorphosed shales and limestones of the Armorican massif (two deposits), of the Central Massif, the axial zone of the Pyrenees, the interior massifs of the Alps (La Plagne), the Maures massif and Corsica.

The deposits are most numerous in the south of the Central Massif. There are about twenty there, arranged in a V-shape on the borders of the massif, from Largentière in the east, through the deposits of the Montagne Noire, to Villefranche-de-Rouergue in the west.

Galena and blende deposits are always closely associated, and also include iron pyrites, mispickel, magnetite, arsenic, gold and an appreciable quantity of silver (1 kg. of silver per ton of ore).[33] These deposits have a very low content of pure metal, around 2–5%, as against contents of 20–30% in North Africa or the United States. The reserves are moreover very limited and they are often badly situated in mountainous regions. On the forty or so known deposits, about ten mines are being worked at present, and others are dormant, awaiting an economic revival so that they can open again for a time. Lead production is 10,700 tons (1964), and that of zinc 16,900 tons. The Pierrefitte zinc bed in the Pyrenees provides 45% of all zinc mined in France.

Tungsten ores are mined in Allier, copper ores in Rhône, gold in Aude and iron pyrites in Rhône, Saône-et-Loire and Gard.

Potassium (formed by the concentration of potassium salts in lagoon deposits) is mined in a large deposit in Alsace, between Mulhouse and Guebwiller. Production amounted to 1,141,000 tons (1964).

Deposits of sodium chloride, which has important industrial uses, are found in Triassic lagoon formations. There are underground workings in Lorraine (Saulnois and valleys of the Meurthe and the Seille; at Varangeville nineteen salt-beds contain a total thickness of 72 m. of rock salt), in Franche-Comté at Poligny and Salins, in the Landes (Dax), in Basses-Pyrénées (Salies-de-Béarn) and in Haute-Garonne (Salies-du-Salat). The production of these mines is far greater than that of the salt-marshes.[34]

France contains many other substances which it would be tedious to enumerate, but which lead to a certain amount of industrial activity and bring (or could bring or have brought) wealth to the regions producing them; at the very least they have endowed these regions with an industrial tradition. These substances are not all of great worth, but they are sometimes very important, even if the deposits are small or isolated.

Tin has been mined at Saint-Renan near Brest. Sulphur was found at Marseilles, Aubagne and the district round Manosque.[35]

Fluor spar (used as flux in metallurgy) is to be found in Provence (Maures–Estérel), in Pyrénées-Orientales, Tarn and Haute-Loire.

Kaolin, a product of the alteration of feldspar, and the raw material of porcelain, is fairly widely distributed (in Morbihan, Côtes-du-Nord, Allier, Indre-et-Loire and Dordogne).

Diatomite, a siliceous powder used as an abrasive and an insulating material, and in silica black, is mined in Cantal and Ardèche.

The talc deposit of Luzenac (Ariège), with 80,000 tons per year, accounts for a fifth of world production (it is quarried to a thickness of 50 m.).

Magnesium is mined in the Basque country.

Asbestos was obtained from Corsica until mining ceased in 1965.

Certain resources are now practically un-exploited, but at one time they went through periods of intensive mining which brought activity and wealth to several districts. This was the case, for example, with phosphate of lime, which ceased to be extracted when the North African deposits began to be worked. The phosphatic beds are found at various levels in the sedimentary rocks of the Carboniferous (Montagne Noire and Pyrenees), the Lias and the Cretaceous (Paris basin), as well as in solution pockets in chalk (Amiénois). Renewed exploitation of such deposits is at the mercy of international political and economic circumstances.

C. Mineral Waters

French territory is extraordinarily rich in mineral waters. These waters come either from very ancient deep-seated juvenile waters or from ground water which emerges naturally at springs or is trapped in one spot after a long journey through faults and joints.

These mineral waters appear, generally speaking, in regions where the basement rocks have been modified by volcanic activity, as in Auvergne, or by recent folding, as in the Pyrenees. But they are also found in the Alps and the Paris basin, where the Triassic and Liassic rocks outcrop or are found near the surface, as at Vittel and Forges-les-Eaux.

These waters are very varied in nature and effects. There are radioactive waters from Luchon and Plombières; saline (chlorinated) waters from Dax and Salins; sulphate waters from Vittel and Bagnères-de-Bigorre; sulphuretted (calcic) waters from Aix and Enghien; sodium waters from Cauterets, Luchon, Uriage and Challes; alkaline waters from Vichy, Royat, La Bourboule and Évian; and ferruginous waters from Forges-les-Eaux.

27. By reason of their structure, the Pyrenees have a much greater mineral wealth than the Alps.
28. Sand has a great variety of uses, and not all types can be used for the same purposes: there are building sands, foundry-sands, river-sands.
29. 1960: 67·7 million tons.
30. A deposit has recently been discovered at Julos (reserves 15 million tons).
31. 1929: 678,000 tons; 1938: 649,000 tons; 1955: 1,493,000 tons.
32. After the U.S.S.R., Jamaica, Surinam and British Guiana.
33. This accounts for the place-names Argentière and Largentière.
34. The salt-producing centres of Salin de Giraud and Aigues-Mortes accounted, in 1958, for almost 90% of the total production of all French salt-marshes.
35. The sulphur production of Lacq (see p. 205) has dealt a death blow to these deposits.

II

CLIMATE

1. CLIMATIC ADVANTAGES OF FRANCE

These advantages have been shown in broad outline in the first chapter. It is often said that the French climate possesses the characteristics which are universal in France: moderation, a happy mean in all things and a perfect balance between opposing influences. This is true; taken as a whole, France has neither prolonged and severe winters, nor very dry summers, nor torrential rains. France owes these characteristics both to her situation and to the lay-out of her relief.

A. Situation

The latitude of France, between 42·5° N. and 51° N., means that most of the country lies in the southern half of the temperate zone *sensu stricto*, and that part of it is on the northern fringe of the subtropical zone. The dividing line between the temperate and sub-tropical zones (a temperature of 6° C. for the coldest month of the year and of 20° C. in July on the western side of continents) passes through southern France. Both Aquitaine and the Mediterranean region belong to this subtropical *midi*.[1] It is not always realised that France belongs to two climatic domains, because the subtropical climate is regarded as a subdivision of the temperate zone.

France has two seaboards, close to each other, and this gives her from the climatic standpoint a situation that is unique in Europe. To the west, France is at a high enough latitude to derive full benefit from the warm waters of North Atlantic Drift. To the south, the Mediterranean basin brings its reserves of humidity and its moderating influence to areas in latitudes which would otherwise suffer the rigours of a desert climate.

B. The Distribution of the Relief

The distribution of the relief leaves France especially open to climatic influence from the west. France has great advantages over the Iberian peninsula with its high relief, over the upland western margins of the British Isles (Welsh mountains, Pennines) and over the western seaboard of the United States, where the mountain barrier restricts oceanic influence to a narrow coastal zone. But climatic influences from the north, east and south also find sufficiently favourable conditions to enable them to penetrate a long way inland.

Nevertheless these climatic advantages do not imply regularity or uniformity of climatic factors. From the very fact of her advantageous situation, France is constantly in the path of disturbances associated with the polar front, is subjected by turns to air masses of different origins and comes under the influence of meteorological centres of activity with sharply contrasted characteristics. The price that France has to pay for her advantages is a climate made up of a succession of weather types, and liability to climatic disasters and abnormal conditions. Though the annual and monthly averages show the French climate to be a temperate one, that should not make us forget the realities of the particular day's weather or month's climate.

1. Climatic conditions in the south of the Central Massif are more complex.

2. ELEMENTS AND FACTORS OF THE CLIMATE

A. Temperatures

The distribution of temperature clearly shows three influences acting in varying degrees (whether we are concerned with temperatures reduced to mean sea-level, with observed temperatures or with the range of temperature) (fig. 22):

1. The influence of latitude. Average temperatures for the year decrease from 15° C. (Côte d'Azur) to 9° C. (Lille). In the intermediate seasons (spring and autumn) the isotherms follow the parallels in all except the coastal regions.

2. The influence of the oceanic margins. The respective importance of the latitude and the Atlantic seaboard varies according to the seasons; the oceanic influence is at its maximum in winter when the warmth of the water counterbalances the effects of latitude; then the isotherms of 6°–8° C. surround the coasts from the Cotentin to the Basque country. The Channel plays a less important part owing to its epicontinental nature. But the oceanic influence has a clearer and more durable effect on the range of temperature; the annual range isopleths tend to follow the meridians and coastlines; the annual range of temperature amounts to 10° C. at Brest, 14° C. at Nice, 16° C. at Paris, 19° C. at Strasbourg. France, then, has neither the very small range of the pure oceanic climate (Valentia 4·7° C.) nor the excessive contrasts of the true continental climate (Warsaw 21·3° C.).

3. The influence of the relief is predominant in the pattern of true isotherms, even if the other two influences can be seen in the temperature as a whole. In January most of the land to the west of the pre-Alps, the Jura and the Meuse has a temperature equal to or above 0° C.; only the higher parts of the Central Massif are not thus favoured. In July, apart from the higher parts of the Alps, the Pyrenees, the Jura and the Central Massif, temperatures rise above 15°, the highest mean temperature for this month being 24° C.

The pattern of these actual temperatures emphasises the regional contrasts already suggested by the analysis of the relief. In the plains of northern and western France the temperature curves are simple; large areas have regimes of uniform temperatures, without any marked contrasts attributable to the relief.

In the part of the country with strongly differentiated relief, isotherms are crowded together and show finger-like shapes corresponding to the valleys or lowland corridors (the 20° C. isotherm advances as far north as Chalon-sur-Saône in July). As a result, neighbouring districts have very different climatic conditions, hills contrasting with lowlands and ridges with valleys. Warmer and cooler *pays* are found side by side and interwoven, each with its own regional or local climate.

Regional differences in temperature, which do not exist in northern and western France, are very important here. Even in Lorraine differences are observed between cuesta dipslopes and subsequent vales or depressions. The valleys and the enclosed and isolated basins of the Central Massif are affected at night by the well-known phenomena of temperature inversion.

An important element of the climatic conditions of a region is the duration of frost, which is determined by altitude and distance from the sea rather than by latitude. Only the coastal regions of the Atlantic and the Mediterranean have on average less than a month of days with frost. Above 1,000 m., top-soil and water are frozen and the snow lies on the ground for more than three months; during this time frost and snow prevent agricultural activity and make communications difficult, so that the way of life and living conditions must be adjusted to the long cold spells. But

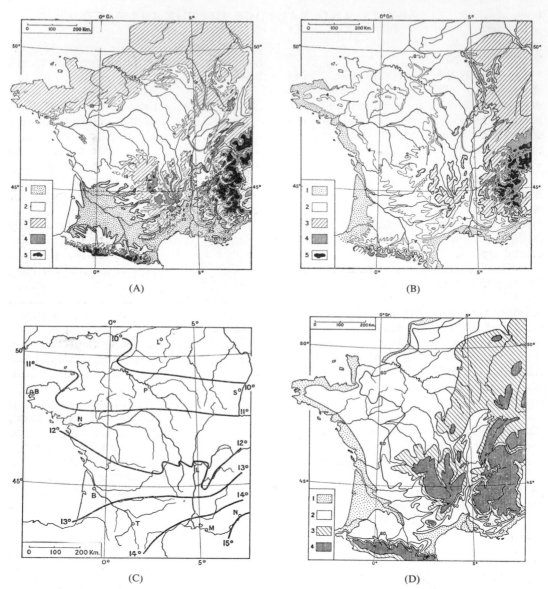

(A)   (B)

(C)   (D)

Fig. 22.   Temperatures.   (Source: E. De Martonne, *Géographie Universelle*, A. Colin, Vol. VI)
A. January: Actual mean temperatures.
1. Over 6° C.   *2*. 6° to 0°.   *3*. 0° to −5°.   *4*. −5° to −10°.   *5*. Below −10° C.
B. July: Actual mean temperatures.
1. Over 20° C.   *2*. 18° to 20°.   *3*. 15° to 18°.   *4*. 10° to 15°.   *5*. Below 10° C.
C. Mean annual temperature.
D. Number of days with frost.
1. Less than 40 days of frost.   *2*. 40 to 80 days.   *3*. 80 to 100 days.   *4*. More than 100 days.

even Lorraine has more than 80 days with frost.

In eastern France, Languedoc, Provence and the Rhône–Saône corridor, especially south of Valence, there are warmer regions set between the highlands which overlook and enclose them, and which themselves have three months or more of frost.

The seasonal distribution of frost is as important as its duration. In the whole of western France and the low-lying oceanic regions frost is strictly limited to winter. Farther inland, on the other hand, at altitudes over 800 m. in the northern Central Massif, and in its southern part at over 1,000–2,000 m., frost can occur in the middle of summer. Intermediate regions are not free from frosts in late spring (May to June) and in autumn (September), these being very harmful to agriculture.

B. Atmospheric Circulation

France, and more generally western Europe, where land areas are small and land and sea are closely interwoven, does not form an air-mass source region but rather a kind of no-man's-land, the possession of which is disputed by pressure systems and air streams, which may originate thousands of miles away. These many and varied meteorological centres of action give rise over western Europe to a frontal and circulation pattern of extreme mobility.

METEOROLOGICAL CENTRES OF ACTIVITY

Low pressures

The Icelandic low is the most constant and most important semi-permanent low-pressure centre. It is a low-pressure zone of dynamic origin intensified, especially in winter, by the warm water of the North Atlantic Drift. It attracts disturbances and air masses from the north (polar air), from the west (polar front) and from the south (tropical air), revitalises depressions and steers them towards Europe, giving them a westerly path.

The Gulf of Genoa low (or Ligurian depression) is established chiefly in winter and during the intermediate seasons; in summer it gives way to subtropical high-pressure centres moving up from the south.

In summer, when central Europe is strongly heated, a central European depression is sometimes established.

High pressures

Western Europe is under the influence of oceanic and continental high-pressure centres. The most important of the *oceanic high-pressure centres* is the Azores anticyclone, part of the subtropical ridge, of dynamic origin, which surrounds the hemispheres with unequal intensity, separating the trade-wind circulation from that of the Westerlies. To be more exact, this is an offshoot of the Azores anticyclone, which has developed in a mass of more or less modified polar air. This anticyclone, owing to its mobility, exerts a profound influence; in winter it does not move beyond the 35th parallel, leaving the western Mediterranean exposed to the polar air masses and cyclones coming from the west. In summer it reaches the 48th parallel, going as far north as the Loire and covering the western Mediterranean. All southern France is then under its protective influence, which shelters it from the mild moist air streams of the Atlantic disturbances. This protection is reinforced, in a more lasting way, by the existence of a high-pressure zone aloft over the western Mediterranean basin.

Independently of the Azores anticyclone, but often appearing to be an extension of it, there are Atlantic anticyclones resulting from outflows of polar air between two families of disturbances. After several major outflows a true North Atlantic anticyclone may be formed to replace the Icelandic depression.

Continental high-pressure centres. These correspond to temporary anticyclones which are thermal in origin; they are formed in the cold season over Scandinavia, central and eastern Europe or Greenland. Continental high-pressure centres are sometimes autonomous; often they are the extreme western advance post of the high-pressure centres reigning all winter over Asia and European

Russia. In certain favourable barometric conditions a continental anticyclone is joined to an oceanic anticyclone (from the Azores) by a ridge of high pressure separating the Atlantic from the Mediterranean. These continental anticyclones result in the appearance over France of cold, dry air currents of particular severity.

FRONTS

These air masses are separated by frontal zones along which warm and cold air come into contact, causing disturbances to form; the most important of these zones are:

1. The polar front separating polar and tropical air; but often the polar front does not correspond to this definition, as the tropical air is replaced by returning polar air which has become quasi-tropical.

2. The arctic front where polar air is in contact with air from the Arctic basin. This front is not confined to high latitudes; it can go as far south as the Mediterranean, bringing together arctic and tropical air.

3. The Mediterranean front separates, in winter, the cold polar continental air from the warm Mediterranean air.

Other secondary fronts appear for short periods, with unequal influences on French territory. Such are the trade-wind front between the oceanic trades and the continental Saharan trades, and the Aquitaine front over the Bay of Biscay between Atlantic air and continental air.

The paths followed by the disturbances associated with these frontal zones sweep over the whole of France, bringing about a succession of air streams from the north-west, the west, the south-west, the south-east and the east. The direction of these paths is determined by the position of the pressure systems at the time.

The constant movement of the pressure systems and frontal zones produces a great variety of patterns over western Europe; in order to clarify this perpetual kaleidoscope, meteorologists have distinguished five source regions from which air masses and winds emanate, singly or combined, to influence the atmosphere over western Europe. These are: the Atlantic–Azores region, the Icelandic–Greenland region, the Baltic region, the Eastern region and the Mediterranean region.

Innumerable atmospheric permutations are possible; their ever-changing pattern appears on day-to-day weather maps. Only a few of the most frequent combinations, or those with the most characteristic climatic influences, will be mentioned:

1. Icelandic low and Eastern anticyclone; a cold-season circulation pattern.

2. Eastern anticyclone and Azores anticyclone, forming the ' barometric col ', analysed above, over central and western Europe.

3. Azores anticyclone alone, spread over the southern half of France, protecting it from the effects of disturbances.

4. Baltic anticyclone, formed in winter and acting as a source region of ice-cold winds.

5. Anticyclone over Greenland and Gulf of Genoa low; the Icelandic low is not in existence in this case.

TYPES OF WEATHER

A weather type is a meteorological situation arising in the course of a certain period and corresponding to a clearly defined barometric situation; each weather type is defined in terms of the temperatures, high or low, and the humidity or dryness associated with it. One type of hot weather (summer) is determined by a system of high pressure over northern Europe and Iceland. A type of mild damp weather (winter) is caused by south or south-west winds originating on the margins of the Azores anticyclone.

M. Mezin identified a succession of weather types between 1926 and 1935, and divided them into 26 classes. The average duration of a weather type is 10 days, but blocking situations can prolong the duration (in winter, cold dry weather can last several weeks). M. Mezin has worked out two very interesting indices:

Index of variability: Ratio of the number

of changes in weather type per month to the number of changes per year. The months of maximum variability are September, December (0·098) and April (0·091); September and April are transitional months, during which weather types, each lasting only a short time, succeed one another at frequent intervals. Months with low variability are July (0·070), February (0·072) and January (0·076), during which high-pressure centres from the Azores or the Continent restrict variations in weather types.

Index of diversity: Number per month of classes of weather types divided by the total number of classes.

The weather types showing the greatest diversity are those of March (0·61), April and November (0·57). Thus the months of the transitional seasons appear again; this index is a scholarly expression of the old saying: ' ne'er cast a clout till May is out '. The months with the least contrasts of weather, on the other hand, are July (0·14), August (0·25), January and February (0·26).

Statistical analysis of weather types makes it possible to describe in their finer shades the factors that govern climate. P. Pédelaborde defined the climate of the Paris region according to classes of weather types studied in daily weather maps over ten years. During this period continental weather types (anticyclones or shallow depressions) accounted for 22·35% of the days, and oceanic types for 77·64%, divided as follows:

Northerly and north-westerly cyclonic weather	25·35%
Westerly cyclonic weather	22·87%
South-westerly and south-easterly cyclonic weather	15·61%
Oceanic anticyclones	13·81%

WINDS

The primary geographical expression of these atmospheric situations is given not by temperature or humidity but by the winds (or their absence). France is a veritable crossroads for winds that blow from the four points of the compass, from the land and from the sea; the mountains, by confining these air streams or forcing them to ascend, change their nature or give them their own individual characteristics.

Long ago the inhabitants gave names to these winds which freeze their young crops and their trees, melt the snow or bring the rain for which they long. The *bise* is the cold wind from the north and the east. In the Aquitaine basin the *cers* brings the rain, and the *autan* coming down from the Pyrenees or the Lauraguais scatters the clouds. The *mistral* is a north wind funnelled by the Rhône corridor. Its effects are formidable; in winter, from January to April, it can blow non-stop for three to nine days as a cold, violent wind causing intense evaporation. In summer it is a hot and desiccating wind, raising clouds of dust.

C. Rainfall

Almost the whole of France has an annual rainfall in excess of 500 mm. Only a few strictly localised zones record lower values; these are found on the coasts of Provence and Languedoc, in the Illiers area along the Loir, on the margins of Beauce and Perche, and in Alsace. At the other end of the scale, only the highest peaks of the Pyrenees and the northern Alps, and a few peaks in the Jura and the Central Massif, have more than 2 m. of rainfall. The rainfall map follows the relief map very closely indeed. The largest zone of low rainfall lies within the limits of a quadrilateral of which the corners are Nantes, Amiens, Mourmelon and Poitiers (fig. 23).

As the rain is brought mainly by winds from the western quadrant, the alignment of relief features and the nature of the slopes are two factors which determine the amount of rainfall; north–south uplands form screens reducing the precipitation on the plains and depressions to the east. The uniform milieux of western France, and the more contrasted environments of eastern France and the mountain areas, where basins, valleys and lowland corridors receive less rainfall than the higher ground surrounding them, once more stand opposed.

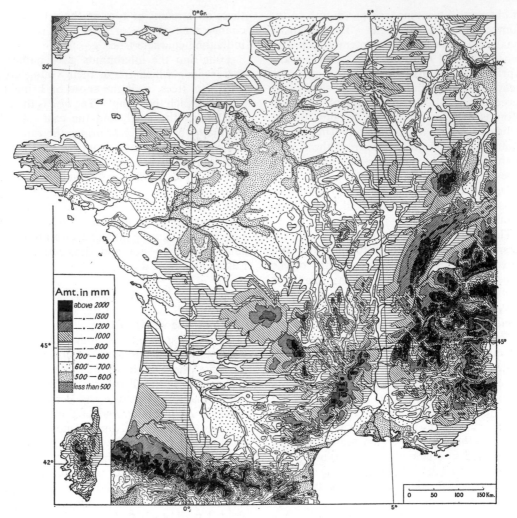

Fig. 23.   Mean annual rainfall.   (Source: E. De Martonne, *Géographie Universelle*, A. Colin, Vol. VI, after H. Gaussen)

SEASONAL DISTRIBUTION OF RAINFALL

Over France as a whole, autumn is the rainiest season, followed by summer and spring.   M. Musset has made a very detailed analysis of the seasonal distribution of rainfall.   By generalising from his typology, three distinct categories can be distinguished (fig. 24).

A.   Here autumn and winter, in that order, are the rainiest seasons.   This type is found in the coastal regions, Mediterranean, At-

lantic and the western half of the English Channel.   These are the seasons when disturbances from the west approach all French coasts most freely, bringing very moist air. Only a portion of the Mediterranean coast is subject to these conditions, which are very close to the pure Mediterranean type of climate.   The western seaboard from the Basque country to Cherbourg displays great climatic unity, but this pluviometric type is especially well developed north of the Gi-

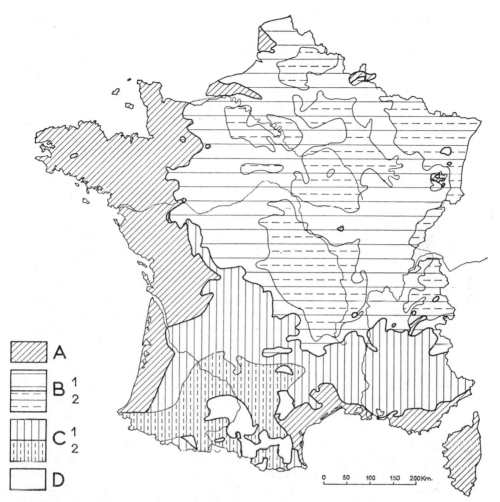

Fig. 24. Seasonal distribution of rainfall. (After R. Musset, *Ann. de Géog.*, no. 292, 1943, map H.T., simplified)

The rainy seasons are:

A. Autumn, then winter.
B. Summer and autumn (B¹ autumn, then summer; B² summer, then autumn).
C. Spring and autumn (C¹ autumn, then spring; C² spring, then autumn).
D. Other types of seasonal distribution.

ronde. These two coastal regions show contrasted types of rain; on the Atlantic coast a fine drizzle continues for whole days, while on the Mediterranean coast more concentrated downpours are characteristic.

B. Here summer and autumn are the wettest seasons, either in that order or reversed.

This type of rainfall distribution is characteristic of most of France, and results from the two influences which intervene, in unequal proportions, as soon as the coasts are left behind: the oceanic, bringing maximum rainfall in autumn, and the continental, making for wet summers and dry winters.

The oceanic influence persists far inland owing to the stepped arrangement of the relief; on the heights of the Ardennes, the Alps and the southern Central Massif, autumn rains, combined with the continental summer rains, show the vitality of oceanic tendencies. In addition, the barrier formed by the oceanic high-pressure centres 'continentalises' all southern France during summer. These summer and autumn rains are stormy by nature, being caused by the convective overturning of moist air above an overheated surface.

C. Here spring and autumn are the wettest seasons. Apart from the area mentioned, a large part of southern France is characterised by the predominance of rain in the intermediate seasons. This type of pluviometric conditions belongs to the northern fringe of the subtropical Mediterranean zone. The dry summers are explained by the northward displacement of the subtropical anticyclones, and the dry winters by the proximity and the persistence of high-pressure centres invading the continent of Europe. This area extends over the Mediterranean region and the Aquitaine basin, except for the coastal zones, the Pyrenees and the southern Alps, the Rhône valley as far as Valence and the southern and western parts of the Central Massif, extending there as far as a line running approximately from Mende through Bourganeuf to Poitiers.

SNOW

Although it is at low temperatures that snow falls and a lasting blanket of snow occurs, the amount of snow depends first of all on the distribution of winter precipitation. Seasonal distribution accounts for the abundant snowfalls on the mountains in the cold season. At Chamonix more than 80% of the atmospheric precipitation in December, January and February takes the form of snow; at height snowfalls can occur in the middle of summer, up to mid-June above 1,000 m. in the Central Massif, and in August above 1,800–2,000 m. in the Alps.

The depth of the snow cover varies considerably according to the place and the year. Averages for 1940–9 show, in the Alps, depths of 2·8 m. at Saint-Pierre-de-Chartreuse, one of the most snowbound winter resorts in the pre-Alps, 5 m. at Mégève, 10 m. at the Hameau du Tour (north of Chamonix) and 47 m. at the summit of Mont Blanc; and in the Central Massif falls reach 1·55 m. at the Chaise-Dieu (1,075 m.) and 2·62 m. at Fay-sur-Lignon (1,160 m.).

Most of France has a very limited number of days with snow. There are more than 20 days with snow on high ground—above 500 m.—in the young mountains and the Central Massif, but also in Lorraine, and on the plateaux of Haute-Saône. How long the snow lies is quite as important to the life and economy of the region as the number of days of snowfall. It obviously depends on the temperature. In the mountains, above 1,000–1,500 m, the snow cover persists from December until the end of April. In the Central Massif the snow cover becomes persistent only from January, and can disappear on several occasions before spring; but the highest parts of the massif—above 1,200 m.—are under snow for 3–4 months. Though the Central Massif has a smaller number of days of snowfall than the Alps, its snow blanket lasts as long, and, most important, appears at more southerly latitudes; the bastions of the southern part of the massif are on the whole more snowbound than the pre-Alps and the southern Alps, the latter being more open to the south and better ventilated.

The great difference in so far as the Central Massif is concerned lies in the annual and seasonal variability and in the very nature of the snowfalls. The vast surfaces of the Central Massif, without any real mountain barriers, and exposed to a variety of weather types, are swept by sudden snowstorms more terrible than the localised falls of the Alpine valleys.

'From the Puy de Dôme to the Causses, a winter seldom passes without some postman or schoolmaster, on his way to or from his own village, finding the road blocked by drifts, then losing his way and disappearing, sometimes a mere step from a farm or a hamlet. At one time a bell was rung at certain difficult points. . . . More useful on the roads were the *montjoies*, large upright stones which accompany the traveller from the Cévennes to Limousin and from the Vivarais to Aubrac, guiding him along a road of which not a trace remains. Sometimes, even, the *écir* (blizzard) is so violent that it is impossible to lead the cattle to drink a few dozen yards from their stable' (P. Estienne).

Whether simultaneous or following one another in seasonal succession, these phenomena combine to give us a definite type of climate which is as important to us as the type of soil or aspect.

Cold, with its resultant frost or snow, is responsible for the length of the growing season, and thus helps to differentiate between good and poor land. The coastal regions and the plains enjoy a long growing season, sometimes uninterrupted, as on the Mediterranean coast; but the mountain areas have only 3–6 months before snow and frost make their soil barren. This short growing season is a feature of the young mountains as well as of the higher parts of the Hercynian massifs. It does not exceed 150 days in the Montagne Limousine, Haut-Livradois and Forez, and is only 100–125 days in Cantal, Aubrac and the Margeride mountains. These natural conditions must obviously influence, directly or otherwise, the way the land is distributed and used.

3. AREAS AND TYPES OF CLIMATE

The first and most fundamental climatic division is that between northern and southern France. Northern France belongs to the temperate zone; influences from land and sea interact throughout the year. Southern France belongs to the northernmost fringe of the subtropical zone, affected by the movements of subtropical high-pressure centres which, in summer, neutralise the influence of the ocean. But the relief pattern is such that the mountains, the Central Massif, the Jura, the Alps and the Pyrenees, cause northern climatic traits, at once temperate and oceanic, to appear in this southern area. Only the lowlands of the Atlantic margin south of the Loire and of the Aquitaine basin, and the whole of the Mediterranean area (including the south of the Central Massif and the southern Alps), have the characteristic features of southern France, namely dry summers and high temperatures.

In both northern and southern France, as one moves inland, a predominantly oceanic regime gives way increasingly to one in which continental tendencies are more marked. The climatic differentiation of France will be examined in terms of a series of representative meteorological stations which will be studied with the help of climograms (figs. 25 and 26).

A. Climates of Northern France

Brest and Strasbourg show the two extremes of climate found in this part of France. The climate of Paris is of a type transitional between these (fig. 25).

BREST

The climogram lies above the monthly average of 50 mm. rainfall; it is circular in shape and shows a contrast between the cold-season months (September to February), which all have more than 75 mm. of precipitation, the absolute maximum coming in October and November with more than 90 mm., and those of the hot season (March to August), which have less than 60 mm. The transitions from one season to the other are very sudden. Variations in temperature are slight, but exist; the considerable drop in temperature between August and November is due to the abundant rainfall.

'In the whole of western France the winters are less cold and the summers less hot than one would expect from the latitude; and this state of affairs

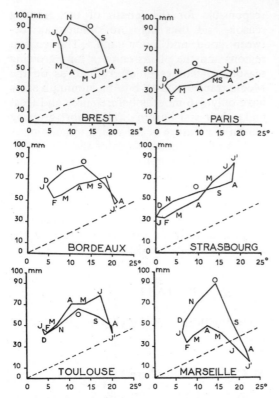

Fig. 25. Climograms of northern and southern France (lowland stations). The broken line corresponds to the relationship $p = 2t$ for the monthly data suggested by H. Gaussen as the criterion of a dry month.

is nowhere to be found more exactly than in Brittany, in particular that part of Brittany, almost entirely surrounded by the Atlantic, that is so aptly named Finistère. Of all these influences two almost contradictory ones stand out. On the one hand there is the strong wind which is so salty near the coast that it burns the skin and leaves a bitter taste on the lips; even in the interior of Brittany it is pleasantly bracing. On the other hand there is a moist warmth in the atmosphere which, together with the grey colour of the soil, imbues the whole countryside with a feeling of gentle melancholy. Brittany is like that: sometimes torn by violent storms, sometimes seeming almost to sleep beneath day-long rain and clinging mist. Only when we reach the main land-mass of France, far from the coasts, do the warmth and the damp begin to diminish' (René Musset).

STRASBOURG

The climogram of Strasbourg, in contrast to the circular pattern of Brest, is elongated in a diagonal direction, and lies nearer to the axes. This pattern is closely related to those of purely continental climates, but differs from them in its steep slope and in the abundant winter rain it shows. It divides naturally into two branches; from January to July temperatures and rainfall increase, and from July to January they decrease. The oceanic influence appears only in the October to December rainfall, which is heavier than that of the spring. The range of temperatures is almost 20° C., but that of rainfall is not much greater than at Brest.

PARIS

Paris represents a mixed type of climate in which both continental and oceanic influences are involved, as the pattern of the climogram clearly shows. The left-hand side, from October to April, is essentially oceanic with a well-marked rainfall maximum in October; the continental influence is expressed in the right-hand part of the diagram, from May to September, with a maximum in June and July equal to the autumn maximum. The temperature range is moderate, 15° C.; the pluviometric range is particularly small, about 30 mm.

B. Climates of Southern France

For reasons stated above, a distinction must be made between lowland and upland stations. Bordeaux, Toulouse and Marseilles are characteristic of the three types of climate found in the plains and on the coast. Their climograms have one thing in common: summer appears as the driest season, giving a downward direction to the right-hand part of the climogram, in complete contrast to the temperate climate of the continental type seen at Strasbourg. In all these three places the intermediate seasons are the rainy ones; the Azores anticyclone accounts for the lower rainfall in summer, and the presence of continental anticyclones explains why it is also lower in winter.

BORDEAUX

The left-hand side of the climogram of Bordeaux is closely related to that of Paris, expressing the strongly oceanic tendency in western Aquitaine during the cold season; there is a clear maximum in autumn, and the anticyclonic block then established prevents any further rise in rainfall. The warm season, on the other hand, shows the Mediterranean influence. Temperatures ($+4.9°$ C. in January) also reflect the latitude.

volves a dry summer and maximum rainfall in winter. Here spring and winter are the rainiest seasons, while the paucity of summer rainfall is accentuated. The climate is purely Mediterranean only from April to September. Farther south, Corsica has this type of climate in its pure form. The difference of magnitude between the two rainfall maxima is remarkable.

HIGH-ALTITUDE STATIONS

Unlike the places previously discussed, these do not give a true picture of a regional type of climate. Differences in situation, altitude

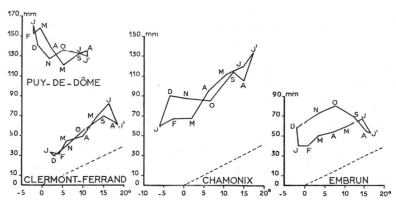

Fig. 26. Climograms of highland stations.

TOULOUSE

As we move farther from the coasts, the oceanic influence becomes blurred; the relative position of the rainiest seasons is reversed, spring having more rain than autumn.

The deep eastward penetration of the oceanic influence, the absence of the excessive rain and wind of the Mediterranean area, 'paler skies, and outlines less strongly marked in a less limpid atmosphere' are the characteristics of 'this quieter, in some way incomplete, South' (D. Faucher).

MARSEILLES

It would not be true to say that Marseilles has a typical Mediterranean climate, which in-

and exposure give rise to a great variety of climatic nuances.

The Central Massif, stretching for a great distance between the plains of northern France and the narrower lowlands of the South, in the very place where every climatic influence meets, makes it very difficult to define clearly types or areas of climate. The climograms of Puy-de-Dôme and Clermont-Ferrand are a good example. In the former one notes, first, the high absolute amounts of precipitation (each of the 12 months has more than 120 mm.), and secondly, the cold-season maximum and the small range of variation between the other months.

A few kilometres to the east, more sheltered than Puy-de-Dôme, which is swept by winds from all points of the compass, Clermont-

Ferrand shows a completely different climogram; the general pattern indicates a continental influence and the downward movement for the months of July and August a slight subtropical influence.

The higher relief in the west of the massif is enough to shift the area of dry summers southwards; this is in evidence only to the south of the river Lot. The axis of the highest relief, marked out by the volcanic massifs of Auvergne, from the Dômes to the Aubrac mountains, forms a sharp division between the oceanic influence to the west and the continental influence to the east. It is even more difficult to define the limit of Mediterranean influence, in spite of the sudden transition, topographically, from the Central Massif to the Mediterranean region.

Chamonix also has its climatic peculiarities. There is very abundant rainfall from April to October, a continental trait; at the same time there is an equally large amount of rain in the cold season, with the maximum in autumn, an oceanic trait. On the other hand, Embrun, in the southern Alps, shows a climogram almost identical with that of Bordeaux, with maximum rainfall in autumn and a sudden dry period in July and August.

Where there are great differences in relief, therefore, climates should be examined locally rather than regionally.

In that part of France with strongly differentiated relief and high mountains, local winds—mountain and valley breezes and pseudo-foehns—and variations or even inversions of temperature are more important than the general climatic regime of any one particular place, which it would be wrong to consider as representative of a regional climate. Intramontane basins, Pyrenean or Alpine valley-floors and south-facing slopes (*adrets* or *soulanes*) have climatic advantages denied to the high plateaux bordering them, to the peaks of high slopes looming over them and to the north-exposed slopes facing them. Bio-geography and human geography depend on this climatic geography and must take it into account.

4. IRREGULARITIES OF CLIMATE AND CLIMATIC ACCIDENTS

Though France really does on the whole enjoy a temperate climate, we should not forget the irregularities of climate which affect every region in France; they take different forms and may last a long or a short time.

Torrential rain concentrated on a restricted space, thunder-storms, gales accompanied by driving rain, heavy snowfalls, all have a spectacular character because of their suddenness, their localisation and their repercussions on human life and economy.

At the beginning of 1958, for example, exceptionally violent thunder-storms raged over Alsace and Burgundy.

'At Strasbourg, enormous hailstones fell on the town, and about thirty passers-by were hurt. Hundreds of cars were damaged. The streets were blocked by tree-branches and electric wires, and by fallen chimneys and tiles. Several were flooded. A large number of roofs were torn off and tens of thousands of windows broken, as well as the glass roof of the central hall of the station. The storm was no less violent at Mulhouse, where the tornado uprooted trees. In various parts of the town the streets were strewn with tiles torn from the roofs. Telephone communication was cut off and traffic brought to a standstill. At Falkwiller the roofs of half the houses in the town were torn off. Near Cernay, twenty-four poplars bordering the Colmar–Belfort road fell across the roadway. Telephone communications were cut off in certain parts of Colmar. Near Liepvre a farm was completely destroyed by lightning. Between Geberschwihr and Hattstatt the vineyards were seriously damaged by hail' (*Le Monde*).

In January 1959 eastern France experienced abnormal snowfalls alternating with fierce squalls.

'*Metz, 14th January 1959.* Following fresh snowfalls alternating with veritable squalls, the situation in the region east of the Moselle nick-named "Little Siberia" has worsened. In the Bitche sector, in fact, none of the snow-ploughs belonging to the Highways Department were able to move, and only a 100-h.p. bulldozer could carry on the work of clearing a way. The snow, which in places was more than 2 m. deep, cut off many travellers both in the Bitche district and in the region of Sarrebourg. They had to hurry to seek shelter in farms, private houses and the luckier ones in hotels, which were soon putting out "Full up" signs. Some isolated travellers were less fortunate, being forced to stay in their cars, shivering with cold, until the snow-ploughs arrived. Road traffic has been blocked every-where, and in many places brought to a complete standstill. Coaches carrying travellers or wor-kers have been immobilised, and some factories have had to close down for lack of staff. Many places were still completely cut off last night, notably Guising, Rimling, Bettviller, Rahling, Achen, Soucht, Lavelette, Landange, Hattigny, Haspach, Dabo and Lahoube. A snow-plough has had to get to work on the railway line from Sarreguemines to Bitche, and the Highways Department say that the main Paris–Strasbourg road is impassable near Strasbourg owing to drifts. The snow-ploughs belonging to the Highways Department have been working non-stop since Monday to try to clear the roads into the villages, but the results of their work are often completely wiped out by the storm. Emergency measures are being taken to meet a situation such as the local inhabitants have not experienced for more than twenty years' (*Le Monde*).

In December 1962 snow 40 cm. deep blocked the points and held up trains for several hours between Toulon and Mar-seilles.

Besides these extremities of weather, seasonal anomalies in temperature or rainfall are not uncommon; the history of French climate is full of abnormally dry or wet summers, and of extremely hard winters, which have very little to do with the seasonal averages. Repercussions on the life of the people and on the country's economy are con-siderable, despite a high degree of technical advancement. Plant of all kinds, and pro-tective measures intended for 'average' condi-tions or for the moderate differences found in

a temperate climate, cannot withstand exces-sive and prolonged anomalies.

Despite their advanced techniques, for example, the fuel and power industries in France are not completely independent of climatic conditions. Particularly mild win-ters reduce consumption of domestic coal, which accumulates at pit-head and depot. Hard winters can hinder the transport of coal and petroleum products by barge, if the canals are frozen. Abnormally wet summers fill the reservoirs and ensure plentiful hydraulic power for peak periods in the winter.

Dry spells

In 1948 Angoulême had a total rainfall for the year of only 596 mm., where a 'normal' rain-fall would be 834 mm.; Dunkirk had 497 instead of the normal average of 795. In the South, while Montpellier had also less than the normal rainfall (1901–30: 755 mm.; 1948: 485 mm.), Lyons showed a total 116 mm. above the average, and Marignane 127 mm. above. From 10th February to 31st July 1949, Paris had 5 mm. of rain as against the average of 93.[2] In 1959, from May to September, the island of Ushant had only 66 mm. of rain as against an average rainfall of 205, Rennes, 110 as against 250, Lorient, 147 as against 320.

These dry periods have important conse-quences, some of them positive, affecting, for example, the tourist industry. The balance of nature is upset; the water-table is lowered, endangering water supplies to towns and in-dustry; springs and wells dry up, river-flow is reduced to a point where navigation becomes difficult and hydro-electric dams are not re-plenished. Meadows begin to look like straw matting, the hay suffers and fodder re-serves for the winter are reduced; farmers then have to buy food for the cattle or else get rid of some of their stock before winter comes. Dry periods also lead to an increase of brush and forest fires.

All these consequences, following upon one another in a chain reaction, finally disrupt the economic structure. In one of the annual pro-gress reports of the plans for modernisation and equipment, the Plan Controller wrote: 'We were obliged to act cautiously owing to the risk of inflationary tensions, accentuated by the dry summer' (1958).

Hard winters

The winter of 1962–3 was, even more than February 1956, one of the hardest winters France had ever known, owing to the combination of persistent cold weather with very heavy snowfalls. This winter had considerable repercussions on agriculture. Almost all the barley sown and more than one sixth of the wheat (800,000 ha.) was destroyed by frost and had to be resown. Half of the vegetable harvest was destroyed. Owing to the lateness of the growing season the normal succession of fruit and vegetable crops was upset; deliveries of different products coincided, and had to be sold at a loss, causing a slump in prices.

But many other aspects of the economy were also affected; canals were frozen for several weeks and roads were snowed up or icy, then damaged when the thaw came, so that the normal rhythm of transport, particularly of coal, was impeded. Building and public-service workers were compelled to be idle for longer periods than the 42 days for which bad-weather pay is guaranteed.

Southern France, which has sharper contrasts of climate and a greater variety of weather types than the north, is exposed to greater risks climatically, and has, moreover, to cope with dry summers. Daniel Faucher has described the uncertainties which confront the farmers on account of the Aquitaine climate:

'Depressions from the Atlantic may linger too long in one place, and the *autan* then blows for days on end, drying up all the countryside around Toulouse. Or they may crowd in swiftly, one after another . . . and downpour follows downpour when sunshine is what is needed. When spring promises well, summer dries up the crops as they stand. If rainfall has been favourable and the harvest is ripening in the bright June sunshine, a violent thunderstorm dashes every hope to the ground. When the time has come to plough for the autumn sowing, but the rain persists and nothing can be done, the earth will be muddy and the corn stunted. . . . In the south we find unpredictable weather while in the north the seasons follow each other in more or less regular fashion.'

The climatic irregularities of the last few years have been particularly troublesome to agriculture in most regions, and a plan for setting up an official body to administer an agricultural disaster fund is under consideration.[3] An agricultural economy moving towards greater specialisation is clearly more sensitive to such calamities than the old strongly autarchic system of mixed agriculture. These climatic extremes, affecting one or more seasons in the year, are not usually isolated phenomena; they form a recurring pattern which is still very difficult to understand owing to the lack of precise statistical observations in the past.

By classifying a very large mass of data, P. Pédelaborde has identified five major climatic phases in the Paris basin since the 5th century A.D.:

1. A warm phase from the 5th to the 10th century.
2. A cold phase with hard winters, from the 11th to the 15th century.
3. A milder period from the 16th to the first half of the 17th century.
4. A recurrence of severe winters from the middle of the 17th century to the 1880s.
5. Another, milder period lasting up to the present day.

The broad climatic framework proves insufficient to define the divisions of the natural environment which the geographer needs. Monthly means or totals, or numbers of days, give only a very approximate picture of this climate which has determined crop systems, division of land and the whole structure of French agriculture. In the realm of local climatology accurate statistics for such things as hours of sunshine or amount of evaporation are practically non-existent or exist only for a very small number of places. Only detailed studies make it possible to appreciate significant contrasts in climate and to distinguish regional tendencies where too generalised observation might give a false picture of uniformity. In the case of the Central Massif, for example, A. Fel has added up the amount of rainfall from December to May which particularly encourages the growth of meadow grass, and has thus shown the contrast between the grass-covered western highlands and the eastern highlands, where grass tends to be scanty.

2. A large number of places show a significant variability of rainfall; examples are Pau (April 1918: 250 mm.; April 1958: 0·2 mm.) and Versailles, where the average for the year is 600 mm., but where 249 mm. fell in 1921, 382 mm. in 1949, 417 mm. in 1953.

3. Thunderstorms, hail, tornadoes and floods must also be considered together with climatic irregularities of seasonal type.

III

SOIL

Between the troposphere and the lithosphere, the presence of life has interposed a third zone, the biosphere. In the upper few feet of disintegrated rock, variations in temperature, rainfall and plant and animal life have combined to form the living, developing world which we call the soil; and in this thin layer are rooted the plants which in their turn will enrich it with their humus. A map of land fertility corresponds closely to a soil map. The topographical and geological diversity of France and its transitional location in relation to climatic influences account for the variety of soil types.

Their distribution and development depend on two factors, that of climate and the oro-geological factor.

1. THE CLIMATIC FACTOR: ZONAL SOILS

Soil types, considered on a global scale, are grouped in major zones corresponding to the climatic belts.

Almost the whole of France belongs to the zone of *Brown Forest soils*. This zone gives place in the north to the *Podzol* zone and in the south to that of *Mediterranean soils*.

Brown Forest soils develop beneath a deciduous forest cover in mild temperate climates, without hard winters, with warm summers and an annual rainfall of between 500 and 700 mm. The warm summers give rise to extensive decomposition of organic matter, more marked than in the case of the podzols, leading to lower acidity of the upper horizon. On the other hand, the lower rainfall gives rise to less thorough leaching; the colloids (iron-clay) are not leached, while the carbonates alone are completely leached or almost so.

The soil profiles appear very homogeneous, with colours varying from pale yellow to dark brown, and with an alluvial horizon that is inconspicuous apart from a lower layer with nodules. On rare occasions this lower horizon may include a true hardpan, when the water-table lies near the surface and drainage is impeded, giving rise to *alios* in the Landes and *grep* in the Toulouse region. Alios is a sandstone formed of quartz sand cemented by a humo-ferric matrix which represents 4–16% of the mixture. This formation has a discontinuous distribution and was built up from material brought in laterally and material rising to root level depending on the variations of the water-table. The bulk of this formation is probably an old soil ante-dating the continental dunes of the Landes. The variety of climates in France explains the diversity of types of Brown Forest soils; the climatic contrasts between Lorraine and Brittany, for example, are sufficiently marked for typical Brown Forest soils to be found in the east of the Paris basin, while in western France they are subjected to more thorough leaching which gives them a podzolic structure (degraded Brown Forest soils). In western France podzolisation is not purely a matter of climate; it is assisted by changes in plant growth, particularly afforestation with resinous trees and the degradation of the vegetation cover into moorland. Brown Forest soils are excellent for cultivation.

Mediterranean soils do not cover a wide area. They are characterised by their colour, red or reddish, which in Mediterranean landscapes contrasts with the whitish colour of the limestone outcrops. This *terra rossa* is found in depressions and on the surface of plateaux; it is a decalcified red clay mixed with coarse quartzose elements. The *terra rossa* also develops on parent material other than limestone, in the Mediterranean climate. Its origin is still disputed; it may be a clay resulting from decalcification still in progress, or it may be an old soil indicative of former climatic conditions which appear to have been tropical rather than subtropical. But it cannot be considered as a true soil; it is in fact a starting-point for the development of soil profiles. The redness of the Mediterranean soils is caused by the upward translocation during the dry season of iron oxides which become concentrated. The Mediterranean Red Earths should not, moreover, be confused with their tropical namesakes which are lateritic; they can be fertile, give splendid harvests and bear soils which stand up well to summer drought.

2. THE ORO-GEOLOGICAL FACTOR: AZONAL SOILS

To this zoning, already modified by local variations in climate, altitude and relief, the underlying rocks add important azonal distinctions. Though the climate may remain the same, soils formed on limestone, marl, granite and basalt will not have the same characteristics or the same properties.

A soil profile does not appear directly after the exposure of a limestone or granite outcrop; its formation involves a process of physico-chemical modification which results in the formation of a variable thickness of regolith which may consist of granitic sand or decalcified clay. This modification destroys the coherence of the rocks, causing them to break up and dissolve, so transforming the limestone beds into small fragments among which water can circulate and roots penetrate, making further chemical reactions possible.

Under present-day climates physico-chemical action is greatly reduced and takes a very long time to produce results. But this was not so in the climates that prevailed during the Pleistocene. Under very cold climates peri-glacial action ground down the rocks, mantled the slopes with soliflucted material and fragmented the upper parts of the bedrock (cryoturbation). The soils developed from this surface mantle, and their extension into Mediterranean regions is due to the effect of palaeo-climates.

Limestone outcrops modify types of soil. On pure limestone the soils developed are *Rendzinas* of every type, from typical rendzina and degraded rendzina to calcareous Brown Forest soil. Rendzinas are characterised by the presence of limestone, which prevents the leaching of colloidal elements; they develop especially on the less resistant limestones such as chalk and marls. This family of rendzina soils has developed on the limestones of the Jurassic and on the chalk.

On the wide chalk outcrops intercalated clays and clay with flints bring about differentiation, profiles developing more readily on these materials than on the chalk. But among the soil of limestone regions the principal contrast is that between northern and southern France. The limestone regions of the south are all, in varying degrees, *causses*, limestone plateaux, the surface of which is jagged, chiselled, pitted with solution hollows and swept by Mediterranean rainstorms. In northern France the limestones have a more continuous soil cover.

Limon or *loess* show a particular type of parent material. Loess is a silty earth, neither too clayey nor too sandy, with a variable limestone content (0–33%), and which has silt as its dominant constituent (average diameter 0·025 mm.). It is formed in a peri-glacial climate. Recent work has shown that we have to take into account the nature of the rocks on which these loess

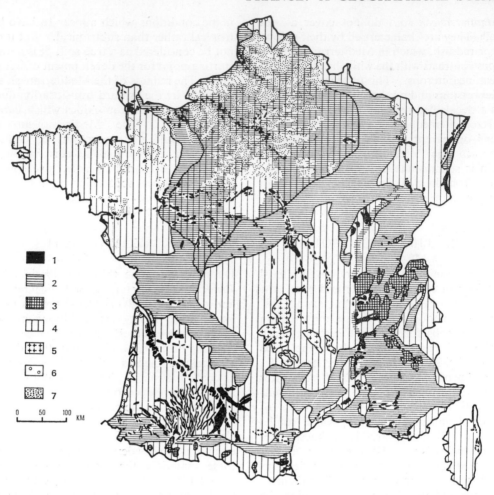

Fig. 27. Parent material. (Source: G. Plaisance, *Guide des forêts de France*, La Nef de Paris)
1. Terraces.   2. Soils developed on limestone (and Mediterranean red earth).   3. Moraines.   4. Siliceous soils.   5. Volcanic soils.   6. Sand dunes.   7. Loess and plateau *limons*.   The superimposition of shadings 2 and 4 indicates that calcareous and siliceous soils form a mosaic.

mantles were deposited; part of the elements entering into their composition seems to be autochthonous.   Like the *terra rossa*, silts are parent materials and not soils.   The upper horizon of loess, when leached and decalcified, gives loam or brick earth.   The lower horizon, enriched, contains small limestone concretions (*Lösskindchen*).

The geological nature of the parent material determines the value of the soil.   On clay and marl the soils are heavy and poorly aerated,

giving thick, sticky mud; they have to be enriched with lime.   Limestone, on the other hand, gives light, warm soil, easy to work, which very early invited cultivation.   Sand, and particularly granitic sand, itself a residual formation, gives light, but very unproductive and infertile soil.   Very often the soil is formed from old residual superficial deposits laid down, for instance, in the Palaeogene cycles of erosion; this gives rise to the most infertile of soils, unproductive, veritable poles of repulsion, such as the deposits which line the Palaeogene surface in the Central Massif. The same applies to the cold lands of certain piedmont plateaux, such as Lannemezan, which are entirely without limestone, their parent materials being derived from the destruction of the granitic massifs of the Pyrenees.

In the case of fluviatile deposits, their composition, that is, the nature of the rocks from which they were derived, determines whether they are fertile or sterile. The alluvium brought down from the Vosges into the plain of Alsace supports a forest cover; the volcanic deposits of the Limagne give rise to black earths.

In the mountain regions the shortness of the period since the most recent uplift of the massifs, and since the disappearance of the glaciers, the vigour of erosion and the brief duration of the warm season have prevented and still prevent the slow development of soil profiles. They are in a skeletal state, regolith rather than soils. Soil formation has progressed unevenly according to the nature of the parent material; loose and relatively heterogeneous materials—fluviatile and morainic deposits—are quicker to give rise to soil. The two main characteristics of mountain soils are the slowness with which they alter and the accumulation of acid humus, which gives them a similarity to podzolic profiles.

Slopes modify this perfect zonal and geological regularity. Typical soil profiles only occur, in fact, on flat ground; on slopes profile development is uneven. In the first place, 'creep' causes the smallest particles to move downslope, truncating the upper horizons of the profile; and in the second place, chemical processes act not only vertically but also laterally owing to the circulation of water. At the foot of slopes which are no longer directly subjected to a linear run-off, the thickness of decomposed material and soil humidity are greater and fertility is increased by the presence of the elements which have moved downslope. This explains the particular fame and the perpetual attraction of the soils formed in these circumstances.

3. MAN AS A PEDOLOGICAL FACTOR

In a country like France, settled from very ancient times, man has exerted a very great influence on the soil; by manuring and improving it, he has succeeded in modifying its structure and composition. The heavy, marshy soil in the interior of Flanders has been enriched by the age-long persistence of Flemish peasants. Drainage by surface or underground channels has also modified hydrological conditions. Irrigation can raise the water-table and modify the conditions in which the soil evolves.

Conversely, man can cause soils to deteriorate and become exhausted, either by intensive cultivation without the use of fertiliser or by encouraging erosive action. There is no need to look for examples in Mediterranean regions; recent research by Vogt has shown that the triennial rotation, which left a whole sector of the agricultural land fallow, exposing it for a whole year to rain and running water, was responsible for accelerated erosion phenomena. This erosion is often referred to in complaint books of 1789. In the same way the loss of agricultural land which has gone on for a century (Part Four), and the increasing areas of waste land, have brought about far-reaching pedological changes through the effects of subsidence, asphyxiation and the encroachment of grass. Finally man can destroy the balance of the soil by raising the water-table unduly; thus the engineering works of Donzère-Mondragon caused a rise in the water-table and sterilised land which was formerly very fertile.

This rapid analysis of pedological factors and soil types should make clear why a soil map is a far more intricate mosaic than a geological map. We see, superimposed on the uniform colour of an outcrop, differences

arising from the processes of decomposition
and modification, the nature of slopes and
soil–water relationships. The nature and the
fertility of soil change over short distances,
from one field to another and sometimes within a field. It is only in the rare districts without pronounced slopes or valleys, such as
Beauce and Santerre, that soil types are homogeneous over large areas.

This prodigious variety of soil and relief in
France, and the close contact and long-standing familiarity of generations of peasants with
the soil, have given birth to the agrarian interpretations of land value which are expressed
in the names given to districts, soils and
slopes. Names salty and full of meaning
show the contrast between light sandy soils,
chalky soils, stony soils, damp heavy soils,
soils that are easy to work and difficult soils.
In the West the heath soil (*terre de lande*),
black, cold, damp and clayey, is contrasted
with the healthy, well-drained *terre de champs*.

It appears very difficult, then, to show
statistically the value of the soils of France.
Excellent soil covers one sixth or one eighth
of the country. Such are the loess soils of
Alsace, Cambrésis, Picardy and Beauce, the
smaller limon patches in Normandy and Brittany, the black earths of the Limagne, the
marly soils of Moselle, Normandy and
Charolais, the alluvial soils of the coastal
marshes or valley-floors, and the soils of
basaltic lava-flows.

Very poor soils (one quarter of the country)
are the mountain soils on too steep slopes, the
'skeletal' soils of the *causses* or limestone
plateaux, and the siliceous soils formed on
detrital accumulations.

Between these two extreme categories are
intermediate types of soil in a bewildering
variety, which have been made suitable for
agriculture by age-long effort, with the help of
techniques for manuring the soil or letting it
rest and recover.

IV

VEGETATION

Charles Flahaut wrote in 1901:

'Research in botanical geography must take into account the action of a large number of factors, none of which begins or ends suddenly. The (present) distribution of species is the result of a series of physical and chemical conditions acting before our eyes, or of geological conditions which existed long before the earth reached its present state.'

Moreover, it is not enough to consider only the combined effect of natural factors in a country like France; man, too, has had considerable influence. The 'natural' vegetation of France is thus the result of very many factors.

1. CLIMATIC FACTORS

Plant life as we know it is, to a great extent, adapted to our present climate, which is, on the whole, favourable to growth in all parts of the country. The growing season lasts, according to locality, from 6 to 10 months if a mean monthly temperature of 10° C. is regarded as representing the threshold for plant growth.

However, plant growth depends in a large measure upon elements which are not always considered when analysing climate, such as the duration of bright sunshine (the evergreen oak needs on average 2,800 hours of bright sunshine a year, the *pin à crochets* (pitch-pine) 2,700 hours, the Norway pine 2,000 hours, the spruce 1,800 hours and the beech 1,700 hours). Spring frosts, wide variations of temperature and winds which desiccate the soil, increase transpiration and bring down trees, all cause ravages on the outskirts of forests.

But present climates, like the present distribution of vegetation, represent mere moments in the long evolution which has gone on in the past, and the vegetation map certainly owes more to palaeo-climates than it does to present conditions (Table IX). France has always been the meeting-place for many types

TABLE IX. POST-WURM PALAEO-CLIMATIC EPISODES

Periods according to Derruau	Tavernier	Climate	Nomenclature	Notes
14,000–10,000		Hot	Alleröd oscillation	
10,000–9,000		Return of cold climate		
9,000–7,000	8,500	Temperate climate, still	Forest-bearing period	Final retreat of the ice
	6,500	cold and damp		
7,000–4,000	6,000	Warm climate of sub-	Climatic optimum	Establishment of deci-
	5,000	tropical type	Post-glacial	duous trees (walnut,
			Campignian culture	then oak)
				Lakes and peat-bogs dry up
4,000–3,000	5,000	Climate tends to become		
	3,000	cooler and damper		
2,500–1,400		Climate warmer and drier	From 1,800 (?)	Lake villages
			Bronze age	
1,300		Rainy phase	Iron age	
			Hallstatt culture	
1,000–600		Dry phase		Retreat of glaciers

D

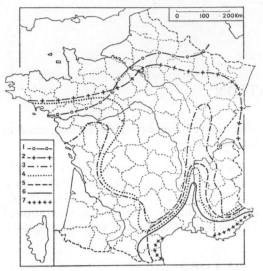

Fig. 28. Northern limit of the distribution of some southern species. (Source: G. Goujon, *Les Relations entre la végétation française et le climat*)
1. Vine. 2. Sweet chestnut. 3. Maize. 4. Evergreen-oak. 5. Mulberry. 6. Olive. 7. *Agrumes* (Citrus fruits)

of climate, and southern heat has always confronted northern cold, while oceanic and continental influences occurred in varying proportions. Botanical species have migrated across France, the northern types during glaciations, and the subtropical xerothermic types during the warm inter-glacial periods. The Atlantic littoral and the Rhône–Saône corridor have played an im-

portant part in facilitating these exchanges, surrounding as they do the southern bastion of the Central Massif.

The temperate character of the French climate, which is simply the result of contrasting situations, and the diversity of relief, have made possible the survival, in sheltered positions and on favourable soils, such as the warm soils developed on the Jurassic limestones, of relics of earlier vegetation formations. We need not be surprised to find, in the Paris basin, residual patches of Mediterranean species; the Montpellier maple, essentially Mediterranean, is found as far north as Lyons and the Gate of Poitou; the same applies to the box and the pubescent oak (*quercus lanuginosa*). Conversely, the survival of the beech in the South and West is a relic of colder periods.

In mountainous regions the climatic sequence has been of even greater consequence, because vegetation was completely banished from the massifs during the glacial periods, either by the actual presence of glaciers or by severe climatic conditions.[1] Plant species withdrew to the base of the mountains and the neighbouring plains; in warmer periods as the ice retreated, they advanced once more up the mountain slopes. Thus the history of mountain vegetation is a very recent one, postdating the Wurm; Table IX gives, in broad outline, the post-Wurmian palaeo-climatic episodes.

---

1. In Cantal, rock-plants of northern or alpine species, such as saxifrages and carex, are found in patches 1,500 m. below the upper limit of the forests, but on rocks facing north or north-east, and in shaded corridors.

2. HUMAN FACTORS

The present characteristic appearance of vegetation in France as seen in the landscape cannot be fully understood without taking into account the intervention of man. This obviously plays a decisive part in the delimitation of plant associations; the forests, which stretched without interruption over almost the whole of the country, have been cleared and now cover less than a fifth of the land surface (17%). The clearing of forest areas

for cultivation, their use as pasture land and the over-exploitation of forests in modern times (for charcoal, ship-building, timber and fuel) have all contributed to the degradation of the forests; coppices have taken the place of woods.

Botanists distinguish three stages of degradation: forest, heath and then grassland, which is the last stage. On the slopes of the Corbières, for example, the natural forest growth is the evergreen oak; deforestation leads to the *garrigue*, and further degradation gives rise to a sort of grassy steppe called *erm*. These stages form the evergreen oak xerosere.

Although the natural surroundings determine which botanical sere shall predominate, the stage of evolution—regressive or progressive—of the sere to which the present vegetation belongs is fixed by the actions of man.

Human intervention finds expression also in the selection of certain species to the detriment of others; as clearing operations have let more light into the forests, the shade-loving beech has been driven out and replaced by the oak; the chestnut has been greatly helped in its propagation by man, because it provided props for the vineyards. And man has also been responsible for introducing new species: orange-trees, agaves, palm-trees and eucalyptus are all imported, while in Brittany the Norway pine has been introduced for the re-afforestation of some heaths.

3. FLORISTIC PROVINCES

Botanically speaking, France is divided into two major floristic provinces, unequal in size, which are subdivided into sub-provinces and sectors (fig. 29):

1. The Euro-Siberian province with its essentially northern characteristics.
2. The Mediterranean province.

A. The Euro-Siberian Province

This is divided into three sub-provinces:

1. The Atlantic or Euro-Atlantic sub-province.
2. The central European sub-province.
3. The montane sub-province.

THE ATLANTIC SUB-PROVINCE

The Armorico-Franco-Atlantic sector covers a large part of France: all western France north of the Charente, the greater part of the Paris basin and central France, excluding the highlands of the Central Massif (above 1,000 m.). Dominant tree species are numerous: the oak in the forests which were formerly cleared, the beech in zones with heavy rainfall (more than 600 mm.), the birch, which, with oak and beech woods, is involved in the reafforestation of heath and waste land. Resinous trees are also present; there are some fine woods of silver fir in Picardy which are a relic of colder climates in the remote past.

The Boreal-Atlantic sector, north of the Somme, possesses on the whole the same combination of forest trees as the preceding sector, but in different proportions; the Atlantic species are less important than the northern ones.

The Aquitaine sector has more clearly defined characteristics on account of its subtropical climate. Atlantic and Mediterranean species mingle there: pubescent oak (*quercus lanuginosa*), tauzun oak (*quercus pyrenaica*), in the areas nearest the sea, cork oak, chestnut and maritime pine.

All the primeval forests of this Atlantic area degrade into heath. Broom, gorse, ferns and heather form one of the most characteristic landscapes of western France. Heathland is a pseudo-natural formation resulting from the degradation of forest; following clearing or accidental deforestation, the sun-loving plants such as heathers and gorse spread, and as they decompose they render the soil more acid and thus make it impossible to re-establish the forest, especially on poor soils. In the Aquitaine sector the heathlands (*touya*) have a rather different composition; they are similar to the *garrigues* in showing some degree of adaptation to the relatively dry summers; box, wild rose and blackthorn are a part of their make-up.

On the foothills of the Basque country the Atlantic oak-wood is replaced by three kinds of heathland: the most widespread consists of bracken and asphodel, often mixed with brambles, the second of gorse, in the lowlands

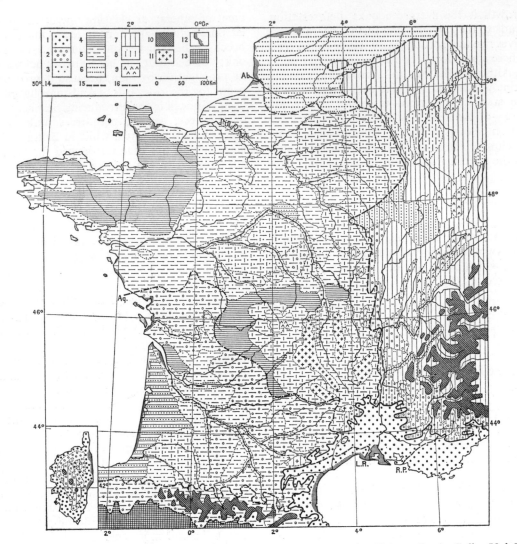

Fig. 29.   The flora of France.   (Source: E. De Martonne, *Géographie Universelle*, A. Colin, Vol. VI, after H. Gaussen)

1. Characteristic Mediterranean flora.   2. Abundant Mediterranean elements.   3. Some Mediterranean or sub-Mediterranean elements.   4. Atlantic flora.   5. Less characteristic Atlantic flora, or Atlantic elements mixed with other elements.   6. Northern Atlantic flora.   7. Central European flora.   8. Central European elements mixed with other elements.   9. Arctic elements mixed with other elements in the Jura and the higher parts of the Hercynian massifs.   10. High mountain flora (Alpine and Pyrenean).   11. Arctic elements (with sub-Alpine elements near the summits) in the higher parts of the Central Massif.   12. Coastal flora (Atlantic and Mediterranean) on saline soils and dunes.   13. Iberian flora.   14. Boundary of the Mediterranean province.   15. Boundary between the Atlantic and Central European sub-provinces.   16. Boundaries of floristic sectors: in the Atlantic sub-province: Aq., boundary of Aquitainian sector; Ab., boundary of northern sector; in the Mediterranean sub-province: L.R., boundary between the western or Languedocian and the Rhodanian sectors; R.P., boundary between the Rhodanian and Provençal sectors.

near the Atlantic, and the third of heather, confined to porous and siliceous soils.

On permeable limestone and chalk soils the shrub type of vegetation is rare; grasslands like the *savarts* of Champagne and the *larris*, with short, sparse grass, predominate.

The plant life of this Atlantic area is given minor variations by two factors: distance from the Ocean and altitude. The Central Massif, cooler, wetter and with a more sharply accentuated winter, differs climatically from Brittany. There, oaks give place to hardier trees like the beech and the Norway pine. The vegetation of the Central Massif does not show a clear succession of altitudinal zones. The whole of the central plateau experiences a climate conducive to forest growth, as is proved by the success of numerous attempts at reafforestation with spruce and Douglas fir.[2] Deforestation has merely substituted what may wrongly be considered as a separate stage of sub-Alpine grassland on the highest parts of the massif, such as Cantal, Dômes, Aubrac, Margeride, Forez and Lozère.

THE CENTRAL EUROPEAN SUB-PROVINCE

This is confined to eastern France and can be subdivided into two sectors: *the Baltic sector* covers northern Lorraine and the Ardennes; there the sycamore, the beech, the hornbeam and the common oak are associated with the ash, the birch, the mountain ash and the larch. *The upland sector* corresponds to the Northeastern ranges, the Vosges and the Jura, prolonged by the northern pre-Alpine massifs; at these moderate heights, and on the lower slopes of the high mountains, beech forests predominate, giving place higher up to firs and spruces.

THE MONTANE SUB-PROVINCE

From about 1,000 m. upwards this sub-province replaces those already mentioned. Its main characteristic is the altitudinal zonation of the vegetation. The montane tier (*étage*) corresponds to the zone of heavy mists, cold and damp; its characteristic species are beech and fir.

The sub-Alpine tier has a cold but bright climate, with a great deal of sunshine; it is characterised by pitch-pines (*pins à crochet*) and larches. Spruce is found at both these stages, but very often at this particular stage spruce plantations represent 90% of the afforestation.

The Alpine tier is that of Alpine prairies; the only trees to be found are stunted, such as dwarf willows, growing close up to the rocks which afford them warmth and protection against the wind.

The upper limit of the forest is very variable, and moreover its present limits are not natural ones; they are the result of man's exploitation both of the forest and of the Alpine pastures. In the Alps the upper limit of the forest varies from one part of the range to another; it lies at 1,800 m. in Chartreuse and rises to 2,300 m. in Haute-Maurienne, reaching 2,500 m. for isolated trees. In the Pyrenees trees disappear at about 2,300 m.; the height of the limit varies from the Atlantic to the Mediterranean.

The mountains reproduce in temperate latitudes the conditions to be found in more northerly regions, with the addition of sunshine; ascent has the same effect as a change of latitude, and we find representative specimens of plants belonging to a very cold climate which go back to the Wurm glacial era (*dryas octopetala*).

Owing to the youth of the relief, and forms of erosion which are peculiar to mountains, shallow basins and gentle slopes are prominent and prove favourable to a type of vegetation belonging properly to peatbogs and marshes, such as sphagnum and other mosses, and rushes.

The botanical differences to be noted between the Pyrenees and the Alps can be explained by the difference of latitude, climatic and ecological differences, and the extent of the Quaternary glaciations. The Pyrenees have more endemic species than the Alps, and more species of tree which are either Mediterranean or originated in the vegetation of the Tertiary era. There are differences even in the interior of each massif, depending on rainfall, slopes and exposure.

In the northern outer Alps, which have a high rainfall, fir and spruce predominate, the limit of the montane forest is low and pseudo-Alpine prairies occupy the sub-Alpine tier. In the southern outer Alps, which are drier, the original afforestation was of beech and Norway pine, but these have disappeared to be replaced by *garrigues* and dry grasses. The climate of the inner Alps is drier and sunnier; Norway pines predominate in the montane tier and larches in the sub-Alpine tier; but the Norway pine is also a colonising tree and many of the pine-woods of the central Pyrenees, the inner Alps and the east of the Central Massif were created in the 19th and 20th centuries on waste land, heathland and abandoned pastures.

B. The Mediterranean Province

Botanically speaking, this province is clearly distinguished from the remainder of France. The summer is the worst season for growth because of its dryness, which kills off plants which cannot stand the hot waterless months. This explains the importance of annuals, which die off in the summer, and of plants with tuberous and bulbous roots, xerophytic plants adapted to dry climates, with spiny, woolly or polished leaves, and aromatic plants.

There are thousands of native species: the parasol pine, the Aleppo pine, the evergreen oak or ilex, the kermes oak (*Quercus coccifera*), the olive and all the families of heathers, cistus and lavenders.[3] In the woodlands, which are rare, the trees are placed far apart, and there is an undergrowth of prickly shrubs.[4] The predominant formations, *maquis* and *garrigues*, are the result of degradation.

Where there is a permanent source of water, either at the surface or underground, the vegetation changes and trees such as poplars, willows, alders and maples grow among green meadows, forming landscapes of lush beauty which result from the association of heat and water.

Paradoxically, it is not easy to trace the boundary of this Mediterranean region owing to the influence of palaeo-climates, contrasts of exposure and the heterogeneous nature of the border zones where mountains alternate with lowland corridors and projecting ridges with valleys; botanists reluctantly acknowledge the value of the olive-tree in defining this boundary (fig. 28).

2. Spruce is an ubiquitous tree which can adapt itself to the most varied conditions of altitude and climate.
3. Corsica, which has been an island since the Pliocene, has a very individual flora.
4. Near Briançon is the only plantation in France of incense-juniper, which is a Mediterranean mountain species.

V

WATER

As we have said in the preceding chapter, valleys are ubiquitous in France, and there is a corresponding abundance of water, the basic element of all life. Water, like soil, is indispensable to man; not only rainwater, which comes irregularly and must be collected in tanks or barrels, but also the steady supply to be found in springs, streams, rivers or wells.

Since France's climatic advantages mean that water in some form or other is normally present everywhere, sufficient attention has perhaps not been paid to it, neither by specialists in the subject nor by geographers. Springs and ground water should, in fact, have formed the subject of strictly geographical research, as each constitutes an essential element in the analysis of every geographical region, no less than relief or vegetation.

1. GROUND WATER AND SPRINGS

As sedimentary rocks outcrop very extensively, and as the permeable chalk, limestone and sands which they include act as reservoir beds underlying large tracts of France, the country is well supplied with ground water. It is hard to imagine the enormous quantities of water which reach these water-tables by percolation: 102,000 m.^{3}/day for the chalk aquifer in the north of France; 153,000 m.^{3}/day for the carboniferous limestone aquifer in the same region, collected from an area of 290 km^2.

In areas of crystalline rocks not all rainwater runs away to be lost in the rivers. A far from negligible part of it feeds superficial bodies of ground water whose volume is a function of the thickness of the sandy layer. In these circumstances the solid rock forms the impermeable bed,[1] though this is not absolutely impermeable, since water can penetrate through the joints in the rock.

The behaviour of these aquifers varies greatly according to the way they are supplied and above all to their volume. Large aquifers vary little; they 'ride out' the dry periods and are rapidly replenished thanks to their extensive catchment areas. On the other hand, in areas of crystalline rocks, three months' drought exhausts the reserves of surface aquifers and it takes three months after the beginning of the rains to restore them.

These aquifers are drained by springs occurring along the junction with an impermeable bed at the base of the aquifer, or by overflow springs when a valley or a depression intersects the upper part of the aquifer. Springs are extremely important geographical elements; they have their own morphology, and a special type of vegetation develops around them. Their soils have a distinctive composition, with intense chemical decomposition and biological action.

As aquifers and springs are closely linked, variations in the former lead to variations in the latter, particularly in springs of the overflow type. The movement of springs downstream is one of the transformations of the natural environment which can be observed within one person's lifetime. There is considerable evidence of these movements, both in place-names and in the siting of villages around a spring which is now several miles downstream.

Not all limestone regions have aquifers. They exist only in strata which are sufficiently jointed and bedded so that a single water-table exists in equilibrium. Often there are local water-tables independent of each other, or individual underground circulations. The depths at which water is struck may then differ strikingly from one commune to another; in karstic regions actual subterranean valley systems take the place of aquifers.

Deliberately or otherwise, man is becoming more and more responsible for what happens to the water-table, especially where there are large engineering works; the building of the Donzère–Mondragon canal (Rhône) seriously disturbed the aquifers, causing the water-table to rise in some places almost to the surface, while in others the soil was dried up because of an insufficient supply of water. The growing need for water has led to greater and greater demands on the underground supplies of water. The wells of village com-munities and the bore-holes made to supply town-dwellers and industry with water have in some regions reached a critical level. Further urban and industrial expansion is impossible from local resources and plans have been made to bring water from distant sources in other drainage basins.

With these plans still unfulfilled, regional water-tables are rapidly becoming danger-ously low; in the north of France, from 1945 to 1959, the chalk water-table fell from +17 m. to +8 m., and from February 1959 to February 1960, from +8 m. to +4·8 m. In Paris and the large towns, mass departures for holidays and week-ends make it possible to restore the water-table and prevent supplies from running out during August.

Experts are predicting that water consump-tion will double in the next fifteen years. There is an imperative need to make a thorough inventory of our water resources and then to decide what steps shall be taken to prevent the water problem from becoming an insoluble dilemma.

1. Patches and depressions in which sedimentary rocks are preserved in the ancient massifs often provide valuable hydrological reservoirs.

2. RIVERS

The hydrological characteristics of French rivers reflects both their courses and their profiles, both climatic and hydrological condi-tions.

A. Factors Determining Regimes and Types of Flow

The regime of a river depends upon a multi-plicity of factors: its long profile gradient, the cross-section of the river-bed, the lay-out and shape of the basin, the nature of the land it flows through, the seasonal distribution and characteristics of the rainfall.

France can be divided schematically into two hydrographic provinces, the boundary extending along a line from the Basque country to the Vosges.

North of this line, gentle slopes, broad basins, gentle long profiles, abundant rainfall with an autumn–winter maximum and the considerable area of permeable outcrops, such as limestone, chalk and sand, give the rivers a very definite regime; the run-off coefficients[2] are below 0·6 or even below 0·4 over much of the area, showing the im-portance of percolation and evaporation; dis-charge is regular, with no very low water; floods are rare and not extensive.

South of this line, conditions are very different. The high relief steepens the river long profiles, the river-basins straddle moun-tains and lowlands, and the distribution of rainfall shows greater seasonal contrasts, par-ticularly in the Mediterranean area. A large part of this rainfall is stored during the cold season in the form of snow and ice, to be released in the spring and summer.

Run-off coefficients are particularly high in mountainous regions, averaging 0·6 or 0·7 and reaching 0·8 in mountain systems. Regimes are not regular, but contrasted, depending on the different ways in which the run-off is derived.

Comparison of specific yields (the ratio of surface run-off to basin surface area), expressed in litres/km.²/sec. brings out the contrasts between the two provinces: those of the Seine (6·7) and the Loire (7·5) contrast with those of the Tarn (14·3), the Hérault (17·8), the Ain (35·4) and the Arve at Chamonix (70).

bined with snow meltwater from March to April.

3. Pluvio-nival regime of the Mediterranean type (the Ardèche at Vallon), with a pluvio-nival maximum in spring and a pluvial maximum in autumn. In the mountains the streams derive their water from the melting of snow or ice.

4. Nival regime of the mountain type (the Romanche at Chazeaux), which is found in almost pure form in basins situated entirely in the mountain massifs.

5. Nivo-pluvial regime (the Fier), where

TABLE X.   TYPES OF RIVER REGIMES

Regime	Jan.	Feb.	Mar.	Apr.	May	June	July	Aug.	Sept.	Oct.	Nov.	Dec.
Oceanic pluvial												
Saône (at Auxonne). .	1·58	*1·95*	1·50	1·01	0·85	0·57	0·42	0·34	0·38	0·76	1·14	1·56
Mediterranean pluvial												
Hérault (at Montagnac) .	1·06	0·94	*1·75*	1·24	0·86	0·48	0·20	0·13	0·65	1·04	1·73	1·89
Mountain nival												
Romanche (at Chazcaux) .	0·25	0·23	0·33	0·73	2·14	*2·49*	2·04	1·52	0·98	0·56	0·42	0·32
Nivo-pluvial												
Fier (at Val-de-Fier) .	0·92	0·94	1·24	*1·52*	1·44	0·82	0·68	0·62	0·68	0·88	1·12	1·14
Oceanic pluvio-nival												
Dordogne (at Argentat) .	1·39	1·41	*1·53*	1·40	1·07	0·69	0·47	0·35	0·40	0·63	1·11	*1·42*
Mediterranean pluvio-nival												
Ardèche (at Vallon) .	1·20	1·25	*1·50*	1·42	0·90	0·42	0·15	0·17	0·45	1·37	*1·67*	1·51
Complex												
Rhône at Lyons .	0·78	0·78	0·95	1·10	1·14	1·21	*1·25*	1·11	0·93	0·92	0·91	0·88
Rhône at Givors .	1·09	1·07	*1·16*	1·15	1·03	0·96	0·93	0·82	0·73	0·85	1·05	*1·12*
Rhône at Valence .	0·95	0·95	1·07	1·14	*1·17*	1·16	1·02	0·84	0·74	0·87	1·02	*1·04*
Rhône at Beaucaire .	0·99	0·95	1·08	1·15	*1·20*	1·14	0·90	0·73	0·70	0·93	*1·12*	1·07

The figures indicate the monthly discharge coefficients: i.e. the ratio of the average monthly to the annual discharge.

In northern and western France the regimes are almost entirely pluvial, of the oceanic type, or, more rarely, of the continental type, extremely homogeneous in character (the Saône at Auxonne).

In southern and eastern France all the other types of regime are found, whether in opposition or in combination (Table X):

1. Mediterranean pluvial regime (the Hérault at Montagnac), exemplified by the mountain streams of Vivarais and the Cévennes, which are like 'wadis' in the summer, and fierce torrents in spring and autumn.

2. Pluvio-nival regime of the oceanic type (the Dordogne at Argentat, on the boundary between the two provinces), where rainfall of the oceanic type, in the cold season, is com-

the cold-season rainfall maximum is transferred to spring, when the snows melt.

The great river systems of France naturally display more complex regimes. The Garonne and the Rhône are good examples. The Garonne is supplied both by the pluvio-nival rivers from the Central Massif and by the nivo-glacial rivers and mountain-torrents (*gaves*) from the Pyrenees.

The Rhône shows a quite remarkable sequence of superimposed influences. Where it enters France its regime is glacial, or more or less nivo-glacial, with maximum discharge in the warm season (Lyons). Below Lyons, the Saône brings a completely new aspect to the regime; flowing from northern France, it has a pluvial regime with a cold-season

*

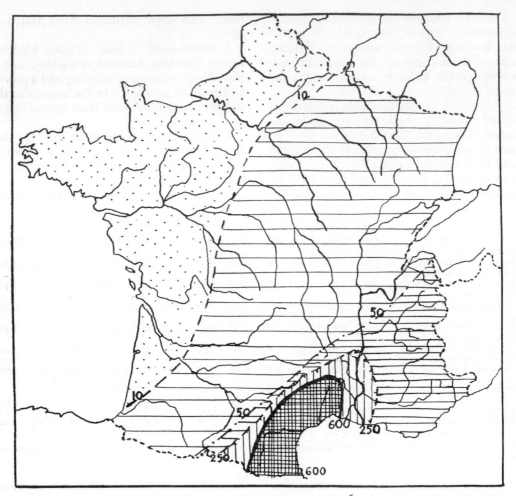

Fig. 30. Importance of floods in France. (Source: J. Corbel, 'Érosion et grands cours d'eau en France,' *L'Information Géographique*, May–June 1962, p. 115)
Ratio of the heaviest floods known to history to the average discharge.

maximum associated with a nival regime with its maximum in spring. At Valence, the Isère confluence reintroduces a powerful nivo-glacial influence, and the highest discharge once more occurs in the warm season. Finally the Rhône is joined by tributaries from the Mediterranean basins, both the Durance and the right-bank tributaries such as the Gard and the Ardèche, with maximum discharges in spring and autumn, which tend partly to equilibrate the regime. Approaching its delta (Beaucaire), the Rhône has two

maxima, in spring and autumn, a major minimum in summer during the normal Mediterranean dry season, and a secondary minimum in January, when the rain is retained in the mountains in the form of snow.

B. Floods

Flooding may be the result of either a climatic irregularity such as exceptionally heavy rain or a sudden heat-wave causing the snow to melt, or the coincidence of one of

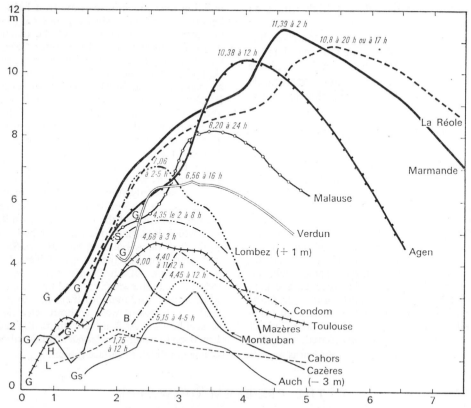

Fig. 31.   The great floods of the Garonne in February 1952.   (Source: M. Pardé, *Ann de Géog.*, no. 329, 1953, p. 20)

'The curves indicate the height reached (scale in metres on the left), during the days from February 1st to 7th (marked on the abscissa, each division representing 12 hours) by the water of the Garonne (G) at Cazères, Toulouse, Verdun, Malause, Agen, Marmande and La Réole, and of its tributaries, the Grand Hers (H) at Mazères, the Save (S) at Lombez, the Tarn (T) at Montauban, the Gers (Gs) at Auch, the Baïse (B) at Condom and the Lot (L) at Cahors.'

these factors with the normal high-water period, or the combination of two exceptional climatic factors, such as very heavy rain at the same time as a period of rapid snow melt.

The seriousness of flooding depends on the long and cross-sectional profiles of the river, that is to say, the speed with which the additional water is carried downstream and the opportunities available for spreading out between the banks and in the flood plain. In fact, the same flood plain is affected every time. It covers 800 km.² in the Saône valley, and 2,400 km.² in that of the Rhône, from Geneva to the sea.

The translational velocity of the flood-water varies considerably according to the river systems. It only takes a few hours in the torrents of the Cévennes; but it is 20–30 hours on the Garonne at Toulouse, and 8–9 days on the Seine at Paris. In quiet regions like the Paris basin, disastrous floods only occur at the meeting of several waves of flooding from different rivers; if these waves are staggered, on the other hand, there is a long period of very high water without flooding.

Often human agency causes bottlenecks and stops the natural flow of the water by confining river-beds between high quays as they pass through towns, or by building bridges with too many piers. Each river has its own type of floods. The Garonne has the greatest floods, rising more than 11 m. above low-water mark at Agen and Marmande (fig. 31). Upwards of Paris, the Seine can rise 3–5 m.

An example: the floods of October 1958 in the South-east

'Parts of southern France are today in mourning as a result of a terrible disaster. Sudden floods, due to heavy rain which swelled tiny streams out of all proportion, have caused damage in the departments of Gard, Hérault, Ardèche and Drôme. We must record not only material damage but also the loss of many human lives. In the department of Gard—by far the worst affected—about thirty people died, according to information which reached the prefecture at Nîmes early this afternoon. In Gard, at Bagnols-sur-Cèze, the Cèze brought all traffic to a halt by cutting off the RN 580 near Codolet. Isolated farms have been evacuated, and most building operations have come to a halt. Workers travelling to the Marcoule nuclear plant had to turn back. In the north of the department, between Bessèges and Molières-sur-Cèze, rivers with normally a very small discharge are in flood. Part of the village of Molières and several houses at Saint-Jean-du-Gard have been evacuated. Bessèges, where the rain began to fall heavily at about 12.30, had to endure hours of suspense. At 3 in the afternoon the Town Hall was flooded. The water was more than a metre deep in many places. Factories had to close down, and for a while the town was completely cut off. The situation was no less serious at Alès, where the Gardon suddenly flooded the lower part of the town. At about 5 in the afternoon the waters of the Gardon covered the Pont Neuf, with its roadway which is 6 m. above the river-bed. All the equipment on a building site at Pré-Saint-Jean was swept away by the water. Riverside houses in the district of La Prairie were flooded. At Pré-Rasclaux the water reached first-floor level in some houses, and many of them had to be evacuated. The town was without electricity for several hours. At 8 in the evening all roads were 1 m. deep in water' (*Le Monde*, 2nd October 1958).

2. The run-off coefficient is the ratio by volume of rainfall to surface run-off.

3. THE PROBLEM OF WATER

The use and preservation of France's water supply becomes more of a problem each year. Some regions have insufficient resources; there is pollution by industry; river utilisation and irrigation projects for agriculture are under consideration. The time has come to formulate a real policy for the use of water, the first draft of which was worked out in 1963. Rivers are classified into four categories according to the degree of pollution, and regional plans for conserving water are to be drawn up. This policy was put into effect by an Act of December 1964 relating to river regimes and water utilisation as well as to pollution control.

VI

CONCLUSION

The ultimate aim of a geographical study is not to analyse one after another the various natural elements, such as relief, climate, soil and water, so much as to show the consequences of the combination of these elements. The distribution pattern and spatial differentiation of each of these elements is determined by its own genetic and development processes, but these are influenced by the spatial patterns of other elements.

Climatic types and vegetation provinces have their own boundaries, defined by purely climatic or purely botanical factors, but also by relief in one case, and by relief and soils in the other. The pattern of relief tends to differentiate between northern and western France, and central, southern and eastern France. The climatic pattern clearly and simultaneously contrasts northern France with southern France, and oceanic western France with continental and montane eastern France.

By superimposing these distribution patterns it is possible to recognise five major regions with no clear-cut boundaries, but with well-defined individual characteristics:

1. A north-western geographical region or domain extending from Vendée to Champagne inclusive. This is oceanic France, with its abundant rainfall, a lowland region with homogeneous landscapes and great agricultural potential. The landscapes are placid and almost all modified by human activity. Only rarely are outcrops of bare rock to be seen; almost everywhere the rocks are masked by a thick mantle of moist, fertile soil, bearing forests, meadows or crops.

2. A north-eastern region clearly defined by the survival of extensive forests everywhere except in Alsace. This is a France of plateaux and wooded limestone cuestas, with poor soil apart from a few fertile areas and with the most severe continental climatic conditions.

3. A south-western region, Aquitaine in the widest sense, a part of western France with distinctive climatic conditions. It is a France of plains, hills and plateaux, 'an incomplete version of the real South' (D. Faucher) but greener, with a greater variety and abundance of trees and grasses, less riddled with rock-strewn surfaces and skeletal soils than the other, the true South.

4. South-eastern France, from the Limagne to the *plans* of Provence, from Roussillon to the plains of the Saône. This is a mosaic of a region with many small compartments full of natural contrasts, scarps and basins, arid or snow-covered plateaux and fertile valleys. The soil and vegetation cover is discontinuous, interrupted by the limestone pavements on the plateaux, the white wall-like limestone scarp faces and gullied hillsides. Productive land occurs in small, isolated and discontinuous patches.

The mountains give rise to a fifth, separate region.

But in these various domains, regional or local combinations of natural factors serve to distinguish a large number of different *pays*. The extreme variety characteristic of France is the essential lesson to be learnt from this analysis. Regional contrasts differ from one area to another, but in every one there are good and bad *pays*, areas that are wind-swept and others that are sheltered, favourable slopes, regions that attract and others that repel.

France may be one whole, but she has a multiplicity of parts, and no simple generalisation can describe her or do other than caricature her. Only long familiarity can help us to grasp all the potentialities and all the facets of an environment, or to understand the significance of soil, aspect or vegetation cover.

We can draw a third conclusion from this analysis: that natural conditions are sufficiently extreme and the ecological balance sufficiently precarious to create serious problems in this country which lies in the calmest sector of the temperate zone and should thus be relatively free from them.

Taking a short-term view, there is not a year in which several climatic, hydrographic or topographical accidents do not remind us of the active presence of these natural elements. Their consequences are all the more serious in a well-peopled, civilised country like France, which is not organised to meet such disasters because they always appear 'exceptional'.

To take the long-term view, we are faced with the problem of preserving the soil and the plant life of France. Vegetation and humus are, in fact, our capital. We must not let them deteriorate and become debased.

In the same way, to safeguard what evidence remains of the biological balance of nature, more and more plans for parks and wild-life sanctuaries are going forward and meeting with an increasingly favourable response. The Camargue, Vanoise, Mercantour, the Cévennes and Aigoual are among the regions which have benefited from these projects.[1]

1. See p. 292.

PART TWO

THE ROLE OF MAN

If some Christopher Columbus were to find an uninhabited France, he would people it in a very different way from the present one.

A. Sauvy

I

POPULATION

The planning and use of land in a country depends first of all on its population. In fact, the course and rate of growth of the pattern of development of an area depends directly on the vitality of its population, on the pressure exerted by high densities of population and by a high rate of increase in population. We have already shown, in the first chapter, the salient characteristics of the population of France: a small population with a high proportion of the older age-groups, a population which showed a slow rate of growth from 1850 to 1946 but one which has become more dynamic since the latter date.

1. GROWTH OF THE POPULATION

The following table (XI) shows the growth of population in France since the beginning of the 19th century.[1]

TABLE XI. GROWTH OF THE POPULATION

Year	Population (in thousands) (Within boundaries at the given date)	(Within present boundaries)
1801 . .	27,300	28,300
1851 . .	35,800	36,500
1901 . .	39,000	40,700
1921 . .		39,200
1946 . .		40,500
1954 . .		42,800
1962 . .		46,520
1968 . .		49,850

A. The Distinctiveness of Demographic Evolution in France

Up to 1850 France shared in the population growth common to all European states, though at a considerably slower rate (29% from 1800 to 1850; Italy 34%, Germany 44%, England 100%). From 1815 onwards the birth-rate was already declining and the rise in the population was more apparent than real; but the break with trends in Europe as a whole appeared in the middle of the century. During those fifty years of urban and industrial revolution the other states maintained or even increased their rates of population growth, while the curve for the population of France began to flatten out, reaching a maximum of less than 42 million in 1911. This figure represented the maximum population of France throughout the first half of the 20th century.

During the same period the other states doubled their population figures for 1850. From 1801 to 1954, when the French population increased by 60%, the rates of increase were respectively 160% in Italy, 190% in Germany, 230% in England and 280% in Belgium and Holland.[2]

But the relationship between a population and its land area can be more accurately expressed in terms of density. The comparisons are revealing despite the differences in

TABLE XII. POPULATION DENSITIES*

	France	Germany	England	Italy
1800 . .	51·3	69·6	43	60·1
1850 . .	66·2	100·8	85·2	80·7
1900 . .	73·8	158·4	151·6	108
1950 . .	76·4	196·3	207 3	153

* Numbers of inhabitants per km.².

land utilisation in the various states (Table XII). The present density of population in France is slightly higher than that of last century, whereas the neighbouring great powers have doubled or tripled theirs.[3]

The causes of this check in the growth of population are many and complex. We must consider first an accidental cause: the loss of human life in war. The First World War brought a loss to the French population of 1,500,000 dead or missing, to which must be added 900,000 wounded with an average disability of 30%. The Second World War meant the loss of 620,000 men, both civil and military. But the consequences of these wars extend far beyond such direct losses:

1. In the lower birth-rate of the war years, causing population troughs (fig. 33).

2. In the increased differences between the male and female sectors of the population.

At the beginning of the 19th century France had just emerged from almost a quarter of a century of revolutionary and imperial wars, the consequences of which partly explain the low population increase of the last century. In addition, the losses of the last two wars became much more serious in their effects on a small population already declining in vitality.

But the fundamental cause of the lack of normal population increase is to be found in the decline of the birth-rate in France which began in the first third of the 19th century. The first indications of this decline came earlier and were more marked than in other European states. The birth-rate fell from 32‰, or 32 per 1,000, in 1801 to 26‰ in 1851 and 22‰ in 1901. The corresponding figures for Germany were 37, 36, 35, for England 33, 33, 29, and for Belgium 35, 31, 28. The figures for France were low in relation to the death-rate, which was higher than in other countries.[4]

The situations in the 19th century and the 20th century are by no means comparable. In the 19th century, to ensure the survival of one child, five had to be brought into the world, as against less than two at present. Although the birth-rate was then low in comparison with the death-rate, we must note that it equalled or exceeded the present birth-rate, through which a recovery in population levels is taking place. In 1881 the birth-rate was 31·7‰; in 1901–10 it was 20·9‰ (1948: 21‰). In 1871–80 the mean annual number of live births was 935,000, in 1891–1900 it was 853,000 (1949: 868,000; 1959: 825,000). A more catastrophic fall occurred from 1905–10 onwards (1911–14, birth-rate 18·6‰).

Much has been written on the reasons for this untimely drop in the birth-rate. All the weaknesses of the French and of French society have been lumped together in a collection of ill-assorted but doubtless complementary causes: individualism, the conservatism of the propertied classes, the decline of religious influence, the emancipation of women, centralisation which 'devitalised' the provinces, the encouragement of one-child families by article 832 of the civil code which made it obligatory to divide the inheritance equally and the lack of legislation for the family. On a larger scale, the transformation of living conditions caused by urbanisation and industrialisation has weighed heavily in the balance.

The most unusual aspect of the fall in the birth-rate in France is its early appearance. It seems that the French, the first to lay the foundations of social equality, were also the first to see the connection between the fall in the death-rate and the prospects that it opened up for controlling births, and between the economic and social opportunities open to them and a voluntary control of births, since the fewer the births, the easier social advancement became. We should also note that the population standstill was probably both cause and effect of the relatively limited effectiveness of the economic revolution in France between 1850 and 1914. There were too few hands to labour and too few mouths to be fed for France to experience an industrial revolution like that in other European countries; and conversely, this comparative stagnation in the economy did not encourage a rapid growth of population.

There was considerable official encouragement for the limitation of families. Jean-

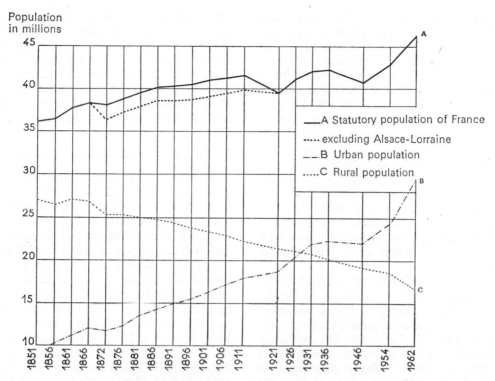

Fig. 32. Evolution of the statutory population, rural and urban, since 1851. (Source: F. Carrière and P. Pinchemel, *Le Fait urbain en France*, A. Colin, Paris, 1963)

Baptiste Say encouraged men to 'accumulate savings rather than children', and forty years later Guizot was matching his 'enrich yourselves' with the advice to be 'discreet in conjugal relations'. We cannot but be amazed at the indifference of those who governed France during this long period of more than eighty years. Not one of them seems to have known or cared about the seriousness of the standstill which the population had reached. Doubtless they feared over-population more than under-population, and were alarmed at the idea that the working classes, the largest and the most dangerous to them, might multiply; we may say that they lacked both foresight and knowledge.[5]

This restriction of the normal growth of the population began earlier than in the other European states, and lasted too long, so that France passed beyond the critical point where the expansion of the population necessary to

ensure normal growth was still possible, and found herself facing senescence and stagnation. In these circumstances it was inevitable that France should become attractive to immigrants. Her density of population was almost static, and this, in contrast with the growing density in the industrial nations of Europe, formed a 'pressure gradient' of increasing strength which encouraged immigration. France, once one of the most densely populated states in Europe, became progressively more under-populated. From 1850 to 1950 emigration exceeded immigration by 8 million in England, 4,500,000 in Germany, more than 1 million in Belgium and Holland, and 6 million in Italy.

Over a period of 150 years (1800–1950) in France immigration exceeded emigration by 5 million.[6] In 1850 there were 400,000 foreign-born in France; they were estimated at more than 1,100,000 in 1914, 1,550,000 in

1921, 2,900,000 in 1931. The foreign-born accounted for 5·75% of the growth in population between 1891 and 1901 and 75% from 1921 to 1931. These immigrants came from adjacent countries; Belgium, Germany, Italy, Spain, but some came from farther afield— central European Jews, Poles, White Russians, Armenians. Overcrowding, unemployment, political, racial or religious persecution were the principal motives. These immigrations had an important part to play through naturalisation, which added to the population of France, and through the employment opportunities taken up by the immigrants, especially in certain regions and in certain classes of employment. Some regions benefited greatly from this influx of foreigners.

French emigration to other countries has remained relatively insignificant during the 19th and 20th centuries. But it has taken place, despite the comparative under-population of France. Emigrants left particular regions for equally well-defined countries of destination: from Brittany they went to North America, from the southern Alps (the Ubaye valley) to Mexico and from Corsica and the Basque country to Latin America. Such movements, even though they were on a small scale, sometimes gave rise to a special organisation.

'The Bretons are going in increasing numbers to seek their fortunes in the United States and Canada. Morbihan leads this movement. In the canton of Gourin, on the borders of Finistère, at the foot of the passes through the Montagne Noire, emigration is taking place very much in the Irish manner. The Compagnie Générale Transatlantique has a permanent agency there, while the Cunard Line and the Canadian Pacific Railway regularly advertise their emigration services. Through the agency of the Compagnie Générale Transatlantique alone (situated at Roudouallec) 302 people embarked in 1957, 205 in 1958 and 240 in 1959. The emigrants mainly go to jobs in the kitchens and pantries in the restaurants of New York' (René Pleven).

Just before the Second World War, then, the demographic situation in France appeared somewhat unsatisfactory. The population increase from 1801 (28 million) to 1936 (41 million) was the result of the following 'balance sheet': on the credit side, increases through greater longevity (16 million), immigration and territorial gains (5 million); and on the debit side, a reproduction deficit (5 million) and losses in war (3 million at least).

B. The Demographic Revival 1946–66

Since the end of the Second World War France has achieved a spectacular demographic revival. From 1946 to 1962 the population increased by 15%, that is to say by 6,030,000 inhabitants, whereas between 1860 and 1946 the increase had been only 2,700,000.

The slow decline in the population of France was halted by the increase in the number of births after 1946, which continued beyond the 'normal' years of increased birth-rate after the war. The birth-rate rose from 16‰ in 1944 to 21‰ in 1947 and 1948. It fell up to 1966 but not to an alarming degree, considering the fall in mortality rates (12·2 in 1951, 10·6 in 1966). This recovery has its origin in the fortunate results of legislation in favour of the family (Families Act of 29th July 1939), but is certainly also due to the changed attitude of the young post-war generations who no longer tried to avoid having children. Since the end of the war France has appeared as a prolific nation with a natural growth of population which is relatively more significant than those of the other European countries. The figures for French

TABLE XIII. BIRTH-RATE (‰)

	1931–40	1946	1950	1955	1960	1966
Germany .	18·2	16·4	15·7	16·0	17·8	17·8
England .	14·9	19·4	16·1	15·5	17·5	17·9
Italy .	23·6	23·0	18·1	18·1	18·5	18·9
Netherlands .	20·8	30·2	22·7	21·4	20·8	19·2
France .	15·5	20·6	20·5	18·6	17·9	17·4
Belgium .	16·0	18·3	16·9	16·8	16·9	15·8

births in the years 1946–66 are in fact among the highest in Europe, and are exceeded only by those of the Netherlands, Italy and the other Mediterranean states (Table XIII).

We must not, however, overestimate the consequences of this sharp rise in the birth-rate. Coming as it did hard on the heels of a century of stagnation, it could only produce a radical change in French population statistics in the long run. The effects of a prolonged decline would be halted only if the large year-classes of post-war years maintained the present high birth-rate. Indeed, the low birth-rate figure for 1967 (16·7) alarmed the authorities as it could mark the end of a period of demographic revival.

Moreover, although the mortality rate in France has dropped spectacularly in the last fifty years, it is still higher than that of many European states. In 1961, 18 out of 25 European states had a lower mortality rate than France (11‰), including the Netherlands (7·5‰), Denmark (9·5‰) and Italy (9·4‰). Part of this difference is naturally accounted for by the higher death-rate of an older population. But two other factors are involved:

1. A much greater preponderance of adult male deaths than in other European states, due to industrial injuries, occupational diseases, various other diseases (tuberculosis), the deplorable housing conditions which too many French people have still to endure and above all to alcoholism.[7]

2. An abnormally high infant mortality rate in spite of the considerable progress that has been made:[8] 1900: 163‰; 1950: 48‰; 1964: 19·4%. The highest figures are found in urban and industrial regions as well as in rural areas, 33 departments showing figures above the national average.

The revival of French fertility has been very effectively assisted by immigration, which has remained significant since the end of the war. From 1947 to 1954 the number of immigrants in the country was 585,000; between 1954 and March 1962 it rose to 1,150,000, including 550,000 foreigners, 450,000 Europeans repatriated from Morocco, Tunisia and other territories, and 150,000 Algerian workers. From 1950 to 1960 inclusive, 443,377 holders of permanent work permits (516,964 accompanied by families) entered France according to official records.

As it is not exactly known how many of these foreign workers have left again, the net immigration rate is estimated at 65–70%. Until 1956 Italians formed the majority of the immigrants; their percentage has since been decreasing in favour mainly of Spaniards, and also of Portuguese. They have been absorbed into five principal occupations: building, agriculture, iron and steel, mines and quarries and domestic work. North African workers are a special case. Most of them were Algerians, who, until Algeria became independent (1962), were considered as French. Their number has risen to more than 500,000 in 1965, representing 20% of the adult male Moslem population of Algeria. But the foreign labour force now comes from other African states; a census taken on 1st July 1963 showed 40,000 coloured workers, mainly domiciled in Marseilles (7,000) and Paris (28,000).[9] Recent agreements have permitted Turkish and Yugoslav workers to enter France.

Immigrants doing jobs which Frenchmen will not take, at least as far as the least skilled occupations are concerned, are too often living in deplorable conditions in shanty towns or slum quarters. Much remains to be done for the reception and care of immigrants. In all, from 10th May 1954 to 7th March 1962 the population of France increased by 8·2%, of which 5·5% resulted from natural increase (+2,350,000) and 2·7% from immigration (+1,150,000).[10] The mean annual natural increase (6·7‰) has never been so high since 1800. Since March 1962 the population has risen sharply by at least 600,000, owing to the mass return of Algerians of French or European stock.

The overall form and indentations of the age pyramid summarise the net demographic variations over a period of rather less than a century (fig. 33). The two very marked recessions correspond to periods of low birth-rate during the two world wars. The unborn children of 1916 would by now have been

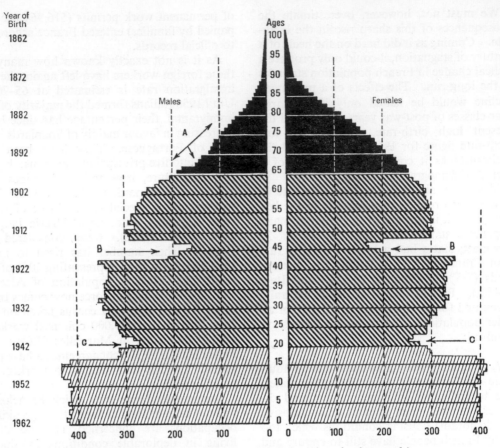

Fig. 33. Age-pyramid as at 1st January 1963 (numbers in thousands).
A. Military losses of the 1914–18 war
B. Age classes reduced by the 1914–18 war
C. Age classes reduced by the low birth-rate of the 30s and by the 1939–45 war

fully active and of an age to assume authority; their absence extends the working life of the older age-groups beyond normal retirement age, and at the same time causes a break between the generations.

On 1st January 1964 the under-20s represented 33·7% of the population, and are increasing regularly year by year. The over-65 age-group which had been continually increasing up to 1958 became stabilised at about 11·9%. Adults, from 20 to 65 years, represented 54·4%, but this proportion is steadily decreasing as the younger age-groups become more numerous.

TABLE XIV. AGE-GROUP COMPOSITION

	under-20	20–39	40–59	over 60
France (1962) .	32·2	27·2	23·0	17·5
Netherlands (1951) . .	38·0	26·7	21·9	13·3
Great Britain (1961) .	30·1	26·0	26·8	17·1
United States (1961) . .	38·8	25·4	22·5	13·2

These proportions are by no means new, and although it is right to stress the importance of the recovery of the birth-rate and the great problems caused by this 'fresh wave' of births, we must not forget that a century ago (1861) the under-20s constituted 35·8%

of the population and the over-60s only 8%. Nor is this distribution of age-groups exceptional in comparison with other states. Table XIV shows the relative magnitude—still a modest one—of the French population revival of the post-war years.

1. Although results of French censuses may on the whole be considered correct, they should not be taken as perfect. In older censuses systematic errors were made in the population of certain departments, such as Corsica, and certain towns, such as Marseilles. Even now the population of Corsica is only very approximately known, and the 170,000 Corsicans living on the island were 268,000 in the 1946 census!

2. There has been a progressive decline in the ratio of the population of France to the population of Europe (including the European part of the U.S.S.R.)—13·5% in 1850, 7·1% in 1950; and to that of the world—4% in 1700, 3% in 1850, 1·5% in 1964.

3. If France had the present densities of population of Switzerland, Italy, Great Britain or the Netherlands, her population would be respectively 75, 100, 125 or 200 million inhabitants.

4. 1821–30, 25·1‰; 1851–60, 23·9‰; 1871–80, 23·7‰ (Great Britain, 21·4‰; Belgium, 22·6‰). 1891–1900, 21·5‰; 1901–10, 19·5‰ (Great Britain, 15·4‰; Belgium, 16·5‰).

5. 'But the French scarcely realised the danger. France imagined that low birth-rates and depopulation would not prevent her from keeping her territory, her colonial empire and her position in the world. She was a rich country then, and numerous foreign states were in debt to her; and, lulled by a false sense of security, she was rousing the covetous instincts of her more crowded neighbours' (Reinhard and Armengaud, *Histoire de la population mondiale* (Paris, 1961), p. 267).

6. The annexation of Nice and Savoie brought almost 900,000 inhabitants to France.

7. The excess of adult male deaths over female deaths in the same age-group (45-59) is 75% in France as against 63% in Italy, 46% in England, 24% in the Netherlands and 13% in Denmark.

8. 1961: France, 25·7; Italy, 40·1; Netherlands, 15·5; Switzerland, 21; Belgium, 31; U.S.A., 25·3. These figures are calculated on common bases in order to permit comparison.

9. From 1956 to 1961, 121,876 foreigners acquired French nationality (47,233 Italians, 24,625 Poles, 24,393 Spaniards, etc.). It was estimated that immigrants and the descendents of immigrants constituted almost one seventh of the population of France.

10. The difference (+130,000) between the two census figures is the result of adjustments and changes of definition.

2. POPULATION DISTRIBUTION AND ITS CHANGES

A. Population Distribution by Departments, and its Evolution Since 1845

Figure 34 shows the basic facts of population distribution in terms of the proportion of the total population in each department in 1962. In that year 63·6% of the population of France was contained in 32 departments, and more than a third (34·1%) in only 8 departments: Seine, 12·1%; Seine-et-Oise, 4·9%; Nord, 4·9%; Pas-de-Calais, 2·9%; Bouches-du-Rhône, 2·6%; Rhône, 2·4%; Gironde, 2%. Conversely, 58 departments together contained only 36·3% of the population. This situation is of course not static. Since the middle of the 19th century the population has shown an increasing tendency to concentration. In 1845, 47 departments each had more than 1% of the population of France; this number declined to 42 in 1872, 35 in 1911 and 28 in 1936.[11] This progressive concentration operated in favour of a few departments which already had high population figures. In 1845, only Seine-Maritime (2·14), Nord (3·20) and Seine (3·85) contained more than 2% of the population.

The most important changes came between 1872 and 1911, and this period saw the appearance of the other population growth centres of today: Bouches-du-Rhône, Gironde, Rhône, Pas-de-Calais, Seine-et-Oise.

The post-war recovery restored, to some extent, the balance of the population distribution. Local accumulations of young people born since 1946 increased the number of departments containing 1–1·5% of the population from 12 to 19. This, however, represents only a slight trend depending for its consolidation on many factors.

In a country like France, populated for so long and with so old a civilisation, it would be useless to try to analyse the present composition of the population without looking to the past to see by what stages the present map, itself a temporary one, was evolved. Considered over a century, population changes in France are the fruit of the combination of two movements: rural depopulation and urbanisation (fig. 32). Some countries have become urbanised without an alarming degree of rural depopulation, where population growth has been vigorous enough to ensure the success of urbanisation. In the context

9,135,000 in 1851 reached 14,311,000 in 1891, 17,380,000 in 1921, 24,089,000 in 1954, 29,375,000 in 1962.[12]

The fact that the two sectors of the population have changed in opposite directions explains the extent to which their respective percentages have been reversed. In 1851 the urban population was only 26% of the total population of France, but the proportion in-

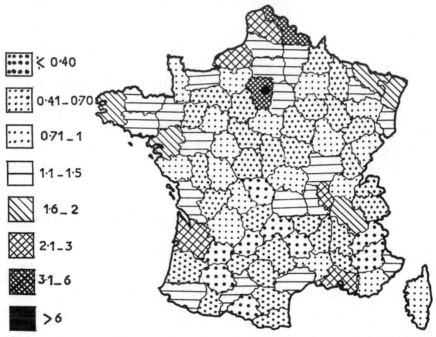

:::::	≤ 0·40
:::::	0·41 – 0·70
:::::	0·71 – 1
▤	1·1 – 1·5
▨	1·6 – 2
▩	2·1 – 3
▦	3·1 – 6
■	> 6

Fig. 34. Distribution of the population by departments in 1962 (in % of the total population of France).

of French demography this type of development was impossible. France, therefore, achieved her industrial and urban revolution by means of man-power recruited from the countryside.

From 1851 to 1962 the population classified as rural fell from 26,648,000 to 17,145,000; from 1891 to 1954 the rural agricultural population fell from 17,436,000 to 9,650,000; from 1921 to 1962 the number of male agricultural workers fell from 4,992,000 to 2,577,000. Conversely, the urban population which was

creased to 41% in 1901, 52·4% in 1936, 56·6% in 1954 and 62% in 1962.

When was the turning-point after which these contrasts became accentuated and the two processes of rural depopulation and urbanisation began to take effect? Up to 1831 the population of all the departments increased. The beginning of the change came between the years 1830 and 1840. We must therefore analyse the two phenomena separately, starting from the middle of the 19th century.

B. Rural Depopulation

Its Extent

It is difficult, without a convenient and accurate base for reference, to estimate the extent of rural depopulation; as each region behaved in a different way, we can give no really satisfactory starting date. It might appear logical to calculate depopulation by reference to the year when the population was at its maximum; but the dates vary from one region to another and even from one canton to another. Above all, this method of calculating exaggerates the extent of the rural exodus by comparing it with a maximum which is often exceptional; these maximum figures, in fact, show over-population, or, to be more precise, an accumulation of rural population. Thus the textile industry occupied tens of thousands of people in Picardy, Normandy, Châtillonnais, Livradois and the South-west. From the days of charcoal furnaces, metallurgy prospered in dozens of little rural centres in the Ardennes, the Argonne, the Hauts-de-Meuse, Basse-Bourgogne, Nivernais and Périgord. Whole cantons specialised in one industry: locksmiths in Vimeu, coppersmiths and ironmongers in the Normandy *Bocage*, spectacle-makers, shoe-makers, glass-makers. The timber industry in its manifold forms provided work for whole villages.

Such accumulations often occurred during the years preceding the beginning of the industrial and urban revolution. At that time, country districts with a high birth-rate supported a population who earned their living by a combination of agricultural work, crafts, industry, public office and services. The various reforms of the Revolution—the sale of state property, the break-up of commons, heathland and forests, changes in agriculture, the end of fallow land and the introduction of new crops—were all favourable to a rapid rise in population and made possible the development of rural industry. When the lack of wool, timber, iron ores or, more generally, of tradition or enterprise—which often occurred when the region failed to become urbanised—

made it impossible to work locally, the surplus working population had recourse to seasonal emigration. Itinerant workmen, such as the masons of Limousin, the chimney-sweeps of Savoie, the hawkers of Oisans, the sawyers of Livradois, travelled the roads all the winter and in summer came back to work on the land. Severely over-populated regions thus appeared about the middle of the 19th century.[13] The map showing density of rural population in 1845 makes it very clear which they are (fig. 35): all north-western France, northern and central Aquitaine, the Limagne, the Lyons region, which stands out remarkably, and eastern France. The population figures for these rural areas are worthy of attention. Nord broke all records with more than 112 inhabitants per km.^{2}; Haut-Rhin had almost 91, the Côtes-du-Nord 81, Puy-de-Dôme 61 and Ardèche 58. At the same time, as the map shows equally clearly, some rural regions were, after 1845, much less densely populated. The pattern of rural population already showed great differences, and Lozère, Hautes-Alpes and Basses-Alpes appear as 'demographic deserts' (*déserts*) with respectively 25, 21 and 19 inhabitants per km.^{2} A zone of lower densities ran across the central part of France, growing wider as it progressed and branching out in the South.

Rural depopulation then spread progressively; from 1850 onwards a number of departments were affected in the West, the East, the Centre, the Alps and the South-west. The map of rural densities in 1872 shows how quickly and how widely it spread in Aquitaine, and on the borders of the West; the departments in the Lyons region suffered equally, while on the other hand the Breton peninsula remained unaffected, like the two departments of the North.[14]

Forty years later the 1911 map no longer shows the close correspondence that can be observed between the maps of 1845 and 1872. Eleven departments have less than 29 inhabitants per km.^{2} The four most affected areas are:

1. In the North-west, Mayenne and Sarthe

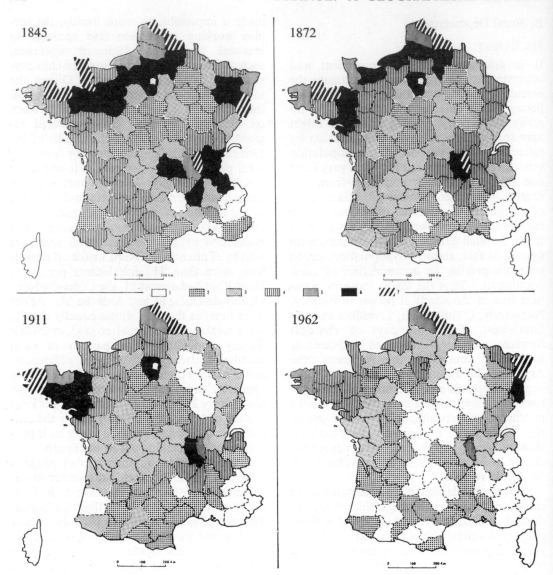

Fig. 35.   Density of rural population (inhabitants per km.²) in 1845, 1872, 1911, 1962 (the population densities of Savoie and the County of Nice in 1845, and Alsace-Lorraine in 1872 and 1911 have not been calculated).

to the south, and Somme, Aisne and Ardennes to the north.

2. The block of departments to the southeast of the Paris basin, extended into Jura and Ain.

3. The block of departments in the Aquitaine basin and the central Pyrenees.

4. The block of departments in the Southeast from Ardèche to Basses-Alps and Bouches-du-Rhône.

The highest depopulation rates are those of Bouches-du-Rhône (40·6), Drôme (34·2), Basses-Alpes (25·9) and Lot (28·6).

But neither the departments of Brittany nor those of the Central Massif appear among those most affected by this depopulation.

From 1911 to 1954 the drain from the countryside continued, and 33 departments had rural populations in 1954 with less than 28 inhabitants per km.². Only Rhône, the departments of Alsace and Moselle, the two northern departments, Seine-et-Oise, Seine-Maritime and Manche, and the Breton departments had relatively high rural populations. Nord was the only department with a rural population density of more than 78 inhabitants per km.².

Analysing this century of evolution, we are struck by the continuity of regional contrasts and of differences in density. There are considerable differences between the 1845 map and that of 1962, yet the regional divisions which could be seen a century earlier are still there in 1962, but less sharply differentiated. The crescent of low population running through central France and spreading out in the South still exists between the more populous regions of the West and the East (from Alsace to Ardèche). Actual differences in population correspond impressively to these differences in density. Between 1906 and 1954 the Central Massif lost 780,000 inhabitants, that is 17% of its population, but all the maps show how differently its constituent departments behave in the matter of population.

Figure 36 shows the progress of rural depopulation in France over more than a century (1846–1954). Forty-one departments lost more than 35% of their rural population. For some of them, the figures are spectacular: Yonne, 88·7; Ariège, 57·2; Basses-Alpes, 56·4; Lot, 56·3; Hautes-Alpes, 55·8; Lozère, 51·5; Meuse, 50·1. But even the lower figures are no less revealing when they relate to departments with less adverse natural conditions, such as Somme (37·9). This rural depopulation is localised mainly east of a diagonal line from Ardennes to Basses-Pyrénées; western France has resisted it comparatively well.

The Factors and Types of Rural Depopulation

The factors

The list of factors contributing to rural depopulation is a long one; it contains both simple and complex factors, and includes economic, sociological and psychological data. The general causes were:

(a) *Industrialisation* of towns and coalfields, which attracted labour to a considerable extent and doomed to disappearance the rural

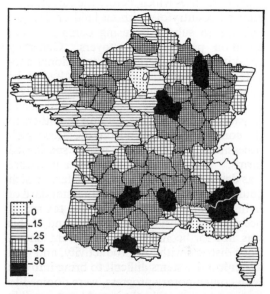

Fig. 36. Percentage changes in the rural population by departments from 1846 to 1954 (*erratum* —Moselle 13·4).

craftsman class and all the industries depending on wood for fuel. All commissions of inquiry and all monographs on the subject record the sudden collapse or the slow decay of a great diversity of trades: textile industries, wood-working, glass-making and charcoal metallurgy, which were at that time scattered throughout many regions.

(b) *Changes in agriculture.* Rural depopulation did not result only from the pull of towns and factories; it was stimulated at the same time within the country districts by changes in agriculture. Crops needing a large labour force contracted or disappeared one after the other—vines, silk-worms, industrial crops (flax, hemp)—while the expansion of pasture land reduced the need for workers. At the end of the 19th century, moreover, agricultural machinery came into wider use, condemning farm-workers to unemployment and causing a 'technological over-population' by its mere introduction into the countryside.

We must also take into account the influence of the disappearance of all the communal practices which, before the Revolution, allowed countryfolk without land or draught animals to subsist by using common land, common pasture and estovers. Generally speaking, in this period the traditional subsistence farming with varied crops had to be adapted, on one hand, to the bulk consignments demanded by the towns and made possible by the railways, and on the other, to the competition of grain from overseas which necessitated larger and more specialised farms. This transformation in agriculture was death to the small subsistence farm which could not provide its owner with a standard of living comparable to that of the towns; it necessitated considerable capital, and if this was not forthcoming, the farm went under. Poor districts with low productivity, and with agricultural systems difficult to bring into line with contemporary progress, were doomed to become poorer still; they could not possibly be integrated into an agricultural economy adapted to supply national and international markets. Since their resources did not increase, the rewards for labour became less and less. All these circumstances encouraged rural depopulation.

(c) Complementary and accidental causes. The drift from the countryside in the 19th century would not have been so widespread if the rail network had not extended progressively over France during the same period. Once the movement had been set going, the new urban civilisation, with its gaslighting, its street fountains on every corner, its trams, its theatres, its true worth and its false reputa-tion, spread its tentacles ever farther to draw in the country people.

The movement was also stimulated by economic crises, either general or purely agricultural; the 1848 crisis contributed to the ruin of rural industries 'by wiping out an age-old form of economy' (C. Pouthas); the slump in agricultural products corresponding to the drop in prices between 1880 and 1896, and the economic crisis of 1930 both initiated new waves of depopulation.

In the 19th century the country districts were seriously affected by diseases attacking a great variety of crops: potato disease in the middle of the century (Lozère was affected as early as 1845), silk-worm diseases which brought about the decline of many communes of the South through the failure of the silk-worm industry, plagues of phylloxera from 1865 onwards, which affected most vineyards, reducing their area to a considerable extent and shaking traditional agriculture to its foundations.[15] The First World War was also an important factor in rural depopulation. Out of 3,700,000 agricultural workers called to the colours, 673,000 were killed, and 500,000 discharged unfit. Many villages received their final blow in the death of ten or twenty soldiers, whose names, carved on a humble war memorial, look out on the derelict houses of a dying village.

Many secondary causes added to the effect of the deep-seated causes of rural depopulation:

1. The railways stretching out across the countryside recruited the necessary labour as they progressed; and these workers followed them to the towns, while the communes which had stations concentrated the population along the main lines, depopulating the stationless communes. For example: 'during the period 1866 to 1936, the total population of the rural communes without stations, situated in a zone stretching for 15 km. on each side of the Paris–Lyon–Méditerranée line (P.L.M.), fell from 1,058,146 to 809,419, a loss of 248,727 which was mainly due to migration. On the other hand the communes with sta-

tions on the P.L.M. line (excluding Paris) gained 1,645,373 inhabitants' (A. Chatelain).

2. State education for all. To a certain extent rural depopulation was encouraged by education and professional training; for the educated countryman was no longer at home in the traditional rural area.

3. Military service which, from 1880 onwards, brought all young rustics into 'urban' barracks and gave them a taste for town life.

4. The increasing number of family and friendship ties between the areas losing population and the growth areas.

To put it more simply and more broadly, there are two civilisations, two 'patterns' of life, bound to the technologies and economies of different ages, that have existed side by side for the last hundred years, the older and more traditional giving way from the start to the pioneer spirit of the other.

A recent survey of the reasons for leaving the countryside was recently carried out with a sample consisting of 92 former agricultural wage-earners, 66 relatives (sons or daughters) of farmers and 7 farm managers, all from the central provinces, and all having left the land less than five years before (80% being under 25 years of age). The most common replies, in order of importance, were as follows: inadequate or irregular pay or returns, no fixed hours, too little freedom, too hard work, lack of prospects in farming, lack of financial help, discomforts of farm life, overcrowded farmhouses. On the other hand, 80% gave affirmative replies to the question: 'Did you like country life?'

Independently of causes connected with the difficulties of adjusting to changes in the agricultural economy, these emigrants were not trying to get away from the country, but from the living conditions to be found there, the bad housing, the hard work and the lack of leisure. Women played a very important part in the flight from the land.

'As a mother she makes it easier for her children to leave, either directly by guiding their decisions, or indirectly by a rigid attachment to the traditional way of life, thus causing a conflict which can be resolved only by the departure of the young people. As a wife she steps in at the moment of marriage. As a daughter, leaving the countryside very early herself, she reduces the vitality of the village community, and in certain regions causes the young men to leave, simply because they are not likely to resign themselves to a celibate life.'[16]

This divorce between two ways of life has increasingly become a separation between two worlds—a phenomenon which we shall meet again in later chapters. All the legislative, administrative and economic actions of successive governments have isolated the world of the country from the urban and industrial world—that is to say, from Paris. For example, social legislation—protection against industrial injuries, restriction of working hours, health and unemployment insurance, family allowances, paid holidays—has all been conceived and calculated in relation to the city wage-earner. It was even more difficult to apply it to small farmers with no conception of a regular wage.

There is no doubt that rural depopulation originated also in the change in working conditions which took place during the first decades of the 19th century. In fact the agricultural revolution of the 18th century, by introducing new crops and making developments in stock-rearing possible, increased the burden of land work; it made country life harder and at the same time suppressed the complementary trades which kept in rural districts workers who were available for occasional help on the land.

Types of depopulation

Districts differ too much geographically and in the factors causing depopulation for it to be possible to group under a single heading all variations in rural population statistics. We can reduce the basic types of rural depopulation to five, of which three are linked with occupation and two are not.

(a) Non-occupational depopulation

1. Depopulation resulting from demographic disequilibrium. A region loses population by an excess of deaths over births, due either to a low birth-rate or a high mortality. The number of young people is insufficient to ensure replacement from generation to generation, and the population inexorably declines, without there having been any real exodus from the country.

2. Non-occupational depopulation (*sensu stricto*). This results from the departure of young people before they have really taken up a trade; sons and daughters who could well have helped their parents in field or workshop, but who had not the occupational status of the farmer, farm-worker or craftsman. This is the type found in over-populated, demographically vigorous regions. It is more logical to see this as a phenomenon of geographical mobility in which there is nothing intrinsically alarming.

(b) Occupational depopulation

1. Occupational depopulation in agriculture is the dwindling of the farming class; this is the real and specific blow at the heart of the agricultural world. The concentration of farms in fewer hands and the elimination of marginal holdings which can only provide a living in combination with other resources, such as those of the '*ménagers*'—'farmers without horses'—in Picardy, represent the purest type of rural depopulation, which completely upsets all social and economic structures.

2. Occupational depopulation among agricultural wage-earners. This is different from the preceding type; this group, together with the following one, has always played an essential part in the spread of depopulation. Agricultural wage-earners were the first victims of technological advances in agriculture, and it is this class which has dwindled the most; there were 2,106,000 paid agricultural workers in 1860, but only 580,000 in 1957. Between 1954 and 1962 the number of male wage-earners decreased by 25·9%. The total number of male persons engaged in agriculture, whether self-employed or wage-earning, dropped from 5,146,000 in 1856 to 5,057,000 in 1921, 4,254,000 in 1936, 3,613,000 in 1954 and 2,582,000 in 1962.

3. Depopulation in occupations other than agricultural. This category, together with the preceding one, has played the most important part in the drain from the countryside, especially from 1870 to 1911. All the crafts and industries scattered throughout the countryside were condemned to death by the concentration of factories and towns in the Industrial Revolution. The hundreds of spinners, seamstresses, weavers, smiths, coopers and all their fellow-workers could offer no resistance; the younger and more enterprising left for the town, while the others fell back on their meagre family property or took day-labourers' work which led them nowhere. In the same way the number of those engaged in the service sector was shrinking. They were having to adapt themselves to new types of clients with new requirements; the farrier and the blacksmith gave way to the mechanic and the many small shopkeepers were succeeded by mobile tradesmen from the neighbouring town.

Of these five types of depopulation some are normal and common; the country districts could not expect to keep children born during a period of high birth-rate, nor craftsmen at a time when industry was developing in the towns, nor people engaged in services whose numbers are related to those of the population as a whole. This is a type of depopulation caused by a surplus, either demographic or occupational. Other types are partly general, partly specific; that is to say that rural depopulation affects some categories of people who could have stayed in the country: farmers' sons who, by leaving, condemned the family farm to extinction, and farmers themselves who have abandoned the land. There is no true rural depopulation unless land values have depreciated or extensive farming methods are adopted in place of intensive methods. As long as the land is firmly held and well farmed, with none left fallow, only 'normal' outward movement takes place, the countryside fulfilling its role as an exporter of labour. But in France rural depopulation has too often, and in too many regions, actually passed beyond the category we may call 'general', to become 'specific'. The reason is certainly to be found in the low population growth of the last hundred years. In certain regions the loss of active workers, or young people not yet working, could be masked by the maintenance of a high enough rate of replacement; the North, Brittany and Alsace are the best examples. The problem was and is quite different for Brittany, which is at the same time over-populated and affected by a considerable exodus, and for the Central Massif or Aquitaine, which are being drained of their essential human capital. 'A surplus has left the Breton countryside, but a sorely-needed labour force has abandoned the South-west.'[17] The regular settling in the South-west of farmers from Italy, Vendée and Brittany as well as those repatriated from North Africa is sufficient proof that some of France's countryside is under-populated.

These five types of depopulation have not all operated uniformly in time. Regional studies all show slight variations and different combinations of factors leading to depopulation.

Rural depopulation has been greatly influenced by environmental conditions. Impoverished mountain regions and those with poor soil have suffered the greatest depopulation. From 1906 to 1954 Livradois and Haut-Limousin lost 50% of their population, Causse Noir 49%, Larzac 51% and the slopes of the Cévennes 42%. The same applies to the limestone plateaux in the east of the Paris basin, and to the mountain regions as a whole.

Mountain areas present a special case among the types of demographic evolution. Collectively, they appear as depopulated zones. But in reality there are several mountain regions to which G. Veyret Verner has called attention with reference to the northern Alps. The mountain zones with the most critical population situation are those of moderate height, below 1,000 m. The middle altitudinal zones have in fact none of the advantages of the plains and none of the assets of high mountains. Their populations are constantly dwindling and gradually growing older. High mountain regions are demographically of two contrasted types according to whether or not they have been saved by the tourist industry. The valleys, unless they have an economy suitable to mountainous zones which has been able to benefit from recent changes, lose their population if they are exclusively agricultural, and show a vigorous growth of population wherever industries are present. In the same way, in the Central Massif, 'upland pastoral areas with moderate densities of population maintain their demographic equilibrium and emigration goes on at a moderate pace; these pastoral areas hold their own, because their population densities have remained more or less adjusted to their economic potential so that a state of balance could be reached between local resources and the dependent population. On the other hand, mountains of moderate height which have both agricultural and pasture land are moving towards a swift decline which is the result of economic poverty, permanent under-employment, absurdly low returns and an agricultural economy which cannot possibly pay at present' (P. Estienne).

There is so much variety in France, however, that the regional pattern does not indicate the real extent of depopulation precisely enough. There have been, and still are, variations not only from one small region to another but also from commune to commune, variations that differ also according to the period under review. In the same region, some communes have remained stable for a century, while others on their borders were affected by a 'torrential wave of emigration' (P. Estienne). Between 1876 and 1962 the communes of a valley in the Ariège district of the Pyrenees lost 69% of their population, but at rates varying between communes from 28 to 94%.[18] In the canton of Rosières-en-Santerre in Picardy the depopulation figures for 1836–1936 range from 26 to 80%. This diversity is reflected in the varying incidence of population. In Brittany 238 communes reached their maxima in 1846 or 1851, 184 communes in 1861 or 1866, 234 in 1906 or 1911, 102 in 1954.[19]   In the northern region (Nord and Pas-de-Calais) during the period 1801–1954, 248 communes reached their maxima between 1806 and 1836, 286 between 1841 and 1851, 297 between 1856 and 1876, 249 between 1881 and 1906, 145 between 1911 and 1931, 45 between 1936 and 1946.

This astonishing diversity can be attributed to the very distinct 'personalities' of the communes, existing from time immemorial. Quite apart from traditions of craft and industry, systems of land tenure, the size of the farms, types of cropping, even the temperaments of the people can explain the juxtaposition of 'strong' and 'weak' *cantons*.   In three cantons of the Somme, 34 out of 63 communes had kept virtually the same number of farms between 1836 and 1936; the whole burden of agricultural intensification had been assumed by the other communes, some of which had lost two thirds of their farmers.

C. Urbanisation

The Growth of the Urban Population

The various types of rural depopulation have made it possible for the urban population of France to increase, even though there has not been a sufficiently vigorous natural growth of population since the middle of the 19th century.

Taking 100 in 1851 as the base, the urban population reached 150 thirty-five years later, 174 in 1901, 191 in 1911, 218 in 1926, 262 in 1954, 323 in 1962.   This represents the urbanisation of more than 20 million people, three times more than the total population increase.   Fed by rural depopulation, urban growth did not take the form of a sudden 'revolution'.   The curve (fig. 32) is relatively smooth.

Since the middle of the 19th century, urban growth in France has passed through three phases:

1. From 1851 to 1901 the towns went through a phase of rapid growth, and urban population increased by 74% (33% from 1876 to 1901); this was the only period of urban 'revolution', especially between the years 1851 and 1866.

2. From 1901 to 1954 urban growth slowed down (50%) and fell to a very low level in the second half of the period (19% from 1926 to 1954).   The growth curve became more irregular.   A very distinct recovery can be seen from the end of the First World War to the thirties, followed by a phase of stability until the Second World War which initiated a period of urban decline analogous to that of the war of 1870.

3. Since 1946, urban growth has been renewed in a very accentuated form (nearly 7 million new town-dwellers between 1946 and 1962).

Compared with other countries, however, this urbanisation appears to be on a modest scale.   France has no industrial and urban concentrations, except Paris, to compare with those of neighbouring states; we have no equivalent to the Ruhr (6,650,000 inhabitants on 8,000 km.^{2}) or South Lancashire (2,500,000 inhabitants).

Urban growth has been very unevenly distributed between the regions (fig. 37).   Its localisation in a small number of departments has contributed to the present high concentration of the population of France.   From 1872 to 1901, 17 departments absorbed 76% of the increase in the urban population, Seine alone taking up 31·25%.   The other departments benefiting from this increase were Nord and Pas-de-Calais (10·04%).   From the beginning of the century the central and south-western parts of the Aquitaine basin, a zone stretching from Lozère to Basses-Alpes, through Vaucluse, Drôme and Ardèche, Normandy and Maine (Mayenne, Eure, Orne), appear as the first victims of the urban revolution.   From 1901 to 1954 the process continued; 21 departments absorbed 79·5% of the urban growth (37·2% in the Paris region: Seine and Seine-et-Oise).   The 7 provincial departments whose urban growth represents more than 2% of the total are: Alpes-Maritimes, 3·31;   Bouches-du-Rhône, 4·36;   Loire-Atlantique, 2·34; Meurthe-et-Moselle, 2·74; Nord, 5·11; Pas-de-Calais, 6·31; Rhône, 2·57. The following eight years (1954–62) confirmed the trend towards urban concentration especially in the Paris region, where 2 departments took 48·6% of the urban growth. Only 4 provincial departments took

very irregularly distributed. In western France, with two exceptions (Ille-et-Vilaine and Haute-Garonne), they are coastal departments with harbours: Gironde, Loire-Atlantique, Finistère, Seine-Maritime. Northern, eastern and south-eastern France contain most of the departments with con-

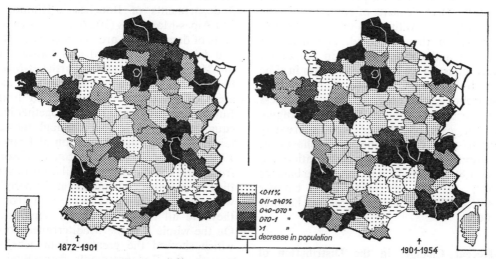

<- 0·11%
0·11–0·40%
0·40–0·70 "
0·70–1 "
>1 "
decrease in population

1872–1901

1901–1954

Fig. 37.   Changes in the urban population by departments (1872–1901 and 1901–54) in relation to changes in the total urban population of France. (Source: F. Carrière and P. Pinchemel, *Le Fait urbain en France*, A. Colin, 1963)

2–3% (Bouches-du-Rhône, Isère, Moselle, Rhône) and only 1 took more than 3% (Nord).

DISTRIBUTION OF THE URBAN POPULATION BY DEPARTMENTS

In 1962, only 22 French departments had a population representing 1% or more of the urban population of France. The 2 departments of Seine and Seine-et-Oise contain 28·8% of France's urban population, and 42·5% live in a group of 20 provincial departments. Nearly three quarters (71·3%) of the urban population is thus concentrated in 22 departments. Three others can be added to this group of departments, each of them containing more than 0·9% of the urban population: Marne, Ille-et-Vilaine and Gard. Altogether 74·1% of the urban population of France is contained in 25 departments. These strongly urbanised departments are

E

siderable urban populations; they can be divided into four groups:

1. The Mediterranean departments from Hérault to Alpes-Maritimes inclusive (9·04% of the urban population of France).
2. The departments of the Lyons region: Isère, Rhône, Loire (6·3%).
3. The 4 departments of Alsace and Lorraine (6·7%).
4. The 2 departments of the northern region (9·8%).

These four groups of departments contain almost a third (31·9%) of the urban population of France. Two characteristics emerge clearly from these figures: the concentration of the French urban population and its 'peripheral' distribution. The 65 other departments share the remaining quarter of the town-dwellers (25·9%). Ten of them have less than 0·25% each of the urban population.[20]

If rural depopulation in France has appeared as a form of evolution in every way harmful to the country, this is because it did not lead to a well-distributed and regionally balanced urban development. In the long history of variations in the peopling of France, we can perceive elements of continuity in the regional pattern, with areas of repulsion and dispersal, on the one hand, and areas of attraction and concentration, on the other. Nevertheless, as we trace the changes in time region by region, very small-scale reversals of these trends can be observed, bearing witness to the variety of influences at work. Languedoc, for example, has passed alternately through positive and negative phases of migration: 1876–1901, net immigration balance 51,800; 1910–11, net emigration balance 19,000; 1911–31, net immigration balance 78,000; 1931–54, net emigration balance 85,000.

D. Recent Changes in the Distribution of Population

The two processes of rural depopulation and urban growth are at present going on in the context of a rapidly increasing population in the country as a whole. Figure 38 shows, by departments, where this increase is located. It records the share of each department in the total increase of population from 1954 to 1962. Fifteen departments returned a fall in population during these eight years (as against 36 between 1936 and 1954). The most compact block is that of the 7 departments of the Central Massif, especially those in the south. But Manche, Orne and Mayenne form a more unexpected group of departments showing a persistent loss of population; Côtes-du-Nord is another. Three south-western departments show similar trends: Dordogne, Gers and Ariège. The greatest losses have occurred in the following departments: Gers (−3%), Ariège and Cantal (−5·5%), Creuse (−5·3%).

More than 60% of the population increase was concentrated in 12 departments, each with an increase of more than 2%. All of these departments are situated north of a line from Montpellier to Le Havre; they fall naturally into five blocks, chief of which is the Paris region, which alone was responsible for more than 30% of the population increase.[21] Second comes Provence, with the 3 departments of Bouches-du-Rhône, Var and Alpes-Maritimes (10·26%). Three other pairs of departments are about equal: Rhône and Isère (6·87%), Nord and Pas-de-Calais (6·7%) and Moselle and Meurthe-et-Moselle (6·34%). These five regions stand out as the areas of most vigorous growth in France. But the four provincial regions together barely equalled the Paris region, although they contained 20·3% of the population of France in 1962. Thirteen other departments absorbed from 1 to 1·99% of the population increase; they are mainly departments on the periphery with either a sea-coast or a land frontier; they are all highly urbanised departments. On the whole it is the Mediterranean region which showed the greatest homogeneity in growth, the 7 departments from Pyrénées-Orientales to Alpes-Maritimes accounting for 14·74 of the increase.

The highest rates of growth for 1954–62 were as follows: Provence–Côte d'Azur region (a development region), +16·9%; Paris conurbation, +15%; Lorraine, +12·4%; Rhône–Alpine region, +10·2%. This population growth results from a combination of natural increase and a positive balance of migration.

How are these two phenomena distributed by departments? They can be measured in two ways: in relation to either departmental populations or the national total. For example, Pas-de-Calais had a natural increase of 9·7% over its total population in 1954. The 122,800 individuals making up this increase represented 5·23% of the total for all departments returning a natural increase. But Moselle, with a departmental increase of 12·5%, represented only 3·97% of that total.

The map of natural increase (fig. 39A) shows a contrast between northern and peripheral France, on the one hand, and southern and central France, on the other. The Gironde and Isère form the points of a huge crescentic northern region, taking in Brittany, Normandy, Picardy, Nord, Champagne, Lorraine, Alsace, the Jura and the Lyons region.

Moselle, 3·97%; Seine-Maritime, 3·59%; Meurthe-et-Moselle, 2·47%; Loire-Atlantique, 2·30%; Bouches-du-Rhône, 2·17%; Rhône, 2·10%. In all, 32 departments showed increases of 1% or more. The weakness, both quantitative and qualitative—de-

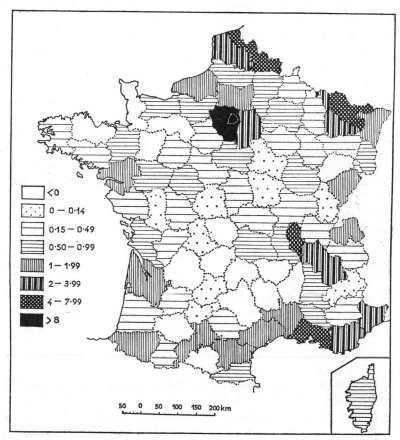

Fig. 38.   Distribution by departments of the increase in the population (1954–62) showing the percentage in each department of the total increase in the population of France.

The highest natural increases occurred in northern France, Doubs and Moselle coming first. Three departments showed a natural decrease: Creuse, Alpes-Maritimes, Ariège. Almost half (46·12%) of the total natural increase was localised in 10 departments alone. In descending order, their gains were as follows: Seine, 11·51%; Nord, 6·68%; Seine-et-Oise, 6·10%; Pas-de-Calais, 5·23%;

mographically speaking—of two thirds of France is evident from this situation.

These figures are significant in another sense. The highest figures, both by departments and as a whole, apply to highly urbanised and industrialised departments; that is to say that urban growth, which was considerable between the last two censuses (19·8%), was ensured not only by the traditional processes (depopulation of rural and agricultural districts, and immigration) but also by natural growth, as the post-war rise in births occurred in urban as well as in rural areas. This has an important consequence: urban growth is now largely 'autochthonous'; it can continue simply by the natural vitality of the town-dwellers, without having to be fed from the country districts as it was in the past. This situation makes it all the more difficult to relieve congested areas and re-establish a balance where sharp contrasts in density of population exist.

movements were in fact more concentrated than they appear to be. More than three quarters (75·24%) of the immigration was absorbed by 10 departments: Seine-et-Oise, 26·79%; Seine, 12·29%; Bouches-du-Rhône, 8·72%; Alpes-Maritimes, 6·06%; Rhône, 5·60%; Isère, 3·80%; Moselle, 3·62%; Var, 3·27%; Haute-Garonne, 3·06%; Hérault, 2·03%.

But in many cases these immigration balances recorded by towns and industrial areas hide a continuing exodus from agricultural regions. Thus, if we except Rouen,

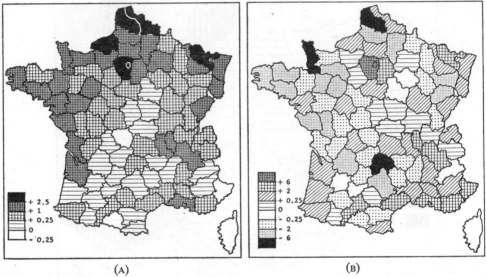

(A)   (B)

Fig. 39. Population change by natural increase (A) or migration (B), 1954–62, in relation to the figures for the whole of France (in percentages).

The map of the increase by migration (fig. 39B) shows quite a different distribution; the area of net immigration (+1,773,800 persons) was mainly concentrated in the urban and industrial regions of 46 departments: Paris region (740,000 net immigrants), Provence (319,000 net immigrants in the group comprising Alpes-Maritimes, Var, Bouches-du-Rhône), Rhône, Isère, Drôme, Vaucluse and the departments of Languedoc. The other departments showing high increases through migration were: Basses-Pyrénées, Haute-Garonne, Pyrénées-Orientales, Moselle, Doubs and Haute-Saône. These migratory

Le Havre, Rennes and Dijon, the departments of Seine-Maritime, Ille-et-Vilaine and Côte-d'Or have lost respectively 25,000, 29,000 and 8,300 inhabitants.

On the other hand, 43 departments show negative balances. They are situated especially in the West, from Deux-Sèvres to Calvados, in the south of the Central Massif and along the diagonal connecting the agricultural departments of Picardy, Champagne and Lorraine, from Pas-de-Calais to the Jura. The highest absolute losses by emigration occurred in Pas-de-Calais (42,000), Manche (39,000), Côtes-du-Nord (28,000), Finistère

(23,000), Morbihan (23,000), and the highest relative losses in Manche (9%) and Mayenne (8·2%). Sixteen departments accounted for more than 67% (67·4%) of the migration deficit of 483,342 persons for the 43 departments together. The departments contributing most towards this emigration were as follows: Pas-de-Calais, 8·6%; Manche, 8·1%; Côtes-du-Nord, 5·7%; Finistère, 5·5%; Morbihan, 4·7%; Mayenne, 4·1%; Vosges, 4·1%; Vendée, 4·0%; Cantal, 3·5%.

These figures provide further evidence of the increasing polarisation within France and the growing dichotomy between its two domains. It is particularly disturbing to find that the departments which have at present a negative balance of migration are in many cases those which have a positive balance of natural increase. There is every reason, in fact, to fear a new phase of depopulation in the regions of the West, which are prolific, but rural and insufficiently urbanised and industrialised. Moreover, the regions which are gaining in population are doing so more by immigration from foreign countries and from North Africa than from other parts of France.

More detailed studies reveal trends which may be of considerable importance for the future of a region; the effect of a migration balance cannot be assessed in quantitative terms alone—it must also be considered qualitatively. An outflow of young people, for example, may be balanced by an inflow of older ones. An outflow of skilled workers may be balanced by an inflow of unskilled labourers, as in the northern region.

The revival of fertility has had two important consequences on rural and urban populations: the change in rural population is no longer negative in the majority of the regions of France, and the high birth-rate in the 'fertile crescent' referred to on p. 133, has called a halt to rural depopulation. In 1954 and in 1962 thousands of rural communes had bigger populations than in 1946 or 1936. Even in less prolific regions such as the Central Massif, 20% of the communes had

bigger populations in 1954 than in 1936. These increases, resulting from growth of the younger age-group (from 0 to 14–16 years), mask a continuation of the process of occupational depopulation.

E. Seasonal Population Movements

Side by side with migratory movements, whether persistent or ephemeral, there have always been seasonal population movements in France. In the past, seasonal migrants came from rural districts where there was not enough food or work for all the inhabitants during the winter; thus chimney-sweeps and hawkers came from Savoie and Auvergne to work in the low countries. Nowadays these migrations are replaced by others: daily movements due to the separation of place of residence and place of work, and seasonal migrations for the purpose of holidays and leisure activities. The extent of these is only now beginning to be realised.

In 1961, 37·5% of French people went on holiday; more than a third of the population left their homes once or twice a year to stay somewhere else. This seasonal exodus occurred first of all in summer, but now tends to happen equally in winter with the development of winter sports. Its incidence varies between the regions and between social and occupational classes. In 1961, 87·3% of the professional people and skilled workers went on holiday, but only 38% of the unskilled and semi-skilled workers, 45% of the public-service personnel and 8% of the farm-workers. In the same year, 75·6% of the inhabitants of the Paris conurbation went on holiday, but only 15·5% of the inhabitants of the rural communes, the percentage diminishing with the size of town. For at least a month Paris ceases to be the overcrowded focal point of the whole country, since almost 4 million of its inhabitants go off to people the 'demographic deserts' of France.

Figure 40 shows how holidaymakers were distributed among the departments in 1961. Their peripheral distribution is very marked, partly because of the attraction of the sea, and

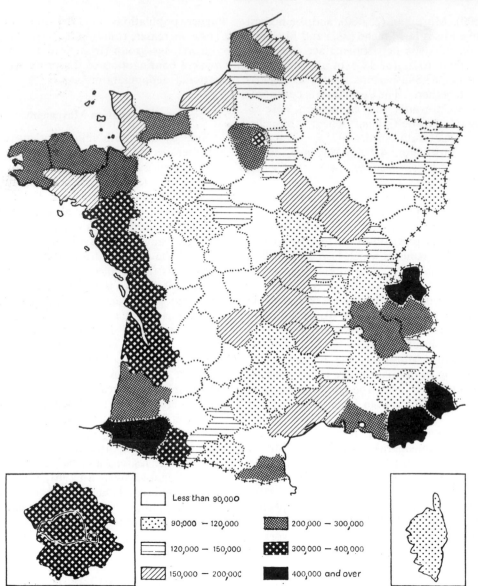

Fig. 40. Holiday visitors in the departments in 1961 (all types of accommodation). (Sources: *Etudes et Conjoncture*, May 1962, p. 415)

partly because the younger mountains which prove more attractive than the ancient massifs are also marginally located. A map showing the distribution of the population of France as a whole in the month of August would be extremely interesting. It would stress the distribution of the French people round the borders of the country. The representation by departments does not clearly show the crowding of holidaymakers along the coast (Pas-de-Calais, for example).

In addition to the sea and the mountains, the countryside itself attracts a large number of holidaymakers, quite apart from the spas.

In this respect the relative importance of the departments in the south-east of the Paris basin and the Central Massif is noteworthy. The growing popularity of country holidays is particularly beneficial to districts which have been hard-hit by depopulation.

Regional concentrations again appear in the distribution of holidaymakers: 10 departments recorded in 1961 more than 300,000 holidaymakers, accounting between them for almost a third of the total: Alpes-Maritimes, 700,000; Var, 520,000; Haute-Savoie, 510,000; Basses-Pyrénées, 480,000; Charente-Maritime, 390,000; Seine, 390,000; Gironde, 330,000; Loire-Atlantique, 320,000; Hautes-Pyrénées, 320,000; Vendée, 310,000. These movements are of great geographical importance:

1. Through the building of weekend and holiday homes, hotels and family houses, through the provision of camping grounds, facilities for sport, games and leisure activities, and the building of roads; they are an important factor in the transformation of the countryside.

2. Through the money spent by the holidaymakers, which represents a substantial investment in the holiday areas.

3. Through the permanent migrations to which seasonal migrations may lead.

F. The Consequences of the Changes in Population Distribution

Between 1861 and 1962 the population of France increased by 9,133,000. Between the same dates the increase in the 8 departments of Seine, Seine-et-Oise, Nord, Pas-de-Calais, Rhône, Bouches-du-Rhône, Moselle and Meurthe-et-Moselle was 10,200,000. Not only was the entire increase concentrated in 7% of the area, but this polarisation deprived the rest of the territory of 1,067,000 people.

POLARISATION AND DEPOPULATION

The consequences of the changes in the distribution of the population are thus twofold: a concentration of towns and industry which is geographically very pronounced, and a decline in population in rural areas which in certain regions has already passed the critical level.[22] But the existence of 'deserted' areas (*désert Français* has become a popular expression in France) is seen less in terms of density of population than of amenities, of living conditions and, in the long run, of men. A region which is becoming depopulated inevitably ceases to attract investments. Amenities (communications and services) gradually cease to pay their way; costs (postal services and upkeep of roads) increase in proportion to the loss of men; the transport systems show a deficit and close down, schools and public services are regrouped; the region becomes more inhospitable and the motives for leaving it increase. The administrative authorities are unwilling to consider bringing electricity and water mains into these districts. One of the consequences of this twofold change—rural depopulation and urbanisation—is clearly displayed by the variations in population of the communes. Table XV summarises their main characteristics. The increase in the number of communes with less than 500 inhabitants goes hand in hand with the turning of much of France into 'demographic deserts'; rural depopulation has greatly increased the number of communes with 200, 100 or even less than 50 inhabitants (there were 92 of the latter in 1891, 591 in 1946, 808 in 1962). An analysis of changes between 1954 and 1962 shows that 'almost all the weight of the demographic recession in country districts has fallen upon villages with less than 500 inhabitants' (R. P. Mols).

But this falling off also affects the category of communes with 500–5,000 inhabitants, communes which are either entirely rural or towns too small to benefit from the spread of urbanisation. Communes with 5,000 inhabitants form a borderline group above which all communes benefit from the concentration of population. Thus, below a certain density of population and a certain degree of diversity of occupations and social groups, in the present state of their standards of living

TABLE XV. COMMUNES AND THEIR POPULATIONS BY CATEGORIES OF SIZE

Size of communes (number of inhabitants)	1851				1921				1954				1962			
	Number	%	Popul.*	%	Number	%	Popul.*	%	Number	%	Popul.*	%	Number	%	Popul.	%
0–300	7,150	19·5	4,839·4	13·5	14,258	37·7	5,556·3	14·2	16,309	43	5,691·6	13·3	16,717	44·1	2,784,065	5·9
301–500	8,354	22·7			7,457	19·7			7,494	19·8			7,238	19·1	2,794,258	5·9
501–1,000	11,955	32·5	8,445·8	23·6	9,065	24	6,242	15·9	7,594	20	5,212	12·2	7,248	19·1	4,994,721	10·4
1,001–2,000	6,517	17·8	8,947·6	25	4,350	11·7	5,946·4	15·2	3,776	10	5,093	12	3,670	9·7	4,999,534	10·5
2,001–5,000	2,262	6·2	6,592·6	18·4	1,828	4·9	5,350·8	13·6	1,841	4·8	5,480	12·9	1,904	5·0	5,738,620	12·1
5,001–10,000	271	0·9	1,939·1	5·4	397	1·1	2,658·6	6·8	518	1·4	3,550·7	8·3	590	1·6	3,994,857	8·4
10,001–20,000	93	0·3	1,393·8	3·9	174	0·6	2,438·3	6·2	250	0·6	3,492·7	8·2	305	0·8	4,143,210	8·7
20,001–50,000	38	0·1	1,272·3	3·5	92	0·3	2,718·6	6·9	146	0·3	4,359·4	10·2	199	0·5	5,948,547	12·5
50,001–100,000	10	—	692	2	33	—	2,306·1	5·9	39	0·1	2,689·5	6·2	52	0·1	3,409,365	7·2
100,001–1,000,000	4	—	607·3	1·7	14	—	3,085·9	7·9	23	—	4,355	10·1	31	0·1	8,751,220	18·4
+1,000,000	1	—	1,053·9	3	1	—	2,906·5	7·4	1	—	2,850·2	6·6	1	0·1		
Total	36,655	100	35,783·8	100	37,669	100	39,209·5	100	37,991	100	42,774·1	100	37,955	100	47,558,397	100

* Population figures in thousands.

and amenities, our country districts cease to be places to live in and become merely places in which to work or sleep: places of work just like factories, and places for sleep analogous to satellite towns or dormitory suburbs.

The drain from the countryside impoverishes rural districts not only quantitatively but qualitatively as well. With few exceptions, those who remain are not the younger nor the more able, that is those who could bring agriculture up to date or furnish the labour required for a factory. Young workers, knowing for certain that they will not find openings locally or within the region, seek a professional qualification which will help them to find a good situation elsewhere.[23] 'The only social advance a peasant can envisage is one resulting from a change of surroundings' (Valarché). This starts off a vicious circle, as rural depopulation leads to more depopulation.

We no longer see the variety of class and occupation which used to exist in the rural areas.

'The big landowners were once the important men of the little commune (mayors, councillors etc.); at the same time as running their own estates, they acted as representatives and leaders. Today the descendants of the big landowners have left the village. The sons and grandsons of country people are engineers, doctors, teachers or run businesses in town, and direct their country estates from a distance, through a manager. In many cases the family estate has been split up, and the old family mansion, the only relic of the past, has become a holiday home' (J. Milhau).[24]

Rural depopulation involves too many factors and casts doubt on too many concepts for it to be easy to make an objective assessment of its economic consequences or to judge it fairly. Some, looking at the question from what they call a human angle, wax sentimental over this desertion of the land, this isolation leading even to the death of the rural communities which were the life-blood of ancient France. The lack of interest in the land is laid at the door of the mechanised, urban civilisation of today. They insist that the

*

strength of France lies in its agriculture, and therefore in its rural areas. Others, with more grasp of economics, see in this depopulation an irreversible and salutary change. The departure of the small farmers increases the area available for cultivation by those who remain, offers them higher incomes and thus more satisfactory living conditions, and allows desirable changes in agricultural systems. They consider that the future of agriculture depends on increasing depopulation.

We are thus faced with a dilemma: should we regret the deserting of a canton such as—to take one example among many—La Trémouille, which, between 1954 and 1962, had a natural increase of only 20 persons, but lost 786 inhabitants by emigration so that some of its communes have less than 10 inhabitants per km.^{2}? Or should we congratulate ourselves that this depopulation has made it possible for the canton to abandon the traditional multi-crop system and specialise in sheep-rearing? 'Thanks to sheep-rearing, these poor heathlands are giving a reasonable return on capital for what is probably the first time in their history: this change was essential for landowners and tenant farmers accustomed to absurdly low returns' (J. Pitié). But the tragedy of the French countryside is that in most regions rural communities do not seem to have turned depopulation to advantage; they have remained set in their agricultural methods, their land holdings (as shown by the cadastres), their traditional outlook. One cannot regard with equanimity—as some people do—the afforestation of vast areas of fallow land, the creation of huge national parks, while all the farming is concentrated on the best land where intensive methods can be practised.

But as things are at present, the problem of populating the French countryside has to be seen in a European context. We have seen that the density of agricultural population is much higher in other countries, and these regions are altogether more populous than France. France is richly endowed by nature, and her soil is on the whole more fertile than that of any other European state. Can she, then, abandon her land to waste and forest? Should she not rather welcome the landless peasants of Holland and Germany, within the framework of Common Market legislation, as planned for 1970? There is no simple answer to this question. We must consider two factors: the ecological factor, that is to say, the conservation of the soil which is our capital, and the economic factor, that is to say, the objectives to be assigned to French agricultural production in the future.

MIXING OF THE POPULATION

The general spread of migratory movements has involved a significant amount of mixing of the population; a large number of Frenchmen have left their birthplaces to settle elsewhere and found a family.[25]   Up to 1881 the census showed more than 85% of the inhabitants to be living in the department where they were born. Since then the percentage has diminished continually; it was already as low as 78·6 in 1911, and fell to 73·8 in 1936 and 68 in 1946. Since the beginning of the century, 700,000 people have left Brittany, 158,000 of them between 1946 and 1954. In 1901 there were 300,000 Bretons living in France outside the departments of Brittany; in 1962 there were 262,000, of whom 70,000 came from Finistère. The mixing of the population varies from region to region; incomers are more numerous in industrial and urban areas, and in low-lying areas near to mountainous regions (Rhône valley).

TABLE XVI. ORIGIN OF THE POPULATION OF FIVE DEPARTMENTS (1946)

Department	% of inhabitants born in the department	% of inhabitants born outside the department and abroad
Nord . . .	81	19
Loire . . .	74·6	25·4
Gironde . .	63·6	36·4
Rhône . . .	55	45
Bouches-du-Rhône .	54·2	45·8

Table XVI indicates the percentages of inhabitants born in the department or else-

where for selected departments of France in 1946. A department like Nord is evidently somewhat unusual; very few people have moved there because its own dense and prolific rural population meets all its requirements for industrial man-power. Whereas the percentage of people born in France but outside the department in which they live merely rose from 7·39 (1901) to 11·76 (1946) in Nord, in Haute-Garonne it leapt from 19·47 to 35·58.

As for Paris, it is the main centre of attraction, where people from all the provinces, especially Brittany, the Centre and the *pays* of the Loire, are found side by side. A recent inquiry into the origins of the population of Paris has yielded some interesting observations, showing that Paris has an especial attraction for the inhabitants of rural communes and small towns.

For every 100 persons migrating to Paris from rural communes, those coming from towns of less than 5,000 inhabitants number 106, those from towns of 5,000–20,000 number 91, those from towns of 20,000–50,000 number 89, those from towns of 50,000–200,000 number 79 and those from towns of more than 200,000 number 44. For 41% of the emigrants the transfer took place directly; for the others there were one or two intervening stages. This mixing, moreover, does not operate in one direction only, as a glance at the population figures might lead us to believe. While a commune is losing some of its inhabitants, it is gaining others, and every drop in the figures represents a difference between two unequal streams of migrants. In a commune with a dwindling population the immigrants are retired people (either returning to the village after all their working life has been spent in temporary migration elsewhere or coming to end their days in a place with an attractive climate), white-collared workers, civil servants and those engaged in public services.[26]   France, then, is covered by a complete and very dense network of migrations. Figure 41 gives some idea of this, though exchanges with Paris and its environs are not shown. The diagrams

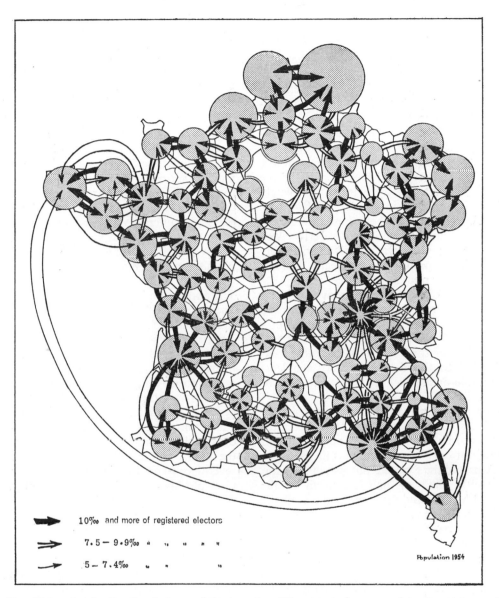

Fig. 41.   Network of migration between departments.   Movements from one department to another of registered electors from 1949 to 1953, excluding Seine-et-Oise (in relation to the electoral roll of the department from which the move is made, on 31st March, 1951).   (Source: Clément and Vieille, 'L'Exode rural', *Etudes de comptabilité nationale*, no. 1, April, 1960)

(figs. 90 and 91) attempt to show the pattern of migration by categories of communes.

G. The Pattern of Population Distribution

The geographer must go deeper than the distribution of population by departments and examine the pattern in as much detail as possible. The division of France into communes (Part Three) facilitates such analysis.

A map of population densities by communes gives quite a remarkable picture of the distribution of the population. Except for the rocky and icebound highest parts of the younger mountains, there is no completely uninhabited region in France. This situation clearly reflects the country's natural advantages and the antiquity of its occupation by man; there was already a scattering of people in prehistoric and early historic times. The conditions under which the peopling took place differed from century to century; different regions attracted 'colonists' at different periods according to their prevailing needs and techniques. Pressure of population in the 16th, 17th and 18th centuries led to the development of the least favourable areas, such as those with clay or poor soils.

First of all the map gives an impression of emptiness; the greater part of the country appears to be very sparsely populated. This is true not only of mountainous districts like the Alps and the Pyrenees but also of the Jura, the south, the west and the north of the Central Massif, and the south and east of the Paris basin; smaller gaps appear in the Aquitaine basin and the west of the Paris basin (Eure).

The second characteristic is the fact that the densely populated zones lie around the periphery. There is a zone corresponding roughly with the Central Massif which seems as though it repelled rather than attracted population. It is shaped like an inverted S stretching from the edge of the Cévennes to the Ardennes. The regions around Paris and Lyons are the only densely populated areas in the interior. All the other populous areas are peripheral, either along the land frontiers (Alsace, the industrial region of Lorraine and Nord) or on the sea (Provence, Languedoc, Roussillon, the Basque country, the West from Bordeaux to Basse-Seine, Haute-Normandie and the Picardy coast).

The third lesson to be learned from the map is the importance of the valleys and the relief. The map might almost be a tracing of the drainage pattern; we can see there all the great valleys, not only those of the four largest rivers but also those of their tributaries (especially of the Garonne and the Seine) and many other river systems, such as the Meuse, the Moselle and the Charente. In regions of contrasted relief, the inland basins, the coastal plains, the interior valleys of the Alps and the Pyrenees, the sub-Alpine trench and the transverse valleys of the pre-Alps are areas of population concentration (Limagne, plains of the lower Rhône, Languedoc, Roussillon). The population is thus distributed in a largely linear pattern.

The fourth characteristic of the map follows on from the preceding one: regions with a uniformly dense population are rare. Only in western France, from the Gironde to Cotentin do we find the population densities to be both very high and also relatively homogeneous, without any clear reflection of the valley pattern. Elsewhere, a similar type of distribution is found in the North, in Alsace, the plains of the Saône and Bresse, and in several cells on the south-west edge of the Central Massif and the Basque country.

THE THREE GEOGRAPHICAL PROVINCES OF THE POPULATION

Without generalising too much, we can divide the country, as far as the population is concerned, into three geographical provinces.

Western France. In this part of France, consisting mainly of plains, there is no strong differentiation between valleys and interfluves; the plains, hills and plateaux between not very deep valleys are all potentially productive. Contrasts in density (density gradients) are diminished by the relative uniformity of the factors underlying the population.

In *eastern, south-eastern and southern France,* zones with high densities are more broken up; the influence of relief is much more decisive, both in the Lyons region and in the Aquitaine basin. The second characteristic of this area is to be found in the many and large gradations of population density. We move suddenly from a very populous coastal plain, valley or inland basin to a hinterland or to an adjoining mountainous area which is almost uninhabited. In Provence, rural communes which have lost half their population in a century are a few kilometres away from urban or suburban communes which have gained more than 100%; such juxtaposed contrasts in man–land associations (*milieux géographiques*) are not found to the same extent in western France. When zones of high density do actually meet, they do so along the line of the valleys.

Between these two there is a *third province* which it would be difficult to delimit precisely, but which shows distinct peculiarities. It corresponds broadly to the inverted S we mentioned earlier. Densities there are on the whole low, even very low, but against this background we can see individual communes scattered like populous 'islands'. The linear arrangement, following valleys or particular relief features, is less apparent. Contrasts in densities are also less. It is a 'spotted' pattern of population.

THE INFLUENCE OF ALTITUDE

In 1954, 450,000 French people (1·05% of the population) lived in communes whose chief towns were situated at a height of 900–2,000 m. and which together occupy 5·5–6% of the total area of France. Of these, 13,449 lived in communes with their chief towns sited at or above 1,500 m., the highest village in France being Saint-Véran (1,990 m.). Population at these heights is very unevenly distributed among the various mountain areas, according to the differing conditions of life. More than half of the people living above

900 m. are in the Central Massif (214,317 inhabitants in 427 communes), where high interfluve surfaces cover a larger area than the valleys, which are too deeply incised to form settlement sites. These people represent 56% of the population of Lozère, 32% of that of Haute-Loire, 26% of that of Cantal.

The Alps come only second, with 171,437 inhabitants living in 414 communes. The reason for this is that the mass of the Alps is dissected and penetrated in depth by valleys whose lower parts have favoured settlement (the 1,000-m. contours extend far up the Alpine valleys). That is why Savoie and Haute-Savoie have only 17 and 18% respectively of the populations of their departments in communes situated at a height of 900 m. or more. In the southern Alps, where the valley bottoms are not so low as those in the northern Alps, there is a more completely mountainous environment. The department of Hautes-Alpes, with 101 communes and 60% of its population in communes situated at 900 m. or higher, comes very near to Lozère. France, on whose territory stands the highest peak in Europe, the western Alps and the Pyrenees, has paid little attention to her older mountains; she has never appreciated the distinctive and truly montane characteristics of the south of the Central Massif. These green plateaux, cut up by valleys, dwarfed by the distant Alps and Pyrenees, have never seemed to her to be real mountains.

Is this population distribution a constant factor in French geography? Or is it the net result of the population movements of the last hundred years?

Comparison with a map of population densities in 1876 shows that at that time there were many more small nuclei of population than there are nowadays. Analysis of the Lyons region, the Aquitaine basin, Lorraine and the northern parts of the Central Massif, serves to emphasise the extent of the changes and to show to what degree depopulation has affected the interfluvial zones, while the valleys form the strong warp threads of the population fabric. The demographic 'deserts', that is to say, the regions which really do lack natural advantages and can only support a very thin scattering of population, are little in evidence and comparatively small. The extent of the thinning out of population to form 'demographic deserts' outside these poorly endowed zones is thus all the more disturbing.   Since 1945, a higher fertility has added significantly to the numbers of young people.   Without a policy to meet this situation it is to be feared that the population mesh will give way again to precipitate a renewed rural exodus and a still higher concentration of population in a few favoured areas.

11. Total number of departments: 86 in 1845; 87 in 1872; 87 in 1911; 90 in 1936; 95 in 1966.

12. For a definition of urban population see Part Six, Chapter I.

13. Begging, which was very widespread in certain rural districts at the beginning of the 19th century, was evidence of this rural over-population.

14. At the same time we must remember that the repopulation schemes for the Landes, Sologne, Bresse and Dombes date from this period.

15. In the Garonne district the vine-growing area fell from 480,000 ha. (1880) to 197,000 ha. (1900).   The vine practically disappeared from certain departments (Aube, 21,000 ha. in 1873; Haute-Marne, 17,000 ha.; Corrèze, 22,200 ha.).

16. Dr. Lutier, 'L'exode rural vu par le psycho-sociologue', *Économie rurale*, January–March 1961, p. 22.

17. Reinhard and Armengaud, *op. cit.*, p. 267.

18. J. J. Lagasque, 'Le déclin d'une vallée des Pyrénées ariégeoises: La Barguillère', *R. Geog. Pyr. et S.O.*, December 1962, pp. 339–56.

19. G. Le Guen, *Norois* (1960), p. 394 (a study going up to the year 1954).

20. Basses-Alpes, 0·14; Hautes-Alpes, 0·14; Ariège, 0·17; Cantal, 0·14; Creuse, 0·10; Gers, 0·15; Lot, 0·14; Lozère, 0·07; Haute-Saône, 0·21; Landes, 0·24.

21. One should add here the department of Oise (1·3%), where the increase, localised in the south of the department, is closely connected with that of the Paris conurbation.

22. Between 1936 and 1962, 540 cantons registered a depopulation above 10%.

23. Aveyron exports 90% of the skilled workers and technicians trained there (the technical colleges at Decazeville alone have 600 students).

24. *Revue Économique*, May 1956.

25. 80% of France's retail cutlers are said to come from Thiers!

26. Burgundy, the country of the middle Loire, western Brittany and the border country between the Central Massif and the Aquitaine basin are considered to be regions where these migrations are a characteristic feature (A. Chatelain).

3. THE DEMOGRAPHIC AND OCCUPATIONAL STRUCTURE OF THE POPULATION

The history of the population has thus helped to intensify the contrasts between the different regions of France.   These contrasts have their counterparts in the demographic and occupational characteristics of the population.

into account the principal factors determining it.

$$VI^* = \frac{\text{Fertility rate}^{27} \times \% \text{ of all aged 20–40}}{\text{Mortality rate} \times \text{index of old age} \left(\frac{>60}{<20}\right)^{\dagger}}$$

A. Demographic Structure

Rather than make a separate analysis of the various demographic factors such as birth-rates and death-rates, we shall consider their results.

VITALITY OF THE POPULATION

G. Veyret-Verner set out to find an index to express the vitality of the population by taking

In 1962 the rate in France was about 3·3. Thirty-five departments have a vitality index above 5.   First come 2 departments, Moselle (10·3) and Doubs (10·7), which rank with the most dynamic states in the world (Japan, 16·8, and Canada, 13·4, in 1952).   These are followed by Meurthe-et-Moselle, Seine-et-Oise, Pas-de-Calais, Calvados, Seine-Maritime and Ardennes.   On the other hand, 55 depart-

* Vitality Index.   † Ratio of the over-60s to the under-20s.

ments have an index below 3·3, 2 of them below 1: Creuse (0·8) and Ariège (0·9).

Figure 42 shows a pattern which is repeated in all demographic maps of France: a 'fertile crescent' stretches from Charente-Maritime to Savoie and Haute-Savoie, taking in all departments to the north of Beauce, which is an outpost of the part of France with a population now ageing and unfruitful, or soon to

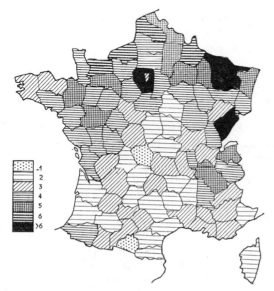

Fig. 42. Vitality indices (1954) for departments and major centres. (Source: R. Balseinte, *R. Géog. Alp.*, 1959, 1, pp. 61–78)

become so. Of all possible divisions of France into two parts, this is certainly the most fundamental and the one with the most far-reaching consequences.

AGE STRUCTURE

Jean Bastié has published a map of regional age variations in the population, according to the 1954 census.[28]

Dividing national and departmental populations into three classes—under 25, from 25 to 64, over 64—he calculated, for each class, how much the populations of the departments exceeded or fell below the national averages, which are: young people, 37·2%; adults, 50·7%; old people, 12·1%.[29] Adults are

below the national average in 64 departments and above it in 23; old people are below the national average in 32 departments and above it in 58, and young people below it in 41 departments and above it in 49. From this comparison the author derived six types of age structure, ranging from type 1, with more young people and less adults and old people than the national average, to type 6, with less young people and adults and more old people than the national average.

The distribution of these types (fig. 43) shows the pattern of figure 42 inverted. The 'fertile crescent' of the 'young' departments (type 1) can clearly be seen, from Vendée to Savoie (25 departments). The 'old' departments (types 5 and 6) form a very large block, consisting of the Central Massif and its northern borders (except Cantal), the Aquitaine basin and the Mediterranean region except Bouches-du-Rhône and Corsica (33 departments). The 'young and old' departments (type 3) form an inverted V between the two preceding groups, from Charente to Ain, with Somme as the apex (25 departments). The 'adult' departments (types 2 and 4) are few: Alsace, the Paris conurbation, Rhône-et-Loire and Bouches-du-Rhône.

Thus the population situation in one third of the departments of France is a serious one; their populations are old and there are not enough young people or adults to ensure their replacement. Leaving out certain departments where the situation can be explained by the large number of retired people, such as Alpes-Maritimes and Var, most of the 'old' departments are rural. It is, then, the agricultural population which shows this senescence. In the agricultural census of 1956, 19·5% of the farmers and farm managers were over 65 (and 5·1% were over 75). Elderly farmers are proportionally most numerous in the southern half of France and in Alsace-Lorraine; more than 50% of them are over 56 in 12 departments of the Pyrenees, the Central Massif, the Alps and Corsica. We need not dwell on the disadvantages of this situation. These ageing rural populations are not receptive to progress and have

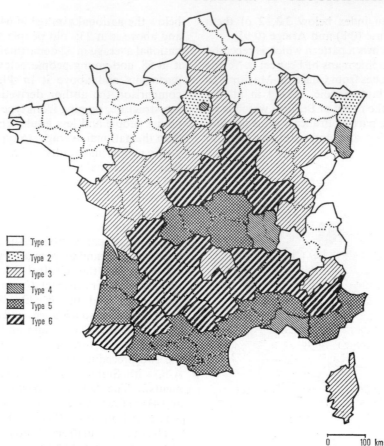

0   100 km

Fig. 43. Regional variations in age structure in 1954 (results of the 1 in 20 sampling). (Source: J. Bastié, *Acta Geographica*, 1958, fasc. 28, p. 15)

Type 1. Young people above national average, adults below, old people below.
Type 2. Young people above, adults above, old people below.
Type 3. Young people above, adults below, old people above.
Type 4. Young people below, adults above, old people below.
Type 5. Young people below, adults above, old people above.
Type 6. Young people below, adults below, old people above.

little interest in the future; obviously they lack mobility and are content to preserve the *status quo* and their existing standards. This situation also accounts for the continued existence of a large agricultural population whose productivity appears inadequate when compared with that of younger countries.

B. Occupational Structure

The working population of France was, in 1962, 41% of the total population. In the last hundred years this percentage has varied considerably, according to the proportion of young and retired people not gainfully employed, and to the number of workers. It was 39·3% in 1856 and 56% in 1921. The actual numbers of the working population were as follows: 14,216,000 in 1856; 20,721,000 in 1906; 21,612,000 in 1931; 19,185,000 in 1954; 19,154,000 in 1962.[30]

Between 1900 and 1950 the working population of France increased by less than 5%, compared with 103% in the United States,

62% in Norway and 38% in Great Britain. From 1950 to 1960 the annual rates of increase of the working population were as follows for various countries: Sweden, 2%; Belgium, 2·5%; France and England, 4%; United States, 7%; Italy, 12·5%; Netherlands, 15%; West Germany, 25%.

The simplest division of the working population is into three sectors:

1. The *primary sector* includes all engaged in agriculture, forestry and fisheries.

2. The *secondary sector* covers all industrial activities.

3. The *tertiary sector* embraces services, commerce and administration.[31]

Table XVII shows the structure of the working population of France compared with that of several other states.

TABLE XVII. THE THREE SECTORS OF THE WORKING POPULATION (%)—1964

	Primary	Secondary	Tertiary
France * . .	19 (20·6)	39 (38·6)	41 (40·8)
Italy . . .	25	40	32
West Germany .	11	49	39
Netherlands . .	10	42	47
England . .	4	47	48
U.S.A. . .	8	31	55
U.S.S.R. . .	38	30	32

* 1962 figures in parentheses.

By these percentages France ranks between countries as different as Italy and the Netherlands. The agricultural sector appears relatively well developed in France, but relatively weak in the economically most advanced states. The secondary sector, oddly enough, appears less strong than in other European states; the tertiary sector is similar to that of West Germany, although it is far behind those of England, the Netherlands and the United States. This comparison indicates no explanations, but it does raise certain problems. Is it the primary sector which, by keeping several million French workers in rural life, is responsible for the other sectors having been left behind, or is it the lack of sufficient population growth of the last hundred years? What are the optimum proportions in which the population could be divided between the three sectors? The re-

cord of changes in the structure of the working population (Table XVIII) shows a considerable decrease of numbers in the primary sector, a slight increase in the population working in industry and transport, a considerable expansion of the tertiary sector and

TABLE XVIII. CHANGES IN THE WORKING POPULATION BY OCCUPATIONAL CLASSES

	1866	1896	1926	1936	1954	1962
Agriculture, forestry and fisheries . . .	47·9	44·9	38·3	35·6	28	20·6
Industry and transport .	30·7	33·7	38·6	36·6	40·5	42·8
Commerce . . .	6·4	8·7	11·8	14	14	13·6
Liberal professions and public services . . .	6·6	7·9	7·7	10·1	17·4	22·9
Private services . .	8·4	4·8	3·6	3·7		

extensive changes between the last two censuses when the primary sector decreased by 25%.

THE AGRICULTURAL POPULATION

The agricultural working population[32] in 1962 was 3,841,000 persons, comprising 1,673,000 farmers, 1,338,000 family workers and 829,000 paid employees, some of whom were the farmers' sons.

It is very difficult to make a statistical break-down of the agricultural working population owing to the variety of different types of farming (Part Four) and the importance of family help. If we take only male workers, the proportion of these to the total male working population of France was 20·2% in 1954. In certain other states the proportions were: Italy (1951), 40·5%; Denmark (1952), 27·4%; Netherlands (1947), 19·7%; Belgium (1947), 13·6%; Great Britain (1951), 6·3%. The male agricultural population includes farmers and farm managers, family workers, full-time wage-earners and seasonal and casual workers. The total is 2,577,000 workers from a total agricultural working population of 3,841,000 (1962).

Considering the distribution of the agricultural working population, we find that France is divided into two very distinct zones by a diagonal line which will become very familiar as we go on (fig. 45). In the North and the East the agricultural population is never as much as a third of the population of a department.   In the South, the Centre and the West, on the contrary, it is more than 44% in 19 departments.   This percentage is lowered only by the presence of large towns in such departments as Gironde, Loire-Atlantique and Bouches-du-Rhône.   There appear to be enormous differences between

and 102,620.   Large urban and industrial populations sometimes conceal a high rural population, and this must be corrected by relating the agricultural population to the area of land occupied.   The map showing the density of the male agricultural working population (fig. 44) gives an appreciably different picture from that shown in figure 45;

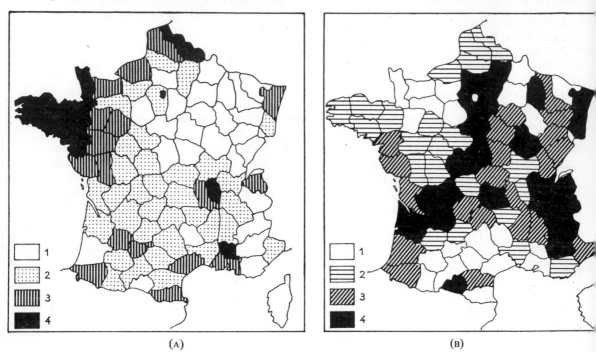

(A)   (B)

Fig. 44.   A. Density of male agricultural working population per 1,000 ha. of agricultural land by departments in 1962.

1. 0–40.   2. 41–60.   3. 61–80.   4. 81–106.

B. Percentage decline in the agricultural working population from 1954 to 1962.

1. 15–20·8%.   2. 21–24·6%.   3. 25–28·6%.   4. 29–39·7%.

departments; in some, such as Gers, 63% of the inhabitants get their livelihood from agriculture, and in others less than 10% (Nord and Bouches-du-Rhône, 8%; Meurthe-et-Moselle, 7%).

But these figures need further explanation. A low percentage does not necessarily mean that the agricultural population is small; Nord and Morbihan have 7 and 42% respectively of their employment in agriculture, but the actual numbers are respectively 61,340

as might be expected, it resembles the map showing density of rural population; we see again the two high-density areas in the South-east and the West, separated by a less densely populated zone.   The predominance of western France is still evident, but it is separated from the Central Massif and joined to the departments in the west of the Paris basin and the North.   High densities also appear in a cluster of departments around the Rhône, in the Rhône valley and in the Mediterranean region, where specialised and intensive cultivation takes place.[33]

These facts invite comparison with the densities of agricultural working population in other countries (Table XIX).

TABLE XIX. DENSITY OF AGRICULTURAL WORKING POPULATION PER SQUARE KILOMETRE OF CULTIVATED LAND

France	.	. 13·4	West Germany	.	26·2
Luxemburg	.	. 22	Netherlands	.	32
Belgium	.	. 23	Saar	. .	44·7

A low percentage of working population in the primary—or more strictly speaking, agricultural—sector is by no means the same thing as a low overall density of agricultural population: rather the reverse. France, with her high proportion (20·6%) of working population in the primary sector, is the least densely populated. These figures give us food for thought when we read categorical pronouncements on the great reduction of agricultural population which ought to take place in this country.

THE INDUSTRIAL POPULATION

The industrial population rose from 5,936,000 workers in 1906 to 6,867,000 in 1954, and 7,323,000 in 1962. This population is very unevenly distributed, the percentages for the departments ranging from 13 to 60%. In 1962 only 16 departments had an industrial working population which was 40% or more of the total working population (Ardennes, Aube, Doubs, Isère, Loire, Meurthe-et-Moselle, Moselle, Nord, Oise, Pas-de-Calais, Haut-Rhin, Rhône, Seine-et-Marne, Seine-et-Oise, Vosges and Territoire de Belfort). These all lie to the east of a line joining the mouths of the Seine and the Rhône.[34]

THE TERTIARY SECTOR

This sector comprises those employed in transport, insurance, commerce, banking and public and private services. If the period from 1850 to 1914 was one of urbanisation and industrialisation, the contemporary period is one of urbanisation and 'tertiarisation'. In quantitative terms, between 1954 and 1962 certain categories of services have

changed by the following amounts: services to enterprises,[35] +53%; communications, +26%; public administration, +25·3%; services to individuals,[36] +21·8%. The departmental proportions of population in the tertiary sector are less varied than those for the other two sectors; they range from 22 to 55%, 68 departments having proportions between 22 and 40%. In 1954 more than 60% of the total working population in the tertiary sector was concentrated in 22 departments, more than 26% of them in the Paris region; a significant indication of the preponderance of Paris in this sector, if we compare this last figure with the corresponding proportion of the total population. Six provincial departments each have more than 2% of the working population of the tertiary sector: Nord (4·4%), Bouches-du-Rhône (3·3%), Rhône (2·8%), Seine-Maritime (2·5%), Gironde (2·5%), Pas-de-Calais (2%).

TYPES OF EMPLOYMENT STRUCTURE BY DEPARTMENTS

Figure 45 gives a synthetic representation of the distribution of the three sectors of the working population in 1962. Three groups are distinguished.[37]

Group I: Departments which are plainly agricultural

There are 27 departments characterised by an absolute predominance of the primary sector (between 38 and 64%) and weakness in the secondary sector (between 13 and 28%).

(a) In 17 of these more than half of the working population is engaged in agriculture.[38]

(b) In Haute-Loire and Orne the secondary sector is slightly more developed than in group (a).

(c) In 8 departments agriculture is still the main activity, but there is no longer an absolute majority of people engaged in it (35–41·5%).[39]

In these three groups the tertiary sector is often more important than the industrial sector.

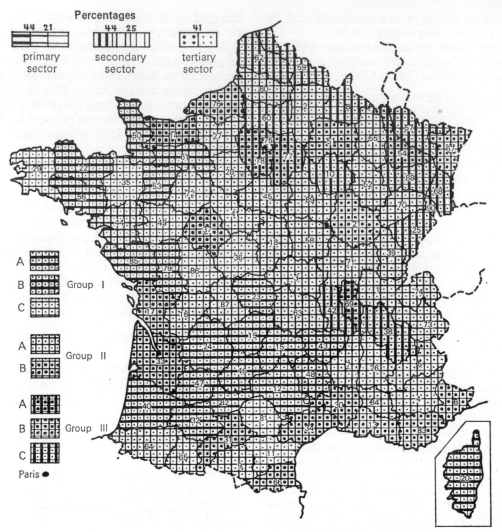

Fig. 45.   Types of employment structure by departments (1962).

Group II: Departments showing an even balance

(a) In 31 departments the percentages for all sectors of the working population are fairly evenly distributed, with 21–44% in the primary, 25–44% in the secondary and 22–41% in the tertiary sectors. These departments have many and varied towns and industries. This type of departmental employment structure became very widespread between 1954 and 1962 as a combined result of a high concentration of agricultural population and industrialisation in the provinces.

(b) In 9 departments the tertiary sector plays a more important part, and neither of the other two sectors ever exceeds 44% of the total.[40]   These are mostly departments where viticulture, market gardening and tourism account for the expansion of tertiary occupations.

Group III: Departments where industrial and tertiary sectors predominate

In this group the primary sector is in the minority with less than 21%.

(*a*) In this sub-group secondary and tertiary activities are both highly developed. This is so in 5 departments: 3 departments in the Paris region, Meurthe-et-Moselle and Rhône.

(*b*) In this case the tertiary sector is the only dominant one, with industrial workers less than 44%. These departments are Bas-Rhin, Seine-Maritime, Bouches-du-Rhône, Alpes-Maritimes, Var and Côte-d'Or.

(*c*) There are almost exclusively industrial departments where the working population in the secondary sector represents 49–59% of the total working population. Eleven departments belong to this category: Nord, Pas-de-Calais, Ardennes, Oise, Moselle, Vosges, Belfort, Haut-Rhin, Doubs, Loire, Isère, all of which are industrial departments, but without large towns.

The map is a synthesis of all the contrasts we have observed so far. Western and south-western France, from the Seine estuary to the Rhône delta, that is, the agricultural part of France, appears economically very homogeneous. Only a few departments do not conform to the general pattern because they have their large towns and ports: Loire-Atlantique, Gironde, Haute-Garonne, Pyrénées-Orientales and Hérault. Western France is differentiated much more by demographic contrasts than by employment structure. The eastern half of France appears much more heterogeneous. It can be broadly divided into seven zones, from north to south:

1. The industrial departments on the northern and eastern frontiers, from Pas-de-Calais to Belfort.

2. A belt of departments from the Somme to the Vosges with a more or less balanced structure.

3. A new belt of industrial departments from Seine-Maritime to Doubs, Côte-d'Or having more tertiary than secondary employment.

4. A group of balanced, more or less agricultural departments, from Loiret and Puy-de-Dôme to Savoie.

5. The three departments of the Lyons region: Loire, Rhône, Isère.

6. A heterogeneous block of departments astride the Rhône or in the southern Alps.

7. The departments on the Mediterranean coast, where the tertiary sector predominates.

FOREIGN WORKERS

Though foreigners represent only 4·2% of the working population of France, their concentration in certain economic sectors enhances their importance. The great majority of them come from countries with a low standard of living, have no professional qualifications and do unskilled manual work. They are farm labourers,[41] miners, dockers, lumbermen, labourers in building trades and public works and in the heavy and chemical industries. Out of 70,000 lumbermen, 40% are foreigners; all the 'high-lead' lumbermen are Italian.[42] The 6,000 labourers employed in rice-planting in the Camargue are almost a hundred per cent foreign, mainly Spanish. The percentage of areas under sugar-beet on which hoeing and picking is done by foreigners rose from 20% in 1955 to 40% in 1957. But foreigners also work as farmers (41,200 in 1955), especially Italians (36·6%), Spaniards (27·2%) and Belgians (17·3%), or as craftsmen and tradesmen, tailors, morocco-leather dressers, furriers and jewellers.

THE MOBILITY OF THE WORKING POPULATION

To enumerate the working population is to give no more than an approximate picture of its real distribution. It is, in fact, very mobile, and there is an ever-increasing separation between the worker's place of residence and his place of work. This mobility is tending to become general as towns grow and spread (Part Six), but it exists also between departments and even between regions. In Paris, 770,000 suburban residents arrive for work every morning; their long, tiring and costly journeys greatly reduce the length of time they spend at home.[43] Frontiers are no obstacle to these daily migrations. In the North and East, thousands of people living near the frontiers go to work in the neighbouring state every day. Thirty thousand Belgians come into the department of Nord every day, especially to the textile mills of Lille, Roubaix and Tourcoing, and to work in building. More than 7,000 workers from Alsace (1966) are employed in Baden-Württemberg, 5,200 inhabitants of Haut-Rhin work in Switzerland, 7,000 people from Moselle have their jobs in Saarland.

The enormous growth of the towns and the absence of any co-ordination in the siting of factories and houses are causing increasing segregation of industrial and residential areas, with unfortunate results from every point of view, whether sociological, economic or psychological.

The siting of factories in large and small provincial towns leads to a great deal of daily commuting over a wide area. For example, 73·4% of the 8,000 workers at the Renault factory at Le Mans come from the town itself, 6·4% from suburban communes and 20·2% from rural areas within a radius of 25 km. In addition to daily commuting, temporary and seasonal migrations have not quite disappeared; mountain-dwellers still come down to the vineyards of Bas-Languedoc for the grape harvest, and the sugar-beet areas still attract a large labour force of Bretons, Belgians or Italians (from 1950 to 1960, 457,118 seasonal workers entered France).

27. Number of births per 1,000 women between 20 and 40 years of age.

28. J. Bastié, 'La composition par âges de la population française et ses variations régionales', *Acta Geographica*, June 1958, no. 26, pp. 11–15.

29. As the strength of each class varies with respect to the others, and from department to department, the author recognises that the method would have been improved by calculating the percentage differences in the total strength of the group and not of the entire population.

30. The total working population includes those looking for work, and soldiers stationed in the territory on the day of the census (208,000 and 550,000 respectively in 1962).

31. This division has the merit of simplicity, but its faults and inadequacies cannot be ignored; the nature of individual jobs and the conventions used by different statistical services combine to cause confusion and make exact comparisons difficult.

32. The agricultural population—or population whose livelihood depends on agriculture—means the total body of people belonging to farmers' households, agricultural wage-earners and retired farm-workers.

33. Statistics for mountain regions give a false impression, as Alpine pastures are not included in agricultural land.

34. See figures 78 and 79, p. 339.

35. These are essentially enterprises working for other enterprises (accountancy, publicity, estate agency, cleaning, health services, security).

36. Health establishments; nursing homes, hospitals, clinics; legal staff; churches; private tuition and sport; associations; liberal professions except architects and quantity and land surveyors, who are classed under 'building and public works'.

37. We have adopted the method used by P. Fournier to analyse the working population in 1954, but the statistical classes used are different.

38. Corrèze, Creuse, Cantal, Lozère, Aveyron, Dordogne, Lot, Lot-et-Garonne, Tarn-et-Garonne, Gers, Landes, Manche, Côtes-du-Nord, Morbihan, Mayenne, Vendée.

39. Ariège, Aude, Hautes-Alpes, Finistère, Ille-et-Vilaine, Indre, Tarn, Vienne.

40. Gironde, Haute-Garonne, Pyrénées-Orientales, Hérault, Gard, Marne, Calvados, Indre-et-Loire, Charente-Maritime.

41. From 1921 to 1939, 1,138,000 foreign agricultural workers—mainly seasonal workers—entered France. From 1946 to 1957, 430,000 entered France, 120,000 of whom have remained permanently.

42. 'Should the source of Italian labour suddenly dry up, the Alpine timber industry would be largely thrown into chaos' (Leroy, *R. Geog. Alp*, 1957, Part III, p. 550).

43. It has been estimated that 3,300,000 hours are so wasted every day in the Paris conurbation.

4. POPULATION PREDICTIONS

It is obviously of very great interest to calculate what the population and its demographic and occupational structure in a country is going to be in a more or less distant future. Such predictions are necessary for investment planning and to anticipate future needs for school building, the training of teachers and the provision of jobs and housing. In the sphere of town and country planning, forecasts are equally or even more important. In fact policies of land use, decentralisation and urban expansion must be worked out in terms of the expected growth of the population.

Predictions can be made in two different ways:

1. From a demographic point of view, by making use of all known statistical data and of trends revealed by statistical correlation to attempt to project the population curves into the future. These methods use census data as their starting-point and make forecasts first by taking account of the natural development of the population (annual births and deaths), and then by advancing various hypotheses based on these figures. These hypotheses concern the biological behaviour of the population, in terms of maintained, increased or decreased rates of change. Variations depend on the number of young people reaching child-bearing age—which is easy to calculate —but also on economic and psychological data which are more elusive and unstable. For example, the continuance of the population recovery after the 'normal' period of two or three years after the war was quite unpredictable.[44]

But two other categories of factors affecting variations in population are partly missed by such predictions:

(*a*) Emigration and immigration movements of French people and of foreigners. On the national scale, an emigration and immigration policy allows a certain check on these movements. It is hoped, however, that such controls will cease to exist under the free circulation of labour envisaged by the Common Market countries.

(*b*) Demographic 'accidents', that is, unpredictable events. The return of 600,000 French people from Algeria in the space of a few weeks was never foreseen or even thought of. The smaller the area for which predictions are made, the more uncertain they become. On the departmental or municipal level, in fact, the factor of emigration and immigration often has more influence than natural population growth; and this factor cannot be very accurately predicted.

2. Economic and geographic planning needs another type of prediction, based not on observed past tendencies but on the optimum prospects for the future. For example, demographic predictions indicate probable changes in the agricultural working population, but the figures give no indication of the regional variations in the optimum agricultural population. In the same way, predictions tell us what the population of a certain town will be in ten years' time; but it is just as important to know what the optimum population of the town would be. Economic forecasting must obviously be even more subject to approximations and factors that defy accurate assessment than the methods just described, but its importance cannot be denied. These approaches are complementary; demographic predictions will help us to tell what the population of a region is likely to become, and economic predictions will help us to relate it to the potentialities of the region and thus to begin to formulate a policy.

A. Total Population Predictions

In 1950 the projected population for 1970 was 46·5 million inhabitants; in 1955, 46–46·5 million inhabitants were forecast for 1971. In 1956 a fresh estimate, lower than the preceding ones, gave 45·9 million for 1971, but in 1960, starting on a new basis, the predicted figures were appreciably higher: 47·4 million for 1966, 49·3 million for 1971. In March 1962 the population was 46·2 million, and the entry of refugees was bringing it up to the figure predicted for four years later. Later predictions based on the 1962 census have allowed us to estimate more precisely; taking into account the decrease in the death-rate and the maintenance of fertility, *but excluding the effects of migration*, France should have 49,837,000 inhabitants in 1970 and 56,000,000 inhabitants in 1985. From 1965 to 1980 the population of France is expected to rise by 11·6%. This rate of increase places France between the Netherlands (25%) and the German Federal Republic (5%). At the end of the century, if there are no unforseeable upheavals, the population of France should be between 60 and 70 million.[45]

There are obvious difficulties in predicting the regional distribution of this future population. Calculations based on the population of 1st January 1963 have been made in three ways: in terms respectively of natural change only, natural change plus internal migration and natural change plus internal and external migration. If internal migration alone is taken into account, only four regions would show a positive migration balance by 1st January 1968: the Paris region (+1,070,000), Provence–Côte d'Azur (+250,000), the Rhône–Alps region (+140,000) and Alsace (+10,000). Brittany would show a loss of 11·5% of its population, Basse-Normandie 12·4% and Languedoc 6·7%. The inclusion of external migration in the calculations accentuates the tendencies in the Paris, Provence–Côte d'Azur and Rhône–Alps regions, and compensates for those in Lorraine, the Centre, Aquitaine and Franche-Comté. The predictions indicate that regional imbalance is likely to increase, and stress the urgent need for a national planning policy. Within the framework of the total population predictions, the urban proportion will continue to increase. Between the beginning of 1963 and the end of the century the increase

in the urban population should be of the order of 20 million persons, that is, a rise of 75% over the 1962 figure.

B. Predictions by Age-groups

The following predictions have been made on the basis of the 1962 census:

TABLE XX. POPULATION PREDICTIONS BY AGE-GROUPS

	1963	1970	1985
0–19 years	33·4%	32·9%	32·3%
20–64 years	54·8%	53·9%	55·1%
65 and over	11·8%	13·4%	12·6%

If the young age-group remains about one third of the population of France, the elderly group will increase appreciably up to 1970 without any change in the active adult population and become a still greater burden.

C. Working Population Predictions

Any calculation of the working population depends above all on the number of young people of school age; but there are two factors which may cause these numbers to vary:

1. The age of entry into the working population, which depends on the percentage of children receiving the different types of education, raising the school-leaving age, the school-building policy followed by the Government and variations in the length of military service.

2. The age of leaving the working population, that is, retirement age; this age also is subject to variations and closely bound up with government action. Though a 'bulge' of young people may cause a scarcity of employment, this may be partly compensated by raising the school-leaving age and lowering the age of retirement. Moreover there are other factors, such as variations in the percentage of women working and the entry or departure of foreign workers, which can influence the number of the working population.

The Fourth Plan had forecast an increase of 930,000 in the number of jobs available.

These jobs would be filled as follows: 180,000 by the natural increase in the population, 290,000 by immigration, 190,000 by a reduction in military service and 270,000 by people transferring from the agricultural sector to the other sectors. The mass repatriation of the Algerian French completely upset those predictions by throwing 250,000 active persons on the employment market. Moreover, the scale of increase appears quite modest compared with the increases in other countries during the last few decades (see p. 134). The annual increase in non-agricultural employment was 4% in the German Federal Republic (1948–58), 3% in the Netherlands (1948–57) and in France 0·7% (1949–59) and 1·5% (1959–65). 'The increase in the number of jobs which France is expected to have between now and 1970 is thus much below that of the highly developed capitalist countries during the last ten years' (A. Sauvy). On the whole the variations between them appear very slight. Here again we find a clear case of demographic recovery taking place in a population of insufficient numbers. Some experts even think that the objectives proposed for the French economy are too high in view of the slightness of the increase in the working population of France. The burden imposed by the non-working population is expected to become heavier and heavier. This predicted working population sets a double problem: that of its apportionment among the various types of employment, and that of its localisation.

OCCUPATIONAL STRUCTURE

For 1965 the Fourth Plan had predicted the following distribution of the working population between the three sectors (Table XXI). The projections appeared modest and even to have been exceeded already in the primary sector; it may also be questioned whether the tertiary sector should not have been expected to develop more rapidly.

In more detail, the Fourth Plan attempted to calculate the changes in numbers expected to be engaged in the various branches of employment between 1962 and 1970. Decreases

were anticipated in the numbers employed in agriculture (−920,000), the coal mines (−51,000), domestic services (−66,000).

TABLE XXI. WORKING POPULATION PREDICTED FOR 1965 AND RESULTS OF THE CENSUS OF 1962

	1962 (Estimate)		1965 (Forecast)		1962 (Census)	
	Numbers in thousands	%	Numbers in thousands	%	Numbers in thousands	%
Agriculture, fisheries, forestry	4,510	24·1	4,100	20·9	3,849	20·4
Industry	7,092	37·6	7,460	38	7,323	38·7
Tertiary sector	7,208	38·3	8,060	41·1	7,734	40·9
Total	18,840	100	19,620	100	18,906	100

Jobs in textiles and clothes, timber and furniture would be stagnant. The categories of employment expected to increase the most would be building and public works (+353,000), manufacture of machinery and mechanical equipment (+200,000) and of electric equipment (+127,000). These changes in occupation will obviously entail substantial changes in professional qualifications, so creating a society appreciably different from the one we know, with different needs, tastes and outlooks, which will modify the various aspects of the country's organisation. For example, between now and 1975 the number of engineers should increase by 50%, doctors by 50%, technicians and draughtsmen by 65%, while the number of unskilled workers will not vary a great deal.

AN EXAMPLE: Predictions for the agricultural working population:

Demographic methods

In order to estimate, in 1961, the agricultural working population of 1970 (all persons gainfully employed at that date being born before 1955), R. Pressat first applies to each age-group of the agricultural population the mortality rates of the whole population of France (since the specific mortality rates of the agricultural population are not known). Thus he calculates, in 5-yearly age-groups, how many of the new workers will be living in 1965 and 1970. By noting the contrasts, favourable or unfavourable, between departments, he predicts whether the agricultural population of a department can be expected to diminish, remain static or increase. He then applies to these numbers the rates of loss from agriculture, determined on the following theoretical basis for the whole country: out of 100 sons of agricultural workers, 85 are working in agriculture at 15–19 years of age, 75 at 20–24, 68 at 25–29, 63 at 30–34 and 60 at 35–39. Finally, the total number of persons leaving agriculture for each department is adjusted to allow for unusual trends observed between 1946 and 1954.

Economic methods

By these methods we must be able to determine the threshold populations at which full employment, an adequate living wage and the most economic use of the land are attainable. The density and distribution of the agricultural working population, the average income from the land and the extent of waste and fallow land are all taken into consideration, as well as the types of crop grown and stock reared, and the available markets. P. Coutin has calculated the desirable size of the agricultural population at which each worker can be employed to the best advantage, by setting up norms for the area to be cultivated *per capita*. For arable land the figures vary between 17 and 24 ha. per man. For permanent grassland the norms are 18 ha. per man in the West, 25–30 ha. in the Central Massif, 40 ha. in the Pyrenees and 30–80 ha. in the Alps. For other branches of agriculture, P. Coutin suggests norms of 4 ha. for fruit and vegetable growing, 4–6 ha. for vines, 2 ha. for flowers and 100–125 ha. for forests. The results show the male agricultural working population so calculated to be a million less than in 1954. In predicting the optimum male agricultural population for 1985, P. Coutin arrived at a figure of 1,800,000 men aged 18–60 working an average of 2,000 hours per year; these men would be assisted by an approximately equal number of women devoting about 1,000 hours per year to agricultural work. The agricultural population in 1985 would thus be 3,600,000–3,800,000 persons. These figures are very

near the present strength (1962) of the agricultural population, so that from this point of view the decrease in the agricultural working population should come to an end from now onwards.

It was this type of forecast, economic rather than demographic, that led the formulators of the fourth plan to find out 'not how many men will probably be released from agriculture in the course of the next few years, but how many men in each region would be able to leave agriculture without doing it any harm if sufficient non-agricultural posts were available to them'.

The direction which research is taking shows an encouraging development in official attitudes towards the problem of the agricultural population. It has in fact been too long regarded either as subordinated to the needs of the other sectors of employment, as a 'residual population, remaining after the other sectors have taken whatever is necessary and sufficient for their development' (L. Malassis), without taking into account the permanent under-employment from which it suffered, or by reference to the advantages of a large rural population.[46]

LOCALISATION

It is extremely difficult to forecast the working population by regions, as it is not possible to take into account movements of population between regions. For example, labour released by agriculture is assumed to be available for other employment within the same department, since future movements into other departments cannot possibly be foreseen. The labour commissions for the Plans have attempted to make a two-sided appraisal of the regional availability of labour by taking into account several factors, such as normal movements, the lowering of employment rates among elderly people, the resorption of unemployment and of the under-employment of women, internal and external migration, the decrease in the agricultural working population, changes in the school-leaving age, and by considering also regional changes in employment, and the application to the regions of the national forecasts for various types of employment.

The map (fig. 46) shows a division of France that is now familiar. Taking no account of internal migration, it is in the northern crescent where, in theory, the largest increases in the working population will agricultural jobs and is of fundamental interest. It represents, in fact, the combined result of the post-war increase in population and the contraction of the agricultural working population. It helps to pinpoint the overcrowded zones for which a special land utilisation policy seems to be urgently required. The departments which have the

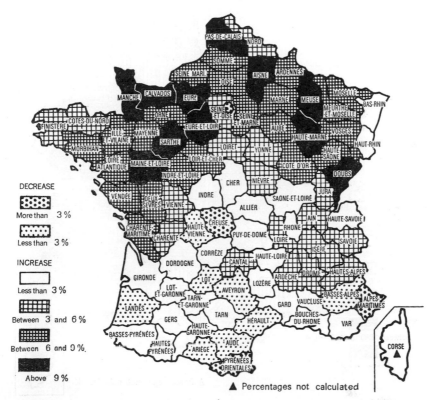

Fig. 46. Changes in the working population. Forecasts for 1960–70. (Source: R. Pressat, *Les Besoins en emplois nouveaux en France par département jusqu'en 1970*)

occur. Taking no account of external migration or of raising the school-leaving age, the working population should increase between 1962 and 1970 by 13·8% in the Paris region, 13% in Picardy, 12·4% in Haute-Normandie, 11·4% in Lorraine, 9·8% in Champagne, 9·4% in Nord, and should decrease in Limousin (5·8%), Brittany (3%) and Auvergne (0·2%).

Figure 47 shows the need for new non-largest surpluses are in fact those which are very little industrialised or urbanised. Unless steps are taken in time they will be the scene of a fresh exodus from the country districts in the next few years. The problem appears to be most crucial in the West where some 350,000 new non-agricultural jobs will need to be created (1960–70). That is why, during the preparation of the Fifth Plan, it was considered a major objective to raise the

percentage of new industrial jobs to be created
in the West compared with those in the
country as a whole from 20%, as it was
between 1954 and 1962, to 35–40%. Even if
this target is reached, western France will
only be given a quarter of the jobs in industry
(and two thirds of those in agriculture).
Moreover, the Paris region's share of the

plains the anomalies which have appeared in
some areas. In a place where a surplus of
labour had been forecast, a new factory had
trouble in recruiting workers because all this
potential labour had either left the district or
had found work in a neighbouring region and
did not wish to give up the advantages to be
gained by moving there. Conversely, a new

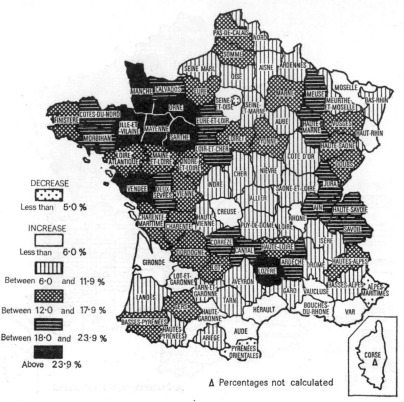

Fig. 47. Needs for new non-agricultural jobs (1960–70). (Source: R. Pressat, *Les Besoins en emplois nouveaux en France par département jusqu'en 1970*)

total employment in France is expected to
rise from 19% (1954) to 23% (1970), a situation described in one report as 'a disturbing
prospect'. Whether it is a question of types
of employment or labour potential, we have
to remember that statistics, which are always
rigid, are being applied to human beings
whose motives, outlooks, individual or collective reactions and mobility can elude the most
scientific methods of prediction. This ex-

factory set up in a region without a labour
surplus might find that simply by coming it
had brought together a body of workers who
were only waiting for such an opportunity to
change their occupation.

It is useless to try to find out the optimum
population which France could support, but
taking its potentialities into account, it is
certain that in the context of Europe, France
appears as a comparatively empty space

among the dense populations of central and northern Europe. We can logically predict that immigration movements from the most densely populated and overcrowded countries will increase, for 'it is less expensive to find or create employment in an under-populated than in an over-populated country. It would be more expensive, for example, to reclaim new polders in Holland than to reclaim some bay, lake or marsh in France'.[47]

44. The projections made by the League of Nations before the Second World War gave France 40,300,000 inhabitants in 1950 and 36,920,000 in 1970.

45. The migration balance with foreign countries will continue on the credit side during this period; it should rise to 1,201,000 from 1965 to 1971, and 1,179,000 from 1971 to 1976.

46. 'The balance of a nation is improved by the presence of a fairly large number of peasants' (J. M. Jeanneney, *Forces et faiblesses de l'économie française*, p. 65).

47. A. Sauvy, *L'Europe et sa population* (Paris, 1953), p. 169.

II

MENTALITIES AND CIVILISATIONS

Landscapes are the expression of a civilisation, reflecting the character and inclinations of a nation quite as much as its literature, its painting and its history. Perhaps, however, they are more difficult to read because they do not begin afresh from one century to another; each century leaves its mark, often confused or almost imperceptible. Yet we cannot deny that the way the land is used is closely linked with the psychology of its inhabitants and their social, juridical and political traditions. A landscape is readily identified as English, Swiss, Dutch or Italian, because in each case we can recognise some particular feature or combination of features: some distinctiveness of the rural landscape or architecture, a certain neatness in the siting of houses, the harmonious way in which they blend with their surroundings, even a beautiful lawn. It is harder to identify a typical French landscape. One is more apt to find affinities with other types of landscape, Flemish, English, Germanic or Latin. There appear to be two reasons for this curious situation: the Frenchman's attitude towards his country, which expresses his psychology, his mentality; and the position of France herself at the crossroads of so many civilisations.

1. THE FRENCH OUTLOOK

To her inhabitants, her children, France is a person, a chattel, a homeland, an idea to possess, admire and defend. She is never to them a mere space or territorial organisation, she is an anthropomorphic concept rather than a nation defined in geographical or spatial terms. To the French, France appears as a rich person blessed by the gods, immortal, who will always emerge victorious from all trials. This personalised conception can hardly favour an attitude of healthy curiosity towards problems which are purely territorial, that is to say, geographical in the strictest sense.

A Frenchman is quick to believe in miracles; he believes in them because his history is full of rebirths, resurrections and astonishing recoveries. This idea of France, together with her wealth, her low population and a solid basis of Christian religion, has kept firmly rooted this belief in a miracle to solve all problems. French civilisation did not spread in a visible, geographical way, as did British civilisation; it exported ideas, not ways of life or models of land development. But no man can be content merely to idealise his country or make of her an entirely spiritual thing; inevitably, he must leave his mark upon the land he occupies and humanise it.

What ideas and concepts have attended and still attend this meeting of man and nature? It is a difficult question, particularly in the case of France. The heterogeneous nature of the population—Nordic, Alpine and Mediterranean—and the wide variety of environments and ways of life have militated against the formation of a uniform, easily analysed mentality. In a mixed population like this, very widely differing temperaments have arisen and exist side by side. Some of the traits of the French temperament and civilisation described below are permanent, while others seem rather the heritage of our history.

A. Intellectualism

The French temperament is essentially intellectual. Love of theory and reflection for its own sake, and readiness to sacrifice everything for it; love of the rigorous expression of thought in a logical manner, of the analysis of realities more for the satisfaction of the mind than for practical application; these are the marks of the French temperament. Action is of less interest than the moments which precede and follow it, for these are 'richer in intellectual possibilities'.

The French are thus disinclined to think in concrete terms and to adapt their ideas to the exigencies of real life; an effective partial reform can never please them as much as a general theory which is attractive but inapplicable. This explains the paradoxical situation of French planning today. A planning theory on a global scale has taken shape in France; its concepts, the ideas which have inspired it, the methods by which it is put into practice and its adaptability are increasingly attracting the attention of the nations of the world. The French are satisfied with this first stage of the 'intellectual' elaboration of the plan, and are less anxious to find out whether its terms and conditions are consistent with reality and if the methods of application and control are as advanced as the theoretical ideas. 'France is the land of impressive, bold and penetrating declarations but also of laborious and half-hearted attempts to put theory into practice' (Ch. Morazé).

This characteristic habit of confusing theory and reality, thought and action, crops up in many situations; the 'planner' who is sometimes in a position of responsibility will even refuse to recognise a very real situation because in theory it is not possible, because juridical and economic principles or even his own proposals make it inconceivable. It may be a little exaggerated to say so, but the French live on fiction and are content with this.[1] The Frenchman tends to be a man of thought rather than of action, and that is why he is often content to produce one single work, and even to invent without reaping the benefit of his invention. France is the land of admirable achievements, of original experiments carried out once only; the model hospital centre, the progressive school, the *avant-garde* work of art, the pilot scheme in agriculture or the boldly planned new town are not the beginning of a series; they are and remain prototypes.

B. Respect for the Letter of the Law

The juridical spirit of the French is well known; laws and the law are on their side, and for protection and reference they have a whole armoury of regulations which for them constitute law and order. Salvador de Madariaga has an excellent description of this trait of the French temperament:

'Order in France is official, imposed from above, though accepted below; it is an intellectual, artificial, over-regulated system in which every action is forestalled by a complicated mass of written rules created to deal with every possible contingency. The French tendency to intellectualism immediately takes possession of the field, sets limits to any possible action and adds a carefully drawn-up network of principles to which every future action must be adjusted. This is the Law. These principles, in their perfect regularity, have naturally little contact with the irregularities of real life. In order to keep a tighter hold on everything that exists or is done, French intelligence adds to the network of the law an even subtler network: that of rules and regulations.'[2]

Obviously this double network of laws and regulations invites routine and inertia; it confines the whole country in a strait-jacket of edicts and regulations which make normal evolution and adjustment to new situations difficult, if not impossible. Since new situations necessitate a second look at the regulations, the natural reaction would be to call in question the principles underlying them and, in fact, the whole structure of the law. That is why, in the middle of the 20th century, the Code Napoleon is still the basis of French law.

When territorial divisions have to be reviewed, and the regrouping of communes, urban districts and estates carried out, this is not considered in the light of the present situation, but becomes a matter of lofty principles, both political (liberty) and judicial (property rights). What is more, the mere existence of a law or a regulation is felt to be the expression of a tangible reality, even if it is applied badly or not at all; 'in the 20th century, France still thinks that the proclamation of a law guarantees its execution' (Ch. Morazé). The French lack the English gift for flexible organisation, more or less spontaneous and always empirical, which keeps in touch with reality and takes human failings into account. The Frenchman cannot organise, so he tends to draw up rules instead.

These two characteristics of intellectualism and feeling for the law explain the success throughout the world of French ideas and examples; they are so general and abstract as to appear universally applicable. We can explain in the same way the predilection of the French temperament for clearly defined categories, and the preference for administration of the 'vertical' type with all its sectors clear-cut and homogeneous. A Frenchman is less at home in 'horizontal' organisation on a geographical basis, which is the very essence of land utilisation and of the understanding of problems on a regional or global scale. This same feeling for the law, associated with logic and a taste for abstractions, too often turns into a formalism which by-passes the real problems, and instead issues petty regulations which, like the rules governing planning permission for building, try to appear rigorous, but are actually absurd.

C. Individualism

There is no need to emphasise the individualism of the French temperament. It can be seen in the landscape, in the patchwork of small plots and in the eagerness to make a house, wherever possible, unlike all the others. France loves individual initiative and individual responsibility. André Sieg-

fried saw in this one of the reasons for the slightness of the industrial revolution in France:

'The revolution in favour of the machine took place very tentatively in France . . . Tradition and habit counsel individual production in small enterprises where initiative can have a free rein. Tradition and habit tell the peasant not to specialise, but to have personal and complete knowledge of all his land.'[3]

These characteristics appear in the Frenchman's relationship with nature. He does not, like the Englishman, seek to blend with the natural setting. Carrying his logical, Cartesian doctrines to their extreme conclusion, he levels everything, wiping out every trace of natural vegetation, and creates parks and gardens in the French manner which provide an entirely artificial setting.

We find this characteristic also in the absolute contrast between the two worlds of town and country. The Frenchman living in an industrial city or town, though he may be the grandson or great-grandson of country people, has lost all personal contact with nature, and considers that he has taken a step up in the world by comparison with those still living in the country; nevertheless there survives in him a solid core of peasant mentality. The French temperament shows a certain lack of understanding of geographical reality. Not versed in natural, historical and sociological contingencies, the Frenchman imagines only too often that foreign elements from no matter what distance can be transplanted straight into any region of France and give benefit at the mere passing of an Act or issuing of an edict.

D. Conservatism, Protectionism and Malthusianism

Other characteristics may appear less permanent, a more direct heritage of recent historical and economic conditions. Individualism and reverence for the law have combined to form the turns of mind which have dominated French thought for the last few centuries: conservatism, protectionism and Malthusianism. This conservatism and Malthusianism is not an unchanging aspect of the French temperament, as the whole of French history proves; it is the logical result of a century of demographic stagnation. The renewal of the population almost man for man from one generation to another raised no problems of expansion, investment or employment; France had the illusion of being governed when she was simply being administered. But this period left a psychological mark. The French turned towards protection—the defence of the rights they had acquired. A. Sauvy has clearly shown this quest for 'statutes' which would protect against any change which might endanger their interests.

At the economic level, protectionism made France into a 'national reserve' sheltered since 1800 from competition; for decades all government action has been, and still is in certain spheres, based on the protection of the little man—the small shopkeeper, the small farmer, small and medium-sized firms, without any motivating force or clear recognition of the irreversible nature of change and without any attempt to move with the tide of evolution and at the same time to lessen its negative effects.

E. Stability

The French have always disliked uprooting themselves; their recent history shows none of the pioneer tradition which makes the Americans into perpetual migrants crossing the continent in search of more congenial employment. This trait, of course, varies regionally; there are districts from which emigration is a matter of tradition. But most often the move is forced upon people by their economic situation. Recent closures of mines and factories have shown the difficulty and sometimes the impossibility of re-employing miners and factory workers within a radius of a few hundred kilometres of their former work. The Frenchman loves his native village; if he leaves it he comes back

F

again and again, during the holidays and on retirement.

Not all these traits are entirely negative; far from it. It would be ridiculous to close one's eyes to the qualities which go with them: a sense of justice, respect for the individual, a questioning attitude towards the dehumanising influence of new ways of life and the love of one's native soil. But at a time when frontiers are opening, when population is increasing in a way undreamed of by earlier generations and when all economic and territorial structures must needs come under review, the French still find it hard to emerge from the inertia bred of their daily routine. All this carries a double risk; the persistence of the traditional French turn of mind, with its individualism, its conservatism and its exaggerated respect for the law, would cause France to be left behind in the dynamic movement of progress; possible excesses of the younger generation might arise from a conflict with a society in which the weight is on the side of age, and whose psychology can hardly be expected to change without the appropriate education.

F. The Tendency to Centralisation

Paradoxically, this land of France, which has no geographical or racial unity, has for centuries been subjected to a degree of political and administrative centralisation such as has rarely been seen elsewhere. Political and administrative centralisation was certainly the price to be paid for the unification of France, which is open to so many different civilisations and ways of life, so full of regional contrasts and conflicts, and with so many lively 'peripheral' regions around its coasts and its frontiers. But in France it fell on fertile ground. Two of the characteristics of the French temperament, intellectualism and respect for the law, paved the way for the growth of a Parisian bureaucracy ready to seize all initiative and hedge it about with regulations.

This centralised administration has become in effect the rule of Paris. From Paris come all the laws and regulations, all the orders drawn up to the smallest detail which are applied in the various parts of France. 'Bureaucratic guardianship means that the whole mass of local problems converges on Paris, dilemmas are multiplied and urgent problems become insoluble abstractions, so that we take fifteen months to make a botch of what could be settled in a fortnight' (Roger Secrétain).

This centralisation grafted on to the image of a personalised France has fostered the notion of ministerial power and of an abstract state to which the French offer alternately their bitter criticisms and their earnest requests. The power of this State has become in some way independent of its territorial position, and it appears as manna from heaven, a permanent source of subsidy, investment, restitution and rescue for which no return is required. This twofold state of mind explains the success of some of the French planning ventures.

The centralised administration and the bureaucratic control exercised from Paris have had some serious consequences:

1. The country has come to be treated as if it were completely uniform, since all the laws and regulations issued in Paris could be and had to be applied in every commune, without any regard to regional peculiarities.

2. Those holding responsible positions in the provinces have tended to lose all initiative and to regard any semblance of originality in thought or action as sterile because it could bear no fruit. This produced a complete effacement of the leading personalities in the regions, rendering discussion impossible in the absence of responsible regional *élites*.

3. The most energetic provincial executives have been attracted to Paris, and capital, though largely of provincial and rural origin, has been redistributed from Paris.

France has thus been oddly 'deregionalised'; the associations and professional bodies to which Frenchmen belonged were structurally of the vertical type; their members had only rare contacts with those of other organisations living in the same town or the same region, and remained unaware that problems could exist, still less be solved, at regional level.

1. 'The whole of our philosophy of life today, beneath its false show of realism, is encumbered with doctrines. We imagine we are firmly rooted in reality, while in fact we are building castles in the air. . . . We are trying to make concrete elements from mere words' (J. Chappey, *La Révolution économique du XXe siècle*).
2. *Anglais, Français, Espagnols* (Paris, 1952), pp. 52–3.
3. Preface to the work by P. Combe, *Le Drame français* (Paris, 1959), p. III.

2. CIVILISING INFLUENCES

These psychological aspects, together with those bequeathed by the country's history and demography, would not be sufficient to explain the lack of characteristic and coherent features in the landscapes of France. One would have thought, on the contrary, that they would in the end have produced a certain uniformity of appearance. In fact at the root of this diversity lie certain ethnic factors, and, more generally speaking, many currents of civilisation whose frontiers and spheres of influence overlap on French territory.

France, being unusually placed in Europe, is a meeting place of Atlantic, northern and Mediterranean civilisations. Broadly speak-

ing, France comprises four entities with contrasting personalities whose boundaries are fluid but exist beyond dispute. Northern France contrasts with southern France, and Atlantic France is distinct from continental France.

A. Northern and Southern France

This division, or at least that between the North and the South, has been recognised from very ancient times, so clear and so numerous are its component factors. The fundamental opposition is that between the countries of common law and those of statute law [4] (Roman law), between the *langue d'oïl* and the *langue d'oc*, between the Mediterranean peoples and the Franks.

The criteria which help us to define northern and southern France are not confined to these essential traits, though they spring from and emphasise them. They include differences in the structure of the rural landscape which find expression in the contrasting patterns of open fields and bocage; differences in the crop rotation system, triennial in the North and biennial in the South; and the presence of trees in the fields in southern France. As far as houses are concerned, the most important contrast is in the roofs; in the North these are steep (45°) with flat hooked tiles; in southern France the round tile (or hollow, or Roman tile) gives more gently inclined roofs (30°). The dividing lines between northern and southern France are far from simple; they vary according to the criterion we are considering. The map shows some wide divergences; the main boundary lines fall between the 45th and the 47th parallel. Angoumois, Auvergne, Bourbonnais, Charolais, Burgundy and Franche-Comté are common-law districts. Saintonge, Périgord, Limousin, Gévaudan, Velay, Forez, Beaujolais, Mâconnais and Southern Jura are statute-law districts.

The language boundary is the one which follows the juridical one most closely, though it diverges from it considerably in the East, by-passing the Jura and running north to Belfort. The agricultural boundary also diverges, following a line from Le Havre to the southern Jura. The boundaries do not run side by side until we reach the Saône plains. The map showing the distribution of roof styles is stranger still, and shows that flat-tiled roofs penetrate far into the Central Massif, Aquitaine and the Alps, while a surprising island of round tiles appears in Lorraine and eastern Champagne, from Châlons-sur-Marne to Lunéville. This island is probably evidence of the strong influence of Roman military colonisation in districts adjacent to the *limes*. [5] This question of the boundary between North and

South has been the subject of careful research in some parts of France, such as the Grande Limagne, studied by M. Derruau, and the southern Jura, by A. Lebeau. These studies reveal the complexity of the problem, but also its great interest. [6]

In the very remote past this boundary between North and South certainly coincided with a forest barrier which separated them everywhere except near the ocean. Brenne, Sologne, Bourbonnais, Nivernais, Bresse and central Jura formed a belt of wooded country, often marshy and infertile, with, here and there, areas of less dense forest and better land. At the beginning of the second milennium Northerners cleared and settled these forest areas, so that the linguistic boundary became established on their southern margins. But it is difficult to make any pronouncement on the primitive origins of this division, its causes and chronology, and whether it is a phenomenon of prehistoric or historic times.

The geographer will once more observe that this major contrast in the human geography of France rests upon a natural contrast. These boundary lines crossing central France coincide in fact with the transition from the humid climates of northern France, damp all the year round, to the subtropical climates of the South, with their dry summers. Northern and southern influences may have reached the limits of their effectiveness at the boundaries of their respective climaxes.

B. Western and Eastern France

The delimitation of the dividing line between North and South is further complicated by the contrast between East and West. This contrast is in fact of quite a different kind from that between northern and southern France, and arises from the individualisation of certain traits of the Atlantic coastal regions. Recent studies by Flatrès have revealed the existence of an Atlantic culture, the common features of which are found from the north-west of the Iberian peninsula to Norway,

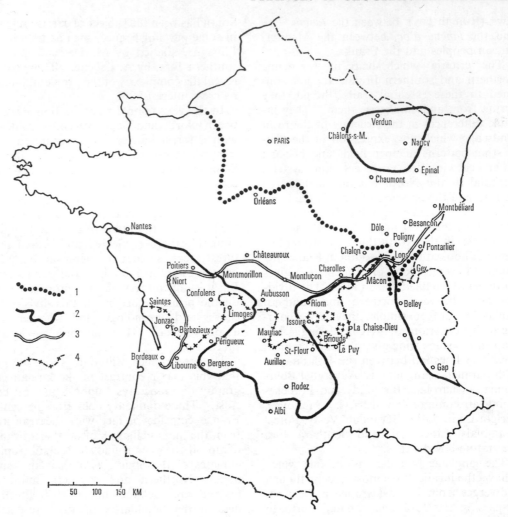

Fig. 48. Boundaries of northern and southern influences. (Source: Dion, Jeanton, Deléage and Lebeau: map drawn by R. Lebeau, *R. Géog. Lyon*, 1948)
1. Southern limit of open-field farming. 2. Northern limit of flat roofs and hollow tiles. 3. Limit of *Langue d'Oïl* and *Langue d'Oc* or Franco-Provençal dialects. 4. Limits of areas of statutory law and of common law.

through Aquitaine, Brittany, Ireland, Cornwall, Wales and Scotland; these are Celtic regions with an indisputable unity of civilisation despite the great contrasts of climate and soil resulting from the wide range of latitudes at which they lie. But the sea, with its ameliorating effect on climate, its fertilising effect on the soil and the greater ease of transport and commerce which it brings, has had a unifying influence which explains why this Atlantic culture is fairly strictly localised.

The main characteristics of this civilisation are:

1. Unity of the agricultural system, which has many distinctive features, including the persistence of a given crop for several years thanks to the use of marine fertilisers, different methods of crop rotation according to the quality of the soil, the bringing of heathland into temporary cultivation, and its use as pasture, as in the Basque *touya* and the *landes* of Brittany.

2. The small size of territorial units; the basic cell in agriculture is that of the farm or small group of farms. Hamlets never reach the size of the Picardy or Lorraine villages.

3. The duality of rural settlement. Along this Atlantic seaboard we find, in modern landscapes as in those of former times, both dispersed settlement and nucleated settlement with hamlets (the Breton 'villages').

This Atlantic region shows everywhere the profound influence of the sea. Along the coast a mixed economy has developed; the men are both farmers and sailors. But even inland the influence of the many ports and the long-standing relationships with foreign countries have made for a greater individuality of approach and made men's minds more inquisitive, more open to new ideas.

4. Statute law is Roman law, fixed by the Theodosian code; common law is fixed by tradition in the Germanic manner.

5. These tiles were still manufactured and used at the beginning of this century.

6. M. Derruau has given evidence for a southward displacement since the 15th century of the roof-type boundary.

III

THE NATIONAL AND REGIONAL PLANS

The French economy today represents a new type of organisation, combining the features of a free economy with those of a planned economy in a way which is unique in western Europe. A free economy was characteristic of France until the Second World War. It was under liberal capitalism, with freedom of investment and competition, that France achieved all her industrial and urban transformations after the middle of the 19th century. The balance of the economy depended on that of supply and demand, and its organisation on the idea that the general interest could be identified with the sum of individual interests, and that to satisfy one was to satisfy the other. However, this economy was not averse to tariff protection when an international contingency threatened the supposed equilibrium. At present this free economy persists in the wide sector of private enterprise which is master of its own investments, profits and location.

Since 1945, however, the French Government has set up in opposition to private enterprise a sector of public enterprise whose considerable and growing power gives it a controlling interest in a large part of the French economy. More than half of the country's investments are directly or indirectly controlled by the State, which has at hand, moreover, numerous opportunities to intervene in the form of fuel prices and railway freight rates, credits and subsidies or contracts offered to private enterprise. There are many links between the two parts of this economic organisation; but at the same time production is not sufficiently well co-ordinated to eliminate expensive competition.

This alliance of two economic structures could be considered as the marriage of two tendencies which appear all through French history: a tendency towards state intervention, which was already evident under the monarchy in the policies of Sully and Colbert and in the Reflections of Vauban, and later at the time of the Revolution, and the First Empire; and a tendency towards liberalism, which is traditional in the commercial and industrial middle classes but has never been entirely independent of the State.[7] The will to plan has, however, never been so marked in French economy as in the years since the war; and it has never before moved in the direction of so pronounced a strengthening of state control, totalitarian rather than socialist in nature.

This change in outlook was given its impetus by the nationalisation policies of the post-war period, but it is the result of several factors:

1. The widespread destruction resulting from four years of war, which meant that resources had to be used judiciously and initiatives co-ordinated.

2. The demographic recovery which, together with the new technical revolution and the end of protectionism, made it necessary to forecast and guide economic growth, and check unbridled competition.

3. The independence movements in the colonies which led people to fall back upon the mother country and brought to the attention of officials, entrepreneurs, holders of capital and senior executives in industry, the relatively underdeveloped condition of France and its considerable potentialities.

Since 1945, France has lived in this strange climate of ambivalent policies, partly authoritarian and partly liberal, initiating activities and taking options in which national and public interests were unequally considered, and favouring the development of private enterprise 'without risks'. The interplay of political forces has led to some curious manifestations of this situation; for example, Air-France, the state-owned airline, has to face competition from private airlines which are directly or indirectly subsidised by the State. Six thousand kilometres from Washington and four thousand kilometres from Moscow, Paris seems to be trying to combine American free enterprise with Soviet authoritarianism into a 'concerted' economy, an undertaking of a kind that is very characteristic of the French temperament.

In January 1946 a decree was issued instituting a planning council and a central planning office (*Commissariat général au Plan*) to deal with the Plan for Modernisation and Capital Equipment, inspired by Jean Monnet. The aims in view were many and ambitious: 'to increase production in France and its overseas dependencies, and their trade with the rest of the world, to raise productivity everywhere to the highest level so far attained, to ensure full employment, to raise the standard of living of the population, and to improve housing conditions and the life of the community'.

It would, however, be a mistake to think French planning only so far as it concerns modernisation and capital equipment. In 1950 the Minister of Reconstruction and Town Planning, M. Claudius Petit, made a statement to the Government with the object of drawing up a national development plan. The object of this plan was to ensure 'a better distribution of man-power in the light of natural resources and economic activities, not merely for economic purposes, but to promote the welfare of the population and the fullest possible life for all'. This proposal expressed a trend of thought inspired by Raoul Dautry, the Minister of Town Planning in 1945, by J. F. Gravier, whose book *Paris et le désert français* had awakened public opinion, and by such architects and town planners as Le Corbusier and G. Bardet.

Though these two complementary aspects of planning were completely different in aim, and were originally quite unconnected, they drew progressively nearer to each other, began to overlap and finally merged. The essential factor in this evolution was the reawakening of interest in the regions, whereas in the early stages planning was undertaken only at the national level and by categories of activities.

7. 'French capitalist activity depends on the State' (Ch. Morazé).

1. THE PLANS FOR MODERNISATION AND DEVELOPMENT

'A plan is the act of a collective body, in which the decisions of its individual and corporate members are made subordinate to definite objectives with a deadline for completion' (P. Bauchet). Planning has been introduced under more favourable circumstances in France than in other European states. Post-war France was bled white and ruined, but rich in her soil and her children. For the first time for decades, France had to look into the future and decide on the distribution of its budgets, on schools and houses to be built, on jobs to be provided. The outlook of the French was also favourable: the search for long-term objectives, the simul-

taneous expansion of dozens of economic and social sectors, the attractive combination of economic and social aims could only take place in a nation of intellectuals, keenly interested in abstract thought for its own sake.

A. Objectives and Achievements

THE FIRST PLAN (1947–53)

This covered the period 1947–53 even though it had been intended in the first place to span a period of four years. But the terms of the Marshall Plan and the wider objectives put forward by the Organisation for European Economic Co-operation led to this extension.

The objectives of the Plan were easy to define in the immediate aftermath of the war.[8]

'The economic resources of France were limited . . . Every possible advantage had to be taken of existing means; key resources had to be increased to the maximum, and the liquid assets of the nation had to be used according to a system of priorities which met immediate needs' (Jean Monnet).

It was a plan for restoring order, and thus concentrated on six sectors which were judged to be the most critical: mining, iron and steel, agricultural machinery, electricity, transport, cement.[9] But these sectors were at the same time the ones where intervention was easiest, as the public powers could act upon them either directly, in the case of nationalised enterprises, or indirectly, by tariffs, subsidies and tax reliefs. The Plan also made it possible to control and direct the considerable aid given by the United States of America immediately after the war, which made possible public investments amounting to 7,000 million francs. The objectives of the Monnet Plan were achieved one year later than scheduled. Industrial production had increased by 71%, agricultural production by 21% and the standard of living by 30%. Though the targets were achieved in basic sectors, with the exception of coal, the manufacturing industries, which were neglected in this First Plan, suffered set-backs; the tractor industry, for example, declined by 15%.

THE SECOND PLAN (1954–7)

There was no continuity between the first two plans. Although the second was drawn up at the end of 1951, it did not get under way until 1954, spanning the four years 1954–7. The objectives of the Plan were much wider this time, affecting the national economy in its entirety. Its mission was to reconcile the necessity for expansion with monetary stability. It laid emphasis on the basic measures to be taken in order to achieve a balance of payments, increase productivity and lower cost prices in the face of international com-

petition. These actions were to be taken without aggravating the inflation from which France was then suffering.

But the Plan drew attention to the paralysis affecting the whole of France's economy; individuals, professional bodies, banks and the public authorities themselves were all concentrating on giving 'first priority to achieving security and holding on to the positions they had acquired'. The plan called for special efforts with regard to housing, agriculture, manufacturing industries and colonial products.

The results obtained during the Second Plan were quite remarkable, sometimes exceeding the target (Table XXII). The basic targets

TABLE XXII. PERCENTAGES OF TARGET PRODUCTION REALISED UNDER THE PLANS

	First plan % realised	Second plan % realised	Third plan % realised
Coal	96	97	100
Electricity	95	105	100
Steel	115	84	102
Aluminium	87	100	103
Chemical industries	—	142	115
Cement	105	—	99
Grain	88	116	88
Meat	94	100	117
Sugar	70	90	118
Housing	—	111	106

were often passed in the chemical and electrical industries (the consumption of fertilisers went up by 30%, electrical plant by 90%), building and social welfare. Investment targets were exceeded on the average by 10%, particularly in the oil and nuclear power industries. But certain sectors failed to reach their objectives; the machine-tool industry achieved only half the planned growth, 20% instead of 40%.[10] Above all, this expansion did not take place in the conditions of financial and commercial stability for which the Plan had hoped. Imports increased considerably, while the increased demands of the home market slowed down exports. The financial burdens imposed by events in Suez and Algeria also fell heavily on investments.

THE THIRD PLAN AND THE INTERIM PLAN (1958–61)

The fate of the Third Plan was very different from that of its predecessor. Intended to span five years, the Plan was not in fact published until February 1959 owing to the political events of 1958. This situation had serious consequences, since for a whole year major projects (Électricité de France, for example) had to be shelved.

The Third Plan set out to meet two pressing and closely connected needs, namely the balance of payments and the need to adapt the economy to new political and economic trends. The Common Market, which was launched by the signature of the Treaty of Rome (1952), was intended progressively to lower customs barriers. At the same time liberation movements in the colonies robbed the French producers of important preferential markets. It was thus of prime importance to place the national economy in a position to withstand the liberalisation of trade and to place it on such a footing that exports could be increased while imports decreased. The Plan gave priority to investment in sectors which could best achieve these objectives. It favoured industries which would help to reduce imports, assisting the exploitation of the natural gas field at Lacq, a synthetic rubber factory and industries which produced finished products for export, such as the motor-car industry, the aircraft industry (Caravelle) and various other industries (electrical, etc.).

This modernisation and increasing specialisation of the economy had to be carried out with no increase in the working population and a large increase in the non-working population. The young people reaching working age during these four years were born in the war years when the birth-rate was low, while children born since the war needed schools and teachers in ever-increasing numbers. To facilitate this economic growth, a liberal policy was adopted with regard to foreign capital, following the report of the Rueff Committee. The labour crisis due to the de-

mographic recession and to the Algerian war, the financial crisis of 1957, the political events of 1958 and the measures of financial recovery decided upon as a result of the Rueff–Armand Plan had in fact had considerable repercussions on the progress of the Third Plan. They had caused a prolonged stagnation of the economy (the annual growth in the national product in 1958 and 1959 was 2·5%) and slowed down investments, particularly in the private sector.

The result was a delay in the realisation of the Third Plan. 'Certain public investments, such as those in waterways, sea-ports and telecommunications, are behind schedule to an extent which will not directly slow down expansion, but which will lead to higher exploitation costs than could be foreseen. In agriculture, mechanisation and the development of stock-rearing are also somewhat behind. The progress of the engineering industries has slowed down . . . We must therefore expect a year's delay before reaching the general production target of the third plan' (Annual report on the implementation of the 1958 plan). To deal with these delays, a surgical operation was carried out in May 1960. An interim plan—or 'little plan'—was substituted for the last three years of the Third Plan; its essential purpose was to stimulate investments in order to regain the anticipated 5·5% expansion. This plan extended over the last months of 1960 and the year 1961. The overall rate of growth to be attained was fixed at 5·5% for these two years. But the rates varied widely between different sectors of the economy: 75% (1960) and 40% (1961) for natural gas, 20 and 15% for artificial fibres, 12 and 11% for cars, 10% for electrical goods and chemicals, 3–4% for agriculture and 4–5% for leather industries.

In order to reach these targets, the overall quarterly increase of wages and salaries was limited to 1%, and above all, credit transfers were imposed, and investment facilities encouraged. The rates of increase of directly productive investments in private enterprise were foreseen as 8 and 9%, while in the public sector reductions (−2 and −1%) were budgeted for. On the whole, this little plan made it possible for the objectives to be attained. Investments reached the rate of growth provided for in the third plan (28·1 %), though social investments made more progress than investments in production. The objectives for basic industries were achieved except in the coal industry, and greatly exceeded in the chemical and aluminium industries.

THE FOURTH PLAN (1962–5)

With this Plan, French economic planning, reached its maturity. Founded on experience gained from the three preceding plans and the searching reappraisal which they had entailed, the new Plan benefited from much better preparation, a clearer definition of aims, a wiser application of techniques and more foresight in decision-making. The Plans for Modernisation and Capital Equipment were followed by a Plan for 'Economic and Social Development'.

The plan was prepared by twenty-eight commissions concerned with modernisation, operating in the vertical plane (by sectors), and in the horizontal plane (finance, labour, productivity, research, regional plans), bringing together representatives of the administration, professional bodies, workers' and peasants' trade unions and experts. Unlike previously, great progress was made: the 'physical' and financial coherence of the work of the commissions was reviewed, and the investment and employment forecasts were made at regional level. The Economic and Social Committee (*Le Conseil économique et social*) and the Supreme Council for the Plan (*le Conseil supérieur du Plan*), which was instituted in 1961, were asked for their opinion. This Fourth Plan was, for the first time, submitted to Parliament, which gave its approval after numerous interventions and after the Government had adopted a corrigendum concerning the Rhône–Rhine link and regional policies.

The Fourth Plan was published in the official gazette of 7th August 1962. The context in which it appeared was characterised by three fundamental changes: rising numbers of young people and an increase in the working population necessitating the creation of more than a million jobs; the extension of the Common Market by the adoption of new measures for unification between the member countries; and the completion of the liberation of the colonies, particularly the granting of independence to Algeria. The overall objective of the Plan was to 'develop the economic means at France's disposal' in order to accomplish 'the great tasks that lie before the nation'; that is to say—and the order is significant—aid to the non-metropolitan territories of France, the structural readaptation demanded by European integration, military commitments, East–West competition, the advancement of the Third World and improvement in the standard of living.

The starting-point of the Fourth Plan was the choice of the annual rate of expansion to be expected of the French economy, which might be anywhere between 3 and 6%. The relatively ambitious rate of 5·5%, that is to say, an expansion of 24% in four years, was finally chosen. The preamble to the Plan emphasised the priority given to investments over consumption. The main effort was to be concentrated on collective capital works of a social character, in relation to both urban and rural areas, cultural activities, sport, science, schools and universities. Expenditure on education, urban development, health and sport were to increase by 50% in four years as against 23% for housing. This choice of priority investments, however, left out two important sectors: housing (350,000 houses per year) and the transport infrastructure. The Fourth Plan also provided for an expansion of agriculture, the member states of the Common Market being expected to open their home markets to French produce.

THE FIFTH PLAN (1966–70)

This, the first five-year plan, was prepared on the same lines as its predecessors. A general report on its main proposals was approved by

Parliament at the end of 1964. The Plan differs from the others in that its predictions relate to a much longer period (1985) than the duration of the plan itself, and in its increased concern for the regional approach.[11] For so long a period, many contingencies must be allowed for: the entry of new members into the European Economic Community, the removal of trade barriers on a world-wide scale, development of the social services, collective projects and building, and the cost of the armed forces. 'The chief objective is to put our economy on a sound competitive basis that will guarantee its continued independence, to ensure that it maintains a balanced expansion and to make it the foundation of a real and lasting social progress.'

The report anticipates major structural changes in industry just as much as in the rural sphere, and calls for the necessary mobility of labour. The planned growth rate is 5% *per annum*, that is, 25% *per capita*, allowing for population increase. In order, at the same time, to preserve the financial stability of 1965, the Plan prescribed a whole series of measures aimed at reducing home consumption by encouraging a savings drive for several years: 'the motive power for expansion (ought) to be switched gradually from consumption to productive investment and exports in order to meet the requirements for a balanced growth'. Another innovation is the provision for a number of 'warning signals'.

B. Strength and Weakness of the Plans

French planning has provoked a great deal of comment and the most contradictory judgments have been passed upon the Plans. Let us examine in turn their value, their ambiguities and the criticisms made of them.

VALUE

The value of the French Plans lies first of all in the tools they have forged or inspired and in the new spirit they have awakened in all groups participating in the economic and social life of the country. The *Commissariat au Plan* gave birth to the public accounting service. Without the Plan we should never have dealt with the mass of statistical data which now exists, whether national or regional, and whether relating to the population as a whole or to its different sectors. Planning has given us well-founded, well-directed action and a policy of structural change, in place of a disorganised series of day to day measures and only the semblance of a policy of controls. The Plans have made for awareness of interdependence and so strengthened the bonds between professions and classes on both the national and regional level. They have provided a rhythm of progress and directions to be followed in the light of requirements which many trade unions were unable to work out, and 'constitute a model market study which all firms would do well to follow' (A. Chalandon). Thus considered, the value of the French Plan is absolute; it is a complete source of economic information; it 'reduces uncertainty and replaces the rule of the market in all cases where the latter is unattainable, weak or out of date'. In short, it is a 'forward-looking scheme for the coherent development of the economy' (P. Massé).

In the second place, the value of the Plans lies in their effectiveness. The data given in the tables show that on the whole the targets have been attained or even passed. Obviously one may wonder whether the expansion of the French economy in the last fifteen years is really connected with planning because countries which lack it have had higher rates of expansion.[12] Although it is impossible to decide how much of this expansion is due to economic liberalism and how much to planning, there can be no doubt as to the influence of the national Plans. They have given an impetus to all kinds of activity, not only those concerned with the economy, helping them towards a coherent, balanced development, and setting up targets for the future which the traditional economic and administrative machinery in France was quite incapable of anticipating. Like all other plans, these too have to face unforeseen risks. The amount of private investment, variations in foreign trade and such accidents as the severe winter of 1962–3 or the sudden return of the French from Algeria are unknown quantities which affect the national Plans in various ways, modifying their targets or the conditions in which they are carried out.

CONTRADICTIONS

The concept of planning usually presupposes the existence of two conditions: an authoritarian organisation of the economy—a plan is drawn up so that it may be fulfilled—and objectives defined in terms of a particular political and economic orientation. A plan 'cannot exist without some kind of political and philosophical guidance behind decisions on economic policy, the distribution of incomes, the attitude towards the Third World. . . . Unless such decisions are made, we have reason to fear that certain plans may be no more than a veneer covering traditional economical and sociological realities, and bring the very idea of planning into disrepute' (P. Bauchet). Plans of the French type fulfil none of these conditions. The Plan is anything but 'imperative'. Numerous epithets have been used to define it: concerted, indicative, normative, inciting, directing, flexible. The first contradiction of French planning is its introduction into an economic structure of the liberal capitalist type. The odds appear to be against the reconciling of economic planning and free enterprise.

In its present state the Plan is more than a forecast, as accurate as possible, of the economic and social position for the next four years; it is less than an 'imperative' plan imposing definite objectives and ways of achieving them. According to the sector of the economy in question and the means of exerting pressure or encouragement at the disposal of the public authorities, the Plan may be purely indicative at one point, and virtually imperative at another. An annual rate of expansion is indicated by the Plan, but firms, workers and consumers still have the liberty to produce, invest, consume or claim their rights as they will. In the spheres of coal, electricity and railways the State has complete control, so that the Plan's objectives can be attained without much difficulty even though some tendency to autarchy may appear. In the sphere of private enterprise the pressure brought to bear by the State depends on the means at its disposal: fiscal or financial pressure or government regulations. But if the interests of particular firms conflict with the general interests, the execution of the Plan may be endangered.

Hitherto the French Plans have not attempted to rest upon any ideological foundation. A very timid attempt in this direction was outlined in the preamble to the Fourth Plan.[13] One can expect these contradictions in French planning to become accentuated. On the one hand, planning procedures will become more and more specific, and the thought behind them must needs become clearer. On the other hand, in the context of the Common Market and the western world, liberal capitalism is weaving a network of international investments and interlaced interests; and there is no reason to suppose that these are going to be altered for the benefit of the French national Plan. It seems inevitable that the French Plan should become simply a part of a greater plan for all Europe. Every year the French economy becomes more deeply involved with the Common Market in an international context. The fixing of prices for agricultural products and the free circulation of capital, merchandise and workers will progressively deprive French governments of the means of control and intervention which planning demands. Investments and economic policy must thus be co-ordinated; in 1962 the Common Market executive recommended the adoption of a 'European programme' in the French style, indicative rather than imperative. These first steps in European planning have met with strong opposition.

Planning is subject to yet another contradiction. Research done with a view to the further elaboration of the Plans is showing up discrepancies, contradictions and structural anomalies which invalidate or at least slow down all measures designed to remedy their effects. Thus the Plan must inevitably involve decisions of a political order. But the Plan was conceived in respect of political, economic and social structures which it cannot and does not claim to upset.[14] The *Commissariat au Plan* can only be a technical body at the disposal of a political power. This position is bound to lead to contradictions. Thus the targets set for agriculture lead the planners to budget for a surplus, in the last year of the plan, of 5–6 million tons of cereals and 45–60 million hectolitres of milk, without indicating how this surplus is to be absorbed or suggesting a basis for a really ordered agricultural economy.

CRITICISMS

Criticisms of the French Plans refer to their formulation and their execution. Some say that the conditions in which a plan is formulated make it rather like a recording studio, the objectives being in the end no more than compromises reached by agreement between the various parties concerned with the French national revenue. The Plan cannot bring forward measures inconsistent with free investment and employment, or measures needing large transfers of capital, particularly of revenue. To a certain extent the Plan is not a plan at all but an optical illusion, since it cannot use any compulsion or sanction. Its authors are the first to realise these limitations; one paragraph of the Fourth Plan draws an apt distinction between targets which it seems desirable to reach, and forecasts, that is to say, the figures which will be reached without intervention by the process of free expansion. Some forecasts are not necessarily 'targets', the production of wheat, for example; but here one finds critics who want a target figure for everything. These criticisms apply equally to the industrial sector where the targets are all too often no more than the forecasts of the trade unions.

Another criticism made of the French Plan is that it is not democratic; on the one hand, it does not make equal provision for the various professional and social groups, and on the other hand, it is too much preoccupied with the economic aspects and too little with the social aspects of the situation. Above all, no attempt is envisaged to change the existing social structure nor the distribution of incomes. Finally, consumer goods, such as motor-cars and electrical appliances, have the highest rates of expansion. Social items, such as housing, receive adequate attention but are not scheduled for major expansion. Certain critics observe that the share of the total national product devoted to the different sectors is just as important as the choice of expansion rates. For example, an increase of 50% for capital equipment connected with the social services is envisaged, but this represents only 1·2% of all investments. François Perroux rightly concludes that 'the purely indicative planning in France, by means of social concessions which may seem to be very timid, stimulates, stabilises and strengthens the capitalist type of decentralised economy'.

The chief problem connected with the French type of plan is to find ways and means of implementing it. For most sectors it offers little more than a statement of aims and intentions. The French planners, in fact, rather than have recourse to direct or authoritarian methods of implementation, have used psychological and above all financial incentives. The State acts through the intermediary of:

1. Credit: since 1955 the chief means of providing credit has been the Social and Economic Development Fund, which has replaced the many types of government stocks which formerly existed. This takes the Plan into the sphere of finance. The fund makes it possible to allocate the credit required to implement the Plan through the Budget, and determines programme details, for it controls practically half of the public funds intended for financing investments. Moreover, the State can use the guarantees granted to borrowers and interest bonuses.

2. Prices: by price control and indirect taxation.

3. Investments: the control and distribution of public investments are indicated, and represent an important part of the Plan's objectives. Private investments fit harmoniously into the plan only because this reflects the intentions industrialists have expressed through the commissions on modernisation. The State can, however, influence them by means of medium-term credit.

4. Various incentives: subsidies, loans, guarantees, bonuses, tax rebates, orders and contracts; the State has a whole armoury of incentives, but its variety probably reduces its efficiency, and the objectives appropriate to each of these methods do not necessarily coincide with those of the Plans.

But these controls are not very effective, and above all their effect is uneven. They act differently on different enterprises according to their output and financial situation. The Plan has no means of influencing directly self-financing firms; it can do nothing about uncompetitive firms or decisions to close factories. What is more, the Plan's finance is not guaranteed by the system of annual budgetary votes. Quadrennial targets not only have to be split up, but they can be called in question every year, which breaks the continuity of the Plan. One attempt to remedy this defect is the passing of special Acts remaining in force for several years, which constitute a guarantee of continuity of investment.

The implementation of the Plan suffers from a *lack of co-ordination*; the targets set for the various sectors presuppose perfect co-ordination of measures of various kinds affecting a large number of services and administrations. This co-ordination is seldom achieved owing to the lack of liaison between the different individuals holding the executive power, particularly the all-powerful Ministry of Finance.

P. Bauchet has given a very clear assessment of the experience of national planning in France:

'After sixteen years the French planning organisation has acquired a new status which appears to be satisfactory in many respects; it is more than an advisory instrument, though less than an executive authority. But the balance between the exercise of powers of arbitration and the use of consultation with the groups involved is unstable. The centrifugal forces of administration and pressures by individual interests constantly obtrude, threatening to degrade it to a mere advisory service of the executive.'

From one plan to the next, French planning has been active within a changing political and economic framework. After 1965, with the desire to limit the means of state control and also some evidence of a return to market machinery, many observers felt that planning was no longer a 'pressing need', and spoke of the 'deplanification' of the French economy.

8. 600,000 killed, 300,000 disabled, 215,000 industrial and commercial enterprises and 610,000 agricultural concerns put out of action, entire towns destroyed, the rail network and marshalling yards disorganised.

9. Motor-fuels and nitrogen were added later. Agriculture, housing and teaching were deliberately neglected.

10. Hydro-electric production also failed quite to reach its objective (24·5 thousand million instead of 29).

11. The report singles out western France, which should receive 35–45% of the anticipated new jobs, the North Sea–Mediterranean axis of eastern France, and the Paris region.

12. From 1950 to 1959 the gross national product of France rose by 4·3%, as against 7·5% in West Germany, 5·7% in Italy, 5·1% in Holland, 2·6% in Belgium and 1·2% in England.

13. 'We may think that the consumer society foreshadowed by certain aspects of American life is turning in the long run towards the satisfaction of futile desires which can only bring unhappiness. Surely it would be better if the ever-increasing abundance for which we can hope were put at the service of a more complete idea of man' (P. Massé).

14. 'The observation of F. Perroux that the French Plan fits into a context of reform by evolution, not revolution, appears to agree with the facts and at the same time to reflect the respect of the technicians for the opinion of the political majority' (Pierre Massé, preface to *Le IVe Plan français*, by François Perroux (Paris, 1962)).

2. REGIONAL PLANNING AND NATIONAL DEVELOPMENT

Up to a very recent period—after the last war—France, above all a whole composed of many regional parts, ignored the existence of disparities between these regions, the reality of regional problems and the need to reorganise economic and social problems on a regional basis, and neglected to consider conflicting regional interests and rivalries.

The reasons for this attitude are clear:

1. Political and administrative centralisation. Seen from Paris, the seat of all power, France appeared as a uniform expanse over which the capital shed its rays of roads and railways. This centralised power, delegated to one representative only—the Prefect—in each department, meant that there was no longer any regional spokesman with whom discussion would be possible and fruitful. Regional solidarity and feeling were greatly weakened.[15] All administrative bodies and trade unions were connected vertically with Paris, never coming into contact with other bodies or other trade unions at the regional level.

2. The demographic and economic stability of the pre-war years. In a dynamic setting of continuous growth, contrasts between regions stand out sharply, but they become blurred in a context where there is no vitality and no competition. Before 1939 rural depopulation and the exodus from Brittany were in being, but in a population with a lower birth-rate the numbers involved were far smaller than they have been for the past fifteen years. The lack of dynamic population growth and economic protectionism eliminated the problems of capital equipment costs and of locating new factories.

3. The absence of statistical records and research at the regional level. Before 1939 the notions of regional economies and of under-equipment and underdevelopment in the regions were completely absent from the French vocabulary.

A. Regional Disparities

Awareness of these regional problems dates from the fifties and grew all the faster for having been so long delayed. It was the result of the renewed population growth. The large numbers of births led politicians, academics and business executives to look into the question. The conclusion reached was that demographic and economic expansion occurred in very different places, so that the provision of schools, professional training and jobs would soon present problems. Suddenly all the inequalities and lack of balance between the regions and between the various social and economic sectors within each region were perceived and analysed and their repercussions on daily life became apparent. These disparities take many forms, and there is not one regional problem but many:

1. The problem may be demographic, due to excess population and lack of jobs, as in Brittany, Normandy and the northern region, or caused by long-standing and excessive depopulation, leading to abandonment of the land, ageing of the population and under-development, as in the Central Massif and Aquitaine.

2. It may be economic, due to the persistence of traditional methods of agriculture based on small self-sufficient units, as in certain parts of the Central Massif, Alsace and Lorraine; to difficulties relating to prices and markets in the case of specialised and intensive farming, as in areas growing sugar-beet, early vegetables or vines; to a lack of sufficient variety of industries, as in the industrial zones of the North, the Loire basin and Lorraine; or to the stagnation of former industrial centres which owed their existence to coal and steam and even water power.

3. It may be social, due to too low an average income in the region, or large differences between the various income-groups;

or to insufficient capital equipment or under-development of the health, education and administrative services.

4. Finally, it may be geographical, due to a congestion or concentration, causing a lack of balance prejudicial to both sides, or, as in the Paris region, raising costs excessively and creating insoluble problems of ordered development; to an obsolete system of land utilisation which slows down economic and social change and leads to the persistence of impossible living conditions, as in the slums and industrial areas; to lack of urbanisation so that the people leaving the neighbouring countryside cannot be rehoused; or to a lack of an adequate infrastructure.

Very often these regional problems are closely linked and the seriousness of the problem in any one case depends on the sum of the various types of deficiency. One only needs to run through these various points to realise the extent of the problems of Brittany or northern France, for example.

GEOGRAPHICAL INEQUALITIES

Every regional problem has two facets; one might say two natures. From statistical observations and predictions which show up weaknesses, it appears as an 'absolute' problem; but considered in relation to the national average and to other parts of France it is a 'relative' problem. As M. Roncayolo observes:[16]

'Though modern societies accept, more or less readily, a certain amount of social inequality, geographical inequality has appeared to be one of the most unacceptable evils ever since the crisis of the thirties. . . . Geographical inequality extends over a definite radius, within an actual area, to an entire community or society; it emphasises and increases differences in income by the cumulative effects of lack of public and private capital equipment, and unfavourable attitudes of mind.'

The facts

In any comparison of the statistics and their discrepancies by departments or regional divisions, there emerge in France as a whole considerable inequalities in population (Chapter I), employment (fig. 45), capital equipment, salaries and incomes (fig. 49), standards of living and of consumption. Figure 50 shows the inequalities in regional incomes per inhabitant in 1958. Taking the average for France as 100, the indices range from 68·7 for Brittany and 69·9 for Poitou and Charente to 159·6 in the Paris region.[17] These inequalities remain if we disregard the num-bers engaged in agriculture, the Paris region being still far ahead of other highly urbanised regions.

If these regional inequalities are mapped, there emerges a division of France into two halves lying roughly on either side of a line running from Le Havre to Marseilles. This division appears on many different types of map; to the north of this line lie the industrial regions, more urbanised, more dynamic and richer. To the south of this line the southern and western districts of France seem the very antithesis of those to the north; rural and little urbanised, poor and with few industries. Until the 18th century this half of France 'breathed through its Atlantic seaboard, where all industrial and commercial activity was orientated towards the sea and the great ports' (F. Crouzet). For a long time these two halves of France were more or less in equilibrium, because the sea-routes, being easier than land-routes, and links with the colonies counter-balanced the centralising influence of Paris. The disequilibrium, became more marked from the middle of the 19th century, when maritime trade declined and the industrial and urban revolution concentrated all development on the Paris region, northern France and a few coalfields. Stendhal was already stressing 'the gloomy situation of that part of France which stretches from Montpellier to Poitiers and from Bayonne to Clermont', and Michel Chevalier, less conventionally, was drawing a contrast between eastern and western France, with a dividing line running from Paris to Perpignan.

Even within this division into two zones, there is a complementary phenomenon, the

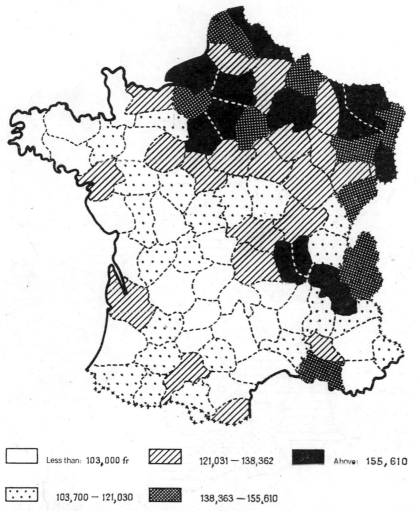

Fig. 49.   Average income per head of population in 1952.   (Source: Jean-Marie Jeanneney, *Forces et Faiblesses de l'Économie française*, A. Colin, 2nd ed, 1959)

concentration of work and wealth in a small number of departments.   A large number of maps in *L'Espace économique français*, published in 1956 by the I.N.S.E.E., bring this out very forcibly.   In 1955, for example, 48·4% of the 3,176 million francs of taxable profits was put down to the account of 7 departments; 12 departments provide 45% of the gross national product.   But over and above the inequalities between the more and less favoured departments, that is, between the

North and the South, there is the much greater inequality between the Paris conurbation and the provinces.   Paris takes for itself the lion's share of the wealth, the *élite*, the most highly skilled and most lucrative work, most of the head offices and the investments, and is in possession of almost all discretionary and financial power.   It is the head, the heart and the lungs of France (in 1959 the department of Seine alone accounted for 48·4% of the tax receipts of France).

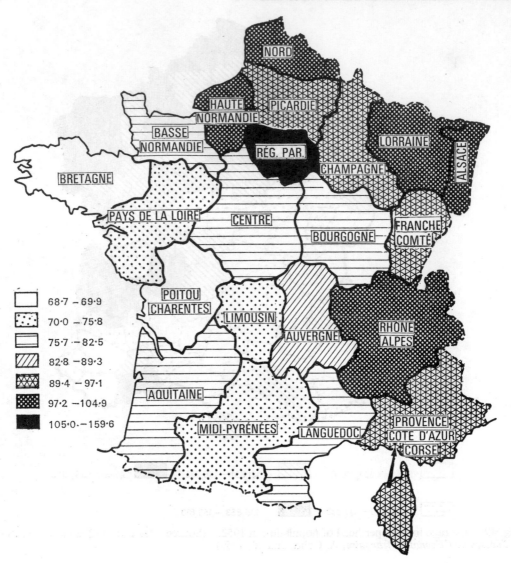

Fig. 50. Indices of regional income per head of population for the planning regions in 1958 (France as a whole = 100). (Source: *Études et conjoncture*, 1961, p. 388)

The causes

There are many.   First of all they depend on the *vigour of economic life*.   After a long period of stagnation, the regions discovered that they had not advanced at a uniform pace in terms of capital equipment and industrialisation.   The realisation suddenly came that in this period of great economic and technical upheaval, the role of activities which had hitherto been considered a part of their heritage, a basic element of their life, had to be reexamined.   The northern region, for example, which had benefited more than most from the industrial revolution of the last century, now discovered that it was attracting few new industries. These are going to other regions which were left out a century ago. These phenomena are not indeed new, they had simply been forgotten; the 19th-century industrial revolution had caused the same upheavals when coke-fired blast-furnaces and the metallurgy of coal and iron ore condemned to death the regions where traditional metal-work had been carried on for centuries, such as Nivernais and the plateau of Langres. The underdevelopment of certain regions can be explained by this decline in local industry, whether recent or of long standing. In the same way the regions suffer from *delay in the development of infrastructures and capital investment*, where the State has not made sufficient investment for their needs and progress. The modernisation of the road system and waterways, as well as the building of schools, sports grounds and training centres, come under this heading.

Lack of regional capitalisation. The centralising influence of Paris has also affected the capital resources of the provinces, by draining them away and taking the initiative in their use away from regional officials and businessmen.

Attitudes of mind. It is always difficult to assess the part played by psychological influences, but it is certain that they exist. The outlook of the *bourgeoisie*, like those of Bordelais, whose interests are rooted in the land and trade with the colonies or England, can certainly explain their lack of interest in industrial questions. In some cases the spirit of initiative seems to have died down in other regions after periods when it flourished. Social psychology also explains certain refusals to adapt to new conditions which threatened to upset traditional structures, as in the textile industries.

Concentration and polarisation. The pattern of the main road and rail routes, dating from the 19th century, has contributed to the lack of regional balance. It finally disorganised those regions whose focal points—ports and large cities—were linked with Paris but had no road and rail network serving their surrounding districts. The Atlantic ports in particular were cut off from their hinterlands; the waterways which were the most important traffic routes before the railways were put in the shade. The concentration of men and activities in Paris and a few large provincial cities has continued to increase and lead to the creation and extension of the French 'population deserts'.

REGIONAL PROBLEMS IN THE EUROPEAN CONTEXT

France's position in a Europe in which frontiers have come to mean less and less is fundamentally altering the problems of her internal organisation. The central axis of all Common Market Europe is developing along the Rhine flanked by Lorraine and the Ruhr and broadening out in Flanders and the Netherlands.

France, with Paris as its traditional hub, is thus relegated to a marginal position, Paris itself being separated from the prosperous regions of the North and 'industrial Lotharingia' by sparsely populated rural areas such as Picardy and Champagne; areas such as the South-west are even more remote, since Paris is no longer the most important focal point, and there is as yet no counter-poise in Spain or Britain. Conversely, the frontier regions of the North and East, which had suffered in the past from their situation on the periphery, now find themselves in an advantageous position. Eastern France is thus very differently placed from the West, since Alsace and Lorraine form a direct link with the great economic heart of continental Europe, and holds a remarkable trump card in the Rhône-Saône corridor, which offers an invaluable route to the Mediterranean.

Paradoxically, it is in the international context that regional problems loom largest and are followed with the greatest interest. In fact the real problems of European integration occur at the regional level, and it is there that the repercussions and consequences of common policies in such matters as transport, power and agriculture are felt; such policies may well aggravate existing inequalities.

B. Action on Regional Problems

This growing awareness of regional problems and of the lack of regional balance in France has led to action on a considerable scale, though belated compared with regional policies carried out even before the war in certain states (the 'depressed areas' of Britain date from 1931).[18] The initiative stemmed from the regions themselves, with the creation of regional research groups (*Comités régionaux d'études*), completely unofficial bodies which started at Rheims in 1943 and increased in number during the fifties. At the beginning of 1958 there were 166 of these groups, each dealing with the affairs of a town, a canton, a department or a much wider area. These committees, created by public-spirited men, had the merit of awakening the more backward provinces, of arousing public awareness of the present and future problems by studies of varying worth and of bringing together men who had hitherto been working in isolation, not realising that they could integrate their work at regional level. The disadvantages of these committees were implicit in their merits; public figures, politicians and the representatives of certain financial interests tried to take them over, with varying degrees of success. Faced with this wealth of committees, in whose formation it had no part, the Government officially recognised the most representative of them, from 1955 onwards, as Committees on Economic Expansion.

The Regional Development Associations (*Sociétés de développement régional*), which also began in June 1955 on the occasion of an important series of decrees devoted to land utilisation, are private financial organisations, but they enjoy a minimum dividend of 5% for twelve years guaranteed by the State and subject to certain controls (minimum capital 2,500,000 francs). Their role is to provide the regions with a substitute for the former local and regional banks by participating in the investment programmes set up by industrial enterprises. At present there are about fifteen Regional Development Associa-

tions in existence, but they have given rise to anxiety on account of:

1. The control of local capital by a minority and the predominating influence of the merchant banks which have notoriously 'avoided mutual competition and shared out their spheres of influence'[19] (M. Byé).

2. The small amount of capital.

3. The conditions under which the benefiting companies were chosen.

4. The financial rather than regional or social interests of the companies.

In fact, this regional action could not succeed without the participation of the central authority upon which the duties of arbitration, guidance and assistance necessarily fell.

Regional Action Programmes

These programmes were created by the series of decrees of 30th June 1955 of which they formed the most important elements. They represent the regional application of the Plan for Modernisation and Capital Equipment, and have a threefold objective:

1. 'To direct the economic and social development of the different regions, particularly those which suffer from unemployment or insufficient economic development.'

2. 'To co-ordinate for this purpose the action of the various administrative bodies, especially those concerned with public investments.'

3. 'To guide individuals, professional organisations and local bodies in the use of the various forms of incentive and assistance by means of which the State may decide to stimulate local development.'

One of the first merits of this programme to appear was that it led to a regional division of France. Twenty-one regions were defined by regrouping departments in blocks of two (Nord and Alsace) to ten (Midi–Pyrénées). These divisions were far from perfect, but they had two advantages: they restored some economic importance to regions based on the old French provinces, and they provided a regional basis on which the innumerable administrative divisions could be progressively fixed, thus giving for the first time a certain coherence to the administrative map of France. The first programme to be published was that of Brittany (1956). These plans were worked out in Paris by co-ordinating committees; provincial requests generally played an active part in them by the intermediary of the committees on economic expansion, but the officials in Paris were often afraid of pressure from public figures and local or regional groups, and kept their contacts to a minimum.

The content of these programmes was standardised by general request; it consists of three parts:

1. An inventory of the situation and problems.

2. A statement of measures to be taken on operations which have been fixed or are to be encouraged.

3. An announcement of general objectives.

Two Examples of Regional Action Programmes

The Languedoc region. The titles of different chapters in the first two parts are very revealing. The basic *data* for the region, which consists of four departments (Aude, Gard, Hérault and Lozère), are as follows: physical conditions—irregular relief, an uncertain climate, soil of uneven quality; human factors—the attraction of the lowlands and the depopulation of the mountainous hinterland, causing simultaneous emigration and immigration, an ageing population and a deteriorating standard of living, a preponderance of monocultural vine cultivation and a natural dependence on trade rather than production.

The *objectives* are then broadly outlined:

1. To compensate for the more adverse physical conditions (by reforestation, for example).

2. To conserve and make the best use of human potential (by employment and housing policies, education and social provision).

3. To diversify agricultural production and to regularise the resulting income by reorganising the market in wines for current consumption; in the plains, by irrigation (Bas-Rhône–Languedoc canal); in the hill zone by an attempt to improve and step up the production of quality wines; in regions of polyculture, by the classical methods of increasing yields; on the coast, by the development of fisheries; in Lozère and the other highlands, by establishing a balance between woodland arable and pasture land; and in the whole region, by structural reform and by education.

4. To promote industrial development, by reviving certain traditional industries; by giving a stimulus to a few centres of expansion, such as Alès, Sète, Montpellier, Narbonne and Bagnols-sur-Cèze; by establishing the region as a 'playground', improving communications and assisting the tourist industry.

The northern region. The programme for the Nord–Pas-de-Calais region was, more than the others, prepared by the Regional Expansion Committee, after a very far-reaching consideration of all the economic, social and administrative representations that had been made. The peculiar character of the region derives from its strong economic vitality, despite a rather obsolescent organisation and a large population growth. The programme fixes five objectives: to increase the range of industries; to reconcile regional agricultural potential with national needs (this formula covering the problems of wheat, potatoes and sugar-beet cultivation); to improve professional training and promotion prospects; to reorganise housing; and to improve the communication network. The programme distinguishes between the 'main geographical divisions': the Lille–Roubaix–Tourcoing–Armentières conurbation, the coal, iron and steel zone, the ports and the agricultural districts.

Judgments on these programmes have on the whole been very severe, and they have been the subject of many complaints. The problems have been tackled from the economic angle or more rarely from the demographic point of view without any idea of true synthesis. The geographical outlook on national development is absent or incorrectly stated. The measures proposed are too often no more than a collection of pious hopes, projects buried for years in departmental head offices or plans already under way. The programmes lack real dynamic force, in that they have no executive power, not even of co-ordination. Even the style is cautious, full of careful phrases like 'it should perhaps be . . .', 'it might be possible . . .', 'it is to be recommended . . .'. As they were completely divorced, right at the beginning, from the elaboration of the national Plans, it was hard to see how they could be made to accord with them and thus become reality.

These criticisms are often accurate, but they must be modified by the following remarks: that these programmes were drawn up at all is remarkable in a centralised country such as France. The first programmes could not be expected to be perfect; such as they were, they meant that people had become aware that regions existed. They constituted an inventory of the strong and weak points of these regions which is not without interest to the central authority, but which also interests the regions themselves. These programmes—and the grievance is in itself an important one—were not conceived at all in the light of a policy of regionally differentiated growth, which is why analysis by sectors of work predominates over geographical analysis.

People in positions of responsibility have noted the drawbacks of this dissociation of economic development from the regional aspects of national growth. For this reason it was decided in 1960 that the regional development plans, which had been made the responsibility of the national development department of the Ministry of Works, but which had never seen the light of day, should be incorporated in the programmes still to appear, and quickly published for those which had already appeared.

'MIXED' AND LAND DEVELOPMENT COMPANIES

These committees, Regional Development Associations and action programmes are not enough to define and carry out a truly regional policy which demands political decisions and arbitration between the different regions, without which the region having the most powerful committee would have the advantage. Side by side with these private organisations, therefore, the State has established 'regional' organisations, though not the same number in every region. The pioneer and model for these organisations was the *Compagnie Nationale du Rhône* (C.N.R.), set up between 1922 and 1934; it had three objectives connected with the utilisation of the river; to turn it into a modern waterway, to exploit its hydro-electric potential and to make its water available for irrigation. The development of seven regions was put into the hands of 'mixed' companies, that is, companies financed partly by public bodies and partly by shareholders.

The *Compagnie Nationale du Bas-Rhône–Languedoc* (1955) aims to transform the rural economy of the vine-growing region of Languedoc by introducing a greater variety of crops. Its most important work is the irrigation of 200,000 ha. between the Rhône and the Pyrenees by means of a large canal taking water from the Rhône, and supplemented by the rivers flowing to the coast. The work of this company affects the entire economy of the region, the infrastructures and capital equipment.

The *Société pour la mise en valeur de la Corse* was formed to reclaim, develop and irrigate 50,000 ha. in the malaria-infested plains of eastern Corsica.

The *Compagnie d'aménagement des Landes de Gascogne* (1956) was formed to reclaim 200,000 ha. of forest destroyed by fire and to substitute a more varied rural economy for the exclusive exploitation of the pine-forests.

The *Société du Canal de Provence*, by means

of a canal taken from the Verdon, is to irrigate 50,000 ha. and supply with water the town of Marseilles and the industries of the Étang de Berre.

The *Compagnie d'aménagement des coteaux de Gascogne* (1960) is to irrigate the slopes of the Lannemezan plateau, using the water of the Pyrenean mountain streams issuing from the Néouvielle massif.

The *Société des friches et taillis pauvres de l'Est* was formed to reclaim and redevelop 150,000 ha. of cultivable land, at present lying waste, on the limestone plateaux of twelve departments in the eastern part of the Paris basin.

The *Société d'économie mixte et d'étude pour la Communauté de la Loire et de ses affluents* (1962) covers eight departments. Its aim is to regularise the regime of rivers in the Loire basin by building barrage-dams, and to make this water available during dry periods, for irrigation, to make navigation easier and to develop industry.

Side by side with these companies, all similarly constituted, circumstances have given birth to organisations or institutions with different structures: the *Commission d'aménagement de la région de la Durance*, founded in 1951 by the Ministry of Reconstruction and Town Planning, to make possible the building of the Serre–Ponçon dam, and the *Association pour l'aménagement des marais de l'Ouest*, which groups syndicated associations under the *Génie Rural*. In this way larger and larger tracts have been taken over by organisations, often possessed of considerable authority and resources, which tend to unify these areas. Hydraulic and agricultural projects predominate, so that a tendency towards a river-basin structure appears. These companies have, however, met with variable success.

The *Land Capital Equipment Companies* are also 'mixed' companies, formed to carry out major infrastructural projects and the building of large housing estates. The majority of these depend on the powerful Central Association for Land Development (*Société Centrale pour l'Équipement du Territoire*).

ECONOMIC MISSIONS AND CODER

The administrative reforms of 1964 had important effects on regional action. They made the Prefect of a region the representative of the *Commissariat au Plan*, established a small but competent and effective 'economic mission' near his office and created a Commission for Regional Economic Development (CODER), a consultative regional assembly.

CRITICAL AREAS, REDEVELOPMENT AREAS AND AIDS TO INDUSTRIALISATION

The Government, unable to assist all the regions in France which, for one reason or another, were in real or potential difficulties, tried to limit its action to a few selected regions. Thus twenty-six 'critical areas' were defined (January 1956) and then eight 'redevelopment areas' singled out for special attention (March 1959). The criteria for the former were the existence of serious industrial unemployment, either actual or threatened, or of a surplus labour force coming from agriculture. The latter were areas with a vulnerable economy which had been hit by periods of slump. The redevelopment areas thus defined were, among others, those of Avesnes-Fourmies (Nord), Béthune (Pas-de-Calais), the Vosges valleys (Vosges and Bas-Rhin), Montpellier, Sète and Béziers (Hérault) and Limoges (Haute-Vienne); they were all former critical areas, to which were added those of Calais, Saint-Nazaire–Nantes and later (1961) Brest. Industrial enterprises which were established, enlarged or converted in these areas benefited from various tax reliefs, and especially from a capital-equipment grant of 15–20% of the sum of investments.

In actual fact this dual experiment was not very successful for several reasons: the limits of the specified areas were too restrictive and open to question, the criteria were ill-chosen and aid was given to firms which had no need of it. The Firestone plant at Béthune cost the Treasury more than 10 million francs. In 1964 these areas were superseded by a system of differential industrial development grants for all areas, ranging from those receiving no assistance at all to those receiving tax reliefs and 20% development grants.

C. Regional Development

PLANS AND REGIONAL DEVELOPMENT

The First Plan did not contain one paragraph alluding to the disparities between the French regions. In the Second Plan there appeared some arrangements for the development of depressed areas or those in a state of crisis. The regions thus enumerated were: the Gascony Landes, Languedoc, the Durance basin and the marshes of the Atlantic coast. But concern with the regions remained limited to these individual cases. The Third Plan gave a very general outline of a balanced development to take place throughout the country. Regional growth was, however, an essential part of the Fourth Plan, which was committed to an experiment in 'regionalisation' presented as 'a hopeful attempt'. The long-term objectives of this attempt were: liaison between national and regional plans, definition of the objectives of regional policy and practical participation by local authorities in decisions connected with the Plan.

In the Fifth Plan the symbiosis effected between the two levels of planning is described as 'the beginning of an era':

'In future the two concepts, national development and regional action, will automatically be taken into account in the making of decisions which hitherto would have applied only to particular sectors. A holistic approach to planning and national development permits the inclusion of provision for regional development in medium-term plans. Consequently, planned development should not consist merely of remedial measures designed to mitigate the effects of spontaneous growth; it must have dynamic objectives of its own.'

Two kinds of regional policy are defined by the Fourth and Fifth Plans in terms of the situation of the various regions:

1. A policy of partnership for strong regions.

2. A policy of leadership for weaker regions.

The *policy of partnership* applies to regions 'where agricultural, industrial and commercial expansion is occurring spontaneously and with sufficient vigour'. The State will confine itself to developing the infrastructures for the public services and capital equipment of all kinds to the required level, and giving some financial assistance to this 'autonomous' expansion, without undertaking any large-scale intervention. A typical case for this course of action is the Rhône valley, where the Government considers it sufficient to give support to private enterprise. Other regions thus treated are the East, Aquitaine and the South (where priority is given to the tourist industry). In all these cases the State is to intervene through limited public or semi-public investment—the 'scattering' of credit or priority investments, a little at a time.

The *policy of leadership* is intended for less favoured regions; state action will here 'change its character and become a policy of leadership, involving bolder anticipation of events and more substantial aid'. These areas, where the State has to 'strike the first blow', are, according to the Plan: Brittany and adjoining departments; the southern border of the Central Massif, that is to say, a crescent-shaped area with its extremities situated at Angoulême and Valence and its centre in the vicinity of Carcassonne; and the Nord–Pas-de-Calais region. In all three cases it is considered that in view of present or threatened unemployment, the State should intervene without waiting for the classical incentives or the efforts of private enterprise to take effect. The course of action recommended for the three selected areas obviously differs in each case, taking into account the current economic situation. In the Nord–Pas-de-Calais region, the obsolescence of the industrial structure and the radical transformations that are needed for such activities as the coal-mines are expected to set some difficult problems in future years. The objectives are simple: the creation of new industrial activities and the modernisation of the old towns. The case of Brittany is still more serious. During the summer of 1961, when the creation of a special redevelopment area at Brest was announced, the Government had tried to polarise Breton activity at three centres: Brest, for the Breton core of Brittany, Rennes and Saint-Nazaire–Nantes for the eastern and southern zones. The Government appealed directly to private enterprise, the major banks and organisations promoting the industrialisation of Brittany, encouraged the establishment of the electronics industry in the departments of Brittany and held over the region the threat of direct state intervention if private initiative should fail; and in this way tended to make Brittany a 'test case' for the policy of regional development.

The Fifth Plan made the division between the two sectors less rigid: 'Regional development policy must find a practical compromise between [the two types of policy]. In the first place it must give every opportunity, within a context of stiff economic competition, to strong regions whose potentialities can benefit the whole country. Secondly, it must try to promote development in weaker regions, to develop initially with outside aid but thereafter on their own.'

But the essential question, which was not solved in 1961, was that of the complete linking up of the re-equipment plan and the regional programmes, which remained a mere catalogue of requirements as long as the investments provided for were not regionalised. Since 1962 a procedure of 'operational regional compartments' has been instituted. These compartments give expression at the same time to the regional aspect of the national plan and to the quadrennial arrangements for the implementation of the regional plans. They define, in the context of the regional programmes, the speed at which the programmes will be carried out, the order of priority of the operations and the methods of financing them, and permit the regional breakdown of the Budget, which was first attempted in 1964. But this enterprise shows how extremely difficult it is to apply such

measures in a country which is politically, administratively and financially centralised, and we find in the regional compartment system the sum of the faults of the plan and of the regional programmes as well as the sum of their good qualities. Certain leading figures in Brittany have proposed another procedure, namely a special Act to deal with planning in Brittany. The text of this Act (*Projet de IIe plan breton et de loi-programme*) has been worked out by M. Phlipponneau, a geographer, and is a very complete document.

P. Bauchet has clearly revealed the defects of the Plan from the point of view of spatial reorganisation:

'In making economic decisions, geographical considerations have been taken into account only in rudimentary fashion, despite the analysis of labour movements by regions, and the localisation of certain branches of activity. We cannot yet decide on the best location for most branches of activity, or choose between moving men to industries or moving industries to reserves of man-power.'

INSTITUTIONS OF REGIONAL PLANNING

On 15th February 1963 a series of decrees appeared in the Official Gazette creating, in particular, a General Delegation for National Development and Regional Action, and a National Development Commission (*Commission Nationale d'Aménagement du Territoire—C.N.A.T.*). This institution put an end to the duality which had existed from the beginning between the *Commissariat* for the Plan, on the one hand, and the *Conseil Supérieur* for public works and the National Development Board of the Ministry of Works, on the other.

'This delegation will be an organisation for co-ordination and encouragement. In terms of the general objectives stated in the Plan, its role will be to prepare and co-ordinate the necessary data for governmental decisions on national development and regional action, and to see that all technical administrative bodies co-ordinate their respective actions in this sphere and use every means at their disposal to attain the objectives which collectively cover more than the activities of

any one body. The Delegate-general is responsible for execution and application of the
plan, but the *Commissariat*, assisted in its work
by a National Development Commission, is
responsible for development research and the
integration of its findings in plans for economic
and social development.'

The first report of the C.N.A.T. was published
in September 1964. The report and publications of the C.N.A.T. revived the chief
recommendations of the national development plan which had been proposed in 1961
but not adopted.

The substance of the plan

The justification offered for the Plan is similar
to that for the social and economic development plans, but with two changes in orientation: the former looks farther ahead than the
four- or five-year periods of the latter—'in
1985 France will be a country with 60 million
inhabitants'—and takes a predominantly geographical point of view. 'France suffers . . .
from an increasing lack of economic and
demographic balance. Her capital is the
only true metropolitan centre. Two thirds
of the country turns its back on the more
advanced parts of Europe, and the technical
and economic backwardness of these areas is
becoming more pronounced as their former
prosperity fades.'

'If a great and effective effort is not soon
made to remedy this lack of economic and
demographic balance, it will be practically
impossible to offer new jobs to young people
except in limited areas (the Paris region and
about twenty departments already associated
with the most highly developed part of
Europe) unless they look farther afield, in
foreign countries.' The north-eastern part of
France will be absorbed into a Europe dominated by Germany, while the regions on the
periphery, losing more each day of their
wealth in goods and men, are more and more
deserving of the epithet of 'French population
desert'. 'According to whether or not a clear
and courageous land development policy is
undertaken in time, France will either become
part of the powerful zone of Europe or will

separate from it and join the depressed areas
of the South.' The introduction to the report
brings out clearly the twofold lack of balance
of the country: 'that of the North-east in
comparison with the South-west, and that of
the country as a whole compared with the
Paris region'.

The Plan traces 'for two decades the general
outlines of a balanced development of the
population and economic life of the country
as a whole'. Its preoccupations are expressed
not in terms of economic growth but of different types of development:

1. Development of the urban framework.
At present this is inadequate, badly distributed with a poorly developed hierarchy (cf.
Part Six); its equipment is inadequate and its
planning is archaic. The plan endeavours to
work out a hierarchy comprising: metropolitan centres, regional centres, principal
urban centres. One conclusion emerges from
all the studies and research carried out; that
this policy presupposes the development of a
small number of regions round a few powerful
regional capitals each of which is a true
provincial metropolis. This action should
not only give new life to the French provinces
but also counterbalance overdevelopment in
Paris. Analyses readily distinguish eight or
nine metropolitan regions around Paris:
Lille, Nancy, Lyons, Marseilles, Toulouse,
Bordeaux, Nantes and Clermont-Ferrand.
But this list at once raises problems and
excites strong reactions because Rennes,
Rouen, Le Havre, Dijon and other towns have
been excluded (cf. Part Four).

Lack of urban development in the provinces
during the last hundred years and the uneven
distribution of the towns make this question
of selection and promotion a very delicate
problem. Roads and railways are insufficient, and these towns often function in-
adequately, if at all, as regional capitals.
What is more, it is not certain that the
provincial centres command wide enough
spheres of influence to cover the country completely. The zone which Paris dominates as a
regional capital is considerable, Lille, Cler-

mont-Ferrand, Nancy and Rheims being the nearest major centres. Undoubtedly the urbanisation of France needs a solution better adapted to its own particular characteristics.

2. *Development of industry*, considered in terms of localisation (and thus decentralisation), diversification, size of factories, labour movement, balance between male and female labour, and relations with rural areas.

3. *Development of agriculture*, the chief needs being improvement in agricultural management, collective and individual capital equipment, the creation of rural centres, the consolidation of land holdings and large-scale regional development.

4. *Development of communications*. Here the emphasis is on freeing the road and rail networks from their absolute dependence on Paris by creating inter-regional and cross-country links or by modernising them where they exist.

Finally, the Plan pays special attention to *land-ownership reform*. 'If this problem is not quickly solved, not only will no ordered development plan be applicable, but before very long there will be an insuperable obstacle to all effective action on the part of the public authorities in every sphere, and the country will lose all hope of playing a useful part in technical and economic progress, and will condemn itself first to stagnation, then to recession.' The question of land ownership, because of the existence of excessively large private estates and of speculation in land, bedevils all proposals for urban development, the establishment of publicly owned factories and the protection of sites.

OBSTACLES AND DIFFICULTIES OF REGIONAL PLANNING

After more than a decade we have to point out that the many statistics published on the national development policy have shown very little change in the essentials of the problem; the results of the last census are sufficiently convincing proof of this (see p. 119). Many reasons can be given for this mild setback.

The initial delay. We have had to wait fifteen years, ever since the Liberation, for regional planning to be accepted as one of the two branches of the French planning system, on the same level as economic planning; and further, for the realisation that the latter presupposed the former. Leaving aside its most devoted supporters, regional planning in the beginning appeared to be a mere pastime or whim of a few experts in the field of human studies, town planning, sociology and geography, who had taken upon themselves the task of reconstructing France and her regions; it seemed in any case less urgently necessary and more 'theoretical' because it was more social than economic. Costs are less easily estimated in social than in economic terms, so that the regional aspect of development is often less easy to recognise as a fundamental one. We tend to underestimate social and cultural needs and to ignore differences in outlook and significant regional differences.

The extent of inertia. Since the industrial revolution, France has undergone no re-planning in the light of internal population movements, technical progress or regional contrasts. At present the same deficiencies are appearing simultaneously in all the regions, and may be expected to reach their climax in the very near future. 'Because of the very fact of these accumulated delays, the need for a national development policy is too great for any regional discrimination to be possible. Needs are imperative over the entire country, regardless of varying states of progress . . . we must pay the price of our neglect in the past' (P. Lamour).

The present situation has become so unbalanced in favour of the Paris region that the planners can find no 'hooks' in the provinces on which they can safely hang a policy for restoring equilibrium. Compared with Paris, no town carries sufficient weight; and thus Paris acts as a sort of magnet, to its continual advantage. Some points of view in favour of Paris, which appear disconcerting at first sight, are thus understandable even if one does not share them. Any plan aimed at restricting the growth of Paris for the sake of an uncertain growth in the provinces is seen as an attack on the development of the country as a whole and on the immediate profits to be derived from it.

This inertia is present not only in actual deeds but also in states of mind. A policy of growth can exist only if it is desired, demanded and properly thought out and applied; and those in authority in past generations have not necessarily felt the benefits of regional planning. What is more, the consequences of such policies may be harmful to their interests and to those of the region; so naturally there is opposition.

Handicaps arising from the objectives. As regards objectives, over and above these uncertainties about methods, there is the fact that a policy presupposes a philosophical theory of national growth centred on the satisfaction of human needs and aiming at an optimum distribution of the population; but it is almost inevitable that priority will be given to the satisfaction of economic needs. One must take constant care not to lose sight of the reality of regional planning; it 'cannot be equated with town planning which is its local version, applying to the limited area of a town or a group of closely linked communes, nor with economic planning which it uses as an instrument, nor with decentralisation which is a means of action, nor with land development which is the final outcome' (Pierre Randet).

Though the merging of these two modes of action, economic planning and regional planning, holds out hopes for better synchronisation, we have equal reason to fear changes in the spirit underlying development plans. They form a long-term 'geography of the future' based on permanent decisions and an unchanging basic purpose, very different from economic action which is necessarily short-term because it has to take the national and international situation into account. The prospect of high returns which will not only be short-term but also tangible, and expressed in terms of finance, is likely to carry more weight than that of far-distant returns calculated partly in terms of social improvement.

Regional planning demands considerable persistence and a strong conviction in order to resist the opposing influence of those who would willingly accept a general impoverishment of France for the advantage of a few urban or regional centres or of a few lowlands and valleys. Though France really does need some strong focal points, together with a closer and more modern infrastructure, her past history and her present natural conditions do not appear to make it desirable to reduce the area of land inhabited and exploited; in the first place, because of the value of capital invested in the smallest of her cantons and represented by fields which many generations have manured and protected against erosion, by buildings and by communications; in the second place, because the population recovery is increasing the number of young people in some of these regions, and a policy to keep them in the region appears desirable; and in the third place, because we cannot prejudice the future of a region when we do not know what its assets will be in twenty-five years.

Action to be taken through regional planning can be seen in terms of location, scale and interrelationships.

Locations for urban development, towns, factories or agricultural enterprises are usually determined by theories as yet scarcely defined, which, applied to reality, come into conflict with numerous social and political situations.

Scale. Progress in regional planning is hindered by a lack of satisfactory replies to questions which are or should be asked as to the optimum size for towns, urban centres, housing estates, villages and farms.

Interrelationships. National planning is not achieved by simply juxtaposing or superimposing measures for agriculture, town planning, industry and transport. Planning means having a coherent vision which takes into account all the country's diverse elements. Administrative and educational decentralisation is only one of the aspects of such a policy; if people are trained, steps must also be taken to find employment for them.

The building of a motorway should not be undertaken only to link two widely separated towns; it should transform the regions it crosses, break their isolation, feed the towns and inject fresh life into them.

We would say that the result of a real policy of national development would be to define the appearance of France in the year 2000, or, more exactly, the progressive landscape changes which are to be desired. Development plans should give a preview of the spatial organisation of the country, which is very different from simply defining the course of a motorway, or planning the building of a university or the extension of an urban development zone. One cannot discuss national development without defining the broad lines of this man-made geography, or without making and justifying the choice between the possible alternative distribution patterns of population density, industrial establishments, infrastructures and regional farming types in the France of tomorrow.

Handicaps arising from methods. The difficulties are no less great from the point of view of methods. It is, in fact, easier to act on economic structures and mechanisms than on areal patterns. For example, it is easier to influence the price of agricultural products than to speed up the consolidation of land holdings, or, going further still, to start off a really radical reform of a region's agriculture.

National planning needs more precise methods, better co-ordinated from the point of view of time and space, and thus more authoritarian and apparently more coercive because they affect more people and the structure of spatial organisations; it demands arbitration between regions, and differential measures appropriate to each region, which is repugnant to the French temperament. The methods adopted in regional planning are often confused with those of regional economic planning; they are legislative and financial in nature, and cover a very wide sphere. But they have the disadvantage of being too widely dispersed, which can result either in precipitate actions that ignore other measures affecting exactly the same locality or in scattered and badly co-ordinated actions.

Experts increasingly raise objections to this method of taking action at many widely dispersed points. Instead of this they propose a system of 'centres of attraction'. In a small number of places an organisation providing for housing, training and jobs is set up quickly and with careful co-ordination. This provides a strong attraction, and the living and working conditions of the whole of the town concerned and its sphere of influence are thereby transformed. The first decisions, taken in 1963, fell far short of this kind of co-ordinated action. Thus, of the first grant of 120 million francs to the *Fonds d'intervention pour l'aménagement du territoire*, the 44·5 million francs released was used for the financing of three establishments for technical education, sports grounds and youth centres, part of the automatic telephone equipment of the Mediterranean coast, the fight against mosquitoes in Languedoc, etc.[20] Nevertheless, year by year, the substantial size of grants from the fund, the growing awareness of the benefits derived from a national planning policy and the very specific localisation of interventions have given appreciable help to the West, the South-east, the Centre, the East and the North.

15. The only expressions of this feeling to survive were of the 'autonomist' type, associated with a conservative attitude of mind which could only serve to accentuate centralisation.

16. Roncayolo, 'Inégalité géographique en France', *Les cahiers de la République*, January 1963, pp. 56–67.

17. The index represents the ratio for each region: one thousandth of the French income over one thousandth of the French population.

18. All too often the only form of regional action known to the central authority was the non-recoverable subsidy without guarantee obtained by the most politically influential regions.

19. 'The Regional Development Associations generally act as a screen for the big organisations in Paris' (P. Bauchet, *La Planification française, op. cit.*, p. 68).

20. The forerunner of the *Fonds d'intervention* was the *Fonds National d'Aménagement du Territoire*, created in 1950 to grant loans to towns and to chambers of commerce.

3. INVESTMENTS

Every country both produces and consumes its revenue; the work of its inhabitants, whether in agriculture, industry or commerce, endows it with a certain wealth in the form of income, profits and salaries. The needs of these same inhabitants absorb the whole or part of this income. Their expenses are partly consumer expenses, food, clothing, rent, recreation and taxes; and partly investments, such as the building of a house or factory, or the buying of a field or the tools of a trade—a tractor, a car or a combine harvester. Such investments entail changes in spatial organisation either directly or indirectly by altering the means by which such organisation is achieved. Investments are made by individuals, local or departmental bodies (such as communes and departments), the State and private associations (commercial and industrial firms). Private investments may be French or from foreign countries.

Apart from their normal resources, the State, collective bodies and firms depend upon the savings of individuals and bank capital to finance their investments. Savings, taxation and self-finance thus provide the bulk of investments. The Frenchman is a born saver; money-boxes, savings banks and the *lessiveuses* of the last war are intimately associated with the outlook and way of life of the French. The Frenchman's idea of fortune—thrift, rather—is more static than dynamic, more Latin than Anglo-Saxon; he is not interested so much in created wealth, invested in factories, houses or commercial enterprises, as in money as such. He wants cash, and prefers an investment which assures a regular return to a long-term speculation. The accumulation of wealth, combined with this state of mind, explains why the French were universal creditors before 1914.

Self-finance is the essence of private investment; it is the most direct type, and consists of the use of part of the profits for investments which will ensure the continuation or expansion of the firm. But the disadvantages of this method become more and more evident as economic planning develops.

'Self-finance is an extra cost paid for by the consumer, that is, mainly by the wage-earners. It is a short cut to inequality because it gives the shareholder, in the form of greater wealth, what should go to the consumer in the form of price cuts, and at the same time this wealth is concentrated in the hands of a few. It can also cause a lack of economic balance, or even a recession, in so far as it breaks the traditional circle of savings and investments. Finally, self-finance, by leaving enterprises in full control of their own decision-making, increases their independence with regard to the plan' (A. Chalandon).[21]

In a liberal economy, foreign investments always represent a variable part of total investments. The fact that a country attracts foreign capital is a sign of economic health and a privileged position among other states. Such investments represent a considerable contribution to be added to national investments, but at the same time they are a danger. Interests held abroad in a national firm represent an alienation of the agricultural, industrial and commercial capital of the country. Economic decisions are taken by head offices thousands of kilometres away, without consideration of national interests or of the economic course laid down by a plan.

Finally, in default of appropriate legislation, the fruits of this foreign investment, by being repatriated, can pass out of the hands of the State; thus, in order to attract foreign capital, France has adopted a more liberal legislation since 1958; foreigners can repatriate the product of sales and services, incomes from investment and interest. By their financial power, big foreign companies bring about large concentrations with numerous consequences, such as the closing of factories, changes in the range of production and shifting of head offices.

The problem is made more delicate still by the progressive building up of the Common Market. In order to cover a market of the size of Common Market Europe, foreign firms can choose between member states without being troubled by differences in price and exchange because these are to be brought into line; nor are they troubled by customs duties, which may no longer exist in 1970. The determining factors, then, are geographical—situation and environment—social and financial. Thus there is keen competition to attract capital, which will give rise to employment and financial returns. In 1964 the sources of investment were as follows: public funds, 18·5%; the stock market, 8·8%; medium-term credit, 7·8%; loans from specialised bodies, 14·6%; own resources (autofinance and dividends from other resources), 50·3%.

A. The Amount and Financing of Investments

A considerable mass of investments arose from the industrial and urban changes of the last century; the great period of 1860–1913 saw the exploitation of mines and the construction of rail networks, canals, urban dwellings and factories. But French savings already looked abroad. Loans to Russia, in South America and elsewhere, absorbed a large part of liquid assets, to the detriment of France herself and the stockholders. It has been estimated that from 1892 to 1913 French capital abroad represented between a third and a half of total savings.[22] In 1913 French credit abroad rose to 45,000 million francs, about 13,500,000 million old francs (1955). Thus there was set off an imperceptible but progressive process of reduction in home investments, which reached its climax between 1929 and 1936; capital equipment and infrastructures were not renewed or modernised; legislation on rents prevented any extensive replacement of private houses; the population standstill and economic protectionism made it unnecessary to adopt a policy of development and thus of investments.

Immediately after the Second World War, widespread destruction of the infrastructure, factories and towns called for considerable and immediate investments, adding to the pre-war backwardness. The Marshall Plan, from which most European nations benefited, brought to France $3,000 million in cash and in kind (such as ships and locomotives). Of this sum, only $209 million were loans (these were paid back by 1962); the importance and the salutary effect of this aid cannot be denied.[23] The amount of investments is calculated in relation to the national product; a more realistic picture of productive investments is obtained if we leave out administrative investments and housing.

From 1949 to 1955 France allotted on average less than 20% of the value of her gross national product to investment expenditure; from 1956 to 1963 she allotted a little over 20%. During the same period in Germany, Italy and Holland, this proportion varied from 22 to 25%, reaching 35% in Japan; experts consider 25% to be the threshold level, so that France suffers from under-investment, both in absolute terms and in relation to the great industrial nations. This under-investment is accentuated by the fact that the growth in investments often involves those sectors which are not directly productive, as in the case of water schemes for tourism and winter sports resorts.

The stabilisation plan (1964–5) led to a further fall in investments during the last few months of the fourth plan, especially in investments by firms.

Foreign capital invested in France amounted to 739·2 million francs in 1960 and rose to 2,090·6 million francs in 1964; the United States and neighbouring states in Europe, such as West Germany, Great Britain and Switzerland (through which U.S. capital also passes) are the principal investors, the United States taking a firm lead. Table XXIII indicates

TABLE XXIII. U.S. INVESTMENTS IN FRANCE AND THE COMMON MARKET
(in millions of dollars)

	France	Common Market
1950	217	637
1957	464	1,680
1958	546	1,908
1960	741	2,208
1962	1,006	2,644
1964	1,446	5,398
1965	1,584	6,256

the accrued amount of U.S. investments in France and in the Common Market.

But this internationalisation of investments does not only concern private capital; from its foundation until 1961, the *Banque européenne d'investissements*, created within the framework of the European Economic Community, financed twenty regional undertakings, representing $154 million.

B. The Distribution of Investments

Table XXIV shows the allocation of investments for 1963 and how they were financed. It will be noted that investments are

of France has been carried out in the last hundred years by the introduction not only of machines, techniques and engineers but also of capital, from England, Belgium, Germany or farther afield. Some of the iron-mines in Lorraine, for example, have been the property of foreign interests for a long time: Belgian iron and steel companies, such as Providence (6,850 ha. and 4,500,000 tons) and Cockerill Ougrèe (5,590 ha. and 4,677,000 tons), and companies from Luxembourg and the Saar. Similarly, powerful foreign aluminium firms (Aluminium Ltd. of Canada and the Swiss company A.I.A.G.) hold large interests in the bauxite deposits.

TABLE XXIV. FINANCING OF INVESTMENTS IN 1963 (%)

	Amount of in millions of francs	State	Financial establishments	Medium-term credit	Stock Market	Other resources redeemable and self-financing
Fuel and power . . .	10,103	49·4	1·8	0·8	14·1	33·9
Including						
Electricity . . .	4,253	37·4		1·7	31·3	29·6
Oil . . .	1,371	7·3	3·3	0·9	5·2	83·3
Coal-mines . . .	977	6·1				95·0
Iron and steel . . .	2,406		7·6	2·1	21·8	68·5
Chemicals	2,755		8·8	1·4	29·1	60·7
Mechancial and electrical industries	5,775		4·0	3·1	16·6	76·3
Building and construction materials	3,224		2·1	4·7	5·5	87·7
Transport	6,934	20·4	8·4		15·7	56·3
Agriculture	4,517	10·7	63·2	6·0		20·1
Agricultural industries .	2,050	1·9	12·3	1·9	11·6	72·3

financed in very different ways according to their source. The private sector predominates in the major industries—except the chemical industries—commerce, and the mineral-oil industry. Foreign capital comes from the creation of subsidiary companies, branches and shareholding companies, and the granting of licences. Very often this capital is used to take over existing companies which come under the control of American, English or German companies.

But although the presence of foreign capital in France has become more obvious since the Liberation because of the quantities in which it has poured in and the spectacular takeovers of French enterprises, it has always been one of the characteristic elements of French economy; a large part of the industrialisation

Investments in the private sector can be influenced only indirectly, by credit, various monetary advantages, differential tariffs or bargains made with the authorities. But such action is limited in the last resort, and M. Claudius Petit could write in 1959: 'The State appears to have no influence on investments in the private sector, even when they co-operate to reach the targets of the Plan.' This freedom left to investors has led to changes, but also to duplication and waste, and to decisions contrary to the national interest; logically, investments favour sectors where short-term returns are assured, neglecting those where returns are long-term or poor. The public sector, that is to say, the State and various collective organisations under its sway, largely controls fuel and power, and, to a lesser degree, transport and the large sector of investments known as 'non-productive'. Public investments (as part of authorised programmes) in 1962 and 1963 are shown, divided into broad sectors, in Table XXV.

TABLE XXV. DISTRIBUTION OF
INVESTMENTS IN THE PUBLIC SECTOR
(in millions of francs)

	1962	1963
Agriculture	1,233	1,556
Industry	73	112
Fuel and power . . .	1,285	1,472
Cultural and social . . .	2,838	3,567
Transport and communications	2,799	3,268
Housing	3,484	3,798
Overseas and miscellaneous (excluding Algeria)	1,184	1,355

Note that the sums thus provided for can be balanced in the Budget and not laid out in their entirety during the fiscal period.

In fact, as Table XXIV shows, the sources of finance cut across one another; though some sectors can invest in a closed circuit, most need to have recourse to loans, for example, from public funds. The possibilities for self-financing in agriculture appear to be limited, which explains the large amount of indebtedness among farmers. As it is impossible to satisfy all demands and needs at the same time and in the same place, we have to establish an order of priority for investments, and to make selections; that is to say, an investment policy is necessary. When the total of investments from public funds falls below the critical minimum because of the calls of other political items on the Budget, the State finds it necessary either to reduce investments considerably (in 1958 the whole hydraulic programme of the E.D.F. was cancelled) or to have recourse to borrowing, or to transfer investments either into the hands of the private sector, which has now been done for housing and motorways, or into the hands of local public authorities. This policy of 'debudgetisation' has become very important since 1965.

It would seem logical for certain investments to have absolute priority; the building of roads, hospitals, schools, houses and

G

research centres, the improvement of electricity and other services, the modernisation of ports, slum clearance and the expansion of centres of higher education are essential to the progress of a nation. In fact, under a capitalist regime, even one which is subject to a certain amount of planning control as in France, basic investments take second place to the satisfaction of consumer needs. People think more about the profitability of an investment than its absolute necessity. Even in governmental and administrative circles, investments are decided upon according to questionable standards of economic value and the prospect of returns; an investments policy presupposes that the general trend will remain constant, not be decided afresh by the budget vote every year. Selection of investments, too, depends on the date of their realisation—short-, medium- or long-term— and the period in which they will give maximum returns.

Where demographic and economic growth are at a standstill, investments are required only to renew, on the same scale as before, infrastructures and capital equipment reaching the end of its useful life. Where there is expansion, the problems are much more complex; investments must be adapted to the needs of a growing population which is becoming at the same time richer, and therefore more demanding; its needs are no longer the same. In the case of long-term investments the choices of those in authority are complicated by technical factors. It is not possible accurately to predict progress and methodological revolutions which may occur in housing (new materials), transport, foodstuffs and conditions of work. For this reason it is desirable to allow for a positive margin with respect to contemporary norms. Motorists in Paris in the 20th century owe the fact that they can still circulate to the enterprise of Haussmann, those in Versailles to the policies of Louis XIV. Projects which at the time appear risky, too expensive or out of proportion to contemporary needs can turn out to be excellent investments some decades later.

Conversely, the fact that in the past essential investments were not made but repeatedly postponed or made on a niggardly scale has proved a heavy burden for present society, which has to requisition and demolish in order to rebuild. On the whole, failure or delay in investment is much more costly than anticipation; it is to be preferred that present generations should inherit an invested capital, the legacy of past generations, than that they should first have to invest in what their fathers ought to have created before they can turn towards the future. The choice of investments implies a policy of co-ordination; they must be complementary, not contradictory, let alone competitive; any policy of agricultural investment which is going to speed up the reduction in agricultural population in the fairly near future must be linked with a policy for absorbing immigrants from the country into the towns by providing houses and training schemes for other occupations. To sum up, it falls to the State to make investments without returns or with long-term returns only, and to see that long-term investments are carried out.

C. Location of Investments

The final aspect, a very important one for a geographical analysis, is that of location. Whether public or private investments are in question, the first condition of their being made is that they should pay dividends; the money invested should bring the greatest possible return within a reasonable time. Obviously investments are more 'productive' in a well-equipped region with strong urban development, a satisfactory infrastructure and a high concentration of consumers, whether factories or individuals. Thus, for example, 1,000 million francs invested in the expansion of the iron and steel industry in Lorraine or the North will in the short run be more remunerative and more productive than the same amount used to prospect and exploit the iron-ore deposits in Brittany.

Investments, infrastructures, capital equipment, factories and men thus tend gradually to become more concentrated, and a small number of growth and development centres arise. This has the effect of increasing regional contrasts between regions of growing

TABLE XXVI. REGIONAL DISTRIBUTION OF PUBLIC INVESTMENTS (1967)*

Planning regions	% Population 1962	Francs per head	Regional ranking
1. Paris region	18·2	201·94	1
2. Rhône–Alps	8·6	161·84	3
3. North	7·9	104·82	20
4. Provence–Corsica	6·7	147·16	4
5. Loire region	5·3	118·05	17
6. Brittany	5·2	120·75	16
7. Aquitaine	5	114·75	19
8. Lorraine	4·7	117·66	18
9. Basse-Normandie	2·6	125·35	13
10. South–Pyrenees	4·4	142·02	6
11. Central France	4	130·92	9
12. Picardy	3·2	126·38	12
13. Languedoc	3·3	126·44	11
14. Poitou and Charente	3·1	135·78	7
15. Burgundy	3·1	124·26	14
16. Haute-Normandie	3	143·34	5
17. Alsace	2·8	175·65	2
18. Auvergne	2·7	131·43	8
19. Champagne	2·6	121·82	15
20. Franche-Comté	2	98·81	21
21. Limousin	1·6	129·44	10
Total or national mean	100	143·78	

* Regionalised credits in 14 sections of budget.

population and those where it is dwindling, between rich regions and poor regions. Below certain threshold levels an absolute disorganisation of the region ensues; paralysis strikes at its very nerve-centres.

The history of the years 1900–40 is one of reduced investments in the provinces and particularly in rural areas; in this sphere the centralising influence of Paris has been decisive; the Parisian banks have drained away capital from the provinces. Ministerial decisions taken in Paris determine the use and localisation of this capital. In a sense the flow of agricultural capital into the towns has probably been more serious than that of the inhabitants. It is hard to imagine the colossal amount of rural savings transferred abroad through loans and investments during these decades. The farmers were never encouraged in any way to invest in the work of their own communes.

Since investment of any kind is the motive power behind area development, it would obviously be interesting to analyse its volume for each region, department or commune in the same way as population densities are studied; but until recently it was practically impossible to know the exact amount of investments made in a given region. The first study on the regionalisation of investments was carried out and published by the Economic Council in 1962. A greater step forward came with the publication by regions of part of the 1964 budget.

Table XXVI shows a number of percentages and amounts which help to drive home the great disparities between regions in the ratio of investments to population. Whether we are considering the sum of investments, their apportionment or their regional and local distribution, the necessity for co-ordinated action becomes more and more obvious; otherwise we shall run counter to all policies of planning and development. A real investment policy is called for, based on a national investment bank. A partial but significant step was taken in December 1962 by the creation of a committee on agricultural investments, attached to the Ministry of Agriculture. But this fundamental question of investments will soon have to be considered and dealt with on a European scale; both public and private investments can then be co-ordinated, and concerted action taken to help such regions of Europe as may be underprivileged or in difficulty.

21. *Le Monde*, 30th May 1962.
22. Money lent or borrowed abroad in relation to the total savings was as follows: 1892, 36·8%; 1895, 59·2%; 1904, 66·3%; 1910, 58·7%; 1930, 5·03%.
23. Among the beneficiaries of Marshall Aid were the rolling-mills of Sollac and Usinor, numerous steel-works, thermal power stations, dams, refineries, ports and the railways.

PART THREE
THE INFRASTRUCTURES

I

THE ADMINISTRATIVE INFRASTRUCTURE

The basic administrative infrastructure is the overall pattern of administrative divisions which provide the framework for local government—communes, cantons, *arrondissements* and departments. These were defined at the beginning of the 19th century, and often followed the lines of older divisions—the parishes, bailiwicks (*bailliages*), *généralités* and provinces of the *Ancien Régime*, and even the *civitates* and the *pagi* of ancient Gaul. Their limits and their dimensions are determined by a mixture of natural and historical frontiers and purely artificial lines which were drawn to form administrative areas appropriate to the transport facilities of the day, since no commune could be more than a day's journey from the chief town of the area.

1. DEPARTMENTS

The geographical role of the division into departments has been a very important one although it has been little analysed. The departments have caused the selective development of certain towns by giving greater opportunities for growth and for the expansion of tertiary functions, administrative centres or *préfectures*. France may now regret that she has no large regional capitals, but the responsibility for this rests with the ninety-five departments, each of which favoured the growth of a small 'big town' with a limited sphere of influence. Road and rail networks, and in fact all the life of the districts, have these prefecture-towns as their focal points. Despite their small areas (the average area of a department is 6,130 km²), the administrative services of the *préfectures* have not been uniformly beneficial to all parts of their departments. Owing to the lack of intermediate towns, and of Members of Parliament or powerful department councillors, border areas a long way from the department-town often had less in the way of investments or capital equipment than nearer districts.

The departments have been greatly criticised on account of their irrational pattern and their anachronistic small size. These characteristics have created anomalies that have led to excessive costs and conflicting interests. The largest provincial town has one of the smallest departments (Rhône, 2,859 km.²), and the department of Isère, which extends right up to Lyons, is not at all concerned with the extension of the town on to its territory. Vienne, which is 25 km. from Lyons, comes under Grenoble for administrative purposes. Certain departments such as Nord, with its elongated and 'wasp-waisted' shape, have a particularly unfortunate irregularity; but the division of Seine-et-Oise into six departments (1964) may be the beginning of a policy to adjust the departmental divisions to the new demographic conditions. Many efforts have been made to establish a more suitable administrative hierarchy. The planning regions (*régions programmes*—Part Two), which form a basis for all regroupings of administrative areas, answer this need, but all these attempts at reform inevitably harm those towns that survive only by reason of their administrative functions (such as Privas, the department-town of Ardèche), towns which would dwindle to nothing if local government were concentrated in fewer and larger units.[1]

1. Even if they lost their administrative functions, the departments should be retained for statistical purposes; otherwise we should be unable to make comparisons with over a century and a half of statistics.

2. COMMUNES

The way in which an area is divided for administrative purposes, in particular its smallest unit areas, is of considerable importance in its spatial organisation. In the case of a long-inhabited country such as France, the communes correspond to ancient divisions. Each commune represents a historical functional unit—the farmlands of the primitive communities which cleared and began to cultivate the land. These tracts of land formed the basis of parish boundaries, mostly fixed before the year 1000, at the end of the great christianising movement of the later Middle Ages. Then later on, new parishes were formed in the large forested areas that remained uncleared, but they covered comparatively small areas and were of short duration.

It is first and foremost within the framework of the communes that the French people live and plan their way of life and their activities. Here investments are localised and here the decisions of higher bodies are put into practice. French society as a whole is divided into as many rural or urban communities as there are communes. Finally, like all phenomena which, small in themselves, occur uniformly over a vast area, the communes express in their own ways the many natural and human influences which determined their sizes, their boundaries and their shapes.

The first thing to be noticed about the network of communes is the small size of the units. In 1962 France was divided into 37,954 communes, with a mean area of 1,428 ha. and a mean population of 1,224. These means obviously conceal a great variety of areas and populations—which is the second characteristic of the French system of com-

munes. The two largest communes in France share the Rhône delta: Arles (70,820 ha.) and Saintes-Maries-de-la-Mer (36,952 ha.). The smallest communes are Mont-Dauphin (2·16 ha.) in Hautes-Alpes, and Castelmoront-d'Albret in Gironde (2·82 ha.). Classification according to size gives the following table (for 1954):

Less than 100 ha.	104
From 100 to 249 ha.	1,050
From 250 to 499 ha.	5,291
From 500 to 999 ha.	11,994
From 1,000 to 1,499 ha.	7,630
From 1,500 to 1,999 ha.	4,336
From 2,000 to 4,999 ha.	6,707
From 5,000 to 9,999 ha.	768
From 10,000 ha. and over	119

Table XV[2] gives the classification of communes according to population; the communes of less than 500 inhabitants, which represent 63% of the total number of communes, have only 11·8% of the population. At the other extreme, 36·8% of the population live in the communes of more than 10,000 inhabitants, and 18·4% of the population are in thirty-two communes. This situation shows up the paradox of a population whose distribution has been completely transformed while the administrative divisions remain unchanged.

A. Large and Small Communes

It was not until 1958 that a precise picture of the network of French communes was provided by a map drawn up in the cartographic laboratory of the *École Pratique des Hautes-Études*. Diagrammatically, a line drawn from the bay of Mont-Saint-Michel to

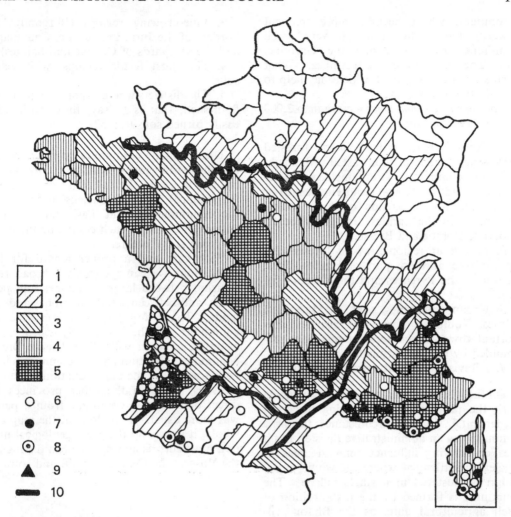

Fig. 51. Mean areas of communes by departments (in 1936). (Source: A. Meynier, *Ann. de Géog.*, no. 295, 1945, p. 163)

1. From 7 to 10 km². 2. From 10 to 15 km². 3. From 15 to 20 km². 4. From 20 to 25 km². 5. From 25 to 44 km². Very large communes. 6. From 10,000 to 15,000 ha. 7. From 15,000 to 20,000 ha. 8. From 20,000 to 30,000 ha. 9. Over 30,000 ha. 10. Limits of the zones of large and of small communes.

Grenoble by way of Orleans, Morvan and the Rhône valley separates the part of France with small communes to the north from that with large communes to the south, but the main interest of the map is that it demonstrates from a new point of view the extraordinary variety of France (figs. 51 and 52).

In the South-west, for example, there are very marked contrasts; the large communes of the Pyrenees are interspersed, even within the mountain range itself, with clusters of very small communes. On the margins of the Pyrenees, from the Basque country to Roussillon, there is a very dense network of communes leaving little room for large communes, which become more frequent towards the north, although very small communes reappear along the Garonne, from Toulouse to the Bec d'Ambez. What correlations can we make which may help to explain these contrasts?

The *very large communes*—more than 2,000 ha.—correspond to:

1. Forest areas, either where forested communes are sharply contrasted with neighbouring communes (Fontainebleau, Locquignol-Forêt de Mormal and Haguenau) or where the forest extends over the whole region, as in the Landes, Sologne, Vosges, Morvan, Dombe and Bresse.
2. Mountain regions, where forests also appear (the northern part of Hautes-Alpes, Provence, the Pyrenees and the Vosges—fig. 52).
3. Urban communes, such as Marseilles, Nîmes, Toulouse, Paris, but also less important towns which were at one time surrounded by belts of farmland.
4. Alluvial zones, salt marshes and polders.

On the whole, the large communes coincide with the parts of France having dispersed settlement.[3] In these circumstances the large commune as an administrative division has a weaker unifying influence than in areas of nucleated settlement where the whole population is clustered in a single village. The commune is formed by the juxtaposition of such agricultural units as the Breton 'villages', hamlets and isolated farms. In Brittany the parishes took shape after the population was established, and the *bourgs* themselves are more recent than the communes. Large communes (1,000–2,000 ha.) predominate in the Armorican massif and the Central Massif.

The *small communes* correspond to:

1. Intramontane valleys (Grésivaudan).
2. Fertile depressions between plateaux or mountains less favourable to agriculture, such as the marginal depression of the Morvan, Limagne and Balagne (Corsica), and the basins on the edges of the Central Massif.

3. Vine-growing regions (Burgundy, the borders of the Jura, Languedoc, Champagne and the vineyards of Cognac and Saintes).
4. The most fertile regions, with loamy soils.
5. The districts where primitive agriculture flourished, that is to say, those with light, easily turned soils (fig. 52).

These small communes correspond to regions with many villages, forming 'a cellular fabric in the full sense of the word' (E. Juillard) with one nucleus to each cell;[4] the commune was the basic unit of agricultural life, and in each commune there was only one social centre.

With care and a proper regard for fine distinctions we can recognise a broad relationship between large communes and poor lands, and between small communes and rich lands. There are many exceptions; the tiny communes of the Normandy *Bocage*, for example, contrast with the extensive Breton communes; in Aquitaine the communes have been formed by the amalgamation of several parishes, while in the other provinces the direct descent of a commune from a parish was more usual. If we look at the map as a whole, it shows up the great geological units in a most surprising way; we can distinguish the Vosges, the Central Massif, and so on.

B. The Shape and the Boundaries of Communes

'Both large and small communes are shown on the map in shapes which are often confused and fantastic, bearing witness to the heated conflicts which took place when the boundaries were being fixed' (A. Meynier). The shapes of the communes are extraordinarily varied; in flat areas with homogeneous terrain, where the modification by man of the environment was not determined by physical factors, the communes have more or less regular circular or polygonal forms. We must not forget that many French communes originated in forest clearings; but also

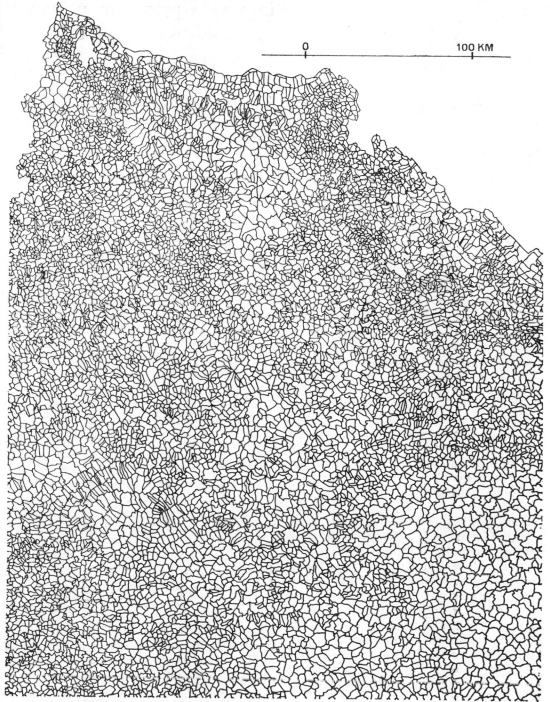

0   100 KM

Fig. 52.   Extract from the map of French communes: the North-east.   (Source: *Annales* (E.S.C.),
No. 3, 1958, full-page map)

North is to the left; the map stretches from the Paris region (N.W.) and the Bourbonnais region (S.W.)
to the boundary of the eastern region.

that the form of individual communes closely reflects variations in relief, so that the greater the degree or morphological differentiation, the more distinctive in shape are the communes, and the more uneven is the pattern they form. Communes stretch from the dip-slope of a *cuesta* to the subsequent depression at its foot to include a strip of forest, the favourably exposed slopes, some arable land and natural meadows along the watercourse, as in the Côtes de Lorraine.

Some features directly determine the shape of the commune by fixing one or more boundaries—a river-bank, an estuary, a break of slope, a ledge on a hillside, the edge of a plateau or a crest-line. The 'good' communes in the valleys thus contrast with the communes on the plateaux, which are often of limestone. In this connection rivers play a decisive part; small streams flow across the communes, but as soon as the valley broadens and the width of the river makes it an obstacle, it becomes a boundary line. The courses of a great number of rivers are thus shown up on the commune map. The Loire and the Allier can be traced from Roanne and Clermont-Ferrand; so can stretches of the Rhône, and most of the Saône and the Garonne. In marshy regions the canals fix the boundaries of the communes, giving them regular shapes; in mountain regions the communes coincide almost exactly with the river-basins. In the ancient massifs a commune stretching across a plateau is naturally bounded by the rivers flowing along the bottoms of the incised valleys. These controlling lines often lead to the creation of regular strings of communes which can be picked out on the map, as on the coasts of Normandy, the Garonne estuary, the banks of the Rhine and the Côtes de Lorraine. Sometimes the communes throw out a 'tail' to reach a river, a belt of meadowland (Blénod, in Lorraine) or woodland (Villacourt, near Blénod). Natural features are not the only ones to influence the shape of communes; throughout France the straightest boundaries correspond to Gallo-Roman roads.[5]

C. Variations in the Pattern of Communes

This pattern of communes is far from static; some of them are disappearing and new ones are being created.

Communes may disappear:

1. Through the effects of war: the wars at the end of the Middle Ages and the Thirty Years' War brought about the complete destruction of villages in the North and East. Villages in Lorraine and Champagne laid waste by the First World War were not rebuilt. Thus the network was once even finer in these regions.

2. By the incorporation of communes: the growth of towns inevitably leads to the remodelling of the commune system by the joining of suburban communes to that of the city. In 1840 eleven communes were brought within the new boundaries of Paris; in 1859 Lille annexed four communes, and Brest incorporated four recently. In rural districts certain tiny and almost uninhabited communes were joined to a neighbouring commune.

Some communes were formed at the expense of existing ones:

1. In tourist regions: spas or winter-sports centres, originating in a hamlet or even an uninhabited area, claim the right to local self-government when their interests diverge from those of the former urban centre.

2. In industrial areas: in Lorraine new communes were formed for new industrial areas. Saint-Nicolas-en-Forêt, near Thionville, was formed in this way in 1957.

3. In urban districts: the problem of the creation of communes is liable to be particularly acute where there are large built-up areas having no natural bond with the centre of the commune on which they stand, especially when this centre is some distance away and poorly equipped as a service centre.

Variations in the number of communes are not easily noticeable and take place over long periods. Normandy had 4,295 parishes in the 14th century, 4,297 in the 18th, 4,102 communes in 1794 and 4,407 in 1936. The regions with large communes and dispersed settlement show the greatest variations, by subdivision or by the raising of hamlets to the status of parishes or communes.[6]

The most profound alterations in the network of communes took place under the Revolution; a municipality was established in every commune, but very often new communes, sometimes very small, were created. For example, the *arrondissement* of Rodez, which had 140 communes in 1936, had 326 in 1793, such increases accounting for the attainment of a maximum number of 44,000 communes at this period. But from 1800 onwards their number was reduced to about 37,000.

Considered as a whole, the commune system shows a remarkable stability. In a century the number of communes changed from 36,835 (1851) to 38,000 (1954). The French temperament, the long history of the individual communes and the resulting differences in their characteristics have all helped to restrain attempts at consolidation. Only an intimate knowledge of these communes can help us to understand the contrasts between them. The inhabitants of a village are, more often than not, known by some nickname or other description, friendly or otherwise, applied to them by the inhabitants of neighbouring communes. In the course of the centuries every commune has acquired a personality, having been taken in charge by officials and influenced by teachers and priests with varying temperaments. Political opinions likewise differ from one to the other, so that projects for reforming the commune system are bound to come up against difficulties and resistance. Yet it seems archaic and an obstacle to progress that France should be cut up into tiny scraps like this. We need not go so far as to take the administrative systems of the newer countries as a basis for comparison, but we can see that in the other European states the system is much looser. These states, confronted with similar situations, do not hesitate to modernise their administrative divisions, as was done by Great Britain in 1945, by Sweden in 1946 and by the Netherlands.

Table XXVII shows the position in France as compared with other countries.

TABLE XXVII. COMPARISON OF COMMUNE SYSTEMS OF FIVE EUROPEAN STATES

Country	Number of communes	Average population of communes	Average area (in ha.)
Netherlands	1,014	11,801	3,205
Italy	7,810	6,460	3,854
Belgium	2,670	3,479	1,146
Western Germany	24,156	2,294	1,027
France	37,962	1,251	1,449

The archaism of the French system is all the more striking because the country is sparsely populated, and urbanisation and the exodus from the countryside have completely altered the distribution of the population. The population of the communes with less than 2,000 inhabitants represented 62·1% of the population of France in 1851; but in 1962 it amounted only to 32·7%. In the 1962 census there were eight communes entirely uninhabited, although the administration had not abolished them.[7] In 1962, 3,415 communes had less than 100 inhabitants (3,025 in 1954) and 14 departments each had more than 100 communes (Doubs, 202; Meuse, 159; Somme, 119; etc.).

As a result, administrative areas are split up into tiny units, and redistribution of land involving a region or a large number of communes becomes very difficult. Excessive fragmentation splits the population into tiny groups whose numbers and social or occupational diversification are reduced to a minimum. The consequences of this fragmentation are felt at every level: administratively, in the difficulty of setting up a municipal council or finding a competent mayor; educationally, in the large number of one-class and one-teacher schools. In 1957, 15,816 primary schools had less than twenty pupils. It is impossible to undertake public works at district or cantonal level, and difficult to pick out a commune to serve as centre for a region. Fragmentation is accentuated by the existence of more than 35,000 'sections of communes'. In large communes where there are several nucleations the inhabitants have often gained a sort of semi-autonomy in electoral and sometimes in administrative matters, by the creation of these sub-sections within the commune. There are no less disadvantages for urban communes. Towns which have spread on the territory of several communes suffer from the large number of different administrations and the difficulty or impossibility of co-ordinating the plans drawn up for each commune.

Several projects for mitigating this excessive fragmentation have been considered.

1. Abolition of tiny communes with less than 50 inhabitants (there are about 500 of these).

2. Abolition of communes whose budget is less than 10,000 francs for at least three years (there are 2,500 of these).

3. Abolition and regrouping of communes with a budget of less than 300,000 francs.

It has been calculated that in order to have adequate municipal finances (apart from the balance of local taxes) the minimum population admissible is 800 inhabitants. There are 7,000 communes in France which fall short of this figure, but the difficulties in the way of such projects can well be imagined.[8]

For urban communes inter-communal syndicates have been set up to standardise public works, such as water mains, sewers, education and fire services. But this is only a palliative. Since 1959 a policy of creating districts has been encouraged. The districts are groups of communes, none of which is abolished, under the authority of a district council whose duty is to plan, put in hand and supervise all public buildings and works.

At the beginning of 1967 there were 67 districts with 454 communes and 2,200,000 inhabitants. The method seems to be applicable to rural communes, and a few rural districts have already appeared. Since 1967 a different and more adaptable system than the districts has been initiated in large towns: that of urban communities. These are compulsory for certain regional centres and optional for all other towns of more than 50,000 inhabitants; urban communities are public authorities responsible for public services, building and works in an urban area as a whole. The Council of the Community represents all the communes, so that a system of administration on two levels is being developed.

2. See p. 126.

3. But the south of Beauce has nucleated settlement and large communes.

4. But Manche has small communes and dispersed settlement.

5. The boundaries of the communes are so firmly fixed that they even bear witness to changes in the courses of rivers, or the cutting off of meanders, as in the case of the Rhône between Loriol and Pouzin.

6. Brittany had 1,299 parishes about the year 1568, 1,310 about 1585 and 1,379 about 1677.

7. Five communes in Meuse, one each in Doubs, Isère and Hautes-Alpes.

8. Under the Consulate and the Empire a number of too small communes had already been changed into hamlets.

II

THE ENERGY INFRASTRUCTURE

1. THE ENERGY BALANCE OF FRANCE

The development of a country and the life of its industries, its towns and its entire population are inseparable from the existence of sources of power. Crises such as that of Suez in 1956, or simply strikes of gas and electricity workers, give some idea of how much our civilisation depends on its fuel and power. The growth of production and consumption of power is the best indication of the economic growth of a country. Problems relating to the availability of the various sources of power and the installation of plant for their production thus play an important part in 20th-century France.

The sources of power which meet this growing demand are themselves constantly changing; in the first half of the last century wind and running water were still in the lead. Then came coal, the life-blood of the industrial revolution. Since the beginning of the 20th century its supremacy has been challenged by hydro-electricity, but natural gas has entered the picture in its turn, followed by nuclear energy. The key feature of the fuel and power economy of France is a growing deficit. In 1950 the production of energy from primary (internal) sources met 67·5% of the consumption, but this had fallen to 50% by 1964.

Both production and consumption are growing at a remarkable rate. From 1949 to 1960 the total consumption of power has increased annually by 3·7% (while the gross production within the country has increased by 4·6% per year). The consumption of power, which was 88·1 million T.E.C. in 1950, reached 170 in 1966; electricity consumption in 1966 was 107,300 million kwh., whereas it had been 31,000 million in 1949 and 17,200 million in 1930. Since the war, technicians have expected electricity consumption to double every ten years. The consumption of power in France has not only grown rapidly but has also changed radically in structure. Table XXVIII clearly indicates these changes, as well as estimated consumption to 1975. The changes are:

1. The decreasing importance of coal.
2. The growing importance of oil.
3. The very recent appearance of natural gas among French and European sources of power.

TABLE XXVIII. CHANGES IN FUEL AND POWER CONSUMPTION, BY SECTORS OF PRODUCTION FROM 1929 TO 1975

(in millions of tons in coal equivalents (T.E.C.))[1]

	1929 %	1938 %	1955 T	1955 %	1965 T	1965 %	1975* T	1975* %
Solid fuels	92·1	83	70·9	65 2	70	41·1	57·8	23·5
Oil products	5·2	8	27·1	25	74	43·4	136·1	54·2
Natural gas			0·5	0·5	9	5·2	22·5	9
Hydro-electricity	2·7	9	10·2	9·3	17·1	10·1	23·2	9·3
Nuclear electricity					0·4	0·2	10	4
Total	100	100	108·7	100	170	100	251	100

* Estimates, assuming a high rate of growth.

4. The stability of electricity other than thermal electricity.

5. The use of nuclear energy.

The present structure of power sources in France could not, in fact, be analysed statistically; it represents the position at only one point of time in a surprisingly dynamic programme of plant expansion, and can only be understood in the light of future power consumption. The annual increase in total demand for power is of the order of 5·5%.

The expected increases in the consumption of electricity are very large: 74,800 million kwh. in 1960, 108,000 million in 1965, 218,000 million in 1975. The apparent consumption of electricity per head of population in 1960 placed France at a fairly low level, 1,642 kwh., which is behind West Germany (2,259), and very far behind Great Britain (2,450), Switzerland (3,520) and the United States (4,650). The consumption per family for domestic use in 1959 was only 530 kwh. in France, similar to that of Italy (460) and Portugal (497), compared with 788 for

Germany, 894 for the Netherlands, 1,902 for Great Britain and 3,585 for the United States. France's demand for oil products is expected to rise from 25 million tons in 1960 to 59 million tons in 1970.[2]

The main factor in French fuel and power policy is the inadequacy of resources within the country and this is bound to become more acute. Only 42–45% of power requirements will be met from primary sources in 1970 and 39–52% in 1975. We shall have to look further afield not only for oil products but also for coal, which will have to be imported in large quantities, particularly in such grades as coking and steam coal, of which not enough is mined, or which are produced at too high a cost. Imports will need to rise from 15 million to 19–25 million tons.

Another feature of the geography of energy in France is the uneven distribution of production and consumption. Regional inequalities which have been analysed in the preceding chapters reappear in energy patterns.

1. The factors for conversion into T.E.C. are: 1 ton lignite = 0·6 tons coal; 1 ton petrol, kerosene and fuel-oil = 1·5 tons; 1,000 m.[3] of natural gas = 1·33 tons; 1,000 m.[3] of manufactured gas = 0·6 tons; 1,000 kwh. of electricity = 0·125 tons. 1 watt is the motor power producing 1 unit of energy (1 joule) per second; 1 kilowatt (kw.) = 1,000 watts (unit of power); 1 kilowatt-hour (kwh.) = work done during 1 hour by a machine with a power of 1 kw. (unit of output).

2. We should note, however, that the demand for power grows more slowly than industrial production. This is a consequence of the increasing efficiency of energy utilisation, increasing mechanical efficiency and the increased importance of industries which consume smaller amounts of power.

2. COAL

Figures for coal production in France are as follows: 1 million tons in 1820, 10 million tons in 1862, 20 million tons in 1886, 30 million tons in 1897, 31 million tons in 1912, 52 million tons in 1926, 46·5 million tons in 1938, 47·1 million tons in 1946, 60 million tons in 1958. Production has declined since and was estimated at 52·9 million tons in 1966. Nearly all the production is mined by the *Charbonnages de France*, a state-owned enterprise.

Coal-mining is a very old industry. Coal was mined at Decazeville from the 15th

century onwards. The northern coalfield has been worked since 1734,[3] that of le Creusot (Blanzy) since 1769 and the Grand'-Combe since 1809. The Moselle coalfield was opened up much later, at the end of the 19th century, when the discoveries of Siemens, Gilchrist and Thomas made it possible to use the phosphoric iron ores of Lorraine. It did not really rise to prominence until after the last war. In 1948 coal deposits with a reserve of 250 million tons were discovered at Lons-le-Saulnier, but not worked.

A. Coalfields

The coalfields of France are very different one from another:

1. In their situation, which can be described as peripheral and northern. The following coalfields can be distinguished:

Northern coalfield (length 100 km., width 5–15 km.)

Lorraine coalfield (length 30 km., max. width 20 km.)

Coalfields of the eastern Central Massif: Blanzy–Le Creusot (length 60 km.), Loire (Saint-Étienne) (length 30 km.), Cévennes.

Coalfields of the south and south-west Central Massif: Carmaux (length 6 km., width 1–2 km.) and Decazeville.

Auvergne coalfield: Saint-Éloy-les-Mines, Brassac-les-Mines,[4] Meissex,[5] Champagne.

Alpine coalfield: La Mure.

Provençal coalfield: Gardanne.

2. In their production.

Table XXIX shows the relative production of the various coalfields.

thick beds of unproductive coal measures which are often displaced and caught up in the folds and fractures of the Hercynian zone. The daily yield (in kg. per coal-face worker in 1966) clearly reflects the differences in mining conditions:[6]

Lorraine	3,453
Auvergne	2,343
Loire	1,877
Nord–Pas-de-Calais	1,707

3. In the variety of qualities and potential uses of the coal produced: anthracite in Dauphiné and Auvergne; coking and flame coals in Aquitaine and Lorraine; anthracite and semi-anthracite in the North, Loire and Blanzy; lignite in Provence and the Landes. The quality also varies within each coalfield. In the Decazeville–Aubin coalfield the content per ton mined was found to be: 400 kg. of stone, 230 kg. of waste and 360 kg. of a friable coal containing 35% volatile substances, very gassy and not suitable for coking; at Carmaux, on the other hand, the coal is of good quality and cokes well.

TABLE XXIX. COAL PRODUCTION BY COALFIELDS IN 1929, 1960 AND 1966

	1929		1960		1966	
	Millions of tons	%	Millions of tons	%	Millions of tons	%
Nord–Pas-de-Calais	34·9	65	28·9	50·6	25·3	47·8
Lorraine	6·1	11·3	14·7	25·8	15·5	29·4
Blanzy	2·8	5·1	2·6	4·6	2·2	5·1
Loire	3·8	7	3	5·3	2·1	4·9
Cévennes	2·2	4	2·6	4·6	1·9	3·6
Aquitaine	1·9	3·5	2·1	3·7	1·7	3·2
Provence	0·9	1·6	1·3	2·3	1·6	3·0
Auvergne	1·1	2	1·1	1·9	0·8	1·5
Dauphiné	0·3	0·5	0·7	1·2	0·8	1·5
Total	54	100	57	100	52·9	100

Thus, until just after the Second World War, France had for all practical purposes only one large coalfield, that of the North, unlike the other great coal-producing countries. In the coalfields as a whole, conditions for mining are difficult; the coal seams are deep (average depth 480 m.) and not very thick: thus North, 1·06 m.; Lorraine, 2 m.; Centre and South, 2·26 m. (average 1·59 m.). They are separated by

B. The Rationalisation of Production

The mean daily output (per coal-face worker) in France was 1,229 kg. in 1938, and rose to 2,140 in 1966.[7] During the same period the number of workers in the industry fell from 242,483 to 143,128 and workers at the coal-face from 161,220 to 101,734. These figures testify to the success of the efforts made by the *Charbonnages de France* to modernise the various coalfields. Since 17th May 1946, in fact, almost all the coalfields have been nationalised and taken over by the *Charbonnages de France* (= National Coal Board) and divided into nine *houillères de*

TABLE XXX. MODERNISATION OF THE 'CHARBONNAGES DE FRANCE'

Types of equipment used in the mines as a whole		Equipment in use at the beginning of the years			
		1938	1946	1952	1962
Bonneted lamps .	. No.	0	0	60,000	142,844
Coal-face Equipment					
Loco-tractors .	. No.	900	680	1,770	1,799
Conveyors (belts and scrapers) .	. km.	92	45	395	565
Metal props .	. No.	3,000	80,000	466,000	779,334
Loaders . .	. No.	6	52	503	718
Short-wall cutting machines. .	. No.	95	91	406	
Planes and misc. .	. No.	0	6	35	206
Underground Electrification					
Electric motors .	. No.	0	250	4,419	18,307
Electric conveyors	. No.	0	96	1,000	6,672

bassins (colliery districts). An immense task has been accomplished, starting from a serious situation which was aggravated by a shortage of investments before the war, by delays in plant expansion and by destruction due to the war itself. These results have been obtained by:

THE CONCENTRATION OF COAL-WORKINGS

In the collieries of the Nord–Pas-de-Calais coalfield the number of pits was brought down from 125 before the war to 59 at the end of 1960 and 41 pits in 1966. This concentration has been made easier since the coalfields, which were formerly split up into the concessions of several companies, have come under a single management. Modern pits have a capacity of more than 2,000 tons per day. In the smaller coalfields concentration amounts to a stoppage of production. Underground working at Decazeville ceased in 1966.

MECHANISATION

Mechanisation has been made possible by underground electrification. Extraordinarily ingenious machines (such as cutters, scrapers, Marietta continuous miners, walking pit-props) have mechanised the driving of mine-

levels and the breaking down and removal of the coal. The fully automated mine, or, more exactly, coal-cutting without miners, is not yet a practical possibility, but experiments show that it is a possibility for the future (see Table XXX). Mechanisation is most difficult in the northern coalfield owing to the geological conditions; 60% of coal produced is still cut with the pick.

C. Coal as a Source of Energy and the Coal Crisis

Coal is a heavy product and a source of power that can be transported and stocked. Chronologically, it was the first great source of energy after wood. The coal output is shared among four groups of consumers: industrial use, 27%; coal-processing industries, 26%; domestic use, 25%; electricity, 22%.

But for some years coal has been going through a crisis:

1. Because of the structure of coal production; the coalfields do not produce enough anthracite, semi-anthracite and coking coal, and they produce too much flame coal and low-grade products. It is therefore necessary to import high-grade coal, anthracite and coke or fines for coking. Our imports in 1964 reached 19,713,000 tons, coming mainly from Western Germany, the Netherlands, Belgium, the U.S.S.R., the United States[8] and Great Britain. Before 1940 these imports were larger: 29 million tons in 1913, 35 million tons in 1930 and 22 million tons in 1938.

The difficulties are emphasised by the inflexible nature of the mining industry; it takes several years to sink a new shaft, and the investments and other work necessary may spread over several decades.

2. Because of competition from other sources of energy.

From 1938 to 1960 the traffic of the S.N.C.F. (*Société Nationale des Chemins de Fer Français* = French Railways) rose from 48·6 to 87·8 million traffic units, whereas the consumption of energy by the railways fell from 9·4 to 5·8 million T.E.C. and that of coal from 8·9 to 2·9.[9] The consumption of *Gaz de France* fell from 5·1 to 3·6 million tons between 1950 and 1959. The quantity of coal necessary to produce 1 kwh. fell in fifteen years from 1 kg. to 400 g.

A. Delion has pinpointed the essential causes of this loss of ground:

'The price per calorie of coal tends to rise steadily, partly because the beds are slowly becoming worked out and thus mining costs are becoming higher, and partly owing to the need to recruit a large labour force which increases in cost with the improvements in living standards and social welfare, while at the same time improvements in productivity gradually become less effective. In terms of efficiency, prices no longer work out in favour of coal, as mechanical methods of using it cannot achieve as high an output efficiency as other sources of power. Costs of using coal are also affected by the greater flexibility of the fluid sources of energy which sometimes completely do away with the need for stock-piling, lend themselves to automation and can be stopped and started instantly, thus cutting running costs, not to mention their psychological advantages, such as cleanliness and the absence of the need for handling.'[10]

Rightly or wrongly, coal is not considered as an element of the industrial civilisation of the 20th century. However, although the direct use of coal in industry, in the home and for railway engines has declined, other outlets are far from being closed. Consumption by thermal electric power-stations, iron and steel works and municipal heating installations continues to rise. The coal situation is worsened by the conditions of distribution. The principal coalfields are marginally located with respect to the rest of France, and transport by barge is limited to northern and eastern France. The development of seaports has led to competition with foreign coal, which is imported, thanks to advantageous freight charges by sea. For this reason the consumption of coal is highly regionalised.

Public authorities are particularly interested in coal production because it represents a source of power produced within the country which can supplement in a crisis the other sources of energy which are always liable to fail. What is more, coal is a source of energy involving a large labour force which is disinclined to move or to change its employment. In fact, work in the coal-mines has undergone fundamental changes. Only a few years ago work in the mines was an honourable and well-paid occupation; now the French are increasingly giving it up and leaving it to unqualified foreigners. The essence of the problem lies in the co-ordination between coal and hydrocarbons; we must 'give to both of them sufficient outlets for oil and natural gas to develop normally and for the coal workings not to be condemned to too swift a regression, which would cause irremediable harm' (R. Combey and S. Marchand).

In 1965 the Government set up production targets. These extended and reinforced the plan to protect the mines which had been drawn up in 1960, and provided for a reduction of about 10% in the production of the mines. The 48 million tons to be extracted in 1970 should comprise 23 million tons from Nord–Pas-de-Calais, 14·5 from Lorraine and 10·5 from the central and southern coalfields. In addition the price of fuel-oil is controlled so as to avoid too keen a competition with coal.

Since the European Coal and Steel Community (E.C.S.C.) was set up in April 1951, coal has become a problem at Common Market level. The Treaty of Paris envisaged a Common Market in coal and steel to benefit consumers and national bodies while at the same time looking after the long-term interests of producers and workers. In fact, the policy of the E.C.S.C., which is very liberal and rests on pure economic theory, has run up against a large number of difficulties. In 1962 the E.C.S.C. experts, starting from a situation of over-production of coal, provided for a rigorous cutting down of production. Assuming that the European economy remains liberal and open to American coal, the total coal production of the Common Market countries should fall from 230 million tons to 160 million in 1970 and 125 million in 1975, and that of France from 57 to 23 million in 1970. Even if France cannot cope with so large a reduction, the need to close some of the mines and to reconvert entirely or partly certain coalfields remains.

Coal as a source of energy is obviously going to have to face tougher and tougher competition. The inflexibility of its production and its high transport costs will become more and more evident from year to year in comparison with the flexibility of other sources of power. But for economic and social reasons, as long as working conditions allow,[11] coal will play an important part in French economy. From being a direct source of power, however, it will tend more and more to be used in thermal electric power-stations and as an industrial raw material. This development was confirmed in October 1966 by the creation of the company *Charbonnages de France-Chimie*.

3. The extension of this coalfield in Pas-de-Calais was not discovered until the 19th century, and its exploitation dates from 1847 to 1853.

4. Reserves estimated at five years in 1961.

5. Reserves estimated at two years in 1961.

6. In 1960 the corresponding yields of the two principal coalfields and of some foreign coalfields were as follows: Lorraine, 2,380; Ruhr, 2,185; Saar, 2,055; Limburg, 1,830; Campine, 1,790; Nord–Pas-de-Calais, 1,560.

7. Mean daily output per worker has increased more in France between 1938 and 1960 than anywhere else.

8. Imports were 16,300,000 tons in 1959, 15,967,400 in 1960, and 17,150,000 in 1965. This recourse to imports does not preclude the existence of large stocks; 8 million tons at the end of 1958, 12 million at the end of 1959, 14 million at the beginning of 1960 and 6,273,000 at the end of 1964.

9. 11·3 in 1929.

10. 'Le plan d'adaptation des charbonnages français', *Revue française de l'Énergie*, January 1962, p. 234.

11. Down to a depth of 1,200 m. the certain, probable and possible reserves are estimated at 4,400 million tons, of which 1,800 million tons are certain or probable; this means seventy-three or thirty-one years' supply respectively at the present rate of working. More than half these reserves are in Lorraine.

3. OIL

In 1964 France consumed 44 million tons of oil and exported almost 9 million tons of refined products. Production within France only meets a small percentage of these needs. France must therefore look further afield for supplies and pursue a policy of imports of crude oil (62,752,000 tons in 1966) for treatment in refineries.

A. Production within France

Until the post-war years the only oilfield in France was at Péchelbronn in the north of Alsace. This produced 75,000 tons in 1929, 80,000 tons in 1938 and 70,000 tons in 1948. Production ceased in 1963. French and foreign capital was being used entirely in the refining industry and there was no interest in prospecting in France itself until after the war. In June 1947 the Esso-Standard Company applied for a licence to drill in the Parentis area (Landes); the first indications of oil were obtained in 1953 and the first impregnated core was brought up on 25th March 1954. The oilfield is a brachyanticline running east–west, 10 km. by 3, situated 1,000–1,500 m. deep in Neocomian limestones. Thirty-seven bores have been made and twenty-nine wells are at present in production (1,276,000 tons in 1962). Outside the Parentis oilfield about sixty exploratory bores have been made, some of which have turned out to be productive: at Mothes (May 1953, producing 68,000 tons in 1962), Lugos (75 m.[3] per day), Lucats (July 1956), Parentis deep (March 1957), Cazaux (sixteen wells producing 270,000 tons in 1962) and Mimizan (1959).[12] The total production of the Landes oilfields was 2,258,000 tons in 1962.

Later, oil was discovered in the Paris basin. The deposits are located between Gien and Meaux, in Brie: Coulommes (February 1958), twenty-nine productive wells, and Saint-Martin-de-Bossenay (March 1959), in the Fontainebleau area: Chailly-en-Bière (October 1958) and Chartrettes (February 1959), and Chateaurenard near Gien; their production is relatively small, 473,000 tons in 1966. At present almost all the sedimentary regions of France are covered by research and prospecting concessions. Though at first they were limited to the south of France, they now cover the most northerly districts. Production in France itself is thus growing rapidly: 151,000 tons in 1950, 885,000 tons in 1955, 2 million tons in 1960, nearly 3 million tons in 1966.

B. Sources of Supply

The exploitation of the oil deposits first of the Sahara and secondly of Gabon made a great difference to imports of oil. This oil from the French zone (France, the Sahara and Gabon) satisfied only 7% of the demand in 1958, but 35% in 1966, so that France made a considerable saving in foreign exchange. Of the 65% of oil imported from countries outside the French zone, 49 came from the Middle East, Iraq and Kuwait being the largest suppliers.[13] These huge quantities of oil are transported by a large fleet of tankers. On 1st January 1967 France had the seventh largest national fleet of oil tankers with 3,700,000 tons (total gross tonnage).[14] The growing importance of oil from the Sahara has resulted in a rapid shortening of the sea routes, so that the capacity of the French tanker fleet is in excess of needs.

C. Refineries

Before 1928 France had only five small refineries;[15] the development of the refining industry dates from the law of 1928 which re-established a protective tariff on oil imports.[16] In 1938 the refineries were capable of producing 8 million tons a year; but all plant was destroyed during the war. Under the impetus given by the Monnet Plan, and the considerable increase in demand, the refining industry developed very rapidly. Refinery capacity rose from 8 million tons in 1938 to 13 million tons in 1950, 43,600,000 tons at the end of 1961 and 79 million at the end of 1966. Thus France ranks sixth among the oil-refining powers of the world, and fourth in western Europe; this is the result of her threefold maritime outlook and the excellent routes through her territory.

The list of refineries is as follows:

	Production capacity on 1st January 1967 in thousands of tons per year
Mediterranean group. . .	*21,530*
Berre (Shell Berre) . .	6,000
La Mède (C.F.R.) . . .	6,400
Lavera (B.P.) . . .	4,400
Fos-sur-mer (Esso-Standard) .	3,000
Frontignan (Mobiloil) . .	1,730
Basse-Seine group . . .	*31,800*
Gonfreville (C.F.R.) . .	10,600
Petit-Couronne (Shell Berre) .	9,200
Port Jérome (Esso-Standard) .	4,800
Notre-Dame-de-Gravenchon (Mobiloil) . . .	3,600
Grandpuits (U.G.P.) . .	3,600
Basse-Loire and western group .	*5,500*
Donges (Antar P.A.) . .	4,300
Vern-sur-Seiche (Rennes-Antar)	1,200
Gironde group	*5,000*
Bordeaux (Esso-Standard) .	2,600
Ambès (U.I.P.) . . .	1,900
Pauillac (Shell Berre) . .	500
Northern group	
Dunkirk (B.P.) . . .	*5,500*
Eastern group . . .	*9,850*
Herrlisheim (S.R.S.) . .	3,850
Reischtett (C.R.R.) . .	3,700
Feyzin (Rhône-Alpes) . .	2,300

The location of the refineries has undergone modifications very recently, to keep in step with the predicted increase in demand and with the appearance of an economically united Europe. Unlike the older sites, which were all on the sea-coast, the refineries are now located in the heart of the continent and joined to the oil ports by pipelines. This is the case with Feyzin, near Lyons, and the two new refineries near Strasbourg, at Herrlisheim and Reischtett; these refineries not only serve eastern France but also export to Switzerland and Germany. A new generation of inland refineries was born in 1965 with the opening of refineries near Rennes and at Grandpuits near Paris (1967) and the building of a refinery between Metz and Thionville. The fifth plan predicts a refinery capacity of 100 million tons in 1970.

D. Pipelines

Pipelines are an inseparable part of the oil economy. They can be used for two purposes—the transport of crude oil and that of the finished products.[17] Until 1962 the pipelines for crude oil were of little importance—223 km. in all. One half (115 km.) discharged the products of the oilfields in Aquitaine and the Paris basin, and the other half transported the oil from the ports (Le Havre and Lavera) to the refineries of Basse-Seine and the Étang de Berre. The network of pipelines for transporting the refined products is localised entirely in Basse-Seine. A 243-km. pipeline, dating from 1953, joins Le Havre to Paris. This pipeline does away with expensive handling and transports more than forty-five different commercial grades of eight basic products.

In 1958 a South European pipeline company was formed to build and exploit a pipeline from Marseilles—Lavera to Karlsruhe via the valleys of the Rhône and the Rhine. It came into service at the end of 1962. This pipeline is 782 km. long and 36 cm. in diameter, and carries crude oil from Lavera to the new refineries of Strasbourg and Karlsruhe. In 1966, 21 million tons passed through this pipeline to Switzerland and Germany. The refinery at Grandpuits is supplied with crude oil from Le Havre by a pipeline 250 km. long. There is a project to build a pipeline for refined oil up the Rhône valley; this will serve Dijon, Annemasse, Grenoble and Saint-Étienne. The development of these pipelines is due to the economies which they effect: the cost per ton-km. by pipeline is thirty to forty times less than by road (and three times more than by sea).

E. Oil Companies

Oil is the only source of energy in France which is not entirely under government control. Private companies, and in most cases subsidiaries of foreign companies prospect, drill, refine and distribute. The Government therefore looked favourably on the creation in 1960 of a new oil company: L'Union Générale des Pétroles (U.G.P.). Its founder members are three companies in which the State is majority shareholder: the Régie autonome des Pétroles, the S.N. Repal and the Groupement des exploitants pétroliers. Together with the Caltex company (U.S. group), the U.G.P. founded the Union Industrielle des Pétroles, which owns the Ambès refinery. The Entreprise de recherches et d'activités pétrolières (E.R.A.P.) was created in 1966 from the fusion of the Régie autonome and the Bureau de recherches du pétrole. These companies are intended to create a basic network which will progressively control up to 15% of the French oil market and channel the oil produced in the Sahara.

12. The reserves of Parentis are estimated at eighteen to twenty years and those of Cazaux at twelve years.
13. Imports of refined oils are small. These are allocations within the Common Market or the result of trade agreements, such as that with Russia.
14. The six largest fleets were those of Liberia, Norway, Great Britain, the United States, Japan and Panama.
15. At Courchelettes (Douai), Colombes, Le Havre, Blaye and Merkwiller (Péchelbronn).
16. The law exempts crude oil for refining from duty and gives the refineries special concessions. The refined oil is then subject to lower duties than imported products.
17. Excepting heavy oils.

4. GAS

The structure of the gas industry is a peculiar one. The production of gas is relatively independent of consumption, as gas is both a product and a by-product at the same time.

A. Production

Gas is a by-product of blast-furnaces, coking plants and refineries. Part of the gas thus produced is consumed on the spot by the industries themselves.

Gaz de France, an organisation created as the result of the nationalisation measures of 1946, took over from a large number of companies which produced and distributed gas; the French gas industry has thus undergone great changes. Earlier, the ugly black shape of the gas-holder, always in the most unfortunate position, was inseparable from even the smallest town; the gas-works, constantly supplied with coal, was the symbol of one of the first amenities of urban civilisation. There were 546 of them in 1946. The nationalisation of 615 gas companies out of 724 and the progress made in the distribution and transport of gas have made it possible to close most of these decrepit and unproductive works (more than 420 have been closed in the last fifteen years), and either to connect the networks with large central gas-works or to build modern gas plants.

Gaz de France thus satisfies the demand by producing and buying gas. In 1964 gas production was 12,157 million therms produced from the treatment of coal (31·5%), natural gas (50%) and oil hydrocarbons (18·5%). This production represented 54·5% of the gas available to consumers. The percentage is decreasing (it was 84% in 1947) because the exploiting of the natural-gas deposit at Lacq has led *Gaz de France* to buy large quantities of gas. In 1961 the national corporation bought gas from different producers as follows: coal-gas, 5,525 million

therms[18] bought from coking plant connected with mines or iron foundries in France and the Saar; oil-refinery gas, 1,427 million; propane and butane, 571 million; imports, 255 million; gas from non-nationalised gas-works, 16 million; natural gas, 7,663 million.

B. Natural Gas

The production of natural gas was 110 million m.³ in 1946 and rose to 7,000 million m.³ in 1962. The gas comes from two gas-fields which are near together but very different in size.

1. The Saint-Marcet and Charlas field; this was first worked in 1942.

2. The Lacq field. At the end of 1951 a bore-hole reached the pocket known as 'Lacq deep', at 3,500 m. depth; there was a violent eruption of natural gas, and a huge reservoir of gas was found to exist; the recoverable reserves are estimated at 200,000 million m.³ or about thirty years' supply. Production began in 1957 and is stable around 5,000 million m.³. Considerable technical difficulties had to be overcome. Some arose from the nature of the occurrence: its depth (3,000–5,000 m.), its high temperature (140° C.) and its pressure (670 kg. to the cm.²); others from the high content of carbonic acid gas and more particularly of sulphuretted hydrogen (15%). After the necessary treatment the gasfield yields annually 4,750 million m.³ of purified gas, 260,000 tons of petrol, 125,000 tons of propane and butane and 1,400,000 tons, or more than three times the French consumption, of sulphur.

The distribution of gas from Lacq has set considerable economic problems. Its discovery gave rise to great hopes in the South-west; this source of energy was going to promote active industrialisation in the quadrant of France which was least favoured. Economic calculations dashed these hopes to the ground. Investments were enormous

(1,150 million francs) and fixed expenses represented 90% of running costs. It was therefore necessary to find regular markets for very large quantities; and it was more profitable to dispose of the gas to a small number of very big consumers served by gas pipelines as large and as short as possible, rather than to a scattering of small factories. From 1956 onwards it became clear that with no consumers already on the spot, the whole of the gas produced at Lacq could not be rapidly disposed of in the South-west. It was therefore decided to bring it out of the Aquitaine basin, and a network of distributing pipes was quickly constructed to the large-scale consumer regions; 3,800 km. of gas pipelines go out from the underground store of purified gas at Lussagnet (Landes).[19] This network serves the paper mills of Angoulême, and a branch from this town serves the Atlantic coast as far as Vannes, reducing imports of American coal in this area, and supplying the electricity power-station of Nantes–Cheviré. From Roussines an eastward branch goes on one hand to the Lyons region (Le Péage) and on the other to Le Creusot and the Saône plain. The main branch goes to the Paris region, where the gas chiefly supplies thermal electric power-stations and private users.

In 1961, out of a total of 4,100 million m.[3] of natural gas extracted, more than 1,800,000 was distributed in the South-west, half of this being consumed by the two thermal electric power-stations of Artix and Ambès. A little over 50% of the 950 million m.[3] distributed by Gaz de France went to the Paris region, 9% to western France between Angoulême and Vannes and more than 15% to central France between Lyons and Dijon. Natural-gas sales were distributed as follows: industry, 40%; power-stations, 34%; public and domestic use, 24%; motor-fuel, 2%. Chemical industries take the greater part (61%) of industrial consumption. We may well imagine the repercussions of the arrival of gas from Lacq in coal-bearing regions such as the coalfields of the Central Massif, and the reactions which this distribution policy provokes, conflicting as it does with the policies of industrial decentralisation and national planning.

The natural gas of Lacq is, moreover, a good example of the financial and legal complexity of the French economy; public and private interests are inextricably mingled in its exploitation. The field is worked by the *Société Nationale des Pétroles d'Aquitaine*. The gas is distributed in the South-west by the *Société des Gaz du Sud-Ouest*, which is controlled by the S.N.P.A. (35%), the *Régie autonome des Pétroles* (35%) and *Gaz de France* (30%). Outside the South-west the situation is even more complex. *Gaz de France*, which owns the network of gas pipelines, lets it to the *Compagnie française du Méthane* (S.N.P.A., 50%; Gaz de France, 50%). This company sells the gas to private enterprise, but also to *Gaz de France*.

But Lacq is not merely an unusual discovery, modifying the system of fuel and power in France for a few decades. Other fields, near or distant, make it certain that natural gas has come to stay.[20] Those in Algeria were discovered together with rich oil deposits. They are immense (that of Hassi R'Mel is said to contain more than 800,000 million m.[3]) and their resources are far more than the potential markets in North Africa are likely to require. This sets the problem of the transport of the gas to the European market. There are two possible solutions:

1. Transport by submarine pipelines; pipes have been laid experimentally in the Mediterranean at a depth of 2,500 m.

2. Transport by methane tankers in liquid form at very low temperatures.

The *Compagnie Algérienne de Méthane liquide* (C.A.M.E.L.) set up a liquifying plant in 1962. Since 1965 the methane tanker, *Jules Verne*, has journeyed between Arzew and Le Havre, where a methane port equipped for the storing, pumping and re-gasification of 425 million m.[3] a year has been built. Pipelines carry the gas to the underground reservoir of Saint-Illiers. Since 1968 Algeria has been selling 1,500 million m.[3] of gas per year to

France. These plans relating only to Saharan gas were upset by the discovery in 1963, and immediate exploitation, of a large gasfield in the northern Netherlands, in Groningen.[21] After southern France, all the northern half can thus be supplied from the methane port at Le Havre or by gas pipelines. From 1967, 5,000 million m.[3] of Dutch gas will be supplied annually to *Gaz de France*, the agreement stretching over twenty years; the gas arrives in France near Bavai and is distributed by pipelines in the North, Lorraine and the Paris region.

C. Transport

The transport and distribution of gas is carried out by a network of feeders which has been developing very rapidly since 1947. The length of the transport network was 2,332 km. in 1947 and 10,728 in 1961, and its main pipes link the coking plants in Lorraine and the Saar with the Paris region (1954), Saint-Étienne to Clermont, Roanne and Vichy, and also the north with the east, Cannes to Mentone by way of Grasse and Monaco. The distribution network has grown from 35,115 km. (1947) to 52,000 at the end of 1965. Since 1958 the underground gas reservoir at Beynes, 40 km. west of Paris, has stored the gas brought from the coking plants of Lorraine. It can hold 340 million m.[3], the equivalent of 550 giant gasometers of the classic type. Storing the gas set some technical problems. It is located 300 m. below sea-level in a 'geological trap' in the form of an inverted basin, made absolutely impervious by a layer of very plastic clay. The gas is stored at the expense of a water-table, which it pushes back into a bed of fine homogeneous sand of the Wealden series, 30–35 m. thick. The Beynes reservoir includes twenty-three wells scattered over the countryside or hidden in the forests. More recently a policy of systematic planning and prospecting for these reservoirs has been put into effect; gigantic natural gasometers are regulated daily and seasonally, at Saint-Illiers near Mantes (800 million m.[3] in 1965) and

Chémezy between Blois and Tours (1,000 million m.[3] in 1968). Gas from the Netherlands will be stocked in two reservoirs near Compiègne and Nancy. The complex geological structure of the South-east does not provide for favourable sites; meanwhile the possibility of creating reservoirs by the solution of salt beds is also under consideration.

D. Consumers

In 1967 sales of gas from plant owned by *Gaz de France* amounted to 31,000 million therms (17,968 million in 1961). The annual volume of sales is strongly influenced by climatic conditions; severe or long winters and cool autumns cause a higher consumption of gas.[22]

Distribution among the various uses in different regions is as follows:

TABLE XXXI. CONSUMPTION OF GAS (1967)

Region	Total (in millions of therms)	Domestic %	Commercial %	Industrial %
Paris	10,984	68	19	13
North	2,815	47	7	46
West	4,142	59	16	25
East	2,301	60	15	25
East Central	3,593	69	16	15
South-west	4,490	65	24	11
South-east	2,235	80	17	3

The chemical industry is clearly the principal consumer of gas, followed by the following branches of industry: production and manufacture of metals, mechanical and electrical industries, glass-works, cement works, foodstuffs industries (such as bakeries, and biscuit factories).

France is thus divided into three main zones for the production and transport of gas.

1. North of a line Caen–Chartres–Auxerre–Colmar the gas is drawn mainly from coking plants, supplemented by refinery gas and natural gas from Lacq, Algeria and the Netherlands. The transport network is very dense, leaving few isolated gas-works. In addition, the northern network is linked with that of Belgium, and the eastern one with that of the Saar. In the few gaps left there are some gas-works or propane works.

2. Mediterranean France depends on gas from the refineries of Sète and the Étang de Berre, which distribute it to the towns of Languedoc and Provence.

3. Between these two, all the rest of France had nothing until the last few years except isolated gas-works and propane works. Gas pipelines were practically non-existent or at least very limited (around Quimper, Vannes, the Nantes–Saint-Nazaire link, Decazeville, Rodez, Carmaux, Albi); the installation of the pipelines from Lacq completely altered the system in this region, and there was soon a very dense network.

18. 1 therm = 1 million calories (the calorific value of 1 m.³ of gas can vary from 1 to 10).
19. The natural reservoir of Lussagnet, with a capacity of 500 million m.³, is situated in Miocene sandstone at a depth of 600 m.
20. Other large deposits were discovered at Meillon, near Pau, in 1965 and at St. Faust in 1966.
21. From 1970 onwards its production (between 7,000 and 10,000 millions) is expected to exceed that of France (6,000 millions); the reserves are said to be 1,100,000 million m.³, some six times greater than at Lacq.
22. Seasonal variations in sales are considerable and are on the increase; the ratio of the highest monthly consumption to the lowest was 2·1 in 1960 and 3·7 in 1967.

5. ELECTRICITY

Electricity occupies a very special place among sources of energy.

1. By its extraordinary growth; at the beginning of this century its production in France was only 310 million kwh.; in 1920 it was 5,800 million kwh., reaching 22,000 million kwh. just before the outbreak of war in 1939. In twenty years (1946–66) production multiplied more than five times (Table XXXII).

2. By its wide diffusion and the variety of its uses; it represents a source of universal energy, driving a wide range of motors, from electric razors to locomotives or rolling-mills; it lights, heats, refrigerates, drives, produces goods and provides entertainment.

3. By the unique way it is distributed; it needs no storing, but on the other hand its transport network is nowadays a feature of every landscape.

4. By the irregularity of its consumption; its wide diffusion, its variety of uses and its flexibility in use causes the consumption of electricity to have sharply defined troughs and peaks. These variations are hourly (about 8 a.m. and 5 p.m. are peak hours), daily and seasonal. This calls for a very flexible system of production and distribution.

5. By its two means of production.

Table XXXII shows relative importance of thermal electricity and hydro-electricity. France is unusual in being a country where the two types of production are more or less balanced, whereas the electricity produced in a country is more often predominantly thermal, as in Great Britain and Belgium, or predominantly hydraulically generated, as in Scandinavia and Canada. The variations are

TABLE XXXII. PRODUCTION OF ELECTRICITY
(in 1,000 million kwh.)

Year	Total production (million kwh.)	Thermal electricity						Hydro-electricity					
		Total		E.D.F.		Other		Total		E.D.F.		Other	
		Prod.	%	Prod.	%	Prod.	%	Prod.	%	Prod.	%	Prod.	%
1952	40,569	18·3	45·2					22·2	54·8				
1954	45,570	21·3	46·8					24·2	53·2				
1956	53,829	27·9	52					25·8	48				
1958	61,599	29·3	47·7	12·4	42·4	16·9	57·6	32·2	52·3	23·8	74	8·4	26
1960	72,118	31·8	44	14·8	46·5	17	53·5	40·3	56	30·6	76	9·6	24
1961	76,489	38·2	50	19	49·7	19·2	50·3	38·2	50	28·6	74·9	9·5	25·1
1962	83,093	47·3	57	26·1	55·3	21·1	44·7	36·7	43	26·9	75·3	8·9	24·7
1963	88,300	44·9	50·8	25·1	55·9	19·8	44·1	43·4	49·2	32·9	75·8	10·5	24·2
1964	93,800	59·1	63	35	59·2	24·1	40·8	34·7	37	26·7	76·9	8	23·1
1966	106,100	54·4	51·3	34·3	63	20·1	37	51·7	48·7	38·9	75·2	12·8	24·8

caused partly by the effect of dry summers on hydro-electricity, but more especially by the policies of *Electricité de France* (Table XXXIII).

TABLE XXXIII. ELECTRIC POWER
INSTALLED ANNUALLY IN
POWER-STATIONS

	In thermal electric stations* (in 1,000 kw.)	In hydro-electric stations (in 1,000 kw.)
1954 . . .	408	592
1955 . . .	513	0
1956 . . .	625	106
1957 . . .	605	470
1958 . . .	1,055	0
1959 . . .	1,500	260
1960 . . .	795	607
1961 . . .	269	806
1962 . . .	675	247
1963 . . .	708	472
1964 . . .	528	345
1965 . . .	1,011	246

* Including nuclear stations from 1963

It can be seen that in every year (except 1954 and 1961) thermal electric power was in the lead. There are several reasons to explain the choice of this type of electricity.

1. The growing scarcity of sites for big hydro-electric power-stations.

2. The higher cost of hydro-electric plant and the longer time before it can be put into service.

3. The necessity to make northern France reasonably independent in power production for some time.

4. The desire to find a market for the lower-grade coal produced by *Charbonnages de France*.

5. The development of sources of energy other than coal in thermal power-stations: blast-furnace gas, natural gas, fuel-oil.

Although production of electricity was nationalised at the time of the Liberation, *Electricité de France* is not the only producer. The producers are:

For thermal power-stations, the *Charbonnages de France*, and some big industrial combines, such as iron and steel works, paper-mills and refineries. For one thing, they already possessed suitable sites, and for another, technical problems arising from the use of certain qualities of coal could more easily be solved within the nationalised coal industry.

For hydro-electric power, the *Compagnie Nationale du Rhône* (9,100 million kwh. in 1966), electro-chemical and electro-metallurgical industries, paper-mills and the S.N.C.F. The S.N.C.F. has nineteen power-stations with a total capacity of 502,000 kw. These are situated in the valleys of the Pyrenees, where investment by the S.N.C.F. was an established practice. The bulk of electricity production was provided, on 1st January 1966, by 1,460 hydro-electric power-stations and 60 thermal power-stations of a capacity greater than 50,000 kw.

A. The Location of Thermal Power-Stations

On 1st January 1967, the installed capacity of all thermal power-stations combined was 14·6 million kw. The distribution of thermal power-stations corresponds to two factors. They are found either at production sites, such as coalfields, lignite mines, coal ports, refineries or iron and steel works, or at centres of consumption, along waterways, and always near water, which they use in large quantities for cooling.[23] From one year to the next, coal products, such as grains, fines and coke-dust, provide 64–70% of production. In 1964, 57% of French production was accounted for by the northern region (32%) and the Paris region (25%). The thermal power-stations of the North are situated on the coalfield, but also outside it, as at Comines. In the Paris region the power-stations are on the rivers by which the coal comes from the North: the Oise at Beautor, near Chauny and Creil, and the Seine at Porcheville, near Mantes and Montereau, all around Paris.

The distribution of thermal power-stations has been changing markedly for some years, now that the South and South-west are playing a more important part. The use of fuel-oil from the refineries and natural gas from Lacq has in fact made possible the setting up of power-stations at Nantes–Cheviré (1953), Lacq and Bordeaux. In the

Maritime North-west, power-stations have been established at Yainville (between Rouen and Le Havre) and Dunkirk (between the refinery and the iron and steel works). These power-stations use two or three types of fuel; refinery gas, fuel-oil and blast-furnace gas at Dunkirk. Power-stations are being run more and more on natural gas together with other fuels. In the South-west the Arjuzanx power-station is sited directly on a small lignite deposit.

Thermal power-stations, thanks to rapid technical progress (the life of a power-station being about fifteen years), can now produce more than the largest barrages. The mean output of a group of turbines is at present 125,000 kw. and that of a thermal power-station is 500,000 kw.

Thermal power-stations are now a part of the French landscape, with their batteries of two to four chimneys emitting a light smoke out of all proportion to their size, their brick or concrete buildings in the shape of a parallelopiped, their cooling towers and their coal dumps.

B. Hydro-electricity

On 1st January 1967, the installed capacity of all hydro-electric power-stations combined was 13·3 million kw., comprising 500 stations of more than 1,000 kw. among which only 150 were of more than 20,000 kw. The inventory of hydro-electric sites gives an aggregate plant capacity of 80,000 kwh million at maximum output, the best areas potentially being the Jura and the northern Alps (25,000 million kwh.), the Central Massif (12,000), the Pyrenees (10,000) and the southern Alps (10,000); the Rhône and the Rhine have respective capacities of 9,000 and 7,000 million kwh.

Planning policy for hydro-electricity is governed by three principles: that a rational development must be related to the abundance and potentialities of the sources of energy; that cost price should be fixed at a fair average level, as certain kwh. cost much more than others; and that the average

selling price of *Electricité de France* must not compete with that of other producers. The task of providing current at peak periods has fallen to hydro-electric power, so that there is a tendency to build 'peak' power-stations with a generating power out of proportion to their average production.

Hydro-electric plant can be classified according to various criteria:

1. Height of fall: stations with a high fall (more than 200 m.) situated in the high Alps and fed by means of penstocks;[24] stations with a medium fall (20–200 m.); stations with a low fall (less than 20 m.) on the large rivers.

2. The way the fall is engineered: by diversion canal—a feeder running laterally to the river or a headrace carrying the water from an intake on the mountainside above the power-station, or by barrage reservoir creating an artificial head of water.

3. The nature of the current produced: base-load (Donzère–Mondragon), variable-load, peak-load (Serre–Ponçon) or mixed (Génissiat, Seyssel).

BASE-LOAD POWER-STATIONS
Power-stations on rivers

An artificial fall of a few metres (26 m. at Bollène) is created either by a barrage which raises the water-level directly above the power-station or by an embanked headrace which carries the water at the higher level up to the point where the fall is desired. The reservoirs of these power-stations are practically non-existent, since they are filled in less than two hours, and the water supplying them is used immediately. They produce 60% of the total number of kilowatts. The Rhône and the Rhine, which are harnessed at numerous points, provided most of this electricity. In 1960 the Rhine produced 4,250 million kwh. from a total of four power-stations. From Kembs to Vogelgrun, the four barrages—Kembs (1932), Ottmarsheim (1952), Fessenheim (1956) and Vogelgrun (1959)—are on one single diversion canal, the Grand Canal d'Alsace. Farther downstream, a looped series of diversions has been or will be built for each power-station so as not to infringe German riparian rights.

On the Rhône downstream from Lyons intermittent looped diversions are generally used. By this means, alternating reaches of river and canal regularise the course of the river and make it navigable, and at the same time raise the level of the water in the artificially embanked canals to feed the turbines. Seven power-stations are in operation; moving downstream, they are: Génissiat (1937–47), 1,700 million kwh.; Seyssel, which is only a compensating dam to make up for the water locked up at Génissiat, 180 million kwh.; Pierre-Bénite (1966), 480 million kwh., the main purpose of which is to keep the river navigable to Lyons; Beauchastel (1963), 1,200 million kwh.; Baix-le-Logis-Neuf (1960), 1,200 million kwh.; Montélimar (1958), 1,670 million kwh.; Donzère–Mondragon (1952), 2,000 million kwh. Two other power-stations are in course of construction or planned: Bourg-les-Valence (1968), 1,060 million kwh.; Vallabrègues, 1,200 million kwh.

VARIABLE-LOAD POWER-STATIONS

Power-stations fed by lakes or seasonal reservoirs

The barrages of these power-stations receive the overflow at periods of high water—taking more than 400 hours to fill—and let it out at periods of low water, thus evening out production season by season. These are the strings of power-stations in the valleys of the Alps, the Central Massif and, to a lesser degree, the Pyrenees. The autumn rains in the Central Massif or the summer rains in the northern Alps are stored for the winter months. In the Mediterranean regions the spring rains serve to generate power in summer, as well as for irrigation, as at Serre-Ponçon.[25] Hydro-electric installations of this type are nothing like those of earlier days. The picture of an isolated dam across a river, depending on particularly favourable natural conditions, has given place to that of an overall plan with engineering works

placed at intervals down the river. Valley barrages are giving way increasingly to very bold schemes in high or very high mountain areas. The power-stations are supplied by intakes from other basins, collecting water from glaciers, lakes and torrents, which underground canals through the mountains carry to the reservoir or directly on to the turbines. Pumping is being used more and more for filling the reservoir. Small power-stations are replaced by canals to concentrate the water upon a few large well-placed power-stations. This method does away in many cases with the main valley dam, which, in well-populated areas, creates delicate financial and social problems through the requisition of land and the drowning of villages, as at Tignes and Serre–Ponçon.

The Roselend–La Bathie complex as an example

Since 1961, the underground power-station of La Bathie, a few kilometres from Albertville, has added a capacity of 500,000 kw. (700 million kwh. per year). The turbines are driven by water confined in a penstock with a fall of 1,200 m., drilled through the mountain. This penstock is fed by a tunnel more than 12 km. long and more than 4 m. in cross-section, from the 160-m.-high dam at Roselend in Beaufortin.

The Roselend lake, at an altitude of 1,800 m., is in turn fed by about twenty piped torrents, some on the right bank of the Isère and others in Beaufortin. This water is brought through 40 km. of tunnels and 7 km. of canals (fig. 53).

Power-stations fed by sluice systems

These power-stations have smaller storage capacities (between 2 and 400 hours supply); they regulate the flow by collecting the water by night and releasing it in the daytime. They also are situated in the mountains, but farther downstream. Large amounts of water pass through the turbines; in 1964 these power-stations accounted for 26% of the installed capacity and 24% of the production. One example is Génissiat, which uses a head

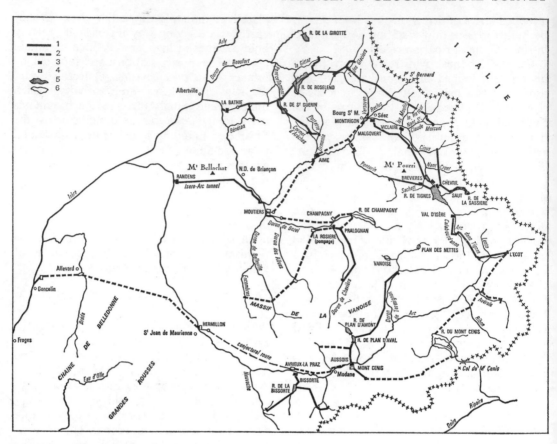

Fig. 53. Hydro-electric development in the upper Isère valley. (Source: J. Ritter, *Ann. de Géog.*, no. 365, 1959, pp. 40–41)

1. Diversion, either existing or under construction. 2. Projected diversion. 3. Power-station, either existing or under construction. 4. Projected power-station. 5. Reservoir, in use or under construction. 6. Projected reservoir.

of water 5 m. in cross-section and amounting to 12 million m.³. This quantity can be accumulated in 16 hours and can drive the turbines for 5 hours.

A large part of this production is provided by river-basins in mountains which are well supplied with both rain and snow. The Isère valley alone provided 4,000 million kwh. in 1959; and to this we must add the contributions of the Drac (2,200 million) and the Arc (1,500 million). In the Pyrenees the Gave de Pau accounted for 30% of the production of the whole mountain range. The most powerful hydro-electric stations are:

La Bathie–Roselend (Isère), 500,000 kw.; Serre–Ponçon (Durance), 336,000 kw.; Baix-le-Logis-Neuf (Rhône), 198,000 kw.; Chassezac, 163,000 kw.; Marckolsheim (Rhine), 156,000 kw.

At the present rate of construction, all the possible hydro-electric sites will be exploited in twenty years. We must therefore expect a decrease in the part played by hydro-electricity in the total production of energy. But we cannot ignore the possibilities afforded by new techniques of construction, such as power-stations fed by pumped water like those already installed in Scotland and

Luxembourg. These make use of water in a virtually closed circuit, in which the water passes from a higher basin through turbines to a lower basin whence it is pumped during off-peak hours from the lower basin to the higher. The map of hydro-electric production could be radically transformed as a result of this development. The site of Revin, in the Ardennes, has been set aside for an initial installation of 300,000 kw., to be exploited in 1969.

C. Tidal and Nuclear Energy

After long years of research and vacillation, the lack of adequate installations in western France led *Electricité de France* to undertake in 1960 the construction of the Rance tidal power-station. A few kilometres south of Dinard, the Rance estuary is crossed by a barrage which contains 24 turbine sets over which the water passes in both directions. Since 1967, with an installed capacity of 240,000 kw., the station has provided 540 million kwh.

NUCLEAR ENERGY

The first nuclear electricity in France was produced on 26th September 1956 at Marcoule, in experimental reactors whose essential purpose was to produce plutonium.[26] *Electricité de France* has drawn up a programme of nuclear power-stations; the reactors will use natural uranium as fuel, graphite as moderator and carbon anhydride under pressure as the cooling fluid. This programme, within the frame of the fifth plan, provides for an output of 2·5 million kw. plus a further 1·5 million kw. if required, and further development at the rate of 200,000 kw. per year. The first nuclear power-station was established at Chinon (E.D.F. 1–2–3). The Loire provides the necessary enormous quantities of water and the installation is leading the way to the development of the electricity potential of western France.

After the three Chinon power-stations, the following stations were built: the Monts d'Arrée power-station at Brennilis, of a different type (uranium, heavy water and gas) and a 70,000-kw. potential (1966); the Ardennes power-station at Chooz, near Givet, which is worked jointly with the Belgian producers within the United States–Euratom agreement (242,000 kw. in 1966); the E.D.F. 4 power-station of Saint-Laurent-des-Eaux (Loir-et-Cher) and E.D.F. 5 on the Rhône (Bugeyl), 30 km. above Lyons. Fessenheim will follow.

D. Consumption of Electricity

In 1966 the consumption of high-tension electricity was 72,700 million kwh., and of low-tension electricity 21,400 million kwh. Losses had risen to 8,100 million kwh. Total consumption (utilised power) thus reached 109,000 million kwh.

The industries consuming the most current (high-tension) are the metallurgical, engineering and electrical (electro-metallurgical, iron and steel, electro-chemical), and the fertiliser, paper and cardboard and spinning and weaving industries.

E. The Electricity Grid

The production capacity and consumption of electric power are far from balanced at regional level. But this lack of balance, which is easily explained by the uneven distribution of consumers, is aggravated by a lack of balance between the types of production. The Alps produce very little electricity in winter, so that current has to be imported from other regions. There are consequently some very complex accounts for electricity existing between the various regions. Three regions show a debit balance: the Paris region, which is the biggest centre of consumption in France, the Alps and the Lyons region, and the West. Three regions export electricity: the South-west, the South-east and the Centre, which, by reason of its low population and lack of industry, is the great provider of power. It imports 2,405 million kwh., but exports more than 5,000 million kwh. A policy of industrial development in the South of France would thus upset all this system of regional interdependence and compel northern France to be self-sufficient.

These exchanges of electricity are carried out by means of a network of power lines, interlinked in such a way as to be able at any moment to pass on the current available in one region to another region. Despite all appearances the transport of electricity is expensive, on average 12–13% of the final price. Three grids, with different voltages, cover France; this is the result of technical progress which enables electricity to be transported at higher and higher tensions.

1. A grid at 150,000 volts,[27] which was 729 km. long in 1923, 6,500 km. in 1940 and 8,500 km. in 1964. It is non-existent in western France, as this particular tension is already out of date.

2. A grid at 225,000 volts, which was 168 km. in 1927, 2,421 km. in 1940, 12,270 km. in 1960 and 15,800 km. in 1964.

3. A grid at 380,000 volts, which was begun in 1947 and reached 3,000 km. in 1964. It has three main branches: from Malgovert–Génissiat and Serre–Ponçon to Paris, from Bordeaux to Paris and from the Dordogne power-stations to Paris.

These three branches are interlinked and radiate outwards from Eguzon, Chaingy and Monistrol in the Centre, Lyons, Génissiat and Bollène in the South-east, Creney and Saint-Avold in the East and Vendin in the North. The fact that most of the lines converge on Paris serves yet again to emphasise the enormous amount of power consumed in and around Paris.

Around these foci of production, distribution and consumption the delicate yet bold silhouettes of the pylons, joined by cables which seem almost to touch the ground, are becoming the most prominent features of the landscape in many places. Pylons are be-

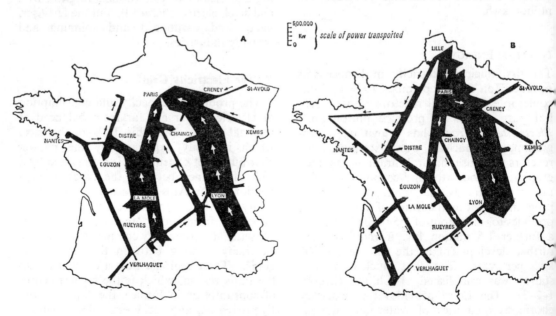

Fig. 54. Flow maps of inter-regional movements of electric power. (Source: E.D.F. *Résultats techniques provisoires 1962*). Arrows denote direction of circulation of power.

A. Power sources mainly hydro-electric; 23rd May 1962, 10 a.m.
B. Power sources mainly thermal; 24th October 1962, 3 a.m.

coming the symbols of our electricity-dominated civilisation; they are everywhere, even on the sides and summits of mountains. The electricity using these lines does not move one way only. It can be reversed, in response to the changing balance of regional supply and demand (fig. 54).

The maps show diagrammatically two very different situations:

1. On 24th October 1962, in a poor season for hydro-electric generation, transfers of electricity were made from north to south; the whole grid drew its power from the North, the East, the Paris region and the Atlantic power-stations.

2. On 23rd May 1962, on the other hand, when the snow-melt and the beginning of the melting of the glaciers provided an ample supply of water, power supplies moved from south to north over the whole grid from the hydro-electric sources. Thermal power-stations reduced production to a minimum.

Electric current knows no frontiers. It is in fact in the interest of countries on different meridians to be interlinked so as to benefit from the staggering of peak hours. Since December 1961 the British and French grids have been linked by a direct current cable. In 1966 France exported 1·9 million kwh. and imported 4·9 million kwh., the exchanges being made with all neighbouring countries.

23. 100 m.³ per hour for the station at Ansereuilles, south of Lille.
24. The record for height of fall is held by the Portillon power-station in the Pique valley (Pyrenees) with a fall of 1,336 m.
25. In 1964 these power-stations were responsible for 35% of the installed power and yielded 20% of the production, but their contribution is particularly valuable.
26. Group G2 at Marcoule was connected to the grid on 22nd April 1959.
27. The original grid at 110,000–120,000 volts, 1,400 km. long in 1946, has practically disappeared.

6. THE FUEL AND POWER PROBLEM OF FRANCE

In the space of a few years the fuel and power budget in France has changed. The discovery of the Lacq gasfield, the development of refineries and pipelines and the prospects opened up by the importation of natural gas and by nuclear energy have invalidated all present and future forecasts and brought competition into the very heart of the coalfields and their market areas.

The fuel and power problem stems from the fundamental differences between the various sources of energy.

Table XXXIV shows the considerable differences in man-power and productivity. The transfer of a quantity of power production from coal to another source is thus equivalent to six- or seven-fold reduction in the man-power directly employed in production. The formulation of a fuel and power policy is one of the major factors of French political economy. It is based on a certain number of constants: the need to find the least expensive way of buying energy,

the need for a secure source of supply and the social repercussions of the choices made. With the economic unification of Europe, the

TABLE XXXIV. MAN-POWER AND PRODUCTIVITY OF THE VARIOUS SOURCES OF ENERGY

	Man-power in production	Productivity per worker in T.E.C.
Coal-mines (miners, office staff, technicians, foremen, coal-face and surface engineers) .	225,000	240
Coal imports (screening + packing) . .	3,800	1,500
Hydro-electricity . .	5,800	1,600
Oil (research + production + refining) .	38,000	1,500
Nuclear (construction + prospecting and mining	4,500	

problems of fuel and power no longer exist purely on the home front. Future needs are so large,[28] technical progress so rapid and economic and political considerations so

H

important that a common policy for fuel and power is indispensable.

At the beginning of 1962 the European parliamentary assembly defined the principles of such a policy: low cost of supply; security of supply; gradual and co-ordinated substitution of sources of power; long-term stability of supply; free choice for the consumer; unification within the Common Market (in 1970 the completion of economic union should bring standardisation of charges). Until coal-mining began and the steam engine came into use, energy was available at widely dispersed locations: wood fires from the forests, or the force of the wind and the flow of streams and rivers harnessed by thousands of wind- and water-mills, led to the creation of numerous small-scale production and consumption sites. With the industrial revolution, the coming of coal destroyed this pattern of power utilisation at isolated, dispersed sites. The difficulty and expense of transporting coal favoured the concentration of men and industry. The coming of electricity changed the system of energy distribution hardly at all. A few centres simply developed near to hydro-electric sites, and western France appeared more and more at a disadvantage.

In the last twenty years the situation has changed significantly, and the next twenty can be expected to reinforce the changes. The sources of energy have become more varied; gas has taken its place beside fuel-oil, and tidal power together with nuclear power is developing for the future. The production and transport of power are becoming increasingly international, and this trend is bound to continue. These new factors will give more equal opportunities to the various regions of France. Production of energy will become more varied and at the same time more mobile. It will no longer be confined for several decades to a small number of powerful coalfields, as it was from the beginning of the century until recently.

28. The E.E.C.'s demand for energy, which was 461 million T.E.C. in 1960, would be 700 million T.E.C. in 1970, 850 in 1975. It is estimated that in 1975 imports will meet more than 50% of the fuel and power needs of Common Market Europe (without taking into account the possible discovery of new energy resources).

III

THE TRANSPORT INFRASTRUCTURE

The influence of natural conditions on the trunk routes has already been made clear; looking at the networks of various periods, we find corridors fitted by their natural advantages to carry roads: the Alpine passes, the Lauragais, Poitou, Burgundy and Vermandois gates (cols), the Toul gap, the Morvan crossroads, the Rhône and Rhine valleys, and the Saône plains. On the other hand, regions unfavourable to the establishment of a dense communications network can be seen on all the maps: the southern Alps and all the south of the Central Massif in particular.

Climatic conditions do not impede road traffic on a large scale. Obviously snow closes the passes in the Alps, the Pyrenees and the Central Massif. But powerful mechanical devices make it possible to clear snow rapidly from the roads. There are still some 'difficult' areas in the Central Massif, owing to the relief and to the dispersed distribution of population. On the main routes traffic may be interrupted for short periods; the situation is more difficult on the secondary roads. Villages and hamlets may be completely isolated for weeks in Aubrac, on the plateaux of Velay and Vivarais, on the Causses and in Margeride, and in the Lacaune and Espinouse uplands. Modern roads along hillsides or in cuttings are more easily blocked than the ancient trackways which followed crest-lines. However, one exceptionally severe winter, such as that of 1962–3, is enough to cause considerable damage to the roads, block the waterways and make long stretches impassable for weeks.

But these natural conditions have had little influence on the overall pattern of communication. The distinctive feature of both roads and railways is their convergence on Paris. The trunk roads, the main railway lines and the principal motorways all start from Paris.

1. THE ROAD PATTERN

A. Growth

The roads radiating from the capital are one of the most familiar features of the map of France. The radial pattern is very old; it goes back to the days of political unification. Since Louis XI, the road network has been a centralising influence deliberately used as such by the central power—monarchy, Empire or republic. As far back as 1690 Colbert was writing: 'We must, moreover, consider the highway from the Provinces to Paris as the principal and most important one because of the constant communication between the Provinces and the capital of the Kingdom, which is virtually the only centre of consumption.'

The whole history of France is reflected in the building and the gradual integration of the road network. It is a combination of routeways of all kinds—feudal, royal, monastic, trade and military.

'Whether royal, imperial or national, the road grows when the State is strong, and dwindles when it is weak. And yet it has profited from internal crises, such as the insurrection of the Camusards, the Chouan rising and the troubles of 1848. Alpine roads gained more from the Napoleonic wars, those of the Pyrenees and the Landes from the same wars and the League of Augsburg, while the Spanish war brought new life to the roads of the North and East' (H. Cavaillès).

The great traffic routes gradually took shape from the routes of the royal mails. This radiating network of roads took the place of the old feudal and Gallo-Roman network which was very differently planned. The main axis of the latter was pushed over towards eastern France, from Marseilles to Trèves, with a branch from Langres to Boulogne. Side roads left the main axis at Narbonne, Lyons and Châlons, going west-wards to Bordeaux, Nantes, Brest, Paris and Rouen, and eastwards to Italy and the Rhine. Lyons, the capital of Roman Gaul, was the main centre from which these roads radiated. When Paris, instead of Lyons, became the centre, the road network was subjected to what Vidal de la Blache calls a 'torsion'; it moved away from the great north–south Rhône–Rhine–Netherlands axis, to the ad-vantage of the entire northern half of France.

The road network very soon attracted the attention of the central authority. Sully, Surveyor-General at the beginning of the 17th century, Colbert, who created the post of Highways Commissioner at the end of the century, then the Highways Department which became autonomous in 1716—these were the men responsible for creating and maintaining the French road network, but the map of mail highways at the end of the 18th century shows that their density was already very uneven, the North and East being better endowed than the rest of the country. The width of the highways de-pended on the amount of traffic they had to bear. Roads were classified, and the *routes royales*, the forerunners of the *routes nation-ales*, extended over a total distance of 40,000 km. The straightness of French roads shows up as clearly in the landscape as it does on the map. This is not only due to the inheritance or the influence of the Gallo-Roman roads. A decree of 1705 laid down that roads should be made in straight sec-tions, ignoring land holdings and relief.

This explains why certain particularly steep slopes are nowadys climbed by roads with one or more sharp bends of recent date, while the original straight section has reverted to a country lane or a short cut.

The French road network is one of the densest and most varied in the world. It consists of 935,000 km. of roads of all categories, 120 km. per 100 km.[2] area, as compared with 50 in Germany and 30 in Italy. We have 16 km. of roads to maintain per 1,000 inhabitants, as compared with 6 in Great Britain, 5 in Germany and 4·5 in Italy. This total consists of 215,000 km. of country roads, 370,000 km. of by-roads, 270,000 km. of departmental roads, 79,655 km. of trunk roads and 346 km. of motor-ways (at the end of 1963).[1]

There is a remarkable shortage of modern roads and motorways which can absorb large amounts of traffic at high speeds; it is a paradoxical fact that this dense network, which has remained very stable over the last few decades, now appears out of date. In the space of a few years the reason for its lack of adaptability has become clear; it is the sudden explosive increase in the number of users. The number of vehicles on the roads was 108,000 in 1913, 236,000 in 1920, 1,500,000 in 1930, 2,300,000 in 1950, 5,080,000 in 1955, 7,292,000 in 1960 and 12,405,000 on 1st January 1968, of which 10,565,000 were private cars and 1,797,000 lorries and vans. The road network is in actual fact far from being completely saturated,[2] but its structure has not changed, whereas there have been huge population movements in the last hun-dred years, as a result of urbanisation and rural depopulation. 15% of the roads bear more that half the traffic, and 5% bear almost one third. This saturation is per-manent in the Paris region, and seasonal along a small number of main trunk roads which the people of Paris use when going on holiday, for the holiday resorts are concen-trated on the periphery of France, in the South (see p. 124) and around a few towns.

However, though the road network may not be completely saturated, road conditions are nevertheless badly adapted to the present demands of motor traffic. The main roads frequently remain narrow (less than 6 m.) and cambered. Of the 79,000 km. of *routes nationales*, only 5,000 allow three-lane traffic and 200 km. allow four-lane traffic.

Since the Liberation, there have been improvements and additions to the road network, made with the aim of keeping a constant regular flow of traffic and eliminating the traffic jams which occur when towns and villages have to be passed through. A large number of diversions and by-passes have been made, as well as short sections of motorway for relieving congestion, as at Marseilles, Nancy and Lille–Armentières. The Motorways Act dates from 1955.[3] The first programme provided for 1,933 km. of motorways, of which 145 had been built by the end of 1960; a new programme has been substituted for it. This caters for three categories of priority; it places the 1,933 km. of the 1955 programme first in order of priority and adds a second group of 585 km. and a third one of 1,040 km., making 3,558 km. in all. At the end of 1966 the motorways totalled 830 km. The fifth plan provides for new building at a rate of 200 km. per year. In 1970 France should thus possess 1,700 km. of trunk motorways and 350 km. of urban relief motorways. Investments in roads are clearly inadequate, while, paradoxically enough, there is an annually increasing gap between the national revenue from road taxes and the money spent on roads by local authorities and the State; the revenue is far in excess of the expenditure.

The layout of the great national and international road routes, and the plans for motorways, clearly show:

1. An excessive centralisation on Paris; priority is given to motorways which will relieve congestion in the Paris conurbation.

2. A scarcity of major cross-country routes; there are none at all between the Brittany–Paris–Lorraine–Alsace and the Bordeaux–Languedoc–Provence trunk routes.

3. The disadvantages of western France in comparison with eastern France.

The present road policy closely follows the lines suggested by past conditions, or at least those of the last few years. Plans are based on the grading of traffic, particularly of traffic between home and work. No one appears to consider the innovating and creative possibilities of a network of motorways without the need to converge on Paris. It would mean that tracts of the Central Massif would be opened up, and its regions more closely linked. Above all, the road network of France would become an integral part of the European network.

4. The peculiar conception of the motorways programme; they are planned only to provide direct links between Paris and the provinces. There is no question of using them to the advantage of the regions they pass through or giving new vitality and opportunities for growth to certain towns. For example, the motorway from Paris to Lille does not serve either Amiens or Saint-Quentin; the first plan for the motorway from Lille to Dunkirk was cut as short as possible, without going anywhere near Béthune or Saint-Omer; the divergence of the motorways from Paris to Lille and Brussels will take place in the open country between Péronne and Bapaume, without benefiting any of the near-by towns.

Faced with the need for considerable sums in investments,[4] the public authorities decided to approve the principle of toll roads on the trunk sections, as opposed to the motorways intended to relieve urban congestion. Apart from the fact that tolls are, in a way, an alienation of public property, the toll system has many disadvantages, the most important of which is the restriction it places on access points and links with the normal road system. These are minimised to keep the number of toll-gates as low as possible, and thus to keep down costs. It is a pity that with all this accumulated delay the Government does not consider building roads with dual carriageways, but on one level, which would be a much less burdensome solution.

The economic integration of Europe poses the roads problem from a new angle—that of setting up a European road system. The Commission of the European Community, in its 'recommendations for the development of the transport infrastructure', has drawn up a map of the major routeways of Europe. But in most cases this amounts to no more than a juxtaposition of the road plans of the separate states. These plans themselves are often very traditionalist, and do not provide for any new arterial roads. On French territory the main European road links are the Netherlands–Brussels–Paris road, which is duplicated by the Lille–Antwerp motorway, and extended to Hendaye, and the Ruhr–Rhineland – Luxembourg – Nancy – Lan-

gres–Dijon–Rhône valley–Mediterranean artery.

Cross-country links are much less adequate; there is a Bordeaux–Toulouse–Marseilles–Nice road, a Le Havre–Paris–Saône valley diagonal and two tunnels through the Alps: the Mont Blanc tunnel, serving the Geneva–Jura–Dijon route,[5] and the 12-km. Fréjus tunnel on the Turin–Lyons route via Chambéry. North-west Europe, the Mediterranean coast and Italy will be joined through Switzerland (the Great Saint-Bernard road tunnel was opened to traffic in 1964) and by the opening of the Zurich–Milan and Innsbruck–Verona roads. The whole of France within the triangle formed by Paris, Bordeaux and Marseilles is completely isolated.

French roads have always been an im-

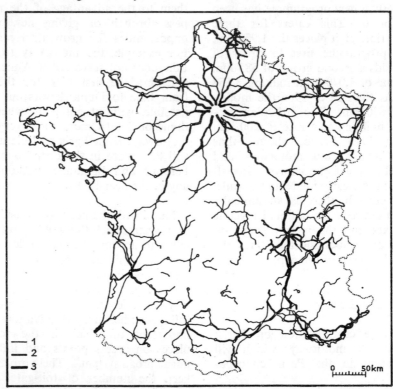

Fig. 55. Development of general traffic on the main roads (1950–55). (Source: J. R. Boudeville, *Les Espaces Économiques*, P.U.F., 1961)
Average daily increase: 1. 500 to 1,000 vehicles. 2. 1,000 to 2,000 vehicles. 3. More than 2,000 vehicles.

portant feature of the landscape with their avenues of trees which could be seen for a long distance, breaking the monotony of the plains. The widening of the roads, and also considerations of safety, have meant the destruction of the lines of trees. Little by little the roads are taking on a new appearance; besides the large amount of land they take in, and the embankments and cuttings involved,[6] the approaches to the roadways are subjected to what the Americans very aptly term 'landscaping'. There are hedges against glare, and plantations of trees and shrubs to prevent monotony.

B. Road Transport

It is difficult to grasp the precise nature of the road traffic because of its heterogeneous composition. There are travellers and merchandise, public transport and private transport, empty vehicles and loaded vehicles. Figure 55 shows the pattern of traffic on the main roads based on the growth of traffic between 1955 and 1960. Its characteristics are interesting from more than one point of view.

1. Traffic is heaviest on the roads radiating from Paris, and linking the capital with the big provincial cities on the Mediterranean coast, in the Lyons region, northern Lorraine and Alsace, the North and Normandy.

2. Cross-country roads bearing a large amount of traffic are scarce. There is the one between Saint-Quentin and Vitry-le-François, and the trunk road from Bordeaux through Toulouse, Carcassonne, Béziers, Montpellier to Marseilles. There is no cross-country road with a large volume of vehicles between Paris and the major cross-country highway of southern France.

Apart from the main arteries of the road network and the regions where traffic is heavy, the distinctive feature of the map is the recurrence of the radial pattern around centres on the major arteries or isolated from all of them, such as Montluçon, Dijon, Rennes. The small size of these star-like patterns and the large breaks in traffic between towns are equally striking. The map thus provides visual confirmation of another known fact: that the average distance travelled on roads is only 40 km. and about 80% of all journeys are of 50 km. or less. Long-distance road traffic is thus the exception. In 1963, however, public and private road transport accounted for 25·5% of all traffic on journeys of more than 50 km., expressed in tons-km. (rail, 63·5%; river transport, 11%).

1. Secondary roads were classified in an Act of 1836: *vicinaux, vicinaux ordinaires, de grande communication* and *d'intérêt commun.*
2. The modernised four-lane road is saturated if there are more than 10,000 vehicles per day; if there are more than 15,000 vehicles a day a motorway is necessary. All the main roads of northern France, which are saturated to this extent, ought to be turned into motorways!
3. The only motorway in existence before this was the one from the West to Paris, built between 1937 and 1942.
4. The Estérel motorway cost 4 million francs per km.
5. The tunnel under Mont Blanc was decided upon in 1949, built between 1959 and 1962 and opened in 1965.
6. For every km. of motorway, 30,000 m.² of land must be acquired in all, and 10,000 m.² for the roadway itself. The average volume of earth to be moved is 1 million m.³

2. THE RAILWAY NETWORK

A. Growth

The first railways were developed in two different regions, initially in the Central Massif, so as to give an outlet to the Loire coalfield, which at that time was the Ruhr of France. In 1827 a single line was opened, with horse-drawn trains, linking Saint-Étienne with Andrézieux on the Loire. In 1830 steam traction was first used instead of horses on the line from Lyons to Givors. In 1833 the Andrézieux–Roanne line became an alternative route to the Loire, which was shallow and dangerous for navigation. Later, some scattered lines came into use especially in the South, such as those from Montbrison to Montrond, Montpellier to Cète and Alès to Beaucaire. But the railways rapidly extended towards Paris, and the famous line from Paris to Saint-Germain, economically unimportant but destined to have far-reaching effects on attitudes towards the railways, was opened in 1837. At the end of 1841, however, France had only 573 km. of railways in service, whereas Great Britain already had 3,800 km. The railway era began with the Act of 1842, which provided for 3,600 km. of lines. This marked the beginning of the gradual construction of the lines radiating from Paris, in imitation of the main road network; this plan had been conceived as early as 1830 by Legrand, the head of the Highways Department. The Paris–Orleans and Paris–Rouen lines were opened in 1843. However, in 1847, when England had 5,900 km. and the German states 5,000 km., France had only 1,900 km., of which 1,250 had been built since 1843.

The real beginning of the French railway system dates from the second Empire. Paris–Strasbourg was opened in 1852 and Paris–Belfort in 1858; the six great companies which were to control French railways until 1938 were in existence by 1859. Their organisation and their activities in connection with transport have left an indelible mark on French economy. The 3,554 km. of lines at the end of 1851 had grown to 8,681 km. in 1858 and 17,440 km. in 1870.[7] Railway construction was continued with energy under the Third Republic, when the Freycinet Plan was carried out; this filled the remaining gaps and joined every prefecture and sub-prefecture to Paris with the railways' ribbons of steel. There were 19,600 km. in 1875, 26,327 km. in 1882, 36,800 km. in 1900 and 43,731 km. in 1910. The railway had then reached the most distant and inaccessible towns; it had reached the south of the Central Massif, where the railway did not penetrate to the plateaux of Chaise-Dieu and Segala in Aveyron until 1902, while the Bort–Neussarges line across the Cézallier

mountains arrived in 1908; and the Alps, where the line from Grenoble to Marseilles via Gap and the Croix-Haute pass was opened in 1878, the Albertville–Moutiers line in 1893, the Cluses-le-Fayet line in 1898 and the Digne line in 1911. After 1918 some 900 km. of rail were laid; loop-lines, tunnels through the Vosges; the line from Nice to Breil and Coni (1928) and the two international lines through the Pyrenees (Somport tunnel, 1928).

To the main system we must add the little local lines or narrow-gauge 'tortillards', serving thousands of communes, no matter how steep the slopes or how tortuous the way. They were built from 1830 onwards in response to electoral as much as economic requirements, and they reached their maximum length of 20,000 km. in 1924. The policy which led to their building meant that there were no great contrasts between different regions:

'Areas with dense networks of railway lines like the North and the Paris region are not extensive, and there are not many areas with very few lines like the southern Alps and part of the Central Massif. This widespread extension of the French railways is a distinctive feature of our country in comparison with others' (M. Wolkowitsch).

Since 1938 the *Société Nationale des Chemins de Fer Français* has taken the place of the companies. It is neither a state department nor a nationalised enterprise, but a limited company differing from other companies of this type only by a few details of its articles.[8]

Competition between road and rail, changes in distribution of the population and also pressure from powerful concerns led to a reduction in the number of lines in use, from 1933 onwards. Lines were closed either altogether or to passenger traffic, as goods traffic needs less upkeep and less security precautions. These closures totalled 5,388 km. in 1938 and 12,000 km. in 1951; they were mainly lines laid under the Freycinet Plan, which would not have been built if the motor-car had then existed. The length of line controlled by the S.N.C.F. fell from 41,200 km. in 1951 to 38,610 km. in 1961. Lines have been closed mainly in areas of gentle relief where buses and coaches can run all the year round without too long a route.

Since the Second World War the S.N.C.F. has undertaken very extensive modernisation of its permanent way and rolling stock. Electric lines, which amounted to only 3,340 km. in 1938, measured 6,890 km. in 1960 and 8,771 km. on 1st January 1968, that is, 32% of the total length of the system. A real little revolution took place about ten years ago, when it was realised that locomotives could be run not only on direct current but also on alternating current with normal industrial frequency (single-phase current at 25,000 volts and 50 cycles), which enabled the installation expenses of lines, sub-stations and overhead cables to be reduced by one third on an average. It was thus possible to make electric traction in general pay better, and in particular the number of lines where electrification was economic could be increased. Electrification has facilitated the provision of links between lines, and electrified lines have been adopted for inter-station links. On lines where electrification is not possible or justified, diesel traction is increasingly replacing steam. At the end of 1967 steam traction was used for only 8·5% of the traffic of the S.N.C.F. (66·2% in 1953) as against 74% electric (31%) and 17·5% diesel (2·8). These technical changes have meant great changes in the locomotive stock. There were 2,140 steam locomotives in 1966 as against 15,200 in 1938; the number of electric locomotives or self-propelling coaches rose from 1,100 to 2,670, and that of diesel coaches and locomotives from 670 to 3,840.

B. Rail Transport

Passenger traffic (Table XXXV) reached its absolute maximum of travellers in 1925 (802 million passengers travelling a total of 29,800 million passenger-kms.); but in terms of passenger-kms. the traffic each year exceeds that of the preceding year; this development proves that rail traffic is being maintained and even increased, despite the considerable development of motor transport. This traffic can be divided geographically into two distinct categories: suburban and long-distance.

There are many factors favourable to passenger traffic: for suburban traffic there is the outward movement of the population, the improvements in rail services due to electrification and the increasing traffic problems in towns; for the main lines there is increased travel on business (the 'business trains' which start from Paris) and the development of tourist travel, for example, in connection with winter sports. Car-ferry trains and sleepers, 'round-trip' tickets and parking space at railway stations all help to explain why passenger traffic is maintained and even increased. Passenger traffic is subject to considerable seasonal irregularities. This traffic takes 12,100 coaches (32,000 in 1938).

The breakdown of goods traffic, and its development, are shown in Table XXXVI. Railways remain the principal mode of transport for heavy goods and bulk consignments over long distances.

TABLE XXXV. S.N.C.F. TRAFFIC

	Passengers carried (in millions)		Volume of passenger traffic in thousands of millions of passenger-kms.		Goods (taxed)	
	Total	Paris suburbs	Total	Paris suburbs	Millions of tons	Thousands of millions of ton-kms.
1929	765	356	28·2	5	223	41·8
1938	540	250	22·1	(17%) 3·7	132	26·5
1960	570	318	32	4·5	227	56·9
1962	579·6	318	35·8	(13%) 4·6	231	59·8
1964	608	350	37·8	(14%) 5·3	248	65·3
1966	629		38·4		232·7	64

*

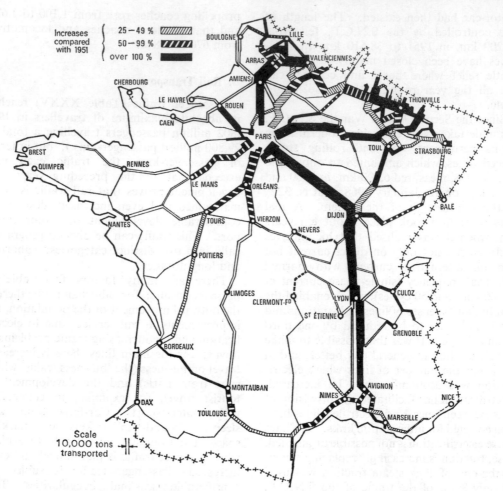

Fig. 56. Goods traffic of the S.N.C.F. in 1960 and its development 1951–60.

The transport of some classes of goods increased greatly between 1938 and 1962: chemical products (+361%), hydrocarbons (+204%), metallurgical products (+183%), quarry and earth products (bauxite, pyrites, forge scale and blast-furnace slag) (+162%), ores (+115%). Other goods have had smaller increases: foodstuffs (+73%), building materials (+57%), mineral fuels (+29%). Finally, others have diminished: animals −26%), sugar and beet (−20%), timber (−8%), retail and bulk merchandise (−4%). Three quarters of the tonnage sent by rail in full trucks is now sent off from private branch-line junctions. This traffic was car-

ried in 346,000 goods waggons of all types in 1964 (472,000 in 1938). This traffic is very unevenly distributed. At the beginning of

TABLE XXXVI. RAILWAY GOODS TRAFFIC
(tonnages dispatched, in millions of tons)

	1964	1963	1938	1929
Mineral fuels . . .	46·8	51·2	37·1	60·3
Ores	} 74·2	39·6	19·7	31·9
Metallurgical products .		30·6	10·3	20
Building materials . .	18·1	15·4	8·7	
Ameliorators and fertilisers	15·7	14·7	7·4	10·5
Hydrocarbons . .		10·4	2·9	
Chemical products . .		8·5	1·5	
Cereals and non-perishable goods . . .	8·3	7·7	6	
Bulk, retail and parcels .		7	7	
Quarry and earth products .		6·8	2·3	
Beverages . . .	6·3	6·1	2·8	
Fruit and vegetables, perishable goods . . .		5·2	3·4	
Timber for building, vegetable fuels . . .		12	4·8	8·2

1963 the electrified lines, amounting to 20% of the total length, carried 64% of the traffic. Traffic is increasingly concentrated on low-land lines, with their straight tracks and easy gradients; these lines have especially bene-fited from technical improvements increasing journey speeds. For example, the express route from Bordeaux to Strasbourg used to pass through Périgueux, Limoges and Mont-luçon; now it goes via Paris.

7. The Mont Cenis tunnel, linking the Italian and French systems, dates from 1869.
8. Its duration is forty-five years, and the State holds 51% of the capital.

3. WATERWAYS

A. The Network

French waterways classed as navigable amount to 15,228 km., showing how favour-able natural conditions are, from the point of view not only of relief but also of climate and hydrology. But only 8,460 km. are actually used, of which 3,635 km. are natural water-ways, such as rivers and lakes, and 4,825 km. are canals. Considering these figures, it is not easy to imagine the vital role of French rivers before the days of modern roads and railways. At a period when neither the state of the roads nor the horse and cart stage of transport technology permitted the transport of heavy loads, the 'moving roads' were used to the full, despite steep slopes and inade-quate flow; in the 17th and 18th centuries the upper Dordogne, the Lot and the Tarn carried to Bordeaux the wood, coal and ores of the Central Massif.

The French waterways have two salient characteristics: their extreme geographical concentration, and their outdatedness, which has recently begun to be remedied. The greater part of the waterways, and the most important ones, appear to the east of a line running from the Rhône delta through Roanne and Orleans to Le Havre. Only in the North and East of France is there a real network of navigable waterways linking the valleys of the Rhône, the Rhine, the Seine, the rivers of Flanders and the Meuse; in the South there are only isolated river-basins unconnected with each other, and a few canals, such as the *Canal du Midi* and the canal from Nantes to Brest.[9]

These sharp contrasts can be partly ex-plained by natural conditions; in the Paris basin and its approaches open to the North, East and South-east, links between river-valleys were easily made;[10] in these river-basins, with their oceanic pluvial or modified oceanic regimes, a regular flow of water was very easy to obtain. In the Loire and Garonne basins, on the other hand, summer droughts made it necessary to build expensive dams and reservoirs. But the waterways system can above all be accounted for by economic and political conditions. The waterways, in the present sense of the term, were contemporary with the Industrial Revo-lution and more particularly with its early stages, when the towns began to develop under Louis XIV. At that time the towns were fortified, the first factories appeared and the transport of heavy goods, such as coal, wood and stone, increased.

Until the middle of the 18th century the rivers were used in their natural state. However, a few canals had been cut; the Briare canal (1604–43), joining the Loire to the Seine by the Loing valley, was the first canal to be built in France across a water-shed. The *Canal du Midi*, cut between 1666 and 1687, connected the Garonne with the Mediterranean.

Canals dating from the 18th century are the Loing canal (1733), the canal running alongside the Somme (1724–35), the Crozat canal (Saint-Quentin–Chauny, 1738), the Neuffossé canal between the Lys and the Aa (1774) and the Central or Charolais canal (1783–92). These were mainly short junction canals. Just before the Revolution, 1,000 km. of canals were in use. The network developed in the 19th century, particularly under the Restoration and the July Monarchy, owing to the need to serve the rapidly growing industrial areas and to provide links between them, so that iron could be carried to the coal and vice versa, and so that the industries in the towns could be supplied with coal and with building materials. Between 1815 and 1830, and between 1830 and 1848, the length of canals was twice doubled. Among the canals built at that time we may mention: the Saint-Quentin canal (1810) between Saint-Quentin and Cambrai, the Rhône-Rhine canal (1790–1832), the Berry canal (1835), the Marne–Rhine canal (1854), the Coalfield (or Saar) canal (1866), the Eastern canal (the canalised Meuse) (1878), the Burgundy canal, which was planned in 1727 and opened in 1883 and the canal from the Sambre (Meuse) to the Oise (1889). This system too is based on the same desire to converge on Paris, a tendency favoured by the natural convergence of rivers in the Seine basin, even though the links thus made do not really correspond with the direction of the traffic. For example, the Marne–Rhine canal was of little use because 'the Rhine could bring nothing—not even by a detour—to a town like Paris, standing on a great river flowing into the Channel. As for Lorraine, this canal reversed the natural direction of the traffic' (C. Précheur). This waterways system considerably accentuated the contrasts between the well-endowed regions of the North and East, and the poorly endowed West and South.

Certain gaps in the system of waterways are rather difficult to explain; in the North of France, for example, the bad connection between the Sambre and the Oise may be attributed either to economic reasons (to prevent Belgian coal from reaching the Paris region) or to strategic reasons (it would be a natural invasion route). More abnormal still is the absence of a junction between the Sambre and the Scheldt, whereas the canal from Condé to Mons has joined Valenciennes to the Belgian Borinage since 1807. But the Mons coal-mines were controlled by French

capital, while the northern coalfield had to be protected from coal from the Charleroi coalfield. Since the 1880s the waterways had been losing ground owing to the competition of the rapidly developing railways, which, it appeared, were quite capable of taking over from them the transport of heavy goods. For more than a century the waterways were to fall into disuse and become out of date without any chance of modernisation. Practically no large-scale work was done on the waterways during the first half of this century.[11] Improvements to traffic facilities were undertaken only on the Rhine (the Grand Canal d'Alsace, 50 km., begun in 1928 in order to avoid the most dangerous section of the river) and on the Rhône (C.N.R.).[12]

Since 1942 the French waterways have been classified into three categories:

1. The large waterways taking barges of 600 tons and more. These include the Seine and the Tancarville canal from Corbeil to Le Havre, the Rhône from the sea to Lyons, the Saône as far as the confluence with the Doubs, the French part of the Rhine, the Meuse downstream from Verdun; there are 1,300 km. of them.

2. The heavy traffic canals which can be made to take barges of 600 tons with a draught of 2·2 m.

3. The main waterways, defined by the Freycinet Act in 1879, open to barges of less than 600 tons with a draught of 2·2 m.

This classification cannot hide the truth that the whole system is out of date and uncoordinated. Most French canals can only take barges of 250–280 tons, according to whether they are self-propelled or not, with a draught of 1·8 m. Over the frontiers of France, on the other hand, a system of waterways is developing which can take barges of 1,350 tons or more. German, Belgian and Dutch barges cannot pass through most of the French canals. Even the barges of the Seine, the Rhône and the Rhine find the rest of the network inaccessible; conversely, ordinary barges cannot venture into some large waterways, such as the Rhône and the Rhine, because their flow is too fast. These small shallow canals are interrupted by a very large number of locks which increase expenses and journey times and also slow down the rate of turn-round. On the Marne–Rhine canal (270 km.) from Vitry-le-François to Saverne there are 153 locks, one for every 1·7 km. The size of boat a canal can take is determined by the size of the smallest lock, and these are often 38·7 m. by 5·13 m.

The waterways are not only out of date; the systems for supplying the canal reaches are very often quite inadequate, especially for junction canals between river-basins. Water shortage caused by drought is a major obstacle which either halts navigation completely or causes a reduction in the draught which can be taken. We have also to reckon with fog and frost, particularly noticeable on canals with stagnant water. In 1954 on the Marne–Rhine canal between Strasbourg and Gondrexange navigation was impeded for 201 days; for 53 of these it was completely stopped. For more than fifty years France has had no waterways policy. It even seemed as though this method of transport was considered obsolete. We have to admit that the railways opposed this modernisation, since this state of affairs gave them a virtual monopoly of heavy goods transport.

Immediately after the last war, then, all this delay had to be made up. The modernisation of the waterways was urgent, and the situation was all the more serious since the economic integration of Europe showed up the French system as being utterly out of date.[13] The French network was becoming part of the European network, which had to be organised and integrated.

Modernisation included:

1. The completion in 1965 of the *Canal du Nord*, which shortens the journey from Béthune to Paris by 45 km. and cuts out twenty-three locks. But this canal is not large enough for international traffic, no doubt intentionally with a view to the protection of French inland water transport.

2. The canalisation of the Moselle. Since 1964, barges of 1,350 tons have been able to reach Metz.

3. The construction of a large canal for barges of 1,350 tons from Valenciennes to Dunkirk on the basis of existing canals (1968).

4. The continuation of improvements to the Seine basin upstream and downstream from Paris.

But the chief task is to provide a better link between the Mediterranean and the North Sea by enlarging and improving the main waterway between the Rhône and eastern France. This has raised enormous problems and considerable interests are involved; when the fourth modernisation plan was being discussed in the *Assemblée Nationale*, the Government issued a corrigendum mainly devoted to this link. A marked advance was made in the improvement of the Rhône for navigation when the various barrages of the *Compagnie Nationale du Rhône* came into service. The barrage of Pierre-Bénite, immediately below Lyons, raises the water at the Rhône–Saône confluence, and this cuts out the whirlpools which prevented the Flemish barges from coming down the Rhône, and helps the great artery of the Rhône to become an integral part of the European waterways; the opening of the whole of the Rhône waterway planned for 1972 has been put back to 1976 because of increasing absolute and relative costs (e.g. the cost of barrages and the growing gap between the cost price of power generated from them and the price of thermal power).

The key problem is, however, that of creating links between the Rhône valley and the Rhine and Meuse basins draining to the North Sea. There are three possible projects:

1. To link the Saône to the Rhine by way of the Doubs, in co-ordination with the development of the Rhine. To the north of Vogelgrun, the most northerly barrage of the Grand Canal d'Alsace, diversion loops connected with the Rhine will facilitate navigation as far as Strasbourg, from 1970

onwards. North of Strasbourg two other diversions are planned at Gambsheim and Roppenheim. These developments should serve to integrate Alsace more closely into the French economy and to prevent it from 'developing in an extra-French context'.

2. To link the Saône to the Moselle by the *Canal de l'Est*. From Frouard, the upper limit of the canalisation of the Moselle, the development of the *Canal de l'Est* would be continued to rejoin the Saône at Conflandrey. This waterway, about 300 km. long, would be able to take convoys of 3,000 tons. It would include about thirty locks and one or two elevators, one of them as compensation for the 120-m. change of level at the drop into the Saône plain. Nancy would thus be less than five days' journey from the Mediterranean. This way sets some difficult technical problems, such as that of water supply.

3. To link the Saône to the Meuse. On 1st September 1960 the Belgian Meuse was developed to take barges of European gauge as far as the French frontier, where the Meuse is canalised to take 280-ton barges. Adoption of the European gauge would link eastern France with Antwerp. But this waterway has the disadvantage of passing very far to the west of the Lorraine coalfield.

In fact, notwithstanding promises many times renewed at the highest levels, the tasks to be accomplished before this great scheme can really get under way will not be completed for some years. The programmes of the fifth plan only cover the canalisation of the Moselle at a wide gauge from Metz to Frouard and from Toul to Neuves-Maisons, the improvement of the Saône at a wide gauge up to Chalon and the branch to the port of Fos (Fos—Port de Bouc canal). This modernisation and integration into Europe, though doubtless necessary, has and would have the effect of accentuating the contrasts between the two parts of France. For this reason other projects are sought: the modernisation of the *Canal du Midi* would link the Aquitaine basin with the Mediterranean and the Rhône by way of the canal from Sète to the Rhône. A modern link between the Seine and the East of France would be provided by the Aisne.

B. Inland Waterway Transport

Traffic on the waterways has increased more or less regularly: 1890, 24,167,000 tons; 1900, 32,445,000 tons; 1910, 34,623,000 tons; 1925, 37,105,000 tons; 1930, 53,297,000 tons; 1945, 15,271,000 tons; 1950, 42,454,000 tons; 1960, 68,048,000 tons; 1966, 93,456,000 tons. This traffic has not grown in proportions comparable to the growth of road or rail traffic. From 1913 to 1957 it grew by 58% as against 115% for the railways. But this growth, even allowing for the inflexibility of the waterway network, bears witness to the permanence of the waterways' function. In 1964 traffic could be broken down into: *internal traffic*, 58,804,000 tons; *external traffic*, 26,814,000 tons; of which 11,490,000 tons were loaded in France, 9,097,000 tons imported and 6,227,000 tons in transit.

Table XXXVII shows the principal cate-

TABLE XXXVII.   TRAFFIC ON THE WATERWAYS (in thousands of tons)

	1930	%	1953	%	1960	%	1966	%
Coal	16,848	31·6	13,319	26·3	12,435	18·2	9,600	10·4
Minerals and building materials .	20,624	38·6	19,336	38	26,283	38·6	44,892	48
Fertilisers and ameliorators . .	2,004	3·8	1,628	3·2	2,282	3·3	2,209	2·4
Manufactured metal goods . .	752	1·4	1,969	3·9	4,146	6·1	4,688	5
Raw materials for metallurgical industries .	2,976	5·6	1,787	3·5	2,715	4	1,885	2
Miscellaneous industrial products .	2,057	3·9	1,795	3·5	2,461	3·6	2,461	2·6
Agricultural products . . .	4,624	8·7	3,328	6·5	4,864	7·1	7,003	7·5
Hydrocarbons.	1,603	3	5,655	11·1	10,479	15·4	17,640	17·6
Miscellaneous	1,809	3·4	1,853	4	2,383	3·7	3,068	3·3
	53,297	100	50,670	100	68,048	100	93,456	100

gories of merchandise in this traffic; heavy and bulk products predominate. But the composition of internal and external traffic differs considerably; heavy goods (minerals, building materials, mineral fuels and hydro-

TABLE XXXVIII. TRAFFIC ON THE MAIN SECTIONS OF THE WATERWAYS

(in 1962, in ton-kms.)

Saint-Quentin canal	722,500
Scarpe–Douai	707,000
Seine through Paris	675,000
Scheldt: Cambrai–Etrun	616,000
Seine: Paris–Argenteuil	440,000
Seine: Argenteuil–Oise	396,000
Sensée canal	209,000
Oise lateral canal	179,500
Haute-Deûle	170,500
Aire–Bassée canal	160,000
Scheldt: Etrun–Condé	118,000
Marne–Rhine: Toul–Laneuveville .	108,000
Seine: Saint-Mammès–Paris . .	105,900
Seine-et-Oise–Cléon	94,000
Canalised Saar	93,000
Saint-Quentin–Cambrai	92,000
Seine: Cléon–Tancarville . . .	85,000
Oise: Joinville–Seine	68,000
Marne–Rhine: Laneuveville–Gondrexange	59,500
Rhine	57,500
Iron-mines canal	39,559
Canalised Moselle	28,000
Coalfield (Saar) canal	25,600
Marne–Rhine: Vitry–Toul . . .	24,000
Marne–Rhine: Gondrexange–Rhine .	21,500

carbons) make up almost 82% of the internal traffic; they represent only 60% of goods entering and 26·4% of those leaving at the frontiers. Manufactured metal goods, minerals and building materials, agricultural products and fertilisers and ameliorators make up the bulk of the exports. The traffic does not vary greatly in composition; the proportion of mineral fuels has diminished considerably while that of oils and metal goods has increased. This traffic is very unevenly distributed; 75·5% of the total tonnage loaded in France is consigned in four

main directions: Paris (31%), Rouen (8·1%), Lille (23·9%) and Compiègne (12·5%).

Table XXXVIII gives an idea of the amount of traffic on the busiest sections of the waterways.

The average distance over which goods are transported varies little from one year to another: 136 km. in 1930, 159 km. in 1950, 157 km. in 1960.

Inland ports. If the canal is the poor relation of the various means of transport, the inland ports are even less generally known. In comparison with the sea-ports,

TABLE XXXIX. TRAFFIC OF INLAND PORTS IN 1962 (in tons)

Ports	Total traffic
Ports in the Paris conurbation:	
Total	17,807,000
Paris	3,520,000
Gennevilliers	1,619,000
Saint-Denis	876,000
Boulogne–Billancourt	645,000
Strasbourg	5,983,000
Rouen	5,185,000
Port-Jérome	1,562,000
Le Havre	3,115,000
Gonfreville–Orcher	2,098,000
Dunkirk	1,951,000
Lyons	1,803,000
Bordeaux	1,604,000
Nantes	1,462,000
Denain	1,120,000
Gayant–Mines d'Aniche . . .	917,000
Lille	814,000

they pass unnoticed, as they lack the striking scenic elements, the enchantment and the mystery of those gateways to the open sea. Nevertheless, the traffic of the river-port of Denain is equal to that of Boulogne-sur-Mer, and greater than that of Dieppe or Lorient.

Table XXXIX gives a list of the main inland ports of France.

9. The Nantes–Brest canal is interrupted at Guerlédan.
10. The chief difficulty was the Burgundy gate—the total change of level along the Burgundy canal is 298 m.
11. The Metz–Thionville section of the Moselle iron-mines canal (30 km.) was opened in 1931.
12. The Rove tunnel, 7,120 m. long, joining the port of Marseilles to the Étang de Berre, was begun in 1911 and came into service in 1926.
13. The Berry canal was closed in 1955.

4. SEA-PORTS

'France has no inborn instinct for the sea,' the *Journal de la marine marchande* wrote not long ago. Nevertheless, the part played by sea trade in the economic development of France from time immemorial cannot be denied; but this development has, in a way, been forced on us by history, the building up of a colonial empire, and the multiple sea-boards. France has never been a seafaring nation in the same way as England or the Netherlands. For a century and a half the protectionist policy has relegated activity in the ports to the fringe of the country's economic life.

A. Maritime Transport

In 1964, 70·2% of France's imports (81·3 million tons) were imported by sea, while only 24·3% of her exports (17·9 million tons) were exported by sea. The weight of goods entering and leaving the ports is thus very unequal, over four to one. In 1967 the goods traffic of French sea-ports was 171,182,000 tons.

Table XL gives a breakdown of the import and export trade.

TABLE XL. GOODS ENTERING AND LEAVING SEA-PORTS

Year	Total	Petroleum products	Coal	Other goods
Imports (in thousands of tons)				
1950 . . .	28,443	14,427	3,482	10,533
1960 . . .	54,510	33,333	2,656	18,521
1962 . . .	74,143	47,174	4,480	22,489
1964 . . .	108,900	75,980	6,774	26,146
Exports (in thousands of tons)				
1950 . . .	12,731	2,871		9,860
1960 . . .	19,040	6,105	159	12,776
1962 . . .	29,219	10,494	824	17,601
1964 . . .	32,350	10,056	802	21,492

Petroleum products and natural gas make up an increasing part of this trade, mainly as imports (1960: 46·5 million tons, 52·5%; 1967: 118 million tons, 69%). They make up 87% of imports and 27% of exports at Le Havre, 82% of the total trade of Bordeaux and 82·9% of that of Marseilles (Table XLII).

Owing to the development of the coastal areas and the peripheral concentration of population and industries, a large amount of coastal trade between the French ports is only to be expected. In reality, this national coastal trade is not very extensive, and it varies very much from one year to another (3,720,000 tons in 1959 and 4,860,000 tons in 1960). It consists of the redistribution of petroleum products, coal and cement. The shipment at Bayonne of sulphur from Lacq has lately increased the range of products transported between the French ports.[14] One of the causes of the small amount of coastal trade is probably the protection belatedly given to sailing-boats by an Act passed in January 1893.

Passenger traffic by sea has always been important because of France's situation (British Isles, North Africa), her separation from Corsica and her colonial possessions. In spite of political changes such as decolonisation, and technical developments resulting in competition from the airways, this traffic has been maintained at a high level (around 5 million passengers were embarked or disembarked in 1966, the passenger traffic with Great Britain amounting to 3,877,000).

B. The Mercantile Marine

Ships sailing under the French flag have carried 59% of international trade by sea. On 1st July 1967, the French merchant navy, with 1,538 ships totalling 5,577,000 gross registered tons (g.r.t.), was the tenth largest national fleet, coming between the Netherlands and West Germany, and the third of the five sea powers in the E.E.C. This fleet consisted of 640 ships over 125 tons (g.r.t.), comprising: 50 passenger ships, 141 oil tankers, 15 vessels for the transport of gas or sulphur, 37 for minerals and bulk products, 39 banana and polythermal boats and 359 other cargo-boats. The oil tankers are of increasingly heavy tonnage. Little vessels of 10–15,000 tons are being progressively replaced by huge ones of more than 100,000 dead weight tons.

C. The Port Structure

Owing to her long coastline and multiple seaboards, France has a large number of ports, on the sea and on river estuaries. In 1966, twenty ports handled a trade of at least 300,000 tons; but only thirteen of them handled a trade of 1 million tons or more (Table XLI). Two important groups of

competition is bound to get worse with the development of the Common Market, the disappearance of customs barriers and the establishment of the great European systems of transport.

The French ports are handicapped: (*1*) by their number—sufficient credit cannot be allocated to each one; (*2*) by their management—the State helps them much less than

TABLE XLI. TRAFFIC OF THE PRINCIPAL SEA-PORTS (1966)*

Ports	Imports	Exports	Total	Oil Products	Passengers
	Goods (millions of tons)				
1. Marseilles group	54·9	7·4	62·4	55·5	813,600
2. Le Havre	26·7	2·9	29·6	25·9	368,280
3. Dunkirk	12·2	3·9	16·4	7·1	281,520
4. Rouen group	6·8	5	11·8	4·2	
5. Nantes–Saint-Nazaire group . .	8·6	2·3	10·9	9·4	
6. Bordeaux group	4·5	2·8	7·4	4·8	8,040
7. Sète	3	0·6	3·7	2·3	
8. La Rochelle	1·7	0·5	2·3	1	
9. Caen	1·5	0·5	2·1	0·5	
10. Bayonne	0·5	1·4	2		
11. Boulogne	0·8	0·4	1·2		728,274
12. Calais	0·9	0·1	1·1		1,922,440
13. La Nouvelle	0·6	0·3	1	0·6	
14. Brest	0·7	0·2	1	0·2	

* Imports: liquids and solid goods in bulk, general merchandise, fishing products.
  Exports: liquid and solid goods in bulk, general merchandise, provisions.

ports are far in advance of the others, with 61% of the total traffic: Marseilles–Saint-Louis, with 37% of the trade, and Le Havre–Rouen, 24%. These are followed by Dunkirk, 10·6%, Nantes–Saint-Nazaire, 6·9%, Bordeaux, 4·7% and Sète, 2·8%. These port groups between them share more than 85·5% of the total trade. The rest of it is shared between about fifteen ports, five of which each have more than 1% of the trade: Caen, Bayonne, Calais, La Rochelle and Boulogne.

Tonnages appear small as compared with those of the other great European ports (1966): Rotterdam (130·3 million tons), London (92·5), Antwerp (58·6), Hamburg (37·4). But in spite of their number, our ports are far from taking the whole of France's sea trade. In 1959, for example, 53% of French exports to foreign countries outside Europe went from foreign ports. Antwerp, Genoa and also Rotterdam and Hamburg benefit from these indirect exports. This state of

in other countries; and (*3*) by their sites—ports on estuaries and small inlets cannot take ships of steadily increasing tonnage. Only Le Havre, Marseilles and Dunkirk can take cargo-boats of 30,000 tons; Bordeaux and Nantes cannot take cargo-boats of 10,000 tons fully laden.

The first signs of a port policy appeared in 1964 with the creation of six autonomous ports on which capital investment will be concentrated.

This policy attests to the growing importance of the ports in the national economy. The period of protection is over and trade with the rest of the world is constantly developing; coal, coke, minerals and oil brought into the ports by ships of ever-increasing tonnages compete advantageously with French coal and iron. In this phase of expansion in sea commerce, France is rediscovering the advantages of her situation at the western extremity of Europe and fronting on two seas.

Her possession of good port sites with deep sea approaches tends to favour her to the detriment of ports that are more continental in location or situated on shallow seas permitting access only to vessels of shallow draught. The extension of the port of Marseilles into the gulf of Fos, and the extension docks at Le Havre and Dunkirk are the first three priorities of this new port policy.

14. At Calais, the artificial textiles factory *Filés de Calais* receives its sulphur from Lacq via Bayonne, by coasting vessels.

5. AIRWAYS

The growing internationalisation of investments and of industrial establishment brings with it the need for greater ease of international communication. Directors of American firms, for example, when choosing a site for their factories, take into consideration the proximity of an international airport. Air transport is thus becoming a major element in spatial organisation. France has the advantages of her position at the centre of the land area of the world, of the attraction of Paris, of the quality of service of her airways companies and of her connections with her former colonies.

The two airports of Paris, Orly and Le Bourget, handled 5,527,000 passengers in 1964, placing Paris second after London and before Frankfurt-am-Main and Rome. These aerodromes, particularly Orly, have already reached saturation point. There are plans to establish a new airfield at Roissy-en-France, near Gonesse, served by the Northern motorway (to open in 1972). But Paris is not the only international aerodrome; in the provinces Nice, and to a lesser degree Lyons, Lille, Bordeaux and Le Touquet, fulfil the same functions. Finally, France has since 1960 been progressively building up a network of internal airlines (*Air Inter*), either permanent or seasonal, which are showing themselves more successful year after year (1960: 16,000 passengers; 1967: 1·5 million). Though most of them radiate from Paris, some, such as the Lille–Lyons, Bordeaux–Lille lines, short-circuit the capital to good effect.

6. TRANSPORT SYSTEMS IN FRANCE AND EUROPE

Until the last few years the road and rail networks radiated symmetrically from the Paris nucleus. Thus a certain harmony, on the map at least, existed within the hexagonal shape that is France. The great arteries of circulation starting from Paris fanned out into the provinces towards Marseilles, Hendaye and Bordeaux, Toulouse, Strasbourg, Lille and Brest. They appeared to meet the needs of the country quite satisfactorily, since Paris is the social and administrative centre and the principal market in the country. The integration of France into the greater economic entity of Europe, together with political changes in the former French colonies, fundamentally altered this balance. The whole system of intercommunication has shifted bodily towards the Rhône–Rhine axis, and towards the vast core area of population and industry of north-western Europe. Every year trans-continental movement becomes more important.[15] At the same time the ports of southern France have lost much of their trade as the old economic structure, which owed a great deal to the colonies, fell to pieces; the liberation of the colonies has led to the reorganisation of economic exchanges on a new basis. There are other reasons too, such as competition from the airways which take to Orly the passengers who used to disembark at Marseilles, Bordeaux and Le Havre.

Philippe Lamour has clearly expressed the consequences of this situation:

'At present the greater part of France is not directly connected with the rest of Europe. What is more, large tracts of France turn their back on Europe, and look towards the Atlantic or Spain, from which they have nothing to gain. Others, situated along the natural axes of European economic life, are cut off from the main body by "cols", like that between the Rhine and Rhône valleys, which isolate rather than link the major growth areas.'

15. In 1960, exchanges between France and the rest of Europe increased by 5·5 million tons of imports and 11 million tons of exports; 40% of French imports were from Europe, and Europe received 78·5% of French exports.

7. TRANSPORT COSTS

Geographical distance is measurable in terms of mileage and the varying difficulty of communication associated with relief and slope variations, but economic distance, one of the factors in the cost of any manufactured article, is not directly proportional to geographical distance. Transport costs can artificially lengthen or shorten distances through the structure of tariffs and the methods by which they are calculated. Changes in rail tariffs show the different possible policies. For a long time, from its creation to the 30s, the railway enjoyed a virtual monopoly, as the roads did not yet compete with it for goods traffic as they do today. As the means by which the whole countryside was opened to modern economy, and by which a real national economy was created, the railways' tariff structure was very simple. Tariffs were made uniform without taking into account the actual running costs of the different lines. For slow goods traffic, freight charges were fixed according to the value of the goods carried. There was thus a twofold equalisation of charges, between the 'rich' lines of the plains and industrial regions and the 'poor' lines, and between light but expensive goods and heavy cheap ones. Upland areas of accidented relief benefited from these tariffs, as it was not too expensive for them to receive fertilisers, agricultural machinery and industrial raw materials, and to dispatch agricultural produce and manufactured goods.

In 1951 the S.N.C.F. instituted a new differential tariff policy. Freight charges were adjusted to transport costs by means of an index system applied to stations; departure and arrival stations were divided into several categories, and given index numbers inversely proportional to their size and importance (Lyons, index 2; Saint-Pol-de-Léon, index 6). The freight rate between two stations was determined by the sum of their indices. For a given distance, the cheapest journey was that between two large stations, and the most expensive was between two small stations. There were in addition reductions for bulk consignments and for full truck loads. Thus geographical factors came into play once more; the great trunk lines had the advantage over secondary lines.

In 1962 a revised system was instituted, replacing the station indices partly by distance weighting factors (from 0·8 to 2) depending on the cost of travel, and partly by a new classification of goods. As a result of this reform, some towns have been brought nearer to each other, and others more widely separated in relation to real distance; rail transport was given an advantage for long journeys and put at a disadvantage for short journeys. For example, charges from Paris to Marseilles have been reduced by 15·5%, from Paris to Strasbourg by 13·2% and from Paris to Bordeaux by 13·5%, but on the Paris–Rennes line the reduction is only 6·5% and from Paris to Brest there is an increase of 4·8%. In this way some of the major lines of communication are singled out and given every advantage; tariffs are based on whole lengths of line rather than on individual points. It is easy to imagine the repercussions of this reform on the location of industry, the overhead costs of firms and the relations between towns.

Freight rate differentials are a vital element of the transport system. Since several types of transport have existed side by side—rail, road, canal, air—fierce and completely uncontrolled competition has gone on between them, each trying to increase its own share of traffic at the expense of the others; many plans for co-ordination have been made without a satisfactory solution being found. Large vested interests are at stake, not only those of transport firms and organisations but also those of the firms supplying them with fuel and equipment.

The last railway tariff reform offers a compromise solution, by arranging for the traffic to be shared, long-distance traffic to go by rail and short-distance traffic by lorry; but in the past this competition which existed especially between road and rail was an obstacle to the smooth development of both regional and departmental transport systems.

PART FOUR

THE RURAL LANDSCAPE

The ancient and powerful structure of our French countryside, the land-owning system on which it is based, the variety of its soils, and all its enchanting beauty . . .   G. ROUPNEL

Because of their wide areal extent in comparison with the more restricted areas of towns and industrial regions, rural environments have received a great deal of attention from geographers, but not for this reason alone.   They form an ideal subject of study for two other reasons:

(*a*) The variety of rural landscapes in France is a remarkable characteristic which has provoked many research projects over a long period.

(*b*) It is in the analysis of the spatial patterns of rural areas that the distinctive contribution of geographical methods can be displayed to the best advantage.

Rural landscapes show, better than do urban ones, the dual influence of man and nature. In the use of land by peasant communities we can see—easily or with difficulty—the fascinating struggle between human societies and natural geographical surroundings which has been going on in France for centuries.

The first chapter shows how the land was appropriated and divided into farms.   The second chapter reviews the types of land use and types of farming.   The third chapter examines the various elements of the rural landscapes.

I

LAND-OWNERSHIP AND FARMS

The explanation of rural landscapes must be sought to a large extent in the history of the social classes to which the present owners of the land belong.

R. DION

1. LAND-OWNERSHIP

The appropriation of land is the first phase of geographical development. Before the industrial revolution, when the population was mainly rural, the chief source of income was the soil. The lord of the manor owed his power to the produce sold by the serfs who worked on his land, or the rent he received from his peasants; the fortunes of the burghers in the towns often depended on the income from their country estates; while those who worked the land have always striven to own the plots they tilled.

A. Landowners

A survey which appeared in 1965 estimated the number of agricultural landowners at less than 4 million. The present structure of rural land-ownership in France is very complex, reflecting the entire history of France since the Middle Ages. Seven categories of landowners can be distinguished: the State and public bodies, communes, private companies, the nobility, the upper middle class (*bourgeoisie*), lower middle and working classes, and the peasantry.

LAND OWNED BY THE STATE AND PUBLIC BODIES

The State and public bodies own a considerable part of the land, largely consisting of forest. The State forests at present cover 1,650,000 ha., divided into 1,108 '*séries*'

(management units); the State owns 15% of the forests of the Alps, that is 156,000 ha.

But independently of this, welfare bodies, savings banks, Public Assistance and similar organisations also own a great deal of land. For example, about twenty savings banks own more than 6,000 ha. between them; the social service centre at Clermont-Ferrand possesses 163 ha. in the black earth country of Limagne; the civic welfare home at Strasbourg owns 5,000 ha. split up among 240 communes.

LAND OWNED BY COMMUNES

The thousands of French communes all own agricultural land, pasture and forests. Forests are owned by all the 11,293 French communes, and together cover more than 2,430,000 ha.; they cover a particularly wide area in the east of the country (42% of the French Alpine forests) and in Corsica. In Haut-Bugey, for example, 22 communes own more than 90% of the forests situated on their land and 34 more than 70%. In fact, 3,764 of these forests are the property of *sections de communes*:[1] this is frequently the case in the Central Massif owing to the fragmentation of settlement into small hamlets.

The communes which own extensive wooded areas derive from them large incomes which enable them to carry out various public works. In 1956 34 communes of the department of Isère received more than

30,000 francs from the sale of timber from their forests. A smaller number of communes received between 150,000 and 300,000 francs (for example, Saint-Pierre de Chartreuse and Villard de Lans).

Besides the land owned by the communes, some is owned by associations within the communes. There are very many of these in the Alps and the Pyrenees. These associations, each belonging to a valley, a district or a syndicate, are long established. They also own collectively certain Alpine pastures.

LAND OWNED BY COMPANIES

In areas of extensive farming the land belongs to limited companies, whether family concerns or otherwise, and these are generally industrial concerns like the sugar companies. In the South the 'Salins du Midi' company is one of the largest landowners; it owns 2,300 ha. in the department of Hérault alone.

LAND OWNED BY THE NOBILITY

This is the heritage of pre-Revolutionary France; it has survived in many rural areas where there is little urban development and where the nobility is still powerful: in central France (Indre, Cher, Allier); in Sologne, Berry, Nivernais, Bourbonnais; on the borders of the Armorican massif (Maine, Anjou), the central West (Vendée) and central Brittany. But fragments can be found all over France, in the Paris region, Boulonnais and elsewhere. Some communes still belong entirely to one family; an example is Épinay-Champlatreux in the Plaine de France. This estate is largely forest.[2]

LAND OWNED BY THE URBAN MIDDLE CLASS

French townsmen have kept a strong attachment to the land, which explains their interest in owning and maintaining country estates. This type of land-ownership is an ancient one, which was already highly developed under the *Ancien Régime*. The burgesses were among the main beneficiaries of the share-out of communal property and the sale of national estates; medium-sized bourgeois estates became much more common as a result of the Revolution. The areas where a large amount of property is owned by townsmen are obviously the most urbanised ones, where there has been for centuries an urban middle class whose interests are closely bound up with the countryside and the land which they work through tenant farmers. The land in the Pays de Caux, for example, which lies between sea- and river-ports and is also near to Paris, is largely in the hands of business men from Le Havre and Rouen, lawyers from Rouen, ship-owners from Fécamp and stockholders from Paris.

In Marquenterre (thirteen communes between the Somme bay and Authie) three fifths of the land belongs to people who do not cultivate it: 420 landowners from the towns of Picardy, the North, Paris (16th and 17th *arrondissements*), Normandy, Touraine, Brittany and Maine.

This type of ownership has been maintained principally in districts where the capital in the towns has not been drawn into industry. From 1830 onwards, and still more after 1850, a large number of estates belonging to townspeople were sold up, as their owners wished to invest in industry. However, the retreat from the land of the urban middle class varied very much from one region to another. In Languedoc, for example, the industrial and commercial middle class, as new industrial regions emerged, abandoned its traditional activities, such as the textile and chemical industries, and commerce, to buy land and develop the cultivation of the vine.

It is in fact probable that the financial and geographical concentration of large-scale industry and big business is a contributary cause of the return to the land of the small-town bourgeoisie.

The North, the great wheat-growing areas of the Paris region, the Loire country, Sologne, Touraine, Languedoc, Bordelais and, more generally, areas directly influenced by towns are the areas where land-ownership by the urban upper middle class is most strongly developed.

Forests and dunes are often sought after by city men, such as bankers and industrialists, for whom they become status symbols, and are used for such purposes as shooting. Thus the forests of the Paris region were taken over by the bankers of the Second Empire, and in the same way the bourgeoisie of Lyons bought land in the Dombes. In order to maintain these burdensome estates, farms were attached to them.

But the exception proves the rule: townspeople have never been able to gain a footing in the country when they have been faced with a close-knit peasant population, firmly entrenched and engaged in intensive farming with a steady market; this is the case in Alsace, highly urbanised though it is.

Side by side with the traditional type of land-ownership by the urban middle classes, another form has been developing for about fifteen years: ownership by agricultural concerns which are not in the hands of country-folk. The landowners are cattle dealers whose aim is to integrate all branches of the meat trade, cattle-food manufacturers, canning trusts, veterinary surgeons and even industrialists and members of liberal professions who are dabbling in farming, putting managers in charge of their estates. It is a new form of 'speculative' investment in land by urban owner-occupiers.

THE SMALL-SCALE HOLDINGS OF NON-RESIDENT LANDOWNERS

Side by side with these estates owned by the nobility or speculative holdings of the upper middle classes, every commune in France has some part of the vast army of petty non-resident landowners. They are clerks, industrial workers or members of the middle classes whose parents, or even great-grandparents a century ago, were countryfolk whose descendants joined in the exodus from the country but at the same time held on to a few plots of land.

Land owned by townspeople who do not live on it makes up, when taken as a whole, a large part of the area of rural communes in many parts of the country. A quarter of the vineyards of Languedoc is owned by 3,000 town-dwellers. To Montpellier, Nîmes

and Béziers belong 120,000 ha., of which 42,000 are under vineyards: 450 Parisians own 65,000 ha. in the region. R. Dugrand estimated the property income of Béziers in 1950 at 150 million francs (1963). R. Brunet has studied the property belonging to townspeople in 369 communes of Gers (500,000 ha.): the inhabitants of Auch own 5,515 ha. outside the town itself; those of Condom, 2,112 ha.; of Toulouse, 4,525 ha.; of Paris, 2,591 ha.; of Bordeaux, 948 ha. This town-owned property generally falls within a more or less clearly defined 'landowners' zone', with radii of 18 km. at Auch, 15 km. at Condom, 80 km. at Toulouse, although Paris and some provincial towns have 'landowning colonies' at a considerable distance.

LAND OWNED BY PEASANTS

This is at present 60% of all cultivated land. From before the Revolution of 1789, a large amount of land has been peasant-owned, in contrast to the situation in other European states. Sometimes feudal rights were a heavy burden on this property of the common people and the peasants had continually to defend themselves against the encroachments and demands of the nobility, but nevertheless property could be transmitted by sale or inheritance.

The proportion of land owned by peasants increased from one third in northern France to more than a half in southern France. It increased under the Revolution; it was the farm-labourer class, already well provided for, who received the greater part of land shared out or sold. These workers built up their farms at the expense of the state lands and thus founded virtual dynasties of landed proprietors.

Small peasant-owned holdings are to be found everywhere, but especially in:

(a) The East (Lorraine, Champagne, Franche-Comté, Burgundy, Alsace), all, except Alsace, regions with little urbanisation.

(b) The South-west, where Roman law, involving the splitting up of an estate among the heirs, predominates, and Provence.

(c) The Central Massif and its borders (Velay, Cantal, Limousin, Marches, Limagne, Morvan, Poitou, Quercy).

(d) Large valleys with rich soil enabling small but very productive farms to be established.

(e) Mountainous districts.

B. The Development of Land-Ownership

Between these various groups of land-owners, the struggle for the possession of land has taken different forms according to the period and the region; it quickly became confined to the peasants and the town-dwelling nobility and bourgeoisie. With the development of towns, a well-to-do class was formed, independent of the nobility and fundamentally rural; this class strove for the ownership of land against both peasants and aristocrats.

From the 15th to the 18th centuries, nobles and bourgeois bought a large number of little peasant holdings, and built up estates consisting of one or several farms. In the 19th century, on the other hand, the peasants had their revenge; their possessions doubled in 150 years.

The growth of the population and the over-population of country districts caused a splitting up of estates in the regions affected; small peasant holdings were formed, which were made to pay by more intensive farming.

The peasant who can buy his land acquires a security, a priceless insurance which he often prefers to investing money or equipment in land which is not his own; the acquisition of land also enables him to enlarge his farm and make sure of an inheritance for his children. For many farmers, buying land is in fact the only way of being able to settle their sons.[3] In the last few years the re-wooded lands of 'dry Champagne' have been bought, cleared and put under extensive cereal cultivation by the sons of large-scale farmers in the central Paris basin.

Tradesmen and minor civil servants, who no longer live on their land or never did, having inherited it from their parents, end by selling it to the farmers. Sometimes the house is kept and used as a holiday residence; but, on the other hand, land owned by towns-men in rural communes is augmented by the sale of plots for building second homes, such as holiday houses and chalets.

New factors can in a few years completely change the structure of property ownership and farming in a region. The return of the French from North Africa is the most recent episode in these abrupt changes; since 1952 they have settled in the Toulouse region, buying farms and amalgamating them into large estates.

Land-ownership by foreigners, formerly limited to a few exceptional cases, is likely to become more general as frontiers are opened. Inevitably, low densities of agricultural population, and especially the existence of large tracts of waste and abandoned land, must attract 'colonists' from parts of Europe too heavily burdened with a farming population.

Since 1959 more and more Germans and Belgians have been acquiring land and putting in tenant farmers. The purchasers are often companies with plenty of capital at their disposal. The Ardennes, Haute-Marne, Seine-et-Marne, Yonne, Loiret, Cher and Indre-et-Loire are the departments most affected.

These circumstances explain the variation in the 'mosaics of land-holdings' from one region to another or from one commune to another; they reflect French society and its history, and make nonsense of any attempt at generalisation. We can take a broad view and contrast the peasant-owned land of Alsace with the Paris region, where townsmen own a large part of the land, or Charente with Languedoc, but contrasting types of land-ownership really exist at the level of the sub-region, the urban sphere of influence, the valley or the plateau.

The variety of natural environments, farming methods and types of land use contribute to the mixture of types of land tenure within regions and communes. Small landowners prefer the valleys to the plateaux, where medium and large estates predominate.

The influence of the physical environment

'. . . really exerts itself only in so far as it is called into play by the demands of those who occupy the land. The most difficult to satisfy of all landowners are . . . the peasants . . . this is understandable because of all methods of farming, the one they generally practise, that of working the land directly by very simple means, is the one involving the most risks. For this reason one of the most fundamental and oldest characteristics of the distribution of rural population in France is the establishment of peasant communities in sites where natural advantages reduce these risks to a minimum. These small farmers need land easy to turn and . . . with the right degree of porosity to counteract both excess and deficient rainfall. They also need places with enough alternative possibilities for every farmer to be able to find or make on the spot all the supplementary resources needed to make farming self-sufficient. . . . The acquisition of land by the middle class appeared later, and they had to be satisfied with the land which the peasant class had not been able to cultivate with any success. There are areas where the owners of small plots readily accepted the offers of the middle class trying to build up estates, and others where they would not relinquish their property' (R. Dion).[4]

These types of land-ownership are found closely intermingled in French rural communes.

The example of the Plaine de France. The Plaine de France is a limestone plateau covered with *limon*, to the north of Paris; it is an area of large-scale grain farming. Its 28 communes show a varied system of land-ownership (1955 figures):

The estates of the nobility, formerly much more extensive, now belong to about fifteen great families whose names are famous in the history of France. The largest amount of land is owned by the Parisian bourgeoisie, 40% of the area; but this category is variously held by middle-class families (17·6%), titled families (12·6%), industrialists (5·2%) and communities (4·6%). Local tradesmen, retired people, who own from 10 to 40 ha., wholesalers, shopkeepers, publicans and skilled workers form the group owning medium-sized estates. The liberal professions and industrialists (from Saint-Denis and Aubervilliers) have large estates, mainly established since 1918. The land owned by farmers is constantly increasing; it was 6% of the area in 1824, 18·5% in 1914 and 27·5% in 1955. Landowners who are not farmers and do not live in Paris own only 18% of the area, as opposed to Parisians and those engaged in agriculture. (After M. Coquery.)

The land of every rural commune in France is thus divided—fragmented, as we shall see, among several hundred owners, some of whom live at the ends of the earth and do not even know that they are landowners, having become so by inheritance, often from distant relatives. These millions of plots are the basic units of land division in France. This heterogeneous nature of land-ownership obviously does not make it any easier to develop a better system of land use.

C. The Price of Land

The value of land is an extremely sensitive barometer whose variations are governed by a very large number of factors, either natural (such as the nature of the soil, climate, aspect, relief and extent of arable land in the area), spatial (transport facilities and distance from large towns) or economic and demographic (pressure of population, size of farms, type of farming and method of sale—by plots or whole farms).

The value of land thus varies considerably from area to area and from plot to plot. In 1966 the average value of a hectare of arable land was 60,000 francs on the northern coast of Finistère and less than 1,000 francs in the Causses and Hautes-Alpes; a hectare of grassland was worth from 8,000 francs in Normandy to less than 2,000 francs in Lauragais. Meadowland generally has a higher value than arable land because it needs more specific qualities of soil, climate and situation. However, in the last ten years the prices for arable land have tended to climb as high as natural meadowland prices. Vineyards have a much greater range of prices, from 6,000 francs for a vineyard producing *vin ordinaire* in the Centre to 300,000 francs for one of the great vineyards of Champagne or Burgundy.

Prices for orchards vary considerably, from less than 10,000 francs (Poitou, Charentes) to 40,000 francs (Loire valley, Isère). Market gardens do so too, according to their situation: in a purely agricultural area their prices are similar to those for orchards, while in an urban area their prices compare with those for building land (100,000 francs per ha. on the coast of Var, 500,000 francs or more in the Paris region).

All observations confirm that land values have been dropping for a century. Between 1862 and 1939 this depreciation, in real value, was estimated at two thirds for meadowland and four fifths for arable land. In 1908 the price of 56 quintals of wheat was needed to buy a hectare of land; in 1953 the number was 32.

There are many reasons for this: 'the splitting up of property ownership caused by the rural leases statute, heavier conveyance charges, the growing gap between the prices of agricultural and industrial products, increased costs of building and building repairs, the growing amount of capital invested in farm equipment in relation to that invested in land, and the growing attraction of transferable stocks' (M. Dunant).

Nevertheless, the land is very firmly held; the smallest plot put up for sale is competed for by a large number of buyers, and young farmers cannot find land to farm. Between 1954 and 1958 the settlement of farmers coming from North Africa caused a spectacular rise in land values, of the order of 200–400%, in the South-west.

TABLE XLII. AVERAGE VALUE OF
1 HA. OF LAND
(France: index 100)

1957	In dollars	In wheat units
France	100	100
Germany . . .	400	270
Belgium	400	300
Italy	110	110
Luxembourg . . .	150	110
Netherlands . . .	150	150

Quality for quality, land is less expensive in France than in most of the Common Market countries (Table XLII). This is due to lower densities of rural population and less intensive cultivation.

D. The Structure of Land-Ownership

FRAGMENTATION OF HOLDINGS

These holdings, whether of the peasant, middle or upper classes, are very diverse in structure. Their most usual characteristic is fragmentation into plots. The average area of the French agricultural plot would be about 0·33 ha., similar to the old *journal*. There are many examples of the very small size of these plots. In Loiret, before the reconstitution of estates, 48,000 plots were shared between 2,771 owners. In 15 communes of Eure-et-Loir 17,968 ha., belonging to 3,850 owners, were divided into 49,610 plots.

Since the beginning of the 19th century, the plots have been many times subdivided. The main factor in this development was Napoleon's Civil Code, which abolished the law of primogeniture and substituted equal division between all the heirs. The Civil Code, 'truly a machine for chopping up land', greatly increased the number of small plots and small holdings. In some regions we see the absolute limit in land division; as the plots could no longer be physically divided, the heirs received various exiguous rights; 'At Plougastel, some narrow strips were divided into thirty-two parts, each with a registration number, although only a single plot was concerned. One of them is divided into four parts, respectively twelve, eight, nine and three thirty-seconds. To complicate matters, some of these portions carry only the ownership, others the usufruct' (A. Meynier).

However, it would be a mistake to think that the whole of France is equally subject to this fragmentation of holdings. It is found in varying degrees, being at its greatest in areas of nucleated settlement and open fields with strip-cultivation, in areas of tenant-farming, in densely populated cantons and on islands.

Moreover, even in these regions the plots belonging to one person may be adjacent, forming groups of 'property blocks'. An inquiry in 1891 counted 62 million such 'blocks', with the very small average area of 85 ares.

The land is least fragmented in areas of dispersed settlement where the land is owner-farmed; a farmhouse and the land around it then forms the estate of one single occupier. In the west of the Central Massif, Limousin and Cantal have long clung to the principle of an undivided estate. Some provinces, such as the Basque country and Béarn, have avoided fragmentation of inheritances by retaining the system of primogeniture; this explains the greater average area of estates and farms where owner-farming predominates.

All types of land division can exist, from complete fragmentation into scattered tiny plots to consolidated large estates. Physical factors play as large a part as human factors in determining the types of land division in France. The structure of estates differs greatly according to origin. Some were established in the first place with a view to farming, and their land kept together in one block. In the 17th and 18th centuries, for example, land holdings were consolidated by monastic orders and nobles with a view to dividing it into domains. Other properties were acquired as investments and consist of plots which are not necessarily adjacent to one another. In any case, below a certain size a property is no longer a viable farming unit.

Fragmentation results from various causes, of which those due to the physical environment are not to be neglected. According to the type of land, whether homogeneous or heterogeneous, the system of farming and the course of settlement, the plots can form a coherent block or be scattered. In the South, estates often comprise a collection of plots including some on hill-slopes, some on benches and some on valley bottoms.

CONSOLIDATION OF HOLDINGS

This French system of small plots, split up again and again by inheritance, reached danger point a few decades ago; this 'cadastral fossilisation' was the main obstacle to the modernisation of agriculture. It was natural that a policy of consolidation should emerge to counteract the tendency to fragmentation.

The first consolidation took place in 1770 at Neuville-sur-Moselle on the initiative of the bailiff. But it is only since the end of the 19th century that several laws have been seriously concerned to extend it.[5]

Consolidation is in fact only an element in a more general policy of agricultural and rural development; this policy aims to 'ensure an organisation of farms and estates consistent with the rational utilisation of land and buildings, taking into account especially the nature of the soil and its conservation, agricultural techniques and their development, man-made environment and rural population, the general economy of the area and the particular economy of the land in question'. This development is carried out in three ways: by a redistribution of plots of land and buildings, by exchanges of land and the reallocation of built-over land; by the carrying out of any work needed to promote a rational system of farming, such as work connected with consolidation; and by the development of recoverable uncultivated land, especially with a view to enlarging farms too small to pay, the creation of new undertakings and afforestation.

The principle of consolidation is simple; all the land in a village is redistributed between all the landowners in such a way that each keeps land of the same monetary value as before. The new plots are as few in number as possible, as near as possible to the farm buildings and each has a direct outlet on to a road.

On consolidated lands, small estates are kept near to the villages and larger ones farther out. Conversely, plots whose owners live in neighbouring villages are moved out to the boundaries of the commune.

Land urgently requiring consolidation in France is estimated at 14 million ha., or 40·2% of cultivated land (excluding moorland

and woods). At the end of 1965, 4,690,000 ha. had been consolidated, the annual rate being about 300,000 ha. For some years the State has been financing consolidation to an increasing extent.[6]

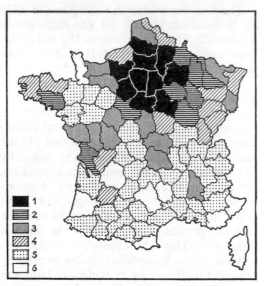

Fig. 57. Area consolidated by 1st January 1962. 1. More than 100,000 ha. 2. From 50,000 to 100,000 ha. 3. From 25,000 to 50,000 ha. 4. From 10,000 to 25,000 ha. 5. Less than 10,000 ha. 6. None.

Consolidation has taken place in 87 departments (as against 46 in 1950), but its progress is very uneven; it is most advanced in regions where open arable fields and nucleated settlement predominates, that is to say, in the Paris basin, where 14 departments have more than 100,000 ha. of consolidated lands, representing half the total amount of such consolidated lands in the whole of France (fig. 57). Outside the Paris basin about 10 departments have consolidated more than 50,000 ha.: Puy-de-Dôme, Morbihan, Bas-Rhin, Drôme, Poitou–Charentes.

The departments in which not one commune has yet been consolidated are: those in which the area cultivated is small (Seine, Alpes-Maritimes, Corsica, Lozère); those in which there is very little arable land (3·2% in

Alpes-Maritimes); departments which are predominantly under either forest (Landes (57%), Dordogne (32·5%), Var (49·1%)) or grass (Manche (63·4%) and Aveyron); and departments like Pyrénées-Orientales, where consolidation would set too delicate a problem owing to the particular type of land use.

In fact we must not neglect the special difficulties of consolidation in mountainous districts, vine-growing districts, regions where bush crops or special crops such as hops are cultivated, and grassland districts, and more generally, where varied relief results in diversity of soil, slope and aspect. Though the consolidation of vineyard and orchard areas raises great problems, it is not impossible. Aspères commune (Gard) is the scene of a two-stage consolidation; arable plots are immediately consolidated, but the consolidation of plots carrying vines is deferred, as the transfers have to take place when the vineyards are being replanted.

But the worst obstacles are still psychological, and it is due to this that consolidated communes and communes resisting consolidation often exist side by side in the same area; moreover, the agreement of all landowners in the commune is in fact necessary, which explains the slowness with which reform can sometimes be effected. In many cases too the concentration of farms, the changes in land holdings and private agreements either make consolidation irrelevant or bring it about themselves.

The actual distribution of consolidation is not without its dangers; it emphasises and adds to the contrast between the agricultural country of the North and that of the South, and acts to the relative disadvantage of districts already backward.

In consolidated communes every new division of holdings on decease must be submitted to the departmental Commission on Consolidation, and made in such a way that 'the new holdings created shall be developed under conditions similar to those of the original holding which has been divided'. For the consolidation process is never finally completed; after fifteen to twenty-five years the fabric which has been so painstakingly woven together is disrupted by the unequal dynamism of the farmers and by sales and divisions of land through inheritance.

Consolidation is, in fact, an undeniable step forward, but it cannot avoid a serious inherent contradiction: the aim is to improve farming through changes in land holdings. Such a policy can be completely successful only in areas where farms and land holdings are co-extensive. This is rarely the case in France. Specialists feel more and more that consolidation can only be effective as part of an overall policy for the reorganisation of the agrarian system and the rural landscape.

1. Part Three, Chapter I, p. 190.
2. The largest private estates in France consist of forests (2,000 landowners possess more than 200 ha. of forest) and areas can reach several thousand hectares: Forêt d'Othe, 15,565 ha.; Grand-Orient, 15,000 ha.; Arc and Chateauvillain, 11,000 ha.
3. 'The supposed love of the peasant for his land is more often than not, in overpopulated districts, no more than the reflection of the peasant's love for his family' (L. Malassis).
4. *Ann. de Géog.*, 1951, pp. 28–9.
5. Laws of 26th June 1865, creating *Associations syndicales*, 27th November 1918, 30th October 1935, 9th March 1941 and an order of 20th December 1954.
6. The State is responsible for 80% of the costs and the owners of the land bear the rest.

2. FARMS

The 10% sample survey of farm structure in 1963 recorded 1,900,000 farms with an average area of 17 ha. of usable agricultural land.

The numbers of farms and farmers cannot coincide exactly, because one farmer may have several farms, and, conversely, one farm may be held jointly by several farmers, even by people not engaged in agriculture.

These farms differ in their types of tenure, their size and their use of the land.

A. Types of Tenure

The type of tenure means the nature of the legal bond between both the farm and the farmer and the land. The classification of farms according to the type of tenure is given in Table XLIII; we see that the various types of tenure are found in France, but that none of them predominates overwhelmingly as in other states. 'It is no mere chance that in France, the crossroads of Europe, we find such balanced development of the Anglo-Saxon system of tenant-farming, the owner-occupation of central Europe and the share-tenancy (*métayage*) of the Mediterranean regions' (H. de Farcy).

TABLE XLIII. TYPES OF HOLDING (1963)*

Types of tenure	Number of farms	% of farms
Owner-occupation alone . .	865,900	45·6
Tenant-farming alone . .	352,700	18·6
Métayage alone . . .	39,600	2·0
Associated types† Farmer owning farm buildings	518,400	27·3
Associated types† Farmer not owning farm buildings	122,600	6·4
Total	1,899,200	100

* Source: Ministry of Agriculture (10% sample survey).

† This distinction was introduced in 1955 because of the growing number of those who are owners and tenant-farmers at the same time.

OWNER-OCCUPATION

This type of farming satisfies the farmers' need for occupational security, freedom and continuity. It is in accordance with the traditional outlook and temperament of the French to be master of one's own land, to own a place in the sun and to pass on a tangible capital to one's children. However, it needs considerable investment and diverts capital from improvements which would increase productivity. The peasant runs into debt in order to buy his farm or plots of land and pays a heavy mortgage which prevents him from buying equipment and becoming mechanised. Moreover, owner-occupation is not *conducive* to flexibility in the size of holding, nor to mobility of the farmers: the son succeeds the father, not from choice or because he is fitted for it, but by inheritance.

Owner-farming is the most widespread method of farming in almost the whole of France, except in the North-west and in the Paris region. It predominates overwhelmingly in the southern half of France, from Charente-Maritime to Haute-Savoie; in 26 departments owner-occupation represents more than 68% of all farming. It is particularly widespread in areas of small farms; in 1946 the average area of these farms was 12·9 ha.; in 1955, 87·7% of these owner-occupied farms had an area of less than 20 ha. In fact this system tends to adapt farm size to that of the owner's family.

Métayage

This is a very ancient type of tenure, the principle of which is theoretically sound. It is the pooling of two contributions; the owner provides the capital, that is to say the land, buildings, live-stock and equipment; the *métayer* contributes his work. The farming is also shared, as the owner directs the work of the *métayer*, selects the farm products and advises on buying and selling. In the typical *métayage* agreement each party shares equally in buying and selling, profit and loss. The result is the utter dependence of the *métayer*, who is subjected to constant supervision and control. Frequently the owner, if he does not reside there permanently or is not technically competent, delegates his authority to a representative or bailiff; three people, that is to say three families, thus live off the same land.

The origin of *métayage* is still disputed. According to Dr. Merle, who analysed the phenomenon in the Poitou Gâtinais, farms of this kind were founded by noble, and later bourgeois, families on the basis of peasant holdings. These, he says, were bought, or held by virtue of seignorial rights, and were grouped into *métairies*, which were given to the most hard-working or the most docile

tenants. The system developed on the model of the Italian system.[7]

Métayage is unfavourable to technical and economic innovations because of the tenuous links between lessee and lessor. Farms worked by *métayage*, apart from the specialised *métairies* of the South-east (arboriculture, market gardening and vine-growing), carry on the traditional *polyculture* (mixed cropping), to render them as self-sufficient as possible, cash crops being confined to one or two easily controlled products like meat. On the other hand, *métayage* 'solves the credit problem in agriculture' (J. Milhau) and makes it possible to grow crops that are subject to considerable variations in yield.

Though *métayage* may act as a brake on agricultural progress, the areas where it is carried on have been able to develop particular types of farming under favourable conditions. Their relatively large size allowed large mechanised farms and large fruit orchards to be established more easily than would have been possible in areas where farms are owner-occupied and smaller in size. *Métayage* works well in a 'traditional' social and economic context, but it is facing increasing difficulties. At the end of the last century it was already beginning to give way to tenant-farming, because of the general commercialisation of French agricultural production. There were 198,000 *métayers* in 1929, 138,000 in 1942, 72,000 in 1955 and 51,550 in 1963. The proportion of land worked by *métayage* fell from 13% (1882) to 6·3% (1955).

Métayage is still found extensively in Berry, Bourbonnais (Allier), Limousin, Vendée, Charente, the Aquitaine basin, Mayenne and Var;[8] but it is changing rapidly as a result of the Act of 1946 which improved the position of the *métayer* by allowing him two thirds of the profits.

TENANT-FARMING

Under this type of tenure the owner lets a farm or plots of land to a tenant by contract, for a rent calculated on a predetermined contractual basis, giving up all rights to the produce from the land. Once the rent is paid, the tenant is an independent agent, unlike the *métayer*.

Tenant-farming is becoming more and more important, but it is not proportionally as important as it is in neighbouring countries, such as England, where 85% of the farmland is tenant-farmed, or in Belgium (66·2%) and Holland (56%). It predominates in the plains of northern France, the Paris region, western France and Bresse, but the position varies from region to region. In western France a landowner often has several tenants, his estate being divided into several tenant-farms; in the Ile-de-France, on the other hand, a farmer always rents plots of land from several landowners.

Tenant-farming allows more effective use of capital than on owner-occupied farms; the tenant has the chance to invest in equipment and improvements to the farm buildings instead of spending everything to buy the land. But there are also disadvantages. If the tenant is not sure that his lease will be renewed, he neglects the use of fertilisers; thus when there is a succession of tenants the land becomes exhausted and the buildings fall into disrepair. In fact, instability is the main handicap of tenant-farming.

The tenant-farming statute of 1946 attempted to remedy this by granting an automatic right to the renewal of a lease except in two circumstances when the tenant can be evicted, namely for bad farming 'of such a kind as to injure the farm', or in the event of the taking over of the farm directly and personally by the owner or one of his children who has attained his majority. In addition the statute provides that the outgoing tenant shall receive an indemnity in proportion to the improvements he has made to the farm, such as buildings improved or built, plantations and improvements in cultivation. Such indemnities are to be paid by the owner, not by the new tenant. Unfortunately these clauses can easily be altered or their instructions changed. On the other hand, the statute makes it difficult for the tenant-farmer to join organisations and

I

associations that entail collective investments and long-term agreements.

Some farmers are in a special, more privileged position, which allows them more initiative, when they are tenants of a member of the family, father or father-in-law.

ASSOCIATED FORMS OF TENURE

The distinctive types as described above are too clear-cut to give a fair picture of the types of tenure. In many areas tenant-farming and owner-farming are closely linked, the farmer being also the owner of part of the fields and very often of the farm buildings (in 1955, 73·2% of French farmers were both owners of their buildings and tenants of the land). This is the characteristic situation in the North-east, in Picardy and Artois, districts where nucleated forms of settlement permit buildings and land to be independent of one another. Some tenants are even owners of other farms. In eleven communes in the west of the Pays de Caux, for example, out of 7,417 ha. of land belonging to non-farmers, 1,184 ha. are worked by tenants who have bought not the farm they work but another farm into which they have in their turn put a tenant.

Apart from *métayage*, which is declining, the structure of land tenure is very stable. Owner-occupied farms covered 59·8% of France in 1882 and 55·3% in 1955; the figures are respectively 27·2 and 38% for tenant-farming. For about ten years tenant-farming has appeared to be expanding at the expense of owner-occupation since the farmer, in considering how to apply his investments, has to choose between buying equipment, which is the principal necessity if he is to keep his farm in good condition and make it pay, and buying land, which means that he must forgo all modernisation.

But within these general tendencies regional differences reappear and make simplification impossible. The demographic and economic situation in the past, as well as contemporary conditions, all help to explain why the pattern of development should be completely reversed as between one district and another;

in the Pays de Caux, for example, owner-occupation is making progress, while tenant-farming is increasing in Ouche.

B. Farm Size

Table XLIV shows the proportion, in numbers and in area, of the different classes of farms according to size (1963).

There is no doubt that France appears as a nation of small farmers, but nevertheless it is not a country of small farms. In fact, though 49% of the farmers have less than 10 ha., their farms represent only 12·2% of the cultivated land, while a quarter (28·7%) of it is worked by 5·6% of the farmers on farms of more than 50 ha.

The standard division of farms is into small (less than 10 ha.), medium (10–50 ha.) and large (over 50 ha.) farms. But the value of statistical grouping is relative; a market garden of 20 ha. may be a large concern, while 30 ha. in the Causses may constitute a small farm.

TABLE XLIV. NUMBER OF FARMS AND AREAS FARMED, BY SIZE CLASSES (1963)*

Size classes (ha.)	Number Farm	%	Total area (thousands of ha.)	%	Average area (ha.)
less than 1	94,010	4·9	55	0·1	0·58
1–1·99	153,740	8·1	} 1,200	3·7	2·75
2–4·99	300,160	15·8			
5–9·99	364,020	19·2	2,700	8·4	7·39
10–19·99	484,980	25·5	7,000	21·9	14·43
20–49·99	393,900	20·8	11,900	37·2	30·12
50–99·99	84,900	4·5	5,500	17·2	64·70
100 and over	23,470	1·2	3,700	11·5	158·11
Total	1,899,180	100	32,055	100	17

* Excluding Seine.

So we must also be very careful in classifying farms on the basis of statistics alone. The category of holdings of less than 5 ha. includes a minority of true agricultural units: flower farms, market gardens, dairy farms and vineyards. The great majority, on the other hand, are not true farms at all. They may be:

Holdings for retirement or subsistence. These may belong to old farmers who have given up the family farm to one of the children and retire to a small neighbouring farm where they grow a little wheat and keep a cow; or to retired people, whether rural or urban, roadmen or postmen, who like to cultivate a garden, or ex-servicemen attempting to eke out their resources by growing a few crops.

Supplementary or subsidiary holdings belonging to artisans, tradesmen or even workmen or farmers whose children bring in additional wages from outside, or to farm workers.

In agricultural regions which need a large labour force (as in vine-growing) wage-earners often own a patch of ground, resulting in many small holdings of less than 1 ha. They produce potatoes, grain for the poultry, a few pigs, wine or a few special crops (endives in the North). There are also farms oddly called non-agricultural because they are directly farmed by townsmen of very different professions, butchers and cattle dealers who buy rich pasture land and members of the liberal professions investing their capital in specialised forms of cultivation, such as orchards.

A few statistical comparisons will enable us to place France in relation to some other countries (Table XLV).

TABLE XLV. FARM SIZE IN FOUR EUROPEAN STATES

	1–5 ha.	6–19 ha.	20–49 ha.	50 ha. plus
France (1963)				
% number	25·1	46·9	21·8	6
% area	3·8	30	36·9	29·3
Netherlands (1966)				
% number	34·7	51·5	12·7	1·1
% area	7·8	51·1	33·2	7·9
Belgium (1966)				
% number	38·5	50·1	9·8	1·6
% area	10·2	51·1	27·1	11·6
West Germany (1967)				
% number	40·4	46·4	11·7	1·5
% area	9·9	47·6	31·4	11·1

In comparison with these three countries France appears as a country of large farms, small ones being relatively less important in both number and area; but in these countries with smaller areas the revenue per worker is often higher than in France, since agriculture is better organised and developed in them.

There are few criteria for differentiating between farms apart from their areas. Gross yield is difficult to gauge because of the con-

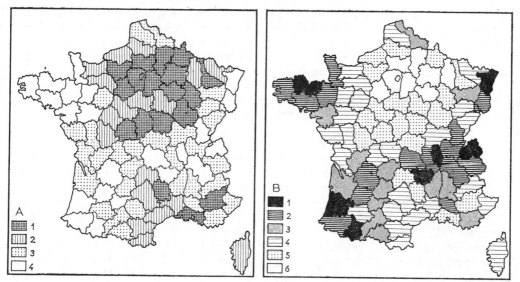

Fig. 58. A. Area occupied by farms of more than 50 ha. (in % of the total farm area in the department, excluding woodland, 1955).
1. 45% and over. 2. 25–44·9%. 3. 10–24·9%. 4. Less than 10%.
B. Area occupied by farms of 5 to 20 ha. (idem).
1. More than 60%. 2. 50–59·9%. 3. 40–49·9%. 4. 25–39·9%. 5. 10–24·9%. 6. Less than 10%.

sumption of produce by the household and the additional income brought in by members of the family, and there is usually no serious attempt at book-keeping; income figures in the *cadastre* give a picture which is out of date. Labour provides some more helpful data; in 1955, 82·1% of farms did not employ any wage-carners, 12·3% employed 1 or 2 and only 0·78% employed more than 5.[9] Table XLVI summarises the main characteristics of the six farm categories distinguished by M. Sebillotte and J. Chombart de Lauwe. Micro-farms, small and medium-sized farms all practise polyproduction agriculture. With the exception of the large farms, they are

family farms; the micro-farms, from 5 to 20 ha., are cultivated without the help of paid labour, while the small farms generally employ one paid worker. This group (from 20 to 50 ha.) plays a major role in the economy in terms of employment, area under cultivation and production, but it is also the most endangered in spite of progress over the last twenty years.

Medium-sized farms are also family concerns; they give priority to stock farming. Large farms are very few and of little economic importance.

The specialised farms of the competitive, capitalist sector of French agriculture are rare

TABLE XLVI. CHARACTERISTICS OF THE SIX FARM CATEGORIES

Categories	Number (thousands)	%	Average area (ha.)	Gross product (francs)	% of gross product	Agricultural revenue (francs)	% of agricultural revenue
Supplementary farms	403	21·2	4	3,400	3·1	2,200	3·7
Micro-farms (<20 ha.)	844	44·5	10·2	13,000	25·1	7,700	32·4
Small farms (20–50 ha.)	380	20	30·2	36,240	31	19,600	31·2
Medium-sized farms (50–100 ha.)	83	4·3	66·3	72,400	13·5	29,610	10·3
Large farms (>100 ha.)	23	1·2	160·9	168,950	8·7	48,000	4·8
Specialised farms	167	8·8	8·4	50,400	18·6	25,100	17·6
Total or average	1,900	100	16·9	23,400	100	12,500	100

and varied: there are vine-growing concerns, large orchards, flower and market gardens, large wheat and sugar-beet farms, rice-growing estates in the Camargue.

The regional differentiation of farm types and sizes is essential to geographical analysis. Figure 58 gives the departmental distribution of two size classes. Figure 58B shows the distribution of 5–20-ha. farms as a percentage of the total agricultural area, excluding woodland. These are particularly numerous in Brittany and in Manche, Alsace, Jura, the northern Alps, the Lyons region, Puy-de-Dôme, Vaucluse, the Aquitaine basin and the western Pyrenees. This distribution corresponds either to areas with intensive production of specialised crops, such as vegetables and fruit, or to areas with a dense agricultural population and traditional farming methods.

Large farms predominate in three regions (fig. 58A):

(a) The Paris region: Seine-et-Oise, Oise, Seine-et-Marne (more than 50% of the area is cultivated in farms of 100 ha. or more), Aisne, Marne, Eure, Eure-et-Loir.

(b) The Centre: Indre, Cher, Nièvre, Côte-d'Or.

(c) The South-east, from Pyrénées-Orientales to Alpes-Maritimes and in Basses-Alpes and Lozère (large farms with extensive sheep-rearing).

Farms of more than 50 ha. represent more than 10% of the number of farms in 22 departments. The regions particularly lacking in large farms are the West, the Basque country, central Aquitaine, the Lyons region and Alsace.

While there is a general tendency in the various regions for a certain type of farming to predominate, there is great variety in every department, even in every commune. Table XLVII gives a few departmental examples.

The geographer is bound to consider the problem of the possible relationships between the physical environment and farm size. Some areas without much topographical variety can support farms of very different sizes. Over the centuries, cropping conditions, agricultural techniques, size of families and rural organisations have determined the range and pattern of farm sizes. In areas of sedimentary plateaux broken by wide valleys, small farms in the valley bottoms, with fields climbing up the slopes, contrast with large farms on the plateaux.

TABLE XLVII. SIZE OF FARMS IN SELECTED DEPARTMENTS

(Proportions in % of the total number—farms of less than 5 ha. included, woodland excluded, in 1955)

	5–9·99 ha.	10–19·99 ha.	20–49·9 ha.	+50 ha.
	%	%	%	%
Aisne	12·5	20·2	27·6	20·5
Aveyron	21·7	26·9	19·1	6·5
Calvados	20·2	23·3	22·3	7·7
Cantal	17·2	29·2	30·4	9·5
Côte-d'Or	14	14·8	22·1	16·3
Loir-et-Cher	15·4	16·9	19·1	7·5
Nièvre	15·6	17	19·1	13

But in accidented areas with numerous incised valleys, such as are often found in France, both in the ancient massifs and in the sedimentary basins like that of Terrefort, the correlation between the basic land form units and farm size cannot be missed. In the words of L. Gachon:

'In Livradois, Combraille and Limousin, there are farms with ten or fifteen plots totalling about 20 ha. This is exactly the average size of a physical unit such as the ridge crest or slope between two valleys, two ravines or two gorges, that is, between two of the thalwegs more or less wide and deeply incised into the crystalline massifs. Farm units tend to coincide with physical units, since whatever man's material resources may be, he is not likely, tomorrow any more than yesterday, to be able to restore what running water has cut away. Moreover, if such a levelling up were ever possible, it would be absolutely disastrous. There must be space for forests on high ground or on the steep walls of ravines, space for fields on hilltops and gentle slopes and space for natural meadowland in the valley bottoms irrigated by running water.'[10]

C. The Spatial Structure of Farms

Farms, whether of 5·5 or 200 ha., are made up of plots whose organisation, distribution and form result in some very different spatial structures (fig. 59). The first factor of farm organisation is the estate. Several types of spatial relationships can exist between the estate and the farm:

(*a*) The farm and the estate may correspond exactly. This often happens in the case of the large isolated farms scattered between the villages on the plains of the Paris basin, or the *métairies* and *bordes* of the West and South-west, but also in certain parts of Provence (the '*domaine aggloméré*').

(*b*) The farm may only be a fraction of the estate if this is very extensive; in the West we still find large estates divided into medium-sized farms, legacies of the division of titled or bourgeois estates into properties of a size appropriate to the labour potential of a family.

(*c*) The farm may be made by joining two or more properties.

(*d*) The farm may be made up of a patchwork of plots belonging to different owners; the farmer himself may be one of these owners.

As with landed estates, the local settlement pattern has its influence on the way farms are constituted. In areas of nucleated settlement it is not unusual for plots belonging to the same farm to be dispersed over the whole of the area of the commune, and even farther afield. Dispersal is due to the existence of old communal restrictions, to the varying potential of different parts of the land and to the aim of every farmer to have plots on each of the various types of soil. These plots may be completely scattered, each field or cultivation unit corresponding to a plot, or they can be grouped in such a way as to form 'cultivation blocks' similar to the 'property blocks'.

The disadvantages of this fragmentation and dispersal are obvious; the large number of boundary-stones and boundary-furrows reduces the cultivable area; a field of 1 ha. has 4 m. of boundary-furrows per acre as against 1·26 for a field of 10 ha. However, we must not blame the divisions of agricultural land for everything; it favours multi-

cropping and reduces the risk of bad harvests; and formerly it was adapted to conditions of work on the land.

The degree of fragmentation varies with farm size. While the large farm tends to group all the land round the farm buildings, the small farmer often has a very fragmented property, with the plots several kilometres apart.

In areas of dispersed settlement the dispersal of cultivated plots is necessarily less, as the farm land tends to form a unit together with the farm buildings (fig. 72, p. 311).

Finally, in contrast to the first type, some farms comprise an area of large-scale cultivation, even though they may be made up of plots belonging to different owners. In some regions the pattern of land-ownership no longer has any geographical significance as the pattern of cultivation units is so utterly different. Changes of crops and multiple leases disguise the property structure. The farmers themselves do not want consolidation, because the present situation gives them great advantages in their tenancy. The result is three superimposed systems of holding; a plot is actually the property of X, who in theory receives rent first from tenant Y, though it is cultivated by tenant Z. This is a special situation, for in many areas landowners do not like all their land to be rented by the same tenant in order to make up a farm.

There is no need to stress the role of physical conditions, for they are implicit in the varying agricultural potential of the different parts of the land. When the system of cultivation is varied and plots of arable land, meadows, woodland and heath cannot be next to each other, the farm must necessarily be scattered. Conversely, large plains with land of a homogeneous character and areas of impermeable rock with dense drainage networks lend themselves to the formation of large property blocks.

The process of consolidation tends to make the spatial structure of farming more uniform, by giving farmers larger and less scattered plots—fragmentation is much

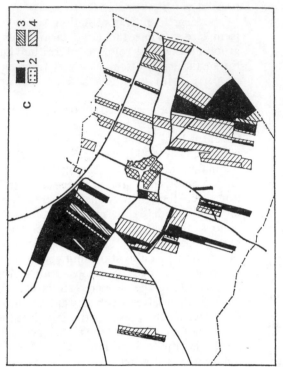

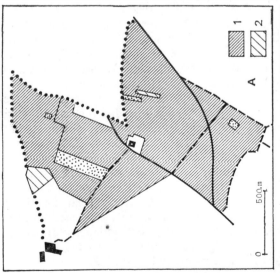

Fig. 59. Estates and farms, examples of spatial structure in Hurepoix. (Source: P. Gueremy, in *Études de Géographie Rurale, Bulletin de Saint-Cloud*, May 1959)

A. A large compact estate on the plateau (120 ha.)

1. Land belonging to the estate.   2. Land let by the owner to another landowner.   Estate and farms correspond almost exactly.

B. A very large estate divided into 2 farms.

1. Farm 1 at Bonnelles.   2. Farm 2 at Pecqueuse.   Note the difference in system of division; this is perhaps the reason for the maintenance of two different farms on the same estate.

C. A medium-sized complex farm on the plateau at Pecqueuse (47 ha.).

1. Land belonging to the farmer.   2. Land taken on hire from another farmer in the commune.   3. Land taken on hire from non-farming owners of more than 10 ha.   4. Land taken on hire from non-farming owners of less than 10 ha.

diminished. But consolidation has its repercussions even on the structure of the farms. The small farmer must rent new land if the land he rented has been put with another property, and sometimes he cannot find small plots suited to the size of his farm.

Consolidation brings many advantages. The farmer whose land has been consolidated saves time because he does not need to travel so far to each plot; he also saves on wear and tear of equipment, and on seed, fertilisers and labour. He has bigger harvests because the headlands and the unproductive borders of the fields have gone. He has more freedom in the use of his plots, which he can divide into fields and temporary meadows at his

the land holdings into large blocks corresponding to the farms (fig. 76, p. 320).

D. Changes in Farm Holdings

CONCENTRATION

Excluding farms of less than a hectare, the change in numbers of farms has been as follows: 3,466,000 farms in 1892, 2,949,000 in 1926, 2,118,000 in 1956, 1,805,160 in 1963. The average size of farms has risen from 8·74 ha. in 1882 to 11·6 ha. in 1929, to 14·1 ha. in 1955 and 17 ha. in 1963.[11]

This concentration of production has affected the different categories of size in different ways (Table XLVIII).

TABLE XLVIII. CHANGES IN THE NUMBER OF FARMS
(see Table XLIV for the 1963 figures)

Size categories (ha.)	1892				1929				1942				1955			
	Number	%*	%†	%‡	Number	%*	%†	%‡	Number	%*	%†	%‡	Number	%*	%†	%‡
Less than 1	2,235,405	39·2			1,014,731	25·6			220,641	9·4			150,260	6·7.		
1–4·99	1,829,259	32·0	52·8		1,146,255	28·8	38·9		615,673	26·1	29·0		642,658	28·4	30·4	
5–9·99	788,299	13·9	22·7	48·2	717,612	18·1	24·4	39·7	503,587	21·2	23·6	32·9	472,084	20·9	22·3	32·2
10–19·99	429,407	7·6	12·4	26·2	593,147	14·9	20·1	32·8	539,879	22·8	23·3	35·3	532,387	23·1	25·2	36·0
20–49·99	335,054	5·9	9·7	20·4	380,373	9·6	12·9	21·1	380,334	16·1	18·0	24·9	375,171	16·5	17·7	25·4
50–99·99	52,048	0·9	1·5	3·2	81,744	2·2	2·7	4·5	77,459	3·2	4·6	5·2	74,901	3·3	3·5	5·1
100–199·99	22,777	0·4	0·6	1·3	23,473	0·6	0·7	1·4	19,510	0·8	1·0	1·3	16,721	0·7	0·8	1·1
200 and over	10,503	0·1	0·3	0·7	8,995	0·2	0·3	0·5	6,632	0·4	0·5	0·4	3,522	0·1	0·1	0·2
TOTAL	5,702,752	100·0	100·0	100·0	3,966,330	100·0	100·0	100·0	2,363,715	100·0	100·0	100·0	2,267,704	100·0	100·0	100·0
Total number of farms of 1 and over	3,467,347				2,951,599				2,143,074				2,117,444			
Total number of farms of 5 and over	1,638,088				1,805,344				1,527,401				1,474,786			

* % of the total number of farms.   † % of all farms of 1 ha. and over.   ‡ % of all farms of 5 ha. and over.

convenience, whereas before consolidation the small size of each plot made it necessary to cultivate it as a whole. Poor land, originally formerly left waste because it was too distant or its plots too small, is now used for arable or grazing or is replanted with trees. But in areas where estates and farms do not coincide, the effects of consolidation are limited, and the plots remain scattered.

There have been some attempts to resolve this contradiction inherent in property consolidation with the aim of improving the agrarian structure. The village of Le Bosquel, 20 km. south of Amiens, which was totally destroyed in 1940, has been the scene of a completely revolutionary experiment. A second consolidation following on the one already made before the war has regrouped

Small farms of less than 5 ha. have been the most affected, falling from 4 million in 1892 to less than 600,000 in 1963. Farms of 5–10 ha. have decreased by 400,000, but they still represent almost one third of farms over 5 ha. Those of 1–10 ha., which covered 21% of the cultivated area in 1921, covered 12·2% in 1963. Farms of 10–100 ha. show a very different tendency—the percentage in the 10–20-ha. category has considerably increased, as has that in the 50–100-ha. category. Between the two, the 20–50-ha. group shows quite a remarkable stability; it represents the typical French peasant holding with 30–50 ha. under cultivation. This stability can also be seen in the percentages of the total area under cultivation. The last group, farms of more than 100 ha., has shown a slight increase since 1955, whereas it had previously been slowly decreasing since 1929.

Farmers have constantly endeavoured to become landowners, and at the same time have tried to enlarge their farms. This movement towards concentration began at varying times in different areas. It was largely under way as early as the 18th century around Paris, and farms of more than 100 and 200 ha. were already numerous in Soissonnais, the 'Pays de France', at the end of the century. The provisions of the Code Rural (1792), which gave the concept of property an absolute value, led to an increase in medium-sized farms, while very large farms were split up and very small ones disappeared. The movement continued with the consolidation of properties resulting from the sale of national assets of the second category (under the act disposing of the estates of the émigrés) and was encouraged by the role of land-tax liability as a qualification for the right to vote. During the whole of the 19th century there was a constant tendency towards the establishment of a peasantry based on medium-sized farms. Since the middle of the century, demographic, technical and economic changes have all been contributing to this concentration of agricultural enterprises.

Rural depopulation, the extent and types of which we have seen, has been the principal factor in this concentration. Small farms and subsidiary holdings, which were workable only if there were other sources of income, have disappeared. An end has come to the thousands of miniature holdings belonging to the brassiers and ménagers whose existence was only possible in a traditional, closed social and agricultural organisation.

The increased average age resulting from the departure of young people and the lack of any new additions to the population is the second major factor in the disappearance of farms, because there is no son or son-in-law to take over from an ageing father. The 1954 census enumerated 440,000 farmers over 65, that is 1 in 5, working 12·6% of the cultivated land (4,061,000 ha.). In 1963, 358,750 farmers over 65 worked 19%

of the land. How many of them will be left in another ten years' time?

A survey carried out in twenty-seven cantons of Finistère showed that 7,000 out of 30,000 farms are run by farmers over 60 years old and without a successor. In Morvan, 1,269 out of 4,181 farms working 23,285 ha. between them are held by men over 65 (55 of them are more than 50 ha. in size). These farms are bound to disappear within the next twenty years for lack of young people. The real problem is the fate of the 23,000 ha. They can be used to enlarge flourishing farms, or become the object of land speculation, or, which is more common, revert to waste.

At Saint-Oradoux-de-Chirouze (Creuse) 'out of 30 farms, 16 are sure of a "normal" renewal of population, which does not mean, however, that these 16 farms are safe from emigration; 24 of them are held by men over 40 who have no children or whose children have emigrated. Thus at least half of the farms are doomed to disappear simply by natural demographic processes' (A. Fel).

But as matters really stand, geographically, economically and socially, agricultural enterprises show the tendency to concentration in many different ways, according to whether it affects an area of tenant-farmers or of owner-occupiers (the former are more mobile, the latter more tied to the land), an area of open fields and villages or of bocage with dispersed farms, flat or broken country.

Depopulation and the winding up of a farm may cause the whole farm, or part of it, or simply a few plots, to be thrown on to the market.

The establishment of farms for retirement often paralyses all normal development of the land, as the farmer abandons the less favourable plots and restricts his cultivated land to a smaller area. The sale of plots is deliberately spread over several years, as the market value of plots is higher than that of whole farms.

In areas of dispersed settlement, where the farm lands are consolidated around the farm-houses, only the nearest neighbours are interested in buying a plot. Moreover, to split up a farm is to 'destroy' it, and people hesitate to do this; only the farms which are too small to pay disappear, and their land is incorporated in one or more neighbouring farms, the only ones willing to buy. In areas of nucleated settlement and open fields, farms can disappear as a whole or by plots, and the same situation obtains, for all the farmers in the village are in the same position owing to the fragmentation and dispersal of plots of land.

In fact, land put for sale interests only a limited number of farmers, not only for financial reasons but also with regard to the size of plots and the situation of their farms. Small and medium-sized plots are more easily negotiated and more sought after; very large plots only interest big farmers.[12] The land of a farm that has been wound up is not sought after to the same degree

'. . . because such a farm only too often has a structure belonging to the 19th century, and the demand is for plots which can be worked in the middle of the 20th century. In every commune can be found sought-after meadows which everyone agrees in valueing at more than 3,000 francs per ha. if they are near to the hamlet, readily accessible, and can be worked mechanically. Conversely, other plots, small, sloping, too long abandoned and inaccessible by road, are "not worth the muck you spread on them"; they are of no use to anyone in the vicinity. Here we can see, to the life, the paralysis of an agrarian system which has developed very little since the period when it was well adapted to a dense population and a 19th century economy. Today we have to salvage what we can from it, and small farms trying to modernise and expand do not always find what they want' (A. Fel).

The physical setting may also prevent farms from expanding. If they are situated at the bottom of steep-sided valleys or, at the other extreme, clinging to the top of an interfluve, they cannot conveniently annex land from which they are separated by over-steep slopes or uncultivated tracts. All these facts explain why the process of farm concentration differs widely from region to region or from commune to commune. Variations in the degree of agricultural concentration among

the communes of the Somme have already been emphasised (p. 118). Side by side there are 'strong' communes with stable agricultural enterprises, and 'weak' communes where farms have dwindled. The former are villages founded by the 18th-century farmers, where the peasantry was strong, and could withstand agricultural crises and changes, or go along with these changes and increase the size of their farms by buying up vacant farmland, thus preventing ménagers and agricultural labourers from stepping in. The weak communes, on the other hand, were inhabited by small farmers, ménagers and artisans, whose holdings have disappeared, as they lacked the resources to expand. In terms of space, these types of commune are characterised by the expansion of the cultivated land of strong communes at the expense of the weak ones, whose farmers could no longer cultivate more than a fraction of their land. Table XLIX gives some examples chosen from the Somme villages.

TABLE XLIX. STRONG AND WEAK COMMUNES IN PICARDY

1942	Area of the commune cultivated by people from outside the commune (in ha.)	Area cultivated by farmers of the commune in other communes (in ha.)
STRONG COMMUNES		
Bouchoir . .	10	265
Beaucamps-Vieux .	2	348
Vironchaux . .	10	151
WEAK COMMUNES		
Folies . .	157	23
Rouvroy . .	155	29
Gouy . . .	136	6
Argoules . .	364	93

Throughout the country every year an average of 70,000–80,000 farms change hands. 50,000 people take over farms, but only about 30,000 transactions are public and subject to the laws of supply and demand; the others are farms taken over either by a member of the family or by the owner of a farm held on lease. Viable farms are less and less concerned in these transactions, but non-viable farms and plots are progressively affected.

This development is still very far from giving agriculture a rational structure. The splitting up of small farms brings more advantage to well-placed farms than to marginal farms which have the greatest need for expansion. Owing to the high price of land, which is rising as a result of speculation, small farmers cannot expand and find conversion impossible. When two properties are united, under circumstances that do not allow the buying of plots, the new farm so formed does not necessarily have the optimum area in relation to the tools and labour available. Concentration often leads to plurality of holdings, that is to say, several farms may fall into the hands of one farmer. He may be a working farmer doubling his land, or a big farmer who will put in a manager to look after the new farm. But the buyer of land put up for sale may not be a farmer. It may be bought by a landowning syndicate, a sugar-factory, a butcher, a cheese manufacturer, a member of the liberal professions, an actor . . . and, whether they control it directly or not, such buyers are acquiring land in increasing quantities.

The expansion of farms competes with the heavy demand for land by urban investors, with a view to speculative afforestation. The fight against plurality of holdings is difficult; there is some necessary and beneficial reorganisation, but very often the consequences are disastrous. The farm on becoming part of a plural holding is in fact dismembered, as the owners let the bare land only and leave the buildings to decay. These practices cause over-bidding in the struggle for the land, and prevent farmers' sons from settling in the same region.

ACTION ON THE STRUCTURE OF FARMS

The concentration of farms is inevitable, but the effects differ according to whether it happens in the traditional manner of a liberal society or with official intervention. In the first case the development is in favour of those possessing capital, who alone are capable of buying land and farms: large landowners, large-scale farmers, non-agriculturalists. In the second case an attempt is made to achieve the best way of occupying and working the land by creating farms which will pay, and restricting their control to farmers.

The formulation of policy for agricultural enterprises always arouses vigorous controversy and high feelings. A few years ago, experts who dared to say publicly that the number of farms should decrease and that accordingly many farmers should go were pilloried and denounced as enemies of the peasants. On the other hand, many defended, and still defend, family peasant farming as the basis of traditional French society, the stronghold of the moral virtues and qualities of the nation.

These standpoints reflect the difficulty of making a dispassionate appraisal of the problem of the future of farms; they also reflect opinions that may be unwittingly or deliberately incompatible. Agricultural populations are confused with rural populations. Small family farms are defended, and the maintenance of numerous farms is extolled as a means of keeping a dense rural population. There is confusion between farm enterprises and family enterprises; the size of the farm is related to the size of the family helped by one or two paid workers, instead of to the optimum size required for economic operation.[13]

Is the objective to maintain a maximum of farmers' families with an income just sufficient for subsistence, or a body of farmers with optimum returns? Even the concept of a family farm is obscure, or at least difficult to define; in fact it is the combination of a farm with a more or less constant area and a family which supplies a labour force varying according to the number of children, their age, their future and the age of the parents.

For some years much research has been devoted to farm management problems. As a result, stress has been put on new concepts like the optimum unit of cultivation or the optimum unit of production in stock-rearing. The idea is to find, for a given crop, the optimum area to obtain the best financial return on capital outlay.

We have already shown the results of an analysis of the area per working man; taking into account the number of working men in a family, we have already defined the minimum area of a family farm (p. 144). This must produce about 18,000 francs per unit of work per year to ensure adequate standard of living for the farmer and a reasonable return on capital. This in turn presupposes:

(a) A capital per worker which varies according to the system of production;

(b) A minimum farm area of 20–25 ha. in good dairy land, 50 ha. in zones of more extensive production, 30–35 ha. in regions of mixed farming. In the South-west, for example, the fruit-producing unit would be at least 8 ha., and at the most 30 ha. (for apples) or 40–45 ha. (for several other fruits). The minimum unit for milk production would be twelve or fifteen cows for a well-organised farm of 15 ha.

The small farm is not irretrievably doomed, but it will pay only with very specialised and very renumerative types of production, such as poultry-farming, arboriculture and vegetable-growing; in the coastal communes of Léon (Nord–Finistère), which specialise in field vegetables, 93–98% of the farms have less than 5 ha. In 1963 the Ministry of Agriculture announced that the Government had 'elected' to maintain about a million farms in France whereas uncontrolled development would leave only 200,000 large farms. The choice appears a courageous one, but it may be that the proposed figure is too high. In relation to the agricultural census of 1963, it presupposes the retention of most farms of more than 10 ha. Whatever the future may bring, in recent years a coherent series of measures have been introduced to help farming in such a way as to allow the concentration of farms to continue, but within reasonable limits, that is to say by favouring the formation of medium-sized farms and by keeping the land in the hands of the peasant class. Since 1st January 1967

the whole government policy of 'remodelling' the production conditions of French agriculture has been entrusted to the *Centre National pour l'aménagement des structures agricoles*.

Increases in farm sizes are facilitated in numerous ways:

The reclamation of waste land. Since August 1962 every plot with a maximum area fixed by law, which has not been cultivated for five years, can be handed over to a neighbouring farmer if he so requests; the only condition is that the area of the applicant's farm must be less than the minimum specified for the region.[14]

The fight against farm sub-division. Anyone who on inheritance wishes to preserve a family farm can do so in one of three ways: it can be kept temporarily undivided; or the whole farm can be preferentially assigned— such allocation is legal for family farms, and is to be extended after discussion to all farms, including large ones; or the farm buildings can be assigned with special rights (pre-emption if sold and priority if let). The beneficiary is obviously obliged to compensate the other heirs. In the same spirit, the supplementary Act of 8th August 1962 provides for the formation of co-operatives: 'civil associations formed between several landowners with a view to amalgamating agricultural properties situated in the same commune or in neighbouring communes in order to release them from joint possession or to create, or preserve, one or more agricultural enterprises, or to secure them, or to facilitate their administration eventually by leasing them out'.

Incentives to retirement for aged farmers. In connection with a *Fonds d'action sociale pour l'amélioration des structures agricoles* (F.A.S.A.S.A.), a law of May 1963 provided that aged farmers freely giving up their farms or ceasing to maintain them 'in such conditions as to facilitate land development' may be granted supplementary retirement pensions known as '*indemnités viagères de départ*'.

Incentives to the transfer of farms. Another

decree provides for compensation and special long-term loans for farmers leaving farms which are too small, to settle on farms considered to be large enough for satisfactory operation. The beneficiaries must furnish proof of competence and undertake to cede their former land, to a neighbour wishing to expand, or to a *Société d'aménagement foncier et d'établissement rural* (S.A.F.E.R.).

Very often, however, these steps may be ineffective or dangerous through not being adapted to regional circumstances. Many texts give as a model a minimum size of 30 ha.; the intention is basically praiseworthy because it tends to be unfavourable to the extension of small farms considered to be uneconomic; under the F.A.S.A.S.A., for example, an old farmer cannot receive his supplementary retirement pension unless the farmer who has succeeded to his land has at least 30 ha. In regions such as Flanders, where the average farm is 16 ha., the system falls down, as a farmer cannot take over the 7 or 8 ha. which an old farmer would be willing to cede to him.

Rural migrations. Lack of balance in the farm structure can be mitigated by encouraging farmers to leave certain areas and to settle in others; since 1949 the *Association Nationale des migration rurales* has contributed to these movements. Periodically an inter-ministerial commission divides the departments into four groups: *départements de départ*, where the market is very limited, average areas of farms too small, and where there is a surplus of farmers (these are the departments of the northern crescent and the Lyons region); *départements d'accueil*, in regions which are under-populated and under-farmed, where waste land and abandoned farms can be reclaimed; *départements d'accueil 'à aménager'*, where farmers can be received only after preliminary works have been carried out. The reception departments are those in the south of the Paris basin (such as Loiret and Yonne), in the Central Massif, the South-west and the 'dry Alps'. Finally, there are *mixed zones* where supply and demand are fairly well balanced, such as the Mediterranean region and Burgundy; departure and reception offices give information, select, guide and help the migrants.

In fourteen years (1949–63) the Association has achieved the following results: 9,000 families settled, 43,000 migrants, 85,000 ha. released in the departments from which they came and 325,000 ha. taken up in the reception departments. The migrants are farmers' sons (33% of the total), farmers working their own land (16%) and also agricultural workers (19·5%). These results, interesting though they are, are very inadequate; much greater financial means would be needed to make such migrations an effective solution.

These rural migrations are not limited to within the country; foreign farmers from member states of the European community are settling in the reception areas. Although this settlement is not yet to be officially authorised before the end of the second stage of the Common Market, the free circulation of capital does in fact lead to farmers settling in France. These foreign farmers do not yet have the right to farm the land which they acquire, without first obtaining authorisation from the head of the agricultural office of the department. In fact this authorisation is almost always granted, partly because the foreign owners can show their resentment if it is not, by refusing to let the land be worked by a French tenant, and partly because the farms they acquire are generally too large for the financial means of French farmers, most of whom want medium-sized farms. Already an organisation in the Federal German Republic called 'Rural settlement in France' is installing farmers and giving them substantial assistance.

Agricultural co-operatives. The Act of 8th August 1962 favoured the establishment of agricultural co-operatives, civic companies for the purpose of co-operative 'working in conditions comparable with those existing on family farms'.

This is an important step towards the achievement of a co-operative agriculture which will succeed in building up large collective farms without upsetting the present system of land-ownership and agriculture. Co-operatives which have already been set up are all in tenant-farming areas. On 13th April 1967, 469 agricultural co-operatives were recognised and 143 were being negotiated; they exploited 60,000 ha. and each contained from two to nine members, family ties being a frequent factor (father, son, brothers).

The commune of Dangers, near Chartres, may be quoted as exemplifying the fundamental changes which are coming about in the countryside: 'Eleven farms are linked in various groups each embracing only a part of them; six of these enterprises are carrying out together a planned programme of work on the soil, manuring and treatment, haymaking and harvesting; five have set up a co-operative which has been able to buy 40 ha. of extra land' (L. Estrangin).

Action on plurality of holdings. Legislation on accumulation of farm holdings provides that any person or body wishing to operate several farms must apply to the prefecture for permission if the area of land involved exceeds the amount specified for the district (120 ha. on the plateaux of Haute-Marne, 25 ha. in Basses-Pyrénées), or if concentration of activity is achieved by reducing other farms below a minimum size fixed for the district.

Action on systems of land-ownership. The key problem, however, is probably that of the relationship between estates and farms. This relationship is becoming progressively reversed. Twenty years ago the tenant-farmer contributed only the many strong right arms of his family, his goodwill and his traditional knowledge; the tenant-farmer of today contributes a working capital, tractors and various machines, whose value may exceed that of the land,[15] as well as his professional skill; he pays the wages of employees other than his own family, and buys seed and fertilisers. Whether the land he occupies pays its way or not depends on him.

This is why an increasing number of tenant-farmers are demanding that the idea of ownership of the enterprise, guaranteeing liberty

and protection of investments, should be recognised. In the meantime all recent legislation tends to favour the farmer; tenant-farmers, for example, have the right to first refusal if the farm is sold.

The *Sociétés d'aménagement foncier et d'établissement rural* (S.A.F.E.R.) were created by the agricultural policy law of 5th August 1960. Their aim is clearly expressed: 'to encourage the strengthening of family farms which are too small or inadequate in other ways, to make them viable and to help them to achieve a balance of both employment and returns; and eventually to set up new family enterprises, well balanced and capable of paying their way'.

The S.A.F.E.R. have rights of pre-emption in case of the alienation, under burdensome conditions, of agricultural funds or agricultural land. They act as landowning associations, buying land, with rights of pre-emption, regrouping it and reallocating it to all whom 'a few extra hectares may save' (E. Pisani).

The S.A.F.E.R. have financial means at their disposal which enable them to oppose the concentration of land in the hands of big farmers or non-resident landowners from outside farming. If, however, prices exceed the ceiling fixed by the S.A.F.E.R., as happens when the property is sold by auction, they lose the land. By 1st January 1967 twenty-seven S.A.F.E.R. had purchased 167,465 ha. and sold 88,535 ha., allowing the creation or transfer of 1,300 farms and the enlargement of 6,000 other farms.

The dissociation of estate and farm tends increasingly to become identified with relations existing between capital and labour in the industrial field. Moreover, to relieve the countryside of the 'burden of land capital' (L. Estrangin) some people are considering the formation of civic land companies which would attract the savings of townsmen, and acquire land on lease. As with shares quoted on the Stock Exchange, the dividends would be of secondary importance, but the capital would appreciate, as land values will probably continue to rise.[16]

In certain areas the farm problem can no

longer be expressed in these terms. Development is such that danger point has been, or soon will be, reached. The problem now is that of land abandonment, for small farms cannot even take opportunities to acquire adjacent areas that are no longer cultivated, because their owners are too old to cope with expansion.

This decline of farms will automatically continue in certain departments, owing to the ageing of the agricultural population (cf. p. 133). The investigations of R. Pressat have shown that 75% of farmers' sons remained on the land. Thus to replace 100 fathers of the present farming generation (age 35–54), 135 sons aged 15–34 would be needed. In 1954 only in eight departments did the ratio exceed 122 young people to 100 active workers: in three west–central departments (Vendée, Loire-Atlantique and Maine-et-Loire); three departments in Normandy (Manche, Calvados and Seine-Maritime); and two northern departments (Aisne and Ardennes). Forty-six departments had ratios between 86 and 112, which means that we cannot possibly be sure of having sufficient farmers in the next generation. Rural migrations are far from restoring a balance: 'in these conditions there will no longer be a single viable farm in these areas, not because the land is lacking, but because the small number of farmers remaining on the land will

make it impossible to provide the technical, economic, administrative, cultural and social services which are indispensable for normal life in them' (Serge Mallet).[17]

This development leads us to reconsider any policy too much inclined towards family farming; the concentration of farms leads to an increase in the average size of farm. At the same time the productivity of agricultural labour is increasing on average by 5% per year.

In these conditions the father–son labour combination, as the standard farming unit, will either be under-producing if labour yield is not doubled within twenty years or will be in a state of overemployment, or virtual unemployment, if this doubling is not achieved. It can be achieved either by more intensive cultivation or by an increase in the area farmed, the latter solution being the more likely. We must therefore find flexible farming systems in spite of the rigidity of structure of land-ownership. The solutions 'lie mainly in giving up autonomy and the absolute independence of the productive unit; and in progressing from an agricultural system made up of autonomous concerns, unconnected with each other, to a better integrated system, probably made up of units of production which are distinct, but bound one to the other, more and more closely, by contract or simply by solidarity' (D. Bergmann).

7. M.Séverac rightly emphasises the distinction between *métayage*, a method of sharing the fruits of the earth, and *métairie*, which suggests an agricultural unit of considerable size.

8. In 1955 *métayage* was the method used in more than 2% of the total number of farms in 35 departments, and more than 10% in 6 departments (Mayenne, Allier, Tarn, Haute-Garonne, Lot-et-Garonne, Landes).

9. In the large farms of Beauce and Soissonnais it is estimated that there is one agricultural labourer for each 18–20 ha.

10. *R. Géog. Alpine*, 1952, p. 286.

11. Comparative statistical analysis of farms comes up against numerous difficulties; the exact number of agricultural concerns varies according to whether or not very small farms are counted; in 1929 all private gardens were counted as farms. It is equally difficult to define the area of farms: in 1929 and 1942–6 woods were included, but in 1955 they were excluded.

12. By creating plots that are too large, consolidation sometimes makes them difficult to sell.

13. The Act of August 1960 does not take sides, giving as one of the aims in view: 'to promote and favour a farming system of the family type which will use modern production techniques to the best advantage and enable labour and farm capital to be used to the full'.

14. Already in 1942 an Act had been passed on 'the confiscation of land which is uncultivated and no longer has any connection with its owner'.

15. It is estimated that in more than half of the departments the value of farm equipment is greater than that of the land.

16. The index of land values based on 1938 is four times higher than that of gold.

17. Conference of the Grand-Orient de France, Paris, 1963.

II

TYPES OF FARMING AND LAND USE

Farms derive their income from agricultural land representing about 60% of the total area of France; this figure places France after the United Kingdom (78%), Holland (70%) and Italy (70%) and before

TABLE L. LAND USE IN FRANCE

1964	Area (in ha.)	% of total area
Arable land	18,543,700	34·1
Areas permanently under grass*	13,280,800	24·4
Woods and forests . . .	11,751,700	21·6
Uncultivated agricultural land .	3,998,500	7·3
Vineyards	1,400,700	2·5
Market and kitchen gardens .	401,100	0·7
Fruit†	345,400	0·6
Other crops‡	237,200	0·4
Productive lakes and ponds .	108,000	0·2
Non-agricultural land§ . .	4,329,900	7·9

* Permanent meadows, grassland, natural meadowland.
† Including true fruit crops and productive olive, chestnut and walnut groves.
‡ Poplar woods, osieries, nurseries and flowers.
§ Built-up areas, and bare rock.

West Germany (58%). But these figures have to be accepted with caution owing to the variety of definitions of what constitutes cultivated land. Table L gives the land-use structure of France by broad categories.

The area of useful agricultural land was 32,190,000 ha. in 1963. But here, as with many other aspects of agriculture, figures give a poor idea of facts, as there is little satisfactory statistical material; for example, fallow land does not appear in the table, and meadows and fields planted with trees are not included in fruit-growing land.

Table LI indicates some points of comparison with the states of Western Europe.

TABLE LI. LAND USE IN SOME EUROPEAN STATES

	Area of agricultural land (in thousands of ha.)	Permanent grassland %	Arable land Total %	Temporary grassland only %	Vineyards and orchards
France	34,069	37·5	62·5	25·4	10·3
United Kingdom	12,569	42·9	57·1	34·5	2
West Germany .	14,250	39·3	60·7	2·6	6·5
Italy . .	16,979	7·2	92·8	18·6	16
Netherlands .	2,310	54·5	45·5	9·5	10

France appears to have the advantage from the agricultural point of view, with 44·7% of the arable land of the European Economic Community, 49·6% of the meadows and permanent pastures and 44% of the forests.

This structure of land use is, however, not stable (Table LII).

TABLE LII. CHANGES IN LAND USE
(in thousands of ha.)

	1910	1930	1938	1948	1957	1960
Arable land . . .	23,680 44·7%	21,790	20,196	18,368	18,735	19,007 34·5%
Areas permanently under grass .	10,062 19%	11,210	11,776	12,301	13,242	13,053 23·7%
Vines	1,685 3·2%	1,590	1,605	1,550	1,467	1,462 2·7%
Woods and forests . . .	9,329 17·5%	10,370	10,775	11,010	11,395	11,435 20·8%
Uncultivated agricultural land and non-agricultural land. . .	6,827 12·9%		(5,679*)	(6,035*)	(4,327*)	8,911 16·1%
Market gardens and other uses .	1,372 2·6%					1,261 2·2%

* Uncultivated agricultural land only.

In fifty years (1910–60) the area of arable land decreased by 10·2%, and that of vineyards by 0·5%. Conversely, wooded land increased by 3·2%, and grassland areas by 4·7%.

We must therefore analyse the factors of this land use and its changes. They depend to a great extent on production methods and types of farming.

1. TYPES OF FARMING AND METHODS OF PRODUCTION

A type of farming is

'. . . a combination of different types of production, implying for each agricultural enterprise a choice between the various vegetable and animal products in which to risk investment, and between the factors of production which will make investment worth while. These factors consist essentially of land, men, energy, and above all means of traction (animal or mechanical), indoor and outdoor equipment and, finally, the varieties of vegetable crops and breeds of animals used' (R. Dumont).

The type of farming is not exactly the same thing as land use; this latter involves analysis of the distribution of arable land and the crops it bears, and the area covered with grass, forest, orchards or vines; it is not concerned with the combination of these elements in the farm economy, nor with their intensity of production; two farms may have the same type of land use and two different types of farming.

A. The Factors Governing Types of Farming

The elements involved in a type of farming are numerous, but the factors determining it are no less numerous; the farmer determines his type of farming in the light of various conditions: physical factors, human factors internal to agriculture (the farmer and his farm) and human factors external to agriculture, such as the market and the State.[1]

PHYSICAL FACTORS

Their influence is self-evident; topography, pedology, climatology and hydrology play their part in making certain crops possible or impossible (at least as profitable investments). The dry summers of the Mediter-

ranean climate preclude meadows and cattle-rearing. The shortness of the growing season in the high Alpine valleys and humidity make wheat unlikely to pay. To a certain extent the application of scientific techniques enables us to disregard this by modifying the natural surroundings or by breeding crops and animals adapted to their surroundings; but such modifications are still rare and involve large investments. Generally speaking the type of physical environment orientates the type of farming. Where there are many slopes and hilltops, damp valley bottoms and sheltered sunny hillsides, or where, as in the South of France, fertile depressions are adjacent to *garrigues* or granitic uplands, conditions are unquestionably favourable to polyculture: 'the tradition of polyculture has been reinforced by geography' (D. Faucher).

HUMAN FACTORS INTERNAL TO AGRICULTURE

The type of farming is closely dependent on the type of farm and agrarian structure. The size of farm determines to a large extent the type of produce; some farms are too small to specialise in particular crops, to adopt complex systems of crop rotation, to keep their animals a long time or to derive sufficient returns from types of production which are in theory the most attractive. In western France small farmers cannot practise the speculative stock-rearing carried on by the big landowners because they have to sell their stock.[2] Broadly speaking, the area of arable land increases with size of farm, while the area of grassland diminishes; the exceptions only 'prove the rule', being the result of specialised intensive cultivation practised on small farms.

The structure of the farm is also a factor; the shape and size of the plots and their spatial arrangement can allow or prohibit a particular agricultural speculation.

Even more important, perhaps, than geographical conditions is the amount of labour available. 'It is the amount of labour available which determines the type of farming in small concerns, while on large farms the type of farming determines the amount of labour' (L. Malassis).

The variety of crop combinations and of stock in any one area is affected by psychological factors and by the very different outlooks of farmers. Each chooses one type of speculation rather than another according to his commercial interests or willingness to take risks, his attitude to his work, his competence and his regard for wealth and the needs of his family. Malassis rightly emphasises the part played by local attitudes of mind: 'family feelings, the quest for security, tastes, the pressure of opinion, and tradition all combine to make agriculture as much a way of life as an economic activity. A part of agricultural activity is quite outside economic logic; the behaviour of a producer interpreted in terms of this logic often appears irrational.'

The type of farming also depends on the technical capabilities and experience of the cultivator; there are some crops and some agricultural techniques which a farmer cannot attempt without professional training. In this respect French agriculture is in a particularly difficult position; only a small minority of the farmers have received some technical training or have studied to a fairly advanced level. The farmer is thus the slave of the past, of the traditions of his region, the example of his father and the experience of his ancestors. One farmer who is ill-prepared for new developments can hold up agricultural reform in a whole district.

HUMAN FACTORS EXTERNAL TO
    AGRICULTURE

The type of farming is clearly dependent on the market and prices. The location of consumers and of food-processing and other agricultural industries, transport conditions, prices and price variations, official guarantees and protection, the regularity or irregularity of the market from year to year are all factors affecting the decisions of the farmer; he can choose, for example, between products with guaranteed prices, such as wheat or sugar-beet, and products of a more speculative nature.

The low degree and geographical concentration of urban development in France have meant that the country districts have no large consumer groups near at hand for the sale of their produce.

It was not possible to vary the farming systems until the development of transport facilities made it possible for agricultural production to become commercialised. Railways, and later roads, enabled the country districts through which they passed to take their part in the circulation of goods; the P.L.M. company (Paris–Lyon–Méditerranée) played a vital part in the transformation of the farming system of Bas-Rhône.

B. Methods of Production

TRADITIONAL POLYCULTURE

French agriculture still bears the deep impression of the self-sufficient polyculture which was the common type of farming before the 19th century. This system depended on the idea that a family farm should be almost entirely self-supporting. It was based on the cultivation of cereals by means of a system of crop rotation, allowing the growing of grain and stock-rearing to be carried on together. This combination of several types of production, adapted to allow the soil to rest as necessary, met almost all the needs of the family, and insured against climatic fluctuations by diversification of production. The system was triennial in northern France, and biennial in the South.

In *northern polyculture*,[3] triennial rotation consisted of an autumn-sown cereal, such as winter wheat, a spring-sown cereal, such as oats, barley or rye, and fallow which allowed the land to rest while at the same time providing grazing for the herds (green fallow);

the spring cereal was made possible by the relatively high humidity of early summer. This rotation was accompanied by collective restrictions which brought about a regular social and community organisation of agricultural life: these concerned common rights and the dates of beginning and ending certain operations.

Southern polyculture was characterised by greater variety and stability. In the South of France, spring sowing was impossible or risky owing to the dryness of the summer months. Only the rotation of wheat and fallow was possible:

'The fallow was the year of rest, for the restoration of soil fertility. Even when uncultivated, this would have had the benefit of manure. The peasant took advantage of it to break up the soil by means of ploughing, often repeated four times; this aeration of the living part of the earth renewed its fertility. In the South, however, it was one of the practices which helped to build up a store of moisture in the soil, which could be added to that available from precipitation during the year of cultivation. Its purpose and result everywhere was the destruction of weeds; southern France, where the winters are too mild, had more need of this than the North. The weeds germinating in spring were in danger of choking cereal crops, which were often too sparse on these poor soils. And finally, these "bare fallows" were not entirely unproductive. In a corner of these resting fields the peasant grew some of his cabbages, beans, peas and other seeds. But above all, they partly made up for the scarcity of pasture for cattle (D. Faucher).[4]

This relatively poor rotation system led to the development of supplementary resources adapted to the natural conditions: heathland and *garrigues* as pasture, vines and fruit-bearing trees, such as chestnuts and olives, are the hallmarks of this southern polyculture, and to these we can add almonds, pears, plums, peaches, apricots and figs.[5]

The southern fallow had not the same value as fallow in the northern regions; during the dry summer months no pasture grew on it; together with the vineyards, uncultivated tracts known as *ermas* and areas of stubble,

the most it could do was to take sheep coming down from the mountains for the winter. In addition there were wild harvests gathered from the uncultivated part of the land; the bark of the holm-oak served for tanning, the *garrigue* gave lavender and thyme, and the kermes-oak provided a dye.

Thus the southern type of mixed farming met the need to insure against a variable climate; farmers produced a little of everything to avoid losing everything. It also responded to the great variety of types of land.

The restrictive effects of crop rotation did not reach the southern regions. The land there was much more heterogeneous, every cultivated plot adjoining a *saltus* (rangelands)—*garrigues*, forests, scrub-covered slopes—where the stock could graze and could move around freely without danger to the fields. The practice of moving the flocks to a distance, by *transhumance*, also avoided having stock-rearing and crops together on the same land.

In reality, the boundary between the two rotation systems was far from clearly defined; two-year rotation is or was found in northern France, either in poor and isolated districts, such as the sandstone Vosges, the plateau of Lorraine, and Morvan, or in particularly fertile districts, such as the *gaigneries* of the Breton *Bocage*,[6] the alluvial plain of the Loire and certain parts of the open country round Caen, the Pays de Caux, Burgundy and the north-east of Alsace.

In the first case the two-year cycle can be explained by the poverty of the soil; in the second case it is more difficult to explain. Physical factors, especially pedology, play their part, together with agronomic factors, such as speculation in the production of cereals for bread-making, and social factors such as the practice of tenant-farming. At the end of the 13th century Alsace turned to a two-year rotation, giving up the three-year rotation in order to satisfy the growing food needs of the Rhineland towns, as winter wheat gives higher yields.

Conversely, strictly localised islands of three-year rotation have been described in southern France, in the mountains, for example. According to D. Faucher, they can be explained by special physical conditions, such as fertile ground which can take cereals two years in succession, or by the availability of large quantities of manure.

THE FIRST CHANGES

The traditional types of farming underwent modification from the 18th century onwards. The changes took place progressively, at different rates in different regions. More scientific systems based on new kinds of crop, and a more specialised and commercial type of agriculture, took the place of the traditional systems or else modified them in the combination of old and new elements.

These changes cannot be attributed to precise dates, even though the expression 'agricultural revolution of the 18th century' is often used. New crops, such as Saracen corn or buckwheat, first grown in the Central Massif in the 16th or 17th century, had in fact been introduced earlier. Some regions had already had their agricultural revolution; one of these was Flanders, where agriculture was transformed from the 14th century onwards, the main developments being in the use of fertilisers, a vigorous working of the soil to drain and aerate it, the abandonment of a three-year crop rotation, the replacement of bare fallow with fodder crops and turnip fields, and, in the 17th century, catch-crops.

The origins of this 'agricultural revolution' go back to the 18th century when the physiocratic movement found a ready audience in the bourgeoisie wishing to apply their spirit of enterprise to their newly acquired estates, and the nobility were attracted to the idea of developing their domains as an answer to rising prices. The principal features of these changes were:

1. The introduction of new plants, such as potatoes and tobacco. Buckwheat and apples were introduced at that time in Brittany, also maize in the South-west. This served as food for men, animals and poultry, and reduced the period of fallow. Beet came in at the beginning of the 19th century, and then colza, completely upsetting the three-year rotation system. The potato helped the development of pig-rearing, thus enabling food production to be carried out on a larger scale.

2. The replacement of fallow-breaks with hoe-crops, such as beet, potatoes, cabbages and Jerusalem artichokes, or fodder crops, such as lucerne, clover and sainfoin. Leguminous fodder crops did away with the need for fallow thanks to their fertilising qualities (fixation of atmospheric nitrogen in the soil), and they favoured the development of stock-rearing, thus increasing the amount of manure.

3. The abolition of the legal restrictions of the corn annual agrarian system. From the second half of the 18th century onwards, enclosure orders allowed individual types of farming to be developed, giving the peasant greater freedom of choice of crops and rotation systems.

The mechanisation of agriculture also made considerable progress from the end of the 18th century onwards, with the introduction of mechanical drills, threshing-machines, Dombasle's all-iron plough and, at the beginning of the 19th century, ploughs with two or three ploughshares. Progress went on unceasingly, with the Brabant plough, single from the middle of the 19th century or double from the end of the 19th century, and the harvester. But these machines came slowly, and by no means generally into use.

The contribution of the 19th century to these developments in agriculture probably consisted less of agronomic innovations than of fundamental changes in the technical and economic framework of agriculture. New systems of communication, such as canals and railways, made the countryside more accessible and enabled it to commercialise its products and send them long distances, and at the same time to receive the necessary fertilisers. Without the Nantes–Brest canal the liming of the siliceous soils of Brittany would not have been possible. Without the railways, fertilisers could not have been sent all over France, either from the North (phosphates from the Ardennes, Boulonnais and Somme) or from the ports (nitrates from Chile and guano from Peru) or from lime-kilns. The use of fertilisers on a large scale in the districts best served and most open to progress dates from the 1850s; but all regions were not reached until half a century later. It was not until the first years of the 20th century that the peasants began to go with their ox-carts to fetch lime from the stations of Limousin.

During the 19th century also, deep digging, drainage works, reclamation of marshland and irrigation operations were carried out on a large scale in many areas.[7]

All this improvement in agriculture pre-supposed considerable financial resources. These were limited, as the commercial side of production was still on a very small scale; but under the Second Empire the *Crédit foncier* and *Crédit agricole* were created, and the country districts at last had opportunities for investment.

This agricultural revolution, which began in the 18th century, thus went on until the beginning of the 20th, the period from 1860 to 1910 being particularly important. But at the very time when agriculture was acquiring the means for development, it entered on a long period of stagnation. Weakened by the exodus from the country which left behind only the oldest and least enterprising, affected by economic crises, either general or peculiar to agriculture, and lulled by a deceptive protectionism, the majority of the country districts of France remained dormant, clinging to their out-of-date traditions. The only regions to escape were those best situated near the large concentrations of consumers, and those with the advantage of fertile soil or of a strong country-born middle class, who were open to progress and had begun to specialise ever since the 1870s.

THE SECOND AGRICULTURAL REVOLUTION

From 1910 to 1946 French agriculture scarcely developed at all. But after the latter date it took a succession of steps forward, which

one can call the second agricultural revolution. Progress affected every aspect of agriculture, biological, technical and human.

The biological revolution

This concerned the improvement of plants, their treatment and methods of cultivation and stock-rearing.

Many results have been obtained by the introduction of new vegetable and animal species, and the breeding of more productive, more resistant varieties. Some labour was saved by the introduction of monogerm seed. For example, a new variety of early wheat, 'L'Étoile de Choisy', caused the yield in southern France to rise from 25 to 40 quintals, turning the whole of the Centre and the South-west into cereal-growing regions. The introduction of hybrid varieties of maize extended this cereal cultivation into northern France, where it took the place of beet grown for distilleries. The law on stock-rearing, passed in 1966, lays stress on the improvement of the genetic level of the livestock as a means of increasing its productivity. Many branches of agronomy have shown similar progress; agricultural zoology, vegetable pathology and phytopharmacy. There is an ever-increasing number of soil dressings, fungicides and insecticides.[8]

The agronomist René Dumont did much to introduce and disseminate a method of 'grass cultivation' which was known in the remote past, but developed in England and Germany during the last war. In permanent pastures, trampled by cattle for decades, the soil is packed down tightly; the grass plants deteriorate and inferior species increase; the growing grass is subject to risks of climate and its yield is poor (1,500 fodder units to the hectare). In short, the traditional methods of grass growing are nothing more than 'bringing the cow to the grass' (A. Voisin). Temporary grassland pasture, previously advocated by Olivier de Serres, is part of a long-term rotation of arable (4–5 years) and grass leys (8–10 years). During the crop-growing years the soil of the plot is broken up and aerated; during the years of pasture it collects moisture. This rotation had been practised for a long time in several regions of the Vosges, and from the Jura to Vendée, but in bad conditions, with seed of poor species, unskilfully mixed. The *fodder revolution* started true cultivation of grass and a rational treatment of pastureland. This entails seeding a plot with rich fodder-grasses which are adapted to the climate (cocksfoot, which can stand up to the dryness of the mean climatic conditions of France, was substituted for ryegrass), and a rotation of arable and pasture on the same plot. It is in fact difficult to keep grassland sufficiently homogeneous for more than four or five years. Rational treatment of pasture means cleaning out the ditches and keeping them clean, piecemeal enclosure of large plots so that the cattle graze successive sections and the grass can grow without being trampled, alternating mowing and grazing, and cutting the grass in moderation.

Finistère and the Lyons region are the areas where the revolution in fodder-growing spread most rapidly and most universally within a few years; almost all their 'normal' farms have adopted the ley system. Similarly when rotation grasses were introduced into Aveyron in the course of the 1950s they caused an absolute revolution in fodder-growing. Whereas rough grazing land cannot support one ewe to the hectare, and permanent grass can take between four and six, temporary grass can take ten, thanks to the increased production of fodder units (10,000 to the hectare).

In the next stage of progress the animals are no longer driven to pasture; the fodder is harvested either green or dried, stored in silos and given to the animals together with artificial food. Free stalling has also become widespread; it reduces hours of work, gives better manure and improves the health of the cattle.

The technical revolution

This involves developments in hydraulics, fertilisers, motorisation and mechanisation. *Agricultural water control.* Twenty years

ago the irrigated areas were very small. Irrigation was considered necessary only in regions subject to extreme summer drought; more often the type of farming was adapted to the degree of aridity.

Now a new policy has been formulated, recognising the value of irrigation in regions which are considered to have a humid climate. The water commission under the plan boldly and rightly observed that 'agriculture cannot afford to continue to take the risks it does, and to remain subject to the caprices of natural rainfall when industry is rationalising its methods of manufacture, planning its production and endeavouring to ensure that those engaged in it shall have steady employment and a steady income'.

The increase in the net returns from each hectare irrigated in a humid area lies between 400 and 5,000 francs. The area irrigated at present is almost 1 million ha., but experts estimate that an area of 19 million ha. could benefit from irrigation. Water control necessitates works of varying magnitude.

Large-scale works involve techniques and resources on a scale requiring action and finance from the State or co-operative organisations. Such are barrages, trunk canals and diversion canals.

It is in the South-east, starting from the Rhône and the Durance, that recent works have been most numerous. On the Rhône the work carried out by the *Compagnie Nationale du Rhône* is transforming the agricultural economy of the valley by allowing the irrigation of vast areas, such as 15,000 ha. at Beauchastel. The Durance too, from the Serre–Ponçon dam, contributes water which is particularly valuable because it is silty. The Canal de Provence, grafted on to the Verdon, will water 110,000 ha. The Crau has already lost its former stony steppe character through the irrigation of more than 18,000 ha. that yield 100,000 tons of hay, in three cuttings per year, for a flock of 250,000 sheep.

But the crowning achievement is that of Bas Rhône–Languedoc, where the aim is to transform the agricultural economy of 170,000 ha. A trunk canal runs for 175 km. from the intake at Fourques (above Arles) to the Béziers region. Its water (75 m.^{3} per sec.) runs into branch canals which can irrigate land up to a height of more than 60 m. The system is completed by a canal using the water of the Orb by gravity. The land-use plan of the *Compagnie du Bas Rhône–Languedoc* was as follows: crops lightly irrigated, 15,000 ha.; minor cereals, 20,000 ha.; rice, 14,000 ha.; fodder crops, 37,000 ha.; orchards, 31,000 ha.; market gardens, 31,000 ha.; industrial crops, 22,000 ha. An intensive and highly commercialised form of polyculture was to be substituted for the sea of vineyards covering the plain of Languedoc, bringing about a general reorientation of agriculture in the area.[9] Another major irrigation project is to be carried out in the hills of Gascony.

Irrigation is increasingly being carried out by sprinkling from a network of underground pipes (one water-point serving 4 ha.); fixed or movable sprinklers of light aluminium or plastic material are run from these pipes. Sprinkling has many advantages; it avoids the costly work of levelling, saves on labour and on water, and is better for the crops.

Small-scale agricultural water control works are those which can be carried out at the level of the individual farm, as their construction and operation are not too costly. The techniques of water use are simple: small barrages and distribution canals and irrigation only by gravity.

These small-scale operations, which are used to develop vast tracts in Italy and Spain, are less developed in France. They are found in the Mediterranean regions and, in particular, in Roussillon, where 44,000 ha. of ploughed fields, meadows, orchards, vineyards and gardens are irrigated.

In Gascony, in Lot-et-Garonne, the technique of hill lakes, hitherto unknown in France, but very widely used in Italy, was introduced in 1958; 300–400 earth barrages collect the water from small river-basins; they can store 35–40 million m.^{3} of water, which is redistributed in times of drought.

Fertilisers. Fertilisers are the main factor in the increase of productivity, even more than the tractor. France has been very backward in this respect; in 1938 her consumption was only 6·6 kg. of nitrate fertilisers per ha. (Germany, 23·6). The consumption of fertilisers rose from 982,000 tons (1949–50) to 3,088,000 tons (1964–5).[10]

In spite of this increase, France is far from reaching the level of consumption of the rich agricultural lands of north-west Europe (Table LIII). The consumption of fertilisers

TABLE LIII. CONSUMPTION OF FERTILISERS

(in kg. per ha. of usable agricultural land, 1962)

	Phos-phorus	Nitrogen	Potassium	Total (France = 100)
Netherlands .	43·5	104·7	54·4	277
Germany .	44·6	43·7	72·9	221
Belgium .	55·7	61·3	100·6	298
France .	30·8	18·1	24·1	100
Italy . .	19·2	16·8	6·1	58

is very uneven from region to region, reflecting partly the types of farming but also the level of technical training of the farmers. The consumption of fertilisers is higher on cereal farms and specialised farms; it is lower on pasture lands, for the increased fodder yield which results requires an overall modernisation of farms and considerable expenditure on additional cattle. In 1965–6 only 8 departments used more than 200 kg. per ha., all but 2 of them being in the northern half of the country. The 20 departments where under-consumption of fertilisers is most conspicuous (<50 kg.) are Savoie, Ariège, Vosges, Doubs, Jura, Corsica and departments of the Central Massif (fig. 60A).

Between 1954–5 and 1964–5 the consumption of fertilisers in kg. per ha. rose from 1 to 4 in Haute-Garonne, Gers and from 198 to 4,000 tons in Corsica. The distribution of areas where fertilisers are most used coincides rather surprisingly with those of tenant-farming (apart from the market-gardening area of the lower Durance and the vine-growing areas of the South).

Motorisation and mechanisation. Motorisation of farms on a large scale is recent in France; it dates from the years just after the

Second World War. The tractor, first imported from America as part of the loans under the Marshall Plan, and later built in the newly reconstructed factories, became the symbol of national recovery; during the year 1948 alone 30,000 tractors came into service. Few farmers have resisted the

soil better and to reclaim old pastures and waste land. But motorisation was applied to small and fragmented farms, whose small size and multiplicity of plots made it impossible to use the tractor rationally and economically.

Full use of a tractor (1,500–2,000 hours per

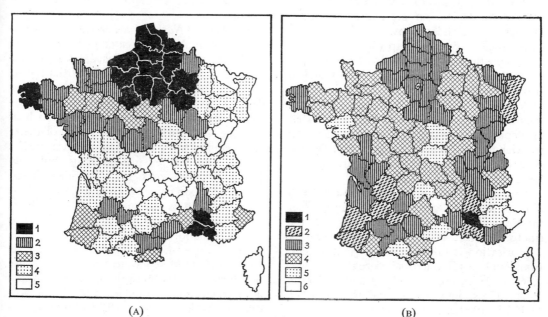

(A)   (B)

Fig. 60. A. Consumption of fertilisers by departments (consumption per ha.—cultivated land, pasture included—of the principal fertilisers: N.P.K. 1958–9).

1. More than 100 kg. per ha. 2. 75–100. 3. 50–75. 4. 25–50. 5. 0–25.

B. Number of tractors by departments (number of tractors per 1,000 ha. of useful agricultural land on 1st January 1962).

1. More than 45. 2. From 35 to 45. 3. From 25 to 34·9. 4. From 15 to 24·9. 5. From 5 to 14·9. 6. From 0 to 4·9.

temptation to possess a tractor, in order to be the first in the commune, or to please a son, or so as not to be thought a stick-in-the-mud. There were 35,000 tractors in France in 1938, and this rose to 44,000 (1946), 120,000 (1950), 230,000 (1954), 425,000 (1957), 625,000 (1959), 890,000 (1962) and 953,000 (1964).[11]

The tractor has often made possible an intensification of farming which is reflected in increased production. They can pull heavier ploughs more quickly and for a longer time, and help the farmer to till the

year) is assured only on large farms and diversity of crops does not help it to be used to the full. A farmer's comment—'We have a tool in our hands which no one has taught us to use'—aptly describes the nature of this motorisation. Thus in all too many cases the farm is over-equipped, as the tractor is too powerful or the opportunities to use it insufficient, while at the same time motorisation brings with it under-employment or hidden unemployment of labour on a family farm.

The efficiency of a tractor is decreased still

more by the division into plots; its optimum return cannot be achieved on plots that are too small and badly shaped, and a great deal of its work is wasted on the roads, going from one plot to another. 'The farmer who has bought a machine to ease his labours, and who feels himself bound to work harder in order to pay for it, begins to realise that true progress depends less on mechanical than on biological considerations.' Motorisation varies regionally; the map (fig. 60B) shows sharp contrasts in the number of tractors per 1,000 ha. of agricultural land, from Corsica, Alpes-Maritimes and Lozère with 13·3 each, to Vaucluse with 67. The North, the Paris region, Finistère, the South-west and a belt of departments running from the German frontier to the Mediterranean except for the Alpine regions, are the areas where there is the greatest density of tractors.[12]

This map of motorisation, compared with that of fertiliser consumption, shows that the French countryside is less opposed to the tractor than it is to biological progress.[13] Motorisation is in fact making great strides. Finistère had 150 tractors before the last war, 2,560 in 1953, 10,700 in 1959 and 21,500 in 1964. Gers had 3,753 tractors in 1950, 11,173 in 1960 and 19,400 in 1964.

Mechanisation of agriculture goes hand in hand with motorisation. Every year the equipment is increased. Machines of all sizes and for many different purposes, towed by the tractor or worked by electric motors at the farm, have fundamentally altered the living and working conditions of farmers and their employees. The number of combine harvesters rose from 200 in 1938 to 10,150 (1953), 42,000 (1959) and 92,200 (1964). The numbers of mechanical cultivators rose from 6,000 (1938) to 120,000 (1959) and 186,000 (1964), and mechanical reapers from 1,000 (1938) to 58,000 (1959) and 98,000 (1964).

Mechanisation has a direct influence on the farming system. It reduces working time and thereby makes possible the introduction of new crops while reducing losses due to the late harvesting of hay and other crops.

Information and organisation

These great changes which have been achieved in about fifteen years would not have been possible without a change of outlook in the farming world, without improved methods of disseminating and popularising new ideas and above all without new forms of professional organisation.

The *Institut National de la recherche agronomique* (I.N.R.A.) was created in 1946. There are 104 experimental stations and laboratories and 22 experimental farms (1,500 ha.) scattered all over France, which belong to or depend on the I.N.R.A. In country districts there are agricultural advisers to help farmers. In 1961 there were 1,500 of them, 1,000 employed by the Government or public bodies, and 500 by private firms, but only 1,000 of these work on a full-time basis. The proportion can easily—and regrettably—be worked out as one adviser to 2,300 farmers as against one to 420 in Germany and one to 240 in Holland.

The *Co-opératives d'utilisation de matériel agricole* (C.U.M.A.) were formed to ensure that farmers can obtain the equipment which is indispensable to modern methods of production, which is too costly to buy and impossible to acquire on hire purchase and to use effectively on one farm alone.

The mechanical cultivation and threshing syndicates which were in existence before the Second World War were the forerunners of the C.U.M.A. Immediately after the war the C.U.M.A. mushroomed—10,000 of them were counted—and these had priority in the allocation of agricultural machinery, which was in short supply. In 1954 only 4,500 were left as a result of the mechanisation of individual farms, and more particularly because serious economic and technical mistakes were made by members of these co-operatives who were psychologically unprepared and economically and professionally ill-equipped for their work.

The movement was then restarted, with a better organisation, on co-operative lines. In 1962 almost 10,000 C.U.M.A. were in operation with 10,000 combine harvesters, 25,000 balers and 15,000 tractors, together valued at 230 million francs, at their disposal.

An hierarchy of C.U.M.A. has gradually come into existence. They range from local C.U.M.A., consisting of small groups of farmers, to departmental C.U.M.A., to which the former are affiliated, and which possess the heavy equipment needed for large-scale land development. The C.U.M.A. are playing a more and more important part in agricultural life by increasing the solidarity of their member farmers and by inducing them to help each other in a way which will make great changes possible in the future.

The *Centres d'études techniques agricoles* (C.E.T.A.) originated in 1944, in the Paris region. There were 530 of them in 1958, and more than 1,000 at the beginning of 1962, involving all agricultural regions and all types of farms. A C.E.T.A. consists of about fifteen farmers and operates on three principles: the pooling of knowledge, the sharing of research work according to the ability of each member and the participation of experts in the work of the group.

All improvements in the farming methods and thus in yields and farm income depend in the first place on an accurate knowledge of farm management and farm economics. In this field French agriculture is very backward. In 1938 only about 300 sets of farm accounts were available; since the war great efforts have been made in the economic analysis of agricultural enterprises, but at the beginning of 1958 only 3,800 had been so analysed.

At present there are agricultural auditing offices and administrative centres in most departments.[14] The administrative centres, in fact, work at departmental level. They are making an economic classification of farms, distinguishing between good farms, which are functioning satisfactorily, average farms and poor farms. Productivity and public relations committees and control areas complete the administrative framework. At the same time the co-operative movement has continued to develop, as the list of 17,000 co-operatives (1966) testifies more clearly than words.[15]

The vertical integration of farms, now becoming more common, is also an important factor in recent progress.

The balance sheet of this second agricultural revolution is impressive. In a few years the face of French agriculture has changed completely. The rise in mean yields provides a somewhat inadequate measure of this progress (Table LIV).

TABLE LIV. THE GROWTH OF YIELDS

Quintals per ha.	Average 1934–8	Average 1953–7	Average 1961–3
Wheat	15·6	22·3	27
Barley	14·5	21·9	26·9
Maize	15·8	24·4	28·7
Potatoes	111	157	156*
Sugar beet	276	304	328*
Mangolds	360	453	416*

* 1962

The increase in yield varies greatly from area to area. Between 1930–9 and 1954–7, for example, yields of wheat increased by 96·2% in Vienne department, compared with 9·3% in Haute-Vienne, 76·1% in Loire-Atlantique and 7·4% in Ardèche.

But this progress is irreversible and new factors of change are appearing on the horizon. Thus 'the structure of agricultural production, particularly in respect of livestock, will be undergoing fundamental changes in the next few years; mass production of animal foodstuffs will enable large units to be created for the production of eggs, poultry, pork and beef' (L. Malassis).[16]

C. The Diversity of Farming Types

The extraordinary diversity of types of farming in France can best be understood by correlating them with production methods, on the one hand, and physical conditions, on the other. It is often tempting to assign a particular type to a region, to speak, for example, of the Caux type or the Santerre type, but there is a risk of confusion between product orientation and type of farming or between land use and type of farming. There are innumerable minor variations even within one region; in fact 'the term "type of farming" can strictly be applied to one farm only. As soon as farms which are not producing exactly the same crops are grouped together, it is no longer justifiable to refer to a common type of farming' (J. Klatzmann).

It is not clear whether present conditions tend to promote regional uniformity in types of farming or, conversely, to accentuate existing differences between farms. On the one hand, it seems that although the farms in some regions might have shown a measure of uniformity in types of farming before the second agricultural revolution, they have done so to a diminishing extent during the last twenty years. Modernisation of farming and changes in agricultural practices do not affect all farms at the same time. Many other factors go to explain why, in the same region, some farms cling to their habitual polyculture, while others more quickly pass through the stages of development leading to commercialisation. These factors are the farming type itself (farms practising highly differentiated forms of polyculture are least susceptible to change because of the rigidity of their systems of crop combination), the age of the farmer, individual and family outlooks, the availability of capital, accessibility to communications, markets and consuming centres, and the type of land. Small farms cannot, for lack of money or skill, switch to more profitable crops quickly enough to take advantage of them before too many others have done the same thing. 'The small farmer in the South-west says he cannot convert his twenty hectares under polyculture all at once into orchards of Golden variety apples, while the great estates established in the region by big landowning companies are still selling them at advantageous prices. He will no doubt get round to it in five years, when the boom in this particular produce is over' (Serge Mallet).

On the other hand, the development of communal organisations and enterprises, from co-operatives to group farming by way of C.E.T.A. and C.U.M.A., should lead progressively to a greater uniformity of types of farming among the farmers of one region.

The same kind of contrast occurs on the regional scale. On the one hand, types of farming are becoming simplified as they become specialised, by the reduction of the number of products from each farm. From the 19th to the 20th century the range of crops was reduced; industrial crops, which occupied an important place in the French peasant's combination of crops, dwindled owing to competition from tropical crops (oils and textile fibres), or synthetic chemical products in the case of vegetable dyes. This specialisation and simplification tends to accentuate the contrasts between regions, as each, once it has escaped from its subsistence polyculture, finds its agricultural 'vocation'.

On the other hand, biological and technical improvements lead to an increasing artificiality in agriculture; the natural suitability of a region for a certain crop, and the different potentialities of rich and poor regions, lose part of their significance as the modernisation of agriculture progresses—mechanisation, plant protection, scientific feeding, fertilisers, irrigation, genetics, information services and publicity all lessen the significance of contrasts between good and bad land, contrasts which were becoming more marked right up to the middle of the 20th century. Thus the Haut Bocage of Vendée harvests 40 quintals of wheat per ha., as much as Limagne; on the light chalky soils of dry Champagne, mechanical digging and the chemical treatment of the soil have enabled as much as 50 quintals per ha. of cereals to be harvested.

THE TRADITIONAL SYSTEM OF POLYCULTURE

The traditional system of polyculture has continued for lack of labour, money and initiative, on the majority of farms. It is found in many forms but with the common characteristic of being a family type of farming combining multi-cropping and stock-rearing.

This form of polyculture is practised by farmers who still have a peasant outlook and whose economic conditions are still at subsistence level.[17] 'For a very long time the chief thought in the minds of our country people was quite simply the fear of being short of food' (A. Fel). This fear was kept alive by periods of war, and particularly by the Second World War, during which the peasants were glad to be able to live on the varied produce of their land, while the townsmen were rationed.

In fact this polyculture is not exactly like that of last century, owing to the commercialisation of part of the production. But the money so gained is still considered as something extra, to be spent in the town market on something the farm does not produce. The French peasant is 'a man of tradition and the heir of moneyless generations' (D. Faucher), and this is the man who today is finding himself caught up in a radical transformation of the techniques of agricultural production and organisation.

But there are instances of traditional polyculture which are, paradoxically, recent, or the result of retrograde development. In the South-west, at the end of 17th century, the *métairies* were on the brink of ruin, as their soil was impoverished by insufficient manuring resulting from the relative scarcity of cattle. They were saved by the introduction of maize, which partly cut out the need for fallow. Polyculture in Aquitaine was then based on three staple products: wheat, maize and wine. But this system of cultivation was soon upset, partly by crises, such as phylloxera and the importation of foreign wheat, and partly by lack of labour, as the three basic products involved a very heavy programme of work for the year. Aquitaine then returned to small-scale polyculture on a self-sufficient, family basis.

In Vivarais, up to the middle of the last century, the rugged, sharply contrasted countryside, with its poor soil and practically no flat surfaces apart from the limestone plateaux, had a very different economy from the present poor farming system. It was a varied economy based on cereals, with vineyards, chestnuts and sericulture. The cereals dwindled as a result of an invasion of foreign wheat, the vines were destroyed by phylloxera, the chestnut trees were decimated by disease

and by competition from manufacturers of tanning extracts, the silkworms were attacked by pebrine and the silkworm industry was dealt a death blow by silk imports from the Far East.

With only a few changes these two regional descriptions would portray the situation in many parts of France. Once more they reveal the responsibility of the past for the present situation of too many farms, and make it easier to understand the reasons for their backwardness.

'These farms (*microfundia*) are too small to specialise in the very select group of crops which necessitate a high level of skill and are subject to more serious risks than polyculture. Their monthly income, including domestic consumption, is no more than 100 to 120 francs, which is sometimes less than 50 francs an hour. These regions which, it cannot be denied, are relatively over-populated are found in Bas-Rhin, Rhône and in the whole of the West from Manche to Charente.'

ADVANCED FORMS OF POLYCULTURE

Side by side with this more or less archaic system of polyculture, there are more intensive types that have benefited from progress and are adapted to the conditions of contemporary agricultural life. Changes on these farms do not normally take the form of a radical change over to commercial agriculture, but rather the introduction of commercial crops side by side with the traditional subsistence cultivation. In some cases the new crops may be in the minority, but in other cases the old traditional crops may be relegated to a few plots, specialised crops having taken the pride of place in the system of rotation. The result is not so much a radical modernisation of the type of farming but an intensification of the polyculture system which permits of a large population remaining in the communes.

The North offers type examples of these intensive and highly developed systems of polyculture. The farming system in Flanders is characterised by a small proportion of the land under grass, and a large proportion of root-crops, legumes and other crops, together with stock-rearing. Rotation systems are very skilful, wheat being grown, for example, four times in eleven years. This intensive polyculture is practised with innumerable minor variations on many farms, and is more or less specialised and more or less intensive according to the importance of pasture. It is the predominant system in the Pays de Caux, and low Picardy, where cereals, roots or legumes and pasture are found together.

In southern France the vine forms an element in this polyculture, apart from the areas of specialised production like Gironde, the hills of Lot-et-Garonne, Vendée and the Val-de-Loir.

In both traditional and advanced forms of polyculture, stock-rearing is subordinated to crops because of its lower yield (7 vegetable calories are needed to produce 1 animal calorie).

Specialisation in stock-rearing is in fact possible only in commercial agriculture because then stock-rearing becomes more remunerative owing to the relative prices of grain and animal products. Some such farms produce milk, others meat.

SPECIALISED FARMING AND MONOCULTURE

Among this widespread polyculture, whether archaic or advanced, stand out the specialised and monocultural types of farming, and specialised stock-rearing; the great cereal and sugar-beet farms of the central Paris basin and the North, the rice fields of the Camargue, the great stock-rearing estates, small market gardens, orchards and flower-farms, and vineyards. But in the sixties these systems of specialised farming have spread widely over many regions. On the fruit farms of Comtat Venaissin,

'the area of one holding is rarely more than 2 or 3 ha. . . . Everything is done to capitalise on local climatic advantages and to accentuate them as far as possible. Sowing is done under glass from January onwards; in March the plants are pricked out in low houses for melons, high and carefully closed ones for asparagus; aubergines, tomatoes and cucumbers ripen at the very foot of the cypress hedges. . . . All these practices demand incessant work, and a meticulous, often individual, handling of plant—every melon grower has his own special tricks of the trade, and to nip off the right melon in the right place at the right moment is an art—and also considerable capital' (R. Livet).

In the vegetable-growing coastal districts of Léon, intensive growing relies on a carefully worked out calendar and the aid of catch-crops. First year: early potatoes lifted from April to June with the first pricking out of cauliflowers in May. Second year: onions and artichokes mixed. Third year: second-year artichokes at full yield. Fourth year: wheat and annual red clover.

Another type of intensive farming is found immediately round large towns.

'In contrast to the tendency to uniformity of crop combinations over large areas of the countryside the restricted areas of urban fringe zones display an extraordinary variety of combinations, related to opportunities for speculation and the existence of a more complex, more advanced technical and social structure. . . . Between the built-up areas we notice first, there are fields of vegetables, market gardens, orchards, the greenhouses of horticulturists and the cowsheds of dairy farmers to bear witness to this variety' (M. Phlipponneau).

There is no typical landscape of suburban agriculture; it is a heterogeneous patchwork. The land plays only a tiny part in these types of farming; what matters is capital, techniques and labour. Tons of manure, chemical fertilisers, waste and drainage from the towns, irrigation, greenhouses and crop selection allow the suburban cultivator to be independent of natural conditions; the land is only a base for his work. Often there are from three to five harvests a year from the same field. We do sometimes see the influence of natural conditions in the location of some enterprises, but quite often this is only a hangover from a period when they really did play a part (market gardens in low-lying plains, and fruit farms on sunny hillsides).

In France, this suburban agriculture developed at the same rate as urbanisation and industrialisation, that is to say to a lower degree than abroad. Small market-garden suburbs exist round every large French town, but it is in the Paris region that suburban farming appears in its most characteristic form.

Poultry farming. The production of poultry, eggs and rabbits in France amounts to 335 billion francs, that is six times the value of the production of sugar-beet, and twice the turnover of Gaz de France. Poultry-farming has developed considerably in certain parts of France in the last few years, both in the form of the poultry farm, as in Bresse, and in the form of specialised battery units of several thousand head, as in Brittany.

Fowl-rearing is an interesting way of making the best use of maize; 1 ha. of maize consumed by laying hens gives a return almost twice as high as that from pork.

CHANGES IN TYPES OF FARMING

Farming types can develop very differently within the same commune. Their flexibility depends directly on the system of land holding and the size of the farm, quite apart from the other factors, such as training, outlook and situation.

Innovations in agriculture are often the result of external stimuli:

(*a*) Immigration. For example, it was the people of Ardèche who came down from their mountains to the plain of Montélimar and planted the peach orchards. The French from North Africa settled in the abandoned or under-developed *métairies* of the South-west, and introduced fundamental changes into the farming systems, thanks to the abundant capital at their disposal and their professional training, by intensifying cultivation and by planting orchards of industrial crops.

(*b*) Incentives. The growing of early potatoes was introduced into Saint-Malo about 1880 by the growers from Jersey; the potato plant spread throughout Finistère because attempts to popularise it in France were favourably received by the head of the Department at the Ministry of Agriculture (and secondarily because there are no green-fly in Brittany). Similarly, some contract cropping was introduced, effecting a complete,

if localised, transformation of the farming system and agricultural economy.

(*c*) Changes in the market. The growing demand for meat and dairy produce since the end of the 19th century explains the development of stock-rearing and the conversion of arable land into pasture. So also the upland types of stock-rearing adapted themselves to consumer demand. At first there was a tendency to abandon the Alpine pastures, which are favourable for cheese-making but not for the transport of milk to the tourist-filled valleys, but now 'milk pipe-lines' again allow the flocks to be taken on to the mountains.

THE GEOGRAPHICAL AND ECONOMIC POSITION OF TYPES OF FARMING

All these conditions explain the uneven, fragmentary character of any picture of the farming type pattern, and the danger of any generalisation. The important issue is their regional distribution. When the majority of the farms in one region practise the same type of farming with comparable intensity and mean productivity, an agricultural region can be defined. Beauce, Santerre in Picardy, the regions of vine monoculture, the market-gardening regions, fat-stock regions and dairy-farming regions are the most representative examples. At the same time the underlying heterogeneity of types of farming must not be forgotten.

The modern specialised agriculture of Périgord, for example, is very localised and very varied in the midst of a region of poly-culture. It embraces the vine-growing around Monbazillac, the production of *foie gras* and truffles, tobacco in southern Périgord, 'white' calves in Ribéraçois, asparagus in Double, walnuts, fruit on the recently planted orchards, apples and peaches in the Dordogne valley below Bergerac and strawberries in the forest of Vergt and on the margins of the Barade forest.

This individual and regional heterogeneity of types of farming, with traditional and progressive farming existing side by side, is a source of great disadvantages. It tends to

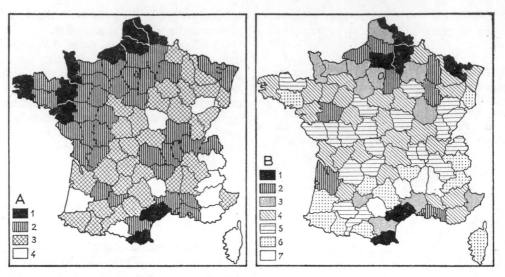

Fig. 61. A. Gross yield per ha. of agricultural land in 1954–5 (in thousands of old francs). Source: *Économie rurale*, July 1956)
1. More than 72.   2. 39–68.   3. 22–38.   4. Less than 21.

B. Average income per person in households where the head is a farmer (in thousands of old francs). (Source: *Structures de la France agricole*, Rennes, 1961 (map 2454))
1. More than 443.   2. 334–443.   3. 246–334.   4. 181–246.   5. 135–181.   6. 106–135.   7. Less than 106.

accentuate regional contrasts; in fact the most notable progress has been made in regions which were already most productive so that the gap between rich and poor regions has been widened.

The two maps (fig. 61) give two evaluations, by departments, of returns from agriculture. The second shows income adjusted to allow for varying size of families (mean income per person in households, the head of which is a working farmer). The departments with the most advanced and specialised farming types stand out clearly; the density of agricultural population has an inverse effect on income distribution.

The first map, compiled by J. Klatzmann, measures the gross yield per ha. of agricultural

land (1954–5). The gross production takes into account the principal products sold and consumed by the family. The gross production per ha. is high in regions of polyculture and intensive stock-rearing (East, West, North), in the rich arable and stock-rearing areas of Normandy, the Lyons region and the Paris region, and in fruit- and vine-growing regions. The differences between the various regions appear relatively clear-cut.

The contrasts, however, go further still; for example, the price of wheat is based on yields from about 20 ha., which are achieved on the least productive and least advanced farms. But this evaluation only represents a really economic return for large farms whose yields are twice as high. In the long run

TABLE LV. COMPARISON OF SOME ELEMENTS IN EUROPEAN AGRICULTURE

	France	Germany	Belgium	Netherlands	Italy
Use of fertilisers in 1963–4, in kg. of fertilising elements per ha. of usable agricultural land .	87·2	186·7	255·6	242	44·5
Average yield (1963–5) in quintals of wheat per ha.	29·7	34·3	30	46·8	20·4
Average milk yield per cow, in kg. (1964) . .	2,622	3,517	3,811	4,177	2,705

these large farms have much to gain from the survival of an out-of-date sector in French agriculture. And what goes for farms goes for regions too.

This heterogeneity also explains the relatively mediocre level which our agriculture has reached in comparison with other nations: the huge number of traditional or as yet incompletely modernised farms weighs heavier than the few tens of thousands of productive farms (Table LV).

Table LVI gives a statistical balance sheet of French agriculture. This gives some cause

TABLE LVI. STATISTICAL BALANCE SHEET OF FRENCH AGRICULTURE

Product		Commercial production in France (thousands)	Consumption in France (thousands)	Extent to which internal demand is covered (%)
Wheat	(quintals)	73,400	55,000	135
Barley	(,,)	27,000	20,000	135
Maize	(,,)	12,000	8,000	150
Sugar	(,,)	1,600	1,400	114
Potatoes	(,,)	4,000	4,000	100
Fresh fruit	(tons)	1,560	1,600	98
Fresh vegetables	(,,)	7,100	7,200	99
Wine	(hectolitres)	58,000	72,000	80
Vegetable oils (tons)		40–60	55–70	72–85
Beef, carcass meat	(,,)	1,150	1,030	110
Veal	(,,)	380	380	100
Mutton	(,,)	136	140	97
Pork	(,,)	1,150	1,050	109
Horsemeat	(,,)	80	100	80
Eggs				98
Milk	(hectolitres)	175,000	160,000	110

for satisfaction, but there is in fact more reason to be surprised at the low quantities of certain products. To seek out the causes of this situation would mean drawing up a balance sheet for every sector of agriculture; we will dwell on only two, which appear to be critical.

If the considerable progress in motorisation, in mechanisation and in agronomy have not produced as much effect as might have been expected, this is because farms are paralysed by obsolete agrarian structures, or by the bad organisation of agricultural land.

On the other hand, rural depopulation and its corollary, concentration of farming, have

enabled farmers to increase their output without having recourse to intensified cultivation; thus concentration has to a large extent come of its own accord.

The types of farming practised on the majority of French farms must therefore change considerably before we have a really modern agriculture. But there is a danger that changes may cause a large number of farmers to increase production simultaneously and thus bring about a sudden overproduction of certain products. The effects of overproduction on the market are disastrous and cancel out the progress which each farm may expect from it. Inter-regional competition even occurs when two regions go over to the same kinds of specialisation at different times. For example, the pea-growers of Brittany have been affected by competition from large farms in the Paris region.

So we are up against the main problem of reconciling the optimum type of farming for an individual farm with the total prospects offered by the agricultural market. The distribution of production must be worked out in relation to overall middle-term demand, and we can see at once the size and the difficulty of this task. In particular,

'is it possible to determine scientifically the best possible location for such agricultural production as a comprehensive analysis has shown to be necessary? It is unlikely. The problem is in fact a very complex one, especially, as is the case in France, when we have no exact inventory of the potentialities of the various areas. If the plan can be made regionally less concentrated, we will, in fact, locate the various types of crop and stock in the areas where they can be produced more or less in the best possible conditions' (D. R. Bergmann).

Finally, modernisation of agriculture must go hand in hand with fundamental changes in commercial organisation, an important topic which has no place in this book.

1. This classification was made by J. Klatzmann.

2. In stock-rearing regions small and medium-sized farms, for lack of land and capital, sell their calves at seven months, at the end of one rearing season, while the large farms sell the animals at eighteen months after two seasons.

3. *Polyculture* is a very common French term for multiple-product farming. It is applied both to 'mixed' (crop and animal) farming, as described here under the heading *northern polyculture*, and to types of farming in

which interculture of crops is a distinctive feature and animals are kept mainly for draught purposes, and referred to as *southern polyculture*. The term polyculture is retained in this text with its comprehensive connotation in French (A. J. Hunt).

4. *La Vie Rurale vue par un géographe*, pp. 48–9.

5. 'As soon as they give some shade, trees are the most efficient users of irregular rainfall' (R. Dumont).

6. Cf. p. 322.

7. From the 16th to the 19th century the conquest of the salt-marshes of western France and Languedoc was waged continuously; the Dutch played a large part in their reclamation.

8. Chemical weed-killers act selectively, destroying weeds without harming the crop. Researches on trace-elements have shown their essential role in increasing yield or even in the introduction of certain crops. Many granitic soils, for example, are deficient in either copper, thus preventing the extension of wheat-growing, or manganese.

9. Within the irrigated zone as planned vines occupy 50% of the area in Gard and 85% in Hérault.

10. The year from 1st May to 30th April.

11. In spite of this rapid mechanisation, France is still behind other countries; the number of tractors per 1,000 ha. of cultivable agricultural land was 70 in Western Germany, 33 in the Netherlands, 31 in Belgium and 26 in France (1962).

12. The power of tractors must also be taken into account; in regions with heavy soils the farmer must have powerful and costly machines whose use is more restricted.

13. This in spite of physical conditions which are often unfavourable.

14. But instead of depending on one single organisation, these offices have developed quite at random; most are independent, and the others are connected either with the departmental federations of farmers' syndicates or with the chambers of agriculture or with the departmental agricultural services.

15. 3,202 dairy co-operatives, handling 52% of the commercial milk, 1,172 wine co-operatives making 37% of the wine, 800 cereal co-operatives taking 82% of the harvest, 450 fruit and vegetable co-operatives handling 20% of the produce, 39 sugar-beet co-operatives, 1,500 co-operatives for farm supplies (fertilisers and cattle-feed) and 11,070 co-operatives for farm services—threshing, insemination and the C.U.M.A.

16. Statistical progress alone is out of step with economic progress. The public authorities, having no definite figures at their disposal, cannot predict or encourage any particular trend in farming. In 1958 the Ministry of Agriculture gave 190 million hectolitres as the milk production for the year; a study by the I.N.S.E.E. on the basis of consumer analysis found it to be 220 million. The numbers of cattle are known only to within a few millions.

17. In 1956–8 the proportion of subsistence production in the total agricultural production was estimated at 17–18% (as against 30% in 1939).

2. LAND USE

The juxtaposition of plots which are similarly or differently employed by all the farmers in a region determines particular patterns of land use. Fields, permanent or temporary pasture, orchards and vineyards, forests, heathland and waste land in different proportions and combinations are the essence of rural landscapes and the natural expression of the constant give and take between types of farming, settlement and natural conditions.

A. Types of Land Use

Three major categories of land use are commonly distinguished: *silva, saltus* and *ager*. The *silva* is the wooded area, utilised and maintained; the *saltus* is under-utilised land which plays a supplementary part in the system of farming—heathland, rough grazing, waste lands; the *ager* embraces all land used for cultivation in the widest sense, that is to say both arable land and permanent pasture, though the distinction tends to become blurred where there is rotation of arable and pasture; sometimes the *hortus*, comprising gardens and market gardens, is differentiated from the *ager*.

FORESTS

Forest occupies a special place in the countryside; it is more or less excluded from land classified as agricultural. There are several reasons for its exclusion: the special characteristics of the ownership (resident or non-resident) of forest lands and of their management (often with the aid of labour drawn from outside the district); and the part played by the State in their administration and exploitation. The forest has no part in the daily routine of a farm, for woodland represents an investment rather than an activity; it is an empty space, only occasionally enlivened by the presence of people.

This situation in which the forest is set apart from the system of cultivation is of relatively recent origin. At one time the forest was much more clearly integrated into the rural economy than it is today. Its many resources were used: wood was used for heating and building, it was 'a vast stable' where the animals grazed, and the peasants gathered acorns; many industries brought life to its clearings.[18]

But there is another reason why the forest occupies a special place in the territory of France. Apart from the Mediterranean areas, the Atlantic coasts and marshy valley bottoms, it once covered the whole country. The present rural landscape with its intermittent and unevenly distributed remnants of woodland has indeed been brought into existence by progressive clearance of the forest.

This is not the place to retrace the steps in the clearing of this vast mantle of forest. The 10th, 11th, 12th and 13th centuries, the 16th, the second half of the 18th and the 19th centuries were the periods when most of this was done.[19]

From 1828 to 1908, 489,000 ha. of forest are said to have been cleared. These clearings were made possible to a very large extent by encroachment on the state forests (117,000 ha. in about 1831–5, and 72,000 ha. in 1868). At the present time clearing projects are being carried out in certain regions, arising from the need to increase the area of open land (Berry) or to introduce new crops (strawberries in Périgord).

Reafforestation has always gone hand in hand with clearing. The planting of the Gascony heathlands with softwoods (from 1857), the reafforestation of the Sologne (from 1859) and reafforestation in mountain areas are some of the major steps in this development, associated with the introduction of softwoods into poor forests and the conversion of coppices into timber stands. The reafforestation policy assumes increasing im-

K

portance. Created in 1946, the *Fonds National Forestier* has reafforested more than 1,100,000 ha. in twenty years. Since the middle of the 19th century, 120,000 ha. have been planted in the Alps. In the southern Jura the area of pine forest rose by reafforestation from 18,000 ha. (1850) to 31,000 ha. (1950). Dry Champagne was the scene of an immense reafforestation scheme covering 112,000 ha. The official policy of reafforestation can, however, be in opposition to the evolution of agrarian structures and the needs of the various systems of culture.

At present eight departments have forests covering more than 35% of their total area: the Landes, 59·7%; Var, 49%; Gironde, 45%; the Vosges, 42%; Haute-Saône, 37·4%; Haut-Rhin, 37%; Haute-Marne, 36·6%; Jura, 36%.

The largest wooded areas are found in north-eastern France, while other departments from Nièvre to Bas-Rhin and from the Doubs to the Ardennes also have large areas. Forests are least extensive in the Armorican massif and in northern France. The Central Massif also appears as a relatively little wooded area, while 20–30% of the Pyrenees and the Alps are wooded (fig. 62).

The present distribution of the forests can be explained:

1. By physical conditions, forests being nearly always confined to poor soils:

(*a*) Siliceous soils: the sandy areas of the Paris basin, the sandstone lower Vosges, Sologne and the Landes.
(*b*) Skeletal limestone soils: the dip-slopes of the cuestas of Lorraine and the plateau of Langres.
(*c*) Clay soils: the Argonne and the clay with flints of Normandy.
(*d*) Stony soils: the Hardt forest.

R. Dion has demonstrated the importance of the old tertiary erosion surfaces that carry alluvial clay–sand deposits and hard-pans as factors in the location of forests: 'the great forests of Haut Perche and the plateaux of Touraine, the desolate heaths of Ruchard to

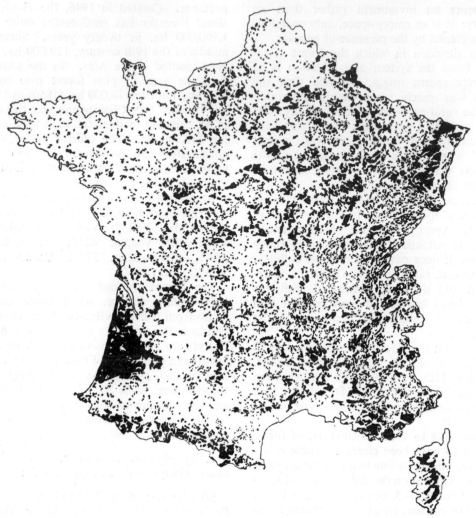

Fig. 62.   Distribution of the French forests.   (Source: G. Plaisance, *Guide des Forêts de France*, **La Nef de Paris**, 1961)

the north of Chinon, the forests and heaths of northern Berry and Puisaye, the forest of Othe . . . the eastern part of the plateau of Brie, between Orbais and Épernay', and the forests of the Landes.

2. By man-made conditions, forests and population being mutually exclusive, so that forests are found in sparsely populated areas. Very often the forests have survived because they formed frontiers between different regions; the forest of Der was a barrier between

the Tricasses and the Cataluni, and the forests of Eu, Bray and Lihons separated Normandy from Picardy.

The location of the forests also reflects their varying functions. There are timber forests and reclamation forests which serve several distinct purposes: to prevent gullying in the mountains or wind erosion in coastal dune areas, to promote the reconstitution of the soil in forest reserves or as suburban and 'green belt' woodlands.

The forest cover takes many forms:

(a) Extensive 'regional' forests: Landes, 1 million ha.; Ardennes, 100,000 ha.; Vosges, 95,000 ha.; Maures, 67,000 ha.; Argonne, 45,000 ha.; Estérel, 26,800 ha.

(b) Large forests: Forest of Orleans, 45,500 ha.; Fontainebleau, 25,000 ha.; Bitche, 20,000 ha.; Haguenau, 15,000 ha.; Compiègne, 14,500 ha.; Rambouillet, 13,600 ha.; Chaux, 13,050 ha.; Othe, 12,000 ha.; Chatillon, 8,870 ha.; Écouves, 7,800 ha.; Eu, 6,905 ha.

(c) Very scattered small woods and forests, distributed according to differences in soils, slopes, field patterns and the pattern of land-ownership; the fragmentation of farm land led to a corresponding fragmentation of wood-land. This has been accentuated by re-afforestation aided by the *Fonds National Forestier* and carried out by non-resident, non-agricultural landowners. An Act of 1954 concerning forest co-operatives attempts to check this piecemeal reafforestation. In order to prevent reafforestation from becoming disastrously entangled with small culti-vated plots an Act of 1960 provided for the demarcation zones where tree planting would be prohibited or controlled.

Like other agricultural products, the pro-duction of the forest has to be adjusted to changing demand; but this cannot be done quickly in the space of a few years, which ex-plains the almost continual time lag between the forests and economic circumstances. One third of the forest is not productive or not regularly exploitable, one third is at present kept as coppice or coppice with stan-dards, producing firewood, pit props and second-rate hardwoods which are less and less in demand.[20] One third is coppiced. De-ciduous trees occupy 68% of the area (30% in Western Germany). The yields are below those of forests in neighbouring countries. Thus France, paradoxically enough, has to import 57% of her needs, particularly soft-woods for paper pulp.

Thus a great and long-term transformation of the French forests must be undertaken; its three elements will be the extension of planta-tions by over a million hectares, the change over to timber trees, the planting of conifers.[21] The optimum percentage of forest would be in the region of 27%.

To this end a law 'for the improvement of the production and ownership of French forests' was passed in 1963. It imposes on landowners (private persons own 65% of French forests, the communes 21% and the State 14%) an obligation 'to ensure the biological equilibrium of the country and the satisfaction of demands for wood and other forest products'. It institutes various *Centres Régionaux de la Propriété Forestière* with the task of encouraging, planning and generally advising on production. Since 1st January 1966 a national forest bureau administers the state-owned and communal forests.

WASTE LAND

The agricultural land of France is far from being completely utilised. Official statistics group together heathland, uncultivated land and non-agricultural land, but this does not give us an idea of the quantity of abandoned land.

Waste land (*friches*) is a vague term. It may be totally abandoned, a former arable field or a former patch of vine or mulberries. But it can also be a field converted, de-liberately or naturally, into grassland grazed occasionally by a few cattle or sheep.

In the landscape, waste land appears as an intermediate stage between pasture and wood-land; grasses, brushwood, bracken and gorse gradually invade abandoned plots, starting from the periphery; the hedges left to them-selves become over-luxuriant, paradoxically giving the waste a *bocage*-like character. 'It is the sight of so many French countrysides being invaded by grasses and shrubs which emphasises the contrast between improve-ment or decay of the land in the space of a single lifetime. . . . In this way, every plot of land which was productive a century ago re-verts to waste if it is not actually in use as a field, garden, vineyard, hayfield, orchard, rich meadow, good pasture or simply a wood, forest or well-tended park' (L. Gachon).

But the history of the waste land is the same as that of the rural population. Is it really necessary to go back to the time when the rapid growth of population in the country necessitated the intensive use of land and of every available plot?

The fact is that waste land covers a large area of France. L. Gachon estimates that only a quarter of the agricultural land area of France is worked over every year; since the middle of the 19th century there has been a great reduction in the area used for agriculture; from 1862 to 1939, according to Paul Combe, the area of heathland and uncultivated land has practically doubled (coefficient 1·93).

Physical conditions contribute to the localisation of waste land, but they are not themselves determining factors. Reduction in the proportion of cultivated land has been particularly marked in certain types of area:

(*a*) Those under steep slopes which were worked by hand when there was a dense rural population and which are not suitable for modern farm implements.

(*b*) Those with soils which are not fertile enough or too hard to work.

(*c*) Those with extreme climatic conditions.

In Corsica, where the area sown with cereals has diminished from 140,000 ha. (1840) to 38,000 ha. (1868) then 10,000 ha. (1914), heathland, waste land and useless land have increased in proportion. On the slopes of the Sancy hills, bracken and scrub have invaded the pastures. Waste land also results from rural depopulation, lack of financial resources and changes in the country way of life and working conditions in agriculture. In general, waste land is the geographical expression of the sum of the changes that the countryside has undergone during the last hundred years. There is a very clear relationship between the extent of waste land, on the one hand, and the amount of rural depopulation and concentration of farming, on the other.

Technical progress has been to a large extent responsible for the increase in waste land, in areas where subsistence polyculture has survived for lack of opportunity to specialise owing to the small increase in demand. In fact, technical progress made it possible to meet the demand with higher returns from areas which are necessarily more restricted.

Excessive fragmentation of holdings also leads to land abandonment; plots which are too small, too distant or too inaccessible for machines cease to be cultivated. When a farm falls vacant, it is sold in plots. The meadows, which are the best land, are snapped up, while cultivated plots and low grade grassland do not attract a buyer. Changes of occupation also lead to more waste land; as the standard of living rises, supplementary wages can be earned, outlooks become more sophisticated and mixed occupations of the industrial worker–peasant type tend to disappear; the peasant becomes a full-time factory employee, and leaves the small amount of land he owns to run to waste. This 'social waste land' is found in densely populated areas where industrial and rural occupations intermingle (around villages and small industrial towns).

Neglect of the maintenance and cleaning of the ditches in polderlands and damp valley bottoms allows marsh vegetation to gain the upper hand, raises the water-table and turns formerly cultivated zones into marshes.

From what has been said, the difficulty of analysing the distribution of waste lands can be appreciated. They are rare or even non-existent in the northern half of France, where they can be observed only on a few hills or slopes which have lost their vineyards. They are most widespread in the North-east. In the thirteen departments of north-eastern France, with the exception of the departments of Bas-Rhin and Haut-Rhin, there are 350,000 ha. of uncultivated land and 350,000 ha. of poor or ruined forests.

The southern half of France has most of the waste land; it is the legacy of an unfortunate combination of conditions, both physical (such as steep slopes and a climate unfavourable to dry crops) and demographic. In the Aquitaine basin, waste land can be explained by rural depopulation with its shattering effect on farming systems. In the hinterland of the Côte d'Azur, waste land is the dominant element of the countryside, amid sumptuous villas and villages repopulated by artists and summer visitors.

ARABLE LAND

The map (fig. 63) shows the proportion of arable land to total area in each department,

tion stops at 1,200–1,400 m., in the northern Alps it stops at about 1,200 m. The limit rises southwards; at Saint-Véran (Queyras) cereals can be cultivated up to 2,000 m. Figure 64 gives a more exact picture of the distribution of arable land, expressed as a proportion of the total cultivated area of each agricultural region. This shows more accurately the extent and limits of the arable areas.

The use of these arable lands varies con-

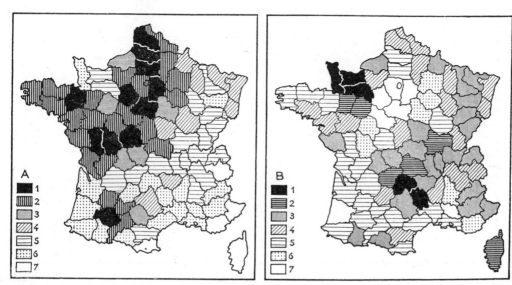

Fig. 63. A. Area occupied by arable land, in % of the total area of each department (1959).
1. More than 50. 2. 43·2–55. 3. 35·8–43·2. 4. 28·5–35·8. 5. 19·8–28·5. 6. 8–19·8. 7. Less than 8.
B. Areas always under grass in % of the total area of each department (1959).
1. More than 50. 2. 37·1–50. 3. 27–37·1. 4. 19·2–27. 5. 12·8–19·2. 6. 8–12·8. 7. Less than 8.

the arable land being concentrated in well-defined areas. From Charente to the North, and from Finistère to the Marne, all departments but three (Calvados, Manche and Orne) show more than one third of their land to be arable. Outside this block only five departments in Aquitaine appear as an arable area. In twelve departments the percentage of arable exceeds 55%.

Elsewhere, arable land covers smaller areas, giving way to forest, meadow, heathland and uncultivated ground. The upper limit for crops varies; in the Pyrenees cultiva-

siderably from one region to another, according to the prevailing types of farming. Departments with very high percentages of arable land correspond with regions practising intensive polyculture, specialising in wheat, sugar-beet and potatoes, and with regions of traditional polyculture in western and west-central France and Aquitaine.

Cereal-growing departments are in northern, central and eastern parts of the Paris basin, all wheat-growing country, and in the South-west where both wheat and maize are grown.

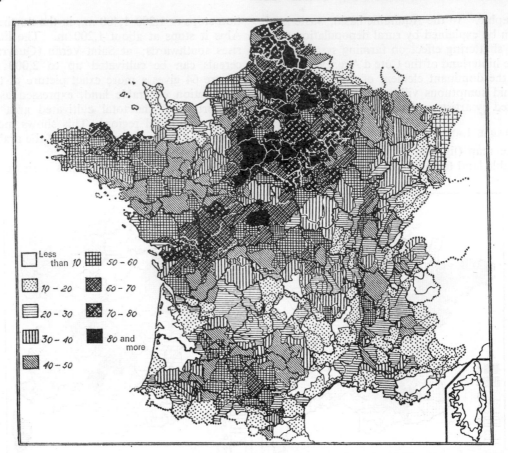

Fig. 64.   Proportion (%) of arable land on farms by agricultural regions, in 1942.   (Source: J. Klatzmann, *La Localisation des cultures et des productions animales en France*, I.N.S.E.E. 1955)

Wheat.   Taking the average of the years 1954–7, thirteen departments contributed 43·4% of the total production of France.   Two departments harvested more than 4 million quintals: Aisne (4,570,000) and Seine-et-Marne (4,082,000). Five produced between 3 and 4 million quintals: Eure-et-Loir, Nord, Oise, Pas-de-Calais and Somme.   Six produced between 2 and 3 million quintals: Côtes-du-Nord, Ille-et-Vilaine, Maine-et-Loire, Seine-Maritime, Seine-et-Oise.

In the West arable land is mainly occupied by root crops and legumes, areas of poly-culture with stock-rearing where there is an adequate labour force (West) or areas where stock-rearing predominates (Normandy and central France).   J. Klatzmann has observed that farming in areas of ancient rocks is characterised by a high proportion of roots and legumes on the arable land.

Arable land has diminished from 25·4 million ha. in 1892 to 18·5 million in 1953.[22] A comparison between 1862 and 1949 shows that the largest reductions are to be found in Normandy, in the North-east, in mountainous regions and in the Pyrenean region of the South.   This reduction has been effected in particular regions in favour of pastures, vine-yards or more commonly waste land, as the least productive and most distant land was abandoned.

'What has in fact happened to most of the former arable land between 1914 and today?

Arable fields were first put down to rotation grasses, then left as natural hayfields (dry meadows or stubble fields), then put down to grass again, finally to become degraded pasture through the invasion of broom, bracken, brambles and shrubs until it becomes natural coppice or is deliberately planted with softwoods' (L. Gachon).

A line from the Ardennes to Pyrénées-Orientales separates an eastern zone of France, where arable land has greatly diminished, from a western zone where arable land has survived better, except in Normandy and Gironde.

In some western departments the arable area has even increased, thanks to the clearing of heathland in connection with the rise in population. The Breton moors, for example, have been reclaimed to a considerable extent since the middle of the 19th century; their area diminished from 976,000 ha. in 1840 to 309,000 ha. in 1938. Since the beginning of the 19th century, 58,000 ha. of heathland have been reclaimed in Morbihan, and of this area 31,000 ha. are at present in cultivation and 5,000 ha. have been planted with trees.

GRASSLANDS

Grassland (*prairie*) is a type of land use which gives a false illusion of uniformity. In 1956–7 of a total area of 17,650,000 ha. under grass, artificial meadow represented 3,370,000 ha. and temporary meadow 1,115,000 ha., that is, 4,485,000 ha. taking part in crop rotation and occupying a large proportion of arable land. The rest was the area always under grass. But this natural meadowland, which occurs in the most varied of geographical contexts, consists of several types:

Hayfields (*prés*) or meadows, which provide hay for the cattle in winter or for stall-fed cattle (5,270,000 ha.). On impermeable ground either crystalline or clayey, the hayfield, when irrigated and manured, provides two harvests of hay a year.

Pasture lands (*herbages*), which are permanent grassland used for grazing but not cut for hay (known as *embouches* in Nivernais

and Normandy, *montagnes* in Cantal and *pâtures* in the North) (2,170,000 ha.).

Grazing lands (*pâtures*, *pacages* and *alpages* or 'Alpine' pastures) are well-drained grasslands where the growth is too slow to yield hay (4,900,000 ha.).

The regions with most grass are western France, especially the three departments of Basse-Normandie, the Central Massif, the North-east and the damp mountain areas. Manche, Calvados and Orne, on the one hand, and Cantal and Lozère, on the other, form two groups of departments with more than half their area under grass.

An analysis by departments can only give a crude idea of the distribution of grasslands; the map (fig. 65) compiled by Klatzmann gives a more accurate representation which is in the main complementary to the distribution of arable land. Thiérache, the Pays de Bray, Basse-Normandie, excepting the plain of Caen, the northern Jura, the northern Alps and the volcanic region of Auvergne stand out clearly.

The best grasslands are established on volcanic soils, on those rich in lime and phosphoric acid, on the clayey and marly soils of the Lias and on the rich alluvial soils of the valleys. At higher altitudes conditions favour grass, as there is more rain and less risk of drought in summer; here is the zone of hay fields.

Areas with little grass stand out clearly on the map (fig. 65): the Mediterranean region with its boundary extending up the Rhône valley to the north of Valence, the Landes, the south and centre of the Paris basin. The limestone surround of the Central Massif, in the North and West, stands out clearly in contrast to the Liassic clay lowlands which support grasslands.

The areas under grass have been increasing steadily since the second half of last century. This trend has particularly affected cool, humid and very well watered areas where wheat grew badly and late harvests were the rule, and those areas which were seriously affected by labour shortage resulting from rural depopulation.

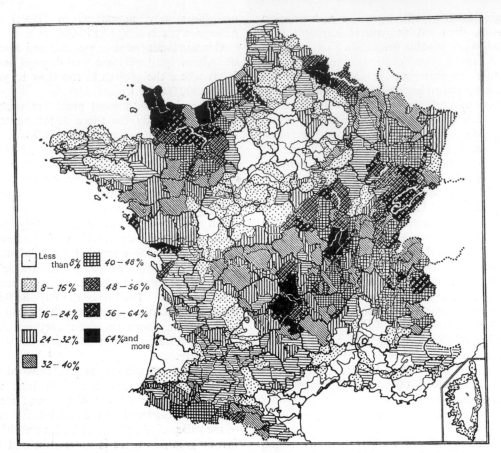

Fig. 65. Proportion (%) of areas under grass on farms by agricultural regions, in 1942. (Source: J. Klatzmann, *La Localisation des cultures et des productions animales en France*, I.N.S.E.E. 1955)

The department of Manche is the one which went furthest in this conversion of arable into grassland, which rose from 92,000 ha. (1852) to 172,000 ha. (1892) and to 408,000 ha. in 1955 (63·4% of the total area).

Permanent grassland has often served as a stopgap. 'To say that a region was ideal for stock-rearing actually meant that it was suitable for nothing in particular. Such areas were often devoted to mixed subsistence farming, coupled with extensive stock-raising' (Séverac). Thus developed what René Dumont called '*prairies abusives*', which are often recognised by their enclosure in barbed wire. They suffer from summer drought, and only yield 1,500 fodder units per ha.,

whereas the temporary meadows of Finistère, for example, yield 7,000–9,000.

L. Gachon has most aptly described the diversity of French grasslands:

'All these degenerate meadows and pastures which now lie useless, exposing to the world their waste, their ant-hills, their scrub . . . It is true that the Normandy grasslands of the Pays d'Auge are not degenerate; they are on marl, and are continually watered by the Atlantic rains. Neither have the meadows of the Jura, Savoie, Cantal and Mont-Dore suffered much deterioration. But there are so many others on the Saône plains, in Bourbonnais and in Aquitaine which are whipped by winter rain, cracked by summer drought and trampled by the hooves of grazing cattle. All these grasslands and stubble fields must now be saved from suffocation, opened up again and ploughed.'[23]

VINES

Viticulture is a very widespread type of land use in France; there are only 17 departments with no vineyards. But in the majority of departments the vine occupies a very small area; it is loved and cherished, but it is a minor element among very varied crop combinations.

The vine covers large areas in a small number of departments only: more than 5% of the effective agricultural area in 25 departments and more than 28% in 6 departments: Pyrénées-Orientales (38·8), Gard (28·9), Hérault (47·5), Var (35·9), Gironde (30·4) and Aude (30·3). Only in 7 or 8 of the 20 departments which produce more than a million hectolitres of wine does the vine constitute the main source of farm income.

But these statistical data give a distorted idea of the importance of the vineyards. They can in fact be divided into those producing high-quality wines (*vignobles de cru*), in Champagne, Burgundy, Alsace, Loire and Bordelais, and those producing ordinary wines (*vignobles de masse*), especially in Languedoc and Roussillon, which contain 27% of the world's area of bulk-producing vineyards.

The origin of the localisation of vineyards has been the subject of patient and intelligent research by R. Dion, which has given rise to an exciting controversy. The central problem is that of the relative importance of physical and human factors in the localisation of vineyards. Few plants need so much care as the vine if they are to bear fruit. 'Damp and dryness are the two enemies of the vine-grower,' says the priest in *La Rôtisserie de la reine Pédauque*. The vine needs dryness, especially for the seventy days from the opening of the buds to maturity, but excessive dryness is harmful. Temperature conditions are also exacting, the plant needing temperatures above 18° C. for the greater part of the growing season. The exposure of the ground to sun and air is equally important. M. Bordas has emphasised the relationship of the vine to the aridity index for July. As long as the index is below 20 the vine can grow and spread out, in Languedoc as well as in the Gironde lowlands. With an index above 20, site conditions become more critical; the vine is restricted to hill-slopes exposed to the south-east. This accounts for the contrast between the linear vine-growing areas in northern France and the widespread vineyards in southern France.

These strict conditions seem to be in contradiction with the wide area which vines have covered at one time or another, all over France, for the vine was once cultivated in Picardy and Normandy. We must note, however, that most of France has temperatures suited to the vine and that the many hillsides, well-sheltered sites and local climates have been favourable factors.

But powerful human causes have encouraged expansion. From Roman times the vine spread out along trade routes and on valley slopes along the rivers. Catholic liturgy—the Communion wine—was largely responsible for its dispersal during the centuries when wine could not be transported. The poorer classes found in the vine a unique opportunity to appropriate and develop land which would otherwise only have been waste land or poor heathland. This is one of the most important aspects of viticulture as a form of land use. 'By means of the vine, the non-Mediterranean part of our country has been associated in more than one way with one of the special advantages of the Mediterranean world, which is to be able, even where there is no arable land, to extract from the soil the essential or scarce food substances yielded by plants whose roots can force up stones or creep into the cracks in the rock' (R. Dion). For the well-off, the nobility, the bourgeoisie, the vine has been a matter of prestige and profit. 'The vine held such an important position among the preoccupations of our ancestors that anyone of rank cultivated it for the honour as much as for the profit; the presence of a castle or of a village enhanced by a few wealthy houses sufficed for the establishment of a vineyard' (R. Dion).

The Atlantic seaboard of France, open to the British Isles and northern Europe, has developed vineyards for export purposes. The vineyards of Bordeaux, first established to meet the needs of the local bourgeoisie, nobility and clergy, were transformed and extended for export purposes as early as the 12th century, thanks to political ties with England and the ports of the Hanseatic League.

'The great vine-growing region established in the Middle Ages in south-western France to satisfy the demands of northern lands coincides more or less with the respective zones of influence of the coastal towns. In Bordelais, the limits of the wine-producing zones are not climatic limits, nor are they the limits of navigability of the rivers (the Dordogne and the Garonne); they are the frontiers of the seneschalsy. ... The upper country, comprising all the provinces of the Garonne basin above La Réole, is not allowed to produce wine for export without being subjected to a vexatious control system, to taxes which are often prohibitive and to the exacting demands of the Bordeaux bourgeoisie. For this reason neither Agenois nor the Gers district of Gascony are vine-growing districts, although climatically they are ideal' (H. Enjalbert).

The rise of the Languedoc vineyards was similarly connected with the development of means of communication (the port of Sète and the *Canal du Midi* at the end of the 17th century, and the main roads from the 18th century onwards). Until 1875 the development of international trade, going hand in hand with that of means of transport, led to the rise of vineyards in coastal regions around the ports, since the vine will grow on a great variety of soils, even on alluvial plains.

It is thus evident that the siting of vineyards has not been determined entirely by physical conditions; men have planted vines only where they knew they could easily dispose of their products, that is to say near sea-ports, along navigable rivers and certain main land routes, or around the great urban centres. What is more, when the necessary physical conditions did not exist around these centres or these main routes, human enterprise made up for it by creating a truly artificial soil, as in Champagne, or by draining the land and by creating a more hardy strain of vine, as in Bordelais.

But it is probably debatable whether the vineyards of Lyonnais, Maconnais and Burgundy can be explained by the presence of a main road alone. Within the areas where vine-growing is economically possible, physical conditions again become determining factors.

The phylloxera crisis and the transport revolution changed the distribution of the vineyards. After the phylloxera visitation, the vineyards came down to spread over the rich land of the plains.[24] Local and regional vineyards whose commercial position, situation and qualities were inadequate have disappeared, so that the total area of vineyards decreased from 2,400,000 ha. (1854) to 1,300,000 ha. (1951).

The viticultural statute of 1934, by giving the monopoly of wine production to vine-growers operating at that time, immobilised the development of vineyards. According to its provisions it is forbidden to plant new vines without first grubbing up the old ones from an equivalent area; there are exemptions for named wines and for the production of table grapes. Acts of 1953 and 1954 tended to favour voluntary grubbing up by compensating the owners. This policy was suspended on 31st July 1957.

B. The Small Rural *Pays*[25]

Arable land, grassland, vines, woods and uncultivated land are very unevenly distributed within the various regions and combine to form a great variety of small rural *pays* (*terroirs*) which present sharp contrasts to the traveller.

Apart from very rare exceptions, in fact, farmers do not determine the elements of their own farming systems. Each type of land use needs special conditions which the farmer must seek in the land at hand, and his freedom of choice varies. L. Malassis has drawn a very apt distinction between land which can be used for one crop only and land suitable for many. The former has its specific use determined by slope, soil or other physical conditions, by technical considerations as in the case of vines and orchards, by economic factors where a change of use would be too drastic, as in the case of marshes, heathland and forests, or by situation, an important consideration for the pasture, garden and formerly the hemp fields which occupied intensively and continuously cultivated plots adjacent to the farm buildings. The latter allow much more latitude in the choice of use, and a varied succession of crops.

Physical conditions determine the way these lands are used. In short, relief governs the local distribution of soils, and of groundwater, just as it modifies the local climate. The more closely we look at the use of land on the scale of the individual hamlet or farm, the more relief must be taken into account.

The smallest unit of land on which the 'slope–soil–water–local climate' complex assumes a distinctive individual character is known as a *terroir* (A. Fel).

The types of *terroir* thus vary from region to region; homogeneous terroirs attracting only one form of land use are the rarest. The extensive monotonous plains of Beauce, Santerre (Picardy) and the Landes are the most characteristic examples of this type, together with the alluvial plains whether of fluvial or marine origin.

Heterogeneous *terroirs* are the most common because contrasts in soil and slope conditions are usual in the natural environment.

In one type, cultivated *terroirs* are discontinuous, separated by uncultivated tracts of heathland, scrub (*maquis*), *garrigues* and used to a greater or lesser extent as pasture; the southern lands belong to this type. The countryside

'... is everywhere made up of discontinuous elements. The arable land commonly occurs in patches surrounded by stony wastes or barren sands. In some areas the relief is broken into ridges and narrow valleys; elsewhere old plateau surfaces are split into narrow strips by intervening deep valleys. The extensive loamy tracts of the North, rich in nourishing soil, are nowhere to be seen and there is an almost complete lack of soil soaked with fine rain, and able to feed large numbers of milk or beef cattle. As far as the soil is concerned, everything here is small, fragmented and diversified in the extreme' (D. Faucher).[26]

In Corsica 'the contrast between field and scrub results from that of hard and soft rock under varying local conditions of altitude, slope, exposure, proximity to the village, etc.' (P. Rondot).

Sometimes the differentiation of *terroirs* depends on the possibility of irrigation. In the Comtat of Basse-Provence,

'Wherever water can be brought, wherever it can be raised at the cost of slight pumping, vegetables, grassland and orchards begin to grow. The main branch of the irrigation canal divides the district into two areas of unequal value. Above it the high ground is devoted to the traditional dry crops. Vines, cereals, almonds and olives remain, along with the old farming system. Below it, the low ground enables more profitable crops to be grown' (R. Livet).

In northern France the forest tracts alone separate cultivated *terroirs* one from another, especially in the North-east.

But the land-use patterns of the *terroirs* differ according to the geological setting. In sedimentary areas the *terroirs* are orientated in favour of particular types of farming by structural and hydrological variables. The strips of meadowland along damp valley bottoms cutting through monotonous tracts of arable land on limestone or chalk plateaux, and the gardens, orchards and cultivated fields on the hillsides between wooded summits and grassy depressions, are the two most widespread types of landscape.

In crystalline or sedimentary areas associated with a high stream density the variety of potential uses of the land depends on the density of major and minor valleys. Here

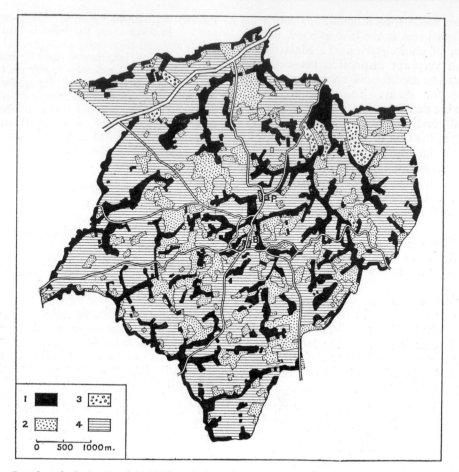

Fig. 66.   Land use in Bulat-Pestivien (Côtes-du-Nord) commune.   (Source: A. Demangeon, *Géographie Universelle*, Vol. VI, A. Colin, 1946)

Distribution: 1. Fields; 2. Heathland; 3. Woods; 4. Ploughed land; B. Bulat; P. Pestivien.
(After L. Fournier, Geographical monograph on the commune of Bulat-Pestivien.)

the terrain units do not form large tracts of uniform type, but are broken up and scattered so that they collectively form assemblages of great variety (fig. 66).   To some extent these offer the farmer as much freedom in his choice of crops as he has in homogeneous *terroirs*, but they are naturally adapted to mixed types of farming.

In the mountains natural conditions determine absolutely the composition and distribution of the various elements of the *terroir*. Altitude, aspect, slope and soil are the main factors in planning the land use of a *terroir*.

Altitude is responsible for the distribution of forests and Alpine pastures and the duration of the snow cover.   The orientation of valleys leads to a distinction between shady hillsides (*ubac, ombrée*), which are wooded, and sunny ones (*adret, soulane*), to which cling the fields and houses.   In the eastern Pyrenees the development of east–west valleys with one slope facing south results in high percentages (60%) of cultivated land, but in the west the percentages are much lower (16% in Barèges); on the shady parts hayfields take the place of crops.   The fields are generally found in the inhabited part of each *terroir*. Sometimes, and this was even more widespread in the past than now, little fields exist in forest clearings at high altitudes. Such are the *germs* or *artigues* in the Pyrenees. They were cultivated by those concerned with the movements of flocks.

Certain regions show unusual types of *terroirs* or of land use which are mostly due to water. One example is the 10,000 ha. of artificial lakes in Dombe, the oldest of which date from the 12th century. For one year out of three a lake is dried up and cultivated; for two years out of three it is under water and provides fish, which are netted when the water is drained off. Others are the 'amphibian' regions of the coast, salt-marshes, and oyster and mussel beds. In every case they provide peculiar landscapes which show up well in aerial photographs.

C. The Balance Sheet and Policy of Land Use

THE BALANCE SHEET

These different modes of land use are combined in varying proportions in different regions by farms practising either similar or dissimilar types of farming.

The result is an uneven intensity of land use which it would be interesting to evaluate precisely. J. Klatzmann has worked out a method of making such an evaluation. Taking as the unit of reference the average gross yield of a hectare under grass, he applies the following coefficients: arable land, an average of 2; cereals, 1·5; root crops, 4; fodder crops, 1·5; dried vegetables, 2; fresh field vegetables, 8; other crops, 4·5; grasslands, 0·6–1·3 (according to the proportions of natural grassland, on the one hand, and cultivated pasture or grazing land, on the other); vines, 5; market-garden crops, fruit and flowers, 10; family kitchen gardens, 6. These values must obviously not be taken as indications of size; they give 'a rough idea of the gross yield per hectare of the main categories of crop'.

The sum of the values obtained, when these factors are applied to the respective percentages of land use, gives the coefficient of land use.[27] The types of land use are divided into five classes: extensive cultivation, coefficient of intensity below 80; slightly intensive cultivation, 80–119; moderately intensive cultivation, 120–159; intensive cultivation, 160–199; very intensive cultivation, 200 and above.

The map thus obtained (fig. 67) is very revealing: against a background of regions with low or average coefficients (80–120) (southern and inner Alps, Corsica, the south of the Central Massif, the Pyrenees, the Landes, Sologne) stand out the regions with intensive types of farming: the North, the Paris region, the West and particularly west-central France, the northern border of the Central Massif, Limagne, Aquitaine, Alsace, Bas-Rhône, Provence and the vine-growing regions.

LAND-USE POLICY

Despite constant changes in the pattern of land use, whether they involve the conversion of permanent grassland into temporary grassland, the grubbing up of vines or reafforestation, the present pattern is too burdened by the influence of the past to be ideal. 'While mountains and slopes preserve too much arable land, the flat lands have a surplus of natural, permanent pasture, which is only too often a form of semi-abandonment of agriculture' (R. Dumont).

With this in view it is desirable to formulate or to hope for the formulation of a policy of land use. 'It is necessary to find the optimum balance between cultivated fields (*ager*), pastures (*saltus*) and forest (*sylva*), taking into account the agricultural potential of the soils and their biological equilibrium, the regional and national markets as well as local demographic conditions' (Michel Cointat).[28]

The balance of field, forest and pasture must first ensure the maintenance of the natural biological equilibrium. We too often and too willingly forget that agriculture is not only a way of exploiting the land; it is also a means of soil conservation. As 'custodian of

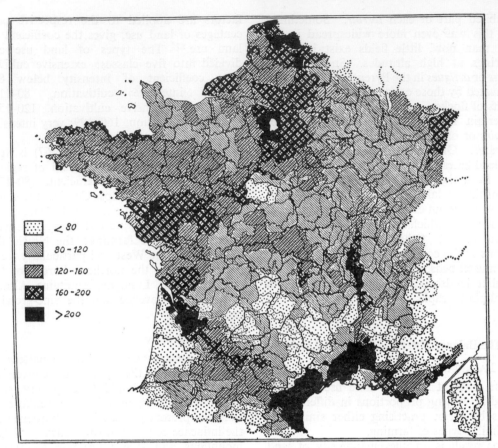

Fig. 67. Map of coefficients of intensity of land use. (Source: J. Klatzmann, *La Localisation des cultures et des productions animales en France*, I.N.S.E.E. 1955)

the humus', agriculture must ensure the perpetuation of the thin covering of soil on which all civilisation rests, despite the considerable technical progress of the last few decades; in this sense agriculture performs the role of a public service.

A first prerequisite for a land-use policy is the definition of the area to be used for agriculture. 'It appears that production could be confined to zones much more restricted than the 33 or so million hectares which are used at present by French agriculture. The delimitation of this excess land, which should be devoted to forests and recreation, is a formidable task which is a preliminary to virtually every improvement in agricultural

planning' (D. R. Bergmann). Everything points to the need for a much more differentiated use of rural areas in which agriculture will not be the only user. Whole valleys of the Alps have already lost their flocks, their pastures and hayfields having fallen into disuse as the tourist invasion has advanced.

The national parks are only one aspect of these changes. In all advanced countries which face the problems of industrial and urban civilisation there is a strong countermovement towards the creation of nature reserves. These reserves serve a threefold purpose: to protect or restore nature in its most picturesque aspects (the sites) or its most interesting ones (the flora and fauna); to preserve natural tracts in a world where people jostle each other at both work and leisure; to allow the rural renovation of regions whose agricultural and industrial potentialities are weak. In this field France was behind many other European or North American countries (Yellowstone Park, in the U.S.A., dates from 1872). But more and more projects are being realised; the first national park (Vanoise) was created in 1963; subsequently the national parks of Port Cros and the western Pyrenees were created (50,000 ha.). Parallel with this, legislation to set up regional nature reserves was passed in March 1967; seventeen reserves are under examination or being established: among them the forest of St. Amand (Nord), the Camargue, the lake and forest of Orient (Troyes), the Mont Pilat massif, the volcanoes of Auvergne, Morvan, Vercors, Grande Brière.

The second element of a land-use policy concerns the allocation of the land to its varying possible agricultural uses, an operation which can be carried out only after a detailed analysis of natural conditions.

'With regard to the large sector of uncultivated land it is necessary to consider how much should revert to forest and how much is worth using for crops or stock. The division should be based, in particular, on pedological studies, which are rarely carried out for lack of specialists and of money. The problem is thus an economic one. A decision to devote an area to forest commits the land for several generations ahead' (D. R. Bergmann).[29]

The problem of restoring a part of the present waste land to cultivation is one which can only increase in extent and immediacy in the near future. France is the only state in Europe with a million hectares of recoverable waste land; the figures have a purely indicative value. This amount of available land in a country with a low density of agricultural population and which is rapidly dwindling can only be a temptation to others, as we have already said. But it is important to know in what ways reclamation of the waste land can be carried out. There is above all a danger that any coherent policy will be blocked by psychological, political and social difficulties. The designation of *terroirs* suitable for the vine and the zones where conversion is necessary, for example, is a relatively simple operation from the technical point of view, but one which no government has dared to attempt owing to the pressures working against it.

The irrigation of certain types of vineyard was made possible in 1963 by the Compagnie du Bas Rhône–Languedoc itself at the very time when the cornerstone of this vast land development enterprise was the conversion of part of the vineyards of the plains to other uses. This situation arose because of the many social, economic and therefore political implications involved in such a reorganisation of the vineyards.

18. These forests were very different from those of today; they were interrupted by clearings, and full of undergrowth; the many ways in which they were exploited had caused them to deteriorate until they were generally reduced to the state of coppice. Mountain coniferous forests were not misused to the same extent as the deciduous forests.

19. The forests from which the (medieval?) landscape was carved were not all natural. Some were the result of spontaneous regeneration following the devastation caused by the great invasions. Research has shown that these forests were populated and exploited in Gallo-Roman times; the same phenomenon was repeated after the disasters of the Hundred Years War when 'the woods came back with the English'.

20. Commune and private forests have the least timber wood; the national forests have only 17% coppice wood, or coppice with standards.

21. This policy presupposes a considerable increase in the staff of water and forest undertakings (there is one engineer for 9,200 ha. as against one for 3,700 in Belgium, and one for 2,000 in Germany).

22. Despite the contribution of Alsace-Lorraine.

23. L. Gachon, 'Les caractères du paysage français', *Bull. Groupe poitevin Et. Géog.*, 1950, 1, p. 15.

24. The first vineyards in Languedoc were located on the stony ground of the Costières of Gard, and the Aspres of Roussillon, the slopes of the *garrigues* plateau and the older terraces of the lower valley of the Hérault.

25. The French term *terroir* here refers broadly to a landscape unit of a lower order than the *pays*. Elsewhere

it is used in an ecological sense to denote 'site', 'land type' or 'land system', but there is no exact equivalent in English.   In most cases the French term has therefore been retained (*Note*—A. J. Hunt).

26. *La Vie Rurale vue par un Géographe*, p. 187.

27. Given that arable land covers 20% of an area, grass 30%, vines 1%, family gardens 1%, other types of cultivation being almost non-existent.   Multiplying each of these percentages by the respective coefficient, we find: $(20 \times 2) + 30 + 5 + 6 = 81$.

28. Report of the conference of the Grand-Orient de France, Paris, 1963.

29. *Ann. de Géog.*, 1954, p. 348.

III

RURAL LANDSCAPES

There is scarcely a feature on the face of the French countryside today which does not find its explanation in an evolution whose roots plunge deep into the twilight of time.

MARC BLOCH

The ownership of the land, the structure of farming and the variety of types of land use all explain the extreme diversity of the rural landscapes of France.

These landscapes are the geographical expression of the many factors we have already analysed. But they are also the reflection of . the ideas of the various groups of human beings as they have affected the spatial organisation of their agricultural land.

1. RURAL SETTLEMENT

The intense humanisation of the French countryside is largely connected with the density of the buildings which are in the words of D. Faucher the 'basis of operations in the large expanse of developed countryside'.

These rural buildings are of many kinds; there are farms, but there are other buildings too, in which the life and work of all the rural non-agricultural population goes on. Almost everywhere the countryside is dotted with manors, *châteaux* and the mansions of the nobility and the bourgeoisie, all bearing witness to a truly 'manorial civilisation'. Of various ages, built on commanding heights for the sake of strategy or scenery, or simply standing in the middle of estates, they give an undeniable charm to the countryside by their buildings which are often architecturally beautiful, their ancient trees and their long vistas. There are several thousands in France, 700 in Vendée alone, 1,200 in Périgord. One or more farms almost always adjoin them.

There are, nevertheless, some unpopulated regions. These are mainly the uplands. The upper limit of permanent rural habitation is very high, between 1,000 and 2,000 m. Saint-Véran, in Queyras, 2,000 m. up, is the highest village in France. But in both the young mountains and the Central Massif the last permanently inhabited dwellings are found between 1,100 and 1,200 m.; the upper limit varies according to the region. The highest settlements in Morvan are not above 750 m. and in the mountains of Limousin a long backbone above 900 m. is left to heathland and forest, but there are farms at 1,000 m. near the headwaters of the Allier and the Loire; on the Mézenc mountains the limit is as high as 1,500 m.

In low-lying regions, the unpopulated areas are the extensive forested areas or heathlands. Apart from the Royal Forests around Paris, which have been preserved despite the fertility of their soils, forests and heaths correspond in most cases to the more forbidding environment. But these 'rural deserts' are rare, for successive phases of rejuvenation and erosion have usually 'opened the way for an agricultural population' (R. Dion), cracking the old hard surfaces and creating new slope patterns and new soils.

Broadly speaking, in northern France soils account for the gaps in the population which are emphasised by great blocks of forest; in southern France height and slope add their influence to that of the soil.

The rural house, whether isolated or associated with others, is an integral part of the complex of fields, lanes, trees and crops, whose long history and slow development have created intensely humanised and harmonious landscapes. It is both the key feature of the rural landscape, because everything is arranged round it, and the one which is most readily understood. It has long attracted the attention of geographers more so than fields. The diversity of the settlement pattern has provided themes for research which have not been exhausted by a long succession of studies.

Settlement problems are fundamental to the most important discussions in geographical research, because nature and man are jointly important as explanatory factors.

Rural settlement more than field patterns has its roots in a very remote past; even though explanations of ethnic origin are no longer accepted, and it does not seem necessary to go back to contrasts in settlement types associated with early civilisations, it is none the less true that rural settlement is rooted in the distant past.

'To make an extreme simplification, it can be considered that the present rural habitation of France developed in the course of two main periods: the first from the widespread destruction of the second half of the 3rd century to the last Barbarian invasions, that is to say until the second half of the 10th century, was characterised by development within closed economy. The second, which is discernible from the 11th century onwards, with the rebirth of trade and the growth of towns, went on until the railway era' (R. Dion).

During these sixteen centuries changes in feudal life, in property ownership, the regional distribution of population, technical conditions, farming systems, social life and ways of dealing with natural conditions have all woven a complicated web of causes and influences.

The ways in which the population is distributed over the countryside vary greatly. The two main types of settlement, nucleated and dispersed, are present but more often mingled than clearly distinct.[1]

There are few regions where rural settlement consists entirely of single farms, or, on the other hand, of villages; the pure types merge in most cases into combinations very difficult to analyse and interpret.[2] Definitions themselves are not without difficulties, for it is not easy to say exactly where nucleation ends and dispersion begins.

The system of administrative units, the communes, is conducive to error. Are large hamlets scattered over a large commune so very different from small, closely spaced villages occupying very small areas? At the other extreme, the very dense dispersed settlement of Brittany has little in common with that of the *pays* of the Causses. The word village itself embraces settlements as different as the little villages of the Central Massif and the large villages of Beauce, Picardy or Champagne.

A. Factors of Dispersal and Nucleation

The earliest settlement was probably concentrated in nucleations, the villages of Alsace being the descendants of those existing in Celtic times. Above all, nucleated settlement corresponds to a communal agrarian system whose juridical characteristics have become deeply impressed on the land; the agricultural area of a village is legally distinct from its administrative area. The medieval *mansus*, strictly speaking, already meant the land which carried the house, the farmyard, the orchard, the garden and the home pasture, the whole often enclosed by hedges or walls. The names vary according to the region: *meix, enclos, curtil, chasal, pourpris, champ de maison* (Bresse), *horts* or *casals* (Aquitaine). Until the Revolution the *meix* benefited from a special legal statute, absolving it from obligations to the community; the boundary walls of the individual *meix* marked the boundary of the village, outside of which it was not possible to build.

The village site itself was often separated from the cultivated land by a physical boundary, a hedge, wall or lane; beyond it lay the 'suburban zone', where crops needing manure and a great deal of care were grown.

The three-year crop rotation practised in villages of the type found in Lorraine or

Picardy 'depends upon renewal of soil fertility during one year's rest helped only by the method of cultivation and manure, in the main provided simply by the flocks passing over it. This is possible on loams containing a certain proportion of calcareous elements, but not on poor sandy soils' (R. Dion). A communal three-year rotation—the three-field system—also requires that the *terroir* should be fairly homogeneous, that it should be easy to get from one part to another and that it should be physically possible to treat all the land to be used as common pasture as a single field.

Recently formed villages are rare; rural agglomerations have often grown up around isolated manor farms or medieval granges (of the 16th century, in Burgundy), the houses huddling within the enclosure of the ancient grange. New villages date from the 17th and 18th centuries; such are the 'planted' villages of Provence and the villages of Lorraine which were rebuilt after wars.

THE STAGES OF DISPERSAL

The primitive isolated dwelling was a rare phenomenon before the 10th or 11th centuries; natural, political, legal and economic conditions all opposed such a settlement form.

Nevertheless, apart from the dwellings of woodmen, hermits, hunters and pig-breeders, certain types of isolated dwelling have been observed in the highlands of Auvergne or in Brie, where some isolated farms have persisted on the sites of Gallo-Roman villas, a great feudal estate having been grafted directly on to a villa.

From the 10th or 11th centuries onwards, dispersed settlement appeared with the extension of clearings and the colonisation of land which had hitherto remained uncultivated, outside zones already inhabited or on the periphery of administrative areas.

The *mas* or isolated farms were established from the 10th to the 13th centuries in Livradois, the mountains of Forez and the Bois Noirs. Lower Nivernais, Bourbonnais, the Varennes of Limagne and Morvan were colonised about the year 1000. In the 10th

century Bresse was still almost continuous forest; it was peopled in hamlets under the direction of the lords of the manor at the end of the century. At the end of the 11th and 12th centuries '*granges*', of monastic origin and established outside the old villages, increased in number.

Dispersed settlements developed in the 13th century, especially from 1225 onwards, in the form of subsidiary farms founded by the lords of the manor and given to settlers. In Brie a dispersal of population followed the founding of the fortified towns (*villeneuves*) for the colonisation of the last uncultivated regions.

In Margeride 'the present pattern of rural settlement was brought into existence just before the beginning of the 14th century by means of a scattering of isolated houses' (A. Fel). Maine was colonised in the same way. In Bresse and the mountains of Beaujolais a number of secondary settlements were founded after 1240.

So there came into being farms, hamlets, little 'villages' with evocative names: Beaulieu, Clairefontaine, Chantecoq, Grange-au-Bois and those with place-names preceded by the article (which was not in general use before the 11th century), those with the names of saints, and also La Villeneuve or Neuville, Francheville or Les Franchises, Les Masures, Les Ouches, Le Clos, Le Plessy and Le Plouy.

The movement to create isolated farms on the boundaries of villages and in the remaining uninhabited areas began in the 13th century and spread in the 14th, favoured by depopulation which eased the pressure within the villages. Thus were created the *bordes*, *métairies* and large farms, with enclosed land and each held by one tenant.

From the middle of the 15th century onwards the movement continued with isolated farms established on land bought by the bourgeoisie—the estates with suffixes in *-ière* or *-erie*, added to the name of the founder. From the 14th to the 17th centuries, monastic granges and shepherds' chalets were built on the high ranges of the Jura.

In the 18th century the rural population grew by 30% between 1715 and 1789. There resulted a great extension of inhabited areas at the expense of heathlands, common land, zones of poor soil and alluvial valley bottoms, where farms, and more rarely hamlets, received evocative names like Les Loges, Le Canada, Le Nouveau Monde, Mississippi and Cayenne.

The last episodes of agricultural occupance date from the 19th century. Large isolated farms were founded on the plateau surfaces (*savarts*) of dry Champagne, in the woods of the clay areas of Haut-Artois and Haut-Boulonnais, on the heaths of Berry and Poitou, the heathlands of Sologne and the plateaux of Touraine; their names, Moscou, Alger, Sébastopol and Solférino, are valuable indications of their period.

THE FACTORS OF DISPERSAL

Through the centuries, the dispersal of settlement was caused by combinations of different factors:

Farming systems

G. Duby has clearly shown the basic causes of dispersal:

'If we ask ourselves why small farmers should wish to settle away from other settlements we can in the first place consider the cumulative effect of assarts. (An assart is a field added to a farm by enclosure of part of the 'waste' or common land—*Note*, A. J. Hunt.) There came a time when, to avoid having to leave work and come back to the village every night, the pioneers built shacks on their most distant fields, and these later became permanent homes. But was it only a matter of adaptation to distance? It is also likely that very often, from the 13th century onwards, as the farmer acquired better tools, he ventured to cut adrift with his household, and thus free himself from the old need for mutual help. Was it not also very often a matter of the soil? It would be interesting to find out whether the last phase of the conquest of new land did not extend over terrain which demanded a different, more individualistic way of integrating cereal cultivation and stock-rearing and one which in fact involved the predominance of the latter.'[3]

It is incontestable that dispersed settlement is more suitable for stock-rearing, with its dependence on short distances between sheds and pastures and on the necessity of keeping an eye on the animals. The early cases of dispersal were often those of farms where pasture predominated, the cow-sheds and sheep-folds being isolated in the meadows.

In irrigated market-gardening areas the system of cultivation itself is an encouragement to the dispersal of farm buildings, because of the constant care and supervision which are necessary. Thus the type of settlement is partly attributable to the farming system.

Land-ownership

The other important series of reasons has to do with social structure and the land. Generally speaking the isolated farm reflects a particular type of rural social structure. It is often derived from a noble or bourgeois domain, or a *métairie*: in Livradois, for example, isolated farms correspond to demesnes, seigniorial property or property in mortmain, while the villages and hamlets correspond to peasant holdings.

In all regions with a strong urban middle class the creation of large isolated farms and large estates by this middle class first appeared in the 14th century and spread in the 17th and 18th. M. Rochefort has shown how the bourgeoisie built up large isolated farms in Auxois and Autunois during that period.

Physical conditions

What was and is the role of physical factors in this dispersal settlement? It is a fundamental question of rural geography, and a very controversial one.

Water. Few subjects have been as controversial as that of the influence of water on the pattern of settlement. The question has become the target of critics of an exaggerated determinism. As a result these critics have been carried away by their enthusiasm and left themselves open to attack.

In the early stages of research, arguments centred on the widespread contrasts between the limestone regions supporting villages and the crystalline or clay regions with dispersed settlement.

The purely hydrological arguments brought forward were simple enough; in limestone regions there is no water on the surface of the ground, springs are rare, but when present are abundant and regular; and the water-tables which can be reached only at considerable depths necessitate deep wells which are difficult to build and maintain. It therefore seemed logical that dwellings should be grouped together in these areas; on the other hand, in areas of impermeable rock the abundance of springs and streams favoured dispersal of farms and at the same time provided many possible sites for meadows.

Anti-determinist critics have found no lack of exceptions to this 'law of water'; two regions which appear in all the literature on the subject are the clay vale of the Woëvre, peopled in villages, and the limestone Causses with their isolated hamlets and farms. In fact, this argument is very superficial, and rests on a faulty analysis of the real position. On the one hand, in the clay regions of Lorraine the villages are of a special type:

'The villages on the damp lands of Lorraine, namely the Woëvre, the lake zone, seem at first sight to contradict this principle. In fact they show it to be correct. For the particular difficulties of the clay soil have made it necessary to reduce the size of the cultivated clearing around the central cluster of homes to such an extent that these villages on the damp soils of Lorraine are mostly reduced to the size of hamlets. Their arable land is confined to small hilltops surrounded by grassy hollows and is all to be found within a radius of 300–500 m. from the church; the number of inhabitants is often far less than a hundred' (R. Dion).

On the other hand, the dispersed settlement of the Causses consists of farms or small hamlets, very far apart, further than the villages of the Woëvre, and clinging to karstic hollows enriched by decalcified soil. Here dispersal is due to factors other than water; even powerful groups of villages would not have been able to sink a well capable of reaching non-existent water-tables! Water cannot be isolated from the other factors; if the type of settlement is adapted to physical factors it is to them as a whole, in the geographical environment, and not to one or two of them alone.

Relief. Broken relief leads to fragmentation and restriction of cultivable land and farms (cf. p. 250). The distribution of the basic unit of rural settlement—that is, the farm or the hamlet—is related to the degree of dissection of the relief, and this does not apply only to the ancient massifs; it has been observed also in the regions of sedimentary rocks. In Terrefort 'the agricultural unit is the ridge between two valleys, when its size is consistent with the work output of one family. On larger ridges, two, three or four estates lie with their fields around the *métairie* or the *borde*, running slantwise down the slope from top to bottom' (D. Faucher).

This topographical differentiation does not act only negatively, by enclosing every unit of rural population on a particular site; it leads to a diversification of land types favourable to dispersion. In order that a farm may stand alone with its fields around it, the various elements essential to agricultural life must be present round the site. 'A moderate but varied relief, where damp and dry soils are found close together, is more favourable to the formation of compact holdings than large expanses of uniform character' (A. Fel) (fig. 66).

The terroirs. The interruption of cultivable land has a similar effect:

'All physical conditions which tend to break the continuity of arable land and divide it into fragments too small to occupy the population of a village, and which put obstacles between these fragments, are unfavourable to the growth of village communities. Such handicaps, when they are not the effect of the relief, result from the combined action of geological and climatic phenomena, and can appear in the most varied environments' (R. Dion).

The dispersal of settlement on the karstic limestone plateaux of southern France is obviously connected with the fragmentation of the belts of arable land in the bottoms of the valleys and dolina; it is hard to see how village settlements could be established there.

In regions of poor clayey or sandy soils where the land is broken up by the relief, manure is provided for the fields by another part of the farm:

'An uncultivated patch at least as large as the cultivated field is annexed to it; usually it is a heath (or *garrigue*) which serves to provide fertiliser. This can be either the earth itself, which the peasant strips off after burning the spontaneous vegetation cover, or manure from the animals for which the heathland provides food and litter. This system makes it necessary to mix uncultivated land and cultivated fields, and thus prevents the formation of large uniform fields of arable land. . . . The village using rotation cropping in its fully developed form could not therefore be established on the sheets of granitic sands surrounding the Central Massif, or on the decalcified clayey soils of the *boulbènes*' (R. Dion).

Soils and the type of terrain. Areas which were colonised late were very often those which were formerly considered to be uncultivable because of heavier, clayey soils which were harder to work and more difficult of access: areas of clays, sandy clays or marls. Such lands were more suitable for pastures than for cultivated fields. Everything, then, combined to limit the administrative area, to split up the population, to keep buildings and fields together as far as possible:

'It is seldom, in a region of clayey soil, that one can walk 2 km. without having to cross water several times. The abundance of shallow streams and the rapidity with which the smallest erosion hollows are enlarged extend and multiply damp depressions which are difficult to cross, even in summer, in the absence of properly made roads. The farmer encountered more than one on his way to his fields if his house was not near by. Impermeable or decalcified soil—and these defects are generally found together in regions which remain uncultivated and covered with forest for a long time—are thus incompatible

with any type of agricultural development that puts long distances between the house and the fields belonging to it' (R. Dion).[4]

It would therefore be absurd to deny that the physical environment has some influence on types of settlement, in the same way as it would be absurd to say it is the predominant or only factor. The physical environment has not, strictly speaking, determined the distribution of the population; human communities or individuals have chosen between the available possibilities. We must not forget that dispersal has often succeeded another type of settlement pattern, or modified its former character. But if some regions have waited centuries before being peopled, that is probably also because their natural conditions did not seem easy to reconcile with the idea of village life.

This mixture of physical and human factors makes them difficult to evaluate in a country which has been peopled for so long a time. From this point of view France is a museum of settlement types.

In *Limagne* the contrast between dispersed settlement in the north and nucleated settlement in the south can be explained by differences in the periods of settlement (M. Derruau).

In the *Jura*, L. Gachon explains the settlement differences between the northern and southern Jura by stressing the geological structure: 'In the northern and north-western Jura we often find synclinal basins covered with fine, deep humus-rich and fertile soils which form homogeneous *terroirs* that are large enough to encourage the development of villages which became the centres of communes. The southern Jura . . . where the agricultural areas are smaller and less homogeneous, often arranged in longitudinal strips or benches formed by outcrops of soft rocks on the sides of the deep valleys, is more suited to settlement in hamlets of a few houses or even isolated farms.'

B. The Dynamic Character of Rural Settlement

The difficulty of analysing and interpreting rural settlement is all the greater because fundamental changes have taken place over the centuries, independently of the extension of inhabited land and the late colonisation of some areas.

The fabric of rural settlement has been modified by an increase or decrease in the density of settlement sites and by changes in types of settlement. To the west of the Dores, in the commune of Saint-Sauves, the number of settlements has increased from thirty at the end of the 18th century to sixty-seven today. At Besse, in less than a century, the number of isolated farms has trebled; in both cases the settlement is related to a very specialised type of pastoral economy.

Positive change in the settlement pattern is often brought about by the intrusion of hamlets or isolated farms among the villages. In areas of village settlement, isolated farms could be established on the remaining un-cultivated land near commune boundaries, on abandoned land, on sites that were often far from favourable or on the wind-swept heights (hence names like Heurtebise and Bellevue).

This secondary dispersed settlement is found to some extent in Lorraine; in the Metz region there are many farms between the villages. Their dates of foundation range over two millennia, as the first are the descendants of Gallo-Roman *villae*, and the last are contemporary with the conquest of Algeria. They correspond, in fact, to relics of the dispersed Gallo-Roman villa settle-ments (place-names in -ey or -y), such as the farms to the north of Scarponne, along the Langres–Metz road; or to villages devastated in war (particularly the Thirty Years War) which could not be entirely rebuilt (such are the communes of Athienville and Arracourt); or to former ecclesiastical estates, or former communes, or secondary settlement on the periphery of existing administrative areas: 'Le Mesnil', 'Malmaison', 'Malhaye', 'Villeneuve' and place-names with the prefix 'Saint', from the end of the Middle Ages; the 'Folies', 'Bellevue', 'Mississippi', 'Petite Pologne' in the 17th and 18th centuries; and 'Magenta', 'Solférino' and 'Alger' in the 19th century.

In the Pyrenees the development of secondary dispersed settlement was en-couraged by the persistence of common land, forests and grazing lands which were enclosed at a late date. The common land in the valleys could carry sheds or barns for cattle or mown hay, and could be locally cleared and enclosed. From the 18th century on-wards this temporarily acquired land became private property, permanently farmed owing to the effect of demographic pressure.

The process of secondary dispersal went on also in areas of dispersed settlement. In Comtat-Venaissin at the end of the 19th cen-tury a dispersal of *mas* and country houses took place among the already dispersed settlements of the 18th and earlier centuries. 'The end of the Middle Ages, and our modern period have both seen a swarm of new farms, slipping rather stealthily among the scattered dwellings which constitute the basic pattern. These farms find it hard to stand up against crises such as wars and economic or demo-graphic upheavals' (P. Marthelot). Never-theless the abandonment and disappearance of settlement sites seem to have been much more important than the appearance of new ones.

From the 14th century onwards, wars, epidemics and climatic disasters put an end to many farms and villages; rural depopulation caused a reduction in cultivated land and the abandonment of marginal farms on land which had been the most recently acquired and were therefore the least firmly held. In Brie and Provence, hamlets began to disappear in the second half of the 14th century; in Artois, Picardy and Lorraine hundreds of villages disappeared as a result of the devastations of the 15th to the 18th centuries, changing the density rather than the type of settlement and preparing the way for later settlement by means of secondary dispersal. In the 15th, 16th and 17th centuries an isolated farm often took the place of a hamlet destroyed in war. The development of the enclosure of land and the farm concentration played decisive parts in modifying the settlement pattern. In the Gâtine of Poitou dispersal in hamlets was succeeded by dispersal in *métairies*, owing to the consolidation of holdings from

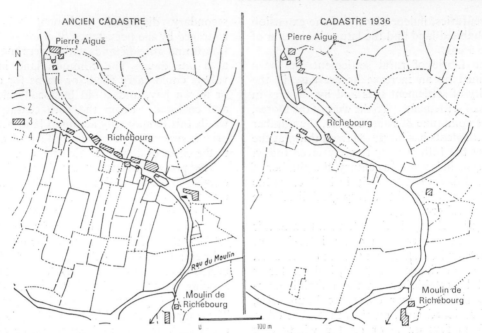

Fig. 68. Transformation of a hamlet into an isolated farm: the example of Richebourg (commune of Sainte-Gemmes-le-Robert, Mayenne). (Source: J. Suret Canale, *Ann. de Géog.* no. 360, 1958, p. 106) 1. Roads. 2. Watercourses. 3. Buildings. 4. Property boundaries.

the 16th century onwards. In the 18th century a new wave of isolated *métairies* came to occupy the interfluves which had hitherto been uninhabited and covered with heathland. This agrarian colonisation was the result of the introduction, from 1850 onwards, of cultivated pastures (fig. 68).

In Provence, R. Livet has pointed out the interesting case of a village which has recently and spontaneously developed in a region of complete dispersal in association with the establishment of small holdings (Rognonas).

The siting of rural settlements can change without changing their character; thus villages perched high on hills have come down towards water supply points, cultivated land and means of communications.[5]

C. Types of Settlement

NUCLEATED SETTLEMENT

The plans of 'villages' are very varied. A. Demangeon devised a classification which distinguished long, compact and radial villages.

The *long villages* are very numerous, developing along a single street with very rare transverse extensions; in plan they may be straight or curved (fig. 69).

In some cases there is a clear relationship between the plan and a specific physical factor; a valley bottom, a hill foot, a spring line, a dyke, the concave bank of an incised meander, an island of solid ground in the middle of a marsh, a narrow spur or interfluve. But in other cases the explanation must be sought elsewhere. Demangeon rightly remarked that this type of village was frequent in eastern and northern France.

Compact villages are more commonly found in the South. They are villages lying in the middle of their cultivated *terroirs*, often colony villages founded by abbots and lords of the manor. They may also be villages with houses clustered together on a defensive site, like the perched villages of Provence, now abandoned or modified.

Radial villages. Instead of remaining in a compact group, the farms in this case are strung out along the roads and lanes which converge in the centre of the village.

DISPERSED SETTLEMENT

From one region to another, even from one commune to another, the type of settlement dispersal varies considerably. Even in regions of true dispersed settlement, a certain amount of variation is introduced by the presence of the *bourg* (commune centre) and of villages of the Breton type, that is, hamlets with a population not exclusively agricultural.

Dispersal in isolated farms. Many areas are covered with a sprinkling of farms which are all isolated from one another; this type of dispersal is found in the Vosges massif, in maritime Flanders, in the Folded Jura, between Nanterre and Saint-Claude, in the molasse hills of the Terrefort of Aquitaine and the highlands of eastern Velay. In certain cases of total dispersal it may happen

that the village centre is completely split up, the church, the *mairie* and the school standing apart from one another, sometimes on different hills.

Dispersal in hamlets. Settlement consisting entirely of hamlets is relatively rare, as these are very sensitive to demographic and economic changes, as in Champsaur and the southern Jura.

In the Central Massif and Basse-Provence, as in many other regions, the hamlets were often initially of the family type, each derived from an isolated and primitive family unit (patronymic hamlets). The splitting up of the family brought, with each generation, a greater dispersal by the creation of new farms, while the old nucleus often reverted to an isolated farm.

A special form of hamlet is often found in the open-field enclaves in the *bocages* of the West. The farmhouses lie side by side, with common dividing walls, under one roof, forming a row, *rangée* or *barre* of three to six units, several rows sometimes being placed parallel to each other. Similar plans are found in the Monts Dore and in Artense,

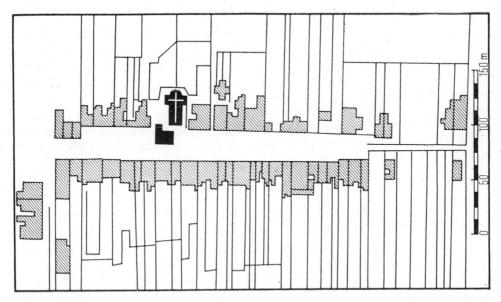

Fig. 69. Plan of Tanconville. (Source: J. Nicod, 'Problèmes de structure agraire en Lorraine', *Ann. de Géog.* no. 322, 1951, p. 343)

where they are known as *barriades*. According to A. Fel, they correspond to hamlets of a primitive family type.

On the whole, the hamlet form of settlement appears to be ambiguous, being related, according to the region, either to nucleated or to dispersed types of settlement.

'The Breton farms, only some tens of metres apart, have nothing to do with each other. The hamlets of Haut-Beaujolais are similar; the houses carefully avoid any common walls, every farm has its well or spring, its yard, its approach road, quite distinct from those of the others. Every farm opens on to its own land, often all together on the same side of the hamlet.... These hamlets, despite the apparent closeness of their buildings, are still collections of very individual farms.... In Basse-Provence, the hamlet still has a few of the characteristics of the true nucleated settlements' (R. Livet).

Mixed dispersal (hamlets and farms). This is the most common type, resulting from the factors already mentioned; the Armorican West has this mixed type of dispersed settlement. The Pays de Caux is another remarkable example of this dual form of dispersal (fig. 72).

Intermediate and mixed types—rural agglomerations ('nebular' villages). Sometimes the term 'dispersed' cannot be used, because belts of uninhabited farmland alternate with belts of farmland with farmsteads. The term 'nucleated' is no more appropriate, because the farms are far from adjoining and appear to avoid each other. The roads and lanes group them in long trails like nebulae. This is the type of rural settlement found in Vimeu and in some of the Breton coastal 'villages'. 'Farther south, on the periphery of the Vôge and around Épinal and Rambervillers, the houses are not always adjacent to one another so that the villages become loosely grouped or "nebular" (transitional to the Franche-Comté type) and towards the east, round Sarrebourg, there are villages in clearings with houses strung out along several kilometres of road, like Schneckenbusch, Buhk and Bertrambois' (Nicod).

Secondary dispersal. The creation at a

late date of settlement in the form of isolated farms or hamlets on the periphery of village lands, in association with recent clearance, has already been referred to. This dispersed settlement has acquired the appearance of high-density settlement because the farms were laid out in sizes appropriate to family labour, if necessary reinforced by a few hired hands. In fact, on the one hand, after the destruction of the Hundred Years War there was a shortage of labour which was unfavourable to the formation of large estates, and, on the other hand, these medium-sized holdings were within the means of the middle class. The 13th–16th centuries, then, saw the origin of the dense scattering of isolated dwellings which was destined largely to establish the pattern of rural settlement until the present day.

Linear settlement (street villages and hamlets). In many cases the rural buildings are strung out for kilometres along a village street; the farms are rarely adjoining, and are usually well apart, separated by pasture fields. Neither the village concept nor the isolated farm concept is really applicable to the linear settlement forms. It is found in polder regions where farms and roads follow the lines of the protective dykes. It is also the form of settlements in many forest clearings dating from the 12th and 13th centuries, such as the 'villages' of Aliermont which stretch uninterrupted for 17 km. and the *boels* or villages of the forest of Lillebonne.

The dwellings of agricultural labourers. Little attention has been paid hitherto to the dwellings of farm labourers. They carried on no large-scale cultivation and worked a few patches of ground in association with the farmers, so they had no need of large buildings. In Lorraine the houses of the labourers stand along short streets at right angles to the main street, in rows cutting across the long field strips. In Flanders, their little houses, like small-scale models, are scattered over the meadows at a distance from the big farms. In Brittany the *pentys* are situated away from the farms 'on heathland covering the steep slopes of the valleys or the open country'. The multiplication of these *pentys* in the last hundred years 'especially on sites avoided by the old farms has greatly contributed to the regularity, on the official survey maps, of the distribution of black dots representing houses, and to the impression of extreme dispersal of settlement created by the maps of Basse-Bretagne' (P. Flatrès).

D. Rural Roads

Although field systems and rural settlement have been the subject of many studies, the third element of the rural landscape, the roads, has been relatively neglected. Their importance should not be underestimated. Between the links of that network of main roads which join regions and towns to each other, rural roads serve villages, hamlets and farms, and give access to the plots of agricultural land. Through their location, density, courses and changes, these roads constitute a basic element in the analysis of rural landscapes. In 1958 there were 650,000 km. of them, comprising 280,000 km. of rural roads and 160,000 km. of farm tracks.

These networks of rural roads are heterogeneous. They include not only roads specially made to serve the various parts of the *terroir* but also old and formerly more important routeways which have suffered decay, such as former pilgrim routes and salt roads. Often the presence of a crossroads or a convergence of lanes in the open country is the only surviving visible relic of a place once inhabited, a village or a hamlet destroyed by war or simply abandoned, or of an old mill, an ancient shrine or a former collecting centre for the harvest.

M. Gautier has outlined the main features of the rural road pattern:

'The thin radial network of the open-field areas is often contrasted with the dense, confused network of roads in the *bocage*—but this view is too systematic and very superficial. The basic pattern of rural roads is the same everywhere: radial patterns around the commune centres and in the centres of the earliest clearings; short branches or cul-de-sacs petering out among the fields; and longer ones from one small centre to another. Over and above these are the very long lanes which are probably the ancestors of all the others, cutting diagonally through the pattern. They are old routeways which are only occasionally used to reach the fields. ... But in the *bocage* a secondary network has grafted itself as best it may on this primary network. It grew up together with secondary dispersal of settlement.'

These roads are themselves an element of the landscape. Some run at ground level, on chalk or limestone and on all hard rock outcrops. Others are sunken roads, several metres below the fields, or are flanked by two banks topped by hedges. The first type of such roads, on the slopes, is made by carts which 'grind away the edges, crushing the earth which falls on the road as dust. Running water carries this debris away, and the road is gradually cut downwards' (M. Gautier). The second type, the *bocage* road, is said to be sometimes the result of ditching by two landowners, the earth taken out being used to form banks on either side. These sunken winding lanes are a great obstacle to the modernisation of agriculture, as they prevent the passage of machinery over a certain size.

Up to the middle of the 19th century most parishes, and later the communes, led an isolated existence, far from the main traffic routes; the roads linked the farms and hamlets to the villages and served the various parts of the *terroir*, but access to towns and between communes was difficult. Insecurity, fords, tolls and customs posts aggravated this situation, which could exist only through the persistence of a self-supporting rural economy and very little urbanisation.

After the first improvements under the Consulate and the Empire, the law of 21st May 1836 took in hand the local road system by allocating special rates, allowance in kind and departmental and State subsidies for their maintenance. In the space of a few years existing roads were straightened, macadamised and connected with the roads of neighbouring communes.[6] The network of local roads amounted to 122,000 km. in 1866 and by 1898 had reached 275,000 km. In

1881 the rural roads were in their turn the object of a statute classifying them as public property, thereby preventing encroachments by farmers and disputes between landowners.

1. As officially defined in 1962, the population agglomerated in the administrative centres of rural communes totalled 9,006,604, and the so-called dispersed population amounted to 8,079,416.
2. In Provence, for example, part of the population is strongly concentrated in the villages, but other settlement is extremely scattered.
3. *L'Économie rurale et la vie des campagnes dans l'Occident médiéval* (Paris, 1962), Vol. 1, pp. 166–7.
4. The quotations from R. Dion are all taken from: *La Part de la géographie et celle de l'histoire dans l'exploitation de l'habitat rural du bassin parisien*, Publicat. Soc. Geog., Lille, 1946.
5. Livet has reconstructed these hill village sites, emphasising some of their climatic advantages: a less severe winter than in the valleys owing to inversions of temperature, and a more bearable summer.
6. This accounts for discontinuities in the course of roads and field patterns at the boundary of a commune.

2. RURAL HOUSE TYPES

In 1960 there were 3,324,000 dwellings in rural communes. They are not all farms or farmers' houses; farm labourers, tradesmen and in general all the secondary and tertiary working population of rural communes occupy some of them; the houses in village centres thus have their own particular characteristics. However, many of these dwellings of people not engaged in agriculture were once farms, which have changed in function as a result of demographic and economic changes.

A. Demangeon has given us both a definition and a classification of rural house types. He stresses the distinctive character of the rural house; that it is not simply a dwelling, but a collection of buildings adapted to specific agricultural functions. A 'farm' includes buildings for people and others for grain, livestock, poultry, agricultural machinery, stocks of fertilisers and seeds, all together on a plot of land of very definite shape.

The different types of farms arise from varied conditions and varied adaptations to them. The rural architecture of France has in fact a rich variety; the farms are the expression of the coexistence of several agrarian civilisations, of the variety of natural environments and of types of farming. But as D. Faucher has emphasised:

'There are very few ways of building a rural dwelling. The units which provide lodging for men and animals, and shelter for grain and tools can either be placed side by side and joined together or superimposed one above the other, or remain independent, placed round an empty space of varying size and shape. Each layout has been adopted in relation to the materials used, the space available and physical conditions, most important of which is the climate.'

Following Demangeon's classification in broad outline, we will distinguish compact houses (*maisons blocs*) and multiple houses (*maisons à bâtiments dissociés*).

A. Compact Houses

These form the simplest type; everything is under one roof—men, cattle, grain and tools. There are many sub-types:

The low compact house (*maison bloc à terre*). All the buildings of this farm are under one roof. It is all on one floor or has only one upper floor, which means that it takes up a great deal of ground. It is found in all parts of France, except the Mediterranean region (though it is found in Corsica), the centre of the Paris basin and of the sedimentary part of Normandy (fig. 70).

The rudimentary, low, compact house (*maison bloc à terre élémentaire*). The typical example is the *bourine* of the marshes of Poitou, a low building with one or two rooms, with earth walls covered with rushes, extended by small buildings for the poultry. But this type is relatively rare in France; as soon as animals and fodder have to be kept under shelter, its size increases and the different rooms, whether for human habitation or not, become individual units with varying layouts.

The long, low, compact house with transverse elements (*maison bloc à terre en longueur*). The house and the farm buildings, such as stables and sheds, are built in a row under the same roof in the case of small farms, and under roofs of different heights in the case of large farms; the house thus consists of juxtaposed units. The typical example is the traditional Breton farm, but others of the same type are the rural houses of Berry, the Toulouse region and the Central Massif, and the *mas* of the Rhône–Provence area. This type of rural dwelling is probably derived from the rudimentary type, sometimes from a shepherd's hut on to which annexes have been built.

The broad, low, compact house (*maison bloc à terre en profondeur*). This is typified by the farms of Lorraine. It is a rectangular block with units under one roof, the habitable rooms to the right, generally including the living-room overlooking the street, a corridor down the centre and the sheds and barns on the left; the stable may be behind the living quarters. The plan of this type of farm in Lorraine is bound up with a very rigid field system with fields divided into strips 6–12 m. wide, perpendicular to the main street (fig. 69).[7]

This arrangement has several major disadvantages. There is no farmyard; the bulky equipment, manure, firewood and poultry were and still are kept in front of the farm in an empty space called the *usoir, barge* or *aisance*. As the *usoir* varies in depth, the street frontages of the houses are rarely in line and often irregular. It is impossible, as the buildings have common walls, to admit light to the middle ones from the side, so that overhead lighting, by means of glass roofs, skylights and small interior courtyards must be used. Communication between the street and the back of the farm is difficult, which explains the absence of pasture, the rest of the long plot being taken up with gardens and orchards.

The massive compact house (*maison bloc massive*). These farms are found in the Basque country, Auvergne, Limousin and the Savoie Alps. The plan is characteristic of stock-rearing areas; the barn and sheds are very large. Climatic conditions, such as the long winter and period of snow cover, have caused all the parts of the farm to be brought under one roof. Hay is often stored on the upper floor (hillsides are used so that this floor can be reached at ground level) above the sheds which, together with the dwelling-house, occupy the ground floor.

The tall, compact house (*maison bloc en hauteur*). This type shows a complete functional specialisation of the various floors. On the ground floor are the animals, the farm implements and some heavy or bulky produce such as timber or wine.

The dwelling is on the first floor, and in the loft on the second floor is the grain, fruit and even hay, hoisted up by a pulley.

This is the characteristic house type of southern France: Roussillon, Languedoc, Provence and Corsica; but it spreads widely over the south of the Central Massif and the Aquitaine basin (Causses du Quercy), goes up the Rhône–Saône corridor and infiltrates into Tarentaise and Maurienne. It is the house of the wine-grower or the sheep-farmer. It is essentially a village house, and the village is often on a particular type of site, either on a hilltop or clinging to the side of a valley. It is usually very inconvenient, as no extension or alteration is possible (fig. 70).

B. Multiple Houses (*maisons à bâtiments dissociés*)

In regions of larger farms with a wider range of cultivation, where the storage of crops requires as much room as stock-rearing, it is not possible to have all the buildings under one roof. This has led to the separation and functional specialisation of the buildings which may include a dwelling-house, a stable, a sheep-fold, cow-sheds, pig-sties, a poultry-house, barns, a dairy and tractor-sheds.

The enclosed courtyard farmstead (*ferme à cour fermée*). In one type of plan for multiple buildings the units are placed round a

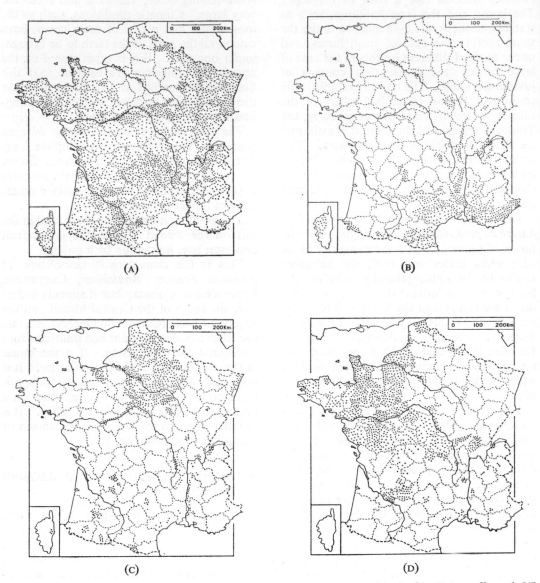

Fig. 70.   Distribution of types of farms.   (Source: A. Demangeon, *Géographie Universelle,* vol. VI, A. Colin, 1946)

A. Distribution of the low compact house.
B. Distribution of the tall compact house.
C. Distribution of the enclosed courtyard house.
D. Distribution of the open courtyard house.

courtyard. It is a very old plan which is found in many regions, and in both isolated farms and villages; the slight variations between them are related to types of farming, farm size and the opportunities afforded by the plots on which the farms are built. The four sides of the farmyard can be enclosed by buildings. Such are the farms of Picardy and Artois or large isolated farms, as this plan also serves as a means of defence. Generally the barn is beside the road over a wide double doorway and has openings into which the harvest can be unloaded without the carts having to go into the yard.

The dwelling-house, with sometimes a small stable, is at the back, with a narrow path giving access to the meadow behind it, at the end of a small garden. On both sides are cow-sheds, pig-sties, the dairy and various types of shelter. In the centre of the yard is the enormous manure heap at which the fowls pick. Sometimes only three sides of the yard are built up or even two (the buildings forming a right angle), the other sides being enclosed by a wall or serving as the farm entrance.

The distribution of this type is highly localised (fig. 70). It is most widely spread on the Tertiaries of the Paris basin, in Picardy, Champagne, Artois and some parts of the North: Cambrésis and the Walloon part of Flanders. It is characteristic of both small and large farms. Outside these areas it is found in areas of extensive arable farming, such as the plain of Caen, the plain of Forez and Basse-Alsace. In some cases the plan appears to have evolved. In fact, although this plan must be the original one for large farms, because the arrangement of buildings on all four sides of a farmyard was necessary for them, we cannot say the same for all enclosed farms. In Picardy a comparison between the cadastral plans or older plans shows that a progressive enclosure has taken place (fig. 71). At the beginning the plot had perhaps only two buildings. The one facing the street comprised the barn and tool store; a second building behind it contained the dwelling-house, stable and cow-sheds.

Sometimes a small building leant against one of the sides without being connected to the other two, thus limiting the risk of fire. With enlargement of the cultivated area and changes of the farming system, such as the addition of more livestock, annexes were built on the remaining sides, thus closing the plan.

The open courtyard farmstead (ferme à cour ouverte). The buildings are spaced out, away from each other, but their arrangement still encloses a more or less clearly defined courtyard. This is the characteristic plan of large farms in the West, Sologne and Berry and Bresse, of the *hofstede* of Flanders and generally speaking of all recently established farms (fig. 70). This plan presupposes a very large plot, and quite often a dispersed settlement pattern. It appears in stock-rearing farms where cattle occupy an important place and must have easy access.

The scattered farmstead (ferme à bâtiments épars). This is a hypertrophied version of the open farmstead. The shape of a courtyard can no longer be distinguished, and the buildings are placed in apparent disorder according to aspect, the demands of life on the farm, successive extensions and the shape of the site. In the farms of Caux the buildings are far apart from each other and scattered over a pasture forming a farmstead (*masure*) enclosed by a broad embankment reinforced with beeches (fig. 72). This is a distinctive solution to the problem of farm planning because it keeps the pasture, the garden and all the buildings within one enclosure. It was probably intended as a protection against fire; but that cannot be the sole explanation for this type. Norman influence has been suggested.

Pastoral summer chalets (chalets pastoraux d'été). The mountain huts or chalets used by shepherds and cowherds in summer must be regarded as outside the classification of types of farmstead. They are temporary homes for men who have left the valleys to care for the flocks on the mountains and hills, and where necessary to make butter and cheese. They are the Alpine chalets, the *burons* of the Central Massif, the *cujala* or *cayolar* of the Basque country and

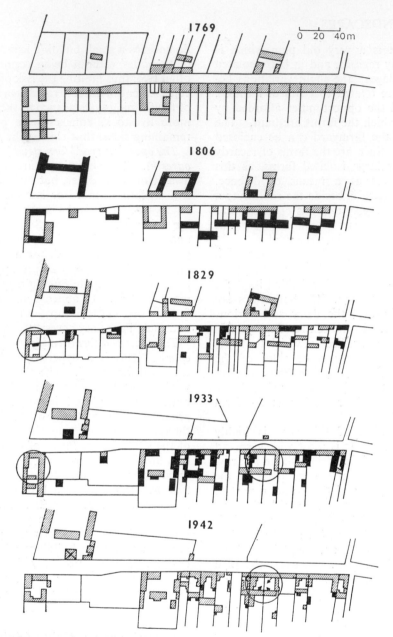

Fig. 71. Plan of a street in the village of Aumont (Somme) illustrating the evolution of rural houses in Amiénois since the 18th century. (Source: R. Coque, 'L'Évolution de la maison rurale en Amiénois', *Ann. de Geog.*, no. 352, 1956, p. 404)

On each plan, new buildings since the preceding one are shown in black. Plan of 1769: Few enclosed courtyard houses compared with rudimentary types. 1806: The appearance of large buildings represents the first stage of evolution towards the closing of the rudimentary types. 1829: The appearance of smaller buildings accentuates the tendency already shown in the preceding period. The 1933 plan shows enclosures resulting from successive waves of building. Further, we may observe the formation of larger farms by grouping, accompanied by a partial reorganisation of the built-up area and the appearance of sheds. 1942: Slight modifications in the same direction.

Béarn, the *cabane* of Couserans and the *horry* of Foix. Their size and equipment vary according to their functions as temporary shelters, milking sheds, barns or cow-sheds.

This variety in the plans of rural houses is matched by an astonishing variety of architectural styles and building materials; galleries, balconies, porches and outside staircases give individuality to every farm, even if it has

or stone, slate, tiles, roofing stone, wooden shingles. At one time local resources determined the nature of the material. 'From the Agoût to the Pyrenees stretches a large area entirely or almost without building stone. The land lacks a solid foundation, and man has no resistant material of which to build his house. He must resort to clay which he mixes with straw and sometimes with fine

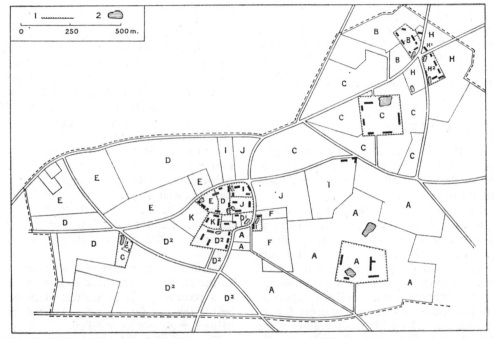

Fig. 72. Settlement and land pattern in the Pays de Caux. (Source: A. Demangeon, *Géographie Universelle*, vol. VI, A. Colin, 1946)

1. Ditches surrounding the *masures*.   2. Pond.

The letters indicating the farmsteads (A, B, C, etc.) are repeated on their lands to show how they are arranged around them. The dotted line represents the boundary of the commune.

originated from one regional 'model'. Differences in architecture and materials often underline social differences; in the South-west, for example, the roofs of the manor houses with their small, flat, steeply inclined tiles contrast sharply with the gently sloping roofs covered with roman tiles of the peasant dwellings.

The materials used for the walls and roofs emphasise this individuality; clay daub, bricks

gravel to give body to the mixture as it dries out' (D. Faucher). This is the *paillebart* of the Toulouse and Marmande regions, the *pisé* of northern France and the Lyons region, and the *torchis* of Picardy.

Lastly, further variety results from varying conditions of slope, aspect, climate, physical environment, by all of which farms have been very much influenced. The rural houses of Aubrac, for example, have had to choose

L

between protection against the cold north wind and the violent south wind; and they defend themselves to a greater extent against the latter.

'The south wind is strong, but the north wind brings the cold. For protection, the house buries itself, and shrinks back against the slope; thick walls protect it against extreme cold and temperature variations. The roof has strong rafters to support thick slabs of stone which no gale can lift and which no weight of snow can crush; in Mende it has a bell-like shape, perhaps so that the heavy and thick falls of snow which could be dangerous can slip more easily to the ground. In the north of Vivarais, so as to leave no loophole for the wind, the massive stone roof goes down to the ground at the back of the house' (P. Estienne).

C. Changes and Facilities

These traditional rural houses were in past centuries man's answer to the problem of planning the layout of rural houses and farm buildings to the best advantage.

But in these days they appear as relics of the past, unrelated to the necessities of rural economy and life in an advanced society. Changes in methods and types of farming have compelled the peasants to adapt their farms, by changing the uses of some buildings or by building on to them. In Bas-Languedoc the introduction of vine monoculture forced the peasant to fix up his wine-making plant in the old cart-shed or in the yard. In the plain of Valence the spread of lucerne cultivation before the First World War made it necessary to build special sheds, and in the same way buildings had to be built for drying tobacco leaves or walnuts.

Recent agricultural techniques demand a recasting of the plan and often new buildings. Stall feeding, which is rapidly becoming more widespread, curtails radical transformation of the old cow-shed and needs much more space, including areas for movement, for resting, for feeding and a milking parlour. But in many cases the plans of the farms are not susceptible to adaptation; the Lorraine type of farm, for example, is unadaptable.

The role of these types of rural settlement as a brake on the economic and social evolution of the French countryside should not be overlooked.

Among the solutions resorted to when building cannot be adapted are the erection of stacks and sheds in the fields, and even the use of the buildings of a deserted farm. Often the only solution is the use of some or all of the buildings of abandoned farms; in such cases the farm spreads out into the village.

In 1962 over three quarters (78·3%) of the rural houses (3,948,000) dated from before 1915; 13·3% (672,700) had been built between 1915 and 1948, many of these being farms that were rebuilt after the First World War. Only 8·4% (426,100) were later than 1948.

It is astonishing how dilapidated, out of date and lacking in comfort French rural homes are. Most farms are actually more than a hundred years old, and particularly in Normandy, on the plateaux of the East, in the southern Alps, on the borders of the Aquitaine basin. It is in the North, Brittany and the Landes that rural buildings are 'youngest'—that is to say about seventy years old!

Certain changes have of course been made. In the Breton countryside the clear-cut lines of a recently built house can often be seen beside the old farm block; some farms are being completely remodelled.

Demographic changes in the countryside and farm concentration are causing houses to become unsuitable in one way or another for the people living in them. In 1961, 36·5% of the houses in rural communes held the normal complement, but 15·2% were overcrowded and 48·3% under-inhabited; 180,000 dwellings had only one room, 638,000 had two rooms, 589,000 had three rooms, 862,000 four rooms, 439,000 five rooms and 316,000 six rooms.

In 1960, 32·5% of the houses in rural communes had no water, and only 21·5% had water, water closets and proper drains; 18,137,000 country people have no running water and must be content with a spring or a well, sometimes even a pond or river. Table LVII gives a picture which is already dated, but which emphasises the great backwardness of rural housing.

Household facilities in rural houses vary greatly from region to region. The maps (figs. 73A and B) show the distribution of two such facilities. The map of piped water supply gives the percentage of rural dwellings with

partments in the Paris region, Lorraine and those of the moderate or high mountain regions.

In mountainous areas there are plenty of springs and streams, and water can be supplied simply by gravity. The concentration of settlement is another essential factor. Piped water supplies have spread much more quickly in areas of village settlement, whereas

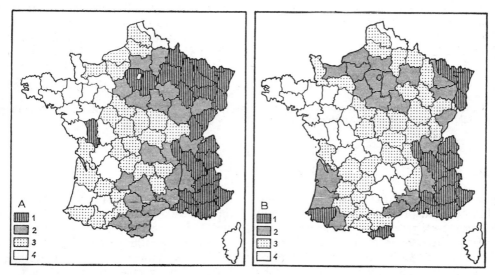

Fig. 73. Piped water (A) and sanitary installations (B) in houses in rural communes (1954).
A: 1. More than 50%. 2. 31–50%. 3. 21–30%. 4. 20% or less.
B: 1. More than 8%. 2. 6·1–8%. 3. 4·1–6%. 4. 4% or less.

a tap inside the house. The eastern half of France appears to have a great advantage over the western half, particularly the de-

TABLE LVII. HOUSING FACILITIES IN RURAL COMMUNES (1954) (%)

	Rural communes		
	Non-agricultural buildings	Agricultural buildings	All France
Water in the house	28·1	24·9	58·3
Water in the yard .	29·8	49·9	23·1
Cylinder gas .	50	41	29·8
Mains gas . .	3·7	0·6	36·4
Electricity . .	90·5	87·1	93
Bath or shower .	4·8	2	10·4
Inside W.C. .	13·5	4	26·6
Outside W.C. .	66·6	64·3	59·8
Central heating .	3·7	1·3	10·2
Telephone . .	6·1	3·6	8

dispersed settlement makes the work much more costly and less economic. In Finistère 1·5% of the communes with less than 5,000 inhabitants have piped water supplies.

The second map, even more than the first, gives an indication of living standards. An I.N.S.E.E. enumeration of houses with sanitary installations included all those possessing a wash-hand basin with running water, but not necessarily a bath or shower. The average for the whole of France is very low: 5·9%. Figures for the departments are even lower. Comparison of the two maps shows that there is no high correlation between the two elements (compare Deux-Sèvres and Aveyron). Sanitary facilities are more closely related to rural standards of living, in terms of incomes and the necessities of the rural way of life.

Improvements in rural housing, and, more generally, changes in the standard of living, play a decisive part in the way of life of farming people and especially of women and the young. 'The Danish peasant has a house as comfortable as that of the townsman, even the doctor or lawyer from the little town near by. When his work is over at 6 o'clock he takes a shower, changes and goes into the sitting-room with his family to listen to music or join with his neighbours in social evenings and study circles.'

Thus a long and costly programme of modernisation must be undertaken to prevent the disequilibrium of town and country becoming worse than it is now, thus maintaining the critical state of under-development in the rural areas.

The fourth plan undertook to reserve 25% of the national housing programme for the rural population. In fact, insufficient effort is being made to modernise and build rural dwellings. Negligence on the part of public authorities is aggravated by that of architects and building contractors, all of whom leave the country-dwellers to do the best they can on their own initiative.[8]

7. The vine-growers' houses on the slopes of Lorraine are longer and narrower than the farms in the marl depressions.
8. Rural housing co-operatives have been created in many areas to guide their members, supervise the work and provide technical and administrative staff.

3. FIELD PATTERNS

The patchwork of fields, arable or grassland, woodland or heath, as seen from any high viewpoint, reflects the influence of the structure of land-ownership, farm structure and farming systems within varied natural surroundings; landscapes, aerial photographs of them, show changes from year to year in cultivation units and crop units according to the systems of rotation; they do not correspond exactly to land-ownership divisions. The tenant-farmer can divide one parcel of land into several parcels of crops or combine two parcels of land leased from different owners into one parcel of crops.

These parcels are classified by their sizes, shapes and combinations. For lack of systematic studies covering the whole of France, the systems of land division are very unevenly understood; the nomenclature itself is not yet standardised and varies with the author.

A. The Sizes of Fields and Parcels

It is practically impossible to know at all accurately how many fields or parcels are used for agriculture in France. According to the first cadastral surveys made between 1810 and 1850, the number of parcels not built over was 126 million in 87 departments comprising a rateable area of 53 million ha., that is to say, an average area of 0·42 ha. (about 1 acre) per parcel. In 1891 the 'presumed' number of parcels rose to 151 million (average area 0·35 ha.). In 1929 the total agricultural area (50 million ha.) was divided into 125 million parcels (average area 0·39 ha.). In 1946 the number of parcels was estimated at 145 million (0·33 ha.).

Although the size of the parcels varies greatly within any one commune, and even more from one region to another in the same department, regional differentiation is clearly shown by a map dating from 1882 of the sizes of parcels by departments. A group of departments with very small parcels is to be found in north-eastern France, and in the eastern and central areas of the Paris basin with extensions into the Jura. The 'large parcels', an entirely relative term, are to be found in the South of France and particularly in the South-east. But they are also found in Normandy, in the Central Massif (except in Puy-de-Dôme, where the average is lowered by the small parcels of Limagne). A broad relationship can be seen between large parcels and mountain regions, and between large parcels and stock-rearing areas, but this must not be overemphasised.

In more detail, the exiguity of parcels is carried to extraordinary lengths. In Alsace it reaches caricature proportions—Bas-Rhin has the French record for exiguity with an average parcel area of 0·17 ha. (about 0·4 acres.[9] In a sample of 61 communes, the average areas were found to be less than 0·1 ha. in 6 communes, 0·1–0·15 ha. in 30 communes, 0·15–0·2 ha. in 16 communes and more than 0·2 ha. (half an acre) in 9 communes only.

The causes of this fragmentation of French field plans are many and go back far into the past. One of the principal causes is beyond doubt the adjustment of parcel size to methods of cultivation in early times. Many parcels have an area of about 0·3–0·35 ha., corresponding to the *journal* (0·34 ha.) or area which one man with a plough-team could cultivate in one day. Communal farming systems accentuated the division into small parcels by scattering the holdings of each farm over several fields. Small parcels are also a feature of certain farming enterprises, such as hillside vineyards, market gardens or small-scale specialised farms.

Field subdivision has been greatly accentuated by multiple inheritance. On a decease, in areas where the land was not grouped around the farm buildings, each field or parcel was divided into as many parts as there were heirs. This whittling down, succession by succession, led to plots so tiny as to be almost uncultivable. More generally still, parcellation is linked with the structure of land-ownership and type of farming. Areas of small owner-operated peasant holdings are those where the cultivation of small plots has been most persistent.

Consolidation of holdings has obviously effected great changes in parcellation, considerably increasing the average area culti-vated per commune, and creating parcels of from 1 to 3 ha.[10] But there are always small and large parcels side by side in any one area or commune. Valleys, hillsides, broken ground and the outskirts of the villages are places where small fields are most common. One or more isolated blocks of small parcels persist even in consolidated areas, corresponding to very small properties.

B. The Shapes and Combinations of Parcels

The size of fields is not entirely a matter of choice; more and more research on the subject reveals characteristic lengths corresponding to old agrarian measures, themselves linked with very ancient farming techniques. The tools used, such as the type of plough and the method of traction, were often the cause of differences in size. The fields were long so that the plough-teams would not have to turn too many times at the ends. The minimum width of 4–5 m. was determined by the extent of the peasant's seed broadcast. In the centre of the Paris basin P. Brunet distinguishes small fields, less than 200 m. long, medium fields, 225–350 m. long, and large fields, longer than 375 m. A length of 250 m. seems to represent the dividing line between small and large parcels. If we can find the original (?) lengths of the parcels we can thus retrace the various stages in land occupance. Fields of 300–400 m. are very common, and this is the optimum length for fields created by the consolidation of parcels.

The classification of parcels according to shape is very complex; from century to century, according to the prevailing natural, social, economic and legal conditions, men have applied much ingenuity to varying field systems. The concept of small fields and large fields is a relative one, and it is difficult to devise a simple classification which can apply to all parts of France.[11]

A preliminary distinction can be made between irregular parcels without geometric shapes and geometric parcels. The former have sinuous, curved outlines and composite polygonal shapes, 'enclosures of complex shapes recalling no simple geometric figure, and often with curving sides' (P. Flatrès, speaking of southern Finistère). In areas of discontinuous farmland the land determines the form of parcels, their outlines being modelled on the contours of the ground; the fields are rarely adjoining.

Geometric parcels fall into several categories, the main criterion of classification being their degree of elongation.

Small square parcels, typical of medieval farm structure, still show through recent parcellation which was often content merely to group them together. They still exist as vineyard parcels in many regions. Parcels under crops which need a great deal of hard manual labour are often square.[12] These chequerboards of small square parcels are common in Basse-Provence.

The large parcels may be square, rectangular or sometimes in T or H shapes, dovetailed into other parcels, and forming a geometrical patchwork of large fields. They are a feature of the rich cultivated plains in the centre of the Paris basin, and of the vineyards of Languedoc. In Brittany 'squat rectangles' (Meynier) almost always correspond to recent enclosure of the heaths (18th and 19th centuries), but they can also result from the sharing out of a property.

Compact fields are also characteristic of Dombe and Bresse (where the land was divided in the 15th–17th centuries into great squares with sides measuring 200 m.). These compact parcels, small or large, are often characteristic of stock-rearing districts.

Rectangular fields can be defined as having a ratio of length to breadth of between three and five to one; they are very common in many regions.

In Alsace (Plaine d'Erstein), in Provence and in the Rhône corridor numerous traces of Roman centuriation can still be identified. If a grid corresponding to the Roman divisions is applied to aerial photographs, incontestable proofs appear: the north–south orientation of the major routes, the width of the parcels (710 m.), the rectangular layout, straight lengths of roads and lines of vegetation. In the Valence region, for example, the Valence–Chabreuil road corresponds to the *Decumanus maximus*.

In the south of Finistère almost all the common lands were divided within the last hundred years into geometric parcels, generally rectangular. Consolidation creates a rectangular field of moderate size (300–400 m.) and of a mean length–breadth ratio of 4 to 2 in response to the demands of motorisation (fig. 74).

Strip-fields, whatever their regional frequency, are characteristic of French rural landscapes. Beyond a certain degree of elongation (when the ratio of length to width exceeds five to one) the parcel becomes a strip. But this pattern can become accentuated (the elongation can be as much as fifteen to one) to the point of creating long ribbons of cultivated land a few metres wide and ten or more times as long (fig. 75, 2).

This division into strips gives the countryside of Lorraine its characteristic appearance. But it also exists in Vimeu, Artois, northern Brie, the plains of Poitou and Charente, the coastal region of the Pays de Caux, the Rhône corridor, the valley of the lower Ain and the great valleys of Aquitaine. All along the coast of the bay of Mont-Saint-Michel, around Saint-Brieuc and on the south-west coast of Brittany the *bocage* gives way to a coastal open-field pattern with small-sized plots, often in strips and sometimes short. Strips, enclosed or otherwise, can be seen throughout southern Finistère.

In several regions of France, blocks of *curved fields* have been observed, ribbon-like strips grouped in 'quarters' or 'bundles', with the curves fitting one into another. Some of these patterns can be explained by the relief, the boundaries of the fields following the contours of the hillsides. But in flat areas other explanations must be sought, and several hypotheses have been brought forward: encroachment on a neighbour's land; the 'natural' deviation towards the right of the ancient ploughs of prehistoric origin (the megalithic fields); solar orientation; even religious ordinance. But none of them is really convincing.[13]

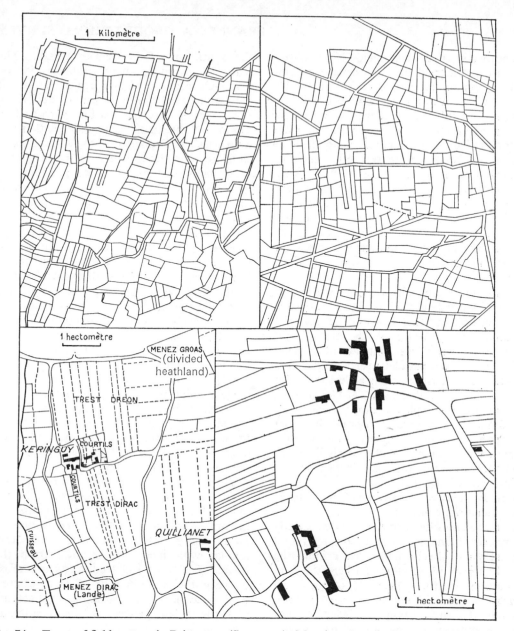

Fig. 74. Types of field pattern in Brittany. (Source: A. Meynier, *Ann. de Géog.*, no. 309, 1949, p. 9)

Top left, most widespread type: rectangular plots slightly curved, with no clear systematic pattern; roads and the long sides of blocks of plots turned in a fairly constant direction (on the whole); plots of unequal size. Tracing of an aerial photograph (North region, west of Dinard). Some roads may not be visible.

Top right, type found on heathland divided since the 19th century: boundaries in straight lines; no predominant direction; numerous plots of more or less uniform size. Tracing of an aerial photograph (area north of Loire-Inférieure).

Bottom left, *méjou* type: enclosed blocks; open parcels. The dotted lines indicate boundaries not marked out on the ground. Linear hamlet (Kéringuy) Scale 1/10,000. After Flatrès, 'Le Pays nord-bigouden', *Ann. de Bretagne*, 1944.

Bottom right, pattern of open-field type: fields in strips and slightly curved. Scale 1/5,000. After Flatrès, *ibid.*

The origin of the strip-fields is not clear. The strip is better adapted to a cereal economy and to communal organisation than to the more individualistic occupation of stock-rearing. In most cases it appears to result from the sharing out of large parcels. This method of dividing a parcel simplifies the placing of boundary marks, equalises soil conditions and obviates the need for new approach roads. R. Bomer gives a good example of the rapidity with which the division into strips can take place. In Grande Sologne, between 1860 and 1910, the broad parcels of the large, decaying farms were bought up and divided into strips by small farmers.

Strips and rectangular parcels are grouped in combinations of which the most frequent is the 'quarter', but they can also be arranged in bundles; in Alsace, in the Outre-Forêt 'most often there are bundles of curving strips, remaining parallel over a length of 3 or 4 km., and thus straddling valleys and hills. Each is cut into several fields 200–400 m. long, but in different places along each strip' (E. Juillard). In several regions there are fine examples of radical divisions into parcels. Some are star-shaped, with parcels like very elongated triangles, radiating from a central point; such is the field pattern at Étang de Montady, between Narbonne and Nîmes. The others are concentric.

In some cases the field divisions are strictly geometric, being laid out according to an overall plan. Such is the case around the *bastide* towns of Aquitaine, where the field boundaries continue the lines of the town streets or are laid out in a radial pattern around it. In Brittany A. Meynier has pointed out many examples of parcels following the direction of alignment of megaliths.

Contrasts in field patterns are found at different scales of geographical observation, between the major provinces of France, between regions or within a single commune. Broadly speaking, the geometric parcels of the plains of northern France contrast with the more shapeless, less well-ordered parcels of part of the South and of the Central Massif. The field pattern in southern France is indeed much more confused and irregular. In the cultivated basins of Provence and the southern Alps 'small irregular fields surround a mixture of broad fields together with some long ones' (P. Brunet). In the communes or small regional units there are frequent contrasts between the parcels on plateaux, on hillsides and in valleys, but such contrasts may also be seen in areas of homogeneous environment.

The reasons for this are to be found in natural conditions as much as in the various systems of cultivation and the structure of land-ownership. Almost always, in areas of open fields with their narrow strips, the marshy areas and belts of land along the banks of even the smallest streams are divided into larger parcels which are more compact and enclosed. In the Mediterranean South the irregular fields of the hillsides and the *garrigues* contrast with the narrower and more regular parcels of the plains. Sometimes the parcels are not symmetrical on the two slopes of a valley; in the hills of Terrefort the large cultivated parcels on the sunny side contrast with the small enclosed grassland parcels of the shady side.

But as soon as the intensity of occupation or utilisation of the land increases, 'social factors take precedence over geographical factors' (J. Sion). In the *garrigue* around Nîmes the parcels become larger and more regular with increasing distance from the town. The most usual contrasts are those between the large parcels of great estates, owner-occupied farms, *métairies* or chateaux, and the small parcels of the small-scale farmers.

The heterogeneous nature of the field patterns often reflects that of the social structure and its past changes, quite as much as physical conditions.

'Referring to a field plan of 1757, where an estate with irregular enclosed fields can be seen breaking the continuity of a strip-field landscape, Marc Bloch shows that there are four possible interpretations: the creation of an estate by one

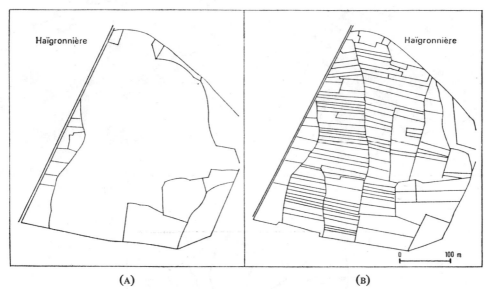

(A)   (B)

1. Example of recent division into strips in the commune of Haute-Goulaine (Loire-Atlantique), 1830–
1961.   (Source: A. Meynier, *Norois*, 1962, p. 140)

A. 1830 Plan.   B. 1961 Plan.

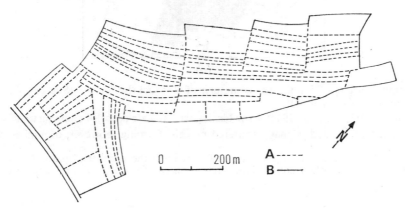

2. Example of grouping of strips at Allerey (Côte-d'Or).   Formation of a large meadow by consolidation
of strip fields.   (Source: M. Rocherfort, *Volume jubilaire offert à E. de Martonne*, Rennes, 1952)

A. Agrarian structure in 1841.
B. Agrarian structure in 1950 (a single meadow).

Fig. 75.   Examples of inverse evolution of land division.

*

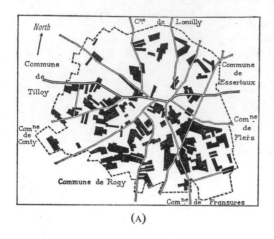

(A)

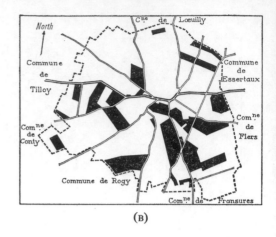

(B)

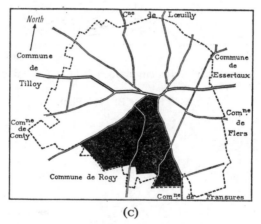

(C)

Fig. 76.   Example of consolidation: the commune of Bosquel (Somme).   (Source: A. Meynier, *Les Paysages agraires*, A. Colin, 1958)

Cadastral plans of 1913, 1934 and 1944.   The black parts indicate parcels belonging to a farm of 180 ha.

A. In 1913 the farm consisted of many scattered parcels, forming, however, a number of cultivation blocks.

B. In 1934 the first consolidation, of the classic type, reduces the number of parcels.

C. In 1944 a second and bolder consolidation has been carried out to the advantage of the farmers (cf. p. 333).

tenant on a part of the land which was brought under cultivation at a late date; the recent creation of this estate by consolidating narrow parcels which originally belonged to different people; a very old seigniorial estate surrounded by the small parcels of the tenants; or the survival of a former agrarian structure with large enclosed fields which were partly replaced by an open-field pattern' (E. Juillard and A. Meynier).

C. Changes

Field patterns are very unstable, even if appearances—that is to say, archaic sizes and shapes—appear to contradict this. Changes in land-ownership, farm concentration, the sharing out of land on inheritance, changes in systems of cultivation and the consolidation of holdings all play a part in their development (fig. 75).

Enclosure may or may not alter the field pattern; where the parcel network is very much split up into strips, enclosure is impossible without grouping some of them together. The introduction of the vineyard into the valleys of the Pays de la Loire led to the fragmentation of fields into small parcels; conversely, the decline of viticulture often led to a considerable modification of the field patterns.

Consolidation of holdings creates a new rural landscape. The parcels are larger and their shape more geometrical; the triangular and axe-shaped forms characteristic of the old systems disappear. No fields remain completely isolated; they are all served by a country road or farm track (fig. 76). The network of roads is completely reorganised, straightened, extended or reduced as necessary, and a grid plan is superimposed on the star pattern radiating out from the village. Progressively, but too slowly, a new field pattern is replacing the archaic system inherited from the past. However, consolidation does not necessarily wipe out the contrasts in field patterns within a commune. Not all of it is in fact consolidated; inhabited areas and their approaches as well as damp meadowland are excluded. Moreover, the structure of land-ownership as well as natural conditions affect the extent and nature of consolidation.

9. Bas-Rhin is followed by Haut-Rhin, Moselle and Meuse.

10. The optimum dimensions of plots have altered rapidly owing to motorisation; before the war, plots of 0·3–0·6 ha. could conveniently be worked by animal traction. The increased average size of plots complicates the process of consolidation in a *pays* with too many small and medium-sized farms.

11. In southern Finistère, for example, P. Flatrès distinguishes irregular, geometrical and regular quadrilateral fields. Analysing the field pattern of Basse-Normandie, P. Brunet distinguishes regular *bocage* with a close mesh of square plots or foreshortened rectangles not more than 150 m. long, regular *bocage* with an open mesh of plots with sides over 250 m. and irregular *bocage* (Pays d'Auge).

12. Some have said that this is so that the workers will not have to move too far away from their wine-bottles, particularly in regions with a warm climate!

13. Observations made in the forest of Paimpont have shown an accentuation of the curve of the fields during the last hundred years.

4. OPEN AND ENCLOSED FIELD PATTERNS

The field pattern is only the substratum of rural landscapes. The main types of agrarian organisation are characterised by the presence or absence of enclosures. Open fields or *champagnes* with villages, on the one hand, and *bocages* or *enclos* with isolated farms and hamlets, on the other, are the two major types of rural landscape in France on either side of a line joining the mouth of the Seine to Lake Geneva (fig. 48). Their study has for a long time occupied the attention of the best scholars, who are fascinated by their sharp contrast and all the factors which go to explain it.

A. Unenclosed Patterns

In unenclosed areas there is no obstacle to break the wide view of a more or less extensive surface without hedges and generally without trees, though sometimes dotted with trees in southern France. Boundary-stones flush with the ground and changes in crops form the only visible boundaries between the plots.

In fact, there are many exceptions to the general contrast between the wide, open landscapes of northern and eastern France and the enclosed landscapes of the rest of France.

THE OPEN-FIELD PATTERN

South of a line from Le Havre to Geneva, open fields of the northern type may be found in the most varied localities. The Limagne, the Rhône corridor and the plains of Charente are the largest open plains of southern France. But the plain of Saint-Flour also has a typical landscape of open fields divided into strips. This same landscape characterises the valley of the lower Ain and the islands of Brière. Some mountain areas and Alpine valleys also have open-field landscapes.

The open field of the Lorraine type corresponds to a form of collective agrarian organisation combining cereal crops and large-scale stock-rearing in districts with few meadows. The communal practices already described could not exist without a strong social organisation, nucleated settlement and the dispersal of holdings, so that each farmer had a share in each field.

Open fields are paramount in limestone regions, with flat surfaces scarcely affected by erosion, and rich, permeable soils. Geologically distinct regions show close relationships between limestone terrains and open fields, as in Boulonnais and the chalk 'headland' of Mélantois between Pévèle and inner Flanders, both of which have clay soil and are regions of *bocage* or pseudo-*bocage*.

Open Fields in Areas of *Bocage*

Isolated groups of open fields have been recognised at the very heart of the *bocages* in the West and the Central Massif. They have special names: *méjous* in Breton-speaking Brittany, *champagne, campagne, plaine* and *quartier* in northern Brittany, *bandes, gaigneries, domaines* in southern Brittany, *versenne, champs, chaumes* in Vendée, *coutures* in Limousin.[14]

These outlying areas of open fields are very often associated with houses joined in rows (cf. fig. 74). In the south-east of Vendee,

'the *gaignerie* is the most prized land for ploughing and arable crops. It appears in the rural landscape as a block of patchwork, always more than 3 ha. in area. It is impossible to confuse it with the hedged fields which cluster around the isolated *métairies*. It is surrounded by a large bank capped by hawthorn, furze and brushwood. It is divided into a large number (20, 30 or even 40) of strips several metres wide which sometimes run parallel to a main axis, and sometimes are grouped into several "quarters". Within the *gaignerie* there are no hedges or ditches. The boundaries between the strips are indicated simply by a furrow called a *raise* or by boundary-stones placed on tile foundations' (A. Bouhier).

On examination the *méjous* are seen to comprise a great variety of types. In southern Finistère P. Flatrès distinguishes single isolated *méjous*, in which the various farms in the village own plots, groups of single *méjous*, separated by enclosures, roads or banks, and *méjous* in the form of extensive open *terroirs* belonging to one or more villages, and crossed by unfenced roads at ground level.[15] These *méjous* of the *bocage* lands of the West are associated with a rural system of open fields with triennial rotation, as in Brittany, or biennial, as in Vendée, but with relatively intensive cultivation; communal farming may be practised or not according to the area.[16] Many hypotheses have been put forward to account for them, attributing them variously to natural factors (location on fertile ground), ethnic factors or conditions of land tenure where land is shared by the nobility and the communes.

Some *méjous* undoubtedly derive from the subdivision into open fields of an ecclesiastical estate which has been sold. In the Vendée *Bocage* the *gaignerie* was the result of clearing operations carried out collectively by small peasant copyholders. At present we can only repeat the conclusion of A. Meynier: 'The open fields, cultivated in strips, of western France, whose date and origin are unknown, generally seem to have been worked in the past by peasant smallholders who, at certain periods and sometimes up to the present day, practised a partly collective system of economy.'

Open Landscapes

Side by side with this open-field pattern generally found in areas of low relief and recalling the open fields of Lorraine in character and organisation, southern France shows a wholly different type of open landscape.

Here we return to the distinctive agrarian system of the Aquitaine and Mediterranean regions. Farmlands are distributed so that the grazing lands are quite independent of the cultivated fields. R. Livet has expressed the problem succinctly:

'It is impossible to find any connection between unenclosed fields and collective practices as we can in the northern regions. In particular, the open-field system, at one time so characteristic and widespread in other regions, is completely unknown in Provence where a patchwork of various crops has always been the rule. It therefore seems misleading to speak of the Provençal open-field system if we give the expression its full meaning, i.e. applying not merely to the appearance of the cultivated land, but also to a complex and coherent set of traditions, rules and customs that are reflected in the way a particular landscape is built up.'

This author proposes to use the more modest and more precise term 'open landscape'.

B. Enclosed Patterns

Enclosed landscapes do not belong exclusively to the *bocage*, although this is the most common and most representative form. The fencing can consist of walls or dry-stone walls. The heaps of stones cleared from the land in Béarn, the Causses du Quercy, on some slopes in the Alpine valleys and in Provence, while forming divisions between the plots, are not necessarily intended to enclose. In slate country (around Allassac, in Corrèze and Redon) slabs of slate stood on end act as walls.

In areas of true *bocage*, there is a difference in type according to whether or not there is an embankment as well as a hedge. The *bocage* landscapes with hedges and no embankments are those of Boulonnais, the Pays de Bray, Thiérache, the west of the Paris basin, Maine, Perche, the west of the Central Massif, part of Aquitaine and the Pyrenean regions. The hedge consists of trees and bushes, generally combined, with the branches of the bushes laid to make them impenetrable. Between Avignon and Carpentras, in the Palud, rows of willows and clumps of reeds form partitions between the meadows; this is an example of an original *bocage* in a Mediterranean setting.

Bocage landscapes with hedges set on embankments are found in Brittany; the earth bank is built with the spoil excavated from the adjoining ditch which promotes drainage and allows the water to flow away. These embankments with hedges are extremely varied: 'low, earth-covered dykes in the *pays* of Quimperlé, low, squat embankments covered with furze in Léon, the bare embankments of recently enclosed heathland, the narrow, high embankments planted with oaks of the loam terrains of north-eastern Brittany, and the embankments of Trégorrois, several metres wide and covered with two or three parallel rows of trees. There are innumerable varieties, of which no detailed list has been made. . . .' (A. Meynier).[17]

The types of fencing vary widely in relation to the fields and methods of land use. In Brittany, for example, every parcel is enclosed, whatever its nature and its use; in Limousin, on the contrary, only meadow parcels are enclosed (*bocage de prés*); the same applies in the Basque country, the central Pyrenees and Couserans, where only the hayfields are enclosed. The enclosures can contain one parcel or a group of parcels giving a 'unit-parcel *bocage*' as against a 'multiple-parcel *bocage*'. In extreme forms the enclosure separates a block of fields from the neighbouring road, or from another block of fields, or contains only occasional parcels.

Each enclosure around the villages of Lorraine is a *meix*; outside the village the *meix* is a walled garden which is always found near farms and other buildings, such as mills and inns.

All regional combinations are possible, and exist in fact; some have enclosures and partly enclosed plots side by side (the borders of the Armorican massif, Bourbonnais and Bresse). Others have zones of *bocage* and fragments of open landscape adjoining within the same commune, as in southern Brittany, or enclosed meadows and groups of fields which are simply surrounded by a hedge, as in the west of the Central Massif.

Pseudo-bocages and pseudo-open fields. We frequently meet with landscapes of false *bocage*. The hedges, though real enough, are not continuous; they do not enclose, but form screens, line roads, pick out the long sides of a strip-field, grow on embankments of cleared stones and mark the thalwegs of the valleys.

In regions with a high stream density this may give rise to a 'pseudo-*bocage*' landscape even if there are no real hedges, as in the *terrefort* of Aquitaine.[18]

R. Lebeau gives a good description of one example of this in the valley of the Oignin to the west of Nantua: 'The hedges, when seen close to, do not enclose. They follow the contours of hillsides and form screens or artificial barriers to hold back the earth.

'On the parallel-sided valley bottoms they outline the long sides of the fields. The cadastral plan shows, in fact, a typical *champagne* pattern; three-year rotation is the rule and communal practices have not entirely disappeared. This apparent *bocage* is not one at all; it is a "pseudo-champagne". During the last century, hedges were allowed to grow everywhere, along screens, on walls of cleared stones and between the parcels, in order to provide firewood. The peasants wanted the hedge for itself, not to enclose land. A field bordered with hedges increased in value.'

In the regions of the lower Rhône the northern boundaries of the parcels are outlined by tall screens of cypress, thuyas and reeds (*canne de Provence*) against the dangerous blast of the Mistral. The cypress hedges are all recent; they date from the Second Empire, at the time when the cultivation of vegetables began to develop. They are 20–30 m. apart and reinforced by rows of reeds, dividing the parcels into blocks like pigeon-holes 'in each of which the comparative stoppage of air currents, the reflection of heat and light, and the regular and calculated distribution of irrigation water create a true micro-climate' (T. Livet).

In other regions the *bocage* or semi-*bocage* appearance is entirely due to the hedges or trees in close proximity to farm-houses and their annexes. The Pays de Caux, for example, without its screens of majestic trees would have a landscape of unenclosed fields. In Flanders the hedges of the farms and their neighbouring meadows are the characteristic feature of the '*bocage flamand*'.

Indeed, open fields, open landscapes and *bocage* are anything but clearly distinct; and composite or mixed landscapes are far more frequent than 'pure' open field or *bocage*. The *bocage* may be limited to the valleys, leaving the higher parts of the interfluves open, or islands of open fields may suddenly appear without apparent reason, like a clearing in the middle of the *bocage*, and sometimes an island of *bocage* may stand out in the middle of an open-field landscape.

THE HISTORY OF THE *BOCAGE*

The *bocage* is not an original form. It is true that as early as the 9th century the Redon cartulary describes ditches and enclosures, and coins of the 10th and 11th centuries have been found in an embankment in Finistère, but it does not follow that the whole of the Armorican West was a *bocage*. From the later Middle Ages onwards the making of temporary enclosures was authorised, but closed and unenclosed fields existed side by side on the same *terroir*. The enclosures were made at very different periods, as the *bocage* progressively invaded unenclosed fields and heathlands in one area, while these remained unenclosed elsewhere.

But most enclosures date from after the 13th century and correspond either to zones peopled at a late date by an agrarian society more individualistic than that of earlier centuries or to enclosures transforming a former open-field system.

The first mention of the *bocage* in the Central Massif goes back to the 15th century. In the 16th century the right to enclose existed in the rural communes of Marche, Bourbonnais and Nivernais.

Much more often the enclosures date from the 18th century in respect of land granted by subinfeudation, and from the 19th, of cleared land. From 1770 to 1777, administrators in most provinces issued orders of enclosure for common land and common pasture, in imitation of England. Thus the *bocage* of Thiérache dates from the 18th century. In the damp valleys of Lorraine the many meadows are surrounded by hedges planted in the reign of Louis XVI for the enclosure of the common pastures.

It was enough for such a region to be attached for purposes of administration to a district where individualism in agriculture was the rule, for the enclosure system to spread easily. Revermont, which became part of Bresse in the 18th century, saw a large number of enclosures in a short time.

In 1847 the sharing out of the heathlands at Saint-Barnabé (Côtes-du-Nord) was accompanied by the obligation to enclose within two years; in Finistère the last enclosures of heathland date from the beginning of the 20th century. The dispersed settlement and the *bocage* landscape of Cotentin are recent characteristics. The region once had nucleated settlement and an open-field agrarian structure.

There are simple monogenetic *bocages*, but more often they are polygenetic and were formed in several stages. The *bocage* of Gâtinais, for example, was formed in two stages, from 1450 to 1720 and after 1850. The hedge first appeared with the *métairie* system, and was put there by the nobility just after the Hundred Years War as a result of widespread consolidation of holdings achieved at the expense of an open-field system based on hamlets. After 1850 the heaths which had hitherto been deserted were colonised and enclosed in their turn.

THE PURPOSE OF *BOCAGE*

Geographers have wondered about the origin of this *bocage* pattern which covers a large part of France. It is a difficult subject for research, for its causes may have evolved in the course of time and ceased to be clearly visible by the 20th century.

The *bocage* as a type of agrarian organisation is a complex system with various functions. The ditch, which is almost always found beside the embankment, has an important part to play in drainage; particularly in very rainy districts with impermeable soil. This presupposes regular and general maintenance of this system of ditches and the embankment may be no more than its result. The embankment with a hedge, or the hedge alone, provides useful protection from wind, drizzle and frost. The hedges prevent the meadows from drying up and help the drainage. At one time they provided indispensable wood, branches, stakes and litter for the animals or food for them in winter.

The large number of trees in *bocage* country too often makes us forget the absence of any real forest in western and central France. The excessive clearing of former centuries had deprived the 18th- and 19th-century peasants of their normal sources of wood supply. The boundary trees of the *bocage* reclaimed from the heath supplied this need (it is often noticed that the plots of farms near woods are less surrounded by hedges); the *bocage* was 'the forest of those who have none'. But these are secondary reasons resulting from the very existence of the *bocage*; we must go further, analyse the part played by physical and human factors in the development of the *bocage* and thus seek out the reason for its existence.

The bocage and the system of cultivation

The first explanation which comes to mind is that of protection; the enclosure or hedge is raised in such a way as to isolate a parcel, a group of parcels or a part of the commune. In every system of cultivation which involves having crops and animals on different parts of the land, the former must obviously be protected from invasion and destruction by herds.

Either fields or pasture may be enclosed, according to which type of agriculture predominates, which type came first and what physical conditions exist. There is twofold protection, both from intrusions from outside and from the escape of the animals from inside.

Adherence to traditional practices in Brittany ended in the enclosure of cultivated lands, for their owners could otherwise not enjoy the right of common pasture. Elsewhere enclosures were made in the middle of common land. In the Pyrenees, for example, the inhabitants could settle in the middle of the common pastures; they first built temporary dwellings and barns which later became permanent homes. These 'bordiers' scattered over the common land of the community enclosed their lands to protect them from the flocks and to affirm their rights to them. The formation of the Pyrenean bocage dates from the 17th century and still more from the 18th, and lasted until the 19th.

The process worked the same way in Brittany and Auvergne; the conquest of the heath was accompanied by enclosures protecting the whole of the cultivated terroir from the animals which freely grazed there. The Lectoure area of central Aquitaine was pointed out by M. and P. Féral as an extreme case of enclosed fields with open meadows transformed into a system of enclosed meadows with open fields. In the Varenne de Lezoux, in Limagne, a former system of enclosed pasture had become completely converted to bocage by the 19th century.

Formerly, forests were also enclosed: this was intended to prevent wild animals from invading the crops, and more rarely to prevent domestic animals from getting into them. These forest hedges were the origin in certain regions, such as Artois and Haut-Boulonnais, of a new type of bocage; when the forests were cleared the residual forest hedges were retained for a long time in areas where communal practices were rigorously observed. The land could then be said to be enclosed by ancient right and was not incorporated in the common land.

Enclosures appear where they are most necessary: around plots bordering common pasture land, along the roads used by cattle, near the land where the common flock was assembled and dispersed, but also round the best grassland.

The progress made by stock-rearing in the 13th century, and the profits to be gained

from it, encouraged bourgeois, nobles, ecclesiastics and the wealthier peasants to make themselves isolated enclosed farms, free from community restrictions.

The connection which is always present between the development of stock-rearing and that of bocage is sufficient proof of the function of the hedges.

'The open-field system of the plain of Chantonnay in Vendée was considerably reduced with the development of stock-rearing; now it occupies only about 50 ha., limited to the best limestone terrain of the Jurassic. There the landscape is open, or rather the hedges trace only a very vague chequerboard pattern, interrupted here and there. This is an area of warm and well-drained soils, often stony, of a fine red-brown colour and of great value in a climate where there is generally no fear of drought' (A. M. Pavard).

In a more general way these enclosures protect against all the encroachments of an agrarian communal society; they are the geographical reflection of individualism. The movement towards individualism in agriculture is a result of technical progress, which allows a certain autonomy, and the wish of the farmers to keep for their own land the benefits of the improvements made possible by manuring and irrigation, and to protect them from damage by animals on the common pasture. 'Bocage became more extensive in less densely occupied regions, where the village communities were looser and less strong. It made progress because the most recently cleared land was worked in a more individual way, and the bias was definitely towards stock-rearing' (G. Duby).

Social factors are clearly inseparable from economic ones. In the plain of Forez two communes established on varennes at the end of the 18th century, Chalain d'Uzore and Saint-Paul d'Uzore, evolved in different directions although they were identical to begin with. At Saint-Paul the persistence of large estates specialising in the rearing of cattle and horses favoured the creation of a bocage of a type resembling English parkland. At Chalain a class of small landowners arose, practising intensive mixed farming; the landscape here is much more open although still crossed by hedges.

There were still powerful forces ranged against individualism in agriculture. The *brassiers* and *ménagers* were justified in defending their rights of common and access to the forest, without which they could not live, but the attempts of nobles to defend free access to their hunting grounds were more questionable.

In a region of open fields the *bocage* could rarely extend over all the area; there was a wide gap between the interests of small farmers clinging to community practices and those of big landowners trying to free themselves of them. The result was a compromise, partly open field and partly *bocage*, and ancient privileges such as rights of way were maintained after long lawsuits.

This protective function of the *bocage* is not universally admitted. A. Meynier brings forward several arguments, such as the ineffectiveness of the hedge—'Cows and horses get through hedges even when they are planted on embankments'—but perhaps he is thinking of badly kept hedges which have ceased to fulfil their function—and the use of the hedge in circumstances when its protective function did not exist, although it was needed to define a legal boundary.

The bocage and the pattern of land-ownership

In some cases the *bocage* has been seen as the visible expression of the appropriation of land. Documents show in fact that ecclesiastic and seigniorial estates were enclosed when peasant holdings were not; the lord of the manor could take open land and enclose it. Unless the tenant could produce deeds in evidence, enclosure implied ownership. The sale of communal property contributed to the creation of a typical *bocage*, which was yet another proof of the affirmation of ownership. In other circumstances the hedge 'legalised encroachment on the waste by its presence alone' (in Margeride); in the Mediterranean *garrigues* 'enclosure was a way of affirming the principle that "possession

is nine points of the law!" . . . it is only in the second instance that it serves to protect the patch of land from damage by sheep and still more by goats, for the walls were low and the goats were ruthless' (Marres).

In fact there is no real need to contrast the two groups of reasons. The hedges of the *bocages*, in the Pyrenees and elsewhere, have a double significance—individual appropriation and protection of the land.

The bocage and the physical environment

What part do physical conditions play in the origin and extension of the *bocage*? They are not sole determinants in any particular case; but as the *bocage* is a system of enclosure of vegetated areas, and as it is linked with an essentially pastoral economy, it would be a paradox to deny its relationship with the conditions of soil, water and climate that favour trees, shrubs, bushes and grass. The *bocage* is really at home only in damp regions with clayey soils and much surface water. 'In the Central Massif the relationship between the humidity of the climate and the distribution of the *bocage* on all the northern and western borders from Morvan to the Montagne Noire is indisputable' (A. Fel). Exceptional locations must be examined with great care, with as much attention payed to physical peculiarities as to the social and economic conditions of the past.

Like all geographical phenomena, the *bocage* changes progressively or retrogressively under various influences. Enclosed parcels and fields were most numerous at the time of the population maximum in the 19th century; the hedges gave the overcrowded country districts the firewood which the devasted common land could no longer provide.

Examples of regression of the *bocage* are numerous, in the first place through the reduction of cultivated land, the concentration of farms, the development of new types of farming in areas that were rapidly becoming depopulated. The old hedges were no longer looked after; large gaps appeared in them which the cattle could easily get through; the gates rotted and were never renewed, and the *bocage* became fossilised. Elsewhere the hedge ceased to be maintained once its function of providing wood was finished, and farmers stopped up gaps with barbed wire.

Very often the hedge becomes a nuisance and is deliberately cut down, and replaced by electrified fences which are almost invisible. The peasants complain that it takes up too much ground which could be used (26% in Vendée), that it breeds weeds and animal pests, that it collects damp, delays the melting of the snow and keeps the sun off part of the plot; the sunken roads, moreover, are impassable for modern agricultural machinery: it is thus necessary to cut down the hedges and widen roads by filling in the ditches.

The first changes in the *bocage* came with the destruction of hedges and embankments, often independently of land consolidation. This movement began at the end of the 19th century, was developed between the wars and speeded up after 1945, more so after 1958 when it was encouraged by state subsidies.[19] Destruction of embankments enabled large areas of land to be recovered, directly or indirectly (2 ha. on a farm of 28 ha. in Mayenne).[20]

But the main origin of the changes in the *bocage* landscapes was the consolidation of holdings. Consolidation in *bocage* areas, which have long been difficult to deal with, has now begun.

The problems of consolidation are clearly different from those of the unenclosed areas. It means the removal of hedges, the levelling of embankments, the use of bulldozers to fill in ditches, the building of an elaborate network of local and farm roads, the widening of existing roads and the creation of large regular fields. Variations in the value of land is greater than in the *campagnes* because of the greater variety of slope, aspect and soil; the texture of topographic variation is much finer.

Nevertheless, consolidation is not more difficult in every respect. More of the land is owner-occupied than in open-field districts, and the fields and pastures of one farm are often already grouped around the farm buildings. The hedge has often survived only round the whole farm, or round a few meadows.

Example. Remungol, a consolidated commune of Morbihan, 40 km. north of Vannes, extends over 2,600 ha. The consolidated area covers 1,990 ha., involving 330 owners. Consolidation raised the average area of the parcels from 1·04 to 4·28 ha., and the number of parcels fell from 1,900 to 465. It involved the building of 20·75 km. of local roads, recognised and properly surfaced, to serve farms and villages, and 21 km. of farm roads, partially metalled, leading to fields, meadows and woods (roads 8 m. wide), and the levelling of 250 km. of embankments (an average of 125 m. per ha.); 250 ha. of land have been reclaimed for cultivation.

'Thus a new landscape is developing, creating wide unexpected clearings in the old *bocage*, opening unlimited prospects on to far horizons. At the present rate we may estimate that in about twenty years the large parcel of open, unenclosed land will be the characteristic element of the Armorican region' (A. Meynier).

The possible consequences of these actions have been questioned in view of their effects on soil, hydrology and micro-climates. It is important not to change this agrarian landscape only in order to eliminate its disadvantages without regard for its advantages, which may be unappreciated or not readily apparent. Hedges have sometimes been removed without sufficient regard for their role in the physical environment: retaining sands on steep slopes or maintaining underground water-tables, acting as wind-breaks, reducing evaporation or sheltering cattle. Selective improvement in relation to environmental conditions and the substitution of large enclosed fields of the English type, for the present jig-saw pattern, seem preferable to the precipitate creation of vast open spaces in western France.

14. The identification of open fields is not easy; a vast piece of land enclosed within a *bocage* surround can be divided into five parcels worked by five different farms, or as five units by one tenant.

15. Many of these *méjous* were enclosed during the last hundred years, without consolidation or after partial consolidation.

16. In Vendée, common land was introduced into the *gaigneries* at a late date, as common pasture on the waste became rarer.

17. The large number of very wide embankments in Finistère is partly explained by the fact that they belonged to the tenants and not to the landowners under the legal statute concerning rights of eviction from landed property.

18. 'The intramontane region (of the Central Massif), where there are practically no hedges, is on the other hand rich in lines of trees. Their function is to supplement the food of the cattle, sheep and goats; the ash is the most widespread of these fodder trees' (A. Fel, thesis, p. 81).

19. In Finistère 27 km. were cut down at Melgven; in Morbihan 135 km. were cut down at Gourin in 1960.

20. It was not only agriculture which encouraged the destruction of the embankments; the hedges were cut down at crossroads at the demand of the Highways Department because they hindered visibility.

5. AGRICULTURAL LANDFORMS

The very long continued radical modification of the physical environment in the course of agriculture has virtually created agricultural landforms: terraces, lynchets and ridge and furrow are the three principal types.

Cultivation terraces are made on slopes that are too steep for normal farming practices. The earth is held in place by dry-stone or masonry walls. The terraces thus formed are long and narrow, following the contour lines. They bear fields, vineyards and orchards; they are comparatively rare in France, but are found in the Cévennes, the valleys of the Causses and Provence, Alpes-Maritimes, southern Auvergne and Corsica.

Many of them are now abandoned and ruined, bearing witness to their situation in marginal environments deserted by man at an early date, or to the decline of the crops with which they are associated, such as the olive and the vine. L. Gachon has pointed out the remains of terraces in the forests of Livradois, Velay and Margeride, proving that in past times, whose dates have yet to be established, cultivated land was more extensive than now.

Rideaux (lynchets and lynchet-type features) are ledges of embanked earth covered with grass or overgrown with bushes, separating two parcels of land. They are found in many regions and are particularly numerous on the chalk lands of the plain of Picardy; their height varies from a few decimetres to several metres.

They have interested geologists and geographers for almost a century, and have been interpreted in various ways. It appears that the different types of *rideaux* have different causes; the very large *rideaux*, several metres high, cannot be attributed to man; at the most he has modified them, taking advantage of natural breaks of slope, land-slip lenses or small fault-scarps in limestone regions.

Smaller *rideaux* or true lynchets are caused by an accumulation of earth as a consequence of down-slope movement resulting from cultivation. At present, owing to the concentration and consolidation of holdings, farmers are removing the lynchets by gradually levelling them away at their extremities.

Headland ridges (called *crêtes de labours* in France generally, *ackerberge* in Alsace and *chepseaux* in Poitou) are longitudinal ridges ranging from a few decimetres in height to as much as 1·5 m. at the extremities of open fields; they form an asymmetrical wave-like topography with wide troughs and well-defined narrow ridges.[21] This type of agricultural landform has been found in Alsace, in the Loire basin, the Saône plains, Poitou, Beauce, the Limagne and more generally on flat ground with clays or fine loams.

'There is no doubt about the mode of formation of these ridges: at each turn the plough throws up fragments of earth from the field on to the *tournaille* or headland. The field is thus slowly dug out while the headlands rise, and finally solifluction gives a regular concave shape to the whole parcel. The speed of this process and the height reached by the headland and the ridges obviously depend on local conditions of climate and soil, and on the initial form of the land, as well as on the type of plough and fre-

quency of ploughing in the field rotation ... it is thought that it took a minimum of ten centuries and perhaps more to form the highest *acker-berge*' (E. Juillard).

21. A headland is a strip of land at the end of the ploughed field left for convenience in turning the plough at the end of the furrows and used as a boundary. The headland ridges (*crêtes de labours*) that result from the process described in the text should not be confused with the ridges of 'ridge and furrow' that may be found within the fields. (*Note*—A. J. Hunt.)

6. THE CLASSIFICATION OF RURAL LANDSCAPES

The difficulty of identifying and classifying the rural landscapes of France will be apparent. Ideally, classification should be based on three criteria:

1. The size and shape of parcels or fields.
2. The presence or absence of enclosures.
3. The continuity or otherwise of the visible field pattern, that is, of the man-made landscape.

P. Brunet and M. C. Dionnet have given us the first maps of the rural landscapes of France. Their classification is as follows: open fields with large compact parcels; open fields with medium-sized compact parcels; open fields in quarters of elongated parcels; open fields in quarters of parcels of long strips; small open fields more or less irregular in shape; enclosed areas with very large parcels; enclosed areas with medium-sized or small parcels; semi-*bocage*; Aquitaine landscape; Aquitaine landscape with large parcels; mixed areas with various field patterns together with forest or heath; outliers of open fields in heathland.

Figure 77 gives a simplified representation of this classification; its complexity can be seen despite the generalisation necessitated by the reduced scale. More detailed maps drawn up for certain regions show very complex patterns which more closely reflect the reality. More simply, we can confine ourselves to defining the homogeneousness and the continuity or discontinuity of landscape modification by man by distinguishing: discontinuous rural landscapes, 'predetermined' rural landscapes and freely developed rural landscapes.

A. Discontinuous Rural Landscapes

In this category the area of land occupied and modified by man is greater than that of the natural landscape which, however, survives in varying degree and interrupts the continuity of the man-made landscape. This is the typical landscape of the great Alpine valleys, where the human elements are arranged in a linear fashion, and become less dense and less clearly defined as we climb the hillsides. It is also typical of plateau regions deeply incised by narrow, steep-sided gorges; here the strips of plateau surface, the flattened summits of the interfluves and the ridge-crests are the developed areas, the chequerboard pattern of the fields stopping at the edge of the valleys. To this group also belong the broken landscapes where the man-made features are interrupted by rocky humps, volcanic cones, quartzite outcrops, hills or escarpments.

To this type also belong the cleared or intermittently cleared forest lands, heathlands where the cultivated areas are separated by tracts of heath and common pasture. These heathland clearings are quite as significant as forest clearings. Both are characteristic of a large part of France. Forest-clearing landscapes are found in the North-east where forest predominates. In the Central Massif, 'east of a line running from western Livradois, along the highlands between the Loire and the Allier to Velay near the source of the Loire, the forest more or less engulfs the patches of agricultural land' (A. Fel).

Rural landscapes with 'heathland clearings' are characteristic of mixed farming areas, such

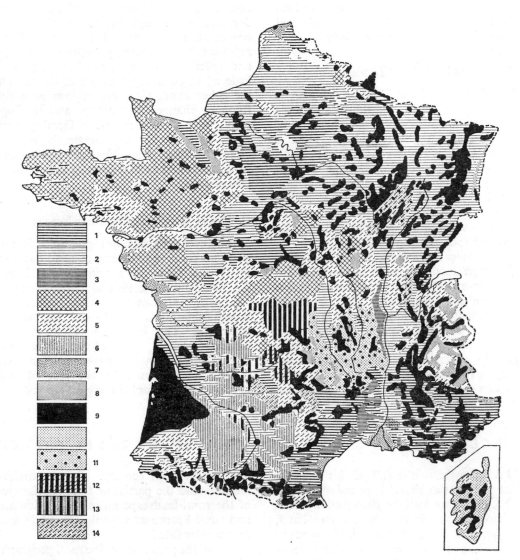

Fig. 77.   Map of rural landscapes by P. Brunet and M. C. Dionnet (simplified map by kind permission of the authors).

1. Open fields in large parcels.   2. Open fields in quarters.   3. Small irregular open fields.   4. Areas of enclosures.   5. Semi-*bocage*.   6. Aquitaine landscape.   7. Marshy areas.   8. Alpine pastures.   9. Forests.   10. Heathland and *garrigues*.   11. Blocks of open fields in heathlands.   12.   Mixture of *bocage* and forest.   13. Wooded Aquitaine landscape.   14. Mixture of *bocage* and heathland.

as the highlands of the Central Massif and the heathlands of the West, but also of regions where the lack of continuity or cultivable land is determined by physical conditions.

B. 'Predetermined' Rural Landscapes

In this category modification by man is complete or nearly so, and the field patterns are interrupted rarely or only by tracts of limited extent. But 'man-made landscape' is a generalised description that requires qualification, because development has been strongly influenced by physical factors that affect the shape and size of parcels as well as their use. In both respects these are affected by slope, relief, lithology, soil and by subaerial and subterranean hydrology.

The organisation and use of land have often been determined by these factors, so that even 'man-made' features have a more or less predetermined character. For example, there are strips of meadowland along streams and rivers, cultivated land is located on the drier interfluves, and in a typical cuesta landscape the different types of land in a commune include part of each band from the crest of a cuesta to the river in the subsequent depression at its foot.

The extent to which man-made features are determined by physical or cultural factors depends on their diversity and on the type of organisation and use of the land. Some regions are comparatively uniform in geology and relief and some types of farming have little effect on the type or use of fields. On the other hand, there are regions in which frequent changes in outcrops and in slope forms, or a particular type of farming, such as polyculture, virtually dictate the type of cultural forms. Such areas are Boulonnais, Mâconnais and certain parts of the southern folded Jura.

C. Freely Developed Rural Landscapes

Wherever geological or topographic factors exert no positive influence, cultural development can take place without restriction. Hamlets, villages, fields and meadows can be established anywhere because pedological, topographic and hydrological factors are irrelevant. This has happened in the rich farming lowland areas of the Paris basin and in some homogeneous crystalline areas of the ancient massifs; the role of man is then determinant in regard to cultural forms.

CONCLUSION—THE SPATIAL DEVELOPMENT OF RURAL FRANCE

Having come to the end of this analysis, which, being too short, is oversimplified, a geographer may well be disturbed by contradictory impressions. On the one hand, he may find the multiple criteria used to evaluate the smallest fragment of rural landscape rather unexpected but admire the close relationship between the countryman and his environment as expressed in successive forms of adjustment through the centuries which have contributed to the present landscape. On the other hand, he may be painfully conscious of being face to face with a lovely relic of the past, and be forced seriously to question the value and efficiency of an inherited agrarian organisation in the second

half of the 20th century. Do the archaic features and the partial or total fossilisation of the rural landscape mean that agriculture and rural France as a whole are condemned to a similar fate?

One of the paradoxes of the rural geography of France probably lies in the fact that those regions which have clung for longest to an archaic form of mixed farming, from which they cannot easily emerge because any attempt at modernisation would destroy the entire rural way of life, are those which have the most beautiful landscapes. They are an expression of the age-old adaptation of the peasant to his environment, a spatial organisation adjusted to an almost closed economy in which each produced his own grain, fruit, wood and sometimes wine.

Our anxiety becomes keener when we see a· rural spatial organisation that is still largely traditional in character having to stand up to the strong winds of change which are now blowing through the rural world, questioning the viability of existing systems of land-ownership and farming, and transforming the methods of cultivation.

These two divergent views of the country-side cannot long continue, and the rural land-scapes must inevitably reflect the new legal and economic structures. But the time lag may be increased by the inertia of the fixed elements of the infrastructure, services, build-ings and roads. Reorganisation of the land only partly affects the elements of a rural landscape; it does not, properly speaking, create a new agrarian structure; settlement forms in particular do not change, as the farm and the hamlet are the elements most difficult to move.

Rural depopulation, the concentration and mechanisation of farms have made out of date a spatial organisation whose roots go back into the Middle Ages. It is the farm sites and the high density of villages in relation to a greatly reduced population which hinder the enlargement of farms, slow up their moderni-sation and make investments less likely to be profitable.

Slowly the idea of a real reorganisation of the countryside is gaining ground. It would create new landscapes which would meet the economic and social needs of a rapidly changing world; 'country-planning' (rural-isme—Louis Leroy) would thus balance town-planning. Such a development would de-pend on the existence of a policy based on clearly defined conceptions and objectives for agriculture.

Rural redevelopment can follow several 'models'. Some experts envisage the reduc-tion, even the abolition, of villages and the dispersal of farms among compact holdings. This is the 'North American' or Danish solution. On the other hand, it is possible to envisage, thanks to the development of com-munications, a much sparser rural settle-ment pattern with the entire farm and non-farm population living in centres of 2,000–5,000 inhabitants, that is, large villages or cantonal towns. Cultivators would travel thence to their farms, all situated within a radius of 15 km. This may seem utopian, but it can become reality with modernisation and specialisation of farming systems. No doubt the diversity of France would allow for flexible and varied adjustments.

The Picardy village of Bosquel, south of Amiens, which was entirely destroyed in 1940, is one of the rare examples of rural redevelop-ment. Consolidation of holdings was under-taken for the second time with the aim of pro-viding farmers with large expanses of land (fig. 76). The farms have been rebuilt with entirely new layouts and arranged in a ring round the periphery of the village centre, each communicating directly with one of its large regrouped parcels of land. The village, which has also been rebuilt, houses the agricultural workers and tertiary acti-vities.

PART FIVE
INDUSTRY

I

INDUSTRIAL STRUCTURE

In 1965 the industrial population of France, with a man-power of 7,900,000, represented 41% of the active population and 16% of the total population. The corresponding numbers for Great Britain were: 12 million, 47·5%, 22%, and for Western Germany: 13,200,000, 50%, 23%.

In 1962 France had 771,316 'industrial establishments', but 339,717 of them employed no labour and 354,518 employed 1–10 wage-earners. Only 75,000 establishments had more than 10 employees, that is, one establishment per 635 inhabitants. By comparison, Germany had one per 462, Belgium one per 583 and Italy one per 659 inhabitants. In terms of density France thus has 1·34 industrial establishments per 10 km.² as compared with 2·51 for Italy, 4·78 for Germany, 5·19 for Belgium, 6·11 for the Netherlands. Of the 75,000 workshops and factories 4,785 had more than 200 employees, and only 506 had more than 1,000. Three features of French industry are apparent from these figures: the relatively low rank occupied by industry in the French economy, the comparatively low density of industrialisation, and the predominance of small and medium-sized establishments.

1. BRANCHES OF INDUSTRY

There are many ways of defining the importance of an industry, according to the point of view adopted: man-power, volume of production, measured either by weight or by value, turnover, area of factory plant. These data provide different but complementary pictures of the various branches of industry. In 1962 industrial firms employing more than 10 workers were distributed between the major branches of industry (having more than 2,000 firms) as shown in Table LVIII.

Table LIX shows the three leading characteristics side by side so that it is possible to compare the relative positions of selected branches of industry.

TABLE LVIII. BRANCHES OF INDUSTRY WHICH INCLUDE MORE THAN 2,000 FIRMS (1962)

Branch	Number of firms	%
Building	19,570	25·8
Clothing and clothing materials.	5,212	6·8
Furniture and wood products .	3,827	5·0
Textiles	3,165	4·1
Metal goods . . .	3,084	4·0
Textile allied industries . .	2,566	3·3
Foundry products, boilers, engines, pumps . . .	2,975	3·9
Chemicals	2,647	3·5
Printing and publishing . .	2,704	3·5
Machinery and machine parts .	2,560	3·3
Electrical industry . . .	2,399	3·1

TABLE LIX. CHARACTERISTICS OF SELECTED BRANCHES OF INDUSTRY

Branches	% of firms (1962)	% of industrial man-power (1962)	% of turnover (1961)
Building, public works	26	18·4	11
Metallurgy, engineering	16·9	32·2	28·4
Electrical industry	3·1	6·3	4·1
Energy industries .	2·4	3·9	11·4
Food industries . .	7·5	7	16·8
Textiles industries .	14·5	16·9	9·2
Chemical and glass industries .	4·1	6·6	8·5
Wood and furniture industries .	5	3·1	2·3

A comparison between man-power and turnover gives some idea of the varying importance of man-power. For every thousand million francs of turnover, there are 52 persons in refineries, 222 in power-stations, 250 in chemical industries, 327 in electrical industries and 700 in coal-mining. The size structure of

engaged in making railway equipment and 44% of those in electrical engineering. At the other extreme, firms with more than 500 workers employ only 29% of the foundry workers, 17% of the machine-tool and tool makers, 12% of the metal-workers. The same variation occurs in the textile industries,

TABLE LX. SIZE OF ESTABLISHMENTS IN DIFFERENT INDUSTRIES (1962)

	From 1 to 10 employees (%)	From 11 to 50 employees (%)	From 51 to 100 employees (%)	From 101 to 500 employees (%)	From 501 to 1,000 employees (%)	More than 1,000 employees (%)
Engineering and electrical industries .	10·4	16·2	8·2	25·5	14·2	27·5
Textile industry	4·8	15·6	12·6	43·6	11·7	11·7
Clothing	21·6	30·1	15·6	28·8	3·5	0·4
Furs and skins	49·9	24·7	11·5	13·9	—	—
Leather industries	17·4	32·7	12·7	28·5	8·7	—
Timber industries	27·7	36·7	14·4	17·5	3·7	—
Paper industries	4·5	18·6	12·4	46·1	18·4	—
Printing and graphic arts . . .	18·2	26·5	12·9	25·1	15·1	2·2
Miscellaneous industries . . .	6·8	16	10·2	29·6	10·8	26·6
Total, secondary industries . . .	10	18·5	10·6	29·9	10·8	20·2

the various branches of industry differs widely, and this is reflected in their density and distribution. Table LX shows the size structure of various branches of secondary industry.

The overall figures are rather striking. 39·1% of the employees in secondary industries work for firms with less than 100 employees; 29·9% for firms with 101–500 employees; and only 31% for firms with more than 500 employees. The engineering and

where establishments with more than 500 employees take 28% of the total labour force, but 78% of the workers in artificial and synthetic fibres, 31% of the jute and rope workers, 28% of the cotton workers and only 15% of the hosiery workers.

In the other industries big factories employ between 10 and 15% of the man-power, except in the fur and hides and timber industries, and in bleaching and dyeing, where they are ex-

TABLE LXI. CONCENTRATION OF UNDERTAKINGS (1960)*

Industrial classes

Petroleum	15%	of undertakings account for	98%	of turnover
Automobiles and cycles	1·3%	”	81%	”
Electrical engineering	6%	”	75%	”
Chemicals and rubber	7%	”	76%	”
Textiles	8%	”	70%	”
Printing and publishing	1·4%	”	46%	”

* Financial year 1960, according to revenue returns for firms taxed on real profits.

electrical industries are by far the most concentrated, 41·7% of the firms having more than 500 employees. The degree of concentration varies considerably, however, from industry to industry, 77% of the automobile, cycle and motor-cycle workers being in factories with more than 500 employees; also 50% of those engaged in making semi-finished non-ferrous metal products, 51% of those making semi-finished steel, 79% of those

ceptional. In all, there are only 855 factories in the secondary or 'transformatory' industries which employ 500–1,000 workers, and only 435 with more than 1,000 workers.

Conditions differ in another kind of industry like building. In a survey covering 224,000 enterprises, the *Fédération du Bâtiment* (Building Industry Federation) found that 112,700 had no employees, 88,480 employed 1–5 workers, 23,000 10–50 and 2,000 more than

50, but only 76 of these employed 500–1,000 masonry workers, and 29 more than 1,000 workers in masonry and joint undertakings. The breakdown in terms of man-power does not necessarily reflect the degree of concentration; a very small number of large concerns often accounts for most of the turnover (Table LXI).

2. DISTRIBUTION OF INDUSTRIAL ESTABLISHMENTS OVER THE DEPARTMENTS

Figure 78 shows the general pattern of distribution of industrial undertakings in the departments (1962), by showing the proportion in each department of the total number of establishments.[1] At first sight there appears to be a very wide diffusion of industry over the whole country. Only 4 departments show very small proportions, having less than cause of disequilibrium in the industrial geography of France. The industrialised departments do not all lie in one zone. It is significant that the list includes 3 out of 4 Breton departments, Dordogne, Alpes-Maritimes and Charente-Maritime, as well as departments which are more traditionally regarded as industrial.

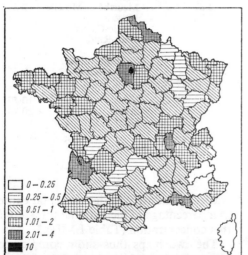

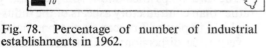

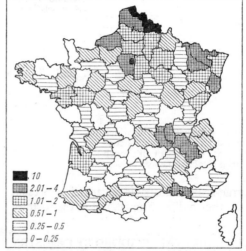

Fig. 78. Percentage of number of industrial establishments in 1962.

Fig. 79. Percentage of number of establishments with more than 200 employees.

0·26% of the total: Hautes-Alpes, Basses-Alpes, Corsica, Lozère.

Some degree of concentration of industry is, however, discernible in this apparent uniformity. Twenty-six departments show figures over 1%, and together contain more than half (57·05) of the industrial establishments; 6 departments have more than 2% each; the department of Seine itself with a figure of 15·7% can hardly be regarded as a

The picture changes entirely when, neglecting the small and medium-sized establishments, the distribution of factories with more than 200 workers is analysed (fig. 79). There is an amazing contrast between the two maps. On the second map France appears, once again, to be divided from Seine-Maritime to Bouches-du-Rhône. Northern and eastern France contribute 78% of all industrial production, compared with 22% from the

South and West. The number of departments possessing more than 1 % of these large industrial establishments is the same, but nearly three quarters of them (74·6%) are concentrated in the North and East. The concentrations of population shown on the population maps reappear on this map: Nord–Pas-de-Calais (14·45%), Isère–Rhône–Loire (7·98%), Seine–Seine-et-Oise (23·73%).

industrial concentrations, but as isolated factories. In 1962 all departments of France, including Corsica, had at least one industrial establishment with more than 200 employees. Charente had 27, Finistère 29, Indre-et-Loire 28, Haute-Saône 27. The concentration would be seen to be even more striking if only the very large establishments were being considered. The following analysis of the value

TABLE LXII. INDUSTRIAL ESTABLISHMENTS IN FRANCE IN 1962

Departmental % of total industrial establishments in France	All industrial establishments		Industrial establishments with more than 200 employees	
	Number of departments	%	Number of departments	%
–1%	64	42·95	64	25·35
1–2%	20	26·75	14	16·54
>2	Bouches-du-Rhône 2·19		Bouches-du-Rhône 2·02	
	Gironde 2·23		Isère 2·52	
	Nord 3·54		Loire 2·27	
	Rhône 2·87		Meurthe-et-Moselle 2·23	
	Seine-et-Oise 3·75		Moselle 2·34	
			Pas-de-Calais 4·05	
			Haut-Rhin 2·27	
			Rhône 3·19	
			Seine-Maritime 3·09	
			Seine-et-Oise 3·55	
	Total 5	14·58	Total 10	27·53
>10	Seine 1	15·72	Nord 10·40	
			Seine 20·18	
			Total 2	30·58
Number of departments in which the industrial establishments constitute more than 1% of all French industrial establishments	26	57·05	26	74·65

Large-scale industry is nevertheless present in the other half of France, not in the form of

TABLE LXIII. VALUE ADDED BY INDUSTRY AS A PERCENTAGE OF THE NATIONAL TOTAL*

	%
Seine, Seine-et-Oise, Seine-et-Marne . .	26
Nord and Pas-de-Calais	13·5
Lorraine and Alsace (4 departments) . .	8
Rhône, Loire, Isère, Bouches-du-Rhône .	10
Seine-Maritime	2·6
Doubs	1·5
Gironde	1·4
Loire-Atlantique	1·4
Haute-Garonne	1
Puy-de-Dôme	1

* The value added equals the sum of wages and social costs, payments to sinking-funds, indirect taxes and profits (after Courtin and Maillet: *Économie géographique*).

added by industry in departments, expressed as a percentage of the national total, confirms this concentration (Table LXIII).[2]

The two maps thus show complementary rather than contradictory aspects of the industrial geography of France: on the one hand, a very wide dispersion; and on the other, a particular concentration in a score of departments. Industry is present everywhere, and the outlines of industrial buildings may be seen in such varied urban and rural environments and in such inexplicable locations that France seems to offer specimen examples of paradoxical industrial location, from the rubber-tyre factories at Clermont-Ferrand to the wrought-iron working of Vimeu, from the umbrella works of Aurillac to the jute factories of Picardy. But at the same time the bulk of French industry is concentrated in one quarter of the departments. These two characteristics reappear into her aspects of French industry.

France is not an industrial power to the degree that England and Germany are, but she possesses factories which put her in the first rank for certain branches of industry. At Noguères (near Lacq), for example, there is the largest aluminium factory in Europe. The Établissements Brissonneau et Lotz, apparently illogically located at La Rochelle, are one of the most modern railway rolling-stock workshops in Europe. Aurillac is a leading centre of the umbrella industry. The leading European plywood factory is at Niort, and grew up from a little timber-processing factory founded in 1923. There were 50 workmen then; now there are 2,500. The largest European ethylene plant is at Lavera, and the largest sulphuric acid plants are at Saint-Fons and Le Havre.

1. Industrial establishments employing more than 10 wage-earners.

2. In 1960 the undertakings in 12 departments together accounted for nearly 75% of the gross turnover of all French undertakings.

II

INDUSTRIAL LOCATION

In the majority of cases, research into the factors governing the location of an industrial establishment in France necessitates an historical study which will often lead back for several centuries and the unravelling of a tangle of causes of all kinds, in which the least logical are apparently the most important.

The geographical and structural dispersal of French industry is the consequence of the antiquity of industrialisation in the country. It is therefore necessary to proceed chronologically and to trace the changes which occurred in industrial locations and to identify contemporary survivals of former locations.

1. LOCATION FACTORS BEFORE THE INDUSTRIAL REVOLUTION

The industrial geography of France under the Old Regime was very different from the present distribution of factories. Industry was still at the craft stage and had rarely reached the factory stage. Motive power and energy were provided by wood, running water and wind. Coal as yet played a minor part.[3]

Industry then existed in numerous locations. Forests furnished wood and charcoal; running water in rivers large or small enabled mills, tilt-hammers and forges to operate. For example, the abundant and fast-flowing rivers passing through gorges in the foothills of the Pyrenees attracted the siting of many 'mills': Catalan (Biscayan) forges, spinning-mills, jet-mills and paper-mills. The purity of its water and abundance of workers made the valley of the Salat a paper-making district from the 17th century onwards. Bas-Couserans was a flax-growing district, so it made and exported linen. Volvestre and the Pays d'Olines made woollen fabrics. Fourteen mills, three saws, five hemp-beaters, one fulling-mill and three forges were working with power provided by the Giffre at Taninges (Haute-Savoie) in 1771.

Metallurgy which served to supply local markets also depended on local resources—surface deposits of iron ore (siderolithic ores derived from Eocene deposits in the Jurassic limestones and ferruginous oolites), wood

from the forests and running water to temper the metal, turn water-wheels and operate tilt-hammers.

Figure 80 shows the distribution of 600 sites inventoried in 1789. The regions with least industry are the Mediterranean South, which had no forests, most of the Central Massif, which was already stripped of its forests, and the Paris basin. The best endowed regions are those where outcrops of ferruginous Jurassic Palaeozoic rocks bore extensive forests, or were near forested areas: Thiérache, a depression in the Ardennes, Haute-Marne, Haute-Saône, Vosges, Morvan, Jura, Nivernais, Bourbonnais (the steel industry at Montluçon used wood from the forest of Tronçais), Bas-Dauphiné, Périgord, Nontronnais, Limousin, the northern and north-western borders of the Central Massif, the Normandy *Bocage*, the Ariège zone of the Pyrenees. There were 1,000 metallurgical establishments in France in 1789—forges, blast-furnaces and tilt-hammers. The departments with the largest numbers were Nièvre (138), Isère (75), Haute-Marne (72), Dordogne (67), Côte-d'Or (55), Ariège (53), Haute-Savoie (50), Haute-Vienne (34), Vosges (33), Meuse (32), Ardennes (27), Landes (24), Jura (24), Doubs (22), Cher (21).

Many parts of France had specialised craft

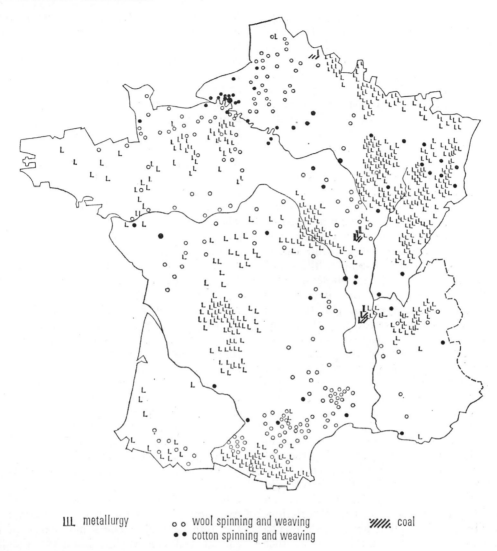

| ⊔⊔ metallurgy | o o wool spinning and weaving | ⫽⫽⫽ coal |
| | • • cotton spinning and weaving | |

Fig. 80. Localisation of industry in France about 1780. (Source: Ch. Morazé, *Les Français et la République*, A. Colin, 1956)

industries: textiles at Tarare and Thizy, lace and cloth in Livradois, glassware in Nivernais, cloth in Maine (fig. 80); the cloth-looms of Haut-Languedoc were located around Lodève, Saint-Pons, Carcassonne and Aubenas in the 17th century. The ribbon trade of Saint-Étienne and Saint-Chamond grew up in the 18th century through the use of Swiss looms. The clockmaking industry of the Jura and the Arve valley was introduced in the 18th century by emigrants from Geneva and Neufchâtel. The precious-stone cutting industry around Saint-Claude was linked to the clockmaking industry of the Pays de Gex. The turners and wood carvers of the Saint-Claude and Oyonnax areas depended upon the presence of box woods on the limestone slopes. The cloth industry had already made the name and

M

fortune of many cities in the 13th century; Arras, Douai, Lille, Cambrai and Saint-Omer all flourished through the workshops of families of weavers, fullers, dyers, welders and traders. In 1492 Amiens acquired the high-warp tapestry, gold brocade and silk indus-tries from Tournai. In the 16th century Valenciennes, Cambrai and Saint-Quentin welcomed weavers from Courtrai, Ghent and Ypres to work at looms for fine-cloth. The silk industry took root in 1536, when letters-patent of Francis I gave the municipality of Lyons privileges for its silk workers.

These origins reveal one of the permanent features of French industrialisation: the fact that foreigners often played a decisive role by fostering industrial development in regions near the frontiers. For example, 'the art of weaving silk was brought in whole with the weavers, the looms, and the material for treating the silk and dyeing it' (M. Rondot). Milling establishments were set up at Virieux, Privas and Aubenas at the end of the 17th century by a spinner from Bologna. The spread of weaving was at all events a new development; under the Old Regime it was an urban industry. An order-in-council authorised the peasants to weave in 1762, and so broke up the weaving guilds.

Heavy industry developed in the 17th and 18th centuries without experiencing the up-surge or spontaneity which characterised it in Great Britain. It is a fact that France did not appear to be a fertile ground for the spread of industry before the Industrial Revolution. It may be questioned whether this was due to psychological causes mentioned in another chapter, or to political and religious causes, as some historians suggest. ('France was not industrial to the same extent that she was not Protestant' (G. Duveau).)

The State founded manufacturing industries right from the start, from Colbert down to Napoleon I. There was an arms factory at Saint-Étienne from 1515, and royal factories multiplied in the 17th century: arms at Tulle, tapestries at Aubusson, cloth at Sedan (1642), Carcassonne and Lodève,[4] and arsenals in Nivernais. The Van Robais family left

Middelburg and settled at Abbeville in 1664. Mirror manufacture was established at Saint-Gobain in 1692; this creative work was en-couraged by royal patronage in the 18th century. Turgot set up the porcelain factory at Limoges in 1771.

The ports were important industrial centres under the Old Regime, for they were favoured by their colonial trade. Bordeaux, Nantes, Marseilles, Le Havre and Rouen all shared in this traffic (triangular trade), and encouraged the development of industries (sugar refineries, soap factories) at the ports which imported raw materials,[5] or at some distance from them. The flour-mills, the cloth trade and the silk trade of Montauban were within the sphere of influence of Bordeaux. Many present-day industrial locations are inherited from these 17th- and 18th-century foundations. The inheritance varies; it may be in the form of industrial infrastructure, labour supply, local specialisation, local or regional capitalisation. The old industrial sites have been kept in use for more than a century by an uninterrupted succession of firms and the adaptation of their activities to the circumstances of their day, and this explains the high incidence of sur-vivals on the present map.

The existence of a textile craft tradition, hemp weaving, flax and wool spinning and weaving, was often at the origin of the siting of industry. The Basque linen woven in factories in Basses-Pyrénées descends in a direct line from the fabrics which have been made on farms in the Basque country from the 16th century. The same is true of the sandal and canvas-shoe industry; the fac-tories at Aliermont (clocks, precision en-gineering, turning, foundries) between the Pays de Bray and the forest of Eu are explained by the fact that clockmakers from Dieppe settled there in the 17th century. The workshops and a factory making buttons and fancy wooden articles at Méru (Oise), still busy in the middle of the 20th century, descend from the workshops of trinket makers (making fans, brushes and frames for binocu-lars) who prospered there from the beginning of the 18th century and supplied Paris and the

Court at Versailles with their wares. Glove-makers, the forebears of those of the 20th century, were working at Grenoble from the end of the 16th century.

The port industries of the 18th century determined the site of industries established in the following centuries: semolina, pre-serves, chemical products. Functional con-tinuity is paralleled by a striking continuity in ownership: 62 of the 289 metal-working companies existing in 1927 originated in con-cerns founded before 1789. But these early industrial developments have also given rise to the founding of new branches of industry at existing locations. These are 'superim-posed' industries, which have made use of the traditional skills of labour, the sites, even the old industrial buildings, and sometimes benefited from the accumulation of capital in the locality or the region. The brass and wrought iron foundries of Vimeu, for example, made use of a labour supply with a textile tradition. However, industry has not sur-vived in all old craft areas: the former textile industries of some parts of the South have disappeared.

3. The first text relating to the working of coal in the Le Creusot coalfield dates from 1510. The *Compagnie des mines d'Anzin* dates from 1756.

4. Cardinal Fleury (who was born in the district) granted Lodève a monopoly of military cloth.

5. About 20 refineries were treating sugar cane from the 'islands' at Nantes in 1788.

2. THE INDUSTRIAL REVOLUTION

The term 'Industrial Revolution' is a con-venient but vague expression covering a series of technical and economic changes which occurred over more than a century.

A. The First Phase

In England these changes began in the 18th century. At that time the first signs of the Industrial Revolution were already percept-ible, but the Revolution and the Empire then isolated France for a quarter of a century from its English exemplar and source of inspiration.

The beginnings of the French cotton indus-try go back to English emigrants; John Kay, the inventor of the flying shuttle, settled in France in 1747 and introduced the carding machine (1771). John Holker founded a cotton factory at Rouen in 1750. In 1770 another Englishman set up blast furnaces at the cannon foundry at Indret. The English Milne family settled at Neuville-sur-Saône in 1779 and introduced the first Ark-wright's waterframe (water-powered spinning machine). In 1781 the Maréchal de Castries, minister for the Navy, 'gave orders to Messrs. Wendel, Touffaire and Wilkinson to travel through different provinces in order to choose a suitable place for establishing blast-furnaces and forges, in which it is proposed to exploit the iron-mines by means of coal'. Mont-cenis (Le Creusot), where there was already a royal glass-works, was regarded as the best place, and in 1782 the king authorised 'the establishment of blast-furnaces to smelt iron by the English method to feed the royal foundry at Indret'. This installation at Le Creusot in 1785 was the first industrial instal-lation of the English type to be set up. The forges of Vierzon were founded in 1780 by the Count of Artois, and those at Montataire near Creil were set up in 1791 by the English-man Taylor.

But history was about to hold back the true beginnings of industrial revolution in France for twenty years. France was handi-capped technically and financially by the absence of a merchant fleet. The French Industrial Revolution was retarded in com-parison with that in England, but it also took place under different conditions. These were less favourable in France: 'the population was strongly attached to the soil, in spite of changes in agriculture, and commercial capi-talism was less developed and orientated towards other sources of profit . . . behind the virtual wall of tariff protection from 1806 to 1860 initiative suffered from a lack of competition which lulled the manufacturers into a treacherous somnolence' (C. Fohlen).

The energy situation was also different; coal was not in fact a new source of energy, quickly developed and giving rise to rapid geographical changes. It played a negligible part until 1850 for various reasons: the habitual immobility of industrialists, whose workshops operated without fear of competition, the standstill of the metal market and the inadequacy of means of transport. France was far from being one large coalfield and her coalfields were peripheral or situated in rugged regions, away from easily utilisable rivers. Above all, the contemporary coalfield map of France only faintly resembled the modern map. The Loire coalfields still produced one third of French coal output towards the middle of the 19th century, whereas the North produced only 23%. All the industrial economy of France was organised about the Loire coalfields, as the early canals bear witness. The coalfields of Blanzy and the Loire basin were regarded, though on a very different scale, as the French Ruhr.

Coal was of secondary importance, limited to the coalfields themselves, to their vicinity and to those few cities and regions which could get coal from them on favourable economic terms; the railway system was very fragmentary until 1860 and a true railway network radiated only from Paris for a distance of about 200 km., linking the North and Basse-Seine with Paris, which was just beginning its industrial expansion. Picardy, Champagne, Normandy and Paris were favoured by proximity to the coalfields of the North. Paris had 50 cotton-spinning mills with 150,000 spindles around 1815; in 1834 Amiens had 43 mills spinning combed wool. The development of the coalfield industrial regions was just beginning and along with it changes in the steel industry and the introduction of the steam engine. In 1815 Chaptal, director of industry at the Ministry of the Interior, decided to set up a coke-fired steel works at Saint-Étienne. He put it in charge of the Englishman Jackson, and also opened a 'Miners' School'.

The first coke-fired blast-furnaces appeared in 1818 at Saint-Étienne and at Pont-l'Évêque, and to the east of Vienne, using ore from La Voulte (Ardèche) and coal from the Loire field. Others followed in quick succession: at Hayange (1822), at Decazeville and Aubin (1826), at La Voulte (1826), at L'Horme (Loire) in 1827, at Ferrière-la-Grande (local ore and coke from the Borinage) in 1830, at Tamaris (Gard) in 1832, at Bessèges (Gard) in 1835 and at Denain (using ore from the Boulonnais) in 1837. The steam engine spread by degrees. It appeared in a cotton-spinning mill at Lille in 1817; in a wool-spinning mill at Fourmies in 1839; and in 1849 at Tarare, where a velvet factory was built and equipped with a steam engine. A flax-spinning mill was opened by the Englishman Maberly in Picardy in 1838; a second one by another Englishman at Pont-Rémy. In 1843 two Scotsmen, the Baxter brothers, founded the first French jute-spinning mill at Ailly-sur-Somme. These steam engines were used only in areas where coal could be easily obtained. This was the case only on or near the coalfields where the first concentration of industry naturally occurred (Table LXIV).

TABLE LXIV. NUMBER OF STEAM
ENGINES

					1834	1838
Nord	.	.	.	.	200	422
Seine	.	.	.	.	173	300
Loire	.	.	.	.	169	225
Seine-Inférieure		.	.	108	221
Haut-Rhin	.	.	.	.	48	80

However, French industry remained largely traditional in its structure and location. Beside these coke metallurgical plants, which were strictly localised, charcoal metallurgy remained general in all the other areas where it had existed for centuries. Haute-Marne was the leading department for iron production in 1815. In 1819 Haute-Saône had 36 blast-furnaces, 43 refining furnaces, 23 tilt-hammer forges, 7 foundries, 4 wire-drawing works. In 1826, for example, Great Britain had 2 charcoal blast-furnaces and 280 coke blast-furnaces, when France had 379 and 4 respectively. In 1820, 65 factories were using steam engines. In 1840 only 41 out of 462 blast-furnaces were using coke. In 1850 the departments of Doubs, Jura, Côte-d'Or, Haute-Marne and Haute-Saône were still the 'land of the charcoal-iron industries'.

Also, because of the lack of coal and means of transport, 'there were a great many water-mills at the time of George Sand and Balzac; flour-mills, tan- and tanning-mills, fulling-mills, water-powered tilts and forges, mills to work circular saws, paper-mills, mills for 'malleting' the ripe, dry clover to husk the seed; mills producing woad, a dyer's colour obtained by crushing plants of the *cruciferae* order' (G. Duveau).

Most streams with a sufficient gradient were virtual industrial streets. Spinning-mills were concentrated along them from the beginning of the century, if they could not obtain coal. More than 1,200 factories were powered by water in the department of Eure in 1862. During the following hundred years and more, these mills created fixed sites and many factories were set up in their old buildings. There were about 30 flour-mills and oil-crushing mills along the little stream called the Airaines in Picardy in 1852. In 1924 the following were still in operation: a flour-mill, a mill for husking hop-trefoil and clover seed, a sawmill, a power-station; and other buildings now contained factories and workshops (velvet, cabinet making).

The most widespread industrial structure during the first half of the 19th century was the *fabrique*;[6] 'a *fabrique* was an organisation of traders who bought raw material or manu-factured products (yarn for warp and weft) and distributed them to workers grouped in little workshops or working in their own dwellings, in the town or in the country. What gave a *fabrique* its unity was its depend-ence on a particular town or city where spinning was usually carried on and where business was transacted' (C. Fohlen). Rheims, Roubaix, Sedan, Amiens and Cholet were all places with *fabriques*. During the decade after 1850 Cholet was the centre of a *fabrique* spread over 120 communes and employing from 45,000 to 50,000 workers.

New processes were already being installed and reinforcing the hold of the textile indus-tries on their existing locations. Cotton took the place of flax in the West from Cholet to Falaise. Flax and hemp gave way to jute in Picardy (1843). Elsewhere wool declined without replacement by other raw materials (Calvados, Manche, Loir-et-Cher, Hérault). It was then that the textile region of the East (Alsace-Vosges) began to expand. Weaving took root there at the beginning of the 19th century, and spinning followed later during the last years of the Empire and the Restora-tion. In contrast to the position in other textile regions, these beginnings were due entirely to the initiative of entrepreneurs, not at all to survivals. Mechanical weaving struck death blows to the domestic weaving industry of many rural areas. The industry became concentrated in Mulhouse, Rouen, Roubaix and Rheims. Nevertheless, although Rheims had 900 mechanical looms in 1860, 22,500 hand looms continued to operate in the surrounding villages.

The Lyons silk trade illustrates the develop-ment of a particular kind of geographical structure in an industry. Silk weaving was mainly an urban craft until 1825. Of the 27,000 looms in operation in 1824, 22,000 were in Lyons and its suburbs. Changes in fashion, foreign competition and crises be-tween 1825 and 1860 led to the number of urban looms being progressively reduced and to the spread of looms over the countryside. After 1837, 18,000 looms were already at work in the villages of Saône-et-Loire, Isère, Drôme and Ain.

The industrial geography of France there-fore had two facets in the middle of the 19th century, and these have persisted down to the present day. Industries retained a character-istically wide dispersal sustained by local traditions, infrastructures, entrepreneurs and pools of labour. At the same time the emerg-ence of coalfields and other areas of industrial concentration became progressively more pronounced. These areas gave birth to the new class of industrial employers in the second half of the century. The nuclei of these bodies of employers were the owners of factories that were already localised, spinners, bleachers and dyers, dealers in textile materials and manufacturing wholesalers. The old *fabrique* sites became centres of the textile industry, where weaving was grouped around the spinning-mills.

Most contemporary industrial centres were already on the map more than a century ago —textile mills or factory centres with locations inherited from old textile foundations. But France has been greatly handicapped in the gestation of new industry by one capital fact: neither the northern coalfields nor the coalfields of Lorraine played a decisive part in these early decades. The whole organisation of industry was orientated towards the coalfields of the Centre.

B. The Second Phase

The second half of the 19th century qualifies as the age of industrial revolution much more than the first half. In the thirty years between 1860 and 1890 the face of industrial France underwent profound and enduring modification. The financial organisations which were about to open up France to the great capitalist companies and to the banks were already established. The new capitalism had both French and foreign roots. Without underestimating the part played by French initiative, once again it is necessary to acknowledge the importance of the contribution of foreign countries not only in the form of capital investment but also through the introduction of technicians and machines, at first illegally, then openly. It was not by chance, nor because of geographical advantages, that industrialisation at that stage reinforced the peripheral character of the distribution of French industries. The English invested at Calais and in the north-west of the Paris basin, the Belgians invested in the valley of the Sambre; Swiss bankers aided the industrialists of Alsace and Franche-Comté.

Industries developed in relation to availability of finance and financial centres; family companies were formed, and built factories in the vicinity of the financial centre. This kind of capitalism permitted the spread and adoption of all the changes which progress and inventions made possible. Coal, the steam engine, the railway and the canal together carried France into a new phase of industrial evolution.

Coal consumption increased from 7·5 million tons in 1851 to 15 million in 1861 and to 21 million in 1869. The number of establishments possessing steam engines increased from 6,543 in 1852 to 22,851 in 1870; the number of those possessing steam engines employed by industry rose from 6,080 in 1852 to 27,088 in 1870 and to 84,000 in 1900. Exploitation of the northern coalfield came about slowly; in 1851 production was strictly limited to the department of Nord and amounted to only 1 million tons. The deposits in Pas-de-Calais came into production in 1854, but output remained below 5 million tons until 1872 and did not reach 10 million tons until 1886. The figure had risen to 20 million tons by 1900, and three quarters of this tonnage came from Pas-de-Calais. This is why the northern coalfield supplied the northern region only for the first three quarters of the 19th century; its peripheral situation was unfavourable for the wider distribution of coal. The building of canals and railways eventually allowed coal to be transported at economically favourable prices while English coal was shipped to the western and south-western ports as soon as they were opened to it without tariff discrimination.

The transport infrastructure, developed during this period, accentuated the disequilibrium between the two parts of France. Wherever canals facilitated the transport of coal and heavy products, industrial sites appreciated in value; old factories began to use coal and turned to new activities. In western France and the South, away from the port areas, coal was hard to obtain and costly. Regions doubly endowed with coal and a dense network of canals and railways were particularly favoured. This was the case in the North.[7]

In each of these areas opportunities for industrialisation were discounted by the railways. Cities and towns—and they existed —which refused to let the railway come through deliberately cut themselves off from the Industrial Revolution. The tariff policy of the railway companies played as decisive a role as did the mere building of the lines. By favouring transport of heavy products over long distances, the freight charges permitted manufacturing industries to be set up far from raw materials and sources of power. The development of heavy industry in the Paris region was largely due to the *ad valorem* charges adopted by the railway companies from the beginning. 'The railway was therefore the instrument which allowed the capitalist system to spread freely, to extend its influence to all forms of human activity and to impose itself in quick succession on all parts of the country, causing all the remains of older economic structures to collapse' (M. Wolkowitsch). This twofold stimulus from coal supplies and transport facilities caused a revolution in the industrial geography of France. A number of small industrial centres disappeared and some of the industries disappeared from particular towns: textiles from Limoges, metallurgy from Poitou and Berry. On the other hand, new industrial centres were founded or developed spontaneously.

Coke was substituted for charcoal in the largest blast-furnaces after 1850, and steel began to dethrone cast iron and soft iron. New steel centres began to appear over the coalfields: at Saint-Étienne, in the Alès coalfield, at Decazeville. In the same way blast-furnaces were installed at Pamiers and Tarascon after the 1860s and were fed by railborne coal from Carmaux, Graissessac and Decazeville. However, deposits of ore remained scattered. An inquiry made in 1858 found that French iron ores made an average journey of 12 km. to the furnaces!

A coastal iron industry developed at the same time. In most cases sites were chosen in relation to the import of iron ore. Those at Boucau (1881), at Pauillac, at Trignac and Outreau (near Boulogne-sur-Mer) and at Les Dunes (near Dunkirk) used Spanish ore from Bilbao and Pyrenean ores. Those at Balaruc, Beaucaire (1874) and Saint-Louis used Spanish and Algerian ores. Conversely, the blast-furnaces at Caen used Norman ore, but English coke. These coastal iron works developed when the industry needed non-phosphoric ore, before the discoveries of Thomas and Gilchrist were put to use; they were not integrated works, for the cast-iron was sent to the steel works in the interior. In some of the old iron-works areas the industry continued to develop by adaptation to new techniques. This was the case in the Bourbonnais–Nivernais area, Haute-Saône, Champagne and Ardenne, coal being obtained either from local deposits, as at Commentry, or brought in without difficulty by canal and rail. The first Bessemer converter was installed in Dordogne in 1858. By 1878 France had 24 converters: 11 in Loire, 7 at Commentry, 2 at Denain. In 1870 the four chief centres of the iron and steel industry were Le Creusot, Hayange, Denain-Anzin and Saint-Étienne. After them came the less important Alès, Decazeville, Saut-du-Tarn, Fourchambault, Montluçon, Châtillon-sur-Seine and Marseilles (fig. 81).

Mechanical weaving spread more quickly after 1860, at the expense of hand weaving. The result was a geographical concentration of weaving in the *fabrique* towns: Cholet, La Ferté-Macé, Flers, Condé, Rouen, Bolbec, Lillebonne, Roubaix, Sainte-Marie (Alsace). Fourmies, at the gates of Champagne and near the northern coalfield, became one of the leading woollen centres. In 1910 it accounted for 47% of French production of combed wool, and factories grew up there like mushrooms: 42 combing machines in 7 factories in 1852, 630 combing machines in 26 factories in 1890, 12 spinning-mills in 1844, 76 in 1875; 51,900 spindles in 1844, 112,000 in 1855, 650,000 in 1867 and 930,000 in 1890. In 1860, 40,000 craftsmen were working in the quadrilateral Dieppe–Yvetot–Bolbec–Totes in

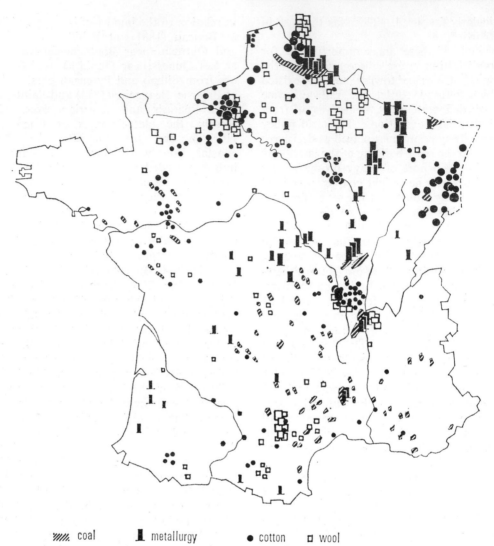

////. coal   ▌ metallurgy   ● cotton   ◻ wool

Fig. 81. Localisation of industry in France about 1880. (Source: Ch. Morazé, *Les Français et la République*, A. Colin, 1956)

the Pays de Caux in association with the spinning-mills and weavers of Rouen.

The process of concentration took place at the same time as the Industrial Revolution. The Franco-British commercial treaty of 1860 and the American Civil War accelerated this process by helping the stronger firms to survive or adapt themselves to the technological changes. There were 233 spinning-mills in Seine-Maritime in 1859, but only 185 in 1869

(47 at Rouen, 24 at Oissel). There were 547 beet-sugar refineries in 1838, but only 288 a dozen years later. The number of combed-wool spinning-mills at Amiens fell from 43 in 1834 to 16 in 1864.

C. The Third Phase

Shortly before the end of the 19th century, the Industrial Revolution entered a third phase with the arrival of hydro-electric power, the beginnings of iron-ore working in Lorraine, new minerals, such as aluminium, and new industrial activities, especially chemical industries. The industrial geography of France was once more modified, and these new factors finally gave it its present features, notably the concentration of activities to the east of the Le Havre–Marseilles line. Until 1848 the iron industry of Lorraine was only the prolongation of that of the past. The Lorraine orefield was not exploited and industrialised until late. There were two main reasons for this: the production of iron between 1840 and 1880 was then considered to be generally sufficient, since English iron products penetrated France after 1860; and the iron companies of the central region disliked the ore, partly because of its composition.

French production of iron ore reached a ceiling of 3 million tons between 1857 and 1881, whereas Great Britain produced 14 million tons from 1869 onwards. The Gilchrist–Thomas process, which enabled the ore of Lorraine to be brought into use, dates from 1881. Thomas steel furnaces were built between 1880 and 1913, and the exploitation of iron ore did not get under way until after that date: 5,448,000 tons in 1900, 22 million tons in 1913, 50 million tons in 1929. Exploitation of the Lorraine deposits severely shook the traditional iron-working centres. Those located on the coast or on surface ore-deposits were forced to decline by developments on an orefield with substantial reserves. The low metal content of the ore made it costly to transport, and so helped to concentrate the industry. Blast-furnaces multiplied in the Lorraine mining area, but the iron industry of Lorraine did not acquire Thomas steel works until 1900. In spite of its advantages Lorraine did not become the scene of really powerful industrial development; 'the low iron content of the ores, the absence of waterways and rail freight charges all assigned a strictly regional role to these deposits of international value' (C. Prêcheur).

The old iron-works regions reacted by specialisation and became centres for secondary metallurgy only.[8] The Barguillière valley in the Ariège zone of the Pyrenees contained 4 Catalan forges, 12 tilt-hammers and 60 nail factories during the 19th century; in 1931 there remained only 2 tilt-hammers and about 15 nail factories; in 1960 only 1 nail factory survived. Exploitation of bauxite deposits in the South-east was stimulated by the discovery of aluminium. The 4 French aluminium factories are situated near the bauxite deposits and lignite mines: at Gardanne, La Barasse, Saint-Louis-des-Aygalades (Bouches-du-Rhône) and Salindres (Gard).

Finally, hydro-electricity, the latest of the new developments, brought a new source of power. The first industrial hydro-electric plant was installed at Lancey near Grenoble in 1869, by Aristide Bergès. One by one the best sites were equipped with barrages and penstocks. The industrial centres in the Alps came into being because the water resources were developed by industrialists at their own expense, and proximity to the generating plants kept the price of electricity low. All the industries which are big consumers of electricity were installed and developed there: the chlorine industry, the electro-chemical industry, the electro-metallurgical industry. The Alpine generating plants were providing them with 500,000 h.p. from 1911 onwards. This is why aluminium factories are located in Alpine and Pyrenean valleys. Before nationalisation, Péchiney had 7 hydro-electric plants in Maurienne and 2 in the Pyrenean valley of Vicdessos.

Wherever it was available under good economic conditions, electricity brought further industrialisation, at the same time permitting a return to a dispersed pattern of location. Thus the silk works in the Lyons region changed directly from manual operation to electric motors, without being forced to concentrate to the degree that steam power would have necessitated. The silk works of Lyonnais had 33,000 looms in 1866, but only 12,000 in 1888, and 4,200 in 1914. In Isère the big factories broke up into small independent works (62 factories in 1880, 357 in 1920).

*

The textile industry played a decisive role in the industrial geography of France in the 19th century by its association with certain other branches of industry. These branches began by being complementary to textiles, but developed and acquired autonomous existence. So, for example, the chemical industries developed from dyeing and finishing, and mechanical engineering originated in the making of textile machinery.

Each branch of industry thus played its part in creating 'poles of industrial development'; one factory led to another as a result of reciprocal needs and secondary consequences, complementary functions, and interdependence. Associations of industries were formed on the coalfields, linking coal, metallurgical, glass and chemical industries. The existence of an unemployed surplus female or male labour was often enough to cause the appearance of new activities, such as the ready-made clothing industry which employed the wives and daughters of miners. Secondary causes, by chance or otherwise, intervened throughout this period of the Industrial Revolution to favour the rise of new industrial foci. The availability of men employed on building railway lines was frequently a factor promoting rapid industrialisation. This happened at Creil after the northern railway system was finished in 1848.

Industrialisation was inhibited along frontiers by war and fear of war. Conversely, the changes in the eastern frontier of France favoured other regions. Immediately after the 1870–1 war thousands of emigrants from Alsace flocked to Belfort, whose factories were established by large Mulhouse firms (*Société alsacienne de constructions mécaniques, Dollfus Mieg et Cie*).

The First World War led to a strong concentration of labour and equipment in cities such as Lyons, where firms took refuge from the danger of invasion (*Ateliers de Delle, Compagnie Électro-mécanique, Hotchkiss*) in order to produce munitions. The shoe industry took root in Limoges during the First World War and replaced the china industry, which was already in a state of crisis. The iron indus-

tries (blast-furnaces of Rouen) and chemical (tar) works of the lower Seine date from 1914, when the factories in the North were occupied by the Germans. The first chlorine factories were built in 1914–18 to meet military needs, namely the threat of mustard gas.

The firm of Brissonneau et Lotz, already mentioned (p. 341), is at La Rochelle because the *Societé des Entreprises Industrielles Charentaises* was financially linked with the Standard Steel Car Company of Pittsburgh. During the First World War this latter firm supplied most of the rolling stock for French railways and the United States Army in France. The parts were landed at La Pallice and assembled in workshops at La Rochelle. The firm was bought by the Pullman company in 1931, passed into the control of the Rothschild Bank in 1947 and was taken over by Brissonneau in 1957.

But these general and secondary causes are not sufficient to account for all industrial locations. 'Personal' factors play a large part in such a country, inhabited for so long, with numerous industrial centres and with more and more diversified industrial activities. The personal factors or causes are:

1. Intervention by politicians in favour of their own constituencies or towns.

2. The simple fact that a man of initiative with enough capital to invest lived on the spot. It is well known that the rubber industry was founded at Clermont-Ferrand because a local industrialist married MacIntosh's niece, and his own factory, a sugar refinery, had been burned down. Mazamet treated three quarters of the world production of sheep skins between 1860 and 1930 because in 1851 an industrialist of that little wool town got the idea of importing some sheep skins from abroad. His initiative, favoured by the abundance and purity of the water, resulted in the unusual development of an industrial centre for the treatment of imported skins 170 km. from the sea.

Recognition should also be given to the part played by local interests and psychological considerations in the uneven industrial

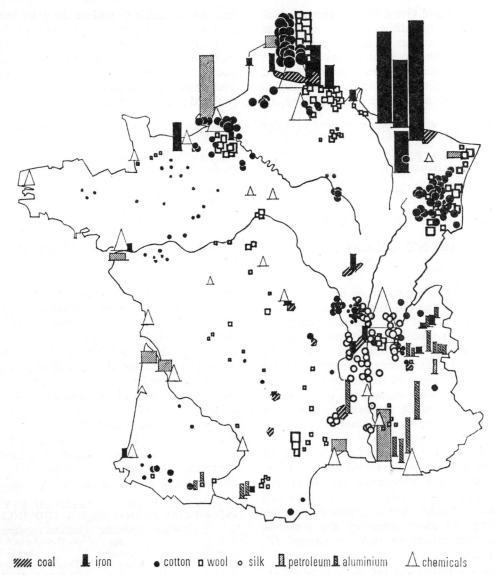

//// coal   **I** iron   ● cotton □ wool   ○ silk **⊞** petroleum **⊞** aluminium   △ chemicals

Fig. 82.   Localisation of industry in France about 1930.   (Source: Ch. Morazé, *Les Français et la République*, A. Colin, 1956)

development of French towns and cities. Just as some places refused to allow railways, so well-established landed ruling classes, anxious to maintain the political and social *status quo,* also refused to allow industries to be founded in some towns. This explains the industrial backwardness of Dijon and many other cities.

The industrial geography of France was clearly outlined on the map by the eve of the First World War. The industrial regions were established, and so were the industrial towns, with their employing classes, working classes, their new landscapes and townscapes (fig. 82).

But the French Industrial Revolution did not have as great an effect as its counterparts in Germany and Great Britain, through lack of abundant quantities of coal and large numbers of workers at a very early stage. Moreover, the Industrial Revolution in France depended on eccentrically located power and mineral resources which lacked good communications to other regions, so

that it was unable to replace the older industrial centres completely. Thanks to local tradition and established communications, these found ways and means of adaptation and survival, so that numerous small industrial centres remained side by side with the coalfield industrial regions.

6. There is no direct English equivalent for this term. Similar units of organisation began to form in England, but they failed to develop because the early arrival of the factory system removed their raison d'être (Note—A. J. Hunt).

7. In contrast to Alsace, Normandy and the Central Massif, the North had no rivers that could be used to produce power because of their low gradients. Before steam, the first mechanical looms were powered by teams of horses.

8. The metallurgical industry of Périgord put up a prolonged resistance to the new industrial regions. The last blast-furnace in Périgord (at Savignac-Ledrier) was not shut down until 1930.

3. RECENT CHANGES IN THE INDUSTRIAL GEOGRAPHY OF FRANCE

This existing complex of industrial sites developed during the last three centuries and the early years of the present century has already been modified since the end of the Second World War. This has been all the more spectacular because French industry was virtually static from 1920 to 1945. In a period of general stagnation, demographic and economic, such as there was until 1939 there was no question of establishing or even extending factories.[9]

Much of the backwardness of French industry today is attributable to the total lack of vitality of the inter-war period; 'from 1918 to 1939 everything took place as if the French elites and public were incapable of comprehending, let alone assessing, the contents, needs and effects of industrialisation' (F. Perroux).

The exceptions are the more noteworthy; the aircraft and munitions factories of the Paris region were decentralised after 1935 for strategical reasons, and so were the factories of O.N.I.A. (*Office National des Industries de l'Azote*—National Office of the Nitrogen Industries). The consequences were important. Thanks to this policy, the south-western and central regions acquired 62 factories, employing 10,000 workers. The establishment of artificial-fibre factories also

dates from the inter-war period. They were founded mainly in the suburban fringe of Lyons, at Décines, Saint-Maurice-de-Beynost, Neuville-sur-Saône, Vaulx-en-Velin, Venissieux, Lyon-Vaise and Irigny. This location is due to many factors: sites suitable for getting water supplies and disposal of effluent; the coal available to factories in Loire, the acids of Saint-Fons, the nearness of the *fabrique* of Lyonnais, which was a better outlet between 1920 and 1930 than the cotton and wool industries of the North and the East.

France was excluded from all the discoveries in industrial technology made in

TABLE LXV. DEVELOPMENT OF NEW INDUSTRIAL PLANTS IN THE PROVINCES[10]

| | Number of permits* | | Predicted employment in these factories | |
| | | For founding | | In the new |
Years	Total†	factories	Total†	factories
1956	905	215	32,698	16,426
1957	993	233	27,315	12,077
1958	1,087	274	38,736	16,491
1959	1,011	253	43,086	19,772
1960	1,359	323	49,040	25,135
1961	1,545	515	68,850	40,045
1962	1,570	466	72,990	37,220
1963	1,680	686	70,480	38,480
1964	2,142	776	86,250	45,200
1965	2,265	802	87,710	37,340

* Permits for industrial establishments with more than 500 m.² or more than 50 employees.

† For new factories and extensions to existing factories.

Britain and the United States between 1939 and 1945, and the consequent setback has been difficult to make up since. For example, continuous-strip rolling-mills were installed in France after the Second World War, but they operated from 1923 in the United States and in Great Britain from 1938.

France experienced a new phase of industrial development after the Second World War. The annual increase in industrial production other than building was 6·9% between 1949 and 1960. This growth was accompanied by factory building and factory extension (Table LXV).

This post-war industrialisation took place under particular conditions:

1. The location factors were no longer the same as they were at the beginning of the century.

2. Financial and technical resources had become more concentrated.

3. Admittance of foreign capital had been accelerated by the setting up of the Common Market.

4. Industrial conversions had modified the aspect of certain towns and regions.

5. A policy of indirect control of the geographical distribution of industry had been introduced.

A. Changes in the Factors of Location

The factors of industrial location were very different, after the Second World War and an interruption of nearly twenty-five years, from those which operated during the three phases of the industrial revolution.

POWER FACTORS

Coal has ceased to be the great supplier of industry; other sources of energy have been developed in competition with it and attract industry. These other sources are mainly electricity and petroleum products.

The use of electricity has become less and less dependent on proximity to places where it is generated, for several reasons: the introduction of high-tension, alternating-current transmission lines with reduced head losses,[11]

the nationalisation of some factories, which deprived them of the use of generating dams built for them in the Alps, and the tariff policy for electricity, which has greatly diminished the advantages of location near to the power-stations. One of the chief consequences has been the downstream shift of the electro-chemical industry of the Romanche, and of Alpine industries generally, towards the valley of the Rhône. New chemical industries, with unlimited prospects, attach themselves directly to sources of energy, the carbo-chemical industry to the coalfields, around coking plants, and the petro-chemical industry around oil refineries and natural-gas bores. The petro-chemical industry did not develop in France until the refineries possessed plants capable of producing the sought-after hydro-carbons by chemical synthesis (catalytic cracking, steam-cracking, catalytic reforming, which together ensure the supply of olefins, diolefins and aromatic hydrocarbons). The products of the petro-chemical industry have many uses: as detergents, solvents, synthetic tannins, resins, polyesters, nylon, tergal, octylic alcohols, carbon black, synthetic rubber, plastic materials.

In general, power is a highly variable factor in industry and affects location to a varying degree. The direct energy used makes up more than 10% of the cost of the products of the following branches of industry:[12] nitrogenous fertilisers, 30%; steel, 25%; iron and steel products, 19%; aluminium, 17%; bricks and tiles, 15·8%; cement and plaster, 15·5%; stone and ceramic products, 14·7%; paper pulp, 13·6%; glass, 12·4%. In most cases, however, power is of minor importance, accounting for less than 2% of the cost of such products as tyres, 1·7%; pharmaceutical products, 1·0%; footwear, 0·2%; motor vehicles, 1·4%; industrial machines, 0·8%.

Power costs are inversely proportional to the elaborateness of the product; marked differences in power costs occur, however, from region to region. In 1961 the cost of transporting fuel-oil varied from −9 francs (Berre–Marseilles area) to +48·5 francs a ton (Saint-Dié area). Thermal units produced from industrial coal cost 30% more at Rheims than at Marseilles, 15% more than at Paris, 20% more than at Strasbourg or Lyons. If we take the price per kwh. under full load in winter at a tension of 60 kv. as an example, the lowest prices are charged in Ariège, Haute-Garonne, Hautes-Pyrénées; the highest prices are paid by consumers in the departments of the West (Brittany and Manche). Until gas arrived from Lacq, the West was therefore always at a disadvantage.

RAW MATERIALS

In many branches of industry 'raw materials' as a location factor seem to be far less restrictive with the development of synthetic products, the recovery of materials from industrial waste and improvements in manufactured products themselves. Manufactured products tend to become lighter, thereby reducing the factor of transport cost. Some sources of raw materials have been superseded. The clearest example is that of iron ore. A new coastal iron and steel industry has been created for the second time, at the expense of Lorraine, by the discovery of very rich deposits in Africa, which can be transported at low cost by sea in ships of 60,000 tons.

The first of these new plants began operations at Dunkirk at the beginning of 1963; the choice of location is explained by the fact that it belongs to the Usinor group and that its site is near other plants on the northern coalfield. Extensive works were undertaken in its construction: part of the site was reclaimed from the sea; the sand of the coastal dune-belt had to be consolidated to support the weight of blast-furnaces and rolling-mills; a dock had to be dredged for ore ships at the port, and water supplies had to be laid on. There are projects for other coastal iron and steel works, Nantes and Marseilles being two possible sites. The site at Marseilles (Fos) was proposed as a means of recompensing the city for its loss of traffic and business after Algeria gained independence.

Water plays an increasingly important part in industrial geography.[13] The demand for it becomes greater and greater, consumption doubling every fifteen years, and more concentrated in a few industrial regions. The task of supplying water to the industrial complex at Dunkirk has posed grave problems, resolved by the decision to build a dam on the Aa at Harchelles. Sites for industries which consume great quantities of water are selected in relation to the availability of water. Thus two rubber and tyre factories—Dunlop and Goodyear—have been built at Amiens, which has abundant water from the chalk, and from the Somme. Valleys with large, regularly flowing rivers and sedimentary areas with abundant ground-water both attract factories. They replace the old industrial regions whose extent was determined by the disposition of coal seams, with industrial valleys which make more use of the advantages of arteries of circulation whose water is used both as a means of transport and as a raw material.

MEANS OF TRANSPORT

There has been a considerable diversification of means of transport during the last twenty years, in comparison with conditions prevailing during the 19th-century industrial revolution. Then, there were only the railways and the waterways, and truck transport came in at a late date. Today there are not only roads but also aircraft, pipelines, overhead-cable railways, and telephones and radio, which permit operation by remote control and rapid communication between factories.[14] Industrial decentralisation and establishments of new factories have been frequent to the west of the Paris region because the motorway to the West allows rapid communication with the capital, where head offices have remained.

The same is true with regard to air links: aerodromes are now one of the infrastructure elements accounting for the location of some of the new factories. Factory managers—especially managers of factories which are subsidiaries of foreign firms—wish to site their plants near international airports (Geneva, Nice, Paris). The tendency for products to become lighter and smaller also reduces the relative importance of transport costs. Transport makes up more than 4% of the cost price (direct and indirect costs) only in the following branches of industry: paper pulp, 12·8%; furniture, 9%; iron and steel products, 7·7%; building materials, 7·5%; mineral chemical products, 4·4%.

LABOUR

Labour costs carry less weight then they used to do in the calculation of location costs in relation to costs of production. The index of labour requirements per ton of metal produced fell from 45 to 21·9 between 1951 and 1959. Whereas, in 1947, 52 man-hours were needed per ton of aluminium produced, only 15·5 were needed in 1955.[15] Labour requirements are small compared with the value of production in the most recent industries, chemical and electronic, and they have little effect on cost prices. For example, the chemical industry employs 230,000 workers for a turnover of 175 million francs.

Labour is theoretically more mobile in the 20th century than it was in the 19th century and has the benefit of varied collective and individual means of communication. However, the political tendencies of the workers have always played a part in the siting of factories. New factory development is restricted in an area where, rightly or wrongly, the workers have the reputation of belonging to the extreme Left, or simply of being militant and demanding. It is partly for this reason that some towns have difficulty in establishing new industries.

INDUSTRIAL SITES

Location factors have changed similarly as a result of developments in industrial technology. Factories get bigger and bigger and require a large amount of space. The large motor works have left the Paris area chiefly because they could not find room for expansion. By moving to the provinces they can obtain large areas of land, including reserves for later developments, which safeguard the future of the industry.

Such changes have not, however, involved the majority of small and medium-sized factories, and the availability of existing industrial buildings has become an even more important location factor than it used to be. Between 1950 and 1960, 472 provincial factories (1,772,600 m.²) which had been shut down were brought back into use.

THE ENVIRONMENT

Environmental factors and amenities claim attention and will continue to do so to an increasing extent. The beauty of the countryside, its use for recreation, facilities for communication with the capital or the nearest large city, university and cultural institutions, the amount of sun and nearness to the sea, snowfields and lakes have now all become factors of industrial location. They are clearly not decisive ones, but, other economic conditions being equal, they turn the scale one way or the other. The strength of location factors does not differ very greatly from one town to another in France, so that these marginal factors become decisive. The existence of attractive 'infrastructures' is becoming more and more a determining factor of industrial location.

RELATIONS BETWEEN FACTORIES

Today, single factories are progressively losing their geographical isolation. The siting of a factory is influenced by the distribution of all the factories situated above it and below it in the chain of production to which it belongs. A motor-vehicle factory cannot lie too far away from all the sub-contracting firms which provide it with factory components and accessories. Financial concentration and reorganisation within a firm have the same effects. A firm has no desire to have its factories scattered over all parts of the country. Quite the reverse; it prefers them to be near the headquarters, or at least in the same region, on the same line of communication. The factories of the Kléber-Colombes group were originally situated at Colombes (Paris) and Decize (Nièvre); its new factories are at Troyes, Nevers, Trilport.

Michelin has aligned its new factories between Paris and Clermont-Ferrand, at Bourges and Orleans.

Broadly speaking, factories are not easily established in an area where there is not an 'industrial climate', where they will be effectively isolated or where their problems will appear unfamiliar. Such isolation becomes very important when any movement of workers and technicians is involved. A factory is becoming more and more a part of a larger organisation, integrated with a complex of ancillary buildings and connections, not only with managements and sub-contractors but also with laboratories and research departments.

INCENTIVES

Since the end of the war, and especially during the 1950s, industrialists have been attracted by many incentives offered by municipalities, departmental, regional and national authorities, which helped them to become established in their respective regions and communes by advances, exemptions from military service, offers of land and accommodation. These incentives were an important element in regional policies, but too many post-war industrial locations were the result of over-bidding by municipalities and chambers of commerce, which, in order to develop their unindustrialised areas, acceded to all the demands made by interested firms and accepted all the financial sacrifices that they entailed.

On drawing up the balance-sheet of post-war industrial locations we must admit that in most cases marginal, secondary and often abnormal factors were the decisive ones, and not the factors that economists prefer to enumerate.[16]

B. The Process of Concentration

The industrial map of France has been altered by strong tendencies to concentration of production in fewer units.

Technological developments necessitate concentration in larger production units, and changes in production which entail the closure of some workshops and the regrouping of others. Thus, in the department of Nord alone there were 3,000 breweries in 1914, but only 139 in 1957. There were 20 French rayon factories in 1950, but only 11 in 1959. Some factories are closed down in some branches of industry because they are below the optimum size to take advantage of technical advances. The aluminium factory at Saint-Auban, Basses-Alpes, had a capacity of 40,000 tons a year, but the threshold production for profitable operation is now 100,000 tons. Likewise, several arms factories were shut down at Chatellerault, causing difficult problems of conversion and redeployment of labour.

The concentration of finance which, as we have seen, has been going on since the middle of the last century has been accelerated during the last fifteen years by the internationalisation of investments and the setting up of the Common Market. Mergers between firms, specialisation agreements, share-taking in French and foreign companies, all have multiplied. They have taken place on the most spectacular scale in two key industries: in steel, Usinor, founded in 1948 by Denain-Anzin and Les Forges du Nord-Est, was merged with Lorraine-Escaut in 1966; and in industrial chemicals, Péchiney and Saint-Gobain concluded agreements defining their respective responsibilities in 1959 when a subsidiary was set up to co-ordinate their research and extension programmes, to conduct their marketing operations and to take charge of new projects. Public bodies encourage these concentrations and associations for they increase the productivity of the factories and their competitiveness on the international front. In 1967 alone there were around 60 cases of the regrouping or merging of companies. These mergers and agreements sometimes result in the creation of a total monopoly, as exemplified by the aluminium industry. All these measures of concentration have important repercussions on the location of industry. Reorganisation plans cause factories to be closed and several manufactures may be brought together in a single factory. The concentration of technical and financial resources must in any case be closely linked. Their incidence depends on the type of manufacture; some types are best adapted to dispersal in more or less autonomous factories, each making a particular product. The Navarre paper-mill concern, for instance, has ten factories scattered throughout France, but Grand-Quevilly produces thin paper for commercial printing, Voiron superfine paper, parchment paper and special papers, Roanne satin and coated paper, Monfourat (Gironde) fine esparto papers, Champ-sur-Drac cardboard, Bristol board and playing cards.[17]

The Thomson–Houston company employs 15,000 persons in very widely spread factories which reflect the expansion of the firm; foundry castings and kitchen ranges have been made in the Ardennes since 1892; domestic electrical equipment, especially refrigerators, are made at Lesquin (near Lille) in a factory which the company has owned since 1900. Electric radiators and kitchen equipment have been made at Jarville since 1918. Six factories were set up in the provinces between 1936 and 1959; at Chauny-Bohain, in Aisne, and at Rheims, Thomson makes copper wire and cables; the company's precision engineering works and factories making sealed compressors for refrigerators are concentrated at Nevers, where they employ more than 2,000 people. An annexe to this factory has been set up at Moulins. The Thomson company built a huge factory at Angers in 1957 for making radio and television sets. In 1960 the company took the decision to transfer its factories producing commercial electronic equipment from Paris, where they had been concentrated up to then. Three factories were acquired for this purpose at Orleans, Aix-en-Provence and Thonon, where transistors, diodes and electronic tubes are produced; another factory was built at Laval in 1962. But Paris is still the unchallenged centre of laboratories for advanced training, technological research and the assembly of complex electronic machines.

The Thomson companies conduct research into radar and make radar equipment at Bagneux and Sartrouville; it makes its Hertzian tubes and radio and television transmitters at Gennevilliers; its high-power tubes are made in Paris itself.

C. Admittance of Foreign Capital

After hesitating and even opposing foreign industrial investments, official circles realised that such an attitude was illogical, since from 1st July 1968 products of factories situated in the member states of the Common Market have been able to enter France without duty. Also generous facilities have been granted since 1965 to foreign companies wishing to build factories or to participate in existing firms. Such is the case with the new factory of semi-conductors built at Toulouse by the Motorola company (Phoenix).

D. Closures and Conversions of Factories

The traditional industries which made their fortunes during the Industrial Revolution—textiles, footwear, glass—experienced some difficult times when faced with young industries in full expansion. Many textile factories shut their doors in the old bastions of the North, the East and Normandy. The glass industry disappeared from Creil, the footwear industry from Amiens and from west of the northern coalfield. In 1954 the cotton industry drew up a fifteen-year plan for conversion and modernisation. Two million spindles were put out of use and nearly 300 factories were closed or converted. Old spindles have been replaced at the rate of 100,000 a year; the number of looms has been reduced by 10% every five years and brought down from 175,000 to 80,000. Altogether between 1952 and 1964 the number of cotton spinning-mills fell from 320 to 238 and that of cloth-mills from 977 to 705. In order to facilitate the modernisation of traditional industrial activities and of industrial regions, 'Associations for Industrial Expansion' have been created since 1966 in Nord, Lorraine, Loire and the

Alès coalfield. Their chief purpose is to encourage the influx of new industries into the coalmining areas. *Charbonnages de France* have been authorised to participate in new industries.

E. The Policy of Indirect Control of the Geographical Distribution of Industry

Ever since the end of the war, governments have pursued a policy that was clearly aimed at producing decentralisation of industry, in conformity with national planning policy as a whole. Its aim was, almost exclusively, to restrict the growing concentration of industry in the Paris region.

Innumerable measures have been adopted for this purpose:

1. In 1954: loans, bonuses and interest allowances to finance decentralisation operations; subsidies to cover the cost of training and transferring personnel.

2. In 1955: the institution of a permit from the Ministry of Building for all industrial buildings of more than 500 m.^{2}.

3. In 1959: this preliminary permit was required for building offices and setting up industries in existing localities.

4. In 1960: the introduction of a premium (50–100 francs), according to zone, for each m.^{2} of factory floor or office space put out of use, and of a tax (100–200 francs) on the establishment of offices and factories, state aid usually being granted in the form of premiums and loans each time that industrial investments lead to the creation of new employment. In 1964 differential scales of assistance towards industrialisation were set up for the whole country.

Such industrial decentralisation operations created 100,000 jobs between 1952 and 1960, that is, 1% of the wage-earners in industry. The result may seem small, but in the French context it deserves careful analysis. Table LXVI shows the balance-sheet of operations since 1950. The industries which agreed to share in decentralisation are mostly expanding light industries. Of the 601 decentralisation

operations carried out between 1950 and 1959, 375 were concerned with the engineering, electrical, electronic, chemical and rubber industries.

TABLE LXVI. INDUSTRIAL DECENTRALISATION OPERATIONS[10]

Starting year of operations	Number	Jobs created At 31st December 1964	At the end of the operation
1950–4	44	23,260	28,505
1955–8	358	71,865	93,960
1959–62	826	88,710	140,810
1963	253	12,180	41,920
1964	196	2,290	21,810
1965	201		19,780 *
1966	215		17,222 *
1967	180		17,262 *

* Jobs created in the next three years.

A breakdown of the 146,000 jobs created outside the Paris region between 1950 and 1959 gives the following results: 40,450 in the motor industry, 16,555 in the mechanical and structural engineering industries, 8,720 in precision industries, 30,400 in electrical, radio-electric and electronic industries, 13,700 in chemical and allied industries, 11,400 in ready-made clothing industries. Out of 785 industrial decentralisation operations between 1950 and 1960 (inclusive), 400 plants were set up at a distance of less than 200 km. (88 at less than 100 km., 179 at 100–150 km. and 133 at 150–200 km.); 385 were installed at distances over 200 km., 348 of them between 200 and 400 km. The new industries were established mainly in a ring of departments around Seine-et-Oise, Seine-et-Marne and Seine, most of them in Eure, Somme, Loiret and Loir-et-Cher. This location pattern shows that, although firms were willing to decentralise their factories, they were not prepared to stretch the umbilical cords which linked the factories to their head offices in Paris, nor to move away from the dynamic areas of the Common Market merely to revitalise the West and the South-west of France (fig. 83).

These impressive and efficacious operations were carried out successfully within their limits. The first steps towards industrial decentralisation were taken between 1950 and

1953, when the Renault company transferred workshops to Le Mans and the factory increased the number of its workers from 3,000 to 9,000; when a Citroen factory was built at Rennes, the Motobécane concern moved out to Saint-Quentin, and Gillette to Annecy. Since 1960 the industrialisation of Brittany has been speeded up, and above all more diversified, for until then only Fougères and Rennes had benefited by dispersal of industry

ties, the faults lay in persuading firms to shift factories into areas without an industrial 'climate' where the population could neither understand their problems nor assimilate them into their society. Municipal councils and chambers of commerce contemplated the coming of factories only from the point of view of the rates. On the other side, some firms looked upon decentralisation only as a convenient way of modernising at the expense

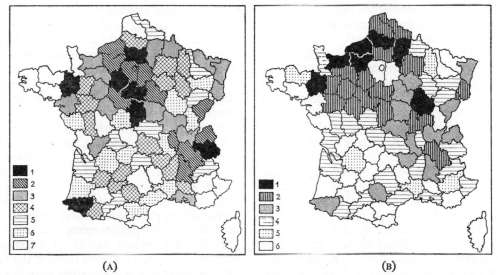

(A)   (B)

Fig. 83.   Factories established or enlarged in ten years: 1950–60 (square metres of industrial floor space per person working in the industry).
1. 4 and more.   2. From 3 to 4.   3. From 2·5 to 3.   4. From 2 to 2·5.   5. From 1·5 to 2.   6. From 1 to 1·5.   7. Less than 1.
B. The result of ten years of industrial decentralisation (number of jobs created).
1. More than 5,000.   2. From 2,000 to 5,000.   3. From 1,000 to 2,000.   4. From 200 to 1,000.   5. From 100 to 200.   6. Less than 100.

from the Paris region. The C.S.F. at Brest, Alsthom at Lorient, Flaminaire at Redon, C.N.E.T. at Lannion, Joint français at Saint-Brieuc and Olida at Loudéac were the spearheads of this industrialisation, which has broken out of the 200-km. circle; but it has also reached smaller centres as a result of sub-contracting.

It cannot be denied that errors were made, both through narrow authoritarianism and through over-simplification of the facts of the problem. On the side of the public authori-

of the State and of taking the maximum advantage of the facilities it offered. The founding of new factories is brought about by the dynamism and the spirit of initiative of a small number of men, who act on their own, sometimes without regard to existing institutions, often in the face of opposition or without help from chambers of commerce and local authorities, which are more anxious to protect their own interests and their majorities than they are to secure a future for their districts or towns. On the other hand, the presence of influential politicians has enabled some towns to secure fast-growing and profitable industries. This is what explains the surprisingly uneven distribution of industry resulting from this policy. Thanks to well-directed efforts, a small town like Château-du-Loir has been able to acquire several decentralised firms: the Promécam company from Saint-Denis, the A.R.O. works and the Rotary company from Ivry-sur-Seine.

Only too often the result of these developments has been a dangerous over-dispersal of industry, a scattering of decentralised firms among too many local centres. Shifts to the provinces were often determined, especially in the early days of the decentralisation policy, by the presence of available industrial buildings or by the designation of problem areas and of areas for special development. Many firms settled in towns affected by the crisis in the textile industry: Amiens, Rheims, Elbeuf. The *Compagnie des machines Bull* set up one of its branches at Belfort, in buildings of the Dollfus Mieg textile firm. At all events, decentralisation of industry led to the building of factories with an aggregate floor-space of 1,632,511 m.² between 1950 and 1959, more than the space obtained by reoccupation of untenanted factories. Local authorities and chambers of commerce gradually became more keen to offer prepared industrial sites to firms willing to leave the Paris region. But the very big firms do without financial help from public authorities and freely put their factories wherever they wish, without submitting to the demands of government planning policy.

The decentralisation of firms was not necessarily accompanied by movement of their employees, although this was the chief objective of the policy, which was intended to slow down the excessive rate of growth of the Paris conurbation. Each decentralised factory took only 7 or 8 employees with it. These were largely administrative personnel, whereas the workers easily found other jobs under the prevailing conditions of overemployment which will last until the numerous post-war generation comes of age. To judge by the rate in recent years, decentralisation is taking less than 2,000 employees away from Paris every year. Decentralised factories have sometimes recovered part of the available labour force, which was either compelled to move considerable distances without gaining any financial advantages or to take up very different occupations than those for which it was trained. This was the case, for example, at Fourmies, but in areas of diversified industries the advantages of zoned wages and work in a large city can keep a labour force permanently attached to its working area. In this case new firms do not find the labour they expect, and often regain only the least qualified, and female workers.

In any case, Parisian industry has not stopped growing, and it absorbs 20,000 work people from the provinces every year. Thus, the number of industrial establishments in the Paris region employing more than 1,000 persons (S.N.C.F. and public administration not included) rose from 135 at the end of 1954 to 155 at the end of 1960, and the number of workers employed by them rose by 63,000. In the city of Paris, over the same period, the number of big establishments rose from 50 (121,300 employees) to 57 (141,200 employees). However, Paris's share of the total amount of *authorised* industrial building fell considerably from 37% in 1955 to 19·5% in 1957, 17·8% in 1959 and 13% in 1961.[18]

F. The Results

All these circumstances, new location factors and changes through concentration, conversion and decentralisation, have led to the rise of new industrial areas and towns on French soil. The preeminence of the old industrial regions has been challenged. The new industrial locations result from the combination of all the circumstances examined above. It is worth quoting examples to illustrate the considerations that may govern the choice of a location.

The Timken company, making tapered roller bearings, had decided to build a new factory (the old one was at Asnières) and to transfer the management there. In order to choose a site for the new plant,

'the company's experts spent a whole winter travelling about France in all directions making inquiries of municipalities and prefectures, and recording the characteristics of each locality in terms of a number of factors which are listed here: firmness of the ground; price of land; prospects for the planning of a properly equipped industrial area by the municipality; date by which this is likely to be done; local situation in respect of building firms and building materials; architects; population; unemployment; availability of labour within a radius of 15 km.; state of industries in the area; level of wages; type of labour in the area; activity of trades unions and employers' associations; political interests of the municipality; hotels having rooms with bath and water closet, availability of accommodation, cultural facilities (schools, etc.); places of worship, entertainment facilities, shopping facilities and cost of living; hospitals and doctors; climatic conditions; fire services; activities of the local chamber of commerce; banks; lawyers and solicitors; post offices; insurance facilities; situation in relation to the Common Market; facilities for transport to other countries by road, rail and air; road transport services; local suppliers and sub-contractors; attitude of the local authorities. After eliminating Saint-Quentin because it had a Communist municipality, Nantes because of extremely conflicting social interests, and then Châlons-sur-Marne, Châteauroux and Saint-Étienne—the remainder of the leading contenders—the Timken company finally chose Colmar. Although Saint-Étienne is situated in a special redevelopment area, the American company preferred Colmar in the belief that its long-term advantages, technical (abundant labour and suitable land) as much as economic (centrality within the Common Market) and financial (willingness of the municipality to sell land on very favourable terms), were financially better than it might have obtained from the French government in the form of subsidies or credit by adopting the other choice' (R. Lemoine).[19]

In 1963 the Renault company had to choose a site for a new factory. Dijon, Nantes and Le Havre were all considered viable after many other possible towns had been rejected. Eventually, Le Havre was chosen for the following reasons: the low freight charges on parts brought from the factories at Billancourt and Flins; the relatively low cost of distributing assembled vehicles; finally, managerial convenience, it being possible to visit all the company's factories in one day by travelling from Paris to Le Havre by way of Cléon and Le Mans.

Which regions have benefited particularly from the present period of industrialisation?

1. The provinces surrounding the Paris region: Normandy, Picardy, Champagne, the Orléanais, Marne, Touraine, Anjou (Radio Technique at Caen, L.M.T. at Laval, Schneider at Le Mans, Thomson and Bull at Angers, Dunlop, Goodyear, Bendix at Amiens). The valley of the lower Seine has particularly benefited by the proximity of the Paris region, for which it is the sea outlet, by the proximity of the port facilities at both Rouen and Le Havre, and of refineries built before the war. Stemming from these, the petrochemical industry has developed at Grand'-Couronne, Port-Jérome (7 factories), Gonfreville (2 factories). Port-Jérome is notable for possessing the first synthetic (Butyl) rubber factory built in France (1959). Other industries have taken root in the valley of the Seine, between Paris and Le Havre.

2. The East of France: Lorraine, Alsace, Burgundy, Franche-Comté. Here the key factor has been geographical position with regard to the economic unification of Europe. After the Treaty of Rome came into force, Alsace received a first wave of industrial developments, mainly of German Saarland firms. Many American firms came later. Besides the Timken company already mentioned, which went to Colmar, Remington-Rand went to Huttenheim (1959: 340 persons, electric razors), Hanserman went to Koenigschoffen (mobile metal partitions), Controls France to Schirmeck (1961: 100 persons, regulating devices), Polymer Corporation to Wantzenau (1962: 170 persons), Pétro-chimie to Woerth-sur-Sauer (1961: 130 persons), Société Minoc to Lauterbourg (1959: 145 persons, chemical products, fungicides, resins). The opening of two new refineries represents the first development of the petro-chemical industry at a distance from sea-ports. Burgundy—and Dijon in particular—have acquired several electronic factories. The Compagnie Générale de T.S.F. (C.S.F.) has set up three concerns at Dijon, mainly employing female workers. Other factories are envisaged at Beaune, Seurre, Auxonne and Genlis.

3. The Rhône valley and the Alpine valleys have greatly benefited from industrial decentralisation and expansion. Besides purely economic attractions, such as the value of the Rhône valley routeway, there were also psychological motives for this: proximity to big French and foreign cities (Geneva and its international airport); the mountain environment with its opportunities for the development of winter and summer tourism. These reasons account for new industrial developments at Annecy (Gillette, Aspro), Cluses, Bonneville, Thonon (Houston), Évian (detergents, Lensbourg) and the swarm of wood-turning workshops in the valley of the Arve. The shores of the Étang de Berre, between the Rhône and Marseilles, have become the site of an important petroleum and petro-chemical industries zone. These refineries are being surrounded by factories producing isopropanol and acetone, dedocylbenzine, carbon black, olefins and polythene. Since 1962 Berre has possessed the second French synthetic rubber factory, where the Société des Élastomères de synthèse produces Cariflex S.B.R.

4. The exploitation of the gas deposits at Lacq has had important repercussions on the industrial development of the South-west. Ugine and its subsidiary S.P.A. have expanded the chemical works which already existed at Lannemezan, by increasing production of ammonia and setting up a methanol plant. O.N.I.A. and the Pierrefitte company have considerably increased their production of nitrogenous fertilisers in their factories at Toulouse and Pierrefitte.

Above all, a big chemical complex has been built up around Lacq. The Société Aqui-taine-chimie was financed jointly by O.N.I.A., Pierrefitte, Saint-Gobain and Péchiney, the Bank of Paris and the Netherlands. The company makes ammonia and acetylene and sends its residual gas to another company, Méthanolacq (Aquitaine-chimie and Kuhlmann), for making methanol. The gas at Lacq has not attracted manufacturing industries. Acetylene is transformed on the spot into vinyl chloride and acetaldehyde, the former then being sent to the factories at Saint-Fons (Lyons) and at Saint-Auban (Durance), and the latter to factories at Péage-du-Roussillon (south of Vienne, on the Rhône) and at Melle. The ethylene is used by the Société éthylène-plastiques for making polyethylenes. Benzine is turned into cyclohexane and manufactured at Péage-du-Roussillon and Chalampé (near Mulhouse).

On the other hand, some regions have suffered 'de-industrialisation', such as the Pyrenees, some of the Alpine valleys, the North, where the mining and textile industries have been affected, and Languedoc.

Examples in Languedoc: 'An enumeration is the best way—dry and monotonous though it may be—to show the relentless ubiquity of the phenomenon: abandonment since 1948 of the lignite mines of La Caunette and La Matte, the coal-mines of Plaisance and the mines at Ceilhes, abandonment of the glass-works at Bousquet-d'Orb and Pont-Saint-Esprit, of the gas-works at Montpellier and Béziers; closure of a score of textiles factories at places like Lodève, Béziers, Clermont-l'Hérault, Montpellier, Sommières and Nîmes; closure of several biscuit factories at Montpellier, basket factories at Brunelle, breweries at Arles and Biterre, liquorice factories and distilleries, cooperages and weighing-machine works, fertiliser factories, icecream factories, taweries, and canneries' (R. Dugrand).

Between 1950 and 1960 the *Direction de l'Aménagement du territoire* (department for national planning) counted 2,800 closed factories. These factories were abandoned by the textile industry (349 establishments), the metallurgical industry (197 old foundries) and by other industries including old mills and distilleries (326 establishments) and sawmills (148 establishments).

Post-war industrialisation had a twofold effect: diversification of industrial activities in over-specialised regions and some hiving-off of factories from the old industrial regions; Parisian and provincial firms have been persuaded to set up new factories or to integrate existing ones by conversion. For example, the Radiotechnique firm hived off an electronic tubes factory to Chartres in 1953 (1,147 persons employed on 1st December 1960); a radio and television factory to Rambouillet in 1954 (842 persons); an electronic components factory to Évreux in 1955 (951 persons); a television and cathode tube factory to Dreux (1,242 persons) and a spare parts factory to Nogent-le-Rotrou in 1956 (592 persons); a semi-conductors factory to Caen in 1957 (1,480 persons).

Too much hope had been placed in industrial decentralisation. It was a mistake to expect it to provide a new equilibrium in the distribution of French industry. This industrial decentralisation policy was too 'liberal' and too 'vague'. It could not save or revive the old industrial areas which were in a state of crisis, nor force developments on areas hitherto untouched by industrialisation. This was the case with industrial centres such as Decazeville, the Lower Loire, and industrial regions such as Berry, the Nivernais and the Cévennes. It is clear that 'state aid will never persuade an industrialist to settle in an area which for one reason or another does not suit him.'

This new industrialisation had not been thought out and co-ordinated within a national development plan to prescribe all the steps that would need to be taken to develop infrastructures, towns and capital equipment on the lines needed to promote the birth of modern industrial areas. The only things that came to life were the zones and areas naturally predisposed to industrial development, whereas other areas continued to decline for lack of development in urbanisation and communications. If works are not started to open up departments, it is useless to count on the private sector to move industry to them, for industrialists do not have 'suicidal tendencies'.

Finally, it was too much to expect of the industrialisation policy that it would either relieve depressed industries by taking up their surplus labour, or absorb the labour potential of the young age-group and the rural areas. In fact, the old industries, the textile factories, laid off large numbers of workers, whereas the young industries, going over to automation, required less labour. That is why the jobs created failed to compensate for those that had been lost, as happened at Decazeville, and at Amiens.

9. No blast-furnace was established in Lorraine between 1913 and 1950.

10. Source: *Bulletin statistique, Ministère de la Construction.*

11. The maximum distances for economic transmission of current are of the order of 200 km. at a tension of 120,000 volts; 600 km. at 220,000 volts; 1,000 km. at 400,000 volts.

12. In 1951—in *Études sur les perspectives énergétiques à long terme de la Communauté européenne.* Bulletin of the European Coal and Steel Community, December 1962, p. 57.

13. Consumption in cubic metres of water per ton of product: butadiene, 1,300; aluminium, 1,300; rayon, 800; wood pulp for paper, 300; steel, 150.

14. Nevertheless, the railways have by no means given ground: there were 7,500 junctions for private branch-lines in 1958, and 9,800 in 1962.

15. The 90,000 tons of aluminium from the factory at Noguères are produced by 450 persons.

16. On the other hand, the location of the oil refinery at Strasbourg was decided after the requirements for the optimum structure of the refining and oil-products transporting industries had been worked out by an Operational Research company using Bull computers.

17. The mean size of enterprises rose from 5·5 employees in 1896 to 13·2 in 1954.

18. Industrial-building permits in the Paris region: 1950–3, 32%; 1953–7, 27%; 1958–61, 17%.

19. *La Vie Française.*

III

TYPES OF INDUSTRIALISATION

The result of this succession of stages of industrialisation has made its mark on the landscapes and on the map in two ways:

1. The industries are unevenly distributed across France, according to their type of production and size structure.

2. The varying regional incidence of these industries gives rise to regional types of geographical distribution.

1. TYPES OF DISPERSION OR CONCENTRATION

The type and degree of dispersion of a branch of industry across France is determined by the nature of the industrial activity itself, the factors of location, the number and size of establishments. The 'commonplace' (*banal*) industries are found everywhere, because they are located in the consuming areas, because their raw materials are widely distributed or easily transported, or because they have not been subjected to localising processes. Such industries are found in all, or almost all, departments, although there are always some areas which attract a measure of localisation. The timber industry is a case in point. There are 14,000 sawmills in France but only 8% of these have more than 20 workers. The food industries are equally very widespread, since they make use of the entire range of local agricultural resources. The general engineering industry, which comprised 9,313 establishments in 1954, only 1,092 of them employing more than 10 workers, is spread over the whole of France, and is solidly rooted in the traditions of the old metal-working areas.

Other industries are less uniformly distributed, being more concentrated in a number of regional foci, but these foci are themselves widely distributed over the country. A few sectors of industry may be cited as examples. Brass-founding is represented by 380 enter-prises, of which 185 employ less than 10 persons (1958). They are spread over 50 departments, but Nord, Rhône, Saône-et-Loire, Somme and the Paris region predominate. The hosiery industry is present in almost all departments, but more localised in a number of areas: Troyes (28% of the workers), Nord (19%), Roanne (11%) and Paris (9%) are the most important. Secondary centres include Oloron, Toulouse, Castres, Grenoble, Ganges, Le Vigan.

In the same way, the footwear industry is largely localised at a dozen centres: Lyons, Romans (18% of the production), the Paris region (13%), Fougères (11%), Cholet, Laval (10%), Nancy (9%), Bordeaux (8%), the North (6%), Alsace (5%), Provence (5%), Limousin (4%). Glovemaking is carried on in 53 departments, but three towns account for 89% of the total production: Millau (47%), Saint-Junien (22%), Grenoble (20%). The fitting and turning industry (lathe-work) is distributed in four areas: Haute-Savoie (45% of the national production), the Paris region (25%), Seine-Maritime (15%), Doubs, Jura (10%). 54% of the electrical industry is located in the Paris region, 12% in the Rhône–northern Alps region, 6% in Normandy, 5% in the North-east and 3·5% in the North. Some other branches of industry have a distribution similar to that of the electrical industry, but with a high concentration in the Paris region, though this does not amount to a monopoly.

Certain other industrial activities are, however, very highly localised, predominantly or exclusively in one or two locations. It is difficult to distinguish between these two types. In cases where there are predominant locations, one town or one area contains more than half of the activity in that branch of industry: 80% of the lens-grinding enterprises are in the Jura; 77% of the production of lead comes from the department of Nord; bobbins for the silk-milling industry are produced almost entirely in three neighbouring departments: Ardèche (50%), Drôme (15%) and Loire (10%). Ardèche and Drôme also possess 80% of the false-grain spindles used in making staple or pile nylon. Beyond a certain figure—and 80% seems a good limit—the degree of localisation may be regarded as exclusive rather than just predominant. Nearly 90% of the wool-combing industry is concentrated in the North, at Roubaix–Tourcoing, which has a capacity equivalent to more than 12% of the world total. Likewise,

90% of the woollen-carpet industry is situated in the North (mainly Roubaix–Tourcoing), and 85% of flax spinning is also there. Most French production of jute yarns and woven fabrics comes from factories of the Saint Frères group in Picardy (Abbeville, Beauval, Vallée de la Nièvre).

Zinc metallurgy is entirely concentrated in four factories, three in the northern region, at Auby, Mortagne-du-Nord, Noyelles-Godault, and one in Aveyron, at Viviez. 80% of the French production of seamless tubes comes from factories on the Sambre and in the Ardennes. Cutlery is localised exclusively in the two areas of Thiers and Nogent-en-Bassigny. 89% of farinaceous food preparations (pasta) come from the Bouches-du-Rhône. The canvas-shoe industry is exclusively concentrated in three centres: Mauléon-Soule and Oloron-Sainte-Marie, in Basses-Pyrénées, and Saint-Laurent-de-Cerdans, in Pyrénées-Orientales. About 90% of the newsprint is produced at four mills located at Corbehem, Essonnes, la Chapelle (near Rouen) and in the department of Seine.

2. TYPES OF INDUSTRIAL AREAS

These industries which are unevenly distributed among the departments are characterised by widely differing locations, ranging from the little isolated workshop in a village to the great factory belonging to a whole industrial complex. All kinds of industrial landscape may be found.

A. Industrialised Rural Areas

French industry has inherited relatively important rural locations from its past, not only the factories situated in local centres and minor regional centres but also the cottage workshops, the little factories scattered throughout the rural communes. This is the case in many regions: in Vimeu, where each commune has locksmiths' workshops, plastic-replica plants and small brass foundries; the

Normandy *Bocage* and Haute-Marne, where the valleys (Marne, Blaise, Rognon) contain many metal-working and engineering factories; the Jura, where there are precious-stone, coopering and casing, and plastics works. The valleys of the Vosges, Choletais, Berry, Cambrésis and Lyonnais, with its scattered textile workshops, are all representative of the other leading type of dispersed industry. These rural industries coexist with factories in the towns of each area and with them create 'industrial nebulae'.

The footwear industry in Dordogne includes about a hundred enterprises (3,500 workers), on the edge of the Charente basin around Nontron and in the valley of the Isle (Neuvic-sur-l'Isle). The clothing industry in Berry (clothing, shirts, lingerie and babywear) employs 10,000 female workers, 8,000 in factories, 2,000 working at home. The workshops themselves are very small. In 1958 only one factory with more than 500 workers was recorded. Half the establishments have less than 10 and a quarter of them employ from 10 to 50 workers. The enterprises are scattered in the towns (Châteauroux, Saint-Amand-Montrond, Argentonsur-Creuse, Vierzon, Villedieu-sur-Indre), in the local centres and in small villages. These workshops belong to craftsmen, the owners of small factories or to large firms like the Boussac company, which controls about a dozen establishments. The beginnings of this industry in the region go back to the middle of the 19th century.

B. Industrial Towns

These are the most common type of industrial centre in France. The name of a town is often associated with a particular product—Amiens velvet, Calais lace, Thiers cutlery, Oyonnax plastic, Troyes hosiery, Millau gloves, Alençon household equipment, Dijon mustard, Valence jewellery.

In these towns industry is developed to a varying degree and the range of products varies considerably, so that the towns themselves may be classified anywhere on the scale from one-industry towns to multiple-industry towns (cf. p. 398 *et seq.*).

C. Industrial Regions

The other forms of industrial distribution may be grouped under this heading, but in fact there are several distinct types:

1. Urban–industrial complexes are the hypertrophied product of industrial town development and result from the coalescense of neighbouring industrial towns with multiple activities or to development outwards from a major urban centre. The Lille–Roubaix-Tourcoing complex exemplifies the former, Lyons and Paris the latter.

At Lyons in 1958, 16,260 industrial estab-

lishments employed 198,000 workers.[20] The corresponding figures for the Lyons urban region, which includes 57 communes, are 18,200 and 214,000 respectively. The sizes of the undertakings were as follows:

14,000 employed less than 6 persons.
1,200 employed from 6 to 9 wage-earners (4·5% of the total).
1,400 employed from 10 to 20 wage-earners (8·8%).
  975 employed from 21 to 50 wage-earners (15%).
  625 employed more than 50 persons, that is, 66% of all industrial employment in the Lyons region.

2. Mining–Industrial areas (*bassins industriels*) developed from exploitation of underground resources. These resources gave rise to a particular kind of industrialisation which completely transformed the pre-existing rural landscape, juxtaposing mines and the industries which made direct or indirect use of coal or ore. The shape and extent of these industrial regions coincide with the coalfields and orefields, sometimes extending to include the workers' residential areas. The principal industrial regions of this type are the iron and steel area of northern Lorraine (218 communes), the Lorraine coalfield (152 communes), the coalfield in the west of the northern region (123 communes), with an extension into the Scheldt basin (119 communes), the Le Creusot coalfield (20 communes), the Saint-Étienne coalfield (59 communes), the Alès–La Grand'-Combe coalfield (45 communes).

3. Valley–industrial areas are river-valleys where conditions favour industrial development in linear form within the limits imposed by the steep slopes of the valley sides. Industrial development in such areas varies in density and continuity from the factory-lined roads of the Saint-Étienne depression, the lower Seine and the ring of factories in the Oise valley to the isolated factories in the Arve, Isère, Arc, the valleys of the Alps and the valleys of the Bruche and the Moselle above Charmes in the Lorraine Vosges.

Other examples are the upper valley of the Aude from Limoux to Quillan, the valley of the Bresle from Aumale to Le Tréport, the Sambre valley and the valley of the Risle.

20. The Lyons agglomeration, by the 1954 definition of the I.N.S.E.E., includes 9 communes.

3. THE SPATIAL STRUCTURE OF INDUSTRIAL AREAS

Industrial geography should not be restricted to consideration of the distribution of factories; it is just as important to analyse the role of the factories in the landscape and to define the relations between them and the other elements of the landscape. Industry is above all conspicuous for its modest demands on land, although these are increasing, as we have seen. In the Lyons region, for example, industrial enterprises cover 2,025 ha., that is, 4·6% of the total area of the region (43,282 ha.). The area occupied obviously varies with the nature of the activity. A recent calculation of the area occupied per worker by industries in the Lyons region gives a minimum of 30·62 m.² for the building industry, which is an outdoor activity, and a maximum of 165·16 m.² for chemicals, figures for other industries being as follows: metallurgy, 62·75 m.²; textiles, 65·44 m.²; dyeing, 94 m.²; constructional engineering and boilermaking, 89 m.²; electrical industries, 39 m.²; hosiery, 19 m.²; printing, 18 m.²; leather, 19 m.²; clothing, 13 m.².[21]

The profiles of factories in the townscapes and rural landscapes of France are astonishingly varied, ranging from the factory with featureless buildings, suitable for a number of activities, as changes and substitutions show, to the spheres and columns of petro-chemical plants, which denote a true technological landscape. But the size structure of French firms causes French industry to be geographically scattered in numerous workshops occupying small areas. In many towns these workshops and little factories are tucked away inside urban blocks, where they occupy the space that originally was not built over, so that they are hidden from view by the rows of houses along the streets.

In fact there are 'industries without factories', branches of industry which have no need of large areas and which owe to their origins a characteristic dispersal among numerous little workshops, and a multiplicity of crafts that makes them elusive and difficult to track down. This is the case with the silk industry of Lyons, which has a very peculiar organisation. It includes several hundred (463) *maisons de fabrique* which have their technical and commercial services at Lyons. These 'houses' send out piece-work to a multitude of mills and workshops scattered over the whole region. Some of the *fabricants* who run the 'houses' own a weaving factory, but most of them have none. All of these factories together employ 55,000 persons, 16,000 of whom are in the 57 communes of the Lyons urban region. Thus, 'a visitor never fails to be disappointed with the Lyons silk industry: a hill called Croix Rousse, some twisting streets, dirty, bare buildings, but no factory. The silk industry manifests itself only by means of dark offices with telephones' (J.-L. Bonnot). In short, the characteristic industry of a city does not materialise in buildings worthy of its importance.

But such intra-urban locations are normal for most industrial buildings, because of their age and continuous use. Before the days of communal public transport, factories were built in towns or on their outskirts, near where the workers lived. Urban expansion soon engulfed them and digested them, so to speak. This explains the extraordinary intermixture of factories with other buildings (fig. 85). The availability of vacant industrial buildings having been the most widespread and persistent determinant of sites for new enterprises, industries have succeeded one another in the old factories without the need for rebuilding.

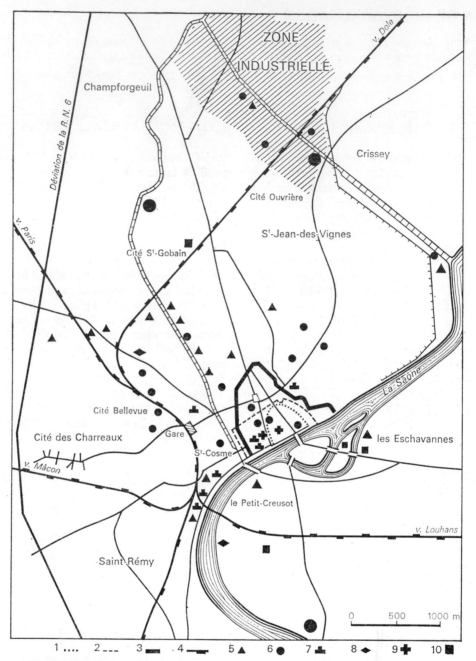

Fig. 84. Chalon-sur-Saône and its industries. (Source: E. Leclerc, *Ann. de Géog.* no. 365, 1959, p. 25)

1. Outline of the 3rd century Gallo-Roman walled Upper town.   2. Outline of the walled Lower town dating from the 14th to 15th centuries.   3. Streets laid out on the 16th-century rampart.   4. Railway. 5. Metallurgical industries.   6. Clothing and umbrella factories, Saint-Gobain glassworks, electric lamp factory.   7. Foodstuffs industries.   8. Timber industries.   9. Printing works.   10. Chemical industries.
    Note the diversity of industrial sites, inside the walls of the old town, along the railway lines, the Saône and the canal, and in the new industrial zone.

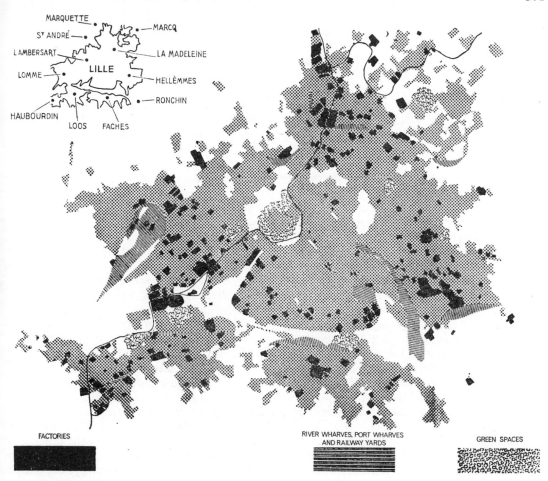

FACTORIES

RIVER WHARVES, PORT WHARVES
AND RAILWAY YARDS

GREEN SPACES

Fig. 85. The industries of the Lille agglomeration in 1959. (Source: *Niveaux optima des villes*, C.E.R.E.S., Lille, 1959)

Some industrial buildings at Angy in the built-up area of the department of Oise (Mouy) were successively occupied as follows: in 1914, by the Leroux chicory firm, evacuated from the North; in 1930, by a footwear manufacturer; in 1950, by a furniture factory; in 1955, by a plastic-brush factory; in 1958, by a girdle factory. The Guilleminot company at Chantilly (photographic films) established its works in an old wool-spinning factory; the Société de la Vieille Montagne at Creil set up in 1915 in buildings vacated by a large glass-works. A large part of French industrial activity thus operates in decrepit factories, in factories which are unchanged and ill-adapted to the technical requirements of the firms and in workshop slums, especially in the centre and suburbs of Paris.

Factories enjoyed more or less unrestricted freedom in their choice of sites according to the nature of their activities, subject to health considerations and water requirements. 'At Lyons, between 1880 and 1914, the silk-dyers were looking for water—they kept well away from each other so as not to lower the water-table below the level of the last hundred years —and the chemical works sought isolation' (M. Laferrère). Dependence on water power also determined many industrial sites, however inconvenient they may have been in other respects.

These out-dated traditional industrial locations, and the diffuse structure of industry associated with them, are yielding to the pressure of changing industrial needs. The fact of their survival has, however, simplified the task of industrial decentralisation. Even at Lyons, a silk factory was opened in 1962 at Saint-Priest. Site requirements have become more and more exacting with the increasing need for large areas (Péchiney covers 130 ha. at Noguères), the rising costs of land, problems of pollution and waste disposal, and the increasing weight of machinery. Designated industrial zones represent a relatively new type of land use in France. They were few in number before the war when they were more often the result of chance rather than deliberate planning. The industrial zone of Saint-Fons, south of Lyons, contains seven chemical factories employing 7,000 persons on 136 ha. of alluvium: Saint-Gobain (1854), Ciba, Rhône-Poulenc, Rhodiaceta, Air Liquide. The industrial zone of Marquette-lès-Lille was established between the two wars by a private company making equipment for railway sidings.

Since 1950 the industrial zone has become a standard element of the land-use pattern (fig. 84). There are large numbers of them, since many communes look upon them as a means of attracting factories, whether decentralised or not. Many of them are only waste land or former pasture lands turned into industrial zones 'solely by virtue of a sign put up at a street corner' (E. Claudius-Petit). Too many of these zones are likewise mere plots, far too small to accommodate big factories, either now or in the future. If a factory needs 10 ha., the manufacturer will look for a site of 40 ha. On the other hand, some industrial zones are big enough and, above all, have been equipped with the indispensable infrastructure (high-tension electricity, water, road and rail services, public transport, care-taking and maintenance services). The industrial zone at Amiens was one of the first to be established (1955) and now has a large group of factories in it. The recent tendency has been to plan several zones for different types of activity. For example, around Bordeaux there are now zones for light industries in the west (Pessac, Mérignac), for 'medium' industries near the Garonne (Bassens, Floirac) and a zone for heavy industry in the Bec d'Ambès.

Finally, the French Planning Commission (*Commissariat au Plan*), imitating many years later the British experiments with trading-estates, decided in 1962 to experiment with prefabricated factories, beginning with ten factories of 2,000 m.^{2} each.

The industrial zone is an interesting compromise form of industrial development between extreme concentration, on the one hand, and extreme dispersal of isolated factories in numerous villages, on the other. It has been proposed, for example, to set up 'industrial bases' in the countryside, which would provide non-agricultural work for the rural populace without obliging them to migrate to the towns. These *points d'appui* would employ about 1,000 workers in 10–20 small or medium-sized enterprises, and would draw upon the labour force within a radius of 20–30 km.

21. After M. Laferrère, '*Lyon, ville industrielle*', thesis, Paris, 1960.

PART SIX

THE TOWNS AND CITIES

It would be a very good thing for beautiful France if, instead of having one centre only, it had ten, all spreading light and life.　　GOETHE

I

URBANISATION

1. THE URBAN POPULATION AND ITS ENUMERATION

We have already analysed the reciprocal development of the urban and rural populations of France (Part Two, Chapter I, p. 110). But percentage ratios alone cannot give an accurate impression of the extent of urbanisation in France. The urban phenomenon itself is not easily defined. A town is at one and the same time a landscape, an economic unit, a population unit, an environment for life and work; it is, even more truly, an atmosphere, a personality, a 'soul'. Though geography is mainly concerned with the distribution of towns and their spatial structure, a geographer can understand neither one nor the other without analysing the various natural, social and economic elements which, through their interaction in time and space, have created the surprising range and variety of urban centres in France.

The statistical definition of a French urban commune is simple: an agglomerated population of over 2,000 in the administrative centre (*chef-lieu*) up to and including the 1954 census; and one with a total commune population of over 2,000 since the 1962 census. This simple definition does not, however, permit comparison with foreign countries, so that it is necessary to assume an arbitrary but uniform criterion. Taking the percentage of population living in towns and agglomerations of more than 20,000 people in 1960–2, the urban population of France is 46·8%, a figure well below those of some other European countries (England and Wales 69%, the Netherlands 56%) and comparable with those of West Germany (47·6%) and the United States (47%). At the same time 51·5% of the urban population of France lives in agglo-

merations of more than 100,000 people, compared with 40% in Germany and 62% in Great Britain.

The density per 1,000 km.[2] of urban communes with 5,000 or more inhabitants is 2·1 in France, 5·2 in West Germany, 6·9 in Italy, 11·4 in Belgium, 12·8 in the Netherlands. Two characteristic features of urbanisation in France emerge from these figures: its relative weakness, and the importance of small towns. There is a similar lack of statistics for the measurement of urbanisation on the regional scale. This actually depends upon figures for the rural population just as much as on those for the urban population.[1]

The writer has devised an index of urbanisation which can be expressed as follows:

$$IU = \frac{\text{Density of departmental urban population}}{\text{Density of departmental rural population}} \times \frac{\text{Department's \% of the total}}{\text{urban population of France}}$$

This index expresses the ratio of urban to rural population (the latter entering indirectly into the regional urbanisation value) weighted according to a department's proportion of the total urban population of France. The map prepared on the basis of this index is very informative (fig. 86). Twenty-nine departments have an index of urbanisation below 0·26, seven of them below 0·09. The great majority of these are in western, south-western and central France; they are departments with relatively high rural population densities, without large towns, without a true urban hierarchy. But the east of France includes

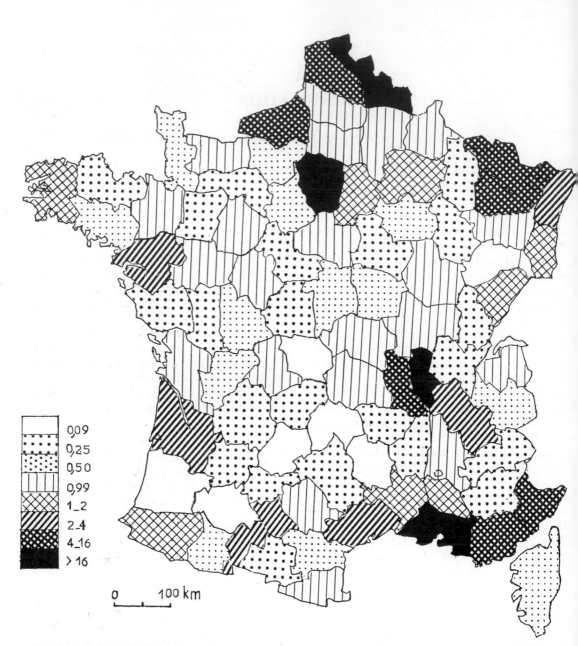

Fig. 86.   Index of urbanisation (1962).   (Source: F. Carrière et Ph. Pinchemel, *Le Fait urbain en France*, A. Colin, 1963)

nine departments in these two categories: Meuse and Haute-Marne, Yonne, Haute-Saône, Jura and Ain, Hautes-Alpes and Basses-Alpes and Ardèche are the very little urbanised parts of this urban and industrial sector of France.

Thirty-five departments have what may be described as average indices of urbanisation between 0·25 and 0·99. Here, towns are more important, both in number and in population, and in some departments the urbanisation index is raised by the lower density of rural population. Some departments appear as highly urbanised solely because there is one large town: Amiens in Somme, Tours in Indre-et-Loire, Caen in Calvados, Dijon in Côte-d'Or, Clermont-Ferrand in Puy-de-Dôme. Only twenty-five departments have indices which put them in the highly urbanised category. The indices are in any case very uneven, ranging from 1 (Gard, Marne) to 71 (Seine-et-Oise). The most highly urbanised provincial departments have the following indices: Bas-Rhin, 2·6; Haute-Garonne, 2·7; Loire-Atlantique, 3·0; Gironde, 3·4; Loire, 4·5; Var, 5·0; Meurthe-et-Moselle, 5·3; Pas-de-Calais, 10·0; Alpes-Maritimes, 12·4; Rhône, 19·1; Nord, 32·8; Bouches-du-Rhône, 38·8. Bouches-du-Rhône has the highest index of urbanisation because the department includes Marseilles and because of the absence of a numerous rural population; a comparison should be made with the intensity of urbanisation of a department with a high density of rural population, such as Nord.

The map gives a very clear overall impression of the unevenness of urbanisation in France, and shows that there are several urbanised regions isolated by 'under-urbanised' zones:

The North and Haute-Normandie.

The Paris region.

An eastern region, clearly bounded by the three poorly urbanised departments of Meuse, Haute-Marne and Haute-Saône.

An axial belt extending from Burgundy (Côte-d'Or) through the plain of the Saône (Saône-et-Loire) to the Rhône-Loire region, and centred upon the two departments of Loire and Rhône, with extensions into the departments of Puy-de-Dôme and Isère.

The Mediterranean region, bounded on the north by a row of little urbanised departments, except in the west, where there is an extension in the departments of Tarn and Haute-Garonne.

The coastal region of Gironde and Charente-Maritime.

The lower Loire region, including Indre-et-Loire, Maine-et-Loire and Loire-Atlantique.

Finistère, Basses-Pyrénées and Doubs complete this picture of 'urban' France. The rest of the country is 'under-urbanised', either absolutely, by reason of the lack of important towns, or relatively, because rural population densities have remained high. The principal 'urban deserts' are: the south of the Central Massif, the southern Alps with inner Provence, and the south-east of the Paris basin. Physical environment is to a large extent responsible for this lack of urbanisation, directly through the restrictions imposed by steep and rugged relief on communication and possibilities for the expansion of towns, and indirectly through the lack of economic resources and population.

Urban growth has been very weak in areas which have suffered most from rural depopulation, except in a few specific cases. In these areas the tertiary sector of the economy had become too large in relation to the needs of a declining population and was itself weakened by the loss of services most conducive to urban development.

1. In 1954 the urban populations of Gironde and Haute-Garonne formed similar percentages of the total populations of the respective departments (54 and 57), but the actual numbers represented 2·1 and 1·28% respectively of the urban population of France.

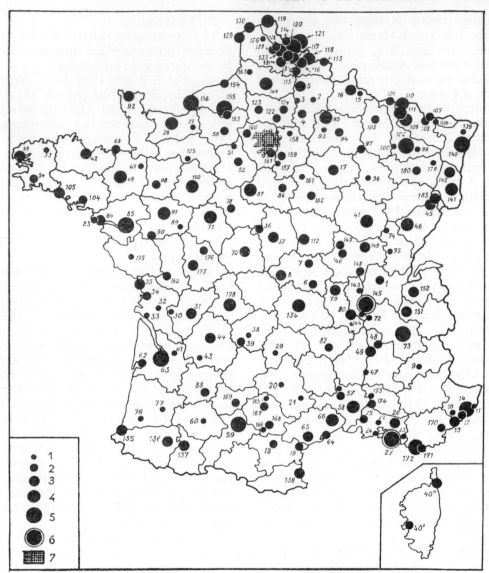

Fig. 87.   Towns and agglomerations with more than 20,000 inhabitants in 1962.

1. Towns with 20,000–30,000 inhabitants.   2. Towns with 30,000–50,000 inhabitants.   3. Towns with 50,000–100,000 inhabitants.   4. Towns with 100,000–200,000 inhabitants.   5. Towns with 200,000–500,000 inhabitants.   6. Towns with more than 500,000 inhabitants.   7. Limits of the Paris urban region (as defined by the I.N.S.E.E.).

AIN: 1 Bourg-en-Bresse.—AISNE: 2 Laon; 3 Tergnier; 4 Soissons; 5 Saint-Quentin.—ALLIER: 6 Vichy; 7 Moulins; 8 Montluçon.—HAUTES-ALPES: 9 Gap.—ALPES-MARITIMES: 10 Grasse; 11 Menton; 12 Antibes; 13 Cannes; 14 Nice.—ARDENNES: 15 Sedan; 16 Charleville.—AUBE: 17 Troyes.—AUDE: 18 Carcassonne; 19 Narbonne.—AVEYRON: 20 Rodez; 21 Millau.—BOUCHES-DU-RHONE: 22 Salon de Provence; 23 Aubagne; 24 Martigues; 25 Arles; 26 Aix-en-Provence; 27 Marseilles.—CALVADOS: 27 Lisieux; 28 Caen.—CANTAL: 29 Aurillac.—CHARENTE: 30 Cognac; 31 Angoulême.—CHARENTE-MARITIME: 32 Saintes; 33 Royan; 34 La Rochelle; 35 Rochefort.—CHER: 36 Vierzon;

2. TOWNS AND THE URBAN HIERARCHY

Towns and agglomerations of 20,000 or more people are the major nodes in the urban network of France and these are very uneven in magnitude and spacing. In 1962 seven departments contained no town with more than 20,000 inhabitants: Basses-Alpes, Ardèche, Lot, Lozère, Creuse, Ariège, Haute-Saône; with the exception of the last-named these departments are all in the southern half of France, and most of them have strong or accidented relief hindering communications.

Lower in the hierarchy, the network of towns with less than 20,000 inhabitants is much more dense. It is these towns, administrative centres of cantons, market towns, sub-prefectures and small industrial centres, that constitute the main fabric of the urban mesh of France within which the towns of more than 20,000 inhabitants are merely local concentrations.

These towns and agglomerations are unevenly distributed. The hierarchy varies from region to region, since the populations of departments differ widely in rank-size distribution among the towns (fig. 87).

The largest town of a department may contain anything from 8% (Boulogne-sur-Mer) to 87% (Toulouse) of the total urban population of the department. By no means does a complete hierarchy exist in every department. In most cases there is a big gap between the size of the largest centre and that of the second largest in the department. Strasbourg (301,400 inhabitants) is followed by Haguenau (21,400), Bordeaux (462,000) by Arcachon (34,350), Marseilles (802,000) by Aix (71,000), Toulouse (329,650) by Saint-Gaudens (11,200).

---

37 Bourges.—CORRÈZE: 38 Tulle; 39 Brive-La-Gaillarde.—CORSE: 40′ Ajaccio; 40″ Bastia.—COTE-D'OR: 41 Dijon.—COTES-DU-NORD: 42 Saint-Brieuc.—DORDOGNE: 43 Bergerac; 44 Périgeux.—DOUBS: 45 Montbéliard; 46 Besançon.—DROME: 47 Montélimar; 48 Romans-sur-Isère; 49 Valence.—EURE: 50 Evreux.—EURE-ET-LOIR: 51 Dreux; 52 Chartres.—FINISTÈRE: 53 Morlaix; 54 Quimper; 55 Brest.—GARD: 57 Alès; 58 Nîmes.—HAUTE-GARONNE: 59 Toulouse.—GERS: 60 Auch.—GIRONDE: 61 Libourne; 62 Arcachon; 63 Bordeaux.—HÉRAULT: 64 Sète; 65 Béziers; 66 Montpellier.—ILLE-ET-VILAINE: 67 Fougères: 68 Saint-Malo; 69 Rennes.—INDRE: 70 Châteauroux.—INDRE-ET-LOIRE: 71 Tours.—ISÈRE: 72 Vienne; 73 Grenoble.—JURA: 74 Dôle; 75 Lons-le-Saunier.—LANDES: 76 Dax; 77 Mont-de-Marsan.—LOIR-ET-CHER: 78 Blois.—LOIRE: 79 Roanne; 80 Saint-Étienne, Saint-Chamond.—HAUTE-LOIRE: 82 Le Puy.—LOIRE-ATLANTIQUE: 83 La Baule; 84 Saint-Nazaire; 85 Nantes.—LOIRET: 86 Montargis; 87 Orleans.—LOT-ET-GARONNE: 88 Agen—MAINE-ET-LOIRE: 89 Saumur; 90 Cholet; 91 Angers.—MANCHE: 92 Cherbourg.—MARNE: 93 Épernay; 94 Châlons-sur-Marne; 95 Rheims.—HAUTE-MARNE: 96 Chaumont; 97 Saint-Dizier.—MAYENNE: 98 Laval.—MEURTHE-ET-MOSELLE: 99 Lunéville; 100 Toul; 101 Longwy; 102 Nancy.—MEUSE: 103 Verdun.—MORBIHAN: 104 Vannes; 105 Lorient.—MOSELLE: 106 Sarreguemines; 107 Forbach; 108 Merlebach; 109 Metz; 110 Thionville; 111 Hagondange-Briey.—NORD: 113 Maubeuge; 114 Armentières; 115 Cambrai; 116 Denain; 117 Douai; 118 Valenciennes; 119 Dunkirk; 120 Lille; 121 Roubaix-Tourcoing.—OISE: 122 Creil; 123 Beauvais; 124 Compiègne.—ORNE: 125 Alençon.—PAS-DE-CALAIS: 126 Saint-Omer; 127 Bruay-en-Artois; 128 Béthune; 129 Boulogne-sur-mer; 130 Calais; 131 Arras; 132 Hénin-Liétard; 133 Lens.—PUY-DE-DOME: 134 Clermont-Ferrand.—BASSES-PYRÉNÉES: 135 Bayonne; 136 Pau.—HAUTES-PYRÉNÉES: 137 Tarbes.—PYRÉNÉES-ORIENTALES: 138 Perpignan.—BAS-RHIN: 139 Haguenau; 140 Strasbourg.—HAUT-RHIN: 141 Mulhouse; 142 Colmar.—RHONE: 143 Villefranche-sur-Saône; 144 Villeurbanne; 145 Lyons.—SAONE-ET-LOIRE: 146 Montceau-les-Mines; 147 Le Creusot; 148 Mâcon; 149 Chalon-sur-Saône.—SARTHE: 150 le Mans.—SAVOIE: 151 Chambéry.—HAUTE-SAVOIE: 152 Annecy.—SEINE-MARITIME: 153 Elbeuf; 154 Dieppe; 155 Rouen; 156 Le Havre.—SEINE-ET-MARNE: 157 Fontainebleau; 158 Meaux; 159 Melun.—SEINE-ET-OISE: 160 Mantes; 161 Corbeil-Essonnes.—DEUX-SÈVRES: 162 Niort.—SOMME: 163 Abbeville; 164 Amiens.—TARN: 165 Carmaux; 166 Mazamet; 167 Albi; 168 Castres.—TARN-ET-GARONNE: 169 Montauban.—VAR: 170 Fréjus; 171 Hyères; 172 Toulon.—VAUCLUSE: 173 Orange; 174 Avignon.—VENDÉE: 175 La Roche-sur-Yon.—VIENNE: 176 Chatellerault; 177 Poitiers.—HAUTE-VIENNE: 178 Limoges.—VOSGES: 179 Saint-Dié; 180 Épinal.—YONNE: 181 Sens; 182 Auxerre.—TERRITOIRE-DE-BELFORT: 183 Belfort.

Conversely, there are departments where towns are very numerous (Nord, Pas-de-Calais, Oise, Moselle). It is therefore neces-sary to examine the factors determining the nature and incidence of urbanisation in France to understand its distinctive character.

3. THE STAGES OF URBANISATION

The urban network of France is very old; most of the present urban sites were already in use centuries ago and possessed an embryo urban centre. They were staging-points on highways, transhipment points, defence posts, small ports, religious centres or places of pilgrimage, or market towns. The early origins of urban development in France were due to the peopling of the country at an early date, the many routeways that crossed it, its position in Europe, its proximity to the urban civilisation of the Mediterranean region and the multiplicity of natural sites for towns. Since Gallo-Roman times, successive genera-tions of towns have grown up in response to the changing military, commercial, ad-ministrative and industrial conditions of the day.

A. The Gallo-Roman Towns

The first urban network in France emerged in the Gallo-Roman period in the form of a relatively dense and well-developed hierarchy of *civitates*, *pagi* and *vici*. It included purely Gaulish towns: Paris, Bourges, Vannes, Arras, Amiens; Gaulish *oppida*, fortress towns, capitals of *pays*, crossroad towns (Bavai), towns either founded by the Romans or developed by them: Lyons, Autun, Nar-bonne, all on the Rhône–Rhine axis and the Mediterranean littoral. Such towns were most numerous in the South of France. Of the 44 stations shown on the Peutinger map as capitals of *civitates*, 26 are prefectures today, 7 are sub-prefectures and only 6 are now sub-towns or merely villages. Later on, towns arose through the concentration of villagers and townsfolk in places of refuge, where they fled from the barbarian invaders; hence Chauny, in a marsh in the valley of the Oise.

B. The Medieval Towns

A second generation of towns and cities dates from the Middle Ages, notably from the 11th and 14th centuries. They originated in three ways:

1. Some towns grew up where there was no pre-existing urban nucleus, at favourable sites, at crossroads, on either side of a bridge, near a mill (Mulhouse), around market places, fairs and staging posts.

2. Other towns grew up around monasteries and castles. There are many towns of mon-astic origin in France: Cluny, Moissac, Brive, Aurillac, Figeac, Bergues, Saint-Omer, Saint-Dié, Fécamp, Saint-Denis, Saint-Brieuc. Most of these towns have remained small, since a site chosen for an abbey was by no means so suitable for a major urban develop-ment. Some of them were once very import-ant, but today they have only the sleepy life of small market towns (*bourgs*) or small historic towns (*villes-musées*). Sometimes monastic *bourgs* which grew up outside a town ended by merging with it (Bourg Saint-Martin at Tours, Saint-Martial at Limoges).

Castle towns are even more numerous, whether placenames indicate their origins or not: Amboise, Chinon, Châteauroux, Niort, Châtellerault, Saumur, Fontenay-le-Comte, Alençon, Épinal, Beaucaire, Salon, Pau, Fougères, Château-Thierry, Châteaudun, Châteaubriant, La Ferté-Milon, Bar-le-Duc, Langres, Nice, Loches, Séverac-le-Château, Montluçon, Sancerre, Chaumont, Langon.

The whole history of France is reflected in the history of its towns; the town protected by a castle was the capital of the little political, economic and administrative unit of the nobleman who wielded sovereign powers over it. Other fortress-towns guarded the frontiers of each feudal state, by the banks of rivers or hidden behind forest marches. Such were Saint-Jean-de-Losne and Auxonne, strongholds on the old frontier between Burgundy and Champagne. Many of the present features of the urban mesh of France derive from the existence of frontiers that are no longer there, for example the twin cities Tarascon and Beaucaire on opposite sides of the Rhône. Towns like these had varied fates. They too were affected by site conditions that in one way or another impeded urban development: a steep-sided, fortified site was not conducive to urban growth.

3. Some entirely new towns were deliberately created by individuals, 'towns which possessed birth certificates' (P. Lavedan). Under the Old Régime the founding of new towns was a convenient device for nobles to increase their numbers of dependents and their revenues. The lords of Beaujeu created Villefranche-sur-Saône; Saint Louis created Aigues-Mortes in 1246; Alphonse de Poitiers founded Villefranche-de-Rouergue in 1256. Villeneuve-le-Roi, in Yonne, Montferrand and Barcelonnette had similar origins. Many of these new towns (*villeneuves*) arose in this way between the Pyrenees and the Central Massif in consequence of the twofold rivalry between the counts of Toulouse and the kings of France and between the French and the English. Bastides and *villeneuves* multiplied between 1250 and 1350 on each side of the frontier between the kingdom of France and English Aquitaine: Mirande (1282), Villeneuve-sur-Lot (1264), Revel (1280). Only a few of these medieval foundations reached city rank: Carcassonne, Montauban (1144), Libourne (1269).

Thus Medieval France already possessed its network of towns with populations that were large for regional capitals in those days. In the 13th century Toulouse and Arras had between 30,000 and 40,000 inhabitants, and Paris undoubtedly had more than 100,000.

C. The 16th and 17th Centuries

A third generation of towns emerged in the 16th and 17th centuries. This was an epoch of monarchical ascendancy, colonial expansion, wars and centralised organisation of the country, which experienced an upsurge of urbanisation, favoured by surpluses of wealth from the countryside and the colonies. Many towns were created, and they were of three types:

1. Fortress towns. During the 16th century: Rocroi, Villefranche-sur-Meuse (near Stenay) and Vitry-le-François (1545), built to replace Vitry-en-Perthois which had been burnt down by the troops of Charles V. In the 17th century Vauban founded many fortified towns: Huningue, Sarrelouis, Longwy in 1679, Montlouis in 1681, Montdauphin (1692–3), Neuf-Brisach in 1698.[2] La Fère is a type example of a town of medieval origin which developed as a military town mainly in the 17th and 18th centuries. It acquired an arsenal in 1666, a school of artillery in 1719 and barracks in 1723 and 1767.

2. Residential towns, the seats of kings and princes. The new town of Nancy (1587–8) next to the old town, Charleville (1608), Richelieu, adjacent to the Cardinal's castle (1635–40), Versailles (1671).

3. Towns of economic origin. These were mostly ports, such as Le Havre (1517–43), and Colbert's creations: Rochefort in 1657, Brest, Lorient and Sète in 1666. Colbert, an early advocate of industrial decentralisation, favoured the establishment of royal factories outside the towns. This could have led to the formation of new industrial towns. Attempts were made at Villeneuvette (Hérault), with a cloth factory, and at La Glacerie, near Cherbourg, but these towns did not develop.

An important stage of urban development in France ended with the 17th century. The previous centuries had established a relatively dense urban network within which the new, planned towns enjoyed privileged status. Henceforth urbanisation continued within the existing medieval and early modern framework by growth rather than by new planting. The only towns founded after that by direct human decision were Pontivy and La Roche-sur-Yon, by Napoleon I, and a few watering places.[3]

Urbanisation was rather different in the 18th century from that in the previous century. It came about in response to a large increase in population, which caused many towns to expand. As defensive walls were no longer needed, most cities were able to expand without hindrance. For example, the population of Lyons rose from 70,000 in 1697 to 115,000 in 1762.

D. The 19th Century

From the middle of the 19th century urban growth in France took place on other foundations and developed completely new features associated with the development of heavy industry, new sources of energy and the new technology. The founding and extension of towns in former centuries, whether by princes, for military and administrative ends or merely as a result of the wealth and dense population of the countryside, were succeeded by urbanisation of industrial origin.

It might have been expected that the 19th century and the early 20th century, as a period of upheaval in the distribution of population and of radical economic changes, would have seen the founding of many new towns. Many towns were indeed created, but only in a statistical sense; every time a census was taken, communes which had been classified as rural at the previous census became urban communes, because their populations had risen above the threshold figure of 2,000 inhabitants in their administrative centres. A large proportion of these new urban communes were, however, situated in the suburban fringes of expanding cities. Thus out of the 31 towns of more than 20,000 inhabitants which were not yet urban communes in 1851, 28 were in the Paris agglomeration, and were really villages being swallowed up by the urban 'metamorphism' of the big city.

The new town concept should be applied only in the case of the appearance of an autonomous urban organism, arising from a village or at a completely new site. Towns of this type have actually been founded during the last 150 years: on the coalfields and orefields, mining or metallurgical towns arose within a few years near the mines, surrounding and sometimes engulfing whole villages, but these creations were strongly localised.

Two other kinds of towns appeared in the 19th century: watering places and seaside resorts, many of which were 'launched' during the Second Empire (Aix-les-Bains, Dieppe, Trouville—Deauville and Vichy); and railway towns which developed around stations, workshops, depots and marshalling yards (Tergnier and La Roche-Migenne, halfway between Paris and Dijon).[4]

E. Since 1945

The first half of the 20th century was a time of demographic stagnation without new urban foundations, since the population contented itself with the building done during the preceding century. In contrast, new urban forms have appeared since the last war, as a result of the demographic revival, renewed factory development and the appearance of new industrial techniques. 'Industrial towns' have grown up around new factories; Saint-Nicolas-en-Fôret in the Lorraine industrial region is a 'Sollac' company town. A town of 2,700 dwellings housing 13,000 people has been built at Behren, where the old village itself contains only 500 inhabitants. Likewise a ring of industrial residential areas together containing 100,000 people has developed around the Étang de Berre. Two new towns typify this kind of industrial–urban development: Bagnols-sur-Cèze and Mourenx. Bagnols-sur-Cèze was a long-established small town of 4,600 inhabitants in 1936, but its population has been increased fourfold by the building of 2,000 dwellings for the workers in the atomic factory at Marcoule. The commune will be turned into a real new town by the progressive construction of three groups of schools, a regional lycée, a sports centre, an open-air theatre, a hospital and a slaughterhouse.

Mourenx is an even more striking example, since the commune itself had only 270 inhabitants in 1936; the new town has been built for workers in the industrial complex at Lacq. The new town principle was adopted after three other possible solutions to the housing problem had been examined and rejected: accommodating the workers at Pau, or in small groups in existing villages, or in three blocks of 1,000 dwellings each to be built round the industrial areas.

Further, we may well question the urban status of these industrial–residential developments as 'new' towns. They have been built exclusively to house the employees of a factory or a group of factories. They have limited functions and facilities, homogeneous social and occupational structures, anomalous demographic structures and sites, and a total lack of integration with their surrounding regions. All these characteristics make them far removed from the normal concept of a town.

Tourism has given rise to more new urban developments than industry has done. Tourist centres have expanded vigorously since 1950, and small towns have sprung up on the coast and near winter-sports centres. At the beginning, the existence of settlements providing 'acquired sites' was often the decisive factor; until a few years ago no one thought of creating a winter-sports station *ex nihilo*, away from all existing habitation, however unsuitable the sites of old villages might be for the exploitation of snowfields. The reasons behind this outlook are to be found in the practice of spreading investments and the dominance of uncoordinated private enterprise. Nevertheless progress was made, Courchevel and Tignes being examples of particularly successful 'new' resorts. Megève is almost as good an example: in 1911 it had only 1,746 inhabitants. Since 1965 the movement has spread and new tourist resorts have boomed, either as a result of private initiative or through the intervention of public bodies (*Caisse des dépôts*); such are Flaine, Avoriaz, Corbier, St. Martin Belleville and Super Bevoluy, in the Alps.

On the Languedoc coastline the resorts of

La Grande Motte, Leucate, Barcarès, with their bold innovations in town planning, are another example of urbanisation related to the exploitation of touristic resources.[5]

In relation to the rate of urban growth during the last hundred years these 'new' towns are unimpressive (see Part Two, p. 118). French urbanisation took place within an urban framework that was shaped far back in the past, and the present urban network is very largely inherited from the pre-industrial era.

But the phenomenon of urbanisation is no longer limited to the growth of towns and the creation of new ones. France is also undergoing an 'exurbanisation', or urbanisation outside the towns, through the freedom of movement provided by the motor-car and the spread of opportunities for leisure. The rural environments of other parts of Western Europe have been deeply 'urbanised' by the growth of towns and their expansion outwards from the old urban nuclei, supported by a vigorous increase in population. This has not been the case in France, where the ruins left by the rural depopulation have certainly not been effaced by a new kind of land use. Until the last few years, France had nothing like the 'rural, non-farm habitat' that is found in other countries.[6] But this phenomenon has now appeared and is developing rapidly in several forms:

1. Rural areas become the places of residence of people who work in towns. These 'dormitory' rural areas are found in the North, in the East, in the Paris region, and likewise in Normandy, the Lyons region, the South-west, the industrialised mountain valleys, and Provence.

2. Seasonal exurbanisation, linked with vacation periods; the villages in the hinterland of the Côte d'Azur, for example, vacated by their inhabitants, have been colonised and redeveloped by artisans, artists and summer visitors. The small farms and huts of the past were the precursors of this phenomenon, and it has only been in the last few years that secondary residential development has taken place on an appreciable scale.

The farmhouses and manor houses around towns, especially large cities, are taken over by townsmen in search of relief from the stress of urban life, for use as permanent, weekend and holiday homes. This temporary kind of exurbanisation is becoming widespread. The western, the southern and the south-eastern (Yonne) parts of the Paris basin have already been greatly affected by it.

2. Henrichemont (Cher), founded by Sully in 1608 to serve as a Protestant stronghold (Edict of Nantes), was never completed.
3. The foundation of La Roche-sur-Yon came from a desire to give Vendée a less ex-centric capital than Fontenay-le-Comte.
4. Lourdes is a very special case of a planted town; its population already numbered 4,000 when the apparitions occurred.
5. Carnoux is an unusual type of 'private new town'. In 1957 some French people from Morocco chose a valley at about 30 km. from Marseilles, between Aubagne and La Bédoule, as the site for building a town to receive their fellow-countrymen who decided to leave North Africa. The project provides for 12,000–15,000 inhabitants, with commercial centres, and an industrial zone. It is run on co-operative lines, membership being acquired by subscription. The site of Carnoux covers two farming estates. The town planner Gaston Bardet is carrying out an interesting experiment around Rennes in creating 'villettes' from rural communes.
6. In the meaning of the United States term 'rural non-farm' population.

4. SITUATIONS AND SITES

French towns are localised in plain and plateau areas and in the lower parts of mountain areas. Only one town of more than 100,000 inhabitants is more than 500 m. above sea-level. That is Saint-Étienne, a coalfield town, and there are only three towns of 20,000–30,000 inhabitants above 500 m.: Aurillac, Rodez and Le Puy. The highest urban centres in France are: Pontarlier (837 m. and 15,782 inhabitants) and Briançon (1,250 m. and 9,879 inhabitants). These facts bring out two points which might otherwise be missed: first, the low altitude of the large Alpine towns, Grenoble, 'capital' of the Alps, being at only 212 m.; secondly, the much more mountainous character of the southern part of the Central Massif. Unlike the Alps, it does not possess broad valley corridors and well-graded valleys, levelled by glacial and river deposits. On the contrary, it is broken into small *pays* by narrow, deeply incised valleys, hindering rather than helping communication. They afford few good sites for towns.

The cities have therefore grown up mainly in the lowest-lying areas of France. On land below 100 m., a quarter of the total area of the country, there are 52% of the population living in towns of 20,000–30,000, 49% in towns of 30,000–50,000, 65% in towns of 50,000–100,000, 37·5% in towns of 100,000–200,000 and 85% in towns of over 200,000 inhabitants (in 1954). Most of these towns are situated on coasts or rivers. It was natural that coasts and rivers should attract urban settlement at a time when water was the chief source of power and medium for communication and trade between towns. At the same time water served as a means of defence, either in the form of moats or as natural defences (cf. Lutetia, the classical city of Paris).

Sixty-one per cent of the French towns are on waterways and seventy-nine per cent of the departmental capitals are on rivers. Out of 165 towns with populations over 20,000 in 1954 only eight were not directly associated with a river or a canal. These included two towns in the Paris region, one being Versailles; three industrial towns, Hénin-Liétard, Forbach and Hayange; two Mediterranean cities, Aix and Nîmes, and a typical hilltop town, Laon. Limoges and Clermont-Ferrand are the only French towns with more than 100,000 inhabitants which are not situated on the coast or a navigable waterway.

The regional diversity of France gives rise to many instances of adjacent *pays* with complementary agricultural and industrial resources and this has encouraged the development of towns along lines of contact between ancient massifs and sedimentary basins, highland and lowland, rich *pays* and poor *pays*, forested areas and cleared areas. 'A great many of the towns of Aquitaine are "contact towns". There is a whole line of them along the western margin of the Central Massif, from Confolens and Nontron to Albi, Castres and Castelnaudary. Another line of towns occurs at the mouths of Pyrenean valleys from Pamiers to Bayonne' (D. Faucher).

There are countless types of town sites.

Valley sites, as distinct from river sites: Pontarlier at the entrance to a *cluse*, Mirecourt at a valley crossroads and many mountain towns.

Sites on estuaries, on rias and on rivers: J. Blache has pointed out the importance of sites established on the outer sides of river bends, at which roads generally converge; this is the case at Orleans, Toulouse, Angoulême, Grenoble, Nevers, Strasbourg, Le Mans, Chalon, Vienne and Avignon.

Defensive sites in valley bottoms: Paris, Amiens, Bourges, Beauvais and the towns of Flanders.

Sites at the edge of areas of easy communication: Lille, which is on the Deûle, but near the chalk spurs of Mélantois.

River crossing sites: Angers, Bayeux, Montereau, Brive, the bridge towns on the Rhône.

Sites which are more or less hilltop sites on meanders and meander cores: Besançon, Cahors, Rodez, Bourges, Saint-Brieuc and Mézières. Curiously, there are few sites at river junctions: Grenoble, Nevers, Lyons, Metz.

Defensive sites of *oppida* set upon well-isolated hilltops, interfluves or buttes: Langres, Laon, Longwy, Avallon, Loudun, Chaumont, Rocroi, Cassel; or on meander cores: Besançon, Poitiers, Vannes, Nevers, Angoulême.

Spring sites: Nîmes, Dijon, Cahors, Orange, Aix-en-Provence, Aix-les-Bains, Vichy, Plombières.

Sites at valley constrictions: Sisteron, Digne, Castellane, Cluses.

Sites at access points to highlands: the towns at the entrances to re-entrants along the borders of the Jura. Such sites on spurs seem to be particularly numerous.

The permanence of site values is one of the characteristic features of French urbanisation, even though the relative importance of the sites has changed considerably over the centuries. The communication infrastructure built up in relation to key sites—bridges, crossroads, ports—has done much to stabilise urban development.

Transfers from one site to another were rare and were made long ago. Aix-en-Provence replaced Entremont (the capital of the Salyens); Clermont-Ferrand succeeded Gergovia; Autun replaced Bibracte, the capital of the Eduens. Cases of 'slipping' or 'creeping' (J. Blache) when towns moved downhill from their defensive hilltop sites were more common: Lyons descended from Fourvière, Annecy from Semnoz and Chambéry from the Lemenc hill. Later, in the 19th century, Albertville developed at the expense of the high-level town of Conflans. More recently still, the railways have often caused towns to migrate downhill towards railway stations.

II

URBAN GROWTH AND TYPOLOGY

1. URBAN GROWTH

The growth of the urban population of France has already been analysed in Chapter I of Part Two.[7] This urban growth has affected cities variously at different periods.

A. Growth from 1851 to 1954

From 1851 to 1954 the coefficients of increase were: 1·9 for urban communes of 5,000–10,000 inhabitants; 2·6 for those of 10,000–20,000 inhabitants; 3·5 for those of 20,000–50,000 inhabitants.

The very small towns or *bourgades* with less than 10,000 inhabitants have benefited hardly at all from the urban development of the last hundred years. Allowing for a margin of about 160,000, there were as many people living in towns of from 3,000 to 5,000 in 1954 as there were in 1851.

Table LXVII summarises the key statistics showing variations in growth by size categories. From this can be seen:

1. On the one hand, the magnitude of urbanisation, amounting to a threefold increase within a century in the number of towns with 20,000 or more inhabitants, and a substantial increase in the number with more than 100,000 inhabitants;

2. On the other hand, a relative stability in the relations between the different categories of towns; whereas the percentages calculated in relation to the total population of France bring out the amount of urban growth, those calculated in relation to the urban population only show less variation, except for large towns of over 200,000, the Paris agglomeration, and towns with less than 20,000 inhabitants.

The case of Paris illustrates these two aspects of development. The population of Paris increased substantially in absolute terms, from 1,242,000 in 1851 to 2,212,000 in 1872, 3,114,000 in 1891 and 4,108,000 in 1931. Its rate of growth between 1851 and 1954 was 3·3 compared with only 2·7 for towns of 20,000 or more inhabitants. But the 'weight' of Paris remained more or less constant in relation to the urban population of France. The population of the departments of Seine and Seine-et-Oise was 21·2% of the urban population of France in 1872, 25·1% in 1901, 27% in 1954 and 26% in 1962.

Growth rates have varied from town to town. Between 1851 and 1954, of the towns and agglomerations with 20,000 or more inhabitants (excluding the Paris agglomeration):

38 had a coefficient of increase between 1 and 2
50 „ „ „ „ „ 2 and 3
32 „ „ „ „ „ 3 and 4
11 „ „ „ „ „ 4 and 5
14 „ „ „ „ over 5

The towns with coefficients over 5 were: Grenoble (5·2), Calais (5·4), Montluçon (5·9), Longwy (11·3), Hayange (9·3), Firminy (9·2), Vichy (8·1), Forbach (7·5), Montceau-les-Mines (6·4), Belfort (5·9), Biarritz (11·1), Creil (7·9), Hénin-Liétard (7·5), Mantes (5·8). These towns are not major urban centres. They owe their high growth rates to specialised functions, twelve of them to industry and two to tourism.[8] These growth rates are clearly negligible compared with those of towns in the Paris region. They include many towns with coefficients over 10, and three over 20 (Aubervilliers, 22·4; Vitry, 20·5; Montreuil,

TABLE LXVII. URBAN UNITS FROM 1851 TO 1962

		1851	1901	1954	1962
20,000 to 50,000 inhabitants	Number	40 (75·4%)	87 (70·1%)	117 (67·2%)	127 (61·65%)
	Population	1,234,562 (35·7%)	2,531,586 (27%)	3,586,265 (22·1%)	3,955,081 (18·3%)
	% French pop.	3·4	6·2	8·3	8·5
	% French urban pop.	13·5	15·8	14·9	13·4
50,000 to 100,000 inhabitants	Number	8 (15%)	22 (17·7%)	29 (16·6%)	38 (18·44%)
	Population	557,941 (16·2%)	1,484,889 (15·8%)	1,932,448 (11·9%)	2,451,532 (11·3%)
	% French pop.	1·5	3·6	4·5	5·3
	% French urban pop.	6·1	9·3	8	8·3
100,000 to 200,000 inhabitants	Number	4 (7·5%)	10 (8%)	17 (9·7%)	24 (11·65%)
	Population	603,639 (17·5%)	1,217,922 (13%)	2,220,882 (13·7%)	3,066,018 (14·1%)
	% French pop.	1·6	2·9	5·1	6·63
	% French urban pop.	6·6	7·6	9·2	10·4
200,000 or more inhabitants	Number	—	4 (3·2%)	10 (5·7%)	16 (7·76%)
	Population	—	1,417,594 (15·1%)	3,593,563 (22·2%)	5,717,680 (26·4%)
	% French pop.	—	3·4	8·4	12·26
	% French urban pop.	—	8·8	15	19·3

PARIS AGGLOMERATION*

	1851	1901	1954	1962
Population	1,053,262 (30·5%)	2,714,068 (28·9%)	4,823,252 (29·8%)	6,454,345 (29·9%)
% French pop.	2·9	6·6	11·2	13·95
% French urban pop.	11·5	17	20·1	21·8

URBAN UNITS WITH 20,000 INHABITANTS AND MORE

	1851	1901	1954	1962
Number	53 (100%)	124 (100%)	174 (100%)	206 (100%)
Population	3,449,404 (100%)	9,366,059 (100%)	16,156,410 (100%)	21,644,656 (100%)
% French pop.	9·63	23	37·5	46·8
% French urban pop.	37·75	58·6	67	73·2

URBAN UNITS WITH LESS THAN 20,000 INHABITANTS

	1851	1901	1954	1962
Number	1,030		1,387	2,333
Population	5,686,055	6,591,131	7,790,261	7,906,331
% French urban pop.	62·2	41·4	32·6	26·8

* According to the conservative definition of the I.N.S.E.E.

20). The coefficients of increase were larger for the smaller urban centres, especially the industrial towns (Briey, 6·75; Thionville, 6·6).

Growth has evidently not been constant throughout the century, for it was most marked during the first fifty years, when the effects of the industrial revolution were spreading most rapidly. By 1901 five of the fourteen towns named above had coefficients over 5. It is important to appreciate the significance of this urban growth in the later decades of the 19th century. Present-day urban growth gives no idea of the rapid expansion which caused, for instance, a rise in the population of Roubaix-Tourcoing, from 76,000 in 1851 to 144,000 in 1872 and 222,000 in 1891, and of Belfort from 8,000 in 1872 to 25,500 in 1891. After 1901 urban growth became both weaker and more strictly localised; the coefficients for most towns for the period 1901–54 lay between 1 and 2; only two towns reached or exceeded 3: Forbach (3) and La

Baule (5). Also, whereas all towns were growing before 1901, several of them have subsequently suffered a slight loss of population: Rochefort and Armentières (0·8), Lunéville, Verdun, Le Creusot, Elbeuf (0·9). Only certain towns in the Paris agglomeration have experienced their maximum growth during this period: Antony (7·9), Aulnay-sous-Bois (13·6), Drancy (40·6), Le Blanc-Mesnil (119), the highest rates being related to industrial development. Comparative studies have shown that growth has varied considerably with the type of industrial specialisation, the closest correlations being found in the case of extractive, metallurgical, engineering and electrical industries (Hayange, Longwy).

Population graphs for towns, for the period 1851–1954 as a whole, reflect wide differences between individual towns. Some have experienced a vigorous and uninterrupted growth since 1851: Toulouse, Bordeaux, Lille, Rennes. For others, growth has been 'interrupted' by a long or short period of falling rate of increase, followed by stability or a slight decline before a revival. Many industrial towns experienced a fall in population, contemporary with the great Depression, between the census of 1926 and that of 1936: Bruay, Saint-Chamond, Le Creusot, Firminy, Hayange. Others experienced prolonged stagnation from 1881 to 1926: Chaumont, Montbéliard, Nevers.

A third category of towns shared very successfully in the general urban growth down to the beginning of the 20th century, but then 'got stuck' until after the war. These were the textile towns of northern France (Roubaix), Alsace (Mulhouse) and the Paris Basin (Saint-Quentin, Rheims, Troyes), and commercial towns in the Aquitaine basin and Languedoc (Cognac, Narbonne). The last group includes stagnant or declining towns, long dormant small towns untouched by the spur of industrialisation right up to the Second World War: Blois, Laval, Lunéville, Rochefort. Five of these towns have been stagnating since 1896: Elbeuf, Sète, Armentières, Fougères, Saint-Dié, mostly one-industry towns.

Administrative functions and industrial localisation have determined this selective differentiation between towns. The arrival of the railway was usually decisive. Thanks to the railways, Le Mans outdistanced Alençon; Vesoul overtook Gray; little *bourgs* became important freight centres: Chasse, Châteaurenard, Charolles.

B. Variations in the Urban Pattern

This growth of towns had important repercussions upon the urban pattern of France (fig. 88). In *1851* the pattern was still very open, and consisted of fifty-eight towns of more than 20,000 inhabitants. Urban life was, in effect, provided by towns with populations below 50,000 (twenty-four from 20,000 to 30,000 and seventeen from 30,000 to 50,000). Towns over 100,000 were six in number and far apart. The towns were irregularly distributed. Whole regions were devoid of them: Normandy, Maine, Brittany, the south-eastern and eastern Paris Basin, the South-west and the Alps. The areas of urban development were northern France as far as the Somme and Languedoc (Montauban, Toulouse, Castres, Carcassonne), the lower Rhône area with Avignon, Montpellier and Toulon as the apices of an urban triangle, the Loire valley from Orleans to Nantes and the Lyons–Saint-Étienne region.

A comparison between the *1851* and *1881* maps shows more clearly than words how France was affected by the urban revolution within thirty years. The number of towns with populations over 20,000 rose to 96 by the addition of 40 new ones. The size categories also changed significantly. The number of towns with populations from 30,000 to 50,000 was unchanged, but the numbers in other categories were doubled. Those which best exemplify the rapidity of urban growth at this period are the 50,000–100,000 and 20,000–30,000 categories.

The salient features of the 1954 urban pattern were already delineated by 1881. The size distribution of towns was, however, very curious. Large towns with populations over

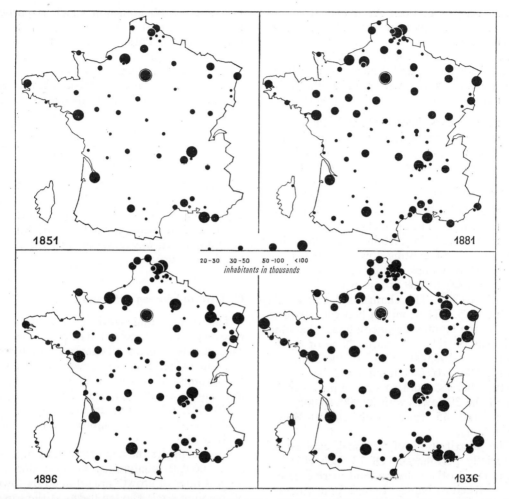

Fig. 88. The urban mesh of France in 1851, 1881, 1896 and 1936. (Source: F. Carrière et Ph. Pinchemel, *Le Fait urbain en France*, A. Colin, 1963)

50,000 predominated north of the line Bcsançon–Nantes, just as they do to the east of the Rhône–Saône axis; towns with populations between 20,000 and 30,000 were few and far between, except in the North, which was in full development as a mining and steel-producing region. In the North-east in particular, towns of more than 50,000 inhabitants appear isolated and lacking in intermediate centres of a lower order. The Loire towns have been joined by Le Mans and Rennes, to make the only group of towns over 50,000

spaced at less than 150 km. In contrast, small towns are much more numerous to the south of the Besançon–Nantes line. Here they are irregularly distributed between the major foci formed by the towns over 100,000 and seven towns of 50,000–100,000 in population.

These small towns are most numerous in two areas:

1. In Languedoc, where the viticultural centres have come to reinforce the traditional urban centres between Agen and Arles, so that twelve towns now have 20,000–50,000 inhabitants.

2. In a triangle formed by Châteauroux, Chalon-sur-Saône and Valence where there are thirteen towns with 20,000–30,000 inhabitants.

Fifteen years later, in *1896*, the urban pattern shows hardly any noteworthy changes in structure, the hierarchy of towns being very nearly the same: 106 in 1881, 111 in 1896. Only 7 have risen to the first category (20,000–30,000 inhabitants): Cognac, Saintes, Vannes, Saint-Brieuc, Lunéville, Saint-Dié and Épernay. The main change during these years occurred in certain size categories. The growth of existing towns exceeded the growth of new ones, mainly to the advantage of the 30,000–50,000 group, which increased from 18 to 30. This change is clearly visible on the map. The contrast between opposite sides of the Nantes–Besançon line is the same as it was on the 1881 map. Nine of the 14 towns over 100,000 and 15 of the 22 towns with 50,000–100,000 inhabitants lie to the north, whereas southern France possesses 18 out of the 30 towns with 30,000–50,000, and 28 of the 45 towns with 20,000–30,000 inhabitants.

The distribution of regional capitals is essentially peripheral. Of 13 such cities, 5 are ports, 3 others are on land or river frontiers. Rheims, Nancy, Lyons, Saint-Étienne and Toulouse are the only big cities in the interior.

In *1926* the urban pattern had barely changed in thirty years. The number of towns had risen from 111 to 128. Most 'new' towns are industrial centres, and several others are the result of a slow increase in urban populations (Auxerre, Bourg-en-Bresse, Dôle, Annemasse).

In *1954* the pattern of urban development again shows no drastic alteration. The map shows, however, two significant changes within the twenty-eight-year period.

1. The appearance of a considerable number of new, small towns (20,000–30,000 inhabitants), a phenomenon which is particularly pronounced around Paris, where the space between Paris and other towns over 100,000 in population has been filled by many towns that did not exist in 1926.

2. The increase in the number of towns with more than 100,000 inhabitants from 19 to 27. Towns in this category, which form the skeleton of the French urban network, have been augmented by Limoges, Dijon, Metz, Brest, Rennes, Le Mans, Angers and Tours.

This analysis confirms the age of the urban mesh. This has developed in its quantitative aspects and has been filled out by the addition of small and medium-sized towns, but the general pattern was established by the end of the last century.

C. Growth between 1954 and 1962

The demographic revival and economic recovery led to a resumption of urban growth. This growth affected all categories of towns, but the higher rates of growth occurred in the groups of towns with 30,000–50,000 inhabitants (+19·3%), and 50,000–100,000 (+20·1%), rather than in those of 20,000–30,000 (+13·6%) or more than 100,000 (+16·5%).

If we consider the agglomerations of more than 100,000 inhabitants, we find that the highest rates of growth are attained by towns of 'medium size'. The ten towns at the top of the list have populations of 97,000–233,000. They are: Grenoble (+44·5%), Besançon (+35·3%), Caen (+35·2%), Dunkirk (+26·3%), Montpellier (+25·5%), Brest (+25·3%), Rennes (+24·9%), Dijon (+24·3%), Orleans (+23%), Toulon (+21·9%), Le Mans (+21·9%). It is the cities in the South-east and the West which show the highest growth rates. The big cities follow, with lower rates: Toulouse (+21%), Lyons (+18·5%), Marseilles (+16·4%), Lille (+8·4%) and Bordeaux, which closes the list (+5·8%). The Paris region comes in the second half, twenty-third on the list, with a rate of increase of 15%.

But the 'Paris complex' has nevertheless taken 46·5% of the total growth of all the thirty-four leading French agglomerations (1,000,600 out of 2,151,700).

TABLE LXVIII. TOWNS WITH THE HIGHEST RATES OF GROWTH BETWEEN 1954 AND 1962 (1954 = 100)

Mourenx	3,124
Behren-les-Forbach	2,200
Faulquemont	342
Guénange	1,052
Fareberswiller	1,416
Folschwiller	378
Uckange	267
Marignane	305
Martigues	200
Port-de-Bouc	197
Poissy	226
Meulan	258
Conflans-Sainte-Honorine	209
Goussainville	206
Trappes	277
Brétigny-sur-Orge	214
Pecquencourt	205
Saint-Brévin-les-Pins	211
Annecy	198
Cluses	234
Bagnols-sur-Cèze	274
Gradignan	205
Lannemezan	288

This confirms its continuing power of attraction; so great are the preponderance and the uniqueness of Paris that, even with lower rates of increase than provincial cities, it still attracts an excessive proportion of the total urban growth.[9] The list of towns with a rate of increase above 200 for the period 1954–62 (Table LXVIII) underlines the importance of the development of new industrial towns and of the communes on the outskirts of Paris and Marseilles. Only Annecy and Cluses are towns in the true sense of the term.

'A comparative study of the growth of towns within the period 1901–36 and 1936–62 confirms that, with certain exceptions, the French demographic revival has not favoured the big cities' (R. P. Mols).

On the contrary, the highest rates of increase were recorded by the medium-sized and small towns. Some of them have gained more than three times as much as they gained between 1901 and 1936. For example: Moulins, Gap, Privas, Carcassonne, Aurillac, Angoulême, Bourges, Guéret, Besançon, Évreux, Châteauroux, Blois, Le Puy, Vannes, Mâcon, Poitiers (Table LXIX).

TABLE LXIX. TYPES OF URBAN GROWTH IN TWO PERIODS COMPARED

	Gains in the period	
	1901–36	1936–62
Bordeaux	74,334	55,725
Lille	70,296	43,889
Nice	141,834	52,131
Strasbourg	66,623	48,410
Toulouse	63,953	114,056
Nantes	58,487	87,327

D. The Growth Process

During these hundred years (1851–1954), urban growth was achieved mainly by immigration, the excess of births over deaths being only a secondary factor. The new townsfolk came from the near or distant countryside, from other towns, or from other countries. Natives of Annecy represented 68·5% of the population of the town in 1838, but only a minority group of 31·1% in 1954, the majority consisting of in-migrants from all parts of France: the Paris region (16·2%), Brittany (3·2%), Lorraine (3·5%). Only 21% of the inhabitants of Moulins in 1954 were born there; 44% were born outside the department. The corresponding figures for Aurillac were 29 and 35%.

Example. In 1886 the population of the small town of Arques (4,567 inhabitants) in Pas-de-Calais comprised: 80·8% born in the commune; 10% born in the department; 7% born in another department; 2·2% born in another country.

In 1960 the electoral population of Arques was as follows: 42·6% born in the commune; 18·5% born in the two cantons of Saint-Omer; 10·4% born in the rest of the *arrondissement*; 9·7% in the rest of the department of Pas-de-Calais; 10·3% in the department of Nord; 5·6% in other departments; 1·5% in another country.

The relay function of towns in the process of urban growth has long been known; small towns represent the first stage of growth, and it is from them that the larger towns draw their increase in population.[10]

Figures 89 and 90 represent the complex of migratory movements between the different

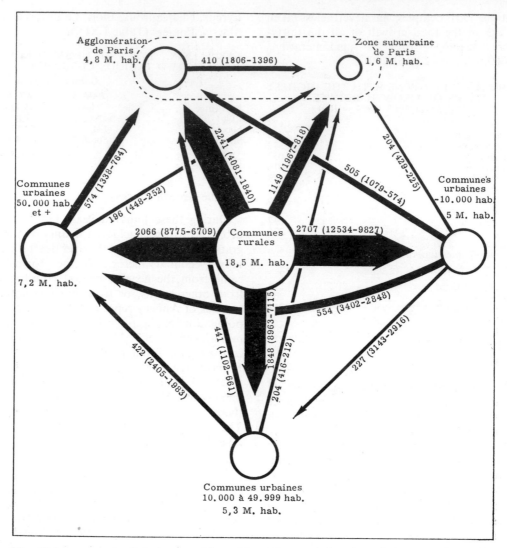

Fig. 89.   Net movements of electors aged from 21 to 29 years (migration of electors registered in 1953 within the categories of communes).   (Source: Clément et Vieille, 'L'Exode rural', *Études de comptabilité nationale*, no. I, April 1960)

categories of urban and rural communes in a breakdown of the movements of electors recorded in 1953.   They show the attraction which towns have for young people in rural communes, and the attraction of towns with more than 10,000 inhabitants for those with less than 10,000, and also the attraction of Paris; the relay function of small towns is thus clear to see.   Another, less often noticed,

phenomenon is that of the return to rural communes of electors between the ages of 45 and 59, although these do not appreciably diminish the townward balance of migration.

The fact that urban populations originate from two sources is generally valid; the population of the Lyons agglomeration, for example, increased between 1954 and 1962 by

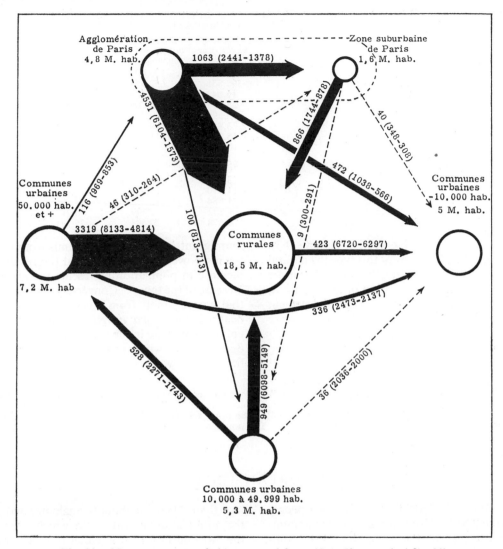

Fig. 90.   Net movements of electors aged from 45 to 59 years (see fig. 89).

an excess of inward over outward migration of 103,002 and an excess of births over deaths of 40,300.   The migration gain by Nice was 52,900 whereas there was a natural decrease of 2,000.   The towns with the highest rates of increase of population by net in-migration, from 1954 to 1962, were: Grenoble (35·7), Besançon (24·8), Caen (23·8), Montpellier (21·5), Nice (20·8), Rennes (18·6), Toulouse (17·2), Toulon (16·9).

But the demographic revival of the post-war period has once again made natural increase important for some towns.   The vitality index, calculated in 1954 for the principal towns of France, reflects widely differing situations.[11]   Some towns had very low rates: Limoges (2·7), Nice (1·5), Saint-Étienne (3·2), Montpellier and Bordeaux (3·7).   Others had very marked demographic dynamism and youthfulness: Le Mans (13·1), Caen (12·5),

TABLE LXX. NATURAL INCREASE AND MIGRATION BALANCE FOR
SELECTED TOWNS AND AGGLOMERATIONS (1954–62)

	Excess of births over deaths	Migration balance of the municipality	Change in the municipal population
City of Paris	118,675	−195,402	−76,727
Paris residential complex	398,856	652,554	1,051,410
Bordeaux	15,643	12,209	27,852
Lille	28,777	4,005	32,782
Roubaix-Tourcoing	16,599	9,789	26,388
Nantes	23,867	19,127	42,994
Nancy	15,224	11,720	26,944
Rheims	10,788	7,508	18,296
Le Mans	11,234	14,506	25,740
Caen	10,690	19,911	30,631
Brest	13,104	13,103	26,207
Dunkirk	11,390	14,024	25,414
Limoges	1,884	12,312	14,196
Nice	−1,882	52,799	50,917
Montpellier	4,678	20,593	25,271

Brest (10·9), Dunkirk (10·3), Nancy (7·3), Rheims (7). In towns of this type the natural excess of births over deaths was either more important than in-migration or as important, in each case representing a substantial element in urban growth. Table LXX gives some examples.

The difference in significance of these two kinds of growth is important; the arrival of 'immigrants' is a sign of dynamism and the town's power of attraction, and the resulting increase in population represents the *specific increase* of the town. Conversely, an increase that comes simply from excess of births over deaths is the *normal increase*, which does not entail an increase in the active population and does not bear witness to a dynamic economic life in the town.

7. Cf. p. 118.
8. To these should be added towns on the Côte d'Azur which were annexed by France at a later date: Nice, 5·5; Cannes, 9; Antibes, 3·5.
9. The city of Paris lost 97,175 inhabitants (−3·4%), the inner suburban ring (*banlieue*) increased by 23·7% and the outer suburban ring (*suburbaine*) by 51·2%. The population of Sarcelles rose from 8,397 to 35,430.
10. Cf. p. 128.
11. For the vitality index, cf. p. 132 and fig. 42.

2. URBAN UNITS

In 1962, 29,550,987 French townspeople lived in 2,818 urban communes in the administrative sense of the term; but these communes corresponded to very different kinds of urban units.

A. One-commune Towns

At the beginning of the recent period of urbanisation, each town identified itself with one commune, and its walls defined the limits of its growth. One-commune towns are still numerous in France; in 1954 they represented 63 out of the 159 towns and agglomerations with more than 20,000 inhabitants. To this first group also belong communes which have less than 2,000 inhabitants agglomerated in the administrative centre, but which possess the attributes of a town, either in form or in their functions.

B. Agglomerations

French communes being very small (cf. Part Three, Chapter I), the growth of towns resulted in their overspill into neighbouring communes. Outlying suburbs became inner suburbs and nearby villages with their rural surroundings were quickly urbanised so that adjacent rural communes were inevitably incorporated within urban areas to form agglomerations.

An agglomeration is one of the easiest phenomena to describe, but one of the most difficult to delimit exactly. It is nevertheless essential to draw up lists of communes included within agglomerations as a basis for meaningful comparison between them. The I.N.S.E.E. worked out an objective method of defining agglomerations for the 1962 census. Several criteria were used: size of population, density, growth rate, proportion of population dependent on agriculture, continuity of built-up areas. Numerical values were assigned for each criterion, the total value for a particular commune indicating whether or not it belonged to a particular agglomeration. The result showed considerable differences in the composition of agglomerations in 1962 from that of 1954. Whereas the index used in 1954 may have been too narrow, that used in 1962 was perhaps too comprehensive. For example, the area of the Lille agglomeration was increased from 12 to 23 communes; that of Grenoble from 7 to 14.

The criteria adopted have the limitations of static properties. They fail to indicate by what kinds of functional relationships and interdependence a commune becomes part of an agglomeration. The criteria suffice in many cases because urbanisation is still very weak and discontinuous in France. They make it possible to define the 'urban quality' of a commune, but they are inadequate in the more heavily urbanised industrial areas and urban regions—when it is necessary, for example, to locate the boundaries of an agglomeration in the northern coalfield of France. The I.N.S.E.E. has thus defined Lens–Hénin-Liétard as an agglomeration of twenty-two communes, whereas these are actually two towns, 15 km. apart, each surrounded by its urbanised zone. Only criteria expressing functions and relationships can help to resolve these problems; daily journeys to work, the attraction of educational, health and commercial services in the commune-centre, the existence of a feeling of belonging to 'the town', are some of the criteria which can be utilised. Broadly speaking the 'mother-commune' contains more than three quarters of the population and almost always more than half; the exceptions occur in special circumstances where, for example, a commune has a very small area (Dunkirk: 24% in 1954), or where there are twin towns (Roubaix-Tourcoing: 41·2% in 1954).

Table LXXI gives the size distribution of French towns according to the commune boundaries and the definitions used in the two recent censuses. The classification by urban communes, disregarding agglomerations as such, stresses the importance of small towns: 83·6% of the communes have less than 10,000 inhabitants and contain 33·7% of the total urban population. The percentages are 85·2 and 21·6% in terms of the urban units defined in 1954. Exactly one third of the urban population of France live in towns of less than 20,000 inhabitants; rather less than a third live in towns of 20,000–200,000 inhabitants and the remaining third live in towns over 200,000 in population, including Paris. Towns of 50,000–200,000 inhabitants contain only 16·7% of the urban population. The 50,000–100,000 and 100,000–200,000 size categories thus seem to be 'under-represented' in France. The 1961 definition of agglomerations yields a larger number of towns in the higher size categories at the expense of the three lower categories; 21·4% of the urban population, compared with a third as defined above, live in towns of less than 20,000 inhabitants. But this definition of agglomerations is inadequate to distinguish between all the types of association between urban communes.

C. Conurbations

An agglomeration is defined as an assemblage of urbanised communes about a single centre (*pole*). When several *poles* exist within an urban complex with the communes clustered around them all, it is preferable to speak of conurbations. The Lille conurbation (767,397 inhabitants) includes the agglomerations of Lille and Roubaix-Tourcoing; the term may be applied to a group of towns such as Biarritz, Bayonne and Le Boucau.

TABLE LXXI. DISTRIBUTION OF THE URBAN POPULATION OF FRANCE IN 1954 AND 1962 BY COMMUNES AND URBAN UNITS

Number of inhabitants	Communes (1954)				Urban units by definition of 1954			
	No.	%	Population	%	No.	%	Population	%
2,000–5,000	1,841	65·3	5,480,076	20·5	775	49·6	2,587,269	10·4
5,000–10,000	518	18·3	3,550,714	13·2	404	25·8	2,792,562	11·2
10,000–20,000	250	8·8	3,492,732	13·0	208	13·3	2,831,189	11·4
20,000–50,000	145	5·1	4,359,380	16·2	117	7·4	3,580,265	14·4
50,000–100,000	39	1·3	2,689,490	10	29	1·8	1,932,448	7·8
100,000–200,000					17	1·0	2,220,882	8·9
200,000–1,000,000	24	0·8	7,205,186	26·9	10	0·6	3,953,563	15·9
Paris Agglomeration					1	0·06	4,823,252	19·5
Total	2,817	100	26,777,578	100	1,561	100	24,721,430	100

Number of inhabitants	Communes (1962)			
	No.	%	Population	%
2,000–5,000	1,904	61·8	5,738,620	17·9
5,000–10,000	590	19·1	3,994,857	12·5
10,000–20,000	305	9·9	4,143,210	13·0
20,000–50,000	199	6·5	5,948,547	18·6
50,000–100,000	51	1·7	3,409,365	10·7
100,000 and over	32	1·0	8,751,220	27·4
Paris Agglomeration				
Total	3,081	100	31,985,819	100

Number of inhabitants	Urban units by definition of 1962			
	No.	%	Population	%
Less than 5,000	685	50·1	2,319,913	7·7
5,000–10,000	327	23·9	2,222,266	7·4
10,000–20,000	155	11·3	2,085,466	6·9
20,000–50,000	115	8·4	3,579,214	11·8
50,000–100,000	43	3·1	2,911,279	9·6
100,000–200,000	23	1·7	3,167,393	10·5
200,000–1,000,000	18	1·3	6,104,747	20·2
	1	0·07	7,813,902	25·9
	1,367	100	30,204,180	100

D. Urban Aggregates

The industrial regions, especially the coalfields and orefields, were urbanised progressively as pits and factories were opened and their service infrastructures established. Villages, small towns and, above all, extensive tracts of open countryside were incorporated in this urban development, without an initial impetus from the expansion of any one or several mother-towns. The pre-existing urban nuclei were usually enveloped by the spread of groups of mining villages and industrial housing estates, without adapting their functions and buildings to the changing pattern of land use. The expression 'urban aggregate' conveniently describes such assemblages of communes which lack a hierarchy and have no organic dependence upon a major urban centre.

E. The Urban Nebula in a Rural Environment

The long history of urbanisation in France and the succession of changes in the factors of urban development have often resulted in the growth of several towns at short distances from each other, without forming a true agglomeration. There are many examples: in the valley of the Oise, La Fère, Tergnier and Chauny together contain nearly 40,000 inhabitants within 15 km., more than the population of Laon or Soissons. On a larger scale, the same is true of Creil, Senlis and Chantilly, of Saint-Raphaël and Fréjus, Tullins, Moirans and Voreppe. This situation often arises from the growth of two towns on opposite banks of a river, like Tarascon and Beaucaire on the Rhône.

F. The Urban Region (an urban nebula in an urban environment)

In the final stage, an entire area may become urbanised, agricultural areas becoming interstitial or open spaces not yet covered by houses, factories or communications. The pattern of urban development may vary greatly according to the size of buildings and the method of growth. This kind of regional urbanisation is rare in France, which, as we have seen, is relatively lacking in major metropolitan areas. The Paris region, the North and also the Côte d'Azur litoral are nevertheless examples of this type, in which urbanised communes adjoin one another.

III

URBAN FUNCTIONS

1. THE COMPOSITION OF THE URBAN WORKING POPULATION

Table LXXII gives a preliminary, overall view of the occupational structure of the urban population of France 1954–62. The figures in the last four columns are relatively homogeneous, and show that the Paris urbanised. Such are Perpignan with 9·4% of its working population in the primary sector, Antibes (18·4), Hyères (25·8), Arles (28·3).

2. Fishing activities are a special case since they are essentially urban activities.

TABLE LXXII. PERCENTAGE COMPOSITION BY CLASSES OF ACTIVITY (1954 AND 1962)*

Classes of activity	1954				1962			
	1	2	3	4	1	2	3	4
(a) *Primary Sector* . . .	27·6	4·5	6·2	0·7	20·6	3·5	4·7	0·6
(b) *Secondary Sector* . . .	*35·3*	*44·3*	*44·7*	*43·8*	*38·7*	*45·1*	*45·7*	*43·9*
Extractive industries . . .	2	2·5	3·5	0·1	1·6	1·8	2·6	1·1
Building, public works . . .	7·2	7·8	8·5	5·9	8·8	9·3	10	7·8
Metallurgy, mechanical and electrical engineering . . .	10·2	14·1	12·2	18·5	12·8	16·1	14·5	19·9
Chemical industries . . .	2·7	3·3	3·3	4·1	1·9	2·4	2·1	3·2
Food industries . . .	2·8	3·2	3·5	2·4	2·8	3	3·3	2·3
Textiles, clothing . . .	5·7	7·5	8·6	5·2	4·7	5·6	6·7	3·4
Other industries . . .	4·7	5·9	5·1	7·6	6·4	6·9	6·5	6·2
(c) *Tertiary Sector* . . .	*35·3*	*48·9*	*47·6*	*52·8*	*40·6*	*51·3*	*49·5*	*55·4*
Transport	4	5·7	5·7	5·7	4·2	5·3	5·2	5·6
Commerce, banking, insurance .	14	19·4	18·4	21·6	15·4	19·4	18·8	20·9
Public services, administration .	17·3	23·8	23	25·5	21	26·6	25·5	28·9
Not declared	1·2	1·6	1·2	2·1	—	—	—	—

* Percentage of:
  1. The total working population of France.
  2. The urban working population of France, including the Paris agglomeration.
  3. The urban working population of France, excluding the Paris agglomeration.
  4. The working population of the Paris agglomeration.

agglomeration does not seriously distort the occupational class structure provided that the occupations are grouped into large classes. The figures for tertiary activities are almost identical.

A. Primary Functions

The primary sector cannot be entirely excluded from a consideration of urban working population, for two reasons:

1. Agriculture is important for certain communes which have not been completely

The way the houses cluster round the docks, the importance of chandlers' stores, fish porters, middlemen, canning and freezing works, transport facilities, the busy activity at certain times of the day and the community spirit, all combine to give fishing ports unmistakably urban characteristics. In 1954 2% or more of the working population of six towns was employed in fishing: Lorient (2%), La Rochelle (3·9%), Sète (4·1%), Dieppe (5%), Boulogne (7%), Douarnenez (24%).

Table LXXIII ranks the seventeen leading fresh-fish ports in 1960 and 1962. Fishing is carried on from 14,206 vessels, 10,800 of which are boats of less than 10 tons. Vessels of more than 10 tons include: 1,305 fresh-fish trawlers, 31 deep-sea trawlers, 3 refrigerator-trawlers, 83 fishwell trawlers, 137 tunny-boats (including 17 equipped with refrigeration),

B. Secondary Functions (industrial)

Considering only towns and agglomerations with 20,000 inhabitants or more, we find that in 1954, 34% of the provincial towns had more people working in the secondary sector

TABLE LXXIII. FISHING PORTS

	Catches			
	Tons		Value (Thousands of francs)	
	1960	1967	1960	1967
Boulogne	120,920	133,854	116,134	143,039
Lorient	47,436	56,198	68,024	93,991
Concarneau . . .	41,282	49,757	55,112	97,126
La Rochelle . . .	23,796	22,917	49,175	64,129
Douarnenez . . .	18,795	17,081	22,555	35,403
Dieppe	17,550	7,759	17,924	—
Les Sables . . .	8,598	9,846	15,135	24,140
Cherbourg . . .	7,685	7,393	9,404	12,574
Le Guilvinec . . .	7,552	11,588	12,086	22,106
Port-en-Bessin . . .	7,352	8,508	7,997	12,321
Saint-Jean-de-Luz . .	6,070	12,169	12,152	23,170
Fécamp	4,517	5,102	3,770	—
Etel	3,624		4,430	
Arcachon	2,948		6,315	
Saint-Gilles-Croix-de-Vie .	2,780		6,009	
Quiberon . . .	2,569		4,630	
Saint-Guénolé . . .	2,530		4,736	
Other ports . . .	43,136		88,629	
Total	369,140		504,217	

147 lobster-boats (including 31 with refrigeration). The distribution of deep-sea and off-shore trawlers between the different ports was as follows in February 1968:

TABLE LXXIV. DISTRIBUTION OF TRAWLERS

	Number	Tonnage	Mean Tonnage
Lorient . .	81	21,934	270
La Rochelle . .	62	15,923	256
Boulogne . .	55	26,288	477
Fécamp . .	27 *	25,990	962
Bordeaux . .	10 †	16,112	1,611
Saint-Malo . .	11 ‡	11,778	1,070
Arcachon . .	3	448	149

* Including 13 for salted deep-sea fish and 1 for salted chilled deep-sea fish.
† Including 8 for salted deep-sea fish and 1 for salted chilled deep-sea fish.
‡ Including 2 for salted deep-sea fish, 1 for chilled deep-sea fish and 3 for salted chilled deep-sea fish.

Only four ports practise deep-sea fishing and go to the Newfoundland Banks in search of cod: Fécamp, Bordeaux, Saint-Malo, La Pallice.

than in tertiary occupations. But in the Paris region the secondary sector was the larger in 66% of the towns.

The difference between the two sectors is generally not very marked, the coefficient being below 1·5. Eleven towns have a coefficient between 1·5 and 2: Vienne, Troyes, Saint-Étienne, Cholet, Fougères, Romans, Saint-Nazaire, Saint-Dié, Roanne, Lens, Villefranche. The coefficients of eleven other towns lie between 2 and 3: Armentières, Elbeuf, Maubeuge, Roubaix-Tourcoing, Hénin-Liétard, Montbéliard, Denain, Montceau-les-Mines, Le Creusot, Longwy, Saint-Chamond. Six others have a coefficient above 3: Forbach, Firminy, Bruay-en-Artois, Liévin, Hayange, La Grand'Combe, the last-named having the record coefficient of 4·7. These twenty-eight towns represent the French family of industrial towns. Note the absence of large cities among them, except for Roubaix-Tourcoing. This twofold numerical weakness, in number and size, of the industrial towns may well seem surprising. The industrial revolution seems to have affected French towns only locally and partially. It did not give rise to great industrial cities such as Manchester, Birmingham in England and Dusseldorf in Germany. In France the industrial towns are strongly localised in the North and the East and grouped within a few areas (fig. 91).

The towns specialising[12] in *extractive activities* are all situated in mining areas; it is nevertheless true that the departments of Nord and Pas-de-Calais stand in a class by themselves with six towns (Hénin-Liétard,

borders of the Jura; Firminy, Saint-Chamond and Saint-Étienne in Loire. They vary considerably in degree of specialisation; only Maubeuge, Longwy, Hayange, Montbéliard and Le Creusot are very specialised.

The *textile towns* are strongly localised in the North, in the East and in east-central France; but with the exception of Troyes the highest degrees of specialisation occur only in the North (Lille, Roubaix, Armentières) and in the Lyons region (Roanne, Vienne, Villefranche, Grenoble).

The towns specialising in *chemical industries*

TABLE LXXV. MULTI-INDUSTRIAL TOWNS (1954)

Towns	% of employed population in secondary sector	Industrial activities	% employed in these activities as a proportion of those employed in all secondary activities
Annecy	53·4	Mechanical + electrical	36·5
		Building and public works	23·2
Cholet	57·2	Mechanical and electrical	24·6
		Textiles and clothing	22·5 + 20·6
		Miscellaneous	18·1
Saint-Quentin	56·6	Textiles	37·2
		Mechanical and electrical	25·4
Montluçon	55·3	Chemical	32·5
		Mechanical and electrical	27·4
Mulhouse	52·4	Mechanical and electrical	28·6
		Textiles	27·2
Villefranche	65	Clothing	34·6
		Textiles	15·5
		Mechanical and electrical	32·1

Lens, Liévin, Bruay-en-Artois, Denain and Douai) in this category as against only one (Forbach) in Moselle. Two more are situated in departments in central France (Montceau-les-Mines and Firminy) and two in Gard (La Grand'Combe and Alès).

The North of France is also outstanding in the *building industries and public works* category, without, however, possessing highly specialised towns. Forbach is an exception, like Brest and La Baule in the West of France, which owe their importance in this respect to reconstruction after severe damage during the Second World War.

The towns specialising in metallurgy, mechanical and electrical engineering industries are grouped within a few departments: Maubeuge, Denain and Valenciennes in Nord; Longwy, Hayange and Thionville in the Moselle departments; Belfort on the

are less strongly localised than those in preceding categories, but many of them are located in the Paris region: Montargis, Melun, Creil, Compiègne, Beauvais, Elbeuf and Mantes surround the Paris agglomeration which, as we know, itself includes nine towns specialising in these activities. Clermont-Ferrand and Montluçon also stand apart and form a smaller but highly specialised group together with Vierzon and Bourges.

Towns specialising in *food and miscellaneous industries* are much more dispersed. Épernay, Douarnenez, Cholet, Limoges in the former category and Corbeil, Essonnes, Fougères and Romans in the other are isolated cases, even though they have a high degree of specialisation.

Some towns appear several times in the lists above; their specialisation is not exclusive, and several branches of industry co-exist

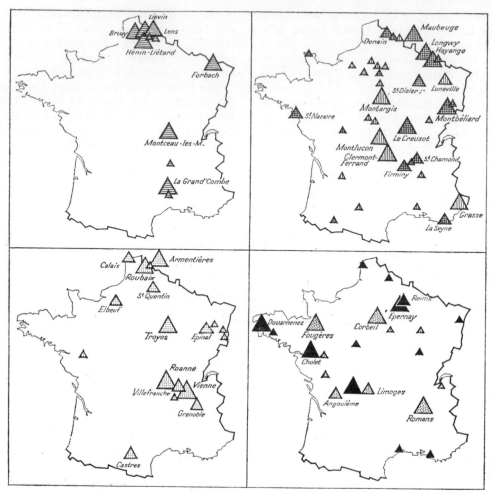

Fig. 91.   Specialised towns, according to departures from the mean (Paris excluded).

in them, giving a more or less satisfactorily wide range of jobs. Table LXXV gives several examples of these multi-industrial towns. But other towns are notable for having developed one activity only, in which almost all the working population is engaged. These are one-industry or mono-industrial towns. Table LXXVI gives several examples of towns and agglomerations of this type, having more than 20,000 inhabitants (1954).

This table shows that mono-industrialisation is essentially confined to the extractive, metallurgical and textile industries, and that it occurs chiefly in towns with less than 50,000 inhabitants—Roubaix, Troyes and Saint-Nazaire are exceptions. Indeed, the smaller the town the higher is the degree of specialisation and the tendency towards mono-industrial character. This is so in the case of Thiers, the cutlery town, Millau, a leather town, and with Mazamet, the sheepskin town.

The index of industrial diversification[13] gives an overall measure of the spread of a town's industrial activities and permits inter-

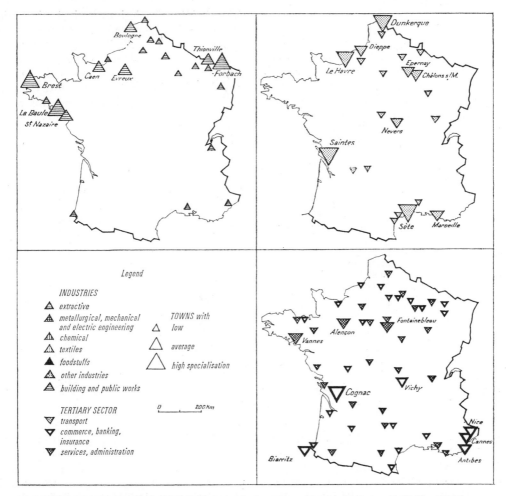

(Source: F. Carrière et Ph. Pinchemel, *Le Fait urbain en France*, A. Colin, 1963)

esting comparisons. The indices of towns with more than 20,000 inhabitants range from 0 to 858, twenty-five towns having an index of 0, and La Grand'Combe being the least diversified of all.

Of the 30 towns and agglomerations with more than 100,000 inhabitants, 12 have an index of less than 100, two of them having more than 300,000 inhabitants: Marseilles and Toulouse. Fourteen have an index between 100 and 300, and the Paris aglomeration is one of these (169). Only four large towns have higher indices: Le Havre, 316;

Toulon, 399; Brest, 490 (all naval bases); and Roubaix, 568. Thus the least diversified towns are those with less than 100,000 inhabitants. Indices above 700 are found only among towns with less than 50,000 inhabitants: Hayange (703), Maubeuge (718), Bruay-en-Artois (769), Le Creusot (785), Montbéliard (791), Longwy (822), La Grand'-Combe (858). The largest number of these undiversified towns are clearly located in northern and eastern France, and their distribution affords further evidence of the contrast between the two halves of France.

C. Tertiary Functions

Tertiary functions predominate in the majority (66%) of French provincial towns (1954). This fact should cause no surprise, since the typically urban functions belong to this sector: commerce, public and private services, administration, transport. The towns differ, however, in the degree of development of the functions of this sector. The

20% (of the population employed in tertiary occupations): Dieppe (2), Nevers (2), Marseilles (2), Brive (2), Béthune (2), Épernay (2), Saintes (33·1), Le Havre (37·7), Sète (31·7), Dunkirk (36·7). In most towns the commercial function does not employ more than 40% of the working population, and this reflects a balanced distribution between commercial activities and service activities. The proportion exceeds 50% in only four towns: Antibes

TABLE LXXVI.   MONO-INDUSTRIAL TOWNS (1954)

Towns	Industrial activity	% of employment in the secondary sector	Population employed in specified activity as % of population employed in the secondary sector
La Grand'Combe	Extractive	81·8	85·5
Hayange	Metallurgical	80·9	73·5
Liévin	Extractive	78	76·1
Bruay-en-Artois	Extractive	75·5	80·2
Longwy	Metallurgical	72·7	80·1
Le Creusot	Metallurgical	72·5	80·1
Montbéliard	Mechanical and electrical	68·7	77·2
Hénin-Liétard	Extractive	68·7	59·3
Montceau-les-Mines	Extractive	68·3	62·9
Roubaix-Tourcoing	Textile	67·1	63·6
Lens	Extractive	66·3	62·1
Armentières	Textile	65·1	62·5
Troyes	Textile	59·5	63·2
Vienne	Textile	58·9	53·9
Forbach	Extractive	76·2	64·8
Saint-Nazaire	Mechanical and electrical	61·7	67·2
La Seyne	Mechanical and electrical	56·2	69·4
Fougères	Leather		71
Romans	Leather		65·1

highest proportions of tertiary, as compared with secondary functions are found in the following towns: Saintes, Laon, Vannes, La Roche-sur-Yon, Châlons-sur-Marne, Montpellier, Narbonne, Hyères, Périgueux, Poitiers.

In comparison with specialised industrial towns, the towns *specialising in tertiary activities* are much more widely dispersed over the whole of France, and generally do not attain a high degree of specialisation. As in the industrial sector, the 'tertiary' towns may be more or less exclusively orientated towards one or other of the branches of this sector. There are transport towns, commercial towns and service towns.

The transport branch is obviously unlikely to occupy majority percentages of the working population. In ten towns of 20,000 inhabitants and more, the percentages are above

(52·4), Vichy (53·4), Cannes (50·7), Cognac (60·6).

Service towns: in forty-six French towns of 20,000 inhabitants or over, the working population employed in services makes up more than half of the working population in the tertiary sector. Forty of these towns are the administrative centres of departments, that is to say, they are so many large or small regional capitals, with developed administrative, school, university, health and other services. The six other towns are: Verdun, Rochefort, Toulon, Aix-en-Provence, Cherbourg, Hyères—military and university towns. The percentages exceed 60% in eleven of these towns: Alençon (65·7), Évreux (65), Hyères (63·2), Vannes (62·8), La Roche-sur-Yon (62·5), Verdun (61·7), Châteauroux (61·6), Rodez (61·2), Rochefort (60·1), Montpellier (60·8), Poitiers (60). It is noteworthy, however, that such high rates do not occur in the biggest towns; the proportion of the working population in the public services decreases with increasing size of the prefecture-towns; it falls steadily from a mean of 30·5% for towns of less than 10,000 inhabitants and levels out at 12·8% for cities with 200,000–1,000,000 inhabitants. The percentages engaged in private services are, on the other hand, much more stable, about 14% (still for prefecture-towns). The percentage of the population employed in national defence (1954) exceeds 10% in four towns: Chaumont (11%), Toulon (12·8%), Châteauroux (13·1%), Verdun (21·4%).

Other towns are remarkable, not for the characteristics of their working population but for the importance of their inactive population. There are towns of people with private incomes, pensioners and the retired. Not all of these are on the Riviera. For example, more than 1,000 retired employees of the S.N.C.F. live at Brive. One sometimes wonders about the 'means of support' of some towns which have no industrial resources, commercial functions or important services. They are landlords of the soil:

'Without industries or creative activities (the town) not only divides, commands, and drains a rural region which it dominates but also largely lives from the returns of capital which it has invested in it' (R. Dugrand).

This study of the urban functions throws into relief one of the characteristics of French urbanisation: the presence in most French regions of towns with contrasted occupational structures. The antiquity of urban development, the juxtaposition of towns of different ages, chance industrial implantations, have led to this heterogeneity of regional urban structures. An old, historic town, such as Douai, with a great past, becomes incorporated into an industrial region. Diversified towns and undiversified towns stand side by side in the same region. In the North, for example, Arras, Cambrai and Saint-Omer are near Béthune, Roubaix, Liévin and Hénin-Liétard. Likewise in the East, Nancy, Verdun, highly diversified towns, are neighbours to the metallurgical and mining towns. This situation, which creates a healthy variety in the urban pattern, also creates difficulties in the comparative analysis of towns and the study of urban hierarchies.

12. The degree of specialisation in each class of activity is calculated in deviations from the mean (that is, a measure of the dispersion of the rates of each city in relation to the arithmetical mean of the terms of the series).

13. $D = \dfrac{\text{Crude index for the town} - \text{Crude index for all towns over 20,000 inhabitants}}{\text{Maximum crude index of diversity} - \text{Crude index for all towns over 20,000 inhabitants}}$

The crude diversification index is obtained by adding up the percentages of collective activities of the branches of industry concerned, ranked in decreasing order and cumulated. The lower the index, the more diversified the industrial activities (cf. F. Carrière and Ph. Pinchemel, *Le Fait urbain en France*, p. 218).

2. THE HIERARCHY OF URBAN FUNCTIONS

From Paris to the little *bourgade* of 1,800–2,000 inhabitants, all French towns fulfil functions which give them a definite rank in the urban hierarchy and spheres of influence of varying extent. Several nomenclatures have been proposed to define the ranks in the hierarchy. P. George distinguishes between local centres (Luçon), regional capitals (Angers), industrialised market towns (Le Mans), industrial towns (Saint-Étienne), large agglomerations, and Paris. J.-F. Gravier

distinguishes small centres (Pontoise, Maubeuge, Sélestat), medium-sized towns (Aurillac, Périgueux), secondary capitals or intermediate towns (*villes relais*) (Le Mans, Brest), regional capitals (Bordeaux, Dijon), and international metropolises (Lyons). J. Coppolani distinguishes *bourgades*, local centres, *villes maîtresses* ('fully-fledged' towns), sub-capitals and regional capitals. The meaning of each of these classifications is self-evident, but it can be seen that there are differences in terminology and difficulty in reaching agreement on definite criteria for the ranking of towns.

A. The *Bourgs* (*villes centres* or minor market centres)

These constitute the first order of towns in France. They occur at about 15–20 km. between two large towns, and are spread along all the roads in the country. They are centres with 1,000–5,000 inhabitants. Their functions are essentially commercial; formerly, all the public squares in these little towns enjoyed animated activity on market days. If the markets have declined in importance and have often become merely a pretext for an outing, the *bourg* has nevertheless retained important trading and service functions; its role has even been extended because traders and craftsmen have moved into the *bourgs* as a result of the spread of motor transport.

The *bourg* contains the stationer, the ironmonger, the drapery store, shoe shops and clothing shops, as well as the doctor, the chemist, the lawyer, the insurance agent, the tax-collector, the local police headquarters, the college and all the occupations linked to the agricultural population served by the town. The economic life of the *bourg* is quite often enriched by some industrial activity. In most cases the *bourgade* acts as the administrative centre for a canton. The exceptions underline the general rule, for they occur only where rail and road services, or situation, have favoured another commune.

Saint-Chély-d'Apchcr, in Margeride, is an example of these little towns of about 5,000 inhabitants (4,790 in 1962). Situated on Route Nationale 9, it is served by the railway, animated by a steelworks and has specialised commercial functions: 7 shoe shops, 5 hairdressers, a fish shop, dairies, pastry shops, jewellers, watch and clock repairers, an optician and wholesalers dealing in foodstuffs, wines and haberdashery. A *Collège d'enseignement général* and two private secondary schools provide this *bourg* with good educational facilities.

B. The Small Towns

These small towns, with 5,000–30,000 inhabitants, are characteristically 'French' with their reputation for being sleepy anachronisms, 'collections of landowners, rural dignitaries and provincial officials' (P. George), their craftsmen, and occasionally a factory or two, and a few workshops. Nevertheless they provide important services for their regions: administrative, judiciary, educational (through possession of a high school), public health (a doctor and sometimes a dispensary or clinic), as well as other services (notary). Their main functions are technical and commercial. Such towns depend entirely on their relations with the surrounding countryside, their market days, agricultural fairs and shows.

But every year they have greater difficulty in safeguarding their functions, first because of the decline in numbers and ageing of the surrounding rural population; secondly because technical progress enables larger towns to extend their direct influence and to dispense with intermediate market-town centres. A by-pass road which removes the motorists' incentive to stop, the closure of a railway line, the relocation of a public service or a court, or a factory closure, any one of these can endanger the biological equilibrium of the town.

'One such small town in the valley of the Lot had eleven middle-class families (*bourgeois*) at the end of the last century. Several of their sons were killed in the war; most of the others entered the magistrature or the army. The daughters married elsewhere. Only two of the eight families which had landed property have kept it, but the members only go there for summer holidays. Only one single descendant of that old bourgeoisie still lives in the town—and he is a bachelor. The factories have shut down; the two former lawyers and two *agents d'affaires* have been replaced by one lawyer. In general, the little town has lost its bourgeois and urban character, and has become a commercial centre, supplying the farmers and handling their produce. It no longer has a social function and the region is as it were beheaded' (Henri Mendras).

But this development may be reversed by bringing in several industries, by encouraging tourists, by improvements in school, health and hotel services.

C. The Regional Capitals

A town in this category is generally the administrative centre of a department. Its sphere of influence generally has a radius of 45–50 km., almost always covering a whole department, but rarely exceeding it. Sometimes two, or even three towns of similar size may be found in one department and share smaller, but usually more populated, spheres of influence. Such are Rouen and Le Havre; Quimper and Brest; Moulins and Montluçon; Montpellier and Béziers; Colmar and Mulhouse; Albi and Castres; Compiègne, Beauvais and Creil; Laon, Soissons and Saint-Quentin; Mâcon, Autun and Chalon-sur-Saône; Calais, Boulogne and Arras. The varying incidence of physical factors (relief and situation) as well as human factors, the second town commonly being an industrial town, accounts for this dichotomy. These towns are small administrative centres (the tertiary towns distinguished above), and economic centres (having chambers of commerce, wholesalers, and their own transport services) quite apart from their industrial activities proper.

Moulins, for instance, with 35,281 inhabitants, has 212 food shops, 300 specialised shops, 88 cafés and about 30 hotels which are explained by the importance of the regional functions of the town, especially for rural areas.[14] Statistical logic may be confounded by the existence, in one functional category, of towns with populations of widely differing sizes. But, whether they have 30,000 inhabitants, like Beauvais, or 130,000, like Valenciennes, these towns perform the same functions, apart from their industrial functions, if due allowance is made for the differ-

ence in size of the populations which they serve. At most, we could distinguish two ranks in this group: towns of 30,000–80,000 inhabitants, and those of 80,000–200,000.

D. The Provincial Metropolis

In the highest rank of the hierarchy, apart from Paris which stands in a class by itself, comes the provincial metropolis. Cities of this rank are distinguished: by their population; by the importance of their provincial functions, which serve a larger area than a department since they have a university, a Court of Appeal, newspapers and the regional offices of professional and trades unions; by the importance of their tertiary functions, ranging from specialist medical services to a theatre, and from barristers to valuers; by the presence of very specialised economic activities serving a wide clientèle, from the regional office of a film-distributor to wholesalers; and by the existence of big stores and luxury shops. These provincial urban functions are fulfilled by towns of varying size, with varying facilities and ranges of activity. Figure 92, drawn according to Reilly's law, clearly shows the anomalies which result from this variation.[15] Several large metropolitan towns stand out prominently: two have more than 800,000 inhabitants (Lyons and Marseilles); two have more than 400,000 inhabitants (Bordeaux and Lille);[16] two have more than 300,000 inhabitants (Toulouse and Nantes).

But these six towns and Paris do not share the whole of France. It is not easy to identify towns of provincial metropolitan status below this level, because of the large number of cities with 100,000–300,000 inhabitants and because of their distribution. France is richly endowed with medium-sized towns with 100,000–250,000 inhabitants which form centres for regions corresponding more or less to the area of a department. Because it lacks the traditional regional divisions of a higher order, France is lacking in very large towns, a consequence of the 'departmentalisation' resulting from the Revolution.

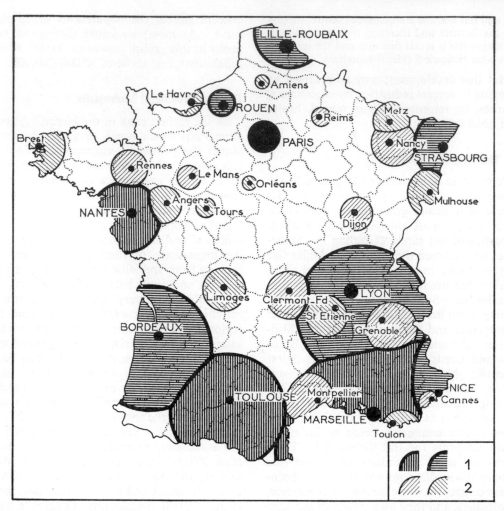

Fig. 92.   Spheres of influence, determined by Reilly's Law, for agglomerations of more than 100,000 inhabitants in 1954.   (Source: J. Hautreux, 'Les principales villes attractives et leur ressort d'influence', *Urbanisme*, 1963)

1. Spheres of agglomerations with more than 250,000 inhabitants.   2. Spheres of agglomerations with 100,000–250,000 inhabitants.   The areas of the circles representing the agglomerations are proportional to their population in 1954.

That is why Rennes could not be considered under present circumstances as the capital of Brittany.   The twin towns of Rouen and Le Havre, Nancy and Metz, and the urban trilogy of Languedoc raise formidable problems of choice in the context of a national planning policy aimed at endowing the regions with single, monocephalic, capitals.   Dijon, an agglomeration of 155,000 people with young

and poorly developed industries, is a good example of the provincial metropolis.   It is the only large town in the centre of the Paris–Strasbourg–Lyons triangle, and stands amidst departments with little urban development or only medium-sized towns.   Its growth is assured by its administrative, commercial and service functions.   It is the administrative centre of the department and of the region (a 'development' region), a university centre, a centre for postal cheques and the site of the regional telecommunications head-office, of a regional military command, an air force base —together these constitute a wide range of services. On the commercial level, Dijon benefits from its crossroads position in the

(2·9), Bordeaux (2·2), Lille (1·6), Toulouse (1·1), Rouen (1·1), Nice (1·4), Nantes (1), Strasbourg (1·1). Likewise, nine cities have more than 1% in the administration and services sector: Nantes (1·03), Rouen (1·07), Strasbourg (1·16), Nice (1·2), Toulouse (1·2), Lille (1·42), Bordeaux (1·9), Lyons (2·69),

TABLE LXXVII. HIERARCHY OF REGIONAL METROPOLITAN TOWNS
(After Hautreux, Lecourt and Rochefort)

1st order   a. Lyons, Marseilles.
           b. Bordeaux, Lille, Strasbourg, Toulouse, Nantes, Nancy.
2nd order   a. Grenoble, Nice, Clermont-Ferrand, Saint-Étienne, Dijon.
           b. Rouen, Rennes, Metz, Limoges, Tours, Montpellier, Rheims.

heart of Burgundy, and acts as a depot for the redistribution of agricultural produce. It is also a railway capital (4,500 railway workers), a staging point and a tourist centre.

Recent studies have attempted to differentiate these 'provincial metropolitan towns' by various criteria: commercial facilities, banking facilities and financial importance, 'ser-

Marseilles (2·7) (in 1954). No matter what criteria be chosen, the list of provincial metropolitan centres hardly varies, and faithfully reflects the distinctiveness in the hierarchy of the largest towns. The disadvantage of these methods is that too much weight is attached to the effects of past growth in attempting to plan for the needs of the future.

TABLE LXXVIII. DISTRIBUTION, BY SIZE CATEGORIES, OF URBAN POPULATIONS AND EMPLOYMENT IN FRENCH TOWNS IN 1962

| | Sizes of towns | | | | | | |
	Less than 20,000 inhab.	20,000– 50,000 inhab.	50,000– 100,000 inhab.	100,000– 200,000 inhab.	Over 200,000 inhab.	Total	Paris agglomera- tion
% French urban working population .	19·8	10·6	8·9	10	50·3	100	30·8
Extractive industries	28·9	20·5	8·8	20·9	20·8	100	1·8
Metall. mech. electr. industries .	17·3	7·1	10·4	9·8	55·3	100	37·9
Chemical industries	16·9	8·9	5·3	8·8	60	100	40·8
Textiles and clothing industries .	23·8	11	10·8	7·1	46·8	100	18·2
Building, public works . . .	22·3	11·7	9·4	10·5	46	100	25·8
Food industries	24·8	11·5	7·3	8·9	47·2	100	23·1
Other industries	24·4	10·7	6·2	7·3	50·8	100	33·1
Transport	14	9·5	8·3	10·8	56·9	100	32·3
Commerce, banking, insurance .	16·7	10·5	8·9	9·8	54·0	100	33·1
Administration and services .	16·1	11·6	9	10·3	53·1	100	33·5

vice' facilities (administration, specialised and unusual occupations, higher education, medical and hospital services), cultural, artistic and sporting facilities, and external influence. Table LXXVII shows the classification resulting from this research.

Towns may also be classified in terms of the proportion of the population engaged in tertiary activities. Nine towns have more than 1% of the urban working population of France employed in the commerce, banking and insurance group: Marseilles (2·8), Lyons

E. Paris

Paris has a threefold place in the urban hierarchy. It is a State capital, it is one of the great metropolitan cities of the world, with functional zones extending beyond the national frontiers, and it is also a provincial capital, just like all the other big cities. This triple role already largely explains its great concentration of activities. The figures given in Table LXXVIII give an idea of this by broad categories of activity. The sphere of

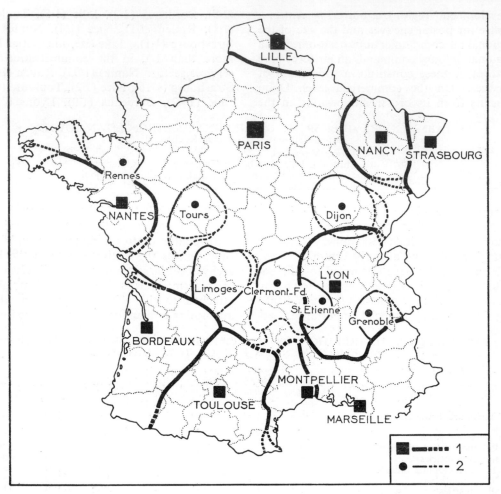

Fig. 93. The main attracting towns and their spheres of influence. (Source: J. Hautreux, article cited, *Urbanisme*, 1963)

1. Main attracting towns and limit of their spheres of influence.   2. Secondary attracting towns and limits of their spheres of influence.

Broken lines have been used whenever the delimitation of spheres of influence is very uncertain, as well as in areas where there are two competing centres.

influence of Paris as a regional capital is very extensive, both because the city has considerable powers of attraction and because no other city is capable of counterbalancing its influence quantitatively.

The map of theoretical spheres of influence determined in accordance with Reilly's law (fig. 92) extends the influence of Paris over three quarters of the whole country and restricts the towns capable of reaching provincial metropolitan status to the periphery, especially in southern France, where the distance from Paris is greatest.   It is interesting to compare this map with a map showing journey times by rail between Paris and the main cities.   The preeminence, the weight of Paris is one of the constants in French civilisation.   Paris was already a 'monstrous' city in the 13th century, already with five or six times as many inhabitants as the largest French towns. But the problem of the too-eminent position of Paris in the French urban network is less a matter of population numbers than of economic power and excessive concentration of the powers of decision, direction and finance.

A study by the *Commissariat au Plan* has assessed the shares of the principal French towns in the turnover of enterprises whose annual turnover exceeds 5 million francs and which have their registered office or administrative headquarters in these towns. The head offices in the Paris region accounted for 82·75% of the total turnover of all large enterprises! After it, very far behind, come Lyons, 2·9%; Marseilles, 1·64%; Saint-Étienne, 1·3%; Lille, 1·21%; Metz, 1·13%; Grenoble and Mulhouse, 0·51–1%; and the other large towns, less than 0·5%. The domination of Paris is overwhelming: the capital contains 14,766 head offices of multiple-branch firms, employing outside the agglomeration 1,329,904 paid workers, while the second town, Lyons, lags far behind (1,325 head offices and 50,763 paid workers). Although Paris delegates some of its industrial functions to the provinces, it remains to all intents and purposes the seat of the entire tertiary sector in France. In Paris live a quarter of the French civil servants, 28% of the doctors, 61% of the artists and 62% of the men of letters.

It is difficult to determine the place of each and every town in the urban hierarchy, since many equivalent criteria are in current use.

Each of these towns exerts a regional influence proportional to its population, its facilities and its communication infrastructure. The whole of France is thus divided into urban regions of unequal size, the typical spheres of influence being embraced by the sphere of influence of a provincial metropolis. Figure 93 was compiled by J. Hautreux on the basis of specified criteria (spheres of attraction), based on the number of telephone calls, of passenger journeys on the railways (S.N.C.F.) and of internal migration.

It shows the importance of Paris as a provincial metropolis, and conversely, the relatively limited spheres of influence of some large towns which suffer from the competition of neighbouring towns (Strasbourg and Nancy, Montpellier and Marseilles).

French towns do not all fit easily into a regional hierarchy. In other words, they do not all qualify for one of the various categories analysed above. The demographic history of France, the antiquity of urban development in France, geographical accidents in the growth of cities and in economic development, have all contributed to the rise of urban 'organisms' of similar size close to one another; or conversely, have hindered the development of a regional metropolis. Towns such as Roubaix, Nice, Saint-Étienne, Vichy, are in some way 'outside of' the urban hierarchy proper, and are superimposed on the urban network. This results in costly and troublesome rivalries.

14. Agricultural fair in January, cattle fair in March, pig fairs, Friday markets.

15. According to Reilly's Law, 'two towns respectively attract the commercial customers of a smaller place situated between them, in inverse proportion of the squares of their distance from it, and in direct proportion of their own populations' (J. Hautreux).

16. Lille and Roubaix-Tourcoing together have more than 800,000 inhabitants.

IV

THE URBAN AREA

1. THE DEVELOPMENT OF THE URBAN AREA

The sites, layouts and street plans of most French towns can only be understood in the light of history. Relict features of the Roman, Gallo-Roman, Medieval and Modern periods are all to be found there, juxtaposed, sometimes superimposed upon one another.

A. The First Stages of Urban Development

These are represented by the ruins and relict buildings which are the hallmark of a town, and bear witness to an importance and prosperity which may no longer exist. The most common monuments of the past are temples, entire quarters, baths and theatres, town gates, arches, towers and walls. In some towns Gallo-Roman town planning is still strongly visible in the groundplan, much more in evidence than in monuments which survive in isolation (the upper town at Boulogne-sur-Mer reflects the plan of Caligula's camp). The lines of city walls, often built against invasions at the dawn of the Middle Ages, still clearly demarcate the original core of the city; inside this line survives the ancient street pattern based on the crossing point of two highways. This first circle of walls likewise exerted an indirect and considerable influence on later urban extensions; it marked the initial zonal boundary between the city, confined within the ramparts, and the suburbs, developing freely outside them.

One such suburb would often become more important than the Gallo-Roman city itself, and, through a shift in the centre of gravity of the urban organism, would become the core of the medieval city (Arras). Through-

out the Middle Ages and modern times up to the middle of the 19th century towns increased in area by successive walled extensions. The first wall often included both the Gallo-Roman city and the first medieval core, suburb or castle: at Strasbourg, the 8th-century wall; at Paris, the wall of Philip Augustus (fig. 94).

Multiple walls were built mainly in the 12th, 13th and 14th centuries. As each new wall was built, a rural area was incorporated into the city, together with its farms, its abbeys, its nobles' mansions, which were until then situated 'without the walls' or 'in the fields'. The network of country roads and lanes and the cultivated fields often provided the framework for the urban plan.[17] The interior of the new town extensions sometimes remained for a considerable time under cultivation or as open spaces (the former parks of monasteries and of the stately homes of nobles and bourgeois), hidden from passing eyes by linear building along the roads. As population increased, these spaces were divided up and built over. French towns have preserved many features dating from medieval and early modern times: narrow, winding streets with no footpaths, or very narrow ones added later; their quaint but charming little squares; the fine façades of a few Renaissance mansions, some monuments, an occasional medieval house, and their irregular street blocks. The walls themselves have either survived wholly or partly intact in towns which did not grow very much, or were demolished in towns away from the frontier during the 18th century or later, to make room for boulevards, inner ring roads replacing the early walls and outer ring roads the later ones.

The foundation charters of new towns often gave exact specifications for urban development indicating the size of property lots (7 m. × 14 m. in Montauban). If these new towns did not all conform to the same plan, there was a distinct tendency towards rectilinear plans. A municipal square occupies a prominent position in the plans of new towns and Marseilles acquired new, well-planned quarters or provided themselves with new streets. That was the great epoch of royal squares: Place Bellecourt at Lyons, Place Louis XIV and Place Louis XV at Rennes, Place de la Liberté at Dijon, Place de la Bourse at Bordeaux, older 'Places Royales', Place Stanislas at Nancy, public gardens and parks (*cours, tours de ville, allées, promenades*). Many French towns have no green spaces or

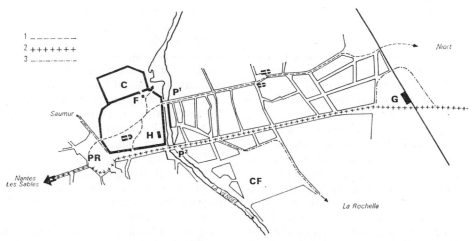

Fig. 94. Elements in the urban development of Fontenay-le-Comte. (Source: R. Crozet, *Villes d'entre Loire et Gironde*, 1949)

C: Castle; F: Fountain; H: Market; P1: Pont des Sardines; P2: Pont-Neuf; PR: Place Royal (Place Viète); CF: Fair ground; G: Railway station.

1. Old road from Niort to Sables or Nantes.   2. Detour from that road, 18th century.   3. Detour about the railway station and road from Saumur to La Rochelle, 19th century.

in the South; from the 14th century, the radial-concentric pattern supplemented the chessboard plan, which was used for fortress-towns and residential extensions.

B. The 18th Century

Most provincial cities bear the stamp of the 18th century, especially its second half. Aesthetic urbanism was then happily linked to practical urbanism, which was concerned with hygiene and circulation in the rapidly growing towns. These developed in accordance with 'plans for embellishment and enlargement'. Nantes, Bordeaux, Rouen, Tours, Lille, Lyons

parking spaces other than those provided by town planners of 200 years ago!

The private town houses of the nobility and bourgeoisie date from the 17th and 18th centuries: 'horseshoe-shaped around an inner court, isolated from the street, drawing upon all the resources of the time for convenience and habitability, with its double row of rooms, one side looking out on to the court, the other on to the garden; the town house with its decorated frontal façade . . . remained the model for all urban architecture down to the 19th century' (Mandrou).

The Marais quarter at Paris still contains many of these old town houses of the 17th and 18th centuries. Most provincial towns of any importance have some, whether they are isolated buildings, whole streets (Rue des Forges, Rue de la Verrerie at Dijon) or quarters. In Provençal and Languedoc towns, the quarters containing such 18th-century town houses, with their decorated fronts, conceal from the passer-by an opulence of architecture which reflects the prosperity enjoyed by the nobility and bourgeoisie of bygone days.

C. The 19th Century

The essential feature of 19th-century urban development is the change in scale. The town spreads without the restrictions formerly imposed by military and geographical considerations. It sends ribbons along outlet roads, and grows around railway stations: the railway and factory quarters are the offspring of this period of urban growth. More generally, buildings containing plant or providing services which were formerly non-existent or poorly developed have led to urban extensions: the school, the *École Normale d'Instituteurs*, the barracks, the hospital. Needing large spaces, they have been constructed on the periphery of built-up areas. During the industrial revolution urban growth occurred under the banner of unrestricted liberalism, and building was regarded as merely another form of business. Towns burst through their ramparts and over their boulevards without any plan. The size and shape of new quarters, new roads and the new building lots were determined solely by private interest, the free play of the market and the need to house thousands of new citizens.

Land was used indiscriminately for blocks of flats, individual houses, factories, gasometers and railway lines and yards, thrown together to make an aimless urban landscape which reflected the economic and social structures of the new order in France. In fact, 19th-century urban development expressed the growth and rivalry of two numerically large social classes—the working class and the bourgeoisie. The form of development of area depended on the social class that lived in it: 'social structure was writ large in urban geography' (F. Bedarida). The middle-class quarters arose in the healthiest, most agreeable areas, which were exclusively reserved for the new class of business bourgeois.

Large mansions, with formal façades and large gates for coaches, concealing large gardens, were built along broad new roads or around new squares: the Chartrons at Bordeaux, the Boulevard Vauban and the Boulevard de la Liberté at Lille, the Cours Pierre Puget and the Cours du Chapitre at Marseilles, the surroundings of Place Bellecour and of the Parc de la Tête d'Or at Lyons. The most widespread kind of building in the bourgeois and business quarters of Paris dates from 1880 to 1910; it was built of stone (limestone) with balconies, seven storeys and about twenty apartments in each.

The rising lower middle class lived in quarters consisting of little individual houses or blocks of flats. These conditions led to a very characteristic pattern of urban development; in order to economise on land as much as possible, buildings were compressed into each lot and the interior courts were reduced to mere wells. The whole of each block was occupied by buildings built one behind the other or by buildings to which access was by private drives, passages and culs-de-sac (fig. 95). Quarters for the workers were built elsewhere, on less attractive sites further from the centre, in joyless streets, uniformly lined with working-class houses or unattractive blocks of flats. These mid-19th-century quarters, which absorbed thousands of country folk, still exist in all the industrial towns: the Croix-Rousse quarter and the workers' housing estates at Lyons,[18] the communes of Wazemmes and Fives at Lille, the Rue des Fumiers at Nantes, most of Saint-Étienne and of Le Creusot.

Before transport systems were developed it was necessary to house as many workers as possible near their work. Maximum density was achieved in filling open spaces, including courtyards and gardens. A special kind of

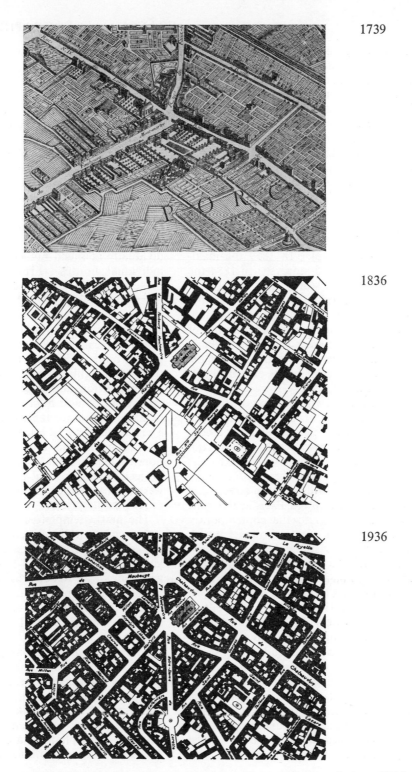

1739

1836

1936

Fig. 95.   Development of the Quartier Saint-Georges at Paris.   Photo: Service technique d'Urbanisme de la ville de Paris.   (Source: Y. Salaun, *Raisons d'être de l'urbanisme*, Vincent, Fréal, Paris, 1948)

workers' housing developed in some towns: the *courées* (houses grouped round court-yards) in the textile towns of the North. Other forms of residential development appeared on the coalfields: workers' housing estates and *corons* (mining villages) like the *cité ouvrière* of Stiring-Wendel, opened by Napoleon III in 1857. However rare, concern for the problems of urbanism nevertheless had some influence upon the ways in which urban growth occurred. One of the earliest steps in town planning was to control the height of buildings. In 1783 a first regulation fixed heights at from 3 to 5 storeys, according to the street. In 1859 the maximum was 20 m. and 5 storeys. In 1884 the maximum number of storeys was raised to 7; after 1902 the permissible height was the width of the street plus 6 m., up to a maximum of 20 m.[19] The Paris town planning act of 1884 fixed minimum areas for courts in Paris at 100–150 m.[2], regardless of the area of the building lot! This explains the extraordinary congestion of buildings.

The best-known town planning of the 19th century is the work of Haussmann; slum areas were completely cleared, and city blocks were defined by a new network of broad, straight streets. Priority was given to the needs of traffic, which had already become the key problem. The width of the streets and boulevards driven through Paris at this time certainly bear witness to the contemporary appreciation of fine views, however much their creation was inspired by military and political considerations. But these measures only created planned façades; the bourgeois dwelling-houses and business houses along the boulevards of Haussmann were built in front of old quarters which retained their narrow and twisting streets and their anti-quated houses behind the façade.

On the periphery of towns, *non aedificandi* zones—where building was forbidden—were set up by military planners in front of the old walls and have often survived as waste land not used for permanent buildings, though sometimes occupied by colonies of huts, forming real shanty-towns (*bidonvilles*).

D. 1900–50

The tendencies of the 19th century were reinforced in the early part of the 20th century. The development of means of communication—tramways, motor-cars, buses, suburban railways, the Paris underground system, allowed cities to spread even further. The suburbs spread into rural communes. The division of land into building lots was characteristic of the whole period 1910–30, especially around Paris. Developers bought large open spaces, laid out streets and building lots as small as possible, and sold them individually at much higher prices as sites for individual houses. From this period date those suburban landscapes, horrible beyond description, which have done so much in our day to discredit the individual family dwelling. The houses of this period might almost be called surrealist—strung out or jostled together, built at different times, each different from its neighbour with pretentious, sham ornamentation and lack of proportion, and all shut in behind high walls. Such chaotic planning could not fail to provoke reactions. The notion of social housing began to appear at the end of the 19th century. Workers' housing associations, 'philanthropic' housing projects and the *Habitations Bon Marché* were all founded to provide decent dwellings at reasonable prices.

The first attempt to introduce town-planning legislation did not come, however, until immediately after the First World War. The law of 14th March 1919 required each town with more than 10,000 inhabitants to draw up a 'development plan', but only one plan was approved between 1920 and 1940! Only one case of genuine town planning between the two wars is worthy of mention—the plan for Villeurbanne, near Lyons. This commune in suburban Lyons was endowed with a centre by the building of a skyscraper (1,450 apartments), a town hall, a theatre.

After 1940 the rebuilding of towns, especially those which had been largely destroyed, gave the town planners a chance to create a new street pattern, to build on new lots and, in short, to work under very favourable conditions. In some cases the old street pattern was retained apart from the addition of a few new transverse roads. Some street plans were redrawn or straightened. The old streets were nearly always widened. Much greater changes were brought about in the most damaged towns: Maubeuge (Lurçat), Le Havre (Auguste Perret), Amiens, Orleans and Brest all show the results of attempts, sometimes courageous ones, at planning. Systematic development thus allowed Amiens, Caen, Le Havre, Boulogne, Maubeuge and Orleans to be rebuilt with profoundly different plans from those of the pre-war era. Blocks of flats have replaced individual houses in the central areas.

Town-planning legislation has also become more specific since the last war. A law was passed in June 1943, but was not put into force until eleven years later. However, although many plans have been drawn up, they have usually had no effect. They are plans for communes, whereas the problems they seek to solve affect progressively larger units as urbanisation continues. The procedures involved in drafting and approving plans are also very long and laborious. Urban expansion has continued spontaneously over the last twenty years by means of derogations and exceptions.

E. Post-war Urban Development

From 1955 to 1960 onwards new building gradually went ahead of rebuilding, leading to various kinds of urban development.

COMPREHENSIVE REDEVELOPMENT PROJECTS

The great demand for housing coupled with the absence of a clear policy for town planning and housing created a problem to which one solution was found and this was soon generally adopted throughout France. This was the solution of the *grands ensembles* or comprehensive redevelopment projects. This term applies to large groups of buildings each built to provide a thousand, or several thousands of dwellings. In the strict sense, the expression *grand ensemble* refers, according to the official definition of January 1956, to projects catering for 30,000–40,000 inhabitants, that is 8,000–10,000 dwellings. But usage has extended it to all groups of several hundred dwellings built within a single estate. The *grands ensembles* of Sarcelles contain 9,000 dwellings; the 'Cité des Sapins' at Rouen has 2,500. At Lyons, those at Bron-Parilly and La Duchêre have 2,607 dwellings (12,000 inhabitants), and at Dijon the Grésilles quarter has 12,000 inhabitants. The location and size of these projects is almost always determined by local circumstances. They have been sited on large open spaces, which were generally divided into a small number of lots so that they could be bought fairly cheaply and would not require excavation or the installation of services on a very large scale.

Two categories of building land meet these conditions: the extreme outskirts of the urban area, at the borders of the town and country, and the empty spaces between lines of ribbon development along roads in the suburbs. In the interior of towns, comprehensive planning is restricted by lack of space, but it is possible on the empty spaces within the built-up area, the former prohibited military zones (*non aedificandi*) and former industrial sites (disused factories). The size of the development areas is determined by the area of each building site and the number of houses that it can or ought to accommodate, this number depending on the profitability of the operation, which varies according to the promoters, the town-planning regulations and the terms of agreement.

The overall plans of the estates built at this period are characterised by uniformity and monotony which can only be explained by the urgency of the need to build and by the total lack of originality and research. The plans set out narrow buildings in lines, in crescents, in cross-pattern, stretched out as far as possible (some are more than 300 m. long),[20] with their fronts rising up in featureless walls to 4, 5, even 20 storeys, divided into identical cells like a honeycomb. Tower blocks with aesthetic pretensions rise above the lower ones. By restricting buildings to 4 or 5 storeys, the contractors avoided the need to provide lifts.

'The breeze-block carried the day. On the exterior it was plastered over and painted with colour that deceived the public for a time until it flaked off leprous-fashion. The whole building is pitted with openings, set at regular intervals, and sometimes further decorated with symbolic balconies. There is nothing to hold the eye, no refuge from the monotony, the only difference between one unit and the next being its number' (F. Choay). This kind of building allows for a good deal of open space, while at the same time creating high densities of population. The street, that characteristic element in the townscape, disappears, and is replaced by open views, green spaces, playing fields or empty spaces.

The arrangement of green spaces around these buildings generally has an air of guilty self-justification, rather than of a well-thought-out and coherently planned and pleasing environment: a few patches of grass, a few rows of poplars, some sandpits, swings and benches, are not enough for the population of the buildings. The impression of artificiality is strengthened by the removal of all natural slopes; the land is levelled, cleared of every sign of older buildings, even patches of greenery and old trees, which would have prevented the rows of flats from being entirely geometrical.[21] Not all *grands ensembles* deserve such strictures; some of them, all too rare, display originality of conception on the part of their architects. Such are the *Courtillières* of Pantin, with their towers radiating in three lines, and the blocks of flats forming sinuous curves in the natural setting of a green valley—the *Grandes Terres* at Marly.

The architect, Le Corbusier, whose creative activity gave the world buildings and towns conceived on entirely new lines, has built community blocks at Marseilles, at Nantes-Rezé and at Briey-la-Forêt since 1945. The originality of these buildings lies in the composition of the dwelling units, which are two-storeyed (maisonettes), in the raising of the

buildings on stilts, and the introduction of certain services in the building itself: a shopping street in the heart of the block, a nursery on the terrace, club-rooms for the young; and in the quality of the design. At first, Le Corbusier's concepts were disputed, ridiculed, but inquiries have shown that the occupants have adapted themselves to these new forms of settlement, and the final verdict seems to be on the whole favourable. At Nantes-Rezé the 294 dwellings (of 1–6 rooms) are inhabited by workers (22%), clerical workers (39%) and administrators and executives (36%).

The high cost of land, together with the need to maximise profits, to minimise expenditure on roads and services, to minimise the net cost of construction, to increase mechanisation in building operations and to conform to a standard architectural style—all these factors explain how in recent years blocks of flats with their towers and barrack-like appearance have gained ground at the expense of individual houses. The proportion of individual houses in all residential building was 36·4% in 1957, 27·1% in 1959, 28·4% in 1960, 35% in 1963. But this policy was contrary to the wishes of the great majority of French people wanting homes. There were several often passionate debates between the supporters of individual houses, and the defenders of collective dwellings. The latter argue that individual housing is more burdensome, takes up much more space, and leads to excessive increases in travelling distance and the extent of the built-up area. The defenders of the individual house lay stress upon its individuality, its superior value as a place for family life because it has more and larger rooms, open spaces and outbuildings, a garden—invaluable for children—and direct access to the street, in contrast to the little, noisy, anonymous flats in the *grands ensembles*.

It is paradoxical that France, the least densely peopled country of Western Europe and one which therefore has no real problem of space, should adopt this policy of building collective dwellings, which the people do not want.[22] The *grand ensemble* phenomenon reflects an elementary and static concept of land-use planning. The French have been accustomed to think of their urban network as stable in its pattern, and do not envisage a policy of urban development in terms of the growth of new urban centres. Urban expansion is conceived without differentiation, in terms of continuous suburbs, and not, as in England, of urban centres which may be near to each other but clearly distinct. This policy of *grands ensembles* is the French solution to the problem posed by the need for more housing. It has not only profoundly altered the urban landscapes but also the traditions of urban life.

It should nevertheless be recognised that this choice has certain merits. Collective housing has fostered industrialisation of the building sector by stimulating prefabrication and standardisation of facilities, by allowing dwellings to be built in series. These conditions have permitted rather low net costs to be maintained, and so made it possible to sell or let the apartments to the less well off. By building in blocks, unnecessary expansion of built up areas has been avoided and the cost of public services (roads and piping) has been kept down. But in most cases, the *grands ensembles* have been open to numerous criticisms—quite apart from architectural and siting considerations.[23] The *grand ensemble* may in no way be defined as a new town. It fulfils the residential function only; commercial, health, cultural and schooling facilities are either totally absent or very inadequate simply because they would have added too much to the builders' costs.

Above all, jobs are not available adjacent or near to these blocks of flats; no centre of tertiary activities, no industrial area is created with them. They result in large volumes of daily movement. A survey at Bron-Parilly (Lyons) showed that 44% of heads of households spent an hour or more travelling to work; 19% spent an hour and a half or more. Students sometimes have a two-hour journey to their school. Finally, the *grands ensembles* have often been planted in or near a suburban area without any plan to provide for them

and to integrate them into the existing urban structure.

All too often the collective housing blocks bear the marks of their financial origins. There have been many examples since the end of the war: there is the H.L.M. (*Habitations à loyer modéré*—Rented housing bureau) ensemble, the LOGECO (*Logements économiques*) ensemble, the C.I.L. (*Comités interprofessionnels du logement*—Interprofessional housing fund) ensemble, the *Caisse des dépôts* ensemble. In these estates the buildings are differentiated according to the areas of their apartments; Block F3 is followed by Block F5; around them or among them there are rows or groups of individual houses, reserved for the largest or best-off families, and appearing to have been set there—out of scale—in order to show that individual housing is not profitable and that it is a luxury which only the privileged may enjoy.

The construction of these block developments, with dwellings built according to uniform specifications, leads to a virtual segregation of the generations. In new dwellings, 62% of the family heads are less than 45 years old; 6% are more than 65 years old, whereas the corresponding figures in old dwellings are 30% and 28%. Of the 8,574 inhabitants of the Beauregard estate at Poissy on 1st January 1960, 1,141 were children under 2 years old! Thirty-one per cent of the inhabitants of the new housing estates at Roubaix-Tourcoing are less than 10 years old, and 53% are less than 20 years old. One of the inhabitants of a *grand ensemble* undoubtedly expressed a most pertinent opinion about these estates when he said: 'It is far from being paradise, but when you have experienced the hell of the slums . . .' The *grands ensembles* are often regarded as transit lodgings, useful for waiting in until it becomes possible to go to a better situated and more comfortable dwelling. 43·7% of the people approached during a survey at Bron-Parilly hoped to move.

Whatever the value of these housing schemes, whether large or small, they have profoundly altered the appearance of French towns. They were often the first to extend outside the traditional geographical sites for towns, by spreading beyond the valley sides up on to the plateaux. Today, the tall outlines of their blocks and towers punctuate the skyline, and mark the advance of the urban front regardless of site limitations. In fact, the towns vary in the suitability of their sites for this new phase of expansion and construction. Many towns originally founded on perched and fortified sites have had to go far afield to find surfaces large and flat enough to accommodate large blocks of buildings. Perched sites, confluences and valley bottoms are particularly unfavourable.

The rate of construction in recent years corresponds to an urban expansion of 6,000 hectares a year. Because of the lack of legislation and rapid legal procedures, speculation in building land has become a serious problem. The very high purchase price of such land far outweighs the reductions in cost obtained by mechanisation of building methods and prefabrication. It leads builders to recoup by increasing the number of dwellings—that is the density—to the detriment of orientation, green spaces, social facilities. Whence the tower-blocks, the resistance to town-planning regulations limiting the number of storeys. In addition, much confusion is created by a multiplicity of building firms all seeking land in the same agglomeration. Year by year, laws and regulations are published adding further to the conditions laid down for the extension and planning of urban areas.

For example, the acts of 31st December 1958 are concerned with: the conservation and creation of wooded areas in communes which are required to possess a town plan; the power to refuse building permits when the buildings are of a nature likely to detract from the character or interest of adjoining districts, sites and natural or urban landscapes, or when the preservation of architectural viewpoints is at stake; the creation of detailed town plans; the control and supervision of all building permits from the aesthetic point of view; the establishment, in 1961,

of a credit fund of 2,360,000 francs to subsidise the preservation of green spaces; greater precision in the records of specifications of building lots of some importance or size, entailing the production of a comprehensive plan and of clauses designed to ensure a measure of architectural harmony. All these measures have good effects.

The Government has tried to diminish the effects of speculation by defining urban development areas. In 1958 it instituted priority areas for urban development (*zones à urbaniser par priorité*—Z.U.P.), and in 1961 it introduced deferred development areas (*zones d'aménagement différé*—Z.A.D.)[24]. In these areas the State and local authorities possess pre-emptive rights when land is offered for sale, and they may also cause a revision of the prices asked (there is a striking analogy with the S.A.F.E.R.). The Z.U.P. permit large housing estates to be built while avoiding uncoordinated building of many small ones. At Rouen, for example, the bulk of the urban growth for the years 1960–75 is localised in five Z.U.P.: the Z.U.P. of Grand-Quevilly, which covers more than half of the commune (6,000 dwellings, including 1,000 individual houses); the Z.U.P. of Bihorel (8,350 dwellings, including 600 individual houses); the Z.U.P. of Saint-Étienne du Rouvray; the two Z.U.P. of Mont-Saint-Aignan and Canteleu. On 1st January 1967, 180 Z.U.P. had been created, representing 24,556 ha. of land to be built on, their surface areas varying between 7 and 800 ha. 'Sensitive areas', in which particularly careful supervision must be exercised over building, have also been defined; they consist of urban sites and landscapes or rural landscapes, which, although neither classified nor protected, ought to be preserved from the abuses of uncontrolled building and subdivision.

MINING SETTLEMENTS

Urban growth has been localised likewise in the industrial regions of the North and the East. Here the classic type of mining settlement has been developed in a modified form, sometimes with a praiseworthy regard for planning principles (orientation with regard to wind, aspect, green spaces), but the essential character—the artificiality—of these creations has not been touched. The pit determines the location, and segregation according to occupation is the rule. The Charbonnages de Faulquemont company has given rise to a 'town' of 15,000 inhabitants, which has no administrative unity and consists of three distinct districts: the workers' quarter, the employees' quarter, the engineers' quarter.

THE NEW TOWNS

Sometimes the scale of a housing project or its location are such that it assumes the character of an urban creation; the term new town applies to a certain number of completed and current projects, among which we may mention Toulouse II, Montpellier-la-Paillade (with 30,000 inhabitants, 10 km. from Toulouse). This 'parallel' Toulouse will be a town of 100,000 on its doorstep. It is in fact a Z.U.P. of 800 hectares, which will have, in the centre, 17,000 dwellings in collective blocks of 14, 8 and 4 storeys, parking spaces for 32,000 vehicles, half of them underground, and on its outskirts it will have a residential zone of small blocks (2,752 dwellings) and individual houses (2,886 dwellings), as well as small factories on the southern boundary. The *ensemble* will consist of five quarters of 20,000 inhabitants each.

Two other 'new towns' are Montereau-Fault-Yonne, and, above all, Mourenx, 4 km. from Lacq. New Mourenx contains 12,000 inhabitants in 3,000 dwellings, divided into 8 groups (80 dwellings to the hectare). At the centre of each group (blocks and individual houses), there is a tower of 11 storeys. A great effort has been made to provide facilities: commercial centres (supermarkets), bathing pools, sports grounds, technical colleges, schools, a church, a wood reserved for children. But this town is not taking shape without difficulty, for it is handicapped by its social and occupational structure, the small number of employers: 1,800 dwellings at the S.N.P.A. (*Société*

Nationale des Pétroles d'Aquitaine), 340 at Péchiney, 300 at Aquitaine-Chimie. The administration and the engineers prefer to live at Pau.

Besides the large-scale building schemes on the outskirts of towns, changes within the built-up areas, though less extensive, are becoming more important every year.

PRIVATE BUILDING

In most of the large French towns, multiple-storey blocks, whether intended for residence, for offices or for general services, are being put up on sites formerly occupied by individual houses. These houses were not necessarily slums. The dominant factor in the siting of the new blocks is in fact the size of the lot, which must be big enough to permit building high enough to be profitable. The secondary factor is the width of the road which controls the building frontage.

The sites of well-to-do town houses of the 19th century, situated along wide avenues, the sites of workshops and factories, and the interiors of city blocks were chosen for this kind of building. At Lille, as in other cities, the big private residences with rooms which are difficult to heat or are useless (the billiard-room) and which were designed for large families with many servants, were abandoned by the younger generations, and were usually only occupied by the surviving grandparents. These were more and more rapidly replaced by buildings of five to eight storeys, containing luxury flats, with all modern comforts, and benefiting from their nearness to the city centre and the existence of a courtyard, divided into individual garages.

These changes carried out inside cities have had the effect of bending the demographic curve, by increasing the population and introducing greater social diversity. At Lille, 20 private mansions formerly occupied by 9 well-to-do families, 6 industrialists, 3 insurance agents, 2 merchants, 1 lawyer and 1 banker, now house 27 industrialists, architects and insurance agents; 28 well-to-do men or women; 19 directors of commercial companies; 18 lawyers, barristers, teachers, inspectors and journalists; 14 engineers, 14 doctors, 12 merchants, 11 representatives, 4 clerks, 30 workmen and 13 concierges.

FACILITIES AND URBAN RENEWAL

The layout of central areas, the administrative machinery, school and health services did not develop at anything like the same rate as the towns themselves. The redesigning of towns and the improvement of central area facilities have been virtually non-existent in most French towns. The pilot-project of the twelve-year plan for the Paris region records an impressive tale of failure and anachronism, and of obsolescence in the public services.

In Paris, 'the distribution, and very often the buildings of the main police stations date from the 1880s; the headquarters for the Halles quarter is situated in an old building at the end of a court cluttered up with packing cases; the space reserved for the public has an area of 6 m.², including the doorway'. In the suburbs, 'the Bagneux town hall was built in 1875 for a town which then had 1,200 inhabitants, but which now has 38,000 . . . La Garenne-Colombes, created a commune in 1910, houses its services in two residential wings and a wine store; Argenteuil town hall is a private house bought about 1890 when the commune had only 10,000 inhabitants, but it now has to meet the needs of 82,000.' 'Apart from a very few hospitals . . . the suburban area is almost entirely devoid of services'; 'the Paris region has only one bathing pool for every 200,000 inhabitants'. The lack of educational facilities is as well known; without proper establishments, the young cannot get technical instruction in particular. This description applies to most of the large towns.

The local authorities in charge of urban planning also have great problems. The central areas of towns, where land is most costly, are occupied by the oldest housing areas. The conditions of normal urban life are made more difficult every year by narrow streets, squares with restricted outlets and narrow shop entrances; a policy of urban renewal took shape during the 1960s, in connection with the fourth modernisation and re-equipment plan. A law of August 1962 introduced the idea of a protected area into legislation for the first time, and went beyond the protection already accorded to historical monuments and sites. The owners of old buildings receive the same assistance for renovating their houses as they would receive for building new ones. Fourteen towns have been designated as the first beneficiaries under this law: Paris (The Marais), Aix-en-Provence, Avignon, Amiens, Besançon, Bourges, Chartres, Lyons, Montferrand, Rouen, Sarlat, Saumur, Troyes, Uzès. This policy is still only in its timid beginnings, and is held back by various considerations: financial (the cost of buying land), economic (high density of shops and workshops), social (the choice between temporary or permanent rehousing) and political (each inhabitant has a vote). The policy has diverse aspects.

If the city blocks in question are very old, unhealthy and without aesthetic value, renovation takes the form of complete rebuilding as in the unsalubrious parts of Paris. One of the biggest operations of this kind now in progress is the reconstruction of the Saint-Sauveur quarter at Lille. But when the central areas of towns are examined with a view to replanning—which generally means clearing them or pushing wide avenues through them —unknown or forgotten artistic gems come to light. Frequently a decline in the class of occupants, unplanned building operations, street repairs, the grime and the patina of time hide such treasures, not in the form of isolated monumental buildings, but as lengths of street. Thus old Lyons has been rediscovered (the Saint-Jean, Saint-Georges and Saint-Paul quarters), and its buildings from the 15th to the 18th century have been found to have vaults and galleries, arcades and balconies, and admirable towers and staircases concealed in their courts. Such buildings are carefully freed of all their useless and ugly accretions— penthouses, workshops, booths—which have accumulated over the centuries, so that the streets and the courts are given back the pleasing appearance of former days (con-demned area number 3 in Paris).

All this recent urban growth has given the new townscapes of French towns a great and often regrettable heterogeneity. The ele-ments of these townscapes which have been erected during the last twenty years are marked by their monotony, the apparent absence of aesthetic intent, the desire to economise and the rarity of new and forward looking ideas. Everything bears witness to a regrettable deficiency in the field of town planning, in spite of an abundance of town-planning controls. These are quite specific, especially in relation to the planning of in-dividual sites. Where they exist, town plans do not have legal enforcement, neither do they give direction to the forces of urban growth. All too often the real aim of these plans is to plan traffic routes. Plans for zoned develop-ment are few and far between. This is why there are so many cases of juxtaposed individ-ual residences and blocks of flats that detract from each other and spoil a whole district.

17. Sometimes a town-planning scheme was linked to such an extension, and a whole quarter would arise in accordance with a well-worked-out plan (Lille).
18. Cité Bergère, Cité du Rhône, Cité de la Part-Dieu, the cités de la Thibaudière and du Prado.
19. Since 1958, the maximum height has been raised to 31 m. (37 m. in outlying arrondissements).
20. The determining factor of this elongation is the saving produced by the use of crane-railway lines that are straight and as long as possible.
21. The Parc de Beauregard, at La Celle-Saint-Cloud, has been devastated.
22. The Ministry of Reconstruction sent out a circular in March 1962, seeking to 'rehabilitate the individual house by integrating it into modern urbanism'; the circular described the advantages in this kind of dwelling and suggests that it be built on the outskirts of the great agglomerations; it requires that the concept of the *grand ensemble* should not be confined to collective housing but should be applied to individual housing as well.
23. The *grands ensembles* have called forth interesting epithets: concrete monsters, hutches for humans, silos for humans, civilians' barracks, tomorrow's slums, the concentration camp universe!
24. The Z.U.P. correspond to short-term investments; the Z.A.D. to medium-term ones.

2. TOWNSCAPES

This account of the different stages in the development of urban environments shows why French towns cannot be reduced to a few types. Founded a long time ago, through the centuries they have acquired varied characteristics, monuments, street patterns, new extensions, buildings and houses, a long succession of modifications which now com-bine to give each town a distinct personality. In some younger countries the urban land-scape is standardised and the towns mirror each other, trait for trait.

In France, as in other parts of old Europe, urban areas came into being slowly and pro-gressively. But variety in the forms of urban development is undoubtedly more accentuated in France than in other countries. English towns and German towns are both more stereotyped than French towns. This diver-sity arises from many causes, referred to several times already, and stemming from the exposure of France to multiple cultural and historical influences. These explain the in-triguing variety of the French urban scene: the Mediterranean town with its roofs of Roman tiles, its tall, closely packed houses and shady walks; the grey, dirty towns of the industrial regions; newer and therefore more prepossessing towns resulting from post-war reconstruction.

There are ochre, yellow, grey and black towns, according to the kind of building materials used (stone towns, brick towns), and different types of façade; towns made distinc-tive by a particular type of house, such as the long narrow houses of the North or the *échoppes* of Bordeaux.

These little low houses, with one storey, with the roof sloping over the front, in soft stone and rounded tiles, were contemporary with the urban growth of the late 19th century, and the urban landscape which they create has a strongly rural air. These *échoppes* at Bordeaux form large crescentic areas on either side of the boulevards of 1863, and extend as far as the Gare St. Jean.

Urban land use has so far been the subject of very little careful, comparative research, which makes it difficult to do a systematic

Table LXXIX reproduces several items from a survey of 1941–2; it gives figures relating to the size of building lots and of spaces within them. The differences between the areas of the lots and the proportion of built-up areas and courtyards are very considerable.

TABLE LXXIX. BUILDING LOTS AND THEIR OPEN SPACES (1941–2)

Cities	Mean area of lots in m.²	Mean area of built-up parts of lots in m.²	Built-up area as % of total area	% of buildings having 1 court-yard of at least 100 m.²	% of buildings having 1 court-yard of at least 500 m.²
Lille	459	68	14·8	4	2
Lyons	701	140	20·0	20	16
Bordeaux . . .	502	104	20·7	5	9
Marseilles . . .	397	101	25·4	8	11
Toulouse . . .	541	112	20·7	17	14
Roubaix. . . .	191	64	33·5	2	3
All towns with more than 100,000 inhabitants .	470	94	20	9	12
Paris	295	210	71·1	10	0·5

study of urban landscapes. There are tall towns (Paris, Lyons, Saint-Étienne), low towns (Roubaix, Toulouse), compact towns and open towns.

The simplest statistics suffice to illustrate any one aspect of towns and to show the individuality of each of them. In 1954 the percentage of individual houses was 9·4 at Paris, 24·5 at Lyons, 45·1 at Marseilles, 52·9

Table LXXX gives a few examples of differences in land use in several northern towns.

French towns frequently have several centres—heritages from their long past: the castle, the old market-place, the Town Hall square, the cathedral or basilica square, the prefecture, the lycées, the railway station, the main street, the law courts—all these form

TABLE LXXX. LAND USE IN SOME TOWNS OF THE NORTH (%)

Towns	Factories	Railway yards and ports	Pits and tips	Green spaces
Arras	2	3·6	0	2·3
Lille	7·5	5	0	4·1
Roubaix . . .	11·9	1·3	0	4·2
Hénin-Liétard . .	6·8	1·3	14·5	0·8

at Bordeaux, 54·3 at Lille, 88·6 at Roubaix-Tourcoing, compared with 50·7 as the average for all towns of over 100,000 inhabitants. The percentage of buildings having less than three storeys was 24 at Paris, 56 at Lyons, 59 at Metz, 60 at Grenoble, 64 at Strasbourg, 73 at Nice, 75 at Perpignan, 79 at Lille and Marseilles, 89 at Toulouse, 90 at Bordeaux and 97 at Roubaix.

part of a town centre which is not very compact and tentacular in appearance, and whose focal point has shifted from time to time (fig. 94). French towns are likewise difficult to classify by their ground plans. Towns with uniform ground plans are rare, and they are usually the stagnant ones; all the others show a variety of plan elements either side by side or in combination.

3. URBAN HOUSING

At the 1962 census the number of dwellings occupied by non-agricultural households (which could, however, be in rural communes) was estimated at 9,308,000. Nearly a quarter of these were more than ninety years old, whereas 20% were built after 1948 (Table LXXXI).

TABLE LXXXI. DISTRIBUTION OF DWELLINGS ACCORDING TO PERIOD OF BUILDING (1962)

Time of building			Number of dwellings in thousands	%
Up to 1871	.	.	2,048	22
1872–1914	.	.	2,970	32
1915–48 .	.	.	2,436	26
1949–53 .	.	.	272	3
1954–62 .	.	.	1,582	17
Total	.	.	9,308	100

A. House Building

Four sets of causes called for special efforts in the sphere of urban housing after 1945.

1. The near stagnation of building before 1945. Between 1920 and 1938, when England and the Netherlands were building 5·2 and 6 dwellings respectively per 1,000 head of population, the rate for France was only 2·1‰. Taxation upon housing rents had the effect of diverting capital away from the building sector; besides, needs were not great, because the population was stable.

2. The age, obsolescence, the lack of facilities in many existing dwellings. Most houses and other dwellings existing in 1945 were more than fifty years old; some industrial towns had hardly budged since the growth phase of the industrial revolution. The numbers of the population remained stationary, and one generation followed another in the same dwelling.

3. The destruction that occurred during the Second World War. This was not localised, as in the First War, in the North and East, but affected the whole country. About 5% of the real estate in France was destroyed during the last war.

4. The population increase since the war.

P

The annual volume of housing construction since the war is shown in Table LXXXII.

TABLE LXXXII. DWELLINGS CONSTRUCTED BETWEEN 1945 AND 1967

1945–9	.	115,400	1959 .	.	320,000
1950 .	.	70,600	1960 .	.	313,000
1951 .	.	74,900	1961 .	.	315,641
1952 .	.	81,400	1962 .	.	309,000
1953 .	.	115,500	1963 .	.	336,200
1954 .	.	162,000	1964 .	.	368,900 *
1955 .	.	210,000	1965 .	.	411,600
1956 .	.	236,000	1966 .	.	413,000
1957 .	.	274,000	1967 .	.	422,543
1958 .	.	292,000			

* Of which 25,000 were second residences.

The figure of 300,000 dwellings, considered to be the minimum required to meet the demand, was not reached until fifteen years after the end of the war; in comparison with foreign countries the French figures seem very inadequate. France built 2,290,000 dwellings between 1945 and 1960, but Western Germany can boast more than 6,000,000 dwellings built in that period, and England 3,700,000. Between 1950 and 1961, 54 dwellings were built for every 1,000 head of population in France, which puts France sixteenth among European countries (Western Europe, 67‰; European Community, 72‰). It should be remembered that reconstructed dwellings are included among the number of new dwellings.

But the number of dwellings built each year does not correspond to the number of dwellings actually made available to the houseless or the ill-housed. The net increase in dwellings between the censuses of 1954 and 1962 may be calculated thus: although the number of main residences built has risen by 2,017,000, that of main residences enumerated in the census has only risen by 1,118,000; 899,000 main residences have therefore altered their function in various ways. Some have been transformed into second residences, others into vacant dwellings, or into premises for professional use (offices). Therefore the actual rate of increase in the number of dwellings has been of the order of 139,000 per annum.

Closer study of the distribution of dwellings between rural communes and urban communes throws into relief the magnitude of the urban growth of recent years. 958,000 of the 1,580,000 dwellings built since 1954 and occupied as main residences in 1960, were situated in urban communes, and 336,000 of these were in the Paris region alone. Considering the net increase in main residences during the same period, we find an increase of 631,000 dwellings in urban communes, and of 260,000 in the Paris region, compared with a diminution of 121,000 in the rural communes.

The two chief obstacles to the development of building were finance and inertia in the building industry. Building costs are notably higher in France than in neighbouring countries (25% higher than in Germany). This is partly due to a better average quality. Other factors are the craft-structure of part of the industry, bad organisation on building sites, abnormal length of time required to complete jobs and the multiplicity of building styles. The fifth plan has fixed a target of 480,000 dwellings to be built in the year 1970.

B. The Builders of New Dwellings

Building is carried out by private persons, by private companies, by local authorities and departmental authorities, and directly by the State. All these contribute very unequally to the total volume. The main problem of the post-war period was to reform the rents system, to make investments in real estate profitable once again. A rent act of 1948 established a basis for a new policy by standardising the method of calculating rents in terms of specific criteria (area, facilities), and by providing for progressive rises in rents up to 1961. Rents were afterwards decontrolled in most urban centres. But this policy of restoring the rents system necessitated a change of attitude on the part of tenants, for whom rents had been a negligible proportion of expenses until then. Moreover, families with small incomes bitterly resented the rise in rents.

These measures for freeing the market in rented housing attracted capital back to building, and the sector concerned with building superior dwellings was abandoned to private capital. After a long period of abandonment, building became a new 'Far West', as the Minister for Building remarked, where large-scale and small-scale promoters, disinterested organisations and speculators all jostled. Housing societies, authorised in 1958, have built about 12,000 dwellings. In March 1962, by the painless method of fiscal reform, the structure of the property market was profoundly altered. Large tax concessions were given to big companies carrying out projects for rented dwellings, while certain exemptions were withdrawn from small building companies. At the beginning of 1963 the Government encouraged the formation of building societies which, being quoted on the stock exchange, would attract savings;[25] but the high price of land and the cost of building caused these companies only to build dwellings for very high rents, which only few could pay.

In fact, the bulk of the building programme is financed by the State and local authorities. In 1965 only 14% of the new dwellings had not benefited from official aid; the communes and departments contributed through the H.L.M.; private enterprises contributed through a levy of 1% on wages, introduced in 1954. These payments are centralised by the C.I.L., which builds dwellings of various kinds for the employees of related enterprises. The State contributes through loans, premiums and the work of its own corporations —the Caisse des Dépôts, the Crédit Foncier; between 1947 and 1957 the State paid out 6,222 million francs in mortgage credits in favour of the H.L.M. (loans at 1%, repayable in forty-five years, and providing 85% of the cost of building).

Because of the social and economic situation in France, the enormous needs can only be met by a housing policy which is treated on the same level as others as a social service. The fourth plan has given the H.L.M. the task of providing one third of the necessary housing. In fact, however, the H.L.M. share is not increasing and tends to diminish, while more costly building has the advantage and increased by 109% in six years compared with a 28·5% increase in the building of rented property through H.L.M. and 85% if it passed into private ownership (Table LXXXIII).

The number of dwellings which it is possible to build every year is not, in the first place, determined by economic or social considerations but by budgetary considerations, since the finance is linked to the distribution of resources among the various sectors of the national budget. Hence the reason why rules for grants, loans and subsidies are becoming stricter and stricter.

State aid to building has been essentially 'aid to the stone'—which means that the State provided capital for building organisations and gave them interest rebates. This kind of aid has helped to lower the quality of building, and encouraged the building of 'austere', if not second-rate, houses. Experts believe that 'aid to the person' would have avoided these unfortunate results, but this exists only under the modest form of dwelling and rent allowances (1961).

Eventual ownership has become one of the main planks of housing policy, since letting, being controlled, does not bring in a fair income. Rented property has always been in the minority. This situation has serious consequences. On the one hand rented dwellings are the only ones available to people with low wages, to young married couples without capital, to slum-dwellers, to those who live in furnished rooms and flats. On the other hand, property ownership leads to immobility of the population, at a time when a degree of mobility could be desired to encourage a better distribution of activities and workers.

Owner-occupier housing is much more extensive in communes of less than 100,000 inhabitants than in large urban agglomerations. In the Paris region, 27·9% of families own their dwelling, compared with 41% in communes of less than 10,000 inhabitants. The number of owner-occupiers is higher in new housing. On examining the distribution of tenure by categories of employment we find that the owner-occupiers belong mainly to the well-to-do classes, whereas tenants are

T BLE LXXXIII. DWELLINGS BUILT, BY CATEGORIES
(in thousands of dwellings completed)

	1958	%	1959	%	1960	%	1961	%	1962	%
H.L.M. for letting	68·7	23·5	82·8	25·8	77	24·3	70·8	22·4	67·4	21·9
H.L.M. for eventual ownership	18·9	6·4	18·1	5·6	18·8	5·9	20·7	6·5	20·8	6·7
Economical and family dwellings	74	25·3	86·6	27·02	89·1	28·4	98·9	31·2	102·1	35·2
Other dwellings receiving state aid	80·4	27·5	87·6	27·03	87·7	27·7	81·4	27·7	73·5	23·9
Non-aided dwellings	25·5	8·7	28·2	8·8	31·3	9·8	31·2	10·1	35	11·4
Reconstruction	24·2	8·2	17·1	5·3	12·7	4	11·8	3·7	8·1	2·6
Total	291·7		320·4		316·6		315·7		306·9	

	1963	%	1964	%	1965	%	1966	%	1967	%
H.L.M. for letting	79·3	23·6	92·6	25	96	23·3	97	23·1	107	25·6
H.L.M. for eventual ownership	22·5	6·7	24·9	6·8	28·5	6·9	30	7·5	31·2	7·4
Economical and family dwellings	112·7	33·5	102·9	27·9	226·9	55·2	201·7	48·6	191·2	45
Other dwellings receiving state aid	79·2	23·6	104·2	28·3						
Non-aided dwellings	39	11·5	41·9	11·4	58·9	14·3	85·4	20·6	93	22
Reconstruction	3·9	1·2	2·4	0·6	1·3	0·3	1	0·2	0·1	0
Total	335·6		368·9		411·6		413		422·5	

much more numerous among the less fortunate: skilled workers, unskilled workers,
48·9%; service personnel, 49·1%; qualified
workers and foremen, 49·7%, compared with
the French average of 41·7%. All in all,
the housing sector takes and will take an
increasing percentage of investments—of the
order of a quarter to a fifth of the total.

C. Location of New Housing

Figure 96 indicates the distribution by
departments of main residences built between
the two recent population censuses (1954,
1962). A particularly striking feature is the
peripheral distribution of departments with
the highest figures. Even more striking is
the degree of concentration. The three
departments of the Paris region have taken
about a third (32%) of newly built housing:
Seine (15·9%), Seine-et-Oise (14·5%), Seine-
et-Marne (1·7%); twelve departments in the
provinces have taken more than another
third, the main ones being: Bouches-du-
Rhône (5·2%), Nord (3·8%), Moselle (3·7%),
Rhône (3·7%), Alpes-Maritimes (2·6%). In
all, fifteen departments have received 66% of
the new housing.

The location of this new housing broadly
coincides with areas of population growth,
since housing responds to the needs of the
new increments which are almost exclusively
in urban areas. The maps showing increase
in housing and increase in population (fig. 38)
are much alike, although they do not correspond completely. Some departments have
gained proportionately more dwellings than
inhabitants: Seine (15·9 and 11·7%), Bas-
Rhin (1·88 and 1·59%). Others on the contrary have changed adversely, since the growth

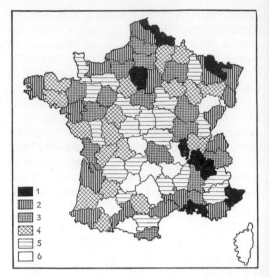

Fig. 96. Departmental distribution of main residences built from 1954 to 1962, in relation to the
national total.

1. More than 2·5%. 2. From 1 to 2·5%. 3. From
0·5 to 1%. 4. From 0·25 to 0·5%. 5. From 0 to
0·25%. 6. Decline.

in their housing has not followed that in
population: Isère (2·54 and 2·81%), Moselle
(3·7 and 4·3%), Nord (3·8 and 4·7%),
Rhône (3·7 and 4%), Seine-et-Oise (14·5 and
16·3%).

D. The Property Capital Situation

French urban dwellings are obsolescent and
poor in facilities. Capital investment in
property has not been increased, so that most
of the houses are dated and their facilities
reflect the epoch in which they were built; in
1960, the age of dwellings was as follows
(Table LXXXIV):

TABLE LXXXIV. DISTRIBUTION OF URBAN DWELLINGS BY PERIOD OF
CONSTRUCTION

	Urban agglomerations					
Period of construction	Less than 100,000		More than 100,000		Paris region	
	Thousands	%	Thousands	%	Thousands	%
Before 1871 .	1,148	27·3	559	18·7	448	16·7
1871–1914 .	1,181	28	934	31·1	1,032	35·3
1915–48 . .	948	22·5	793	26·5	874	29·9
1948–62 . .	933	22·2	710	23·7	529	18·1
Total . .	4,210	100	2,996	100	2,923	100

After Paris, it is the provincial towns with 50,000–100,000 inhabitants which have the most antiquated buildings. Seventeen per cent of those in Paris are more than a century old, compared with 19% for towns of more than 100,000 inhabitants, and 14% for provincial towns of 50,000–100,000 inhabitants. Aix-en-Provence has the highest number of old buildings in this last group: 39% were built before 1850. Next comes Versailles, where a good number of buildings date from the 17th and 18th centuries, then Avignon, Poitiers and Orleans. In the group of over 100,000 inhabitants, Rouen has the most old

desired. In 1961, considering only dwellings occupied by non-agricultural households: 84% had running water, 65% had water closets and 37% had sanitary installations. Tables LXXXVI and LXXXVII bring together the main statistics concerning household facilities and reveal the grave deficiencies of far too many of them. More than a million urban dwellings have no running water; only 19·3% of non-agricultural dwellings have central heating.

The Paris region is no better off. The situation of housing facilities in 1962 was as follows: 3% of the dwellings (100,000) had

TABLE LXXXV. DISTRIBUTION OF BUILDINGS BY AGE IN SOME BIG CITIES (1962)

	Lyons	Marseilles	Brest	Bordeaux	Lille	Roubaix	Toulouse	Paris
Total number of dwellings	278,695	245,312	37,774	142,846	129,407	105,216	99,381	2,528,764
Percentage built:								
Before 1871	24·2	16·9	4·3	24·7	15·6	14·4	20·6	16·1
1871–1914	32·1	34·2	21·2	38·5	39·9	50·2	26·2	35
1915–48	22·5	26	24	22	24·9	18·7	23·9	30·2
Total since 1948	21·2	22·4	50·5	14·8	20·1	16·7	29·3	18·8
Including:								
1949–53	1·8	2·4	15·7	1·8	3	3·5	3·2	1·5
1954–62	17·6	17·7	33·2	11·6	16·5	12·2	24·1	15·7

dwellings: in 1954, 26% had been built before 1850. Bordeaux follows Rouen with 19%. The most recent buildings are in towns which suffered widespread damage during the last war. Most of the existing buildings at Brest were reconstructed after the war. The proportions are: Le Havre, 40%; Caen, 31%; Calais, 21% (Table LXXXV).

Half of the buildings at Lille and Roubaix date from the industrial revolution, whereas barely 3% of the dwellings were built since 1939–40, as against 50% in Brest. It is clear that these rates of obsolescence were greatly modified by the resumption of building after 1954; but since new dwellings are mostly not built to replace old dwellings, the old urban cores of many French towns are still disfigured by insanitary blocks. There are still too many French towns which may be described as museum-towns or slum-towns. At Le Puy in 1955, 5,000 out of 7,000 dwellings were more than 100 years old.

Urban housing facilities leave much to be

no electricity; 15% (500,000) had no water either inside or on the same floor; 45% (1,400,000) had no water-closet in the dwelling; 60% (1,800,000) had no central heating; 66% (2,000,000) had neither bathroom nor shower. The adequacy of urban housing is not measured by facilities alone but by the size and number of rooms, both of which should be all the bigger when dwellings are apartments in collective blocks. But the economic necessities of the post-war period have often caused limitations to the area and number of rooms. New dwellings have a mean area of 65 m.^{2}; 17% of these new apartments have five rooms or more, as against 40% in England and 43% in Switzerland.

Property capital is insufficiently maintained. The *Fonds National d'Amélioration de l'Habitat* (National Fund for Improving Housing) was set up in 1945 to promote large-scale maintenance works by means of subsidies and loans. It is financed by a levy on rents.

THE SLUMS

It is difficult to get an exact figure for the number of slum houses. The behaviour of the occupants plays an important role in the process by which a dwelling becomes a slum. But if we regard those dwellings as slums which are obsolescent and lacking the mini-

crowding;[27] 14% lived in temporarily permissible overcrowding.[28] But at the same time, 15% lived in conditions of moderate under-occupation[29] and 10% in conditions of extreme under-occupation.[30]

Large apartments are actually inhabited by elderly people. Private residences, which once housed large families, nowadays con-

TABLE LXXXVI. FACILITIES IN SOME FRENCH CITIES AND IN TOWNS OF MORE THAN 100,000 INHABITANTS (1962)

Towns	% of dwellings having bathroom and shower	% with a w.c. under the same roof	% with a shared w.c.	% of buildings with running water indoors
Lille	33·4	40·4	15·8	84·6
Lyons	38·7	65·3	15·3	97·9
Bordeaux	38·8	49·6	12·6	91·7
Marseilles	44·4	62·2	15·4	96·2
Toulouse	48	52·5	16·3	95·5
Roubaix	32	37·4	10·1	82·8
Grenoble	60·2	78	7·4	97·9
Nice	56·9	87·1	3·1	96·6
Towns with more than 100,000 inhab.	40·8	56·1	37·6	92·7

TABLE LXXXVII. FACILITIES AND EQUIPMENT BY CATEGORIES OF TOWN AND AGE OF BUILDINGS (1960)

	Towns and agglomerations <100,000 inhab.	Towns and agglomerations >100,000 inhab.	Paris region
Buildings erected before 1915	%	%	%
Dwellings without water	17·9	9·7	13·6
Dwellings with water, w.c. and sanitation	21·5	22·6	25·4
Buildings erected between 1915 and 1948			
Dwellings without water	10	5	6
Dwellings with water, w.c. and sanitation	31	37	45
Buildings erected after 1948			
Dwellings without water	2·5	1·8	1
Dwellings with water, w.c. and sanitation	90	95	95·3
All dwellings			
Dwellings without water	14·8	6	9·4
Dwellings with water, w.c. and sanitation	37·7	41·9	42·8

mum facilities appropriate to the second half of the 20th century, we reach a minimum figure of the order of 450,000.[26]

THE OCCUPATION OF DWELLINGS

Urban housing is badly utilised and figures reveal the simultaneous existence of overcrowded and under-occupied dwellings. The Ministry of Building has clearly demonstrated these conditions. In 1954, 22·7% of French people lived under conditions of severe over-

tain only grandmothers living alone. Severe overcrowding is particularly common in the big towns. It affected 27·8% of Parisians in 1954. The situation seems to have improved by 1961, when 7·8% of French people lived in conditions of severe overcrowding, 9·1% in conditions of temporarily permissible overcrowding. Parallel with this, there was a distinct improvement in respect of under-occupation, since 27% now belong to the fortunate category of moderate under-occupation compared with 15% in 1954. A similar development seems to have occurred in the Paris region. But it is to be noted that apartments with the poorest facilities are usually overcrowded, especially in agglomerations of more than 100,000 inhabitants and in the Paris region, where the proportions of severe and permissible overcrowding are 28 and 32% respectively.

According to recent surveys, there were 33,400,000 living rooms in all housing occupied by non-agricultural families, that is 2·85 living rooms per dwelling. The kitchen was counted as a living room in the 1961 survey, regardless of its size, whenever the household declared that it was used as a 'common room'. That is why the total number of living rooms is said to amount to 39,650,000, that is 3·34 per dwelling, which is an overestimate. New dwellings are generally bigger than the old ones: 20·4% have more than four rooms, as against 9·9% in old dwellings. Towns with less than 100,000 inhabitants are not distinguishable from rural communes as regards size of dwellings. But in towns with more than 100,000 inhabitants and in the Paris region, dwellings are noticeably smaller; 58% have less than four rooms, as against 47% in towns with less than 100,000 inhabitants. Dwellings lacking in facilities are generally small, and half of them have only one or two rooms.

25. The profits reinvested by these companies were exempted from company tax and distributed profits were exempted from the tax on income from real estate.
26. Since 1951 the *Centres de Propagande et d'Action contre les Taudis* (*P.A.C.T.*), or slum-clearance centres, have equipped, improved or made habitable more than 100,000 dwellings in slum areas, thus showing that it is possible to rehabilitate such dwellings.
27. Severe overcrowding: 3 persons or more in one room, 4 or more in two rooms.
28. Temporarily permissible overcrowding: 2 persons in one room, 3 in two rooms.
29. Moderate under-occupation: 1 person in two or three rooms; 2 or 3 in four rooms.
30. Extreme under-occupation: 1 person in four or more rooms, 2 or 3 persons in five or more rooms.

PROSPECTS FOR THE FUTURE

It is clearly difficult to estimate what the urban population and urban growth will be like in France during the next thirty years. If one accepts two relatively conservative forecasts: 70 million inhabitants in France by the year 2000, 70% of them living in urban areas, it can be inferred that the urban population will rise from 29,500,000 (1962) to 52,500,000—which means that the urban population will be doubled. They will be increased by 5 million during the next ten years. The demand for housing is going to increase enormously as the age group born immediately after the war comes of age from 1966–7 onwards. Taking into account the renewal of building property (half of which is to be replaced during the next thirty years) the most conservative estimate of housing needs will require the construction of 9 million dwellings between now and 1980.[31]

The fundamental geographical problem, apart from the carrying through of this vast programme, is that of locating these new dwellings. This problem has two aspects. The first is that of apportioning the new housing between the Paris agglomeration and the provincial towns. 'To prevent the Paris agglomeration from doubling in size, the provincial towns as a whole must be more than doubled in less than forty years.'[32] The second aspect, that of choosing locations for new urban expansion in the provinces, is probably even more important. One course of action is to distribute new building among the existing towns in proportion to the increases expected, while maintaining their relative status in the urban hierarchy. This would operate in favour of the existing urban growth centres. An alternative course would be to give most of the new building to selected towns that have small populations relative to their functions and place in the hierarchy. Yet another alternative would be to devise a true New Towns policy for the Paris region as well as for the provinces.

It is significant of the French attitude towards national planning problems that, except in the founding of urban centres associated with industrial developments, town planning has never envisaged the creation of new towns on the British and Scandinavian models.

'In the last fifteen years, the population of France has increased by 6 million, the equivalent of 20 Bordeaux or 40 Rheims, without a single new town being built. The reason for this sterility is purely political; the towns to be created cannot speak for themselves, because they do not exist. And so the State pays 20,000 francs a square metre to urban landowners rather than 200 francs in a rural area, because the force of attraction of what already exists deprives it of financial foresight and all creative imagination' (A. Sauvy).

The massive urban growth of the years to come combined with the obsolescence and lack of change in contemporary towns make it imperative to adopt a policy for urban development and urban life at the earliest possible date.

31. 600,000 to 700,000 to remedy overcrowding, 2,500,000 new dwellings, 250,000 apartments for repatriates, 100,000 weekend or holiday dwellings, 500,000 dwellings for in-migrants from the countryside, 3–5 million for renovating dwellings which are old, too small or without facilities.

32. '*Avant projet programme duo-décennal pour la région parisienne.*'

CONCLUSION

'One is always wrong about France because one wishes to generalise,' wrote Léonce de Lavergne. The study of the spatial structure of the country does indeed produce a complex picture.

Its complexity is first of all due to the diversity of both natural and human factors which have 'woven' this land and superimposed on it patterns that by no means coincide: a pattern of thousands of valleys, interfluves and slopes which constitute the physical landscape, a pattern of soils, a pattern of local climates, a pattern of communes dotted with settlement units and clusters of agricultural holdings, a pattern of fields and land use units . . . All chapters have led us to the same impressions: of the density, intensity and continuity, but also of the fragmentation, dispersion and intricacy of geographical phenomena in France. Their complexity is seen to be due to the antiquity of human occupance. Nothing—not the relief, nor the soils, nor the settlement, nor the methods of land use, nor the town plans, nor the industrial locations—can be attributed to simple and recent causes.

No part of the French landscape is monogenetic. The pattern of land divisions is rarely consistent with their content—crops, buildings or factories. Neither are the administrative divisions consistent with the patterns of circulation. The heterogeneity and polygenetic character of our landscapes stem from these inconsistencies. If we compiled geographical maps on the same lines as geological maps, differentiating the various categories of phenomena according to their age, we should obtain distribution patterns of great interest showing the progressive formation of landscapes, recent features rarely if ever effacing the older ones completely.

*

An essential feature of the geography of France arises from this diversity and long history of development: the importance of fine variations. 'Everything is finely differentiated and therein lies the distinctiveness of France,' Charles Morazé has rightly said. A further element of complexity has been introduced by recent changes in the spatial structure of the country. The landscapes of France were indeed polygenetic until the years 1945–50, but they were crystallised; few changes were made after 1910 and these were highly localised (consolidated holdings, farms and houses rebuilt in parts devastated by the First World War, and a few new factories). For the last twenty years, however, all the constituent elements of France have felt the winds of change which have already produced transformations, or set them in motion.

It is easy to imagine an immense map of France upon which little coloured lights appear every time that the spatial pattern is altered at any point: ranging from amalgamated communes to new power stations, from motorways to decentralised factories, from new urban extensions to reservoirs, from railway lines to demolished slums. Thousands of such lights would go on to mark the birth of new features, the reshaping of the geography of France.

After fifty years of stagnation, a sense of urgency began to grow in response to the demands of a growing population and increasingly severe economic competition; the extent of the difference between the stagnation inherited from the past and the changes needed today, or in the near future, accounts for frequent laments in the alleged slowness of developments, their fragmentary nature and lack of coordination. All the tasks to be done present themselves at the same time and with the same degree of urgency, which obliges us to establish priorities by sectors and also by regions. Priorities and choices always entail grave consequences, and the thousands of lights on our hypothetical map are certainly appearing in disorderly sequence.

In spite of undeniable goodwill, France has not yet brought its area planning under control, being more accustomed to planning its economy. At present, area planning in France is taking shape in various ways through voluntary efforts, exhortations, public and private decisions, but these lack coherence and a really comprehensive organisation. To be fair to those in power, it must be admitted that such coordination is by no means easy to achieve in France. Ever since her birth as a political unit France has never ceased to be in a state of tension, subject to centralising forces and opposing regionalising forces.

In every chapter of this book we have seen these forces in action. A strongly united and centralised administrative and legislative system neutralises or opposes regionalist tendencies which are deeply rooted in environmental differences and strongly contrasted conditions of social and economic development: France *du Nord* and France *du Midi*; France *d'Oïl* and France *d'Oc*; lowland France and upland France; maritime France and continental France. France epitomises this duality in its broadest characteristics. France *du Nord*, centred upon the Paris basin, without hostile frontiers and with a fine array of converging rivers, contrasts with France *du Midi*, where the huge block of the Central Massif rears up above the plains of Vendée, Aquitaine and the Rhône corridor, keeps them apart, and cuts off the Loire basin from the plains of the South, the Alps and Pyrenees being complementary barriers. By trying to appreciate variations in the structure and resources of the regions, we have been able to discover the magnitude of geographical inequalities between the various parts of the country in spite of, and indeed because of, the effects of a policy which puts all the regions on an equal footing. The regions of France differ profoundly in their landscapes, which symbolise either their 'fossilisation' or, conversely, their 'geographical dynamism'.

The contemporary situation accentuates contrasts between the various parts of France. The founding of a European community with its centre of gravity along the Rhine has favoured continental regions at the expense of the western regions which face the Atlantic and the Channel and lack the counterbalance which Iberia and Great Britain could provide. The north–south alignment of this axis of 'Europe of the Six' is unfavourable to transverse links except those which are already strongly developed, like the lower Seine. These contrasts are reinforced by the continued concentration of the population, through migration, into a small number of cities and a few already favoured regions, the localised concentration of capital, of decision-making and of power around the economic poles, as well as the effects of inertia. Year after year, some regions of France are ageing socially and economically and get dangerously near to becoming the 'deserts' foreseen by J. F. Gravier.

The whole territorial structure of France protests against this trend, for the pattern of regions is so finely divided, and so complex, that there are few regions which seem to be beyond redemption. Some are rich in mineral resources, fertile soils, land potential or their splendid sites, while others are rich in their youthful populations, in capital or in traditions.

The future of the land of France and its constituent regions will depend upon deliberate effort to change its geography by building up, piece by piece, the landscapes of the year 2000, by providing conditions in which the best possible distribution of population can be achieved, and by giving France a truly human geography, through the medium of a genuine policy of national planning.

BIBLIOGRAPHY

A detailed bibliography of the geography of France would fill a large volume; the long productive history of the French geographical schools is responsible for this enormous reservoir of studies. In addition, the bibliography cannot be limited to geographical works. All sciences, natural, social and economic, have contributed to our knowledge of the territory of France, either directly or by the use which geographers have made of their researches.

With a few exceptions, we have not given references to earlier works which have already been mentioned in the bibliographies to works and articles quoted (in particular the three volumes of *Géographie Universelle*) and studies of purely local application.

LIST OF ABBREVIATIONS

ORGANISATIONS, PUBLISHERS, COLLECTIONS

C.A.C., Collection A. Colin (Collection Liz since 1967)
C.R.D.C.G., Centre de Recherche et de Documentation Catographique et Géographique (C.N.R.S., Institut de Géographie, Paris)
C.D.U., Centre de Documentation Universitaire (Paris)
C.N.R.S., Centre National de la Recherche Scientifique
D.A.T.A.R., Délégation à l'Aménagement du Territoire et à l'Action Régionale
F.N.Sc.P., Fondation Nationale des Sciences Politiques (Paris)
G.U., Géographie Universelle (Armand Colin)
I.N.E.D., Institut National d'Études Démographiques
I.N.S.E.E., Institut National de la Statistique et des Études Économiques (Paris)
L.A.C., Librairie Armand Colin
N.E.D., Notes et Études Documentaires (La Documentation Française)
P.U.F., Presses Universitaires de France

REVIEWS

Ac.G., *Acta Geographica* (Paris)
A.F.A.Sc., *Association Française pour l'Avancement des Sciences*
A.G., *Annales de Géographie* (Paris)
B.A.G.F., *Bulletin de l'Association des Géographes Français* (Paris)
B.C.T.H., *Bulletin du Comité des Travaux Historiques et Scientifiques* (section de géographie Paris)
B.S.G.F., *Bulletin de la Societé Géologique de France* (Paris)
B.S.L.G., *Bulletin de la Societé Languedocienne de Géographie* (Montpellier)
H.T.N., *Hommes et Terres du Nord* (Lille)
I.G., *Information Géographique* (Paris)
Méd., *Méditerranée* (Aix-en-Provence)
R.G.A., *Revue de Géographie Alpine* (Grenoble)
R.G.D., *Revue de Géomorphologie Dynamique* (Paris)
R.G.E., *Revue Géographique de l'Est*
R.G.L., *Revue Géographique de Lyon*
R.G.P.S.-O., *Revue Géographique des Pyrénées et du Sud-Ouest* (Toulouse)

WORKS OF GENERAL REFERENCE

BIBLIOGRAPHIES

La Bibliographie géographique internationale, published annually by the *Association des géographes français* under the auspices of the International Geographical Union, contains a particularly detailed section on France; it has superseded the annual geographical bibliography of the *Annales de Géographie*, which has appeared since 1890.

There is no lack of bibliographies useful for a quick survey of recent references; we may mention the *Bulletin mensuel analytique de documentation politique, économique et sociale contemporaine* published by the Fondation Nationale des Sciences Politiques (since 1946) and *Économie régionale*, a selective bibliography published monthly by the Chamber of Commerce and Industry in Paris (since 1957).

GENERAL WORKS

Though there is a considerable bibliography of geographical studies, we cannot say the same of general works. Those which have appeared since the beginning of the century are:
Tableau de la Géographie de la France, by P. Vidal de la Blache (vol. 1 of *Histoire de France* by E. Lavisse), Paris 1903, 395 pp. This is a masterpiece which will never be superseded. The three volumes (vol. VI) of the *Géographie Universelle* (Armand Colin) give a picture of France just before the last war: E. de Martonne, *France Physique*, Paris 1942, 463 pp.; A. Demangeon, *France Économique et Humaine*, Paris 1946 and 1948 (2 vols), 899 pp.

There are two regional approaches to the geography of France: G. Chabot, *Géographie Régionale de la France*, Paris 1966 (1st edition), 433 pp.; P. George, *La France*, Paris 1967, 271 pp.

REGIONAL PUBLICATIONS

Geographers have worked above all at regional level and their documentation can be used on the national level. The eight volumes of the collection *France de Demain*, by the Presses Universitaires de France, edited by F. L. Closon and P. George, 1960–4 and re-edited: 1. P. George and P. Randet, *La Région parisienne*; 2. R. Nistri and C. Précheur, *La Région du Nord et du Nord-Est*; 3. A. Blanc, E. Juillard, J. Ray and M. Rochefort, *Les Régions de l'Est*; 4. J. Labasse and M. Laferrère, *La région lyonnaise*; 5. P. Carrère and R. Dugrand, *La région méditerranéenne*; 6. P. Barrère, R. Heisch and S. Lerat, *La Région du Sud-Ouest*; 7. P. Flatrès, *La Région de l'Ouest*; 8. P. Estienne and R. Joly, *La Région du Centre*.

Regional studies are beginning to be published in the collection Que sais-je: *Les Pyrénées* by G. Viers (1962, no. 995) and *Le Massif Central* by S. Derruau-Boniol and A. Fel (1963, no. 1033). M. Le Lannou, *Géographie de la Bretagne*, 2 vols, Rennes 1952; E. Juillard, *L'Alsace, le sol, les hommes et la vie régionale*, Strasbourg 1963, 80 pp.

REGIONAL THESES

Since the theses of R. Blanchard (*La Flandre*, 1905), A. Demangeon (*La Plaine Picarde*, 1906), J. Sion (*Les Paysans de la Normandie Orientale*, 1909) until the last war, French geographers excelled in this type of work. Since then there has been a tendency to specialise, and we shall mention these theses in the appropriate chapters. Nevertheless the tradition has been maintained: M. Chevalier, *La Vie humaine dans les Pyrénées Ariégeoises*, Paris 1956, 1061 pp.; S. Daveau, *Les Régions frontalières de la montagne jurassienne*, a study in human geography, Lyons 1959, 571 pp.; M. Derruau, *La Grande Limagne auvergnate et bourbonnaise, étude géographique*, Clermont-Ferrand 1949, 544 pp.; M. Gautier, *La Bretagne centrale, étude géographique*, La Roche-sur-Yon 1947, X—454 pp.; P. Veyret, *Les pays de la Moyenne Durance Alpestre, étude géographique*, Grenoble 1945, 596 pp.

REVIEWS

Both national and regional geographical reviews are veritable mines of studies, articles, chronicles, surveys and references which are constantly being renewed.

Les Annales de Géographie were founded in 1891 by P. Vidal de la Blache (Librairie A. Colin); they now appear six times a year. We find there particular reports of inter-university field studies, concise articles on the various aspects of a region by those who have studied them recently. *The Bulletin de l'Association des Géographes français* has published since 1925 the text of papers read at their monthly meetings. *L'Information Géographique*, founded in 1936 by A. Cholley, for the guidance of secondary school teachers, contributes in its five annual issues a collection of original articles, surveys, statistics and reports of recent theses, written by their authors.

The large number of regional reviews is the most obvious proof of the importance of the research done by geographers: *Revue géographique des Pyrénées et du Sud-Ouest* (by the Departments of Geography of Bordeaux and Toulouse), which has appeared since 1930; *Revue de géographie alpine*, Grenoble (since 1913); *Méditerranée*, journal of the Departments of Geography of Montpellier, Aix and Nice (since 1960); *Revue de Géographie de Lyon* (since 1926), the title of which was *Études Rhodaniennes* until 1948; *Revue de Géographie de l'Est*, journal of the Departments of Geography of Besançon, Dijon, Nancy and Strasbourg (since 1961); *Norois*, journal of the Departments of Geography of Caen, Poitiers and Rennes (since 1954); *Hommes et Terres du Nord*, journal of the Department of Geography and Geographical Society of Lille.

STATISTICS

The I.N.S.E.E. publish a statistical year-book, of which the 1965 volume is the 71st: *Annuaire statistique de la France*, very rich in demographic and economic data, accompanied by diagrams and maps, with the addition of series of retrospective statistics (the 1960 volume, new series no. 8, was particularly retrospective), this year-book makes possible contemporary surveys and development analyses. The I.N.S.E.E. published in 1956 (326 pp.), in 1958 (380 pp.), in 1960 (344 pp.), in 1963 (344 pp.), in 1966 (536 pp.) some useful pocket year-books: *Tableaux de l'Économie française*, whose statistics, diagrams and maps enable analyses to be made at department level. The main statistical data can also be found in the *Images économiques du Monde*, by J. Beaujeu-Garnier and A. Gamblin (Paris) which have been appearing since 1956.

ATLASES

The *Atlas de France*, published by the Comité National de Géographie in 1931, and re-issued with new maps between 1951 and 1958, is the basic reference book; several of its maps can be found in the three volumes of the *Géographie Universelle* devoted to France.

The I.N.S.E.E. publishes, under the title *L'Espace économique français*, an atlas which treats at department level almost all available human and economic statistics; 1st edition, Paris 1951, 144 pp. (special issue of the I.N.S.E.E. journal *Études et conjoncture*); 2nd edition, 1955, 120 pp. of text and an atlas (special issue of *Études et conjoncture*); 3rd edition, 1965, 1 (General demography); 1968, 2 (Working population). *Atlas historique de la France contemporaine*, 1800–1965, A. Colin, 1966, 234 pp. (most interesting maps); *Atlas économique et social pour l'aménagement du territoire*, published in sections by D.A.T.A.R., since 1967.

Regional atlases are beginning to be published: *Atlas de la France de l'Est*, Strasbourg, Nancy 1960; *Atlas du Nord*, Paris 1961; *Atlas de Normandie*, Caen 1966; *Atlas de la Région parisienne*, 1967.

PHOTOGRAPHS

A magnificent atlas of aerial photographs has been published by P. Deffontaines and M. J. Brunhes-Delamarre: *Atlas aérien*. vol. I: Alps, Rhône valley, Provence, Corsica, Paris 1955, 192 pp.; vol. II: Brittany, Loire valley, Sologne and Berry, Atlantic regions between Loire and Gironde, Paris 1956, 190 pp.; vol. III: Pyrenees, Languedoc, Aquitaine, Central Massif, Paris 1958, 192 pp.; vol. IV: Paris and the Seine valley, Île de France, Beauce and Brie, Normandy, from Picardy to Flanders, Paris 1962, 192 pp.; vol. V: Alsace, Vosges, Lorraine, Ardennes and Champagne, Morvan and Bourgogne, Jura, Paris 1964, 192 pp.

HISTORICAL CONSTITUTION

Works on historical geography are not numerous. Roger Dion has devoted to the frontiers a very intelligent, scholarly little book: *Les Frontières de la France*, Paris 1947, 112 pp.

RELIEF

GENERAL

Two complementary works: the volume by E. De Martonne, *France physique* (G.U.), already mentioned, contains a mine of information and illustrations which are extremely interesting. Unfortunately morphological theories have evolved so rapidly that we cannot refer to this book without more up-to-date information. This has been provided by J. Beaujeu-Garnier in *Le Relief de la France par la carte et le croquis*, C.D.U., Paris 1953, 348 pp., with very full illustrations and bibliography. On the geological history of France, from which morphological evolution is inseparable: J. Goguel, *Géologie de la France* (Que sais-je, no. 443—4th edition, 1965) is useful. On hypsometry, the essential article is that of E. De Martonne: 'Détermination et interprétation des altitudes moyennes de la France et de ses grandes régions naturelles', *A.G.*, 1941, no. 284, pp. 241–54.

THE MORPHOLOGICAL EVOLUTION OF HERCYNIAN FRANCE

Armorican Massif. A. Guilcher, *Le Relief de la Bretagne méridionale, de la baie de Douarnenez à la Vilaine*, thesis, La Roche-sur-Yon 1948, 682 pp.; M. Ters, *La Vendée littorale, étude de géomorphologie*, thesis, Paris 1961, XIX—578 pp.; H. Elhai, *La Normandie occidentale, entre la Seine et le golfe Normand-Breton, étude morphologique*, thesis, Bordeaux 1963, X—624 pp.; C. Klein, 'Quelques Caractères originaux du socle armoricain', *Norois*, no. 15, 1957, pp. 305–32.

Central Massif. The basic work is still the thesis by H. Baulig: *Le plateau Central de la France et sa bordure méditerranéenne, étude morphologique*, thesis, Paris 1928, 575 pp.; A. Perpillou, *Le Limousin, étude de Géographie physique régionale*, thesis, Paris 1940, 257 pp.; J. Beaujeu-Garnier, *Le Morvan et sa bordure, étude morphologique*, thesis, Paris 1951, 288 pp.

Later evolution. The references given here concern sedimentation, deformations and planations, episodes which are closely linked. *Armorican Massif:* the thesis by S. Durant: *Le Tertiaire de Bretagne* (1960) deals with the numerous deposits scattered over the core of the Breton mountains. M. Gautier, 'La tectonique tertiaire dans le Massif Armorican', *A.G.*, 1967, 414, pp. 168–97. *Central Massif:* M. Derruau, *La Morphogenèse de la Grande Limagne et ses conséquences sur la morphologie des plateaux bordiers*, Grenoble 1949, 185 pp.; P. Bout, *Le Villefranchien du Velay et du Bassin hydrographique moyen et supérieur de l'Allier*, thesis, Le Puy 1960, 344 pp.

Research has been done on Limousin by A. Perpillou, already quoted; by J. Beaujeu-Garnier, 'Essai de morphologie limousine', *R.G.A.*, 1954, no. 2, pp. 269–302, and B. Bomer, 'Le relief du Limousin septentrional', *Mémoires et documents du C.D.C.G.*, vol. IV, pp. 65–96 (it is interesting to read the review by Meynier in *Norois* 1955, July–September, pp. 431–6); L. Gachon, 'L'Évolution morphologique des coulées volcaniques en Auvergne', *A.G.*, no. 296, 1945, pp. 245–73. *Other Regions:* Dubois, *La géologie de l'Alsace*, Paris 1955; E. Juillard, 'Une carte des formes de relief dans la plaine d'Alsace-Bade', *I.G.*, 1949, 3, p. 116.

Structural morphology and differential erosion. M. Derruau, *Les Caractères différentiels des roches du socle dans l'Ouest et le Sud-Ouest du Massif Central français*, Paris 1952, 56 pp. (Travaux Institut Géog., Clermont-Ferrand, 2); E. Coulet, 'Morphologie des Grands Causses', *B.S.L.G.*, 1962, fasc. 1 and 2, pp. 3–62.

River systems. M. Gautier, 'Les Rapports entre l'hydrographie et la structure dans le Bocage Vendéen et dans la Gâtine de Parthenay', *A.G.*, 1958, no. 320, pp. 183–98; M. Ters, 'Permanence et ancienneté des grandes lignes du réseau hydrographique et du relief en Vendée côtiere occidentale', *ibid.*, 1958, no. 359, pp. 1–11; L. Poirier, 'Un essai d'interprétation du réseau hydrographique de la Basse-Normandie', *B.A.G.F.*, 1946, nos. 175–6, pp. 14–23. The hydromorphological data are taken from Ph. Pinchemel: 'L'Étude des réseaux hydrographiques', *B.A.G.F.*, 1950, nos. 208–9, pp. 72–80, and from unpublished research done by F. Damette.

Sedimentary basins. *Paris basin:* there has been a renewal of interest in the Paris basin, inspired by André Cholley, in the last twenty years. The main articles by André Cholley are to be found in his collected works: *Recherches morphologiques*, Paris 1957, VIII—207 pp. vol. I, *La Genèse du Bassin*, 1950, 210 pp.; vol. II, *L'Évolution morphologique*, Paris; 1952, pp. 211–474. Ph. Pinchemel, *Les plaines de craie du Nord-Ouest du bassin Parisien et du Sud-Est du bassin de Londres, étude de morphologie*, Paris 1954, 502 pp.; J. Gras, *Le Bassin de Paris méridional, étude morphologique*, thesis, Rennes 1963, 494 pp. These researches have been synthesised in the 'Carte morphologique du bassin Parisien et son commentaire' by A. Cholley, J. Beaujeu-Garnier, B. Bomer, A. Journaux, R. Musset, Ph. Pinchemel, X. De Planhol and J. Tricart (*Mémoires et Documents* du C.D.C.G., vol. V, 1956, 114 pp., and 1 map of 4 pages at a scale of 1/1,400,000). *Aquitaine basin:* two theses: H. Enjalbert, *Les Pays Aquitains, le modelé et les sols, Première partie, le modelé et les sols*, vol. I, 1960, 618 pp.; P. Fénelon, *Le Périgord, étude morphologique*, Paris 1951, 527 pp.

Quaternary processes and forms. Y. Guillien, 'De quelques Données sur les périodes froides du Pleisto-cène français, cartes, commentaire', *B.A.G.F.*, 1957, nos. 265–6, p. 21, and 'Néoglaciaire et tardiglaciaire: géo-chimie, palynologie, préhistoire', *A.G.*, 1962, no. 383, pp. 1–35; J. Tricart, *Carte des phénomènes péri-glaciaires quaternaires en France, Mémoires pour servir à l'explication de la carte géologique détaillée*, Paris 1956, 40 pp.

Since the 1950s there have been many studies on periglacial phenomena, to the detriment of other aspects of the relief of France. Most often, in fact, these researches analyse deposits or contour forms, and are too exclusively preoccupied with problems of origin. There is no true geographical spirit, except for a few cases. Apart from the theses already mentioned, which all tackle these questions, we shall quote an issue of *R.G.P.S.-O.*, *Morphologie périglaciaire et sols dans le bassin d'Aquitaine et ses bordures*, 1951, fasc. 2–3.

THE MORPHOLOGICAL EVOLUTION OF PYRENEO-ALPINE FRANCE

The Pyrenees. J. P. Mangin, 'Données nouvelles sur le Nummulitique pyrénéen', *B.S.G.F.*, 1959, vol. I, pp. 16–30; F. Taillefer, 'Deux Versants montagneux étroits: le versant piémontais des Alpes occidentales et le versant français des Pyrénées', *R.G.P.S.-O.*, 1955, 3, pp. 190–206, and *Le Piémont des Pyrénées françaises*, thesis, Toulouse 1951, 383 pp.; G. Viers, *Pays Basque français et Baretous, Le Relief des Pyrénées occidentales et de leur piémont*, thesis, Toulouse 1960, 604 pp.

The Alps. The Alps are certainly the region best covered by geographical theses, and the subject of the greatest number of geological and morphological studies. This is due to their problems, and to the inspiration of the great names in geology and geography in Grenoble for the last 50 years. M. Gignoux and L. Moret, *Géologie dauphi-noise*, Paris 1952, 392 pp.; R. Blanchard, *Les Alpes occidentales*, Grenoble, 8 vols, 1936–56. There have been many theses: J. Chardonnet, *Le relief des Alpes du Sud*, vol. I, 1947, 399 pp.; vol. II, 1948, 386 pp.; C. P. Péguy, *Haute Durance et Ubaye, Étude physique de la zone intraalpine des Alpes françaises du Sud*, Grenoble 1947, 315 pp.; J. Masseport, *Le Diois, les Baronnies et leur avant-pays rhodanien. Étude morphologique*, Grenoble 1960, 478 pp.; P. Gidon, 'Essai sur l'orogénie alpine en France', *B.S.G.F.*, 1958, 2, pp. 149–58; G. Masseport, 'Le Sillon alpin, dépression d'érosion ou déchirure structurale,' *R.G.A.*, 1955, 4, pp. 793–820; P. Veyret, 'La Cluse de Grenoble, contribution à l'étude du relief plissé', *ibid.*, 1956, 2, pp. 297–309, and 'Le problème des cluses préalpines: la cluse de Chambéry', *ibid.*, 1957, 1, p. 927.

The Jura. Our knowledge of the structure and orogenesis of the Jura has been completely renewed by the work of L. Glangeaud, 'Les Caractères structuraux du Jura', *B.S.G.F.*, 5th series, vol. 19, fasc. 7, 8, 9, 1949, pp. 669–88; M. Dubois, *Le Jura méridional, étude morphologique*, thesis, Paris 1959, IV, 644 pp.

Provence and Corsica. The latest synthesis, following a very large bibliography, is that of J. Aubouin and G. Mennessier, 'Essai sur la structure de la Provence' in *Livre à la mémoire du Professeur P. Fallot*, vol. II, 1963, pp. 49–98; A. Rondeau, *Recherches géomorphologiques en Corse*, thesis, Paris 1961, 586 pp.; Y. Masierel, *La Provence cristalline et ses enveloppes sédimentaires, essai de géographie physique*, thesis, Gap 1965, 418 pp.; J. Nicod, *Recherches morphologiques en Basse-Provence calcaire*, thesis, Gap 1967, 557 pp.

The fore-plains of the mountains and their borders. A. Journaux, *Les plaines de la Saône et leurs bordures monta-gneuses, étude morphologique*, thesis, Caen 1956, 532 pp.; M. Gottis, *Contribution à la connaissance géologique du Bas-Languedoc*, thesis, Montpellier 1967, 796 pp.; P. Demangeon, *Contribution à l'étude de la sédimentation détritique dans le Bas-Languedoc pendant l'ère tertiaire*, thesis, Montpellier 1958, 397 pp.; review by Marrès, *Med.*, 1962, I, pp. 83–90; Y. Bravard, *Le Bas-Dauphiné, recherches sur la morphologie d'un Piedmont alpin*, thesis, Grenoble 1963, 504 pp.

Climatic morphology, glaciers. F. Bourdier, *Le Bassin du Rhône au Quaternaire, Géologie et Préhistoire*, Paris 1962, vol. I, 364 pp.; vol. II, 295 pp.; R. Vivian, 'Le Recul récent des glaciers du Haut Arc et de la haute Isère', *R.G.A.*, 1960, 2, pp. 313–31; Y. Bravard, 'Les Glaciers de Chartreuse', *ibid.*, 1958, I, pp. 47–63; J. Corbel, 'Glac-iers et climats dans le Massif du Mont Blanc', *ibid.*, 1963, 2, pp. 322–60.

Glacial morphology. The Alps have served as a laboratory for glacial relief. The theories of Paris and Grenoble have been worked over and argued there, but the various explanations in no way change the reality of the forms of relief. P. Veyret, 'L'eau, la neige, la glace, le gel et la structure dans l'évolution morphologique de la région de Chamonix (Massifs du Mont Blanc et des Aiguilles Rouges)', *R.G.A.*, 1959, I, pp. 5–56; F. Taillefer, 'Glaciaire pyrénéen; versant N et versant S', *R.G.P.S.-O.*, 1957, 3, pp. 221–44.

Periglacial morphology. J. Tricart, 'Paléoclimats quaternaires et morphologie climatique dans le Midi médi-terranéen', *Eiszeitalter und Gegenwart*, II, May 1952, pp. 172–88; J. P. Schwobthaler and H. Vogt, 'Aspects de la morphogenèse plio-quaternaire dans le Bas-Rhône occidental', *B.S.L.G.*, 1955, pp. 13–59 and 67–126; F. Taillefer, 'Le modelé post-wurmien des hautes montagnes françaises', *R.G.P.S.-O.*, 1964, 3.

COASTAL RELIEF

There are very many works on coastal morphology and relief of France. Among the articles are: G. Galtier, 'La Côte sableuse du Golfe du Lion', *B.S.L.G.*, 1958, fasc. 2, 3, 4; A. Perpillou, 'Morphologie des côtes du Léon', *C.R.D.C.G. Mém. et Doc.*, vol. IV, 1954, pp. 203–40; M. Phlipponneau, 'La Baie du Mont-Saint-Michel, Étude de morphologie littorale', *Mém. Soc. Géol. et Minéral de Bretagne*, 1956, XI, 200 pp.; C. L. Précheur, 'Le littoral de la Manche, de Sainte-Addresse à Ault', extra issue of *Norois*, 1960, 138 pp.

MORPHOLOGICAL AREAS AND TYPES

Paradoxically, the bibliography is very limited, because at present morphological research is moving away from these problems, and comparative studies are very rare. It would be otherwise if scholars were more attracted to topological research and measurements of forms of relief. L. Gachon has made a very interesting comparative study: 'Les Alpes françaises et le Massif Central', *R.G.A.*, 1955, IV, pp. 685–96.

MINERAL RESOURCES

The sources are mainly geological or economic. The greatest work is still that of A. Lacroix: *Minéralogie de la France et de ses anciens territoires d'outre-mer*, new edition, Paris 1962, vol. I, 723 pp. A great deal of information can be found in: Raguin, *Géologie des gîtes minéraux*, Paris 1940, 613 pp., and in all manuals of economic geography. A metallogenic map of France on a scale of 1/2,500,000 is in course of publication (cf. P. Laffitte and F. Permingeat, 'Maquette d' . . .', *B.S.G.F.*, 1961, vol. 3, no. 5, pp. 481–6).

CLIMATE, SOIL, VEGETATION, WATER

The only general study of the climatology and biogeography of France is to be found in *La France Physique* by E. De Martonne, *op. cit.*

CLIMATE

Climatology is a poor relation of geographical studies. Before the last war the thesis of E. Benevent, *Le climat des Alpes françaises*, Paris 1926, stood on its own. Since then there has been a renewal of interest, but only two theses have been devoted to regional climatic analysis: P. Estienne, *Recherches sur le climat du Massif Central français*, Paris 1956, 242 pp. (*Mémorial de la Météorologie Nationale*, no. 43), and P. Pédelaborde, *Le Climat du bassin Parisien*, 1 vol., Paris 1957, 539 pp., and 1 atlas, 1958, 116 plates. These works reflect the two trends of climatic research as carried out by geographers. The *Mémorial de la Météorologie nationale* regularly publishes climatic studies.

ATMOSPHERIC CIRCULATION

P. Pédelaborde, 'Un exemple de circulation atmosphérique régionale; la circulation sur l'Europe occidentale', *A.G.*, 1953, no. 334, pp. 401–17.

RAINFALL AND SNOW

Since the old, but still useful studies of Angot and Gaussen, French pluviometry has been the subject of an original article by R. Musset: 'La Distribution des pluies en France selon les saisons', *A.G.*, 1943, no. 292, pp. 264–83, one full-page map. The Météorologie nationale has published, in 1966, 13 maps of the mean rainfall for year and months. J. J. Boisvert, 'La Neige dans les Alpes françaises', *R.G.A.*, 1955, fasc. I, pp. 357–434.

SOILS AND SOIL EROSION

The Institut National de la Recherche Agronomique published in 1966 a 'carte pédologique de la France' in two sheets. L. Gachon, 'Un Siècle d'histoire des sols en France, dégradation et réfection', *R.G.L.*, 1950, no. 2, pp. 81–9; J. Nicod, 'Sur le Rôle de l'homme dans la dégradation des sols et du tapis végétal en Basse-Provence', *R.G.A.*, 1951, 4, pp. 709–48; J. Vogt, 'La Dépradation des terroirs lorrains au milieu du 18ᵉ siècle', *B.C.T.H.*, 1957, pp. 111–16.

VEGETATION

Gaussen has made the only comprehensive studies of French plant life: *Géographie des plantes*, Paris 1900 (collection A. Colin, no. 152); G. Plaisance, *Les Formations végétales et paysages ruraux*, dictionary and bibliographical guide, Paris 1959, 423 pp., a very valuable work. G. Kunholtz-Lordat has made some very important contributions to the analysis of the vegetation and the changes made in it by man: *Le Tapis végétal dans ses rapports avec les phénomènes actuels de surface en Basse-Provence*, Paris 1952; G. Plaisance, *Guide des forêts de France*, Paris 1961, 411 pp. (a mine of information of all kinds).

WATER

Ground-water and Springs. Subterranean hydrology is a science on its own, and its specialists in France have published a great deal. Geographers do not appear anxious to take part in their researches or to make their own original contribution to them; nevertheless a geography of ground-water and springs would be just as important as a climatic geography.

R. Colas, 'Le problème de l'eau', *Population*, 1964, 1, pp. 31–54. An example of the problem of water in a highly urbanised and industrialised region is given by G. Waterlot, 'Le Problème de l'eau dans la région du Nord', *B. Soc. Géog.*, Lille 1960, pp. 22–40; I. Chéret, *L'eau*, Paris, 1967, 128 pp.; *Le problème de l'eau en France*, Paris 1965, 53 pp. (N.E.D., no. 3129).

Rivers. French geography is world-famous in the realm of potamology, but owes its fame to one single man, who devoted all his life to it. The work of M. Pardé is indeed massive, and thanks to him, the mechanism of our rivers is well known. On régimes, the description of the basic types can be found in his *Fleuves et rivières*, Paris 1964, 4th edition, C.A.C., no. 155. This can be supplemented by articles by the same author in the different geographical reviews. An interesting cartographical study by J. Corbel: 'Erosion et grands cours d'eau en France', *I.G..*, 1962, 3, pp. 113–16.

Floods and other irregularities. *L'Annuaire hydrologique de la France* gives, every year, the hydrological 'characteristics' for the year. G. Viers, 'La Genèse des crues élémentaires sur les marges du bassin Aquitain', *R.G.P.S.-O.* 1962, 2, pp. 225–46; M. Pardé and Poggi: 'Les Crues de juin 1957 dans les Alpes françaises', *R.G.A.*, 1959, III, pp. 325–74; M. Chartier, 'Les Rivières de la région parisienne pendant la vague de froid de février 1956', *B.A.G.F.*

1957, November–December, pp. 58–65; and 'Contribution a l'étude de la sécheresse, 1959–60', *ibid.*, 1962, no. 307–8, pp. 209–22; J. Tricart: 'Étude morphodynamique du bassin du Gard', *B.C.T.H.*, vol. LXXIV (1961), Paris 1962, pp. 141–326 .

POPULATION

There is a considerable bibliography on the population of France, both general and regional. *Population*, the review of the I.N.E.D., is the best source of information.

GENERAL

Two useful introductions: Huber, Bunle, Boverat and Febvay, *La Population de la France*, Paris 1965, 366 pp.; A. Armengaud, *La Population Française au 20ᵉ siècle* (Que sais-je, no. 1167). M. Reinhard and A. Armengaud, *Histoire générale de la population mondiale*, Paris 1961, 597 pp.; J. Bourgeois-Pichat, 'Évolution générale de la population française depuis le 18ᵉ siècle', *Population*, 1951, no. 4, pp. 635–62; P. Ariès, *Histoire des populations françaises et de leurs attitudes devant la vie*, Paris 1948, 576 pp.

GROWTH AND DISTRIBUTION

Immigration and emigration. A. Girard, J. Stoetzel, L. Bogart, T. Le Liepvré and M. H. de Bousquet, *Français et immigrés*, Paris 1954, 2 vols (I.N.E.D. Travaux et documentes, cahiers nos. 19, 20).

RURAL DEPOPULATION

General studies. P. Clément and P. Vieille, 'L'Exode rural, historique, causes et conditions, sélectivité, perspectives', Ministry of Finance, Department of economic and financial research, *Études de Comptabilité nationale*, no. 1, April 1960, pp. 57–130, Bibliography of 264 issues; P. Estienne, 'Les problèmes de surpeuplement rural, l'exemple de la Combraille', *R.G.A.*, 1950, 2, pp. 301–34; L. M. Goreux, 'Les Migrations agricoles en France depuis un siècle et leur relation avec certains facteurs économiques', *Études et conjoncture*, April 1956, pp. 327–76.
Local and regional examples. Most theses on rural subjects study this question at length. *Plains:* Ph. Pinchemel, *Structures sociales et dépopulation rurale dans les campagnes picardes, de 1836 à 1936*, Paris 1957, 232 pp. (Centre d'Études Économiques, Études et Mémoires, no. 35). *Mountainous regions:* P. Estienne, 'L'étude de la dépopulation en montagne et ses enseignements récents', *R.G.A.*, 1947, 2, pp. 367–78; 'Un Demi-Siècle de dé-peuplement rural dans le Massif Central', *ibid.*, 1956, 3, pp. 463–72; 'L'Émigration contemporaine dans la montagne auvergnate et Vellave', *ibid.*, 1958, 3, pp. 463–94; P. Guiot, Thurins, *Démographie d'une commune rurale de l'Ouest lyonnaise*, Paris 1949, 170 pp. (Cahiers Fondat. Nat. Sciences Polit.).
Y. Bravard, 'L'Arrêt du dépeuplement des Alpes du Sud', *R.G.A.*, 1956, 2, pp. 355–69, and 'Le Dépeuplement des hautes vallées des Alpes-Maritimes, ses caractères et ses conséquences démographiques, économiques et sociales', *ibid.*, 1961, 1, pp. 5–129; M. A. Carron, 'Évolution démographique récente des trois cantons de la Montagne limousine', *B.A.G.F.*, 1960, nos. 294–5, pp. 169–85.

URBANISATION

F. Carrière and Ph. Pinchemel, *Le fait urbain en France*, Paris 1963, 374 pp. (Centre d'Études Économiques, Études et Mémoires, no. 57); L. Chevalier, *La Formation de la population parisienne au 19ᵉ siècle*, Paris 1950, 312 pp. (I.N.E.D. no. 10); J. Bastié, 'La Population de l'agglomération parisienne', *A.G.*, 1958, no. 359, pp. 12–38; G. Pourcher, *Le Peuplement de Paris, Origine régionale, attitudes et motivations*, Paris 1964, 310 pp. (I.N.E.D., Trav. et Doc. no. 43).

DISTRIBUTION

R. Balseinte, 'Notes sur la population française vivant dans des communes dont le chef-lieu est situé entre 900 et 2,000 m. d'altitude', *R.G.A.*, 1957, 1, pp. 155–70.

THE 1962 CENSUS

R. P. Mols, 'L'accroissement de la population de la France selon les régions et l'importance des aggloméra-tions', *Population*, 1963, April–June, pp. 263–304.
Demographic structure. R. Balseinte, 'Valeurs approchées de l'indice de vitalité démographique des départe-ments français et des principales agglomérations urbaines pour l'année 1954', *R.G.A.*, 1959, 1, pp. 61–78: M. Croze, 'La Mortalité infantile en France suivant le milieu sociale', *Études statistiques*, July–September 1963, pp. 163–72.
Population predictions. The general report of the Commission de la Main-d'Oeuvre of the various plans are the most convenient documents: M. Febvay, 'Perspectives d'évolution naturelle de la population par département', *Études statistiques*, October–December 1957; M. Febvay and J. Hayoun, 'Perspectives de la population française jusqu'en 1980', *Études statistiques*, 1960, 2, pp. 143–52; R. Pressat, *Les Besoins en emplois nouveaux en France par département jusqu'en 1970*. Report of the *Haut-comité consultatif de la population et de la famille*, La Documenta-tion française, 1961, 92 pp.; A Sauvy, 'Les perspectives d'accroissement du nombre des emplois en France d'ici 1975', *Population*, 1961, 2, pp. 197–220; F. Gueland-Leridon, 'Perspectives sur la population active française par qualification en 1975', *Population*, 1964, 1, pp. 9–30; M. Croze et F. Cazin, 'Perspectives démographiques régionales en 1970 et 1978', *Études et Conjoncture*, 1965, 4, pp. 85–165.

MENTALITIES AND CIVILISATION

THE FRENCH OUTLOOK

The bibliography on the psycho-sociological aspects of the French is a scattered one. We will mention those works which we have found most helpful. Salvador de Madariaga, *Anglais, Français, Espagnols*, Paris 1952, 270 pp., is a remarkable work; C. Morazé, *Les Français et la Republique*, Paris 1956, 256 pp.; P. Combe, *Le Drame Français, du libre échange au Marché Commun*, Paris 1959, 230 pp. (with an interesting preface by André Siegfried).

CIVILISING INFLUENCES. NORTHERN AND SOUTHERN FRANCE

G. Jeanton, 'Les Limites respectives des influences septentrionales et méditerranéennes en France', *Societé des Amis des Arts et des Sciences de Tournus*, 1937, vol. XXXVII, pp. 125–42 (map for the whole of France); M. Derruau, *La Grande Limagne auvergnate et bourbonnaise*, Clermont-Ferrand 1949 (the fourth part, pp. 405–88, is entirely devoted to the contrast between North and South). R. Lebeau, 'Les contrastes du Nord et du Midi dans la géographie humaine du Jura français', *Études Rhodaniennes*, 1948, nos. 1–2, pp. 93–103, and *La Vie rurale dans les Montagnes du Jura méridional*, thesis, Lyons 1955. The section entitled 'Conclusion: un seuil entre la France du Nord et du Midi' is on pp. 567–72.

ATLANTIC FRANCE

P. Flatrès, *Géographie rurale de quatre contrées celtiques*, Rennes 1957, especially the Conclusion, pp. 561–75, and 'Les Structures rurales de la frange atlantique de l'Europe', *Géographie et Histoire agraires*, Acts of the international conference organised by the Faculté des Lettres at the University of Nancy (2nd–7th September 1957), Nancy 1959, pp. 193–202.

PLANNING

GENERAL

General works are mainly devoted to Plans for Modernisation and Equipment. P. Bauchet, *La Planification française; vingt ans d'expérience*, Paris 1966, 399 pp.; P. Massé, *Le Plan ou l'anti-hasard*, Paris 1965, 251 pp.; C. Gruson, *Origines et espoirs de la planification française*, Paris 1968.

THE PLANS

The text of each of the Plans for Modernisation and Equipment has been published in the *Journal officiel de la République française*, a special issue being devoted to each one. Each Plan has been the subject of annual reports on their carrying out (Paris, Imprimerie Nationale).

REGIONAL PLANNING

The three books of J. F. Gravier, especially the first, set off the 'discovery' of regional inequality: J. F. Gravier, *Paris et le désert français*, Paris 1947 and 1958, 317 pp.; *Mise en valeur de la France*, Paris 1949, 384 pp.; *Décentralisation et progrès technique*, Paris 1953, 394 pp.; since then, there has been a large number of books, articles and reports.

Regional programmes, which later became regional plans for development and land utilisation, were published in the official gazette, and as pamphlets: *Bretagne*, J.O. 1956, no. 1070, 62 pp.; *Poitou-Charentes*, J.O. 1957, no. 1093, 127 pp.; *Corse*, J.O. 1957, no. 1094, 232 pp.; *Lorraine*, J.O. 1957, no. 1103, 181 pp.; *Midi Pyrénées*, J.O. 1959, no. 1128, 232 pp.; *Languedoc*, J.O. 1959, no. 1136, 210 pp.; *Alsace*, J.O. 1959, no. 1138, 233 pp.; *Alpes-Rhône*, J.O. 1960, no. 1179, 336 pp.; *Provence-Côte d'Azur*, J.O. 1961, no. 1185, 340 pp.; *Auvergne*, J.O. 1961, no, 1195, 260 pp.; *Franche-Comté*, J.O. 1961, no. 1206, 286 pp.; *Champagne*, J.O. 1962, no. 1223, 347 pp.; *Bourgogne*, J.O. 1964, no. 1237; *Centre*, J.O. 1964, no. 1243; *Picardie*, J.O. 1964, no. 1246; *Limousin*, J.O. 1964, no. 1250; *Pays de la Loire*, J.O. 1965, no. 1258; *Aquitaine*, J.O. 1965, no. 1263; *Basse-Normandie*, J.O. 1965, no. 1266; *Haute-Normandie*, J.O. 1966, no. 1290.

J. Labasse, 'La Portée géographique des programmes d'action régionale français', *A.G.*, April–July 1960, pp. 371–93; J. R. Boudeville, *Problems of Regional Economic Planning*, Edinburgh University Press, 1966. The first official documents on regional planning were the three *brochures vertes*: *Pour un Plan national d'Aménagement du territoire*, February 1950; *L'Aménagement du territoire, Premier rapport*, December 1950, 100 pp.; *Deuxième rapport*, July 1962, 55 pp. (Paris, Ministère de la Reconstruction et de l'Urbanisme); O. Guichard, *Aménager la France*, Paris 1965, 246 pp.; P. Lamour, *60 millions de Français*, Paris 1967, 305 pp.

Investments. The documentation on this subject is scattered, difficult to interpret and still very elementary at regional level. J. Gervais, *La France face aux investissements étrangers*, 1963, 234 pp ; the financing of regional development, J. Labasse, *Les Capitaux et la région, Étude géographique. Essai sur le commerce et la circulation des capitaux dans la région lyonnaise*, Paris 1955, XVIII—533 pp. (Cahiers de la Fondation Nationale des Sciences politiques, 69); on the regionalisation of the budget since 1963 (budget of 1964): *Projet de loi de finances, documents annexes; Régionalisation du budget d'équipement*, Paris, for each year.

THE INFRASTRUCTURES

THE ADMINISTRATIVE INFRASTRUCTURE

The first study to draw attention to the interest of the network of communes is the article of A. Meynier: 'La Commune rurale française', *A.G.*, 1945, no. 295, pp. 161–79; a remarkable map of the French communes has been published, with comments by A. Meynier, A. Perpillou, E. Juillard, H. Enjalbert, P. Barrère, G. Duby and A. Platier, in *Annales* (L.A.C.) 1958, July–September, pp. 447–87 (1 full-page map).

FUEL AND POWER

The *Revue française de l'énergie* and the *Annales des Mines* are the two basic reference publications. Also the 'Rapports généraux des commissions de l'énergie' for the various plans. A. Gamblin, *L'Énergie en France, Étude de géographie*, Paris 1968, 250 pp.; Y. Mainguy has published in the *Revue française de l'énergie* (1962–5) a series of general and regional articles: 'Éléments d'une géographie économique de l'énergie en France.'

Coal. The official sources are the annual administrative reports of the Charbonnages de France. P. Gardent, *Le Charbon, panorama économique*, Paris 1962, 203 pp.

Oil. The publications of the different companies and unions (Union des Chambres syndicales de l'Industrie du Pétrole, Paris, for example) are among the best sources of information. B. S. Hoyle, 'L'Industrie de raffinage pétrolier en France et en Grande-Bretagne, étude comparée', *R.G.L.*, 1961, 2, pp. 117–37.

Gas. 'Gaz de France' publishes every year a report and a volume of statistics; G. Veyret-Verner, 'Électricité et Gaz de France de 1952 à 1960', *R.G.A.*, 1961, 3, pp. 401–33.

Electricity. *Les Rapports annuels et les résultats techniques provisoires de l'Électricité de France*; A. Bertin, 'Le Barrage de Serre Ponçon, pièce maîtresse de l'aménagement de la Durance', *R.G.A.*, 1960, 4, pp. 625–89.

TRANSPORT

General. R. Clozier, *Géographie de la circulation*, Paris 1963, 404 pp. (Géographie économique et sociale, vol. 3); J. M. Priou, *Les Transports en Europe*, Paris 1963, (Que sais-je, no. 1053); D. Renouard, *Les Transports de marchandises par fer, route et eau depuis 1750*, A. Colin, Paris 1950, 130 pp. (Fondation Nationale des Sciences Politiques, Recherches sur l'économie française, 2); M. Wolkowitsch, *L'économie régionale des transports dans le Centre et le Centre-Ouest de la France*, thesis, Paris 1960, 534 pp.; R. Caralp, 'La Tarification des transports et son aspect géographique', *I.G.*, 1963, 5, pp. 206–17.

Roads. H. Cavaillès, *La Route française*, Paris 1946, 400 pp.; P. M. Duval, H. Jean, G. Livet, L. Trenard and R. Coquand, *Les Routes de France, depuis les origines jusqu'à nos jours*, Paris 1959, 171 pp.; the Ministry of Public Works, Transport and Tourism regularly publishes a traffic census for particular years (main roads). Maps are published showing the volume of traffic on the roads, drawn up on the basis of traffic censuses. The *Institut Géographique National* published one on traffic in 1950, 1955 and 1960.

Railways. H. Peyret, *Histoire des chemins de fer en France et dans le Monde*, Paris 1949, 350 pp.; year-books are easily obtainable: *L'Année ferroviaire* has been appearing since 1947, and is a collection of specialised studies and of statistics (Librairie Plon, Paris); the S.N.C.F. publishes each year a useful booklet: *Activité et productivité de la S.N.C.F.* R. Caralp, 'L'évolution de l'exploitation ferroviaire en France', *A.G.*, no. 322, 1951, pp. 321–36; 'L'Évolution des relations ferroviaires, l'exemple de Toulouse-Paris et de Toulouse-Lyon', *R.G.P.S.-O.*, 1957, 2, pp. 141–65; *Les Chemins de fer dans le Massif Central, étude des voies ferrées régionales*, thesis, Paris 1959, 469 pp. (Centre d'Études économiques, 44).

Waterways. M. Jouanique and L. Morice, *La Navigation intérieure en France*, Paris 1951 (Que sais-je, no. 494). The *Revue de la Navigation intérieure et rhénane* publishes every year *Le trafic sur les voies navigables françaises*. The *Office national de la navigation* publishes a *Statistique annuelle* giving the volume of traffic on inland waterways section by section, and another showing direction of traffic (Ministry of Public Works and Transport).

On the Mediterranean—North Sea links: M. Laferrère, 'Le Projet de liaison fluviale et la géographie industrielle de la région lyonnaise', *R.G.L.*, 1962, 2, pp. 113–29; J. Béthemont, 'Un Problème français à l'échelle européenne', *ibid.*, 1963, 4, pp. 315–56; 'La Liaison Rhin-Rhône, par l'Alsace et la vallée du Doubs, ses caractéristiques techniques et économiques', *Rev. Navig. int. et rhénane*, 1962, 25th May, pp. 375–402; G. Tournier, 'L'Aménagement du Rhône et de la voie méridienne,' *ibid* 1963, 25th Nov., pp. 782–800. On the Atlantic–Mediterranean link: J. Lajugie, 'L'Aménagement de l'axe fluvial Rhône-Atlantique,' *Rev. Jur et Écon. du S.-O.* (série éco.), 1962, 4, pp. 875-96.

Sea-ports. H. Cloarec, *La Marine Marchande*, Paris 1961 (Que sais-je, no. 176); *Comité central des armateurs de France. La Marine marchande. Études et statistiques*, Paris; A. Perpillou, 'Problèmes portuaires dans l'économie contemporaine', *B.C.T.H.*, vol. LXXV, 1962, Paris 1963, pp. 196–217; A. Vigarié, *Les grands ports de commerce de la Seine au Rhin*, thesis, Paris 1964, 715 pp. and atlas.

RURAL LANDSCAPE

The study of the various aspects of the geography of the countryside of France is, together with the morphology, the favourite theme in the researches of French geographers; but economists, sociologists and historians have also made abundant and valuable contributions. It is difficult to follow the plan of the three chapters of Part Four strictly, because all aspects are discussed in the books cited, always in a regional context.

GENERAL REFERENCES

Syntheses, detailed studies of the rural world have come from all disciplines.

History. The most recent synthesis is that of G. Duby, *L'Économie rurale et la vie des campagnes dans l'Occident médiéval*, Paris 1962, 2 vols, 822 pp.; this followed on the masterly work of M. Bloch: *Les Caractères originaux de l'histoire rurale française*, Oslo 1931, new edition Paris 1952, 265 pp.; R. Dauvergne has collected in a second volume the articles published by Bloch after *Les Caractères originaux: II. Supplément établi d'après les travaux de l'auteur*, 1931–44, Paris 1956, 230 pp. (Collection Économies, Sociétés, Civilisations).

Sociology. H. Mendras, *Sociologie de la campagne française*, Paris 1959 (Que sais-je, no. 842); J. B. Charrier, *Citadins et ruraux* (Que sais-je, no. 1107).

Geography. The findings of geographers will be found mainly in general publications: D. Faucher, *Géographie agraire*, Paris 1949, 300 pp. (Collection Géographie économique et sociale), and *La Vie rurale vue par un géographe*, Toulouse 1962, 316 pp., a collection of articles which are very important; P. George, *La Campagne, le fait rural à travers le monde*, Paris 1956, 128 pp. and *Précis de géographie rurale*, 1963, VIII, 360 pp.; R. Dumont, *Voyages en France d'un agronome*, 2nd edition, Paris 1956, 487 pp.; E. Juillard, *Géographie rurale française, travaux récents et tendances nouvelles (1917–63)*, *Études Rurales*, 1964, pp. 46–70.

Economy. J. Pautard, *Les Disparités régionales dans la croissance de l'agriculture française*, Paris 1965, 179 pp.

General Surveys. There are numerous summaries and briefings on the recent development of French agriculture. Among them the most notable are: R. Livet, *L'avenir des régions agricoles*, Paris 1965, 232 pp.; M. Faure, *Les Paysans dans la Société française*, Paris 1966, 366 pp.; L. Gachon, *La Vie Rurale en France* (Que sais-je, no. 242); H. Mendras, *La fin des paysans*, Paris 1967, 361 pp.; J. Boichard, 'Perspectives de l'agriculture française', *R.G.L.*, 1966, 2, pp. 98–127.

Statistics and current information. The Ministry for Agriculture publishes two different documents each year: *La Statistique agricole annuelle* and a *Rapport annuel sur l'état de l'agriculture*. Every two years, the review *Paysans* publishes a special number, 'Tableaux de l'agriculture française', which offers a very useful collection of statistics, graphs and annotated maps. Other reviews: *Annales* (Économies, Sociétés, Civilisations), *Études rurales*, *Économie rurale*.

Regional Studies. The geographical theses devoted to the rural life of one or another region of France have been very numerous and of good quality in recent years; in chronological order they are: Durand, *La vie rurale dans les massifs volcaniques des Dore, du Cézallier, du Cantal et de l'Aubrac*, Aurillac 1946, 530 pp.; E. Juillard, *La vie rurale dans la plaine de Basse-Alsace, essai de géographie sociale*, Strasbourg 1952, 582 pp.; R. Lebeau, *La vie rurale dans les montagnes du Jura méridional, étude de géographie humaine*, Lyons 1955, 593 pp.; M. Phlipponneau, *La Vie rurale dans la banlieue parisienne, étude de géographie humaine*, Paris 1956, 593 pp.; J.-P. Moreau, *La vie rurale dans le Sud-Est du bassin Parisien, entre les vallées de l'Armançon et de la Loire*, Paris 1958, 399 pp.; P. Brunet, *Structure agraire et économie rurale des plateaux tertiaires entre la Seine et l'Oise (Brie, Valois, Soissonais, Caux)*, 1960, 522 pp.; B. Kayser, *L'Arrière Pays rural de la Côte-d'Azur (études sur les conséquences du développement urbain*, Monaco 1960, 593 pp.; G. Galtier, *Le Vignoble du Languedoc méditerranéen et du Roussillon, étude comparative d'un vignoble de masse*, Montpellier 1960, 3 vols of 484, 353, 317 pp.; A. Bozon, *La vie rurale en Vivarais, étude géographique*, Valence 1961, 635 pp.; J. Miege, *La vie rurale du Sillon Alpin, étude géographique*, Paris 1962, 677 pp.; A. Fel, *Les Hautes Terres du Massif Central français*, Paris 1961, 340 pp.; R. Livet, *Habitat rural et structures agraires en Basse-Provence*, Gap 1962, 465 pp.; S. Lerat, *Les Pays de l'Adour*, Bordeaux 1963, 580 pp.; R. Brunet, *Les campagnes toulousaines*, Toulouse 1965, 727 pp.; J. Bonnamour, *Le Morvan, la terre et les hommes*, Paris 1965, 454 pp.; P. F. Gay, *La Champagne du Berry*, Bourges 1967, 556 pp.

LAND HOLDINGS AND FARMING

R. Dugrand, 'La Propriété foncière des citadins dans le Bas-Languedoc', *B.A.G.F.*, 1956, May–June, pp. 133–45. This subject is taken up again in his thesis *Villes et Campagnes*, Paris 1963; R. Brunet, 'Les Recherches sur la propriété rurale des citadins et l'exemple de Toulouse', *B.A.G.F.*, 1957, November–December, pp. 66–75; 'Toulouse et la propriété rurale', *R.G.P.S.-O.*, 1958, pp. 325–42; S. Bonin, 'L'Étude de la propriété foncière, un exemple de méthode cartographique', *Études Rurales*, 1962, nos. 5–6, pp. 136–60; H. Elhaï, 'Recherches sur la propriété foncière des citadins en Haute-Normandie', *Mém. et Doc.*, 1965, fasc. 3, 109 pp., C.R.D.C.G.

CONSOLIDATION OF HOLDINGS

C. Christians, 'Aspects géographiques de la réorganisation agraire par remembrement en France, aux Pays-Bas et en Belgique' *B.S.R.G.*, Antwerp 1960, pp. 64–125; a summary by L. Rieucau, 'Où en est le remembrement rural en France?', *Études Rurales*, 1965, no. 18, pp. 69–78.

TRANSFORMATION OF HOLDINGS AND FARMING

J. Bonnamour, 'Budgets paysans et surface minimale rentable', *I.G.*, 1962, 1, pp. 13–19; J. Madec, *Les structures agraires en France et les sociétés d'aménagement foncier et d'établissement rural*, Paris 1967 (N.E.D., no. 3422).

Types of farming and land use. The fundamental work is the thesis of J. Klatzmann, *La localisation des cultures et des productions animales en France*, Paris (I.N.S.E.E.) 1955, 480 pp., 350 maps and graphs. A. Fel, 'Problèmes des limites entre les systèmes d'élevage, exemples tirés du Massif Central français', *B.A.G.F.*, 1954, nos. 243–4, pp. 97–103.

Techniques of production and cultivation systems. D. Faucher, 'L'Assolement triennal en France', *Études Rurales*, 1961, I, pp. 7–18; E. Juillard, 'L'Assolement biennal dans l'agriculture septentrionale. Le cas particulier de la Basse-Alsace', *A.G.*, 1952, no. 323, pp. 34–45; R. Dumont, *La Révolution fourragère*, Paris 1955.

D. Faucher, *Le Paysan et la machine*, Paris 1954; L.-J. Lapagnot, 'La Motorisation des campagnes dans le département du Lot-et-Garonne', *R.G.P.S.-O.*, 1960, 4, pp. 345–80; P. Flatrès, 'La Deuxième Révolution agricole en Finistère', *Études rurales*, 1963, no. 8, 55 pp.; P. Flatrès, 'Coup d'œil sur les institutions agricoles françaises', *I.G.*, 1963, 3, pp. 93–104.

M. Sivignon, 'Élevage et embouche en Charolais-Brionnais', *R.G.L.*, 1960, 4, pp. 357–79; J. Bethemont, 'Le riz et la mise en valeur de la Camargue', *ibid.*, 1962, 2, pp. 153–206; J. Boichard, 'L'Élevage et la production de viande en Nivernais', *ibid.*, 1965, 1, pp. 47–75; R. Pijassou, 'Structures agraires traditionnelles et révolution agricole dans les campagnes périgourdines', *R.G.P.S.-O.*, 1966, 3, pp. 233–62; J. P. Fléchet, 'L'Évolution agricole de la Dombes', *R.G.L.*, 1967, pp. 39–79.

Agricultural land use.   The already quoted thesis of J. Klatzmann is the basic work: A. Fel, 'Le Climat agricole et les limites altitudinales de l'Occupation du sol sans le Massif Central', *A.G.*, 1955, no. 346, pp. 401–12.   *The Forests: La Fôret française, l'industrie du bois*, Paris 1955, N.E.D., nos. 2071–3; *Les français et leurs fôrets*, Paris 1967; *Atlas Forestier*, 1966, published by the Ministry of Agriculture.   *Fallow and Waste Land:*   L. Gachon, 'Population et friches', *I.G.*, 1948, no. 5, pp. 175–9, and 1949, no. 2, pp. 56–9, and 'Récentes Déprises et reprises humaines sur les massifs anciens du centre de la France', *R.G.A.*, 1952, 2, pp. 265–91.   *The Vine:* R. Dion, *Histoire de la vigne et du vin en France des origines au XIXe siècle*, Paris 1959, XII, 768 pp.; P. Marres, *La Vigne et le vin en France*, Paris 1950, 224 pp. (C.A.C. no. 263).

A. Perpillou, 'Essai d'établissement d'une carte de l'utilisation du sol en France', *A.G.*, 1952, no. 18, pp. 110–15; 'L'utilisation agricole du sol en France et les transformations des paysages ruraux en France', in *Mélanges géographiques offerts à Ph. Arbos*, vol. II, 1953, pp. 189–99; 'L'Évolution de l'utilisation du sol par l'agriculture dans huit départements du Midi de la France', *Mém et doc*, vol. VII, 1960, pp. 121–34, 2 maps C.R.D.C.G.; 'Paysages ruraux du Sud du Poitou', *Norois*, October–December 1954, pp. 391–406; 'Utilisation du sol en Normandie occidentale', résumés of papers, Internat. Geog. Congress, Stockholm 1960, p. 230; 'Utilisation du sol par l'agriculture dans les Alpes du Nord; le cas du département de l'Isère', Actes 85, Congrès Nat. Soc. Sav., Section de géographie, 1960, pp. 169–74; E. Juillard and J.-P. Angrand, 'L'Utilisation du sol dans les départements de l'Est de la France du 19e au 20e siècle', *R.G.E.*, 1960, no. 1, pp. 14–40, 1 map in colour.

RURAL LANDSCAPES

The central problem of all geographical research is the description and explanation of rural landscapes. The general works, the regional studies and the theses already cited analyse this problem.

Comprehensive works are rare: A. Meynier, *Les Paysages agraires*, Paris 1958, 199 pp. (new edition, 1967, collection U2); E. Juillard and A. Meynier published in 1955 a remarkable synthesis, 'Die Agrarlandschaft in Frankreich, Forschungsergebnisse der letzten zwanzig Jahre', *Münchner Geographische Hefte*, 97 pp., no. 9. This text was incorporated in the volume of the symposium *Structures agraires et paysages ruraux*, Nancy 1957, 188 pp.; *Annales de l'Est*, 1957, no. 17, with an important bibliography; R. Dion, 'Réflexions de méthode. A propos de la Grande Limagne de Max Derruau', *A.G.*, 1951, no. 318, pp. 25–33; B. Bomer, 'Paysages ruraux du Sud; bassin Parisien', *I.G.*, 1958, 2, pp. 55–67, and 'Paysages ruraux entre Val de Loire et vallée du Loir' (in 'Géographie et Histoire agraires', Acts of the international symposium at Nancy, *Annales de l'Est*, 1959, mémoire no. 21, pp. 68–78; P. Brunet, 'Problèmes relatifs aux structures agraires de la Basse-Normandie, orientation des recherches', *Ann. Normandie*, 1955, pp. 115–34; F. Taillefer, 'Études sur les paysages ruraux du Sud-Ouest: Verniolles et Unzent (Ariège)', *R.G.P.S.-O.*, 1950, 2–3, pp. 96–126, and 4, pp. 234–57; Dr. Merle, 'Les paysages agraires et l'habitat rural en Gâtine de la fin du Moyen Age à nos jours', *Bull. Groupe poitevin Et. Géog.*, 1951, I, pp. 3–17; P. Brunet, 'Les Paysages ruraux de l'Aquitaine du Sud-Est', *R.G.P.S.-O.*, 1960, 3, pp. 233–76; P. Flatrès, 'La Structure rurale du Sud-Finistère d'après les anciens cadastres', *Norois*, 1957, 15, pp. 353–67, and 16, pp. 425–53; P. Flatrès, 'Les structures rurales de la frange atlantique de l'Europe', Agrarian history and geography, Acts of the international symposium at Nancy, *Annales de l'Est*, 1957, mémoire no. 21, pp. 193–202.

The rural habitat.   We owe the first essays on the typology to A. Demangeon: 'Types de peuplement rural en France', *A.G.*, 1939 no. 271, pp. 1–21 (resumed in *Problèmes de géographie humaine*, Paris 1942, 407 pp.); P. De Saint-Jacob, 'La Structure ancienne du village, habitat et sociologie', *I.G.*, 1948, 5, pp. 188–92; R. Dion has published a remarkable study: *La Part de la géographie et celle de l'histoire dans l'explication de l'habitat rural du bassin Parisien*, Publications Soc. Géog., Lille 1946, pp. 6–80; this article is above all important on account of this results, method and geographical spirit.   A.-M. Pavard-Charaud, 'L'Habitat et les structures agraires de la Grande Brière et des Marais de Donges', *A.G.*, 1948, 306, pp. 119–30; R. Lebeau, 'Carte des formes d'habitat rural de la chaîne jurassienne, suisse et française', *Regio basiliensis*, 1963, 1, pp. 19–34; J. Peltre, 'Du 16e au 18e siècle, une génération de nouvaux villages en Lorraine', *R.G.E.*, 1966, pp. 3–27.

Rural roads.   Marcel Gautier, 'Un Chapitre négligé de la géographie agraire: Les enseignements des chemins ruraux', *I.G.*, 1954, no. 3, pp. 93–7.

Rural settlement.   A. Demangeon made a fundamental contribution to this question: 'L'Habitation rurale en France.   Essai de classification des principaux types', *A.G.*, XXIX, 1920, no. 161, pp. 352–75, resumed and improved in 'Essai d'une classification des maison rurales' (Travaux du 1er Congrès international de folklore), Paris 1937, Tours 1938; both articles were published in *Problèmes de géographie humaine*, Paris 1942, 407 pp.; D. Faucher has taken up this problem again more recently in 'La Classification des types de maisons rurales' in *La vie rurale vue par un géographe*, Toulouse 1962, pp. 237–52, and 'Évolution des types de maisons rurales', *A.G.*, 1945, no. 296, pp. 241–53.

All theses on the subject of rural life provide valuable documentation. On the development of the enclosed courtyard farmhouse in Picardy, see R. Coque, 'L'Évolution de la maison rurale en Amiénois', *A.G.*, 1956, no. 52, pp. 401–17.

Field patterns. All the references already cited, including the theses and articles, devote a great deal of attention to the pattern of land division; in most cases, maps show the diversity of shapes and sizes of land-holdings. It is very interesting to search for ancient field patterns, by aerial photography and new photographic techniques: R. Chevalier, 'Un Document fondamental pour l'histoire et la géographie agraire: la photographie aérienne', *Études Rurales*, I, April–June, 1963, pp. 70–80, 5 figures; M. Gautier, 'Ensembles cadastraux circulaires en Vendée', *Ann. de Bretagne*, 1949, I, pp. 154–64; F. Imberdis, 'Le Problème des champs courbes', in 'Géographie et histoire agraires', Actes du colloque international de Nancy, *Annales de L'Est*, 1957, mém. no. 21, pp. 294–99; R. Livet, 'Les Champs allongés de Basse-Provence', *ibid.*, pp. 383–97; A. Meynier, 'La genèse du parcellaire breton', *Norois*, 1966, no. 52, pp. 595–610; F. Reitel, 'A propos de l'openfield lorrain', *R.G.E.*, 1966, 1–2, pp. 29–51.

Open and enclosed fields. The basic references for the problem of open fields and woods (*bocage*) are printed in the following pages: A.-M. Pavard-Charraud, 'Bocage et plaine dans l'Ouest de la France', *A.G.*, 1949, no. 310, pp. 113–25; A. Boubier, 'Gaigneries et terroirs de hameaux dans le Sud-Ouest Vendéen', *Norois*, 1957, 16, pp. 455–68; J. Bonnamour, 'Paysages agraires aux confins du Morvan et de l'Auxois', *B.A.G.F.*, 1960, nos. 294–5, pp. 158–68; A. Gamblin, 'Le Contact Cambrésis-Thiérache', *Revue du Nord*, 1959, no. 163, livraison géographique no. 10, pp. 33–48.

Agricultural landforms. *The Terraces:* J. Despois, 'Pour une Étude de la culture en terrasses dans les pays méditerranéens', in 'Géographie et Histoire agraires', Actes du colloque international de Nancy, *Annales de l'Est*, 1959, mém. no. 21, pp. 105–17. *Ridge and furrow:* E. Juillard, 'Formes de structure parcellaire dans la plaine d'Alsace. Un indice de l'ancienneté des limites agraires', les crêtes de labours', *B.A.G.F.*, 1953, nos. 232–3, pp. 72–7. *Lynchets:* The basic article is that of L. Aufrère, 'Les Rideaux, étude topographique', *A.G.*, 1929, pp. 529–60; cf. Ph. Pinchemel, *Les Plaines de craie*, Paris 1954, p. 337.

The Classification of Rural Landscapes. P. Brunet and M.-C. Dionnet, 'Présentation d'un essai de carte des paysages ruraux de la France, scale 1/1,000,000, *B.A.G.F.*, nos. 305–6, March–April 1962, pp. 98–103. Presentation of a map published in *Atlas économique et social pour l'aménagement du territoire*.

INDUSTRY

GENERAL

G.-J. Gignoux, *L'Industrie française*, Paris 1952, 190 pp.; the I.N.S.E.E. has defined *Les zones de peuplement industriel et urbain*, Paris 1962, 170 pp. and maps, and published a *Recensement de l'industrie*, 1963; T. J. Markovitch, *L'Industrie française de 1789 à 1964*, Paris 1965–6, 4 vols; *Géographie et industrie*, monthly bulletin published since 1963 with the co-operation of professional groups belonging to the *Conseil National du Patronat français*, provides useful documentation.

STAGES OF INDUSTRIALISATION AND LOCALISATION

The Industrial Revolution is the subject of numerous books: H. Heaton, *Economic history of Europe*, Harper and Row, 1948; T. S. Ashton, *The Industrial Revolution, 1760–1830*, Oxford 1948. Many historical theses have been devoted to the period: C. Fohlen, *L'Industrie textile au temps du Second Empire*, Paris 1956, 535 pp.; G. Duveau, *La vie ouvrière en France sous le Second Empire*, Paris 1946, 605 pp.; P. Leon, *La Naissance de la grande industrie en Dauphiné*, Paris 1954, 2 vols, and by the same author, *L'Industrialisation en France en tant que facteur de croissance économique, du début du 18e siècle à nos jours*, paper of the 1st International Economic History Conference, Stockholm 1960, Paris, pp. 163–204.

INDUSTRIAL DECENTRALISATION

P. George, 'Nécessités et difficultés d'une décentralisation industrielle en France', *A.G.*, 1961, no. 377, pp. 25–36; C. Parry, 'Un exemple de décentralisation industrielle: la dispersion des usines de la Radiotechnique à l'Ouest de Paris', *ibid.*, 1963, no. 390, pp. 148–61.

LOCATION STUDIES

Industrialised rural regions. Besides the theses and regional studies already cited: J. Suret-Canale, 'L'Industrie dans le Bas-Maine', *Norois*, 1956, 2, pp. 249–64; E. Flament, *L'Industrie de la rubanerie dans la vallée da la Lys*, B. Soc. Géog. Lille, no. 5, 1962, pp. 63–75; P. Guichonnet, 'Une originale concentration industrielle, le décolletage et l'horlogerie en Haute-Savoie', *Le Globe*, no. 101, 1961, 63 pp. (Soc. de Géog. de Genève).

Industrial towns. Besides the regional theses already cited and the urban studies cited below: M. Laferrère, *Lyon, ville industrielle, essai d'une géographie urbaine des techniques et des entreprises*', Paris 1960, 546 pp.; G. Viers, *Mauléon-Licharre, la population et l'industrie, étude de géographie sociale urbaine*', Bordeaux 1961, 185 pp. (Institut d'économie régionale du Sud-Ouest, Études d'économie Basco-béarnaise, vol. 2), cf. *R.G.P.S.-O.*, 1958, 2, pp. 97–119; P. Combe, *Thiers, les origines, l'évolution des industries thiernoises, leur avenir*, Clermont-Ferrand 1956, 128 pp.; Leclerc, 'Les Industries de Chalon-sur-Saône', *R.G.L.*, 1960, 2, pp. 121–56.

The industrial regions. G. Veyret-Verner, *L'Industrie des Alpes françaises. Étude géographique*, thesis, Grenoble 1948, 371 pp.; J. Maire and R. Gendarme, *Contribution à l'étude des localisations industrielles de la Région du Nord*, Lille 1956, 107 pp. (Comité d'Études Régionales économiques et sociales, 6e cahier); C. Précheur, *La Lorraine sidérurgique (étude de géographie humaine et économique)*, thesis, Paris 1959, 631 pp., and atlas; R. Haby, *Les Houillères lorraines et leur région*, thesis, Paris 1965, 800 pp., and atlas.

Spatial structure of industrialised areas. The most exhaustively quoted study is that of the industry of Lyons by M. Laferrère, thesis cited above; maps of land use in 17 towns or cities in the North, in Vakili, Pinchemel, Gozzi, 'Niveaux optima des villes', cited below.

THE TOWNS AND CITIES

GENERAL

Naturally a large and important documentation of French towns will be found in general works on urban geography; the most recent are those of P. George, *Précis de géographie urbaine*, Paris 1961, 283 pp., and of J. Beaujeu and G. Chabot, *Traité de géographie urbaine*, Paris 1963, 493 pp.

Comprehensive works on French towns are rare: J. Coppolani, *Le Réseau urbain de la France, sa structure et son aménagement*, Paris 1959, 80 pp.; P. Lavedan, *Les Villes françaises*, Paris 1960, 237 pp., fundamental for the history of the birth and development of the towns of France; P. Dollinger and P. Wolff, *Bibliographie d'histoire des villes de France*, Paris 1967, 756 pp.; F. Carrière and Ph. Pinchemel, *Le Fait urbain en France*, Paris 1963, 374 pp., centred upon statistical analysis of urbanisation, the growth of towns since 1851 and the functions of towns with more than 20,000 inhabitants, according to the data provided by the census of 1954.

REGIONAL STUDIES AND MONOGRAPHS

Studies of the network of towns are also limited and recent; a few have been devoted to them: M. Rochefort, *L'Organisation urbaine de l'Alsace*, Paris 1960, 384 pp.; R. Dugrand, *Villes et campagnes en Bas-Languedoc*, Paris 1963, 638 pp.; Y. Babonaux, *Les villes du Val de Loire*, Paris 1966, 500 pp.; J. Coppolani, 'Agglomérations et conurbations dans le Midi aquitain et languedocien', *R.G.P.S.-O.*, 1957, IV, pp. 337–58; A. Vakili, Ph. Pinchemel and J. Gozzi, *Niveaux optima des villes. Essai de définition des villes d'après l'analyse des structures urbaines du Nord et du Pas-de-Calais*, Lille 1959 (Comité d'études régionales, économiques et sociales, 2ᵉ cahier).

On the other hand, monographs on towns are very numerous, and constitute a framework of research at the individual scale. They are to be found in national and regional geography reviews. We shall give only monographs on cities to which complete published works have been devoted. R. Blanchard, who was the first to outline a methodological framework, has resumed and enriched his publications on *Annecy, essai de géographie urbaine*, Annecy 1958, 201 pp., and Nice, in *Le Comté de Nice*, Nice 1961, 250 pp., pp. 151–218. J. Coppolani has published his thesis on Toulouse, issued in 1954, in *Toulouse au 20ᵉ siècle*, Toulouse 1963, 436 pp.

'La Documentation française' has begun publishing a series of 'Notes et Études documentaires' on the major cities of France and written by geographers: Strasbourg, no. 2993, 1963; Marseilles, no. 3013, 1963; Nice, no. 3106, 1965; Lille, Roubaix-Tourcoing, no. 3206, 1965; Clermont-Ferrand, no. 3221, 1966; Rennes, no. 3257, 1966; Toulouse, no. 3262, 1967; Grenoble, no. 3288, 1967; Nantes, Saint-Nazaire, no. 3362, 1967; Paris, nine volumes since 1968.

The Paris region. The Paris region is a favoured topic for research. The *Atlas de la région parisienne* edited by J. Beaujeu-Garnier and J. Bastié, Paris 1967, is a basic source of information. The publications of the *Institut d'aménagement et d'urbanisme de la région parisienne* are also of great interest; P. Lavedan, *Histoire de Paris*, Paris 1960, 125 pp. (Que sais-je, no. 34); *Paris, Croissance d'une capitale* (Symposium), Paris 1961, 158 pp.

The works of P. Chombart de Lauwe and his team are well known: *Paris et l'agglomération parisienne*, Paris 1952, 2 vols, 263 and 112 pp.; J. Bastié, *La croissance de la banlieue parisienne*, thesis, Paris 1965, 624 pp.; *ibid.*, *Les problèmes d'aménagement et d'urbanisme de l'agglomération parisienne, le schéma directeur*, La Vie Urbaine, 1966, 1, pp. 1–31; J. Beaujeu-Garnier, 'L'Avenir de la région parisienne', *I.G.*, 1966, 2, pp. 47–58; B. Rouleau, 'Le tracé des rues de Paris', *Mém. et Doc.*, 1968, 132 pp., C.R.D.C.G.; F. Mallet, 'Le quartier des Halles de Paris', *A.G.*, 1967, no. 413, pp. 1–28.

URBANISATION

E.-L. Ganshof, *Étude sur le développement des villes entre Loire et Rhin au Moyen Age*, Paris 1943, 79 pp. and 38 plates; J. Blache, 'Naissance et horoscope des villes françaises', in *Pages géographiques de J. Blache*, 1963, pp. 263–77; M. Beresford, *New Towns of the Middle Ages*, London 1967. *Recent urban creations:* F. Malley, 'Une ville neuve à Lacq', *Économie et humanisme*, 1959, May–June, pp. 62–7; R. Balseinte, 'Megève ou la transformation d'une agglomération montagnarde par les sports d'hiver', *R.G.A.*, 1959, 2, pp. 131–224; J. Blache, 'Sites urbains et rivières françaises', *R.G.L.*, 1959, 1, pp. 17–55.

URBAN TYPOLOGY

J. Lefillatre, 'Nouvelle délimitation des agglomérations urbaines utilisées par l'I.N.S.E.E.', Études statistiques, 1961, pp. 3–55.

URBAN NETWORK AND SPHERES OF INFLUENCE

G. Chabot, 'Carte des zones d'influence des grandes villes françaises', *Mém. et Doc.*, vol. 8, 1961, pp. 141–3 and chart, C.R.D.C.G.; a study of zones of commercial attraction is being carried out under the direction of A. Piatier (cf. A. Piatier, 'Les attractions commerciales des villes, une nouvelle méthode de mesure', *Rev. Jur. et éco. du S.-O.* (economic series), 1956, 4, pp. 575–602); J. Hautreux, 'Les principales villes attractives et leur ressort d'influence', *Urbanisme*, 1963, no. 78, pp. 57–64; J. Hautreux and M. Rochefort, 'Physionomie génerale de l'armature urbaine française', *A.G.*, 1965, no. 406, pp. 660–77; P. Lefillatre, 'La puissance économique des grandes agglomérations françaises', *Études et conjoncture*, 1964, 1, pp. 3–40.

TOWNSCAPES

J. Bastié, 'Capital immobilier et marché immobilier parisien', *A.G.*, 1960, no. 373, pp. 225–50; P. Barrère, 'Le paysage girondin autour de Bordeaux', *R.G.P.S.-O.*, 1949, 3–4, pp. 222–52, and 'Les quartiers de Bordeaux, étude géographique', *ibid.*, 1956, 102 pp.; M. Dubois, 'Étude physionomique du quartier des Batignolles,' *I.G.*, 1946, 3, p. 94; G. Pinchemel, 'Cours et courettes lilloises', *Urbanisme et Habitation, La Vie Urbaine*, 1954, January–March, pp. 9–37; Y. Lacoste, 'Un Problème complexe et débattu: les grands ensembles', *B.A.G.F.*, 1963, nos. 318–19, pp. 37–46; 'Les grands ensembles d'habitation', *Notes et études documentaires*, no. 3004, June 1963; P. Clerc, *Grands ensembles, banlieues nouvelles*, 1967, 494 pp. (Travaux I.N.E.D.); C. Précheur, 'Nancy, Rapports de l'actuelle structure urbaine et de l'ancienne structure agraire', *B.A.G.F.*, nos. 235–6, 1953, pp. 106–16; H. Nonn, *Strasbourg, des densités aux structures urbaines*, Paris 1965, 189 pp.; the various numbers of the review *Urbanisme* contain many articles concerning recent city and town rebuilding and replanning.

URBAN HOUSING

F. Bamas, 'État de patrimoine des logements d'aprés le recensement de 1962', *Études et conjoncture*, 1966, pp. 3–58; J. Magaud, 'La situation de logement français', *Population*, 1966, 3, pp. 523–40.

INDEX